CNA^{SM} Study Guide
for NetWare® 5

NOVELL'S

CNA^{SM} Study Guide for NetWare® 5

• • • • • • • • • • • • •

DAVID JAMES CLARKE, IV

Novell.
PRESS

Novell Press, San Jose

Novell's CNA^{SM} Study Guide for NetWare® 5

Published by
Novell Press
2211 North First Street
San Jose, CA 95131

Library of Congress Catalog Card Number: 98-72478

ISBN: 0-7645-4542-6

Printed in the United States of America

10 9 8 7 6 5 4 3 2

1P/QY/QT/ZZ/FC

Distributed in the United States by IDG Books Worldwide, Inc.

Distributed by CDG Books Canada Inc. for Canada; by Transworld Publishers Limited in the United Kingdom; by IDG Norge Books for Norway; by IDG Sweden Books for Sweden; by Woodslane Pty. Ltd. for Australia; by Woodslane (NZ) Ltd. for New Zealand; by TransQuest Publishers Pte Ltd. for Singapore, Malaysia, Thailand, Indonesia, and Hong Kong; by ICG Muse, Inc. for Japan; by Norma Comunicaciones S.A. for Colombia; by Intersoft for South Africa; by Le Monde en Tique for France; by International Thomson Publishing for Germany, Austria and Switzerland; by Distribuidora Cuspide for Argentina; by Livraria Cultura for Brazil; by Ediciones ZETA S.C.R. Ltda. for Peru; by WS Computer Publishing Corporation, Inc., for the Philippines; by Contemporanea de Ediciones for Venezuela; by Express Computer Distributors for the Caribbean and West Indies; by Micronesia Media Distributor, Inc. for Micronesia; by Grupo Editorial Norma S.A. for Guatemala; by Chips Computadoras S.A. de C.V. for Mexico; by Editorial Norma de Panama S.A. for Panama; by American Bookshops for Finland. Authorized Sales Agent: Anthony Rudkin Associates for the Middle East and North Africa.

For general information on IDG Books Worldwide's books in the U.S., please call our Consumer Customer Service department at 800-762-2974. For reseller information, including discounts and premium sales, please call our Reseller Customer Service department at 800-434-3422.

For information on where to purchase IDG Books Worldwide's books outside the U.S., please contact our International Sales department at 317-596-5530 or fax 317-596-5692.

For consumer information on foreign language translations, please contact our Customer Service department at 800-434-3422, fax 317-596-5692, or e-mail rights@idgbooks.com.

For information on licensing foreign or domestic rights, please phone +1-650-655-3109.

For sales inquiries and special prices for bulk quantities, please contact our Sales department at 650-655-3200 or write to IDG Books Worldwide, 919 E. Hillsdale Blvd., Suite 400, Foster City, CA 94404.

For information on using IDG Books Worldwide's books in the classroom or for ordering examination copies, please contact our Educational Sales department at 800-434-2086 or fax 317-596-5499.

For press review copies, author interviews, or other publicity information, please contact our Public Relations department at 650-655-3000 or fax 650-655-3299.

For authorization to photocopy items for corporate, personal, or educational use, please contact Novell, Inc., Copyright Permission, 1555 North Technology Way, Mail Stop ORM-C-311, Orem, UT 84097-2395; or fax 801-228-7077.

For general information on Novell Press books in the U.S., including information on discounts and premiums, contact IDG Books Worldwide at 800-434-3422 or 650-655-3200. For information on where to purchase Novell Press books outside the U.S., contact IDG Books International at 650-655-3021 or fax 650-655-3295.

John Kilcullen, CEO, IDG Books Worldwide, Inc.
Steven Berkowitz, President, IDG Books Worldwide, Inc.
Brenda McLaughlin, Senior Vice President & Group Publisher, IDG Books Worldwide, Inc.

The IDG Books Worldwide logo is a registered trademark or trademark under exclusive license to IDG Books Worldwide, Inc. from International Data Group, Inc. in the United States and/or other countries.

Marcy Shanti, *Publisher, Novell Press, Novell, Inc.*

Novell Press and the Novell Press logo are trademarks of Novell, Inc.

Welcome to Novell Press

Novell Press, the world's leading provider of networking books, is the premier source for the most timely and useful information in the networking industry. Novell Press books cover fundamental networking issues as they emerge — from today's Novell and third-party products to the concepts and strategies that will guide the industry's future. The result is a broad spectrum of titles for the benefit of those involved in networking at any level: end user, department administrator, developer, systems manager, or network architect.

Novell Press books are written by experts with the full participation of Novell's technical, managerial, and marketing staff. The books are exhaustively reviewed by Novell's own technicians and are published only on the basis of final released software, never on prereleased versions.

Novell Press at IDG Books Worldwide is an exciting partnership between two companies at the forefront of the knowledge and communications revolution. The Press is implementing an ambitious publishing program to develop new networking titles centered on the current version of NetWare, GroupWise, BorderManager, ManageWise, and networking integration products.

Novell Press books are translated into several languages and sold throughout the world.

Marcy Shanti
Publisher
Novell Press, Novell, Inc.

Novell Press

Publisher
Marcy Shanti

Administrator
Diana Aviles

IDG Books Worldwide

Acquisitions Editor
Jim Sumser

Development Editors
Kevin Shafer
Kurt Stephan

Technical Editor
Mike Kelly

Copy Editors
Kevin Shafer
Brian MacDonald

Project Coordinators
Susan Parini
E. Shawn Aylsworth

Quality Control Specialists
Mick Arellano
Mark Schumann

Graphics and Production Specialists
Sarah C. Barnes
Laura Carpenter
Angela F. Hunckler
Jude Levinson
Linda Marousek
E. A. Pauw
Chris Pimentel
Brent Savage

Illustrator
David Puckett

Cartoonist
Norman Felchle

Proofreader
York Production Services

Indexer
York Production Services

About the Author

David James Clarke, IV is the creator of the CNE Study Guide phenomenon. He is the author of several bestselling books for Novell Press, including *Novell's CNE Update to NetWare 5*, *Novell's CNE Study Guide for NetWare 5*, and *Novell's CNE Study Set for NetWare 5*. Clarke is an online Professor for CyberState University and cofounder of the Computer Telephony Institute. He is also the developer of The Clarke Tests v5.0 and producer of the bestselling video series, "So You Wanna Be a CNE?!". Clarke is a CNI, CNE, and CNA. He speaks at numerous national conferences and currently serves as the president and CEO of Clarke Industries, Inc. He lives and writes on a white sandy beach in California.

I dedicate this book to all the past, present, and future heroes of ACME. Without their collective imagination and passion the world wouldn't have a chance . . . how about you?!

Foreword

The author of this comprehensive, if not voluminous, manuscript asked me to write a few words in the form of a brief foreword. It boggles the mind what I could possibly have to say about technology invented five centuries after my birth, but why not? — I have done crazier things! As a matter of fact, the evidence against me is overwhelming. So, here we go . . . .

What you are about to experience can best be described as *life changing*. In simpler terms, "the knowledge presented in this guide will significantly alter your perception of network-based communications in such a way that you will permanently modify your behavior towards technology." There you go — life changing.

NetWare 5 provides the means for creating a virtual global community. As such, people anywhere can interact with each other instantaneously. While this concept alone boggles even the largest mind, it slowly gains perspective when you place it in the same company as digital watches, microwave cooking, and daytime television. Now, if you are going to be a successful CNA, and help us save the world, you will need to expand your understanding of Novell technology beyond the local LAN and into the global Web. When I say "Web," I mean the pervasive worldwide communications network known as the *Internet*.

To help expand your understanding of the Novell Internet, the author of this manuscript presents several exciting new technical advancements — many of which dwarf the significance of daytime television. In this guide, you will learn how to install the NetWare 5 operating system, build a global NDS tree, and connect to the network with fellow Webians — using the new Novell Client. In addition, you will architect a virtual city using the NetWare 5 file system, secure the tree with NetWare Administrator, control workstations using Z.E.N.works, and ultimately generate hard-copy output using Novell Distributed Printing Services (NDPS). Stunning!

For the record, I still prefer painting, the sundial, and food cooked over an open flame. However, I am sure that I will eventually adapt to the "virtuosity" of twenty-first century life. After all, we're all in this together, so we might as well make the best of it.

Yours,

Leonardo Da Vinci

Preface

Welcome to your life . . . there's no turning back!

So, do you want to be a CNA? The "superhero" of the cyber-world? Good — because it's time to change the world with the help of NetWare 5. Did I say, "change the world"? Isn't that a little overwhelming? Can't we just start with "help the community?" — No time! We definitely need to *change the world*.

Welcome to NetWare 5 — Novell's Global Electronic Village. To be a successful CNA (and save the world), you'll need to expand your understanding of the Novell LAN beyond the server, beyond the NDS tree, to the "*collective whole*." NetWare 5 is much more than a simple file/print server. It includes numerous intranet/Internet solutions for global connectivity.

In this book, we're going to explore eight different NetWare 5 categories. Here's a quick preview of our "life changing" adventure together:

▸ *Chapter 1: Saving the World with NetWare 5* — We'll start at the beginning. In Chapter 1, I'll introduce the ACME adventure and we'll briefly explore seven CNA techno-tools: Novell Directory Services, connectivity, the file system, security, Z.E.N.works, NDPS, and NetWare 5 Installation. Then, we'll focus our "super powers" on each administrative tool throughout the book . . . starting in Chapter 2.

▸ *Chapter 2: Novell Directory Services* — We'll start by exploring Novell's most highly acclaimed resource management technology: NDS. Novell Directory Services is a distributed, replicated database that helps you manage network resources as objects in a hierarchical tree. Wow!

▸ *Chapter 3: NetWare 5 Connectivity* — Once you've mastered the tree, you need to learn how to access it. NetWare 5 connectivity involves Novell client software, login scripts, and NDS object management. All in a day's work for a NetWare 5 Superhero/Gardener.

▸ *Chapter 4: NetWare 5 File System* — NetWare 5 offers two directory trees: NDS and the physical file system. The file system mirrors NDS in many ways, but also branches off into more down-to-earth territory: physical files. In Chapter 4, we'll learn how to manage the file system using volumes, directories, and files.

▶ *Chapter 5: NetWare 5 Security* — And, of course, with increased resource access and distributed data comes security problems. The trick here is to let the good guys in while keeping the bad guys out. Fortunately, NetWare 5 includes a five-layered security model that restricts access in a number of different ways, such as login authentication, login restrictions, NDS security, file system security, and finally, file system attributes.

▶ *Chapter 6: NetWare 5 Workstation Management with Z.E.N.works* — This is the first stop on our journey through NetWare 5's Global Electronic Village. Z.E.N.works is a desktop-management tool that uses NDS to simplify the process of managing Windows-based workstations. Z.E.N.works is an acronym that means "Zero Effort Networks." So, what does the "Zero Effort" part mean? It refers to the fact that Z.E.N.works reduces the cost and complexity of maintaining network computers by delivering workstation management tasks directly to the user desktop.

▶ *Chapter 7: NetWare 5 Printing (NDPS)* — This is Novell's much-anticipated printing revolution. Novell Distributed Printing Services (NDPS) replaces the queue-based printing system with improved overall network performance, reduced printing problems, and better administration. That's a pretty tough promise to keep — fortunately, NDPS delivers.

▶ *Chapter 8: NetWare 5 Installation* — Finally, you must become a pro at constructing Novell's Global Electronic Village — a.k.a. NetWare 5. The good news is NetWare 5 installation is a GUI odyssey through Java console, auto-detecting hardware drivers, NDS definitions, and licensing. No problem for a modern CNA like you.

So, that covers the top eight solutions offered by NetWare 5. And in a nutshell, that encompasses the technology covered in this book. After all, this is the focus of Novell Education's CNA Course 560 — *NetWare 5 Administration*.

And to aid you during your quest for "life changing" knowledge, I offer a multitude of hands-on and hands-off lab exercises along the journey. I highly recommend that you practice, practice, practice as you read. This is key to NetWare CNAship and "real life" experience. However, please heed this simple warning: Never practice on a production network! There's no telling what these exciting ACME exercises will do to your company's intranet.

Oh yes; I will also present two different types of informational tidbits at key points during your adventure:

Highlights time-proven management techniques and action-oriented ideas. These tips are great ways of expanding your horizons beyond just CNAship—they're your ticket to true nerddom.

▶ . . . . ◀

REAL WORLD

Welcome to the real world. I don't want you to be a two-dimensional CNA in a three-dimensional world. These icons represent the other dimension. In an attempt to bring this book to life, I've included various real-world scenarios, case studies, and situational walk-throughs.

Finally, I'm guessing that at some point, you are going to want to apply all this "life-changing" knowledge to a physical, practical application—a network, perhaps. One assumes that you will act on this guide's technical concepts, philosophies, schematics, exercises, and examples. One also assumes that inevitably at some point, you will need help. Fortunately, the very Web that you will learn how to create can itself provide timely relief. You can e-mail Virtual da Vinci at LDaVinci@iACME.com.

So, get prepared for a magic carpet ride through NetWare 5's Global Electronic Village. Fasten your seat belt, secure all loose objects, and keep your arms inside the ride at all times. There's no limit to where you can go from here!

Ready, set, fly!

Acknowledgments

Saving the world is hard work! But it sure was fun working with all the great heroes of ACME — A Cure for Mother Earth. We all had a wonderful time building Novell's information superhighway, tackling Z.E.N.works, and exploring the nuances of NetWare 5. I emphasize the word "We." I know it sounds corny, but I couldn't have written this book without the help and support of numerous ACME heroes:

- ▶ Human Rights in Sydney — Mary Clarke

- ▶ Labs in NORAD — Marie Curie

- ▶ Operations in Camelot — King Arthur

- ▶ Admin in Rio — Guinevere

- ▶ Crime Fighting in Tokyo — Sherlock Holmes

Let me introduce you to them.

Human Rights in Sydney — Mary Clarke

Human Rights is the "heart" of ACME's purpose. This division has the most profound effect on my work. As I'm sure you guessed, this is where my family comes in. After all, family is everything.

Unless you've lived with a writer, it's hard to understand the divine patience that it takes to accept the crazy hours, crazy requests, and crazy trips. Mary, my wife, deserves all the credit for supporting my work and bringing a great deal of happiness into my life. She is my anchor. Then there's my two lovely princesses: Leia and Sophie. Somehow they know just when I needed to be interrupted — daughters' intuition. Most of all, they both have brought much needed perspective into my otherwise one-dimensional life. For that, I owe my family everything.

Of course, I wouldn't be here if it wasn't for the love and patience of my wonderful parents — Dave and Barbara Clarke — and my endearing sister Athena.

Labs in NORAD — Marie Curie

ACME's mission hinges on innovative technology. Along those lines, I was very lucky to work with such a talented team of scientists and magicians.

It all starts with the other architect of this book — my partner Marie Curie (Cathryn Ettelson). She has been instrumental in all aspects of this project — research, the Mad Scientist's laboratory, exercises, midnight phone calls, and the list goes on. I owe a great deal to this brilliant woman, and I truly couldn't have written this book without her. This is who I'm talking about when I say "we." Thanks Marie . . . I mean Cathryn. Now you can have that week-long vacation I've been promising you for years.

Behind every great book is an incredible production team. It all starts with Albert Einstein (Kevin Shafer) — legendary Development Editor. His flawless organization, quick wit, and patience were instrumental in bringing this book to life. I can say with 100 percent certainty, he is the best editor I've ever worked with. Next, I would like to thank Ada, "The Countess of Lovelace" (Lori Ficklin), who was responsible for bringing my words to life — literally. Also, her husband, Charles Babbage (Richard Ficklin), deserves a lot of credit for making sure I didn't ramble on forever and that the zeroes and ones were in the right order.

And, of course, I would like to thank Sir Isaac Newton (Norman Felchle) for providing the Study Guide with much-needed perspective and readability. He is the cartooning genius of the group. Finally, Michaelangelo (David Puckett) deserves a great deal of praise for creating the beautiful illustrations in this book. I've always believed a picture is worth a thousand words. But his pictures are worth a few thousand more.

Operations in Camelot — King Arthur

King Arthur (Jim Sumser) and his court have done a marvelous job at leading the ACME mission from beginning to end. They are the greatest publishers, editors, desktop publishers, proofreaders, typesetters, artists, and managers in all the land. Of course, the King deserves a lot of the credit because he is the leader and visionary of Camelot. However, we can't forget all the talented heroes that surround the King (and make him look so good).

First, there's Merlin (Kurt Stephan). His bureaucratic wizardy has kept the mission on track and opened doors that seemed forever sealed. And, don't forget the sword incident. Next, Robin Hood (Mike Kelly) gets enormous kudos for being the technical eyes and ears of this manuscript. It's safe to say that he steals from the techno-rich and gives to the techno-poor.

I would also like to honor King Arthur's Court for performing above and beyond the call of duty. Thanks to Brian MacDonald, Susan Parini, E. Shawn Aylsworth, Mick Arellano, Mark Schumann, Laura Carpenter, E. A. Pauw, Linda Marousek, Sarah C. Barnes, Jude Levinson, Chris Pimentel, Brent Savage, and Angela F. Hunckler.

Finally, thanks to IDG Books Worldwide's sales staff, marketing wizards, and bookstore buyers for putting this study guide in your hands. After all, without them I'd be selling books out of the trunk of my car.

Admin in Rio — Guinevere

Now, let's talk about ACME's Administration division — also known as Novell Press. They are truly the future of network publishing.

It all starts with Guinevere (Marcy Shanti). She *is* Novell Press. Guinevere has been a wonderful friend and supportive publisher for many years. I can only hope for greater things in the future. And the dramatic revolution of these Study Guides is due in part to her loyalty and vision — not to mention her uncanny ability to always know what's going on. And, I would also like to thank Guinevere's right-hand woman — Diana Aviles. Diana was wonderfully efficient and incredibly responsive — all with a refreshing positive flair. She's a rock at Novell Press that I always count on for quick and accurate answers. Together, these great people bring Novell Press books to life. ACME would be lost without them.

Crime Fighting in Tokyo — Sherlock Holmes

Fortunately, life is not one-dimensional. And at times it becomes necessary to solve challenging life puzzles and hurdle seemingly insurmountable obstacles. At times like these it's great to have a friend like Sherlock Holmes (Paul Wildrick). He has made puzzle-solving and obstacle-hurdling an art form. Of course, we can't forget Dr. Watson (Steve Romley), who has provided both of us with the tools we need to survive.

In addition, I would like to thank all the magnificent heroes of Sherwood Forest (CyberState University) who have banded together to bring you a plethora of Web-based multi-sensory learning tools. And, thanks to all my extraordinary friends at Diablo Valley College (DVC): Maid Marion (Leslie Leong), Dan McClellan (Friar Tuck), and Matt Anderson (Little John), for being there for me in the very beginning. And to my good friend Rich Rosdal of Clarity Tecknowledgy for always believing in me.

Finally, thanks to golf courses everywhere for giving me a reason to live; Tears for Fears for inspiration; The Tick for being a superhero role model; and Dexter and Dee Dee for teaching me everything I know about people and science.

I saved the best for last. Thanks to *you* for caring enough about NetWare 5, your education, and the world to buy this book. You deserve a great deal of credit for your enthusiasm and dedication. Thanks again, and I hope this education changes your life. Good luck, and enjoy the show!

Contents at a Glance

Contents

CHAPTER I

Saving the World with NetWare 5

In the social hierarchy of needs, the world is pretty out of whack. The Pyramid of Needs states that basic fundamental needs (such as food and shelter) preclude us from enjoying higher needs (such as art, education, and corn dogs). To achieve any semblance of Utopia, we need to make sure that enough people have sufficient resources to satisfy their lowest basic needs — medicine, food, shelter, and peace — so they can fully enjoy the higher needs — like digital watches.

As we'll learn later in this chapter, an organization known as ACME (A Cure for Mother Earth) has been created to make sure we distribute medicine, shelter, and corn dogs to most of the people in the world. As you'll learn, ACME is staffed by the greatest heroes of our unspoiled history. These are the founding mothers and fathers of Earth's Golden Age — before instant popcorn, talking cars, and daytime television. So, how are they going to do it? That's where NetWare 5 comes in.

Welcome to NetWare 5 — Novell's Global Electronic Village. To be a successful CNA (and save the world), you'll need to expand your understanding of the Novell LAN beyond the server, beyond the NDS tree, to the *collective whole*.

Let me explain . . . .

Ever since the beginning of time, people have had an uncontrollable need to communicate. Our nature drives us to exchange ideas, information, and opinions. Without communication, we can't learn. Without learning, we can't grow. And without growth, we shrivel up and disappear. Creativity and communication drive the human race more than any other force. They are essential elements of life.

Networking is the ultimate level of communication. It transcends words and pictures to provide a pathway for thoughts, ideas, and dreams. Networking as it exists today is the result of millions of years of evolution and growth. And the fun is only just beginning.

As we near the end of the 20th century, computers have begun to permeate every aspect of our lives. In the 1970s, they brought us disco. In the 1980s, they converted the "little black book" into an electronic Rolodex. And in the 1990s, computers are in cars, video games, digital watches, and coffee machines. The world is shrinking at an amazing rate. Networking is everywhere. It is essentially the foundation of our future growth.

So . . . what does the future of networking hold?

Undoubtedly the world is becoming a very *small* global village. In the Information Age, humans will become very big fish in a very small pond. With the advent of space travel, we will yearn to share our message with life-forms far, far away. As the galaxy opens up to us, we'll become small fish in a gigantic pond. The next challenge will be to network the galaxy — creating a Galactic Village.

But let's not get ahead of ourselves. Today we're going to explore Novell's solution for global connectivity . . . NetWare 5.

So . . . what is NetWare 5?

I'm glad you asked. It's actually more of a solution than a product. NetWare 5 extends the Novell LAN to include private intranets and/or the globally shared Internet. The great thing about NetWare 5 is that it's fully modular by design. It includes a server-based operating system, Novell Directory Services (NDS), pure IP transport, Z.E.N.works Desktop Management, and a variety of intranet/Internet products. In addition, NetWare 5 is fully compatible with existing NetWare servers, applications, and hardware.

So . . . what's so great about intranets?

Intranetworks (or *intranets*) allow you to leverage existing Internet technology to create a secure private corporate network. Private intranets rely on a common user interface (a graphical user interface, or GUI, browser) to provide access to local and shared information. In addition, paperless communications are encouraged and centrally available. Information can be accessed 24 hours a day. Probably the most exciting feature, however, is the availability of multimedia. That is, data, text, audio, and video simultaneously available through a single browser to everyone on the WAN. Wow!

So . . . what about the Internet?

If your company must extend beyond a private intranet, you may consider surfing the public Internet. The World Wide Web can deliver a variety of information, including product or company data, software updates, press releases, customer support, ordering information, online publications, merchandising, advertising, and/or broadcasting. This is all accomplished using myriad of Internet services — all available within NetWare 5.

So . . . how does Novell do it?

NetWare 5 is Novell's Enterprise solution for building your *Global Electronic Village*. Our ability to save the world relies on the following NetWare 5 CNA and CNE features:

NetWare 5 CNA Features:

1. Novell Directory Services (NDS)

2. NetWare 5 Connectivity

3. NetWare 5 File System

4. NetWare 5 Security

5. NetWare 5 Workstation Management with Z.E.N.works

6. NetWare 5 Printing with NDPS

7. NetWare 5 Installation

NetWare 5 CNE Features:

1. NetWare 5 Upgrade and Migration

2. NetWare 5 Java Console

3. NetWare 5 IP Services

4. Netscape FastTrack Server for NetWare

5. NetWare 5 Application Server

As you can see, NetWare 5 is much more than a simple file/print server. It includes numerous intranet/Internet solutions for global connectivity. In this book, we're going to explore the first seven NetWare 5 categories. That's the focus of Novell Education's CNA Course 560 — *NetWare 5 Administration*.

However, if you're going to grow to become a successful NetWare 5 CNE, you'll need to be an expert in *all* facets of global electronic villaging. For this reason, we're going to extend the introduction to include the additional five CNE features. Then, you can explore *Novell's CNE Study Guide for NetWare 5* to complete your ACME journey. Pretty exciting, huh?

So, surf the Web, sharpen your mind and enjoy the show. Oh yeah, and thanks for saving the world.

NetWare 5 CNA Features

Whether you're a new CNA or just want to surf the Web with NetWare 5, you'll need to become intimately familiar with all seven CNA features. In this first section, we're going to focus on the seven categories that comprise Novell Course 560 — *NetWare 5 Administration*. Here's a brief peek:

▶ *Novell Directory Services (NDS)* — We'll start by exploring Novell's most highly-acclaimed technology, NDS, which is a distributed, replicated database that helps you manage network resources as objects in a hierarchical tree. Wow!

▶ *NetWare 5 Connectivity* — Once you've mastered the tree, you need to learn how to access it. NetWare 5 connectivity involves Novell Client software, login scripts, and NDS object management. All in a day's work for a NetWare 5 Superhero/Gardener.

▶ *NetWare 5 File System* — NetWare 5 offers two Directory trees — NDS and the physical file system. The file system mirrors NDS in many ways, but also "branches" off into more down-to-earth territory: physical files.

▶ *NetWare 5 Security* — Of course, with increased resource access and distributed data comes security problems. The trick here is to let the good guys in while keeping the bad guys out. Fortunately, NetWare 5 includes a 5-layered security model that restricts access in a number of different ways, such as login authentication, login restrictions, NDS security, file system security, and finally, file system attributes.

▶ *NetWare 5 Workstation Management with Z.E.N.works* — This is the first stop on our journey through NetWare 5's Global Electronic Village. Z.E.N.works is a desktop-management tool that uses NDS to simplify the process of managing Windows-based workstations. Z.E.N.works is actually an acronym for "Zero Effort Networking." So, what does the "Zero Effort" part mean? It refers to the fact that Z.E.N.works reduces the cost and complexity of maintaining network computers by delivering workstation management tasks directly to the user desktop.

> ▸ *NetWare 5 Printing (NDPS)* — This is Novell's much-anticipated printing revolution. Novell Distributed Printing Services (NDPS) replaces the queue-based printing system with improved overall network performance, reduced printing problems, and better administration. That's a pretty tough promise to keep — fortunately, NDPS delivers.

> ▸ *NetWare 5 Installation* — Finally, you must become a pro at constructing Novell's Global Electronic Village — also known as NetWare 5. The good news is NetWare 5 Installation is a GUI odyssey through Java console, auto-detecting hardware drivers, NDS definitions, and licensing. No problem for a modern CNA like you.

So, that covers the top seven CNA solutions offered by NetWare 5, and, in a nutshell, that encompasses the technology covered in this book. It doesn't, however, encompass all of NetWare 5. In the next section, we'll discover five more CNE solutions that round out Novell's next-generation information superhighway (which I call the *Infobahn*).

Let's start with a quick look at your life as a NetWare 5 CNA starting with Novell Directory Services

Novell Directory Services (NDS)

NDS is your friend. It may seem a little intimidating at first, but when you get to know NDS, it's actually pretty fun. Really.

NDS has many different names — the Directory, the Tree, the "Cloud," the Sta-Puff Marshmallow Man. In reality, it's all of these things. In more technical terms, it's a distributed object-oriented hierarchical database of physical network objects. Huh? Probably the most appropriate description is the "Cloud" because NDS oversees physical network resources and provides users with a logical world to live in.

So, what does NDS look like? From the outside, it looks like a big cloud hovering over your network. On the inside, however, it's a hierarchical tree similar to the DOS or Windows file system. As you can see in Figure 1.1, NDS organizes resources into logical groups called *containers*. This is like Tupperware gone mad.

▶ · ◀

FIGURE 1.1

A tree in a Cloud —
getting to know NDS

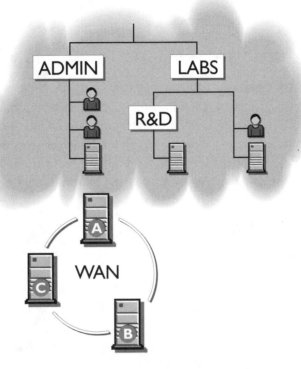

So, is NDS worth it? Well, you'll have to make that decision for yourself. But here are some reasons why I think it's the greatest thing since sliced bread. First, NDS offers a global database for central access and management of network information, resources, and services. Secondly, it offers a standard method of managing, viewing, and accessing network information, resources, and services. Third, NDS allows you to logically organize your resources independent from their physical characteristics or layout of the network. And, finally, NDS provides dynamic mapping between an object and the physical resource to which it refers. So, what do you think? Is NDS for you? Who knows — you might even like it.

Let's take a quick look at some of the key NDS features we'll cover in this book:

- ▶ NDS Objects

- ▶ NDS Naming

▸ NDS Partitioning

▸ Time Synchronization

Let's take a closer look.

NDS Objects

Plant a tree in a "Cloud"—it's good for the environment.

As in nature, the NDS tree starts with the [Root] and builds from there. Next, it sprouts container objects, which are branches reaching toward the sky. Finally, leaf objects flutter in the wind and provide network functionality to users, servers, and the file system. As you can see in Figure 1.2, the tree analogy is alive and well.

The figurative NDS tree

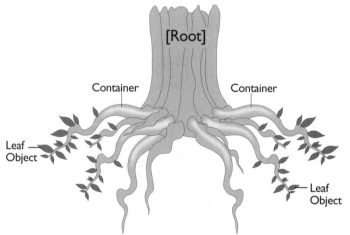

The real NDS tree is made up of special logical objects. NDS objects define logical or physical entities that provide organizational or technical function to the network. As you can see in Figure 1.3, they come in three different flavors:

▸ [Root]

▸ Container objects

▸ Leaf objects

The [Root] is the very top of the NDS tree. Because it represents the opening porthole to our NDS world, its icon is appropriately a picture of the Earth. Container objects define the organizational boundaries of the NDS tree and house other container objects and/or leaf objects. In Figure 1.3, we use container objects to define the ACME organization and its two divisions — ADMIN and LABS. Finally, leaf objects are the physical or logical network resources that provide technical services and WAN functionality. Leaf objects define the lowest level of the NDS structure. In Figure 1.3, leaf objects represent users, a printer, a server, and a group. NDS supports more than 50 different leaf object types, allowing you to manage routers, databases, e-mail systems, and so on. Plus, NDS is open so programmers can add their own objects. We'll discuss these types in detail in Chapter 2.

▶ · ◀

F I G U R E   1 . 3

The real NDS tree

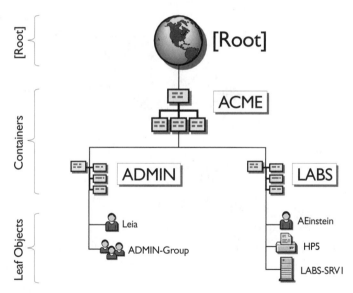

The tree can be organized any way you want, as long as it makes sense. AEinstein, for example, is placed near the resources he uses — the HP5 printer and LABS-SRV1 file server. We'll learn more about ACME later in this chapter. It's time to Save the World!

NDS Naming

NDS naming defines rules for locating leaf objects. One of the most important aspects of a leaf object is its position in the NDS tree. Proper naming is required when logging in, accessing NDS utilities, printing, and for most other management tasks.

The whole NetWare 5 NDS naming scheme is much more complicated than "Hi, I'm Fred." It requires both your name and location. For example, a proper NDS name would be "Hi, I'm Fred in the ADMIN division of ACME." As you can see in Figure 1.4, Fred's NDS name identifies who he is and where he works. This naming scheme relies on a concept called *context*.

▶ · ◀

F I G U R E   I.4

*Getting to know
the real "Fred"*

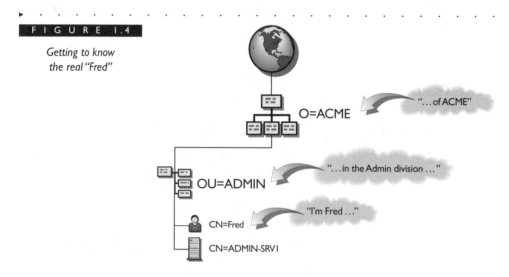

"…of ACME"

O=ACME

"…in the Admin division …"

OU=ADMIN

"I'm Fred …"

CN=Fred

CN=ADMIN-SRV I

Context defines the position of an object within the Directory tree structure. When you request a particular network resource, you must identify the object's context so that NDS can find it. NetWare 5 uses very specific naming guidelines for creating an object's context, and we'll review these in Chapter 2.

NDS Partitioning

Partitioning is the process of dividing the Directory into smaller, more manageable pieces. These pieces can then be distributed near the users who need them.

As you can see in Figure 1.5, NDS partitioning simply breaks the ACME organization into two pieces:

▸ *Partition A* — Known as the [Root] partition because it is the only one that contains the global [Root] object.

▸ *Partition B* — Known as the LABS partition because OU=LABS is the highest container object in that segment. In addition, Partition B is termed a *child* of Partition A, because LABS is a subset of the ACME Organization.

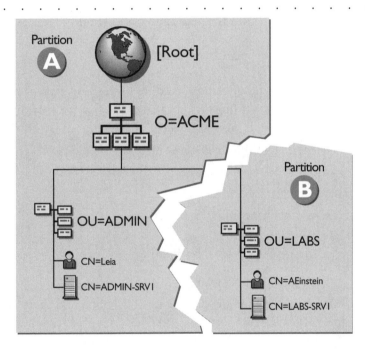

Breaking the NDS tree into two partitions

As a CNA, you have total control over NDS partitioning. You can decide how, when, and where they are created. The good news is, NetWare 5 includes a sophisticated default partitioning strategy. This means you don't have to get involved unless you want to. Many small WANs operate fine without any CNA intervention. There are times, however, when you may want to consider creating additional partitions. We'll discuss them later in Chapter 2.

Time Synchronization

Time synchronization is a temporal assurance scheme that forces all NetWare 5 servers to agree on what time it is. This is particularly important because all NDS background operations and security strategies rely on a time stamp. Time synchronization is accomplished through the use of four different time server types. We'll explore these types in Chapter 2.

In general, time stamps are important for:

▶ Replica synchronization

▶ Messaging

▶ Login authentication and time-based security

▶ File and directory operations

Time stamps report time according to the Universal Time Coordinated (UTC) equivalent. This is a time system that adjusts to the local time zone and Daylight Savings Time. It is also equivalent to Greenwich Mean Time (GMT). UTC is calculated using three values for each time server:

▶ Local time

▶ +/– time zone offset from UTC

▶ – Daylight Savings Time offset

For example, in NORAD, Colorado, the time is eight hours behind GMT. Therefore, if the time in NORAD is 12:00 noon and there is no Daylight Savings Time, UTC is 19:00.

Well, that's everything you need to know about the new-and-improved NetWare 5 "Cloud." Well, not really, but it's a very good start. Remember, every cloud has a silver lining, and this section has yours. Use this information wisely as you expand the horizons of your network.

Now let's continue our discussion of NetWare 5 CNA features by learning how to *connect* to this mysterious network cloud.

For more information about Novell Directory Services, refer to Chapter 2.

TIP

NetWare 5 Connectivity

Once the server has been installed, you are left with a simple directory structure, some workstations, and a few users — a LAN version of a cute little baby girl. Over time, this adorable little monster will learn to walk, talk, and start getting along with others. She will go to school and learn some valuable skills — ranging from how to climb the social ladder to how to deal with integral calculus. Finally, at some point, she will make an abrupt transition to adulthood — buy her first car, get her first job, and move into her first apartment.

In NetWare 5, childhood is dominated by the following three connectivity topics:

- ▸ *Connecting to the Network* — First, you must establish network connectivity using special workstation software. In NetWare 5, this is a 32-bit Windows 95/NT tool called the Novell Client.

- ▸ *Configuring Login Scripts* — Once you log in, these cool new batch files take over. Login scripts establish important network-based configurations such as drive mappings, application support, and printer redirection.

- ▸ *Welcome In* — Finally, the world of NDS and NetWare 5 is open to your users. At this point, they'll need to learn how to browse the Infobahn using NetWare Administrator 32 and a variety of NDS objects.

Let's get connected . . . now!

Connecting to the Network

Throughout this book, we will focus on the "network" as a distributed synergistic collection of computers. Throughout the entire CNE program, we'll learn everything there is to know about how to design, install, manage, and secure the network. However, we have to start somewhere. How about the basics of the workstation-to-server connection? This is the most fundamental platform of local-area networking and wide-area networking.

At its most fundamental level, the network workstation is made up of three fundamental components:

- ▸ Network interface card (NIC)

- Workstation connectivity software

- Local operating system

It all starts with the NIC, which is the hardware component that provides electronic communication between the LAN cabling scheme and local operating system. The local operating system provides a point of access for the LAN user. Without a local operating system (such as Windows 95/NT or DOS), there would be no way to tell the LAN what you need.

The vital connection between the NIC and local OS is provided by a collection of files called the "Workstation Connectivity Software." We'll learn more about the Novell Client in Chapter 3.

Once you've connected to the network using the Novell Client, there's only one task left — logging in. As a CNA, you've already accomplished the hard part — automating the workstation connection. Now it's the user's turn. The good news is our GUI Client provides a friendly login utility for Windows 95/NT users (see Figure 1.6).

FIGURE 1.6

Novell Client GUI
Login Screen

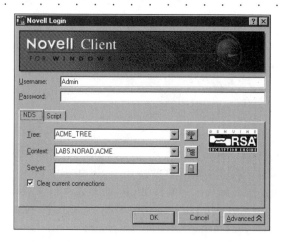

As you can see in Figure 1.6, the GUI login utility provides simple Username and Password input boxes within the native MS Windows environment. In addition, the "NDS" page allows you to specify an NDS tree, server, and/or login context. Similarly the "Script" page allows users to override container and profile scripts with local text files. We'll discuss the GUI Novell client in Chapter 3.

Configuring Login Scripts

Login scripts are the next phase of NetWare 5 connectivity. Once users have been authenticated with a valid username and password, NetWare greets them with login script configurations. In short, login scripts are batch files for the network. They provide a simple configuration tool for user customization — drive mappings, text messages, printer redirection, and so on.

NetWare 5 supports four types of login scripts, which are executed in systematic progression. As you can see in Figure 1.7, there's a flowchart logic to how login scripts are executed. Here's a quick look:

▶ *Container login scripts* — These are properties of Organization and Organizational Unit containers. They enable you to customize settings for all users within a container.

▶ *Profile login scripts* — These are properties of the Profile object. These scripts customize environmental parameters for groups of users. This way, users who are not directly related in the NDS tree can share a common login script.

▶ *User login scripts* — These are properties of each User object. They are executed after the Container and Profile scripts and provide customization to the user level.

▶ *Default login script* — This is executed for any user who does not have an individual User script. This script contains some basic mappings for the system and a COMSPEC command that points to the appropriate network DOS directory.

All four of these login script types work in concert to provide LAN customization for containers, groups, and users. As you'll quickly learn, login scripts are an integral part of your daily CNA grind. In addition, login scripts consist of commands and identifiers just like any other program or batch file. In addition, login script syntax must follow specific rules and conventions. We'll explore login scripts in more detail in Chapter 3.

FIGURE 1.7

*Understanding
NetWare 5 Login Scripts*

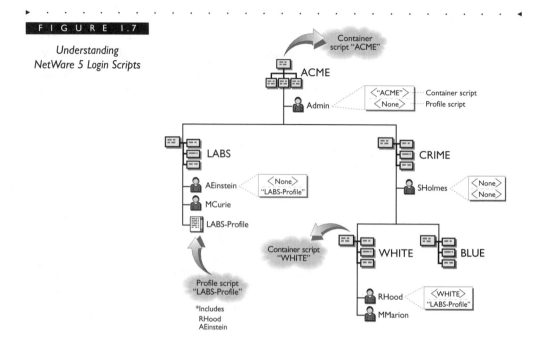

Welcome In!

Congratulations! You've made it into the network.

Now what?

The first thing you should do once you gain access to the NDS tree is "browse." NWAdmin32 (also known as NetWare Administrator 32) is a Windows-based tool that allows you to graphically manage objects and properties in the NDS tree. You can also browse the tree by clicking on specific container objects and expanding their contents. Then, detailed resource information is just a double-click away.

With this utility, you can view, create, move, delete, and assign rights to any object in the NDS tree. Of course, you can only mess around with the objects for which you have access rights. You may restrict access to NWAdmin32 by moving it from SYS:PUBLIC into another, more restricted subdirectory (such as SYS:SYSTEM). Everyday users don't need access to this powerful tree-browsing utility.

If you want to manage the NDS tree, you must load the Novell Client. Once you've done so, you can perform any of the following functions with NWAdmin32:

▶ Create and delete objects (such as users and groups)

▶ Assign rights to the NDS tree and file system

▶ Set up NDPS print services

▶ Set up and manage NDS partitions and replicas

▶ Browse object and property information throughout the tree

▶ Move and rename NDS objects

▶ Set up licensing services

NWAdmin32 runs as a multiple-document interface application. That means you can display up to nine different browsing windows at one time. The primary window is shown in Figure 1.8. It provides a background for viewing one or more secondary windows.

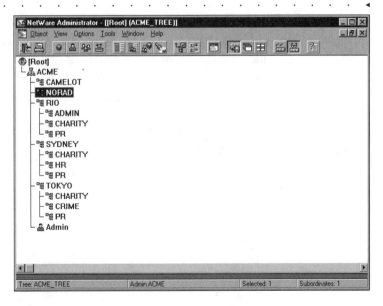

FIGURE 1.8

Browsing the ACME Tree with NetWare Administrator

That completes our brief romp through NetWare 5 connectivity. As you can see, this is a very important part of your life as a CNA. After all, the network is pretty useless without workstations, servers, and connectivity. Fortunately, NetWare 5 offers numerous tools to make these management tasks a breeze.

Now, let's expand beyond the NDS tree, beyond simple login utilities, into the realm of physical network resources. Let's explore the *other* NetWare 5 directory tree.

For more information about NetWare 5 Connectivity, refer to Chapter 3.

TIP

NetWare 5 File System

Just when you thought you had NetWare 5 and NDS figured out, a little voice inside your head whispers, "*there is another . . .*"

Another what? Listen more closely, "*. . . directory structure.*"

Another directory structure? How can that be? You may think that there's only one NetWare directory structure, and it's the foundation of NDS. Well, that's where you're wrong. If you look closely at Figure 1.9, you'll see *two* directory trees — one above the server, and one below it.

The directory structure above the NetWare 5 server is NDS. It organizes network resources into a logical WAN hierarchy. The directory structure below the server is the file system. It organizes network data files into a functional application hierarchy. Pretty simple, huh? The important thing is to separate the two in your mind. NDS handles resource data, and the file system handles application data.

The NetWare 5 file system includes a powerful new high-performance file storage and access technology known as Novell Storage Services (NSS). In this section, we're going to preview three aspects of the new NetWare 5 file system:

▶ NSS Overview

▶ NSS Architecture

▶ NSS Setup

FIGURE 1.9

*The two NetWare 5
Directory Trees*

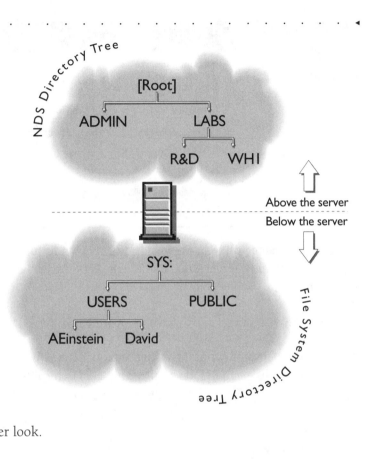

Let's take a closer look.

NSS Overview

NSS is an optional file system that operates independently, yet is fully compatible with, the default NetWare file system. As you can see in Table 1.1, NSS was developed to meet the anticipated storage needs of the next decade. In the table, we compare the key NSS improvements over NetWare 5's traditional, default file system. Take a quick look.

T A B L E I.I	SPECIFICATION	TRADITIONAL FILE SYSTEM	NSS FILE SYSTEM
Comparing NetWare 5's Two File Systems: Traditional Versus NSS	Maximum file size	2GB	8TB
	Maximum volume size	32TB	8 exabytes
	Directory entries	16 million	Trillions
	Volume mounting performance	Several minutes	Several seconds
	Partitions per disk	One	Four
	Volumes per partition	Eight	Unlimited
	CD-ROM support	Additional drivers	Integrated

Unfortunately, there's a downside to this wonderful story. With all its power, NSS cannot fully replace the traditional NetWare 5 file system. Here are a few reasons why:

▶ NSS cannot currently create its own SYS: volume.

▶ NSS does not support the Transactional Tracking System (TTS), software-based disk striping, disk mirroring, Hierarchical Storage Management (HSM), and/or Real Time Data Management (RTDM).

▶ NSS does not support file compression, user restrictions, auditing, or FTP services.

▶ NSS does not support VREPAIR (it uses REBUILD and VERIFY instead).

Many of these limitations will be addressed by future versions of NSS. Despite these current limitations, you may want to create one or more NSS volumes on your NetWare 5 server to gain the advantage of high storage capacities and increased performance.

TIP

While CD-ROMs are automatically loaded as NSS volumes, they are not automatically added to the NDS tree. CD-ROM volumes can be easily created as Volume objects in the NDS tree. Use NetWare Administrator.

NSS Architecture

NSS was designed to make use of the most storage space regardless of its location. To accomplish this, Novell has added an additional abstraction layer to file management. Here's how it works:

▶ *Provider* — An NSS Provider scans the server's storage devices (such as hard disks and CD-ROM drives) to identify and register usable free space. A server's hard drive may provide free storage space from two different places: from a previously defined NetWare partition (using the NSS File Provider, or NWPRV) or from a non-NetWare IBM-formatted partition (using the NSS Media Manager, or MMPRV).

▶ *Consumer* — The NSS Consumer manages registered free space by creating "deposit objects." Consumers use deposit objects to build logical internal file I/O paths to and from network data. As a CNA, you can organize deposit objects into an NSS Storage Group.

▶ *Storage Group* — An NSS Storage Group is a single object representing all the logical storage space residing on one or more server storage devices. Storage Groups are further divided into NSS volumes. These volumes mount and function as traditional volumes, and offer data to users according to the rules of NSS Providers and Consumers.

Clearly, the NSS Solution is much more complex than your traditional tree-based file system. The good news is that most of this architecture is transparent to CNAs and users. All you have to worry about is when to use NSS and how to set it up.

NSS Setup

NSS setup is much simpler than its architecture would suggest. All you have to do is design the NSS volume by identifying its intended purpose and then create it. The trick is that most NSS Storage Groups and volumes use physical hard disk space. Typically, this space has already been allocated to existing DOS or NetWare 5 partitions. If your server's disk drives are already fully partitioned, you have three options for setting up NSS:

▶ *In Place Upgrade* — You may use the NSS In Place Upgrade utility to convert existing traditional NetWare file system volumes (except SYS:) to NSS.

Do not convert traditional volumes that contain files using features NSS cannot support — such as file compression, TTS-enabled files, and/or disk-mirrored drives.

TIP

▶ *Repartition* — You may repartition your server's hard drive to allow for free space. This free space will become part or all of an NSS Storage Group and NSS volume.

▶ *New install* — You can always install a new hard drive into the server and devote it to NSS.

Once you've decided how to utilize NSS, it's time to get on with the show. To create NSS components, start by loading NSS.NLM. Next, select NSS Providers and Consumers. And, finally, create an NSS Storage Group and volumes.

The NWPRV provider is not available in NWCONFIG unless you use the following syntax while loading NSS: "NSS NWPRV." In addition, you can access the NSS Advanced Configuration utility by using the following syntax: "NSS /MENU."

TIP

That completes our jaunt through NetWare 5's second directory structure — the NSS file system. This strange new tree is very different. But once you get past its rough exterior, you'll see that the non-NDS tree shares the same look and feel as the NDS one. They approach life together with a common purpose — to logically organize user resources, except that this time, the resources are files, not users.

For more information about the NetWare 5 File System, refer to Chapter 4.

TIP

Now that we agree that all our NetWare 5 resources should be organized into two logical trees, it's time to start thinking about security. After all, we don't live in a 1960s Woodstock fantasy any more.

NetWare 5 Security

Security in the Information Age poses a very interesting challenge. Computers and communications have made it possible to collect volumes of data about you and me — from our latest purchase at the five-and-dime to our detailed medical records. Privacy has become a commodity to be exchanged on the open market. Information is no longer the fodder of afternoon talk shows. It has become *the* unit of exchange for the 21ˢᵗ century — more valuable than money.

NetWare 5 improves on earlier NetWare security models by adding supplemental front-end barriers for filtering unauthorized users. Once again, the same security goal applies:

Let the good guys in and keep the bad guys out!

As you can see in Figure 1.10, the NetWare 5 security model consists of five different barriers. They are:

- ▶ *Layer 1* — Login/Password Authentication

- ▶ *Layer 2* — Login Restrictions

- ▶ *Layer 3* — NDS Security

- ▶ *Layer 4* — File System Access Rights

- ▶ *Layer 5* — Directory/File Attributes

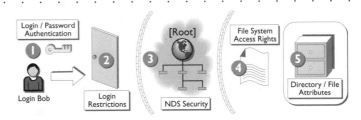

FIGURE 1.10

The NetWare 5 Security Model

As you can see, each layer creates an increasingly strong barrier against user access. Each time you pass through a door, you are greeted with an even stronger barrier. This works much the same way as the opening to the TV show "Get Smart." Maxwell Smart would have to travel through numerous barriers until he finally reached the telephone booth. After entering the correct code, he was allowed access to Control headquarters. Users pass through similar barriers on their way to the ultimate prize — data.

Let's take a quick look.

Layer One — Login/Password Authentication

As you can see from Figure 1.10, it all starts with login/password authentication. Remember, users don't log into NetWare servers anymore — they log into the "Cloud." Or, in the GUI world, the user types in his or her username and password at the Windows 95/NT Login dialog box. First, the user requests access by typing **LOGIN** followed by a valid username. Once this occurs, authentication begins. There are two phases:

▸ *Initialization* — The server and workstation authenticate the session with an encrypted key. You are required to enter a valid password to decrypt the key.

▸ *Background* — NetWare 5 continues to attach the key to all messages to ensure data integrity. This process is known as *background authentication*. In addition, you can enhance background security with a related feature called NCP packet signing. We'll explore both features later in Chapter 5. In addition to authentication, NetWare 5 accepts passwords up to 127 characters. This is a substantial improvement over earlier versions.

Once you have been authenticated, NetWare 5 matches you against a list of global and personal login restrictions. These restrictions allow for conditional access according to a variety of criteria. That's Layer Two.

Layer Two — Login Restrictions

Once you provide a valid login name and password, you are authenticated. Congratulations! NetWare 5 responds with conditional access and NDS rights take over. At this point, I stress the word *conditional* access. Permanent access is made possible by a variety of login restrictions. These login restrictions include:

▸ *Account Restrictions* — These include anything from "Account locked" to "Force periodic password changes".

▸ *Password Restrictions* — These include "Minimum password length" and "Force unique passwords".

▶ *Station Restrictions* — These limit users to specific workstation node IDs.

▶ *Time Restrictions* — These determine when users can and cannot use the system.

▶ *Intruder Detection/Lockout* — This is a global feature that detects incorrect password attempts and locks bad guys out.

Each of these restrictions can be configured by CNAs using NetWare Administrator — a GUI NDS management tool. We'll learn all the details of how and why later in Chapter 5.

Layer Three — NDS Security

Once you enter the "Cloud," your ability to access leaf and container objects is determined by a sophisticated NDS security structure. At the heart of NDS security is the Access Control List (ACL). The ACL is a property of every NDS object. It defines who can access the object (trustees) and what each trustee can do (rights). The ACL is divided into two types of rights:

▶ *Object Rights* — Defines an object's trustees and controls what the trustees can do with the object.

▶ *Property Rights* — Limits the trustees' access to only specific properties of the object.

Here's a great example (see Figure 1.11). Let's say the Group object Admin-Group has rights to the User object LEIA. Admin-Group has the Browse object right, which means that any member of the group can see LEIA and view information about her. But LEIA is shy. She wants to limit what the group can see (reasonable enough). She only wants them to see her last name, postal address, and telephone number. So, LEIA limits the group's rights by assigning the Read property right to only these three properties: Last Name, Postal Address, and Telephone Number. Very cool.

Object and property rights are designed to provide efficient access to NDS objects without making it an administrative nightmare. You be the judge. Users can acquire object rights in a variety of ways, including trustee assignment, inheritance, and security equivalence. Property rights, on the other hand, are a bit trickier. Global property rights can be inherited, but rights to specific properties must be granted through a trustee assignment or inherited using the [I] Inheritable right.

▶ . . . . ◀

Understanding NDS Security

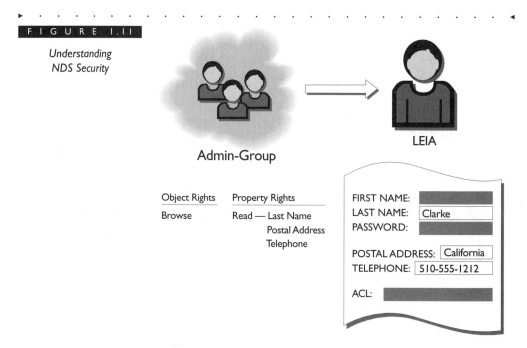

Here's a quick preview of NDS rights assignments:

▶ *Trustee Assignments* — These occur when an object is given explicit access to any other object or its properties. These trustee assignments are administered by adding the user to a host object's ACL property. This is accomplished using NetWare Administrator.

▶ *Inheritance* — This is a little simpler. If rights are granted at the container level, they are inherited by all container and leaf objects within (as long as the [I] Inheritable right is present). This means that rights assigned to the [Root] object, for example, are inherited by every object in the NDS tree. Be very careful. Fortunately, NetWare 5 includes an Inherited Rights Filter (IRF), which can be used to block inherited rights.

> *Security equivalence* — Objects can absorb rights by being associated with other objects. Sometimes the associations are obvious, but most of the time, they're not. For this reason, you should only use security equivalences for temporary assignments, or not at all. In reality, users can inherit rights ancestrally from containers, groups, organizational roles, and [Public].

Regardless of how you acquire object and property rights, the concept of effective rights still applies. This means the actual rights you can exercise with a given object are the combination of explicit trustee assignments, inheritance, and the IRF. The mathematical product of this mess is known as *effective NDS rights* — "modern math." And that effectively ends our discussion of NDS security and moves us on to Layer Four of the NetWare 5 security model — file system access rights.

Layer Four — File System Access Rights

Well, here we are. Congratulations! You've finally made it to NetWare 5 Nirvana. You've passed through three very difficult barriers of network armor and the search is over — your files await you. Ah, but not so fast! Before you can access any files on the NetWare 5 server, you must have the appropriate file system access rights. Once again, another barrier pops up to bite you. Following is a list of the eight rights that control access to NetWare 5 files (they almost spell a word):

> *W* — Write: Grants the right to open and change the contents of files.

> (O) — Doesn't exist but is needed to spell a word.

> *R* — Read: Grants the right to open files in the directory and read their contents (or run applications).

> *M* — Modify: Grants the right to change the attributes or name of a file or directory.

> *F* — File Scan: Grants the right to see files and directories.

> *A* — Access Control: Grants the right to change trustee assignments and IRFs.

> *C* — Create: Grants the right to create new files and subdirectories.

▸ *E*—Erase: Grants the right to delete a directory, its files, and subdirectories.

▸ *S*—Supervisor: Grants all rights to a directory and the files and subdirectories below. This right cannot be blocked by the IRF.

Holy anatomical nematodes, Batman! That spells "WoRMFACES." It's not a pretty sight, but certainly a name you will not forget. NetWare 5 file system access rights are administered in much the same way as NDS object rights. They are granted with the help of trustee assignments, inheritance, and ancestral inheritance. In addition, file system rights are subject to the same rules as NDS effective rights. All in all, NDS and file server security parallel one another—one operating in the clouds (NDS) and one with its feet firmly planted on the ground (file system).

Well, that completes the majority of the NetWare 5 security model. There's only one layer left, and it is seldom used—directory/file attributes. Let's take a closer look.

Layer Five—Directory/File Attributes

Directory and file attributes provide the final and most sophisticated layer of the NetWare 5 security model. These attributes are rarely used, but provide a powerful tool for specific security solutions. If all else fails, you can always turn to attribute security to save the day.

NetWare 5 supports three different types of attributes:

▸ *Security Attributes*—The main attribute category. Some attributes apply to both directories and files.

▸ *Feature Attributes*—Applies to three key features: backup, purging, and the Transactional Tracking System (TTS).

▸ *Disk Management Attributes*—For file compression, data migration, and block suballocation.

Well, there you have it. That's a brief snapshot of NetWare 5's five-layered security model. As a CNA, it's your job to identify network threats and implement appropriate security countermeasures to eliminate them. This isn't easy. You have many factors working against you—including money, office politics, and user productivity. Fortunately, NetWare 5 has a dramatically improved security model for creating and maintaining your impenetrable network armor.

For more information about NetWare 5 Security, refer to Chapter 5.

TIP

Now, let's continue our journey through Novell's Global Electronic Village by exploring one of its most fascinating cyber-cities—Z.E.N.works—otherwise known as the "Zen" of NetWare 5. Stay tuned.

NetWare 5 Workstation Management with Z.E.N.works

First stop—*Z.E.N.works!*

Unlike its name implies, Z.E.N.works has little to do with ancient meditation and wisdom. In actuality, it's a clever acronym for "Zero Effort Networks." While it's impossible to achieve "zero effort" networking, Z.E.N.works does greatly improve the manageability of user access to the Infobahn. Think of it as a highly evolved on-ramp to the information superhighway.

Z.E.N.works is a desktop management tool that reduces the hassle of connecting PCs to small, medium, and large networks. Z.E.N.works leverages NDS to help CNAs manage Windows-based desktops by providing policy-enabled software distribution, desktop management, and workstation maintenance. The beauty of Z.E.N.works is it allows you to achieve all these things without having to visit the user's workstation—no more late night flights to Timbuktu. Darn!

So, how does it do it? Z.E.N.works extends the NDS schema to include workstation objects. These objects allow you to configure and control workstations from within the NDS tree. Then, each time a user logs into the network, Z.E.N.works registers the workstation with NDS. This event can even be calculated. Cool! Once a workstation has been registered, you can configure and control it remotely. This includes tasks such as upgrading software, repairing workstation software problems, and gathering inventory information.

NetWare 5 ships with a "Z.E.N.works Starter Pack." During a typical NetWare 5 installation, a subset of the Z.E.N.works functionality is installed by default. You can install the full Z.E.N.works product from the separate *Z.E.N.works* CD-ROM— which is purchased separately. The automated installation integrates all the features of Z.E.N.works into NetWare 5. To use Z.E.N.works, you must accomplish two tasks: first, install Z.E.N.works components on the server, and second, upgrade the Novell client on each workstation.

Once the kingdom of Z.E.N.works has been installed, you can take full advantage of its three separate realms:

- ▸ *Realm 1:* Workstation Maintenance

- ▸ *Realm 2:* Desktop Management

- ▸ *Realm 3:* Application Management

Let's take a quick look at these three realms and learn what it takes to become king or queen of your Z.E.N.works cyber-kingdom.

Realm 1: Workstation Maintenance

The first realm of Z.E.N.works is the largest. Workstation Maintenance encompasses all the CNA tasks associated with daily user productivity. In this realm, you'll use three NetWare 5 workstation tools: Novell Workstation Manager, NetWare Administrator, and the Novell Help Requester.

Here's what you have to look forward to in the realm of Z.E.N.works Workstation Maintenance:

- ▸ *Policies* — Z.E.N.works includes various *Policy Packages,* which are NDS objects you create to help you maintain workstation objects in the NDS tree. Each package is a collection of *Policies* that allow you to set up parameters for managing workstations, users, groups, or containers. For example, the Policies found in the workstation package help you set up controls that apply to Windows workstations on your network — including printers, desktop configurations, Remote Access Server (RAS), remote control, and login restrictions. Refer to Figure 1.12 for a list of the Policies found in the WIN95 Workstation Package object.

- ▸ *NDS registration* — Workstations must be registered with NDS before they can be imported into the tree and managed as other NDS objects. Z.E.N.works includes a Workstation Registration agent that automatically registers workstations as long as two conditions have been met: the workstation has been updated to the Novell Client for Z.E.N.works and the workstation has been used to log into the network at least once. Once this happens, the agent sends the workstation's address to NDS and places it in a holding tank— NDS registration list. Once a workstation appears in the list, it can then be imported into the NDS tree. As a CNA, you can use one of three methods for automating the workstation registration agent: Novell Application Launcher (NAL), Z.E.N.works Scheduler, or a customized login script.

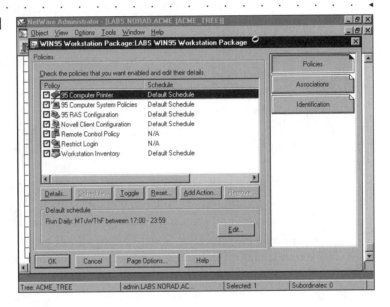

FIGURE I.12

WIN95 Workstation Policy Package in NetWare Administrator

▶ *Remote control* — Once Z.E.N.works has been installed and workstations have been registered with NDS, you can establish remote control access to them by distributing the appropriate User Agents. User Agents allow you to connect and manage workstations using the remote control facility within NetWare Administrator. As a CNA, you have two options for automatically distributing User Agents to Windows 3.x, Windows 95, and/or Windows NT workstations: Terminate-and-stay-resident (TSR) applications or application objects via NAL. Regardless of the distribution scheme you choose, make sure that users have the appropriate NDS and file system rights to accept remote control instructions.

▶ *Novell Help Requester* — The Help Requester utility allows users to notify the help desk or Network Administrator of workstation problems via e-mail or phone. The application provides pertinent information about the user and workstation involved, such as the user's context and the workstation ID. Using NAL, you can push the Help Requester application to all user workstations. When the Application Launcher window opens on a user's desktop, the Help Requester icon appears as a selection. Users can then be instructed to use this utility whenever a problem occurs.

As you can see, Z.E.N.works offers myriad benefits for workstation maintenance in the virtual age. Now let's cruise over to the user desktop and see what it does for them.

Realm 2: Desktop Management

In addition to CNA maintenance, Z.E.N.works offers numerous benefits to the user. This desktop management functionality falls into three different areas:

▶ *Customizing applications* — You can customize the user desktop by enabling two specific Z.E.N.works policies: the User System Policy (in the User Policy Package) and the Computer System Policy (in the Workstation Policy Package). The User System Policy allows you to customize the desktop functions available to specific users. For example, hiding applications such as Network Neighborhood, Run, and Find can help reduce access problems and server traffic. Similarly, the Computer System Policy allows you to customize the Windows properties of a specific workstation. For example, you can use the Properties button to launch a utility that allows you to identify applications that should run when the workstation connects to the network.

▶ *Printing configuration* — One of the most costly and time-consuming aspects of CNA management is printing configuration. Fortunately Z.E.N.works provides a solution that allows you to configure a user's printing environment through NDS. You can even automatically load the correct print driver for a user when the user logs in.

▶ *User profiles* — Desktop settings such as Wallpaper, Screen Saver, and Sounds can be standardized and deployed to every user in the enterprise.

These settings can even be configured so that users cannot modify them. As a matter of fact, most of the normal user-defined preferences set in the Windows Control Panel can be configured using the Desktop Preference Policy in the User Policy Package. Very cool!

If you get the feeling from this discussion that "Big Brother" is watching . . . you're not far off. Z.E.N.works Desktop Management allows Big Brother to tightly control user access and productivity. The good news is *you* are Big Brother!

Now let's complete our brief journey through the kingdom of Z.E.N.works by exploring the final realm—Application Management.

Realm 3: Application Management

Z.E.N.works includes a special version of the NAL that lets you distribute network-based applications to users' workstations and manage them as objects in the NDS tree. Users then access the applications assigned to them using the Application Launcher Window or Application Explorer.

In addition, NAL implements solutions such as fault tolerance and load balancing to guarantee users always have access to the applications they need. Furthermore, if the user deletes application ".DLL" files from his or her hard disk, NAL automatically detects the missing files and restores them when the user attempts to launch the application.

So, what can NAL do for you? Here's a list:

▸ NAL provides multilevel folders to hierarchically order application objects in the NDS tree.

▸ NAL automatically grants file rights to users so they can access the applications assigned to them.

▸ NAL automatically grants NT Supervisor rights to the Admin user so that Admin can handle the Registry settings in Windows NT that require Supervisor rights.

▸ NAL provides an application-suspension configuration to allow you to schedule a time when application access will terminate.

▶ NAL provides the snAppShot utility, which can be used to capture a workstation's configuration before and after an application is installed.

▶ NAL is your friend. It increases user productivity and decreases CNA headaches. Whatever you do, don't miss the benefits offered by Z.E.N.works Realm 3.

That completes our brief romp through the Z.E.N.works kingdom. As you can see, this is a powerfully comprehensive tool for workstation maintenance, management, and control. As a CNA, you should quickly become the king or queen of your Z.E.N.works kingdom. Remember, workstation management is typically a war between user desires and centralized standardization. Whatever you do, don't let your virtual villagers run amuck.

Now let's continue our journey through the seven NetWare 5 CNA features with NDPS printing.

For more information about NetWare 5 Workstation Management with Z.E.N.works, refer to Chapter 6.

TIP

NetWare 5 NDPS

The next stop on our tour down the NetWare 5 information superhighway is printing. NetWare 5 includes a revolution in network printing—Novell Distributed Print Services (NDPS). NDPS is the next-generation NetWare printing service designed to replace queue-based systems. NDPS is the result of a joint development effort by Novell, Hewlett-Packard, and Xerox. With NDPS, network-based printers are independent of servers and printing attributes such as forms and banners are available to every defined printer and user on the network. It sounds better already.

NDPS Printing Features

Here's a quick list of the major improvements offered by NetWare 5 NDPS:

▶ *Plug and print*—Once you set up NDPS, you can plug a printer into the network and it becomes immediately available to all users. This is accomplished using automatic hardware detection.

▶ *Automatic print driver download and installation* — NDPS allows you to select common printer drivers you want to automatically download and install to each workstation.

▶ *Bidirectional feedback* — Clients and administrators can obtain real-time information, such as printer availability, print job properties, the number of copies being printed, job hold, and job completion notification. All this information is displayed using graphical pop-up windows.

▶ *NDS integration* — NDPS offers increased security and easier management via NDS. CNAs can administer all printing devices from a single location.

▶ *Configurable event notification* — NDPS allows you to specify which users, operators, and administrators receive which types of notification.

▶ *Multiple printer configurations* — You can set up a printer with two specific configurations. For example, you might allow all users in a department to print to a color printer using only the black-and-white capabilities, but allow only two or three individuals to use the color capabilities.

▶ *Network traffic reduction* — NDPS turns off Service Advertising Protocol (SAP) and communicates directly with printers.

▶ *Print job scheduling* — NDPS offers much more flexibility in the area of configuring print job scheduling options. For example, you can schedule a job based on the time of day or job size.

▶ *Enhanced client support* — NDPS offers improved functionality for Windows 3.*x*, Windows 95, and Windows NT workstations.

▶ *Backward compatibility* — NDPS clients can still print through the Legacy system, and non-NDPS clients can print through a queue to NDPS-aware printers.

NDPS Printing Architecture

So, how does all this fancy printing work? Check out Figure 1.13. As you can see, NDPS consists of three support components surrounding the heart of printing — the Printer Agent. Let's take a closer look.

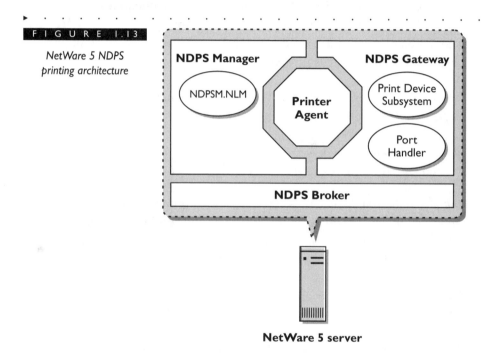

FIGURE 1.13

*NetWare 5 NDPS
printing architecture*

NetWare 5 server

▶ *Printer Agent* — This is the heart of NetWare 5 NDPS printing. Before a printer can be incorporated into NDPS, it must be represented by a Printer Agent. For simplicity's sake, a Printer Agent has a one-to-one relationship with a printer. The Printer Agent combines the functions previously performed by a printer, print queue, print server, and spooler into one intelligent simplified entity. An NDPS Printer Agent can exist in one of three different forms: a server-based software entity representing a computer-based printer (attached to a server or workstation), a server-based software entity representing a network-attached printer, and/or a firmware entity embedded within a network-attached printer.

▶ *NDPS Manager* — The NDPS Manager is a logical entity used to create and manage Printer Agents. It is represented as an object in the NDS tree and an NLM called NDPSM.NLM. You must create an NDPS Manager before creating Printer Agents. A single Manager can control an unlimited number of Agents. The NDPS Manager object stores information used by NDPSM.NLM. This module is automatically loaded when you create a Printer Agent with NetWare Administrator.

▶ *Gateway* — NDPS Gateways allow you to support *unusual* printing environments. "Unusual" printing environments include non-NDPS-aware printers (such as UNIX, Macintosh, queue-based, and/or mainframe systems) and print systems that require jobs to be placed in queues. NDPS currently supports two Gateways: the Novell Gateway and Third-Party Gateways. The Novell Gateway consists of a Print Device Subsystem (PDS) and a Port Handler (PH) component (see the next two bullets). It supports local and remote printers including those using NPRINTER or queues. Similarly, Third-Party Gateways perform the same types of tasks, but are customized by printer manufacturers to support their network-attached printers.

▶ *Print Device Subsystem (PDS)* — The PDS is an NLM that loads when a Printer Agent is created using the PDS configuration utility. The PDS retrieves printer-specific information (such as the make and model of the printer) and stores this information in a central database. As a CNA, you'll need to use the PDS utility when you create a Printer Agent for either of the following: a printer that is not connected directly to the network, *or* a printer that is connected directly to the network, but whose manufacturer does not a provide a proprietary NDS Gateway, *or* a printer running in PSERVER mode. PDS is a critical subunit of the Novell Gateway.

▶ *Port Handler (PH)* — The Port Handler ensures that the PDS can communicate with the physical printer, regardless of what type of interface is used. The NDPS Port Handler supports parallel ports, serial ports, the Queue Management System (QMS) protocol, or remote/network printer protocol. PH is a critical subunit of the Novell Gateway.

► *NDPS Broker* — When NDPS is installed, the installation utility ensures that a broker object is loaded on your network and provides three network support services not previously available in NetWare. Although these services are invisible, you must be aware of them in case the Broker decides to take a vacation. The three NDPS support services are: Service Registry Services (SRS), Event Notification Services (ENS), and Resource Management Services (RMS). SRS allows public-access printers to advertise themselves so they can be discovered or located by CNAs or users. ENS allows printers to send customized notifications to users and operators about printer events, and print job status. RMS allows resources to be installed and accessed in a central location, and then downloaded to clients, printers, or other network entities that need them.

That completes our discussion of NetWare 5 NDPS printing services. Printing has always been and will continue to be one of your greatest challenges as a network administrator. Fortunately, the revolution is upon us. I hope you're as impressed as I am about the improvements Novell has made in the much-troubled arena of NetWare printing.

TIP

For more information about NetWare 5 NDPS, refer to Chapter 7.

NetWare 5 Installation

If you build it, they will come!

At least that's what should happen when you experience Novell's dramatically improved installation procedure. The new install for NetWare 5 was developed using Novell's revolutionary installation architecture called *Novell Installation Services* (NIS). The new install is a Java-based, data-driven object design that will be used for all Novell products in the future.

In addition to NIS, the NetWare 5 installation process introduces *Novell Licensing Services* (NLS), which is a single utility that can be used to license all present and future NetWare products. NLS accomplishes this by tightly integrating with NDS and enabling administrators to monitor and control the use of licensed applications over the network. NLS also provides a basic license metering tool, as well as libraries that export licensing service functionality to developers of other licensing systems. This is all accomplished at the GUI workstation using NLSMAN32.EXE.

You can use the NetWare 5 installation program to create a fresh new Novell server from scratch. NetWare 5 supports both IPX and IP protocols, and automatically detects network and hard disk drivers. During the installation process, you will use a Java-based GUI interface (Installation Wizard). Check out the GUI Install option in Figure 1.14. In addition, if you have several servers with the same hardware configuration, NetWare 5 Batch support allows you to install a single server and then use the same profile to install the other servers. Very cool.

*NetWare 5 GUI
Installation Wizard*

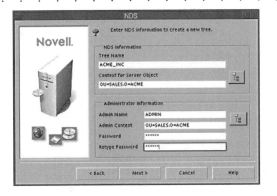

Once the NetWare 5 server is brought to life, you'll notice a few dramatic improvements at the console. The NetWare 5 server console can appear in a GUI environment. Its appearance and operation is similar to the X-Windows windowing environment found on UNIX platforms. The GUI server environment improves installation processes, Java integration, and other server-based management tasks. To use the server GUI console, you must have a VGA-compatible (or higher) video adapter board and monitor. In addition, you'll need a mouse for bouncing around the screen (although you can use a keyboard if you'd like).

The NetWare 5 GUI-based server environment requires additional RAM. Novell does not recommend running the GUI environment on servers with less than 64MB of RAM. We recommend at least 128MB
TIP **of server RAM. It's better to be safe than sorry.**

Whether you're using a GUI- or text-based server environment, NetWare 5 offers a variety of improved console commands. Check them out in Table 1.2. Keep in mind that the legacy commands are retained during an upgrade, but not copied during a fresh NetWare 5 install.

TABLE 1.2	LEGACY CONSOLE COMMAND	NETWARE 5 CONSOLE COMMAND	DESCRIPTION
Improved NetWare 5 Console Commands	INSTALL	NWCONFIG	The old installation program has been replaced with a GUI NWCONFIG command.
	SET	SET	SET commands entered at the console are remembered when you restart the server.
	LOAD	LOAD	LOAD is now optional.
	MONITOR	SCRNSAVER	SCRNSAVER secures the server console with a password. This replaces the "WORM" functionality of MONITOR.NLM. This does not imply that MONITOR.NLM has been replaced, just its screen-saving functionality.
	DOWN and RESTART SERVER	RESTART SERVER	RESTART SERVER combines the previous two-step DOWN and RESTART SERVER process. This simply restarts the NetWare 5 server.
	DOWN and EXIT	DOWN	DOWN replaces the previous two-step DOWN and EXIT process. This unloads all server NLMs, disconnects the server from the LAN, and exits to the DOS partition.
	SERVMAN	MONITOR	MONITOR now provides the functions previously performed by SERVMAN. That is, it allows CNAs to optimize and manage the server from a single menu-based utility.
	(None)	RESET SERVER	RESET SERVER performs a warm boot of the server.

Congratulations . . . you've built a NetWare 5 server. This is your sports car for exploring the Global Electronic Village.

Vro-o-o-o-m!

For more information about NetWare 5 Installation, check out Chapter 8.

TIP

STOP!

That concludes our initial tour down Novell's newest information superhighway. As you can see, NetWare 5 is a powerful tool for saving the world and building a smaller Global Electronic Village. This section focused on the seven main features required for NetWare 5's CNA certification.

In summary, they are:

▶ Novell Directory Services (see Chapter 2 for more information)

▶ NetWare 5 Connectivity (see Chapter 3 for more information)

▶ NetWare 5 File System (see Chapter 4 for more information)

▶ NetWare 5 Security (see Chapter 5 for more information)

▶ NetWare 5 Workstation Management with Z.E.N.works (see Chapter 6 for more information)

▶ NetWare 5 NDPS (see Chapter 7 for more information)

▶ NetWare 5 Installation (see Chapter 8 for more information)

But the Infobahn doesn't stop there. Now we're going to cross a bridge and explore a neighboring cyber-world where NetWare 5 offers a GUI console, Pure IP, Web surfing, and a dramatically improved application server. In short, let's extend beyond the CNA realm and surf the rest of Novell's information superhighway — also known as the NetWare 5 CNE Features.

NetWare 5 CNE Features

If NetWare 5 is going to help ACME build a Global Electronic Village, then we can't ignore *Life as a CNE*. The NetWare 5 CNE Features comprise all the cool advanced technologies that enhance the administrative features we've just discovered. As with any great adventure, the primary players are only as good as their advanced teachers.

Whether you're a continuing CNA or just want to surf the Web with NetWare 5, you'll need to become intimately familiar with the following five CNE solutions. Furthermore, in *Novell's CNE Study Guide for NetWare 5,* you'll explore these technologies and more in great detail. This is the foundation of Novell Course 570 — *NetWare 5 Advanced Administration.* Here's a brief peek:

▸ *NetWare 5 Upgrade and Migration* — We'll start at the beginning. NetWare 5's upgrade and migration procedure has been dramatically improved. It includes a GUI interface, Upgrade Wizard, improved licensing and on-the-fly driver support (via HotPlug PCI and automatic hardware detection).

▸ *NetWare 5 Java Console* — Java supercharges the Infobahn. NetWare 5 includes native support for Java through Java Virtual Machine (JVM), ConsoleOne, and a new Open Solutions Architecture (OSA) initiative. There's nothing like a GUI server.

▸ *NetWare 5 IP Services* — Welcome to *pure* IP! IP is the pavement of NetWare 5's information superhighway (which I call the *Infobahn*). The new Infobahn supports Domain Name Service/Dynamic Host Configuration Protocol (DNS/DHCP) services, IPX compatibility, Service Location Protocol (SLP), and a migration gateway for Internet Protocol/Internetwork Packet Exchange (IP/IPX) interconnectivity.

▸ *Netscape FastTrack Server for NetWare* — Welcome to *Web Surfing 101*! The FastTrack Server allows you to build your own virtual city on the information superhighway. It's fast, full-featured, efficient, and instantaneously global. "Hello, world."

▶ *NetWare 5 Application Server* — To top it all off, Novell has made significant improvements to the speed and reliability of the NetWare 5 core OS. In addition to supporting Java, the NetWare 5 server supports another industry standard, Common Object Request Broker Architecture (CORBA), which enables Internet and intranet users to share objects (such as data and applications) regardless of the platform. To support Java, CORBA, and other open-system applications, Novell has added a multiprocessing kernel, HotPlug PCI, a new I/O technology, better memory management, a new integrated backup engine, and a five-user version of Oracle8 for NetWare. Now, who has the hottest application server in town?

Just when you thought NetWare 5 couldn't get any better, we're going to throw five more mind-boggling features at you. So, without any further ado, let's get on with the show.

NetWare 5 Upgrade and Migration

If you upgrade it, they will come!

NetWare 5 offers three choices for building a modern Global Electronic Village: Installation, Upgrade, and/or Migration. So, which option is for you? Your choice depends on a number of factors — such as the operating system you're currently running, the hardware you have, and which NetWare 5 features you plan to use (such as block size, blocks of allocation, compression, and so on).

The *Installation* process, for example, assumes that you're starting with a "neoteric" server — no users, no files, no communications. The *Upgrade* and *Migration* methods, on the other hand, jump in midstream. Using these options, you will upgrade or migrate an existing server from NetWare 2, NetWare 3, or NetWare 4, all the way to NetWare 5. Keep in mind that the NetWare 5 Upgrade and Migration processes are not "upgrades" in the traditional sense. From coach to first class is an upgrade; Windows 98 is an upgrade; better carpeting is an upgrade. NetWare 5 is a "New Frontier."

Here's a quick look at NetWare 5's new frontier of upgrade and migration:

▶ *Upgrade* — You can also install NetWare 5 on the same machine without losing any existing files. This type of upgrade is called an *In-Place Upgrade*. You can upgrade to NetWare 5 from any of the following previous versions:

NetWare 3.1*x*, NetWare 4.*x*, NetWare 5 or NetWare for Small Business. To begin the upgrade process, simply execute INSTALL.BAT at the server console and choose Upgrade an Existing Server in the first text screen.

▶ *Migration* — NetWare 5 also includes an elaborate migration utility ironically called *Novell Upgrade Wizard* (see Figure 1.15). This GUI migration tool allows you to upgrade NetWare 3 network servers Across-the-Wire to NetWare 5. It will migrate NetWare 3 bindery and volume contents from anywhere on the LAN/WAN. In addition, the Novell Upgrade Wizard will upgrade NetWare 3 printers and queues, has a powerful verification process that pinpoints potential conflicts or errors that may occur, and provides options for resolving those problems before the migration begins. Finally, this is all accomplished using a simple drag-and-drop modeling interface. Your life as a CNA just got a whole lot easier.

FIGURE 1.15

Novell Upgrade Wizard

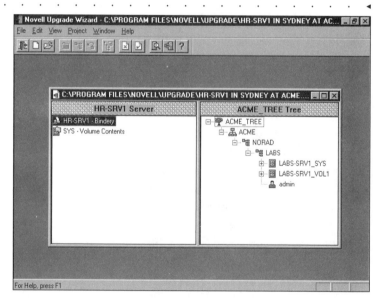

Let's take a closer look.

NetWare 5 Upgrade

I have good news and I have bad news:

▸ *Good News* — The NetWare 5 upgrade process closely resembles the 14 Installation steps we'll cover in Chapter 8.

▸ *Bad News* — The NetWare 5 upgrade process occurs on an *existing* Novell server with all of its bindery/NDS information, shared data, and internal problems.

Fortunately, CNE mechanics are trained to handle the ups and downs of NetWare 5 upgrade (this is not for CNAs). The *in-place* nature of NetWare 5's Upgrade process is both a benefit and a curse. It's a benefit in that it allows you to move existing bindery/NDS and user files to NetWare 5 on the same machine. It's a curse in that it provides limited recovery if (or when) something goes wrong.

The NetWare 5 Upgrade is accomplished in four stages:

▸ *Stage 1*: Getting Started

▸ *Stage 2*: C-Worthy input screens

▸ *Stage 3*: GUI input screens

▸ *Stage 4*: Customization

It all starts in *Stage 1*, where you perform pre-Upgrade tasks and run INSTALL.BAT. Then, in *Stage 2*, you get to attack the text-mode portion of the Upgrade process, including choosing the type of upgrade, selecting regional settings, modifying selected drivers, and mounting the SYS: volume.

Once you've built the foundation frame of your server, it's time to plug in the key functional components. Next, in *Stage 3*, you will build on the text-based platform with some fancy GUI-mode tasks, including loading the Java Virtual Machine (JVM), selecting networking protocols, choosing the server time zone, updating NDS, and installing NLS. Finally, in *Stage 4*, you will finish the Upgrade process by selecting additional products and services, customizing server parameters, and performing post-upgrade tasks — but only if you want to!

The good news is the Upgrade and Installation programs are very closely related—nearly identical twins. This means you will have a big head start as a NetWare 5 CNA.

NetWare 5 Migration

NetWare 5 Migration is the ultimate achievement in "nerdiness." It's probably the most popular installation method for NetWare 5. After all, there are already 5.7 million NetWare servers out there—and no one wants to start from scratch. With migration, existing CNEs can simply transfer bindery/NDS information to the new NetWare 5 Global Electronic Village. The beauty of this system is that they don't have to repopulate it.

The NetWare 5 Migration uses an across-the-wire method for transferring bindery/NDS information and data from one server to another across the LAN. It requires three machines:

▸ A server running NetWare 3.1*x*

▸ A server running NetWare 5

▸ A Windows 95 or Windows NT workstation running the appropriate Novell Client

The NetWare 5 Migration method is the safest upgrade/migration option because the source server remains intact—also known as an "escape pod." You can also use it to migrate all or selected information (which is particularly useful when dealing with a NetWare 3 bindery). Furthermore, this multi-faceted migration option allows you to consolidate multiple source servers to a single NetWare 5 machine.

So, how does it work? Good question. All this fancy across-the-wire footwork is made possible by the Novell Upgrade Wizard—which ironically has nothing to do with the Upgrade process. Here's a quick overview of the NetWare 5 Migration steps you'll learn when you become a CNE:

▸ *Step 1:* Getting Started

▸ *Step 2:* Create a Migration Project

▸ *Step 3:* Implement the Migration Project

▸ *Step 4:* Perform Across-the-Wire Migration

▸ *Step 5:* Migration Cleanup

In *Step 1*, you jump-start the migration process by preparing the source/target servers and installing the Novell Upgrade Wizard. Then, in *Steps 2 and 3*, you can create and implement your Migration Project. The Migration Project is a Microsoft Access Database file (.MDB) that stores your migration configuration settings. In *Step 4*, you will actually perform the across-the-wire migration using the data you configured in the Migration Project database. Finally, the migration ends with some simple housekeeping cleanup chores in *Step 5*.

That's all there is to it. When you become a CNE, you'll be able to install, upgrade *and* migrate servers anywhere in the world. This is a good thing, because ACME spans the globe. Now let's cruise the new world-wide Infobahn with a *supercharged* Java server.

Ready, set, burn rubber.

TIP

> **For more information about NetWare 5 Upgrade and Migration, check out *Novell's CNE Study Guide for NetWare 5*.**

NetWare 5 Java Console

In the previous section, we began our CNE journey by building the NetWare 5 supercar — that's your first CNE responsibility. During this early phase, we breathed life into a cold, hard heap of silicon. Now all we have to do is turn the key.

"Start your engines!"

Consider the NetWare 5 server started. It's a comfortable feeling knowing the server came up smoothly — seeing the familiar "WORM" prancing around the screen, hearing the constant hum of the NetWare NIC, and following the NetWare 5 packets as they bounce merrily along the information superhighway. A successful server startup is one of your most rewarding experiences. Now that the NetWare 5 server is up and running, let's shift our focus from "starting it" to "supercharging" it.

In the past, CNAs and CNEs typically interacted with the server using text-based applications, such as MONITOR.NLM. That was then . . . this is now!

Welcome to the world of Java. Java represents a quantum leap in server modularity. It's an exciting new application-building tool that allows developers to create truly portable and modular NetWare 5 server applications. As a matter of fact, the entire NetWare 5 Operating System (OS) can be managed through Java. This is a good thing.

NetWare 5's support for Java is part of Novell's Open Solutions Architecture (OSA) initiative. OSA is not a specific product — it is a strategic direction Novell is taking to migrate its products and services to open protocols and standards — specifically to Java, Common Object Broker Architecture (CORBA), DNS, DHCP, PERL, and more. By basing future offerings such as NetWare 5 on the OSA initiative, Novell will provide network-aware solutions that are open, manageable, secure, and distributed.

NetWare 5 supports Java through the following features:

▸ Java Virtual Machine (JVM)

▸ ConsoleOne

▸ Java Utilities

▸ OSA Software Developer's Kit (SDK)

Let's take a closer look

Java Virtual Machine (JVM)

Novell's JVM is a set of NetWare Loadable Modules (NLMs) that interprets Java scripts and applications, and executes them on a NetWare 5 server. In NetWare 5, Novell implements JVM at the kernel level, enabling you to develop and run any Java-based application on a NetWare 5 server. According to Novell, this creates the "world's fastest Java server."

Java support on NetWare 5 provides a variety of benefits:

▸ CNEs can run Java applets on the server console.

▸ CNEs can display Java applications in X-Windows style formats, with full mouse and graphics support.

▸ CNEs can run multiple Java applications on the server while it performs other tasks.

NetWare 5 supports Java applications in one of two forms: Java classes and Java applets. Java *classes* are fully functioning applications written in Java, while Java *applets* are programs that require a Java-compatible browser.

NetWare 5 can execute both types of Java applications at the server using JAVA.NLM. Once JAVA.NLM is loaded, NetWare 5 can execute Java classes and applets. Java classes use the JAVA command, while applets rely on the APPLET console command.

ConsoleOne

As part of the OSA initiative, Novell plans to gradually converge all of its management utilities into one platform — Java. In fact, Novell has already started this convergence with the introduction of ConsoleOne.

ConsoleOne is a GUI-based server console utility that provides basic NDS management functions. Future versions of ConsoleOne will provide the same level of functionality — and more — as Novell's NetWare Administrator (NWAdmin), but it will do so from the server. This provides numerous benefits, including performance, security, and central manageability.

Check out Figure 1.16 for a quick look at the NetWare 5 ConsoleOne Java utility.

F I G U R E   1.16
NetWare 5's ConsoleOne Java utility

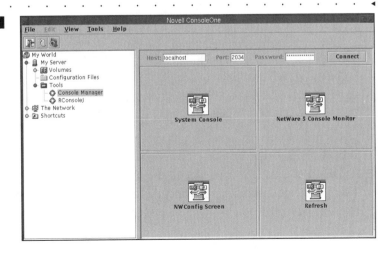

Java Utilities

NetWare 5 gets you started in the realm of Java-based utilities by offering two that can plug into ConsoleOne:

- ▶ GUI install

- ▶ DNS/DHCP Administration

First, NetWare 5 includes a new installation utility that offers an X-Windows looking GUI interface written in Java. As we learned in the previous "NetWare 5 CNA Features" section, this replaces the old text-based installation tool used in previous versions of NetWare.

Second, NetWare 5 includes a Java-based utility for managing DHCP/DNS servers. As we'll learn in the next section, these protocols are part of NetWare 5's IP strategy.

The DNS/DHCP Administration utility can significantly reduce the amount of time you spend managing your company's network. For example, it automates the process of assigning IP addresses to users' workstations and eliminates the problems associated with duplicate addresses. The DNS/DHCP Administration tool can also automate the process of updating host names and it increases security when doing so.

Check out this new Java-based GUI tool for managing NetWare 5's DNS and DHCP servers in Figure 1.17.

OSA SDK

Earlier we learned that Novell has paved the future for open protocol support with its OSA initiative. To align itself with the best Java developers in the world, Novell has included the OSA Software Developer Kit (SDK) with NetWare 5. In addition to the JVM mentioned earlier, the OSA SDK includes Java scripts, Java beans, and Java class libraries. These Java class libraries enable developers to write Java applications that access NetWare services such as NDS, Novell Storage Services (NSS), and NDPS — all of which we explored earlier in the chapter.

The OSA SDK also includes a just-in-time compiler that interprets Java codes. The compiler converts these Java codes into machine code in real time, dramatically increasing the speed at which a NetWare 5 server runs Java-based applications.

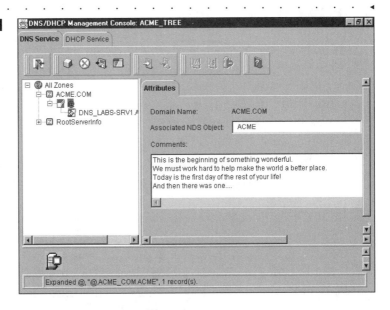

FIGURE 1.17

DNS/DHCP Administration tool for NetWare 5

REAL WORLD

To jump-start Java development efforts, Novell recently announced a $50 million fund to invest in companies developing Java-based applications. Because any of these applications can run on a NetWare 5 server, this fund ensures the development of a potentially huge number of applications for the NetWare platform.

Vro-o-o-o-m!

Now your NetWare 5 supercar has been supercharged. This section focused on the NetWare 5 server as a vehicle for cruising the information superhighway. We learned a little about its architecture and how it can be supercharged using Java GUI support. Now it's time to pour the electronic pavement of the Infobahn using NetWare 5 IP services. See you there.

For more information about Java Console Support for NetWare 5, check out *Novell's CNE Study Guide for NetWare 5*.

TIP

NetWare 5 IP Services

Now that you've constructed and supercharged the NetWare 5 *cruisemobile*, it's time to pour the electronic pavement of our information superhighway. The Internet's main protocol suite is called *TCP/IP*. It consists primarily of *Internet Protocol* (IP), which provides Network Layer routing, and *Transmission Control Protocol* (TCP), which accepts messages from IP and packages them for Internet-based applications. Today TCP/IP is *the* open industry protocol standard for global communications. It is supported by a variety of manufacturers, including Novell, Sun, Apple, DEC, and IBM. TCP/IP offers millions of users immediate access to a complete spectrum of services and information via intranets and the Internet. I guess it's safe to say:

TCP/IP is the foundation of our Global Electronic Village.

In the past, NetWare has only supported the Internetwork Packet Exchange (IPX) protocol. This protocol requires very little user intervention to configure and administer. With the release of NetWare 5, Novell adds native support for the TCP/IP protocol — eliminating the need to encapsulate IPX. While for many this is a great thing, the overhead required to configure and administer IP could prove very time-consuming for CNEs.

Fortunately Novell has included a variety of TCP/IP management enhancements in NetWare 5. Here's a quick look at the CNE topics we're going to cover in this introduction:

▶ Pure IP

▶ Novell DNS/DHCP Services

▶ Compatibility mode

▶ SLP

TCP/IP is a great foundation for Internet connectivity because it provides an open link between your private network and the Internet. Let's surf the 'Net using TCP/IP!

Pure IP

In NetWare 5, all NetWare Core Protocols (NCP) can use the benefits of TCP/IP open connectivity. This gives customers the ability to run in a "Pure IP" environment — *pure* in the sense that the network doesn't retain IP-based encapsulation as in the past. This allows users to select the protocol that best fits their needs. For those who require IP, NetWare 5 will simplify their lives by eliminating multiple protocols and freeing up valuable network bandwidth.

So, what does Pure IP buy us? Good question:

- A single protocol in routed environments requires less hardware and software.

- Pure IP is a much more efficient use of bandwidth, thus increasing performance and lowering costs.

- Less management is required to support a single protocol on each client.

- Pure IP provides a wider range of opportunities for remote user connectivity.

- Pure IP offers better interoperability with today's Internet/intranet solutions.

Although NetWare 5 is Novell's first Pure TCP/IP network operating system, it is not Novell's first TCP/IP solution. For years Novell has been a leading provider of TCP/IP solutions for NetWare, including IP tunneling, IP relay, the IPX-IP gateway, and NetWare/IP. Many of these solutions support TCP/IP by encapsulating it with an IPX packet at various stages of the packet's journey across the network. NetWare 5, in contrast, runs TCP/IP without encapsulation. In short, Pure IP supports TCP/IP applications a little more efficiently than IPX.

Pure IP doesn't come without its fair share of management costs. Fortunately NetWare 5 offers some relief in the form of Novell DNS/DHCP Services. Let's take a closer look.

Novell DNS/DHCP Services

The difficulty of maintaining TCP/IP networks has been called "the best-kept secret around." As more and more companies embrace TCP/IP as the networking protocol of choice, CNEs and IS personnel are looking for solutions to simplify the management of Pure IP. Many who are accustomed to NetWare's relatively effortless IPX-based device naming and addressing scheme are alarmed to find that

TCP/IP does not provide any automatic way to configure IP addresses and other connectivity information. Even sites that have had their LANs connected to the Internet for years are running up against limitations such as the increasing scarcity of IP addresses.

In recent years, two technologies have emerged to solve some of the inherent difficulties of maintaining TCP/IP networks:

▶ *Domain Name System (DNS)* — DNS is a distributed name/address database used to translate between numerical IP addresses and more humane alphanumeric addresses.

▶ *Dynamic Host Configuration Protocol (DHCP)* — DHCP provides a framework for dynamically passing configuration information to clients or service-providing resources on a TCP/IP network.

DNS is widely used on the Internet to translate host names to IP addresses. The Domain Name Space is structured as an inverted tree, much like a file system directory structure. Each node on the tree represents a domain. The end leaves of the tree represent individual host names on the Internet. When you build a Pure IP NetWare WAN, each resource must maintain a unique host name. To automate this process, NetWare 5 integrates DNS with Novell Directory Services (NDS). With NDS integration, each user can automatically be assigned an appropriate DNS server upon login. For example, a mobile user in a distant location might be assigned a DNS server with a faster response time than a desktop user in a local office. DNS/DHCP services eliminate the management overhead normally associated with IP addressing.

DHCP provides configuration parameters to Internet hosts. The server is a host that provides initialization parameters through DHCP, and the client is a host requesting parameters from the server. When a Pure IP NetWare 5 client requests login, DHCP must provide a unique IP address. NetWare 5 uses NDS to help automate DHCP services. You can store IP addresses in NDS. When the user logs into the network, DHCP consults NDS and provides an appropriate IP address to that user. This eliminates the older methods of manually tracking and assigning IP addresses. NDS ensures that DHCP provides managed IP addresses throughout the enterprise.

As you can see, DNS/DHCP Services can greatly reduce your TCP/IP management load. In addition, when DNS/DHCP is integrated with NDS, it allows you to extend your control throughout the enterprise. Here are a few reasons why you're going to love Novell DNS/DHCP Services in NetWare 5:

▸ DNS/DHCP significantly reduces the time for administering IP names and addresses.

▸ DNS/DHCP significantly increases protocol fault-tolerance because configurations are replicated with NDS.

▸ DNS/DHCP completely automates IP address assignment and host name updates.

▸ DNS/DHCP increases security when updating IP addresses and host names.

▸ DNS/DHCP eliminates network problems associated with duplicate IP addresses.

Now that you're thrilled about the prospect of a Pure IP WAN, consider the prospect of updating all your IPX LANs simultaneously. Ouch! Fortunately, NetWare 5 includes significant compatibility with older IPX-based networks. Let's take a closer look.

Compatibility Mode

Just when you thought a Pure IP world would be paradise, consider the cost of upgrading 100 million IPX-based applications and clients to NetWare 5. Oops!

Fortunately, Novell picked up on this little "problem" and decided to do something about it. To accommodate Novell's 100 million existing IPX-based clients, NetWare 5 includes a *Compatibility Mode* option. If you choose Compatibility Mode during NetWare 5 install, you can run IPX-based applications on a Pure IP NetWare 5 server and link IPX segments to IP segments with ease. Novell is hoping that the need for compatibility mode will diminish over time as applications migrate from IPX to Pure IP. However, in the meantime, this option allows users to control both the degree and the rate of change as you migrate from IPX to Pure IP.

NetWare 5 Compatibility Mode consists of three primary features:

▶ *Compatibility Drivers* — NetWare 5 client and server drivers enable you to run IPX-based applications in a Pure IP environment. You can enable the server drivers when you install NetWare 5 and the client drivers when you install Novell's client software on each workstation. Here's how it works. When an IPX-based application makes an NCP call in a Pure IP environment, the client and server drivers ensure that the call finds its way to the TCP/IP stack and is sent over the wire as an IP packet. If, however, the application must access the IPX stack directly, the drivers will accommodate by intercepting the IPX packets and encapsulating them within IP. Very cool.

▶ *Migration Gateway* — The NetWare 5 Migration Gateway provides seamless connectivity between IP and IPX cross-culture networks. In short, it enables you to link IPX segments to IP segments without installing any additional hardware or software. This ensures a gradual transition from IPX to Pure IP. For the most part, the Migration Gateway oversees all activity in both the IPX and IP segments. It can then route any information that needs to be exchanged between them. For an IPX network, the migration gateway uses the Service Advertising Protocol (SAP) to broadcast the segments' services. On the IP side, the Migration Gateway uses the Service Location Protocol (SLP) for service broadcasting. We'll take a closer look at SLP in the next section.

▶ *Bindery Agent* — The NetWare 5 Bindery Agent provides full backward compatibility to the NetWare 3 bindery. This allows IP clients in NetWare 5 to access flat-file bindery data. If you're using IPX-based applications that are dependent on the NetWare 3 bindery, you can integrate them into your network by enabling the NetWare 5 Bindery Agent during install.

Compatibility is a good thing — especially when you're talking about 100 million IPX-based users. Nobody would argue that the future of the information superhighway is based on Pure IP (at least for now). Fortunately, Novell is not forcing us to switch lanes immediately. The more prudent step would be to turn on your blinker, look over your left shoulder, and switch from the IPX lane to Pure IP slowly. Bottom line: The compatibility mode option is your friend.

Now, let's finish our discussion of Pure IP with a quick look at SLP — a new way of broadcasting TCP/IP network services.

SLP

Now that we're living in a Pure IP world, we must change the way users discover things. In the past, NetWare used the SAP method of discovering network services. In NetWare 5, you have three different choices:

- ▸ SLP (Service Location Protocol)

- ▸ DHCP (Dynamic Host Configuration Protocol)

- ▸ Static Configuration

The first and most popular service discovery method will undoubtedly be SLP, which provides automatic resource discovery and registration on a TCP/IP network. Network services such as servers and printers use SLP to communicate with clients. SLP is particularly advantageous because it provides full backward compatibility with network services and applications that rely on SAP-based discovery — such as IPX networks.

SLP is an industry standard protocol defined by the Internet Engineering Task Force (IETF). SLP uses the TCP/IP protocol to allow clients to query the network and obtain a quick list of available network services. SLP does not generate the "chatty" overhead that is characteristic of SAP. In contrast, SLP maintains a registry of all network services in NDS and registers a particular service's availability only once when that service first becomes available to the network. SLP configuration is automatically enabled when you turn on NetWare 5's compatibility mode option.

NetWare 5 also offers the opportunity to use DHCP for network service discovery. DHCP is another standard defined by IETF, and it dynamically allocates IP addresses to multiple workstations on a network. Novell included the DHCP configuration option for companies that already have DHCP servers and DHCP client software installed on each workstation. This is not something you want to try if you're not familiar with the nuances of DHCP management.

Finally, if you don't want to use SLP or DHCP for network service discovery, you can always manually enable IP clients using the Static Configuration option. To do so, simply include the IP address of one or more NDS servers on each IP client. The clients then use the IP address to discover network services instead of using SLP or DHCP.

Well, that's NetWare 5 support for TCP/IP in a nutshell. And we are finally finished pouring the electronic pavement of the information superhighway — for now. Don't worry, you'll get plenty of opportunities to analyze Pure IP in great depth later in this book.

Let's recap. So far we've built the NetWare 5 supercar using a cool new GUI installation. Then, we supercharged the Cruisemobile with Java. Finally, we poured the electronic pavement of the information superhighway using Pure IP, DNS, DHCP, and SLP. So, what's left?

Now it's time to go *cruisin'*!

For more information about NetWare 5 IP Services, check out
Novell's CNE Study Guide for NetWare 5.

TIP

Netscape FastTrack Server for NetWare

Welcome to Web Surfing 101!

The Internet and World Wide Web can be very intimidating at first. But don't let them fool you. The WWW is simply an electronic mechanism for publishing multimedia documents. The analogy of an information superhighway appeals to many because they can visualize themselves cruising the Infobahn at the speed of light. To extend the analogy further, your browser (Netscape Navigator, for example) is a friendly graphical "sportscar" and Web sites are "cities." Each city has a variety of "buildings" that you can visit — Web pages. These multimedia Web pages are published using the HyperText Markup Language (HTML).

In addition, TCP/IP is the "pavement" of the Infobahn and HyperText Transfer Protocol (HTTP) is "cyber fuel." And, finally, the Netscape FastTrack Server provides a "bridge" between your local electronic city and the Infobahn. So, what is the Netscape FastTrack Server and what does it have to do with NetWare 5? Good question.

NetWare 5 includes a fully integrated version of the Netscape FastTrack Server. This server-based application has been specifically optimized for NetWare 5. As such, it includes two major improvements:

- ▶ *Optimization* — The NetWare 5 FastTrack Server has been optimized to take advantage of the kernel enhancements to NetWare 5's core OS.

▶ *NDS-compatibility* — The NetWare 5 FastTrack Server has been fully integrated into NDS, which increases Web Server administration and security. NDS can be used to restrict who can administer the Web Server and what content they can publish.

In addition to these improvements, the NetWare 5 FastTrack Server supports the following Web enhancing technologies:

▶ Lightweight Directory Access Protocol (LDAP)

▶ Common Gateway Interface (CGI)

▶ PERL

▶ NetBasic

So, how does the FastTrack Server work? As you can see in Figure 1.18, the FastTrack Server comprises a set of seven NLMs that run on a NetWare 4.11 or NetWare 5 server. Once loaded, the Web Server publishes HTML documents to corporate intranets or the global World Wide Web (the Internet).

To install the NetWare 5 FastTrack Server, you must complete four steps:

▶ *Step 1: Configure LDAP services for NDS* — Using NetWare Administrator you must create a proxy user with no password and give that user special LDAP security rights.

▶ *Step 2: Install the Netscape FastTrack Server* — Simply run the FastTrack Server Installation Wizard from a client workstation. Follow the bouncing ball.

▶ *Step 3: Bind the FastTrack Server to NDS* — Next, you must replace the default FastTrack directory with the awesome power of NDS. This is accomplished using the Administration Server utility.

▶ *Step 4: Test the bind with NDS* — To ensure that the FastTrack Server is properly bound to NDS, you should compare the user list from Administration Server and NetWare 5's own NetWare Administrator.

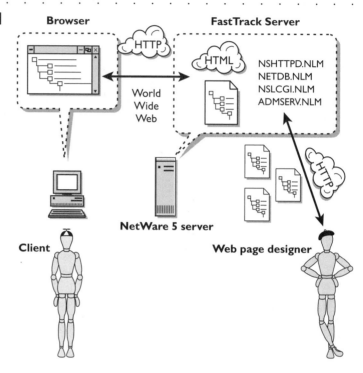

FIGURE 1.18

*Publishing
HTML documents
from the NetWare 5
FastTrack Server*

Once you've installed the Netscape FastTrack Server, it's time for administration. This is accomplished using a special Web-based tool called Administration Server. The Administration Server comprises a series of NLMs running on the NetWare 5 server. This tool helps you manage the FastTrack Server from a single interface — the Administration Server home page. As you can see in Figure 1.19, the Administration Server home page allows you to manage your Web Server from a client browser — preferably Netscape Navigator.

REAL WORLD

Keep in mind that the Netscape FastTrack Server allows you to publish documents locally (corporate *intranets*) and/or globally (the World Wide *Internet*). Without correct security measures, you may accidentally publish sensitive information to every villager on Earth. Be very careful . . . this is powerful stuff!

FIGURE 1.19

*FastTrack Server
management using
the Administration Server
home page*

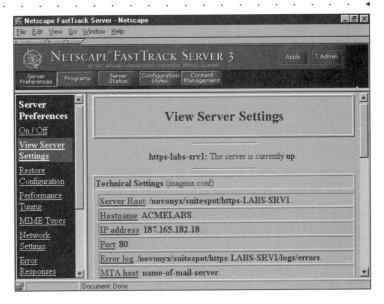

FIGURE 1.19

*FastTrack Server
management using
the Administration Server
home page*

Once you've activated FastTrack's Administration Server home page, you should dive into its most valuable configuration utility — Server Manager, which is a collection of forms you use to configure and control your FastTrack Server. It can be accessed from the Administration Server home page by clicking the button showing the name of your NetWare 5 server. You can use the Server Manager to accomplish a variety of CNE tasks, including:

▸ Modifying basic server parameters

▸ Modifying directories in the document tree

▸ Configuring document preferences

▸ Restricting access

That completes our brief overview of NetWare 5's full-featured FastTrack Server. Don't worry, when you become a CNE you'll get an opportunity to cruise the Infobahn at very high speeds. For now, it's sufficient to understand the basics of Web Surfing 101.

TIP

For more information about Netscape's FastTrack Server, check out *Novell's CNE Study Guide for NetWare 5.*

NetWare 5 Application Server

Our final stop on the whirlwind tour of NetWare 5's CNE features is the Application Server. Once again, I've saved the best for last.

The NetWare 5 Application Server represents a variety of core OS improvements. In short, Novell has retrofitted the server with dual engines, better brakes, and a lightning-quick transmission. The result is the fastest and most reliable server around.

To support these outrageous claims, we're going to explore four different parts of the NetWare 5 supercar:

▸ Core OS

▸ Virtual memory

▸ Supercharged bus

▸ Integrated applications

Vro-o-o-o-m!

Core OS

It all starts with the engine. Novell has made some dramatic improvements to the core OS in NetWare 5. Most of these efforts focus on increasing server-based application performance and reliability. Here's a quick overview of the key core OS enhancements:

▸ *Memory protection* — NetWare 5 segments core OS memory into protected *rings*. At the bull's-eye of NetWare 5 is the "kernel" — which runs in Ring Zero. In order to optimize server-based application performance, you'll want to run NLMs in Ring Zero as well. However, doing so could result in a server crash. Novell counters this threat by advising you to run only Novell-certified NLMs in Ring Zero. Nevertheless, you probably want the ability to run more applications faster without the risk of server failure. Now you can. With NetWare 5, you have the option of installing NLMs at the kernel or in protected memory space. Applications running in protected mode cannot write to any other address space except their own. Hence, when an application running in protected mode crashes, NetWare 5 continues to run.

TIP

Only applications and files stored in the traditional NetWare file system can be loaded into protected memory. The NSS file system does not use protected memory — it runs in the kernel address space (Ring 0) instead.

▶ *Application prioritization* — Just when you thought it couldn't get any better, NetWare 5 allows you to prioritize the applications running on your server. You can specify how many processor cycles you want to reserve for each application when simultaneous applications require more power. For example, you may want the server's financial database application to have priority over an Internet gateway. Just a thought.

▶ *Symmetrical multiprocessing* — Like previous versions, NetWare 5 supports multiple processors. Unlike previous versions, NetWare 5 supports single and multiple processors through the same kernel. In addition, NetWare 5 supports up to 32 processors by default. But that's not even the best of it. A NetWare 5 server with multiple processors can execute individual threads of a multithreaded application on different processors simultaneously. As a result, NetWare 5 gets more done in less time.

Virtual Memory

NetWare 5 further increases server-based application performance by offering as much memory as you need whenever you need it. This is accomplished by using a new feature called *virtual memory*. Virtual memory enables NetWare 5 to store information temporarily on the hard drive when there is not enough RAM to complete an operation. Although this slows down application performance, it does avoid that age-old bugaboo — "insufficient memory" — or even worse, "ABEND".

Let's review some of the advantages and features of NetWare 5 virtual memory:

▶ *Advantages of using virtual memory* — NetWare 5 monitors available memory using the Least Recently Used (LRU) algorithm. Data that has not been used for some time is moved from memory to disk, thus freeing memory for other uses. When the data on disk is needed again, it is moved back into available memory. Because data is swapped on and off the disk, the available memory supports more operations than its physical capacity would usually allow.

▶ *Using virtual memory swap files* — When data is moved from memory to disk, it is stored in a *Swap File*. By default, NetWare 5 creates the first swap file on the SYS: volume. However, you can create swap files on any NetWare 5 volume — only one file per volume, please. In addition, server modules that are loaded into protected address spaces use virtual memory automatically. The modules and the data they access can be swapped to disk. Modules that are not loaded into protected address spaces can still use virtual memory, but the modules themselves cannot be swapped to disk. Swapping the data between memory and disk requires additional system resources, but it increases the memory available for use. The availability of the additional memory improves overall server performance.

▶ *Considerations for using virtual memory* — Here are a few things to think about when using NetWare 5 virtual memory. First, you can only create one swap file per volume. The swap file on the SYS: volume is created by default and it is named _SWAP_MEM. It is placed in the root directory. You can delete this swap file and move it to another volume if necessary. Second, data moved to virtual memory will be stored in any available swap file on any volume. Consider creating your swap files on fast volumes. Third, you can add a swap file to a volume even if the volume is not mounted. Fourth, when you down your server, the swap file is deleted. In addition, it is deactivated when the host volume is dismounted. Fortunately, the swap file is automatically reactivated when the volume is mounted. The exception is the SYS: volume, which automatically re-creates its swap file each time the server is started. Finally, swap files are dynamic. They change in size as data is swapped in and out of memory.

▸ *Managing virtual memory* — Refer to Table 1.3 for some quick tips on virtual memory management. To manage NetWare 5 virtual memory, you must stay on top of swap files. Interestingly, this is accomplished using the SWAP console command. For more information, type **HELP SWAP** at the server console.

TABLE 1.3 *Managing Virtual Memory*	TO DO THIS	TYPE THIS AT THE SERVER CONSOLE
	Display information about swap files currently in use.	**SWAP** Alternatively, from the MONITOR Available Options menu, select Virtual Memory | Swap Files.
	Create a swap file on a designated volume.	**SWAP ADD** *volume_name [parameter=value]* Optional parameters are MIN=, MAX=, and MIN FREE=. These parameters specify the minimum and maximum size of the swap file and the minimum free space that must be left on the volume. Values are in millions of bytes. If parameters are not included, the following default values are used: * MIN = 2 * Max = Free volume space * MIN FREE = 5
	Delete a swap file from a designated volume.	**SWAP DEL** *volume_name* If the swap file is being used when it is deleted, then the swapped data is moved to another swap file.
	Change the parameter values for a swap file on a designated volume.	**SWAP PARAMETER** *volume_name parameter=value* Parameters are MIN=, MAX=, and MIN FREE=.

REAL WORLD

If the overall supply of memory is running low, then swapping will occur more often — *makes sense!* However, if memory is extremely low, the system might spend all its time swapping memory in and out of disk and have no time to accomplish useful work. This is called *disk thrashing*.

In extremely low memory conditions, NetWare 5 will move all the data from a protected address space into the disk swap file, temporarily stopping the modules within the protected address space. After a period of time, NetWare will move the data back into the memory space and shut down another space, moving its data to disk. Without virtual memory, these extremely low memory conditions would cause processes to fail. With virtual memory, the server keeps running, although very slowly.

When disk thrashing occurs, you should add more RAM. Virtual memory cannot compensate for an overall lack of server memory, although it can prevent processes from failing and allow a server to continue to function. The real value of virtual memory is in using a sufficient supply of memory more efficiently, thus improving server performance. Running server applications in virtual memory protects the application and improves server reliability.

That does it for the core OS engine. Now let's put the pedal to the metal and check out the supercharged server bus.

Supercharged Bus

In addition to a supercharged engine, NetWare 5's supercar includes a very quick transmission — also known as *server bus*. Two key features dramatically improve the speed at which instructions find their way from the network to the Core OS. Let's take a closer look:

► *HotPlug PCI* — HotPlug PCI gives you the ability to upgrade or replace network interface cards (NICs) while the NetWare 5 server is up and running. This improves server uptime and eases the burden of costly expansion.

▸ *I2O* — NetWare 5 includes support for an emerging technology known as I_2O. I_2O is an intelligent I/O technology that vastly improves bus throughput and overall system performance by relieving host resources of interrupt-intensive I/O tasks. This allows processors and memory to focus on what they're good at — such as dealing with user requests.

Now that you understand what it takes to build the NetWare 5 supercar, let's take a quick look at some integrated NetWare 5 applications.

Integrated Applications

To show off the improved NetWare 5 application server, Novell has included some very powerful applications with the Core OS. Here's a quick overview:

▸ *New backup utility* — NetWare 5's new backup utility is protocol-independent and adds multiple and repetitive scheduling, Windows 95-based GUI, and autoloader support. It also takes advantage of NDS by allowing central management of backup jobs across the network. All these features save time and money on backup routines by centralizing the system.

▸ *NetWare 5 Management Agents (NMAs)* — NetWare 5 includes three agents (NLMs) to manage the operating system via Simple Network Management Protocol (SNMP). These agents allow any SNMP-based console to manage the NetWare 5 OS via intranet or Internet connections. Some sample SNMP-based consoles include ManageWise from Novell, CA UniCenter, HP OpenView, IBM Tivoli, and SunNet Manager. More than 400 objects and 400 traps are exposed through NetWare 5 NMA.

▸ *Oracle8 for NetWare 5* — NetWare 5 includes a five-user version of Oracle8 for NetWare. The server piece runs on NetWare 5, while the client supports Windows 95 or Windows NT. In addition, this enhanced version has been integrated into NDS. As a result, you can use NDS to control access to your company's database. Furthermore, Oracle8 offers several new features that make databasing in NetWare 5 worthy of praise, including *Oracle Database Assistant* (a creation Wizard), *Oracle INTYP File Assistant* (an integrated

Wizard for creating INTYPE OTT files), *Oracle Web Publishing Assistant* (an HTML Web publishing Wizard that supports Oracle8 data files), and the *Oracle Net8 Assistant* (a Wizard for configuring Net8 client/server products).

Boy, that's quite a deal. You're not only getting an award-winning network operating system, but some great new applications as well. Don't ever say Novell never gave you anything.

STOP!

That completes our exhaustive tour of NetWare 5's CNE-based Global Electronic Village. As you can see, we're cruising the Infobahn in style. In this section, we've expanded our feature discovery beyond the NetWare 5 CNA topics into the realm of Migration, Java, IP Services, FastTrack, and NetWare 5's supercharged application server. Take a deep breath . . . you deserve it.

Now exhale . . .

Just in case you weren't paying attention during the previous 60 pages or so, I've summarized the top 10 NetWare 5 CNA/CNE features in Table 1.4. Knock yourself out.

T A B L E 1.4	FEATURE	NETWARE 4.11	NETWARE 5
Overview of the NetWare 5 Global Electronic Village	Novell Directory Services (NDS)	NDS only	NDS and LDAP support
		Database parsing	Catalog Services
		Context-based login	Blue Sky login
			WAN Traffic Manager
			NDS for NT (sold separately)

TABLE 1.4	FEATURE	NETWARE 4.11	NETWARE 5
Overview of the NetWare 5 Global Electronic Village (continued)	File System	2 GB per file	8 TB per file
		16 million directory entries	Trillions of directory entries
		One NetWare partition per disk	Four NetWare partitions per disk
		Eight volumes per partition	Unlimited volumes per partition
			Enhanced CD-ROM support High-performance access, regardless of file size
	Security	Public-key authentication	Secure Authentication Services (SAS)
			Public Key Infrastructure Services (PKIS)
			Cryptographic services
	Workstation Management	Novell Client 32	Z.E.N.works
		No remote control	Remote Control
			NDS Integration
			Desktop Maintenance
			Workstation Inventory
	Printing	Queue-based printing	Novell Distributed Print Services (NDPS)
		Queues, print servers, and printers	Printer Agents
		Unidirectional communications	Bidirectional communications
			Plug-and-print
	Installation	Text install	GUI install
			NLS Licensing

(continued)

· · · · ·

	FEATURE	NETWARE 4.11	NETWARE 5
T A B L E 1.4	Java Support	JAVA.NLM	Java Virtual Machine (JVM)
Overview of the NetWare 5 Global Electronic Village (continued)			ConsoleOne
			OSA
	IP Services	NetWare/IP Encapsulation	Pure IP
		DNS/DHCP	DNS/DHCP with NDS Integration
		SAP Discovery	SLP Discovery
			Compatibility Mode
	Web Server	Novell Web Server	Netscape FastTrack Server
		FastTrack download	Administration Server Management
	Application Server	Only real memory	Real memory and virtual memory
		No prioritization	Application prioritization
		Uni-processing kernel	Symmetrical multiprocessing
		Four processors by default	32 processors by default
		DOWN server for maintenance	HotPlug PCI
		Standard I/O	I_2O
			Network Management Agents (NMA)
			Oracle8 for NetWare

As you can see from Table 1.4, NetWare 5 is definitely worthy of ACME and their plight — to save the world.

Now it's your turn . . .

You are the final piece in our globe-trotting puzzle. You will become ACME's MIS department. We have recruited you as the architect of their communication strategy. As a NetWare 5 CNA, you come highly recommended. Your mission — should you choose to accept it — is to build the ACME WAN. You will need courage, design experience, NDS know-how, and this book. If you succeed, you will save the world and become a CNA!

All in a day's work.

· ◄

Getting to Know ACME

The world is in a lot of trouble. If we keep abusing the Planet Earth at our current pace, there'll be nothing left in a few decades.

As a matter of fact, the Alpha Centurions have discovered this and decided to do something about it. As it turns out, they are great fans of the Planet Earth and would hate to see us destroy it. They have given us a deadline before which we must clean up our act — or else.

To save the world, we have created an organization called ACME (A Cure for Mother Earth). ACME is staffed by the greatest heroes of all time. They are the founding mothers and fathers of Earth's Golden Age.

We've traveled back in time to recruit the ACME management. Now it's your turn. You will serve as ACME's MIS department. You will build a pervasive internetwork for ACME using NetWare 5. The clock is ticking and connectivity is the key.

In the social hierarchy of needs, the world is pretty out of whack. Almost two-thirds of our population doesn't have sufficient resources to satisfy the lowest basic needs — medicine, food, shelter, and peace — while a smaller percentage takes higher needs — like digital watches — for granted. Something needs to change.

As a matter of fact, the Alpha Centurions have discovered this and have decided to do something about it. As it turns out, they are great fans of the Planet Earth and would hate to see us destroy it. The good news is they are a benevolent and intelligent race. They understand the Pyramid of Needs and recognize that everyone should be able to enjoy digital watches. They have discovered that the top 1 percent of the Earth's population is destroying the world at an alarming pace, while the other 99 percent is just trying to survive. In an effort to save the world, they have issued an ultimatum:

Clean up your act or find another planet to exploit!

They have given us until January 1, 2010, to clean up our act — or else! It's safe to say that the fate of the human race is in your hands. To help measure our progress, the Alpha Centurions have developed a World Health Index (WHI). The

WHI is a balanced calculation of seven positive and seven negative factors that determine how good or bad we're treating the Earth. They've decided that 100 is a good number to shoot for. It represents a good balance between basic and higher needs. Once the world achieves a WHI of 100, almost everyone will be able to afford a digital watch. Here's a quick list of the 14 positive and negative WHI factors:

WHI Positive	WHI Negative
Charity	Crime
Love	Pollution
Birth	Starvation
Education	Disease
Health	War
Laughter	Poverty
Sports	Corruption

Bottom line: The Alpha Centurions have given us a little more than eleven years to increase our WHI from its current level (–2) to 100. We have until January 1, 2010. If we don't clean up our act by then, they will mercifully eradicate all humans, and let the animals and plants live peacefully on the Planet Earth.

 TIP   **Throughout this book, we will use ACME as a global case study for key NetWare 5 CNA management tasks. You will install ACME servers, build their enterprise NDS tree, construct a multi-layered security model, distribute Z.E.N.works clients, and build a comprehensive NDPS printing system. *Pay attention!* ACME may just change your life ... and help you become a NetWare 5 CNA.**

ACME has been designed as "A Cure for Mother Earth." It is staffed by the greatest heroes from our unspoiled history. These are the founding mothers and fathers of Earth's Golden Age — before instant popcorn, talking cars, and daytime television. It's clear that somewhere along the human timeline, progress went amok. We need help from heroes before that time. To vortex back in history and grab the ACME management, we've used a prototype of the Oscillating Temporal Overthruster (OTO). We've hand-chosen only the brightest and most resourceful characters, then meticulously trained each one of them for special tasks. They're a little disoriented, but more than happy to help.

These historical heroes have been placed in an innovative organizational structure. As you can see in Figure 1.20, ACME is organized around five main divisions. They are:

▶ *Human Rights (Gandhi)* — Taking care of the world's basic needs, including medicine, food, shelter, and peace. These tasks are handled jointly by Albert Schweitzer, Mother Teresa, Florence Nightingale, and Buddha. This division's work has the most positive impact on the WHI.

▶ *Labs (Albert Einstein)* — Putting technology to good use. This division is the technical marvel of ACME. In addition to research and development (R&D) efforts, the Labs division is responsible for the WHI tracking center in NORAD. This division is staffed by the wizardry of Leonardo da Vinci, Sir Isaac Newton, Charles Darwin, Marie Curie, and Charles Babbage.

▶ *Operations (King Arthur)* — Saving the world can be a logistical nightmare. Fortunately, we have King Arthur and the Knights of the Round Table to help us out. In this division, ACME routes money from caring contributors (Charity) to those who need it most (Financial) — there's a little Robin Hood in there somewhere. Also, with the help of Merlin, we will distribute all the Human Rights and Labs material to the four corners of the globe.

▶ *Crime Fighting (Sherlock Holmes and Dr. Watson)* — Making the world a safer place. This division tackles the almost insurmountable task of eradicating world crime. It's a good thing we have the help of Sherlock Holmes and some of our greatest crime-fighting superheroes, including Robin Hood, Maid Marion, Wyatt Earp, and Wild Bill Hickok. These heroes deal with the single most negative factor in WHI calculations — crime. This is very important work.

▶ *Admin (George Washington)* — Keeping the rest of ACME running smoothly. It's just like a well-oiled machine with the help of America's Founding Fathers — George Washington, Thomas Jefferson, Abraham Lincoln, FDR, and James Madison. Their main job is public relations under the command of one of our greatest orators, Franklin Delano Roosevelt (FDR). In addition to getting the word out, Admin tracks ACME activity (auditing) and keeps the facilities operating at their best.

FIGURE 1.20

ACME organizational chart

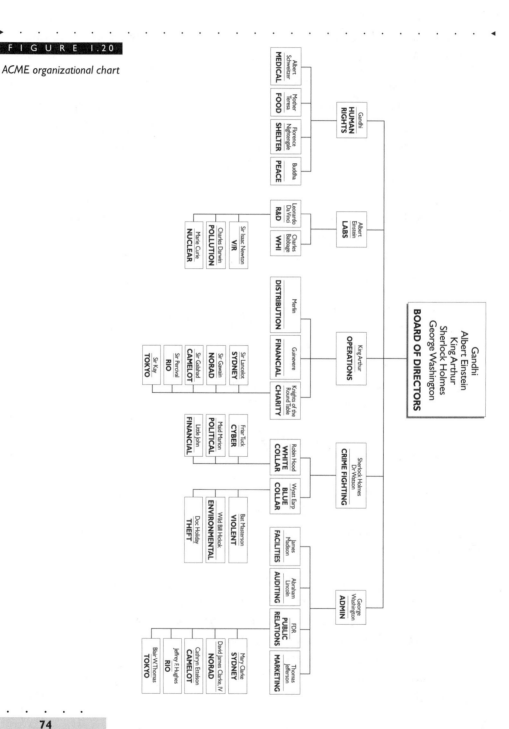

Now it's your turn. You are the final piece in our globe-trotting puzzle. You are ACME's MIS department. ACME has a daunting task ahead of it, so we don't have any time to mess around. I'd like to begin by thanking you for choosing to accept this mission. Now you'll find some NDS schematics included in the next few pages. They are for your eyes only. Once you have read the inputs, eat them! There's other good news — you don't have to save the world alone. The project team is here to help you. Remember, we're counting on you. Be careful not to let these facts fall into the wrong hands. Believe it or not, there are forces at work that don't share our love for the human race.

ACME *Chronicles*

A day in the life . . .

What you're about to read is for your eyes only. This is extremely confidential information. The ACME *Chronicles* is an interactive newsletter that provides a detailed look at the life and times of ACME. This is an exceptional organization created for a singular purpose — to save the world. As you can see in Figure 1.20, ACME is organized around five main divisions:

▸ Human Rights

▸ Labs

▸ Operations

▸ Crime Fighting

▸ Admin

Let's go inside and see what makes them tick.

Human Rights — Gandhi in Sydney

This is the "heart" of ACME's purpose. Human Rights has the most profound positive effect on the WHI. Efforts here can save lives and increase our chances of surviving into the next century. The goal of Human Rights is to raise people from the bottom of the Pyramid of Needs. By satisfying their basic needs (medicine, food, shelter, and peace), we hope to give humans the strength to fight for higher needs (equality, justice, education, and digital watches). This makes the world a better place and dramatically improves the WHI.

All Human Rights materials developed here are distributed every day through ten different distribution centers around the world. The Sydney site is ACME's manufacturing facility for food, shelter, and medical aid. Check out Figure 1.21. In addition, the peacekeepers use any means necessary to thwart global wars. Let's take a closer look at the four different departments of Human Rights.

▸ *Medical (Albert Schweitzer)* — This department is collecting basic medical materials, and training doctors and nurses for field work. Also, ACME is eagerly developing vaccines and working overtime to cure serious diseases. Finally, the medical staff is taking steps to clean up the sanitation of "dirty" countries. This is all accomplished with the help of Albert Schweitzer and his dedicated staff.

▸ *Food (Mother Teresa)* — With the help of her country-trained culinary heroes, Mother Teresa will determine how much Opossum Stew the whole world can eat. In addition, they are developing a series of genetically engineered organisms that will transform inedible materials into food stock. Finally, ACME's Food department has teamed up with R&D to create virtual reality (V/R) programming that teaches people how to grow food of their own. After all, if you give a person a fish, they eat for a day; but if you teach them to fish, they eat for a lifetime (and get a guest spot on ESPN's "Outdoor World").

▸ *Shelter (Florence Nightingale)* — With all the new healthier and happier people in the world, our attention shifts to shelter. Fortunately, Florence Nightingale and her crack construction team have developed a cheap, recyclable, geodesic dome called a Permaculture. It has central heating, air conditioning, water, plumbing, and computer-controlled maid service. The most amazing thing about the dome is that it can be constructed from any native materials — that's cacti and sand in the desert, lily pads in the marsh, and snow in the Arctic. If all else fails, they're edible.

▶ *Peace (Buddha)* — One of the most overlooked basic needs is peace. All the other stuff doesn't mean a hill of beans if you're living in a war zone. Buddha's job is to somehow settle the 101 wars currently plaguing our Earth. He relies on a combination of wisdom, diplomacy, military presence, and fortune cookies.

FIGURE 1.21

The SYDNEY site at ACME

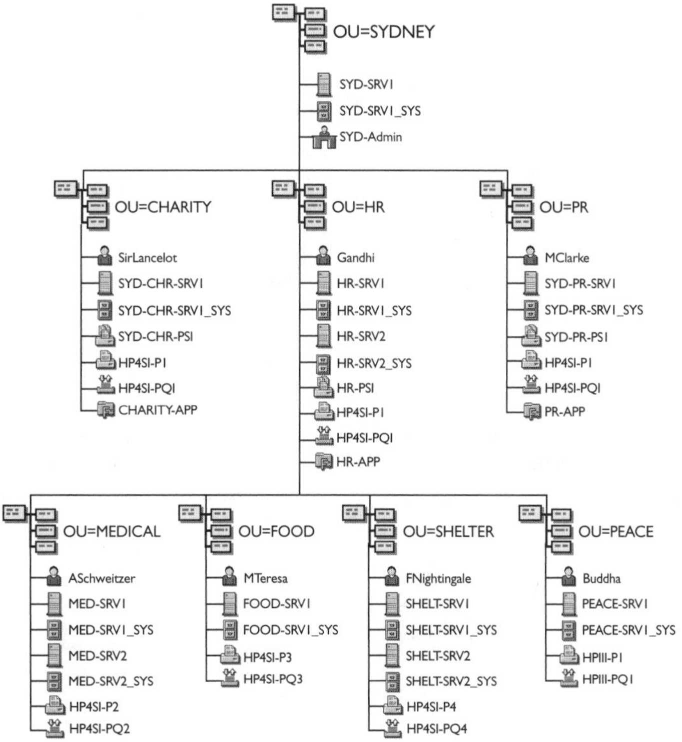

OU=SYDNEY
- SYD-SRV1
- SYD-SRV1_SYS
- SYD-Admin

OU=CHARITY
- SirLancelot
- SYD-CHR-SRV1
- SYD-CHR-SRV1_SYS
- SYD-CHR-PS1
- HP4SI-P1
- HP4SI-PQ1
- CHARITY-APP

OU=HR
- Gandhi
- HR-SRV1
- HR-SRV1_SYS
- HR-SRV2
- HR-SRV2_SYS
- HR-PS1
- HP4SI-P1
- HP4SI-PQ1
- HR-APP

OU=PR
- MClarke
- SYD-PR-SRV1
- SYD-PR-SRV1_SYS
- SYD-PR-PS1
- HP4SI-P1
- HP4SI-PQ1
- PR-APP

OU=MEDICAL
- ASchweitzer
- MED-SRV1
- MED-SRV1_SYS
- MED-SRV2
- MED-SRV2_SYS
- HP4SI-P2
- HP4SI-PQ2

OU=FOOD
- MTeresa
- FOOD-SRV1
- FOOD-SRV1_SYS
- HP4SI-P3
- HP4SI-PQ3

OU=SHELTER
- FNightingale
- SHELT-SRV1
- SHELT-SRV1_SYS
- SHELT-SRV2
- SHELT-SRV2_SYS
- HP4SI-P4
- HP4SI-PQ4

OU=PEACE
- Buddha
- PEACE-SRV1
- PEACE-SRV1_SYS
- HPIII-P1
- HPIII-PQ1

That completes our discussion of Human Rights. Now, let's take a look at the ACME Labs division.

Labs — Albert Einstein in NORAD

Albert Einstein is one of the greatest minds in our history, but how far can he push technology? The U.S. Military has loaned us the NORAD facility in Colorado as a base for technical wizardry. In addition to Research & Development (R&D), this is the central point of a vast WHI data-collection network. Check out Figure 1.22.

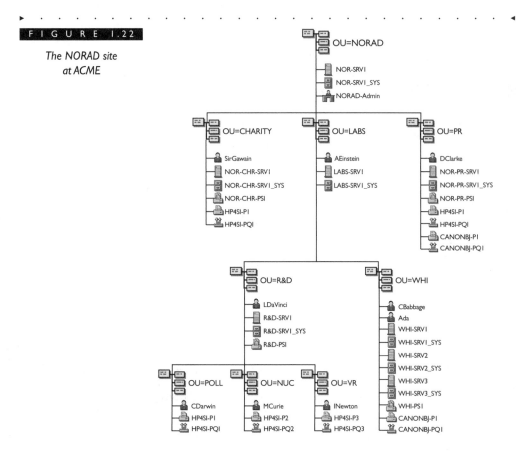

FIGURE 1.22

The NORAD site
at ACME

ACME's R&D efforts are controlled by Leonardo da Vinci and his dream team of scientists. They use technology and a little bit of magic to save the Earth. Current projects include alternative power sources, V/R programming, antipollutants, NDS, and a cure for bad-hair days. Let's take a closer look:

▶ *Pollution (Charles Darwin)* — This department is developing anti-pollutants and methods of transforming garbage into fuel. Also, this group is working to eradicate the world's largest scourge — ElectroPollution. Currently Leonardo da Vinci and Charles Darwin are working on airplanes powered by pencil erasure grit.

▶ *Nuclear (Marie Curie)* — Cybernetic soldiers (Nuclear Disarmament Squads or NDS) are being designed to infiltrate and neutralize nuclear weapons facilities. Finally, somebody's splitting atoms for good.

▶ *VR (Sir Isaac Newton)* — V/R programming is being developed to convince the world that a cure is necessary. The V/R devices will be sold as video games and will help ACME tap the minds of the world. This borders on mind control, but in a good way (if that's possible). There's nothing that brain power and a little bit of magic can't cure.

In addition to R&D, NORAD is the central point of a vast WHI data-collection network. This network is the pulse of ACME. Collection of world data and calculation of the WHI occur here every day. Currently, the WHI sits at −2. And, as we all know, it must climb to more than 100 by January 1, 2010. Charles Babbage and Ada diligently guard the computers and make daily adjustments to WHI calculations. Ada's sacrifice is particularly notable because she used to be the "Countess of Lovelace." But, fortunately for us, she has a soft spot in her heart for mathematics and Mr. Babbage.

Distributed world data-collection centers are scattered to all four corners of the Earth. There are ten ACME WHI hubs — one in every divisional headquarters — and five more scattered to strategic points around the Earth. From each of these sites, world data is sent to NORAD and calculated on a daily basis. The results are distributed to every major newspaper so the world can chart ACME's progress. In addition to the ten WHI hubs, there are hundreds of collection clusters distributed around each hub. Each cluster sends data directly to the closest hub (via dial-up lines) and eventually back to the central site at NORAD.

That completes our journey through ACME technology. Now, let's take a look at the Operations division.

Operations — King Arthur in Camelot

King Arthur and his court will keep ACME financed through charity drives and financial spending. After all, "money makes the world go 'round." Never before has it been more true. In addition, the Operations division handles the arduous task of distributing ACME aid to all the people who need it. Check out Figure 1.23. Here's how it works:

▶ *Financial (Guinevere)* — This is the money-out department. Guinevere handles the distribution of charity contributions, including the purchase of human-rights material, bailing-out of bankrupt nations, and the funding of internal ACME activities. For a more detailed discussion of Financial operations, refer to the ACME Workflow section later in this chapter.

▶ *Distribution (Merlin)* — We're going to need all the magic we can get. This department handles the distribution of human rights materials, medical supplies, doctors, nurses, food, hardware, building supplies, and pre-fabricated geodesic domes. No guns! It also handles implementation of WHI devices from R&D, such as anti-pollutants, Nuclear Disarmament Squads (NDS), anti-hacking viruses, and V/R programming. The latter is handled through satellite TV transmissions and video games. ACME distribution takes place through the same ten hubs as WHI. Think of it as data in (WHI) and aid out (Distribution).

▶ *Charity (Knights of the Round Table)* — This is the money-in department. The Knights collect charity from world organizations and distribute it to the Financial department for disbursement. Each of the five major Knights oversees one of five charity centers — in each of the divisional headquarters. Sir Lancelot is in Sydney, Sir Gawain is in NORAD, Sir Galahad handles Camelot, Sir Percival oversees Rio, and Sir Kay is in Tokyo. I haven't seen such dedication since the Medieval Ages.

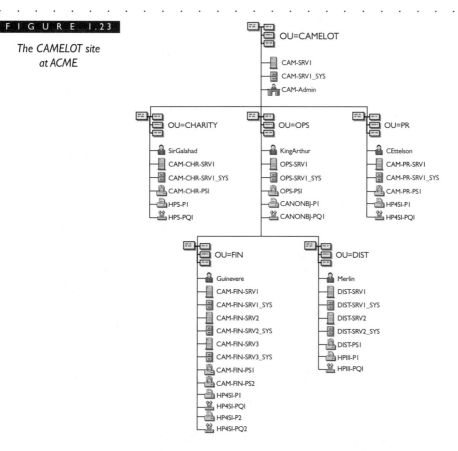

FIGURE 1.23

*The CAMELOT site
at ACME*

Well, that's how ACME's Operations work. Now, let's take a look at Crime Fighting.

Crime Fighting — Sherlock Holmes in Tokyo

Crime has one of the most negative effects on the WHI. Fortunately, we have history's greatest crime-fighting mind to help us out — Sherlock Holmes. With the help of Dr. Watson, he has identified two major categories of world crime (see Figure 1.24):

▶ White Collar

▶ Blue Collar

▶ · ◀

FIGURE 1.24

The TOKYO site
at ACME

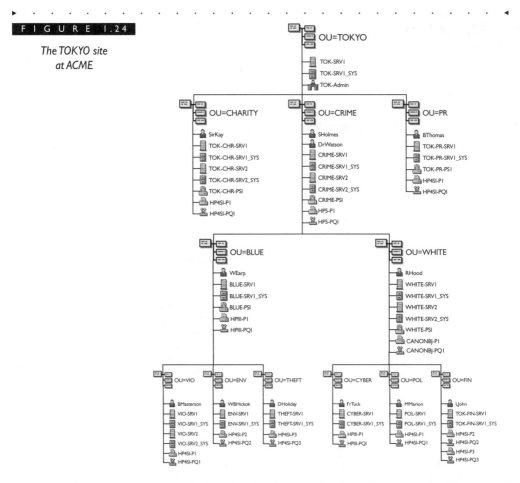

White-collar crimes include cyber-hacking and political espionage. Robin Hood
and his Band of Superheroes direct white-collar crime-fighting efforts from Tokyo.
Here are some of the different types of crimes they're concerned with:

▶ *Cyber (Friar Tuck)* — With the help of the Cyberphilia underground, Friar
Tuck attempts to thwart cyber-crime. Most cyber crimes occur on the
Net, so ACME must constantly monitor global communications. Tuck
also has the help of an offshoot group of guardian angels known as the
Cyber Angels.

▶ *Political (Maid Marion)* — She can charm her way through any politically tense situation. Political crimes are especially rampant in emerging nations, so Maid Marion enlists the help of the United Nations.

▶ *Financial (Little John)* — With some creative financing and the help of ex-IRS agents, Little John thwarts financial crimes throughout the world. These crimes especially hurt the middle class, so he has recruited some key Yuppies as undercover agents.

Blue-collar crimes are a little more obvious — such as violence and theft. This is familiar ground for Wyatt Earp and his band of western heroes. They're not glamorous, but they're effective. Here's a look at ACME Crime Fighting from the blue-collar point of view:

▶ *Violent (Bat Masterson)* — This cowboy is in his element. He thwarts violent crime by getting inside the criminal's mind — literally.

▶ *Environmental (Wild Bill Hickok)* — A great fan of the environment, Mr. Hickok uses his country charm to thwart environmental crimes such as excessive deforestation, toxic waste, whaling, oil spills, ElectroPollution, and forced extinction.

▶ *Theft (Doc Holliday)* — With his legendary sleight-of-hand, Doc Holliday stays one step ahead of the world's thieves.

So, that's what's happening on the crime-fighting front. Now, let's take a close look at the final ACME division — Admin.

Admin — George Washington in Rio

Ever since the beginning of time, humans have quested for wisdom and knowledge. Now we'll need to put all of our enlightenment to good use — or else. A few centuries ago, the United States' Founding Fathers joined a growing group of men and women called Illuminoids. These people were dissatisfied with everyday life on Planet Earth and began to reach above, within, and everywhere else for a better way. The Illuminoids formed a variety of organizations dedicated to creating a New World Order, including the Masons, the Trilateral Commission, the Council on Foreign Relations (CFR), and the Bilderberg Group.

Regardless of their ultimate motivation, the Illuminoids' hearts were in the right place — "let's make the world a better place." The founder of the Trilateral Commission has always claimed they are just a group of concerned citizens interested in fostering greater understanding and cooperation among international allies. Whether or not it's true, it sounds like a great fit for ACME. Once again, we've used the OTO to grab some of the earliest Illuminoids and solicit their help for ACME administration.

George Washington keeps the ACME ship afloat. Along with FDR, he keeps things running smoothly and makes sure the world hears about our plight. In addition, James Madison keeps the facilities running, while Abraham Lincoln makes sure ACME is held accountable for all its work. For years, the Trilateral Commission has been rumored to covertly run the world. Now they get a chance to overtly save it!

Now let's take a look at the four departments that make up ACME's administration (see Figure 1.25):

► *Public Relations (Franklin Delano Roosevelt)* — This department solicits help from the rest of the world by enlisting the help of heroes from our own age — the 1990s. We're not going to be able to save the world alone. The PR department is responsible for communicating our plight to the four corners of the Earth. Department members inform everyday citizens about the Alpha Centurion ultimatum, daily WHI quotes, and requests for charity. There is a local PR office in each major location. See the organizational chart in Figure 1.20 for more details.

► *Auditing (Abraham Lincoln)* — They make sure that everyone stays in line. Financial trails for all charity moneys and complete records of all changes to the WHI are tracked by the Auditing department. Although it's part of the internal ACME organization, Auditing is an independent tracking company that generates bonded reports.

► *Facilities (James Madison)* — This department keeps everyone working, happy, and fed. The Facilities department also organizes field trips and ACME parties. Imagine the doozy they're going to have when we finally succeed!

▶ *Marketing (Thomas Jefferson)* — Educating the rest of the world and soliciting help is another Marketing department responsibility. In addition to advertising, this department develops materials for distributed PR offices. Its goal is to rally all nations around ACME and our cause in order to save the Earth. They also bake really good apple pies and chocolate chip cookies.

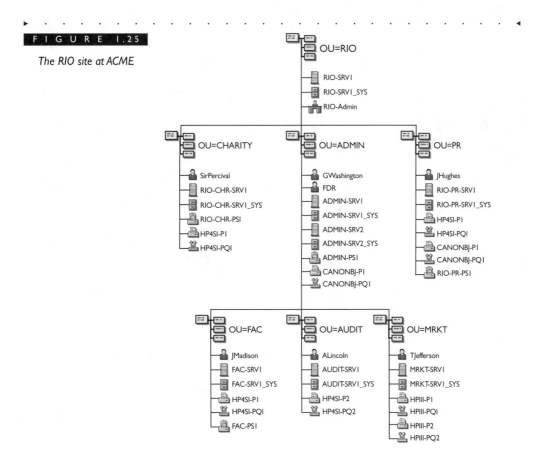

The RIO site at ACME

Well, there you have it. That's everything there is to know about ACME. I hope these *Chronicles* have helped you and the project team to better understand what ACME is up against. This is no normal organization. If ACME goes out of business, the world is either lost or saved — it's up to you.

ACME Workflow

Although it may look complicated, the daily grind at ACME is really pretty simple. It's a combination of workflow and dataflow. *Workflow* describes the daily operations of ACME staff and their task-oriented responsibilities. *Dataflow* describes the daily or weekly movement of data from one location to another. Although the two are not always the same, they should be compatible. This is the goal of ACME synergy.

In this section, we're going to take a detailed look at how work and data flow through the ACME organization. This data has a dramatic impact on NDS design. After all, work and data flow over the WAN infrastructure. Refer to Figure 1.26 as you follow along.

▶ · ◀

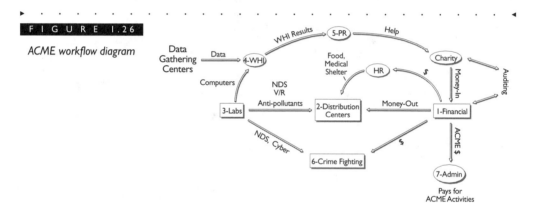

FIGURE 1.26

ACME workflow diagram

Financial

Of course, money makes the world go 'round! The Financial department has two main responsibilities:

▶ Money-in

▶ Money-out

Money-in focuses on funding ACME activities and distributing charities to needy people. With *Money-out*, Guinevere pays for Human Rights materials, Admin work, and Crime Fighting tools. Next, she disburses charity money through distribution centers. Money-in comes from the various Charity activities. All financial activity is audited by the internal Auditing organization.

Technically, this is accomplished from a central database at the Financial headquarters in Camelot. No money changes hands. Quarterly budgets are developed in Camelot and distributed to local banks for Human Rights, Crime Fighting, Distribution, and Admin. Each of these distributed sites sends weekly updates to the central database with the help of local servers.

Distribution Centers

The Distribution department is the hub of ACME achievements. Distribution centers disburse three kinds of aid:

▶ Human Rights materials (such as food, medicine, and shelter)

▶ Money from the Financial department

▶ Exciting inventions from Labs

Each of the ten distribution centers maintains its own distributed database. They move material to local warehouses for delivery to needy people. Weekly summary updates are sent to the central inventory management database in Camelot. The central database oversees the big picture of aid distribution.

If a center runs out of a particular resource, one of two things happens:

1. Camelot updates the center's budget, and they purchase the resource locally.

2. Camelot orders the movement of resources from another distribution center. This option makes sense for finite materials such as special inventions from Labs or medical supplies.

Labs and Their Inventions

This is where the brainiacs hang out. Scientists in the Labs division develop world-saving toys for:

▶ *Crime Fighting* — NDS and cyber-viruses

▶ *Distribution* — V/R programming and anti-pollutants

The Labs division supports WHI and all its technical needs. New product updates are sent to Distribution and Crime Fighting for internal consumption. This is secure information.

WHI Calculations

Labs is also where the WHI (World Health Index) is calculated. Charles Babbage and Ada collect data from data-gathering centers (DGCs) throughout the world. These DGCs are housed in divisional headquarters and distribution centers throughout the ACME WAN. They are:

NORAD	Seattle
Rio	Cairo
Camelot	New York
Sydney	Moscow
Tokyo	St. Andrews

Ironically, the distribution centers send aid out and the DGCs pull data in — from the same ten locations. Daily WHI summary calculations are sent to NORAD each day so the final WHI calculation can be made. Results are distributed to PR daily for inclusion in global periodicals — including the ACME *Chronicles* (an hourly interactive newsletter).

Public Relations

This is the voice of ACME. In addition to distributing daily WHI reports, Public Relations (PR) educates the world and helps solicit money for Charity. PR pulls the daily WHI results from NORAD twice a day. They're also the on-line editors of the ACME Chronicles, which gives them some great financial leads for Charity.

Money-In Charity is ACME's open door. It is the funnel for ACME contributions. There is a charity center in each of the five divisional headquarters. This is how the top 1 percent helps the rest of us. Their motto is:

Spread the wealth, or the Alpha Centurions will eat you!

All money collected by Charity is sent to the Financial department for disbursement. Two of the most important uses for this money are Crime Fighting and Admin. Note that the money doesn't actually change hands. It is deposited in local divisional banks, and daily updates are sent to the central financial database in Camelot.

Crime Fighting

Remember, crime has one of the greatest negative effects on the WHI. The Crime Fighting department relies on the following sources:

▸ Labs' inventions (NDS and cyber-viruses)

▸ Money from the Financial department

▸ The guile of Robin Hood, Wyatt Earp, and their respective heroes

ACME Administration

The ACME staff has to eat. Admin relies on money from Financial to keep things running smoothly. You can't fight bureaucracy. In addition, the Auditing department needs audit-level access to the central financial database in Camelot. They are responsible for tracking money-in from Charity and money-out from Financial.

That's all there is to it. No sweat. As you can see, ACME runs like a well-oiled machine. Someone sure put a lot of effort into designing its organizational structure — and it shows! We're in good hands with ACME.

Good luck; and by the way, thanks for saving the world!

LAB EXERCISE 1.1: ACME (A CURE FOR MOTHER EARTH)

Circle the 20 NetWare-related terms hidden in this word search puzzle using the hints provided. No punctuation characters (such as blank spaces, hyphens, and so on) should be included. All numbers should be spelled out.

```
S  R  M  F  A  S  T  T  R  A  C  K  W  E  B  S  E  R  V  E  R
C  O  N  S  O  L  E  O  N  E  L  E  B  T  H  X  E  S  K  W  T
O  O  S  A  S  C  F  X  H  R  I  R  D  I  Y  L  F  C  R  I  P
M  C  R  L  D  A  P  V  U  I  F  N  X  M  R  V  T  S  R  S  Q
P  V  M  B  P  H  E  B  I  N  D  E  R  Y  A  G  E  N  T  C  J
A  N  Q  H  A  A  C  M  E  R  F  L  C  B  C  B  E  F  O  Z  N
T  M  E  M  O  R  Y  P  R  O  T  E  C  T  I  O  N  R  Q  L  B
I  R  G  H  G  L  E  D  E  R  U  U  E  J  L  T  W  J  X  V  I
B  A  C  K  W  A  R  D  C  O  M  P  A  T  I  B  I  L  I  T  Y
I  G  Y  E  K  G  K  Q  P  C  A  T  S  L  F  G  N  H  I  U  N
L  R  H  W  O  W  D  F  F  K  L  U  W  J  M  Z  J  Y  W  I  V
I  N  O  V  E  L  L  H  E  L  P  R  E  Q  U  E  S  T  E  R  H
T  T  D  C  V  L  K  X  T  W  B  K  J  F  S  I  M  V  I  Y  A
Y  U  R  H  A  R  D  W  A  R  E  I  N  V  E  N  T  O  R  Y  K
M  H  G  N  M  V  W  F  C  O  K  V  U  M  H  H  H  T  R  T  G
O  O  V  Z  M  I  G  R  A  T  I  O  N  G  A  T  E  W  A  Y  S
D  N  E  B  N  U  B  J  X  O  W  M  M  E  V  V  J  E  D  O  W
E  S  E  C  I  V  R  E  S  G  N  I  T  I  D  U  A  B  I  S  M
```

Hints:

1. Organization whose mission is to protect the Planet Earth from Alpha Centurions.
2. Security feature that provides the ability to monitor and record information regarding the use of network resources.
3. NDPS feature that allows NDPS clients to print through the legacy system and non-NDPS clients to print through a queue to NDPS-aware printers.

4. Compatibility mode feature that enables IP clients to access flat-file bindery data.
5. NetWare 5 feature that provides compatibility between IP and IPX protocols on the same network.
6. GUI-based server console utility that provides basic server and NDS management functions.
7. Industry standard that enables Internet and intranet users to share objects such as data and applications, regardless of the platform.
8. Protocol that provides a framework for dynamically passing configuration information to clients or service-providing resources on a TCP/IP network.
9. Optional NetWare 5 product that allows you to create, publish, and serve Web documents to corporate intranets or the global World Wide Web (the Internet).
10. New NDS object used as a central, replicated database for workstation inventory.
11. Generic name for the core of the NetWare 5 operating system.
12. Industry-standard protocol that lets users easily access X.500-based directories such as NDS.
13. NetWare 5 troubleshooting feature that allows applications to be run in protected mode and prevents ill-behaved applications from crashing the server.
14. New NetWare 5 feature that provides seamless connectivity between IP/IPX cross-culture networks.
15. Z.E.N.works feature that allows users to notify the Help Desk or network administrator of workstation problems via e-mail or phone.
16. Initiative that represents the strategic direction Novell is taking to migrate its products and services to open protocols and standards — specifically to Java.
17. Infrastructure for supporting both existing and emerging authentication mechanisms — such as biometric and token-authentication systems.
18. Industry-standard Internet protocol that provides automatic resource discovery and registration on a TCP/IP network.
19. NetWare 5 feature that is not is supported by NSS.
20. Memory-management technique that enables NetWare 5 to temporarily store information on the hard drive when there is not enough server RAM to complete an operation.

**LAB EXERCISE 1.2:
SAVING THE WORLD WITH NETWARE 5**

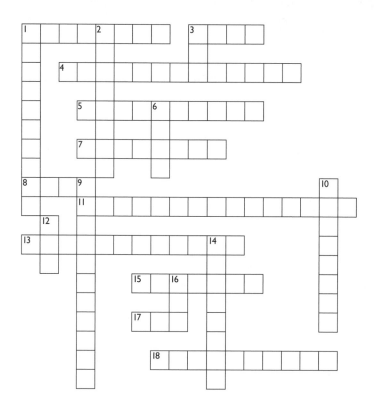

Across

1. Replaces INSTALL.NLM
3. Replaces DOWN + EXIT
4. Replaces DOWN + RESTART SERVER
5. Replacing server NICs on the fly
7. Private network that uses Internet technology
8. Next-generation printing system
11. NDS phone book
13. Provides contextless login
15. Replaces SERVMAN

17. The "Cloud"
18. The "other" file system

Down

1. The ultimate in communication
2. Add-on product for managing NT domains
3. Translates host names to IP addresses
6. No longer required for loading NLMs
9. Replaces the "WORM"
10. Zero Effort Networking
12. Controls the use of licensed applications
14. Surfing location
16. Optional high-performance storage system

CHAPTER 2

Plant a Tree in a Cloud: Novell Directory Services

Welcome to NetWare 5! NetWare 5 epitomizes transparent connectivity. It unobtrusively provides the user with simultaneous access to multiple network resources from a single login — whatever that means.

Simply stated, users no longer belong to servers — they belong to the network as a whole. All resources of the wide area network (WAN) are created as objects in a hierarchical tree, much like files in a directory structure. Users, servers, printers, volumes, and groups are treated equally and given simultaneous access to each other's resources. It's been a long and winding road, but we've finally achieved NetWare 5 Nirvana in true form. This is all made possible through NetWare 5's great wonder — Novell Directory Services (NDS).

NDS is an object-oriented database that organizes network resources into a hierarchical tree — there's that fancy word again. The global NDS tree is fully replicated and distributed throughout the network, providing efficient connectivity and network fault tolerance — which is easier said than done. NDS also features a single login and hidden security system that makes access to any server, volume, or network resource completely transparent to the user. NDS takes care of the complexities of network topology, communications, protocol translation, and authentication in the background, far away from the user.

Think of NDS as a friendly cloud of joy overlooking your network! NDS is simplicity through sophistication.

TIP

NDS enables you to manage network resources (such as servers, users, and printers) as graphical objects in a logical world. In addition, NDS allows you to control the file system (directories and files) through a graphical, Windows-based utility — NetWare Administrator. Clearly, NetWare 5 resource management through NDS is a CNA's best friend.

Every cloud has a silver lining. As a matter of fact, you can probably feel a slight "twinge" even as you read this. You knew that your new life as a CNA would be exciting, but no one prepared you for this. The more you learn about NDS, the faster you'll start growing an NDS tree out of your head. Whatever you do, take this simple advice:

"Keep your head out of the clouds and your two feet planted firmly in the ground."

I'm your friend — "NDS-Head Fred." I'm here to help you deal with this whole cranial gardening thing. As you learned in the previous chapter, NDS is a virtual tree structure that helps you organize network resources. It's also referred to as the "Cloud" because it floats above physical resources — servers, printers, and users. The goal of this chapter is to generate enough neurokinetic energy to stimulate cranial growth in *your* head. In other words, we're going to make you think until it hurts:

▶ *Getting to Know NDS* — We'll start with a brief introduction to NDS and learn how it differs from the NetWare 3 bindery. Then, we'll explore the composition of the logical NDS "tree."

▶ *NDS Objects* — Next, we'll dig up some dirt on NDS roots, containers, and leaf objects. Yes, I said "leaf" objects. These little horticultural heroes form the foundation of NetWare 5 resource management. Get to know them!

▶ *Overview of NDS Management* — Finally, we'll begin our CNA/CNE journey down the path of NDS Gardening with a brief introduction to NDS naming, partition management, and time synchronization. This is great stuff.

So, without any further ado, let's start at the beginning — with an introduction to the NDS Cloud.

· ◀

Getting to Know NDS

NDS is your friend!

It may seem a little intimidating at first, but when you get to know NDS, it's actually pretty fun. Really. NDS is a big Sta-Puff marshmallow man that keeps track of your network's resources. In more technical terms, it's a distributed object-oriented hierarchical database of physical (and logical) network objects. Huh? Just think of it as a huge WAN phone book.

NDS classifies all network resources into numerous different objects. These objects can be organized by function, location, size, type, or color — it doesn't matter. The point is, NDS organizes network resources independently from their physical locations. When a user logs into the network, he or she can access any object in the tree regardless of its location. This type of openness, however, does not come without a price. One obvious problem is security—which is why NDS is controlled by a complex, impenetrable armor known as NDS *access rights*.

So, what does NDS look like? From the outside, it looks like a big cloud hovering over your network. On the inside, however, it's a hierarchical tree similar to the DOS file system. As you can see in Figure 2.1, NDS organizes resources into logical groups called containers. This is like Tupperware gone mad. In Figure 2.1, servers are organized according to function. Then users are placed in the appropriate containers to simplify connectivity. In addition, productivity increases because users are near the resources they use. NDS also creates a global method of interconnectivity for all servers, users, groups, and other resources throughout the WAN. The bottom line is this—users don't access physical resources anymore. Instead, they access logical objects in the NDS tree. This means they don't need to know which NetWare 5 server provides a particular resource. All they need to know is where the server exists in the logical NDS world.

► · ◄

FIGURE 2.1

A Tree in a cloud

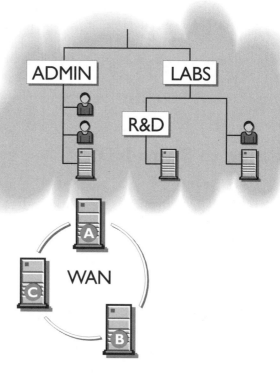

So, is NDS worth it? Well, you'll have to make that decision for yourself. But here are some reasons why I think it's the greatest thing since sliced bread:

▸ NDS offers a global database for central access and management of network information, resources, and services.

▸ NDS offers a standard method of managing, viewing, and accessing network information, resources, and services.

▸ NDS allows you to logically organize your resources independent from their physical characteristics or layout of the network.

▸ NDS provides dynamic mapping between an object and the physical resource to which it refers.

▸ NDS works today and is several years ahead of any competitor with proven reliability, scaleability, and security for enterprise networks.

▸ NDS significantly lowers the cost of managing and administering a network through centralized access and management of all network and operating system resources. In addition, it significantly lowers the cost of connectivity and data synchronization over a wide area network (WAN).

▸ NDS provides increased performance for LDAP access and directory query.

▸ NDS allows in-house and third-party applications to employ LDAP to access various directories — including NDPS.

So, what do you think? Is NDS for you? Before you answer, let's take a moment to get to know NDS. Who knows — you might even like it.

The "Cloud"

NDS has many different names — the Directory, the tree, the "Cloud," the Sta-Puff marshmallow man. In reality, it's all of these things. But the most appropriate description is the "Cloud."

NDS oversees physical network resources and provides users with a logical world to live in. This differs dramatically from what you're used to — NetWare 3.2. As you can see in Figure 2.2, the NetWare 3.2 bindery is server-centric. This means that every physical resource exists within and/or around the server. If Leia wants to access files or printers on multiple servers, she must have a login account and security access on every one. This system makes access and management both repetitive and time consuming. Also, note that nothing exists above the server. The server itself represents the highest level of the physical network organization structure. Users, volumes, files, and printers all exist within each server.

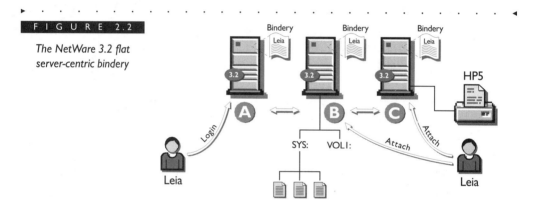

FIGURE 2.2

The NetWare 3.2 flat server-centric bindery

NDS, on the other hand, creates a whole new world *above* the server. As you can see in Figure 2.3, each network resource exists only once as a logical object in the "Cloud." NDS is network-centric in the sense that everything happens in the NDS hierarchy. Suddenly the server has gone from being at the top of the network organizational chart to being a physical object at the bottom. The beauty of this system is that Leia only logs in once and has instant access to all network resources. She doesn't log into each server — she logs into the NDS tree, and it tracks where her files and printers are. All logins, attaches, and access rights are handled in the background by NDS. This is the epitome of user transparency. The beauty is that users don't need to see inside the "Cloud;" all they need to know is that their stuff is there.

The main lesson to learn from the accompanying graphics is the direction of the arrows. In Figure 2.2, the arrows of communication are horizontal. This means that all communication exists within and between NetWare 3.2 servers. If Leia wants access to another resource, she must follow the horizontal communication path to another server by either re-logging in or attaching.

▶ . . . . ◀

The NetWare 5 hierarchical network-centric NDS cloud

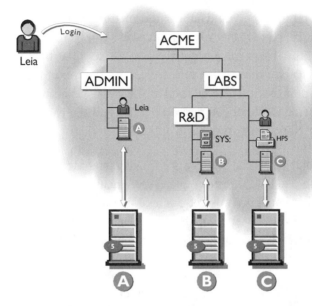

In contrast, Figure 2.3 shows the communication arrows running vertically. This means that communication occurs from within and between the NDS Cloud and its physical resources. The NDS Cloud handles the problem of locating resources and transparently grabs whatever Leia wants. This vertical communication structure makes finding and using network resources much easier for the user. In addition, and this is the part you'll like, it provides a single point of central network management for CNAs.

Let's take a closer look at the differences between NDS and the older NetWare 3.2 bindery.

NDS versus the Bindery

The bindery found in earlier versions of NetWare is a flat-file database that tracks network resources on each server. It's stored as the files NET$OBJ.SYS, NET$PROP.SYS, and NET$VAL.SYS in the SYS:SYSTEM directory. The bindery uses these three files to track network objects, properties, and values. When users need to access a server's resources, they must log in and register with its respective bindery. If the server doesn't recognize them, it disallows access. Then, the administrator must create a special entry with different access security for this user. This is painstaking and time-consuming.

NDS, on the other hand, stores information about network resources in a global database, called the *Directory*. This database can be distributed on all servers in the WAN so that users can instantly get access to what they need. Suddenly, you've been escalated from a lowly bindery user to the top of the NDS food chain. As an object, you exist at the same level as the NetWare 5 server. How does it feel?

Following is a brief comparison of NDS and the NetWare bindery. In each case, focus on NDS's network-centric approach.

- ▶ *Database* — The bindery is a flat-file database consisting of three files in the SYS:SYSTEM directory. Each server retains its own database. NDS, on the other hand, is an object-oriented hierarchical database, called the Directory. The Directory encompasses all objects in the WAN and is distributed across servers. It also consists of database files on the SYS: volume. These files are, however, protected in a special system-owned directory.

- ▶ *Server* — In NetWare 3.2, the server is king of the hill. It houses the bindery and controls all network resources. In NetWare 5, however, the server's importance diminishes quite a bit. It's simply another logical object in the global NDS tree. Network resources are accessed through the "Cloud" — independently from the physical server. But don't get caught up in the logical insignificance of the NetWare 5 server. In the physical realm, it's still king of the hill. After all, NetWare 5 has to be installed somewhere, files have to be stored somewhere, and users have to log into something.

- ▶ *Users* — In NetWare 3.2, users are defined as objects in the server-based bindery. You must create a User object for that user on every server on which the user needs access. In NDS, however, users are logical objects in the NDS Cloud. Each user is defined only once. The system takes care of tracking the resources to which they need access. This is made possible using a concept called context, which we'll explain a little bit later.

▸ *Login* — Bindery logins are server-centric. This means that users must log in or attach to every server they use a resource from — files, printing, or applications. NDS logins are network-centric. This means that users issue one login statement for access to the entire "Cloud." Once they're in, the world is at their fingertips.

TIP

In order for NDS to identify you, you must provide your "full NDS name" at login. This includes your username and "context." There's that word again. A user's full name is a combination of who they are and where they live. My login name, for example, would be DAVID in CALIFORNIA in the USA. We'll talk about this later in the "NDS Naming" section of this chapter.

▸ *Network Resources* — In a bindery network, resources are owned by the server. Volumes and printers, for example, are tracked according to the server to which they're attached. User access to these resources requires login or attachment to the host server. NDS, on the other hand, distributes network resources independently from the server to which they're attached. It might seem strange, but volumes can be organized across the tree from their host servers. It's possible for users to have access to the NetWare 5 file system without logical access to its host server. Very cool. But don't get too carried away. Physical volumes still reside inside NetWare 5 servers. We haven't figured out how to separate the two yet — that's NetWare 7!

As you can see, NDS is a huge improvement over the NetWare 3.2 bindery. NDS is actually not even an improvement — it's a complete revolution. Nothing is as it appears. So, if NDS isn't what you think it is, what is it? Let's take a closer look.

Composition of the Tree

Plant a tree in a "Cloud" — it's good for the environment.

As in nature, the NDS tree starts with the [Root] and builds from there. Next, it sprouts container objects, which are branches reaching toward the sky. Finally, leaf objects flutter in the wind and provide network functionality to users, servers, and the file system. As you can see in Figure 2.4, the tree analogy is alive and well.

▶ · ◀

FIGURE 2.4

The figurative NDS tree

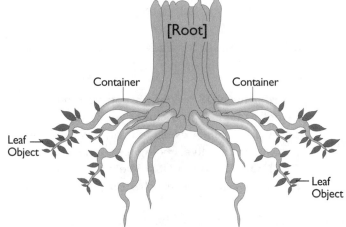

The real NDS tree is made up of special logical objects. NDS objects define logical or physical entities that provide organizational or technical function to the network. As you can see in Figure 2.5, they come in three different flavors:

▶ [Root]

▶ Container objects

▶ Leaf objects

The [Root] is the very top of the NDS tree. Because it represents the opening porthole to our NDS world, its icon is appropriately a picture of the Earth. Container objects define the organizational boundaries of the NDS tree and house other container objects and/or leaf objects. In Figure 2.5, we use container objects to define the ACME organization and its two divisions—ADMIN and LABS. Finally, leaf objects are the physical or logical network resources that provide technical services and WAN functionality. Leaf objects define the lowest level of the NDS structure. In Figure 2.5, leaf objects represent Users, a Printer, a Server, and a Group. NDS supports more than 50 different leaf object types. We'll discuss the most interesting leaves in the next section.

The tree can be organized any way you want, as long as it makes sense. "AEinstein," for example, is placed near the resources he uses—the "HP5" printer and "LABS-SRV1" file server. Remember ACME from Chapter 1? It's time to Save the World!

FIGURE 2.5

The real NDS tree

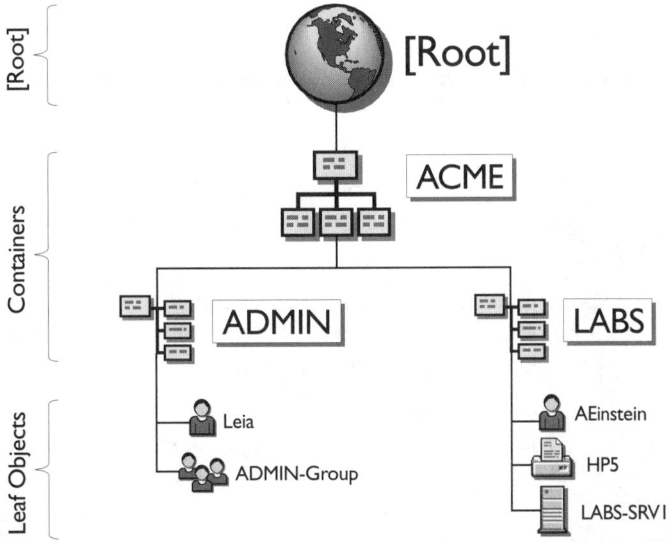

On a more fundamental level, the NDS tree is stored in a fully replicated, globally distributed, object-oriented database, called the Directory. The Directory consists of multiple hidden system files in the SYS:_NETWARE directory on each server. These files are replicated and distributed throughout the WAN to provide fault tolerance and increased connectivity. Although all NetWare 5 servers use NDS, they don't have to contain their own directory database. If a server contains a portion of the database, that portion is called a partition. If a server doesn't have a copy of the database, then it must access it from some other server—which is less efficient. The bottom line is that a NetWare 5 server can contain the entire directory database, pieces of it (partitions), or none at all.

In addition, NDS requires a temporal assurance system, called time synchronization. This means that everyone must agree on what time it is. Time is critical to NDS because NetWare 5 uses time stamps for synchronization, auditing, and NDS security. Time synchronization is implemented by using a variety of different time server types, as you'll see later in this chapter.

Typically, a single network has only one directory. Although it's possible for a WAN to have multiple NDS trees, resources cannot be shared between them. For this reason, Novell is pushing toward a single tree for the whole world. We'll see, but it sure explains the world icon for the [Root].

> **REAL WORLD**
>
> In addition to its own proprietary Directory Service (NDS), NetWare 5 supports another industry-wide directory protocol — Lightweight Directory Access Protocol (LDAP).
>
> LDAP is an industry-standard protocol that lets users easily access X.500-based directories such as NDS. LDAP Services for NDS is a server-based interface between NDS and applications that comply with LDAP.
>
> In addition, NetWare 5 includes an Active Directory Services Interface (ADSI) NDS provider. ADSI is designed to integrate multiple directory services through a well-defined open interface. With ADSI, CNEs can manage resources in a variety of directory services including NDS and LDAP. This product works with Novell Clients for Windows 95 and Windows NT.
>
> Now that NetWare 5 supports both NDS and LDAP, it's safe to say that the Novell virtual cloud covers most of Planet Earth.

Now that you understand the fundamental architecture of NDS, let's take a closer look at its different container and leaf objects. Remember, plant a tree in a Cloud — it's good for the environment.

NDS Objects

When you sprout a cranial conifer and become a Novell CNA, leaf objects and the [Root] will become important to you. I'd like to take this opportunity to help you out a little and explain them more.

As we just learned, the NDS tree consists of three different types of objects — [Root], container, and leaf objects. What we didn't learn is that these objects have specific properties and values. Remember, NDS is, after all, a database.

Here's how it works. An *object* is similar to a record or row of information in a database table. A *property* is similar to a field in each database record. For example, the properties of a Sales database may be Name, Phone Number, and Last Item Purchased. Finally, *values* are data strings stored in each object property. These values define the information around which the database is built.

Let's take a closer look.

Understanding NDS Objects

As we learned earlier, NDS objects define logical or physical entities that provide organizational or technical functionality to the network. They come in three different flavors:

▸ [Root]

▸ Container objects

▸ Leaf objects

As you can see, the tree analogy is alive and well. Figure 2.5 shows that objects come in many different shapes and sizes. They can be physical resources (printers and servers), NDS resources (groups), users or logical tree organizers (containers). We'll take a closer look at some of NetWare 5's most interesting object types in just a moment.

Each NDS object consists of categories of information called *properties*. Properties are similar to fields in a database record that categorize types of information. User objects, for example, have properties such as Login Name, Password, Postal Address, and Description. While the same type of object may have the same properties, the information within those properties can be different. For example, two User objects both have a Login Name property, but one has a value of Leia and the other has a value of AEinstein.

In addition, a unique collection of properties define the *class* of an object. For example, a Printer object differs from a User object in that it has a different set of properties. The Printer object needs to track the default queue, for example, whereas users are more interested in generational qualifiers. NDS uses two different types of properties:

▶ *Required properties* — The NDS object cannot be created until these properties are supplied. When creating an object, you are prompted for required values (for example, Last Name for users and Host Server/Host Volume for the Volume object).

▶ *Multivalued properties* — These properties support more than one entry. For example, the User property called Telephone Number can hold multiple numbers that apply to a single user. Other User multivalued properties include Location and Fax Number.

Finally, *values* are the data stored in object properties. Refer to Table 2.1 for an illustration of the relationship between NDS objects, properties, and values.

T A B L E 2.1	OBJECT	PROPERTY	VALUE
Understanding NDS objects, properties, and values	User	Login Name	AEinstein
		Title	Super-smart scientist
		Location	NORAD
		Password	Relativity
	Printer (Non-NDPS)	Common Name	HP5
		Default Queue	HP5-PQI
		Print Server	LABS-PSI
	NetWare Server	Full Name	LABS-SRVI
		Version	NetWare 5
		Operator	Admin
		Status	Running just fine

Now that you've mastered the subtle differences between NDS objects, properties, and values, let's explore some of the most interesting objects in detail — starting with [Root]. You never know which objects you're going to have sprouting from your cerebellum.

[Root]

The [Root] object defines the top of the NDS organizational structure. Each Directory tree can only have one [Root], which is created during installation of the first server in that tree. The [Root] cannot be deleted, renamed, or moved. The NDS [Root] object is exceptional in that it begins the boundaries of your NDS world. It behaves very much like a container object in that it houses other container objects. The main difference is that the [Root] cannot contain leaf objects.

The NDS Directory tree is sometimes confused with the [Root] object. Unlike [Root], the tree name can be changed.

TIP

Each NDS object has a specific icon that depicts its purpose graphically. The [Root] object's icon is particularly interesting. Because the [Root] object represents the opening porthole to the NDS world, its icon is appropriately a picture of the Earth. As you can see in Figure 2.6, the [Root] defines the top of our tree and houses the ACME container object.

▶ · ◀

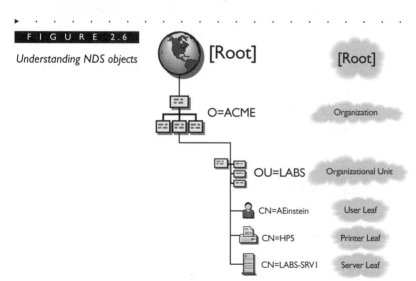

F I G U R E   2.6

Understanding NDS objects

The [Root] can hold only these specific container objects:

▸ *Country* — An optional container object that designates the country where your network resides.

▶ *Organization* — A one-dimensional container that typically represents your company.

▶ *Alias* — A logical NDS pointer to any other object existing elsewhere in the tree. In this case, the Alias can only point to Country and Organization objects. That makes sense.

The [Root] object is exceptional in one other way. It's the only NDS object without any properties. It simply exists as a placeholder for the top of the tree structure. It can have trustees, however. As we'll see in Chapter 5 ("NetWare 5 Security"), certain rights that you assign to the [Root] will be inherited by *all* objects in the tree — which could be a bad thing. All in all, the [Root] is a cool object, but you can't do much with it. Most of your design and management tasks will involve container and leaf objects.

REAL WORLD

You might notice the square brackets ([ ]) surrounding the [Root] object. These brackets designate the object as a special NDS entity. NetWare 5 supports two other such entities — [Public] and [Supervisor]. [Public] is a special trustee that applies security to all other objects in the tree. Users can inherit the rights of [Public] without having to log in. They simply need to attach. As we'll see in Chapter 5, this creates a serious NDS security loophole.

[Supervisor] is a special superuser for bindery emulation. Users from the NetWare 3.2 world can log into NDS using [Supervisor] and inherit all its special rights. [Supervisor] has other important properties that allow you to achieve NetWare 3.2 and NetWare 5 coexistence.

Container Objects

Container objects are logical organizers. They are the Tupperware bowls of our NDS kitchen. Actually the analogy works well — work with me here. The nature of Tupperware is that larger containers enclose smaller containers, which in turn house even smaller ones. Of course, the biggest Tupperware container in the world is the [Root]. Maybe in the future, when NDS takes over the world, we'll all be enclosed in a pale green, airtight, plastic bowl. Finally, Tupperware containers are used to store fruits and vegetables. In NDS, our Tupperware container objects store lettuce "leaf" objects. Sorry.

Here's a quick list of the three types of NetWare 5 NDS container objects:

▶ *Country* — Designates the country where certain parts of the organization reside.

▶ *Organization* — Represents a company, university, or department. NDS only supports one layer of Organization objects, hence, the term "one-dimensional."

▶ *Organizational Unit* — Represents a division, business unit, or project team within the Organization. Organizational Units hold other Organizational Units or leaf objects. They are multidimensional. Cool.

Refer to Figure 2.6 for an illustration of the relationship between the [Root] and container objects. The ACME Organization houses other Organizational Units (including LABS), which in turn house leaf objects (like AEinstein). Let's take a closer look at these three different container objects.

Country Objects

The Country object is optional. It designates the country where your network resides and organizes other objects within the country. You can use a Country object to designate the country where your organization headquarters is or, if you have a multinational WAN, to designate each country that is part of your network. The Country object is also useful if you plan on cruising across the information superhighway. As a matter of fact, many Internet global directory providers (portals) are using the Country object as an entry point to their systems.

As I said a moment ago, the Country object is optional. It is not created as part of the default NetWare 5 installation. If you want a Country object, you'll need to specifically configure it during installation of the very first server. Otherwise, adding a Country later can be a real pain. Also, this object must be represented by a valid two-character country abbreviation. These abbreviations are defined as part of the ISO X.500 standard. Most trees don't use the Country object. Finally, Country objects can only house Organization containers and/or Organization

Aliases. They cannot support leaf objects. Leaf objects must be stored within Organization or Organizational Unit containers.

> **If you don't have any compelling reasons to use the Country object, stay away from it. It only adds an unnecessary level of complexity to your WAN. As a matter of fact, Novell doesn't even use the Country object in their own multidimensional, worldwide NDS tree.**
>
> TIP

Organization Objects

 If you don't use a Country object, the next layer in the tree is typically an Organization. As you can see in Figure 2.6, ACME is represented as an "O." You can use the Organization object to designate a company, a division of a company, a university or college with various departments, and so on. Every Directory tree must contain at least one Organization object. Therefore, it is required. Many small implementations use only the Organization object and place all their resources directly underneath it. Organization objects must be placed directly below the [Root], unless a Country or Locality object is used. Finally, Organizations can contain all objects except [Root], Country, and Organization.

Earlier we defined the Organization as a one-dimensional object. This means the tree can only support one layer of Organization objects. If you look closer at the icon, you'll see a box with multiple horizontal boxes underneath. Additional vertical hierarchy is defined by Organizational Units — they are multidimensional. We'll describe them in just a moment.

Figure 2.7 illustrates the Details screen of the ACME Organization from NetWare Administrator. On the right side of the screen are the many page buttons that identify categories of NDS properties. Associated with each page button is an input screen for a specific set of information (on the left side). The Identification page button (shown here) allows you to define a variety of Organization properties — including Name, Other Name, Description, Location, Telephone, and Fax Number.

Similar page buttons allow you to configure important Organization parameters, including postal information, print job configurations, trustee assignments, and so on. As far as ACME is concerned, the Organization container defines the top of the functional tree.

▶ · ◀

FIGURE 2.7

Properties of an NDS organization

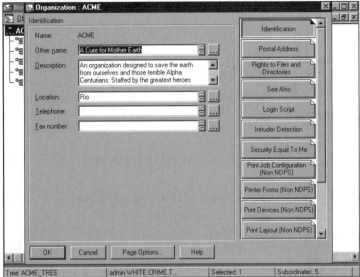

Organizational Unit Objects

The Organizational Unit object is a "natural group." It allows you to organize users with the leaf objects they use. You can create group login scripts, a user template for security, trustee assignments, security equivalences, and distributed administrators. All in all, Organizational Units are your friends.

Organizational Units represent a division, a business unit, or a project team. In Figure 2.6 earlier, the LABS OU represents a division within the ACME Organization. In this container, AEinstein works with his printers and servers. Organizational Units use the exact same properties as Organizations, but in a slightly different way (see Figure 2.7). Organizational Units are multidimensional in that you can have many hierarchical levels of containers within containers. Remember, the Organization can only exist at one level.

Organizational Units are the most flexible Tupperware containers because they contain other OU's or leaf objects. As a matter of fact, Organizational Units can contain any NDS object type except the [Root], Country, or Organization containers (or Aliases to any of these).

Now let's take a look at the real stars of our NDS world — the leaves.

REAL WORLD

NDS supports three other container objects — Locality, User License Container, and Server License Container.

The secret Locality object is like the Country object in that it's optional and not created as part of the default NetWare 5 installation. You can use a Locality object to designate the region where your organization headquarters resides. Unlike Country objects, Locality objects can reside either under the [Root], Country, Organization, or Organizational Unit containers. Keep in mind, however, that most NetWare 5 utilities don't recognize the Locality object. Oops.

In addition, NetWare 5 supports two different types of license container objects: a User License container and a Server License container. These objects are added to the NDS tree when NetWare 5 is installed. They appear as leaf objects in the container that includes the Server object. License container objects can contain multiple license Certificate leaf objects. To manage licenses for users, you use the "Novell + NetWare 5 Conn SCL+500" license container. This is where the initial user license certificates are placed by default. This name is a compound fragment made up of the Publisher, Product, and Version attributes. In addition, the number at the end of the license container object's name indicates the number of users the license certificate accommodates.

Leaf Objects

Leaf objects represent logical or physical network resources. Most of your CNA life will be spent designing, installing, and managing leaf objects — you'll become a vegetarian very quickly. These are the ultimate NDS entities that NetWare 5 users seek.

Because leaf objects reside at the bottom of the NDS tree, they cannot hold other leaves. They represent the proverbial "end of the road." As we learned earlier, each class of leaf object has certain properties associated with it. This collection of properties differentiates the various leaf object classes. NetWare 5 supports almost 15 different categories for leaf object functionality. In this section, we're going to explore the five most interesting categories for CNAs. They are:

▸ User leaf objects

▸ Server leaf objects

▸ Printer leaf objects

▸ Network Services leaf objects

▸ Miscellaneous leaf objects

In this section, we'll explore each of these five categories and identify the key properties of their corresponding NDS leaf objects. So, what's stopping you? Let's get going.

User Leaf Objects

Users are the center of your universe. After all, they are the ones that "use" the network. NDS supports five different leaf objects that help users do what they do. Let's check them out:

User — Represents a person who uses the network. The user can be a beginner, a gardener, or NDS-Head Fred. The only requirement is that every person who logs into the WAN must be represented by a unique User object. When you create a User object, you can create a home directory for that user, who then has default rights to the file system. In addition, you can define default login restrictions using the special Template object. In Figure 2.6 earlier, we learned that AEinstein is a User object in the LABS Organizational Unit. Notice the name designator — "CN." This represents Albert's login name or common name. As you can see in Figure 2.8, AEinstein has a plethora of User-related properties — almost 100, to be exact. The page buttons on the right-hand side identify property categories such as Identification, Security Restrictions, Mailbox, Print Job Configurations, Login Script, and so on.

Template — A new type of object available in NetWare 5 that can be used to create User objects. It's similar in function to the User Template found in earlier versions of NetWare, except that now it offers a dynamic link between Template and User properties. When you define a Template-User link, you can designate default values for User object creation, including NDS rights and file system rights, and a setup script for copying files to each new user's home directory. Refer to the user creation section in Chapter 3 for more information.

FIGURE 2.8

*Properties of an
NDS User object*

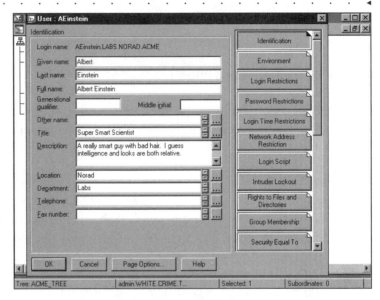

REAL WORLD

NDS is a very powerful database with a lot of valuable user information. Consider using it as a central company database of employee data. If you can't find what you need in the almost 100 default properties, you can always create your own. The NetWare 5 Software Developers Kit (SDK) provides interface tools for modifying and adding NDS properties. This is called "extending" the NDS Schema.

In addition, NetWare 5 introduces a "Schema Manager" for viewing and customizing the NDS Schema directly from NetWare Administrator. CNAs can access this GUI management tool from the Object menu. Check it out . . . it's fun at parties!

Group—Defines an unrelated list of users for the purpose of assigning access rights and other management strategies. Remember, containers create "natural groups" for objects within the same Organization or Organizational Unit. The Group object, on the other hand, allows you to organize users from anywhere in the NDS tree. This is a great management strategy for assigning unrelated trustee rights or login restrictions.

Organizational Role — Defines a position or role within the organization. If you want to assign security to a "position" instead of an "employee," consider creating an Organizational Role. The occupant can change frequently, but the responsibilities of the position will not. Whenever a user occupies the Organizational Role, they "absorb" its security. Some sample Organizational Roles include Postmaster, Chief Scientist, Administrative Assistant, and Coffee Jockey.

Profile — NetWare 5's group login script. The Profile object contains a login script that can be shared by a group of unrelated users. If you have users who need to share common login script commands, but are not located in the same portion of the tree, consider assigning them to a Profile. As we'll see in Chapter 3, the Profile login script executes after the Container login script and before the User login script.

Server Leaf Objects

The NetWare 5 Server is still king of the physical hill. Even though it loses a lot of its significance in the logical realm, NetWare 5 still resides on it, users still log in to it, and printers still attach to it. NDS supports three different leaf objects that apply to the logical server. Let's take a closer look:

NetWare Server — Represents any server running NetWare on your network. The server can be running NetWare 2, 3, 4, or 5. The NDS Server object is created automatically during installation. The only way to insert a server object is to actually install NetWare 5 on the server and place it in the tree. You can, however, create virtual servers using the Alias object. We'll take a look at this strategy a little later. If you create a bindery-based server (NetWare 2 or 3), you'll need to manually create a logical NetWare 5 server object to make its file systems available. Some of the Server object properties can be seen in Figure 2.9. The page buttons provide some interesting informational categories including Identification, Error Log, Supported Services, Blocks Read, Blocks Written, Connect Time, and other dynamic statistics.

FIGURE 2.9

*Properties of an
NDS Server object*

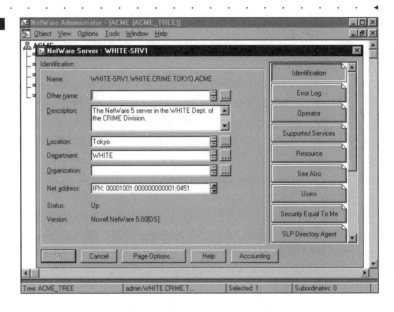

 Volume — Points to a physical volume installed somewhere on the WAN. A logical Volume object is created automatically for every physical volume installed during server creation. NetWare Administrator will allow you to browse the file system using an NDS Volume object. You can create other volumes as logical pointers from different parts of the tree. Otherwise, consider using the Alias object. In the Volume object's properties, you can store identification information such as the host server, volume location, and so on. You can also set restrictions for use of the volume such as disk space restrictions and attribute security. Interestingly, the NDS logical volume is stored independently from the physical server to which it's attached.

Directory Map — Represents a logical pointer to a physical directory in the NetWare 5 file system. Directory Map objects are excellent tools for centralizing file system management. Instead of creating drive mappings to physical directories, you can create them to logical Directory Map objects. Then when the physical location changes, you only have to change the one central object. All drive mappings will then be updated immediately. Pretty cool, huh? Check out the "Drive Mapping" section in Chapter 4.

Printer Leaf Objects

Like previous versions, NetWare 5 queue-based printing relies on three main elements — Print Queue, Print Server, and Printer. Each of these printing elements is represented in the NDS tree as a leaf object. Users print to print queues where jobs are stored until the printer is ready. Once a job gets to the top of the queue, the print server redirects it to the appropriate printer. Sounds pretty simple to me — you be the judge. Here's a quick look at these three critical NDS printer objects:

Printer — Represents a physical printing device on the network. This logical object allows users to find the printers they need — regardless of whether they are using NDPS or queue-based printing. Every printer must be represented by a corresponding NDS object and should be placed in the same container as the users who print to it. Some of the critical printer properties of a Non-NDPS printer can be seen in Figure 2.10 — these include Location, Department, Organization, Assignments, Configuration, Notification, and Features.

▶ • ◀

FIGURE 2.10

Properties of an NDS Printer object

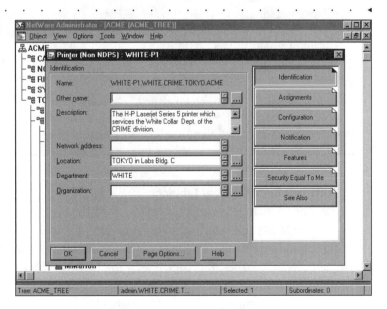

Print Queue — Represents a logical Non-NDPS print queue on the WAN. Every print queue must have a corresponding NDS object. Also, the location of the object in the tree directly impacts users' ability to print. Typically, the queues are stored in the same container as the users and printers to which they relate. NetWare 5 gives you the flexibility to assign print queues on any volume, not just SYS:. It's about time.

Print Server — Represents a NetWare 5 or third-party Non-NDPS print server. Once again, the print server should be placed in the same container as the printers and print queues with which it is associated. Also, make sure your third-party print server software is NDS-compatible. If not, you'll need to create Print Server objects manually for each of your different machines. This is especially important if your users are accessing the network through bindery emulation.

REAL WORLD

As we learned in the previous chapter, NetWare 5 includes a revolutionary printing system called Novell Distributed Print Services (NDPS). NDPS replaces the older NetWare queue-based printing system with a simplified architecture and enhanced services. As a NetWare 5 CNA, you get to choose whether or not you want to implement NDPS printing. The good news is you don't have to if you don't want to!

In Chapter 7, "NetWare 5 Printing," we will explore all the details of this new printing revolution and its corresponding NDS leaf objects. For now, you should enjoy the familiarity of NetWare 5 queue-based printing.

Network Services Leaf Objects

NetWare 5 includes several exciting new object types that are designed to allow CNAs to manage the network more easily and efficiently — saving both time and effort. In addition to the Template object (which was discussed in the "User Leaf Objects" section earlier in this chapter), the Network Services objects include the Application object (which allows you to manage applications as objects in the NDS tree); the Auditing File object (which allows you to manage auditing file logs as objects in the tree), and the License Certificate object (which is used by NetWare Licensing Services to monitor and control the use of licensed applications on the network). Let's take a closer look:

Application — Allows network administrators to manage applications as Application objects in the NDS tree. It requires NDS, which means that you can't run an application associated with such an object if you are using a Bindery Services connection. A new NetWare 5 utility that utilizes this object is the NetWare Application Launcher (NAL) — which allows users to view available applications and double-click on an icon to launch the associated application. The advantage of this object for users is that they don't have to worry about drive mappings, paths, or rights when they want to execute an application. We'll learn more about Application objects and NAL in Chapter 6, "NetWare 5 Workstation Management."

Auditing File (AFO) — Represents an auditing log file that can be managed as an NDS object. This object is created by an auditing utility such as AUDITCON when auditing is enabled and is used to manage an auditing trail's configuration and access rights.

License Certificate — License Certificate objects are created when the NetWare 5 server is installed. All License Certificate leaves are installed into a License container. These objects contain information about the product such as the Publisher, Product name, version, how many licenses the certificate allows, and whether additional licenses are available. Each license included in the certificate allows a *licensed connection* to be made. A licensed connection is initiated when a user requests a network connection by logging in. When the server receives the request, it checks to make sure a licensed unit is available in the license certificate stored in NDS. If a license unit is available, the server allows the client to complete the network connection.

Miscellaneous Leaf Objects

No list would be complete without the final category — miscellaneous. There are five NDS leaf objects that don't fall into any other category. They're dominated by the Alias object, which points to any of the other NDS resources. In addition, there are Workstations, Bindery objects, Bindery Queues, and, of course, the Unknown leaf object — whose icon, interestingly enough, is a user with a paper bag over its head. Just kidding.

Let's check them out:

Alias — A logical pointer to any other leaf or container object in the NDS tree. Think of it as an NDS "chameleon." When you create an Alias, it assumes the icon form of its host object. Although it may look like there are two AEinstein users, only one really exists in the tree. The other is a fake pointer. The beauty of the Alias is that it allows you to distribute objects outside of their parent container. If, for example, users in Admin need access to information about AEinstein, you can place an Alias of him in the Admin container. This way, he appears to live there, but in reality it's simply a logical pointer to the real Albert Einstein in OU=LABS (see Figure 2.11). Be very careful with the Alias object. In many cases, you can't tell an Alias from the real Albert Einstein. If you delete or rename an Alias, nothing happens to the host. But if you accidentally mistake the host for the Alias and delete it, all of its Alias objects disappear into Never-Never Land. Actually, they become Unknown leaf objects.

Workstation — Represents a non-server network computer (workstation) on the WAN. This object provides an excellent facility for managing and accessing distributed network workstations through NDS. This is also an excellent opportunity to integrate NDS and your inventory database. A plethora of Workstation properties are available to you, including Description, Network Address, Serial Number, Server, Owner, and Status.

Unknown — Represents an NDS object that has been invalidated or cannot be identified as belonging to any of the other leaf classes (for example, when an Alias becomes invalidated because the user deleted the Alias's host). If you have any Unknown objects, you may want to research where they came from: It's probably a bad sign.

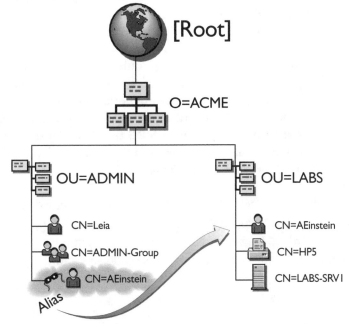

FIGURE 2.11

*Understanding
the Alias object*

[Root]

O=ACME

OU=ADMIN

OU=LABS

CN=Leia

CN=ADMIN-Group

CN=AEinstein

Alias

CN=AEinstein

CN=HP5

CN=LABS-SRV1

B *Bindery* — Represents an object placed in the NDS tree by an upgrade or migration utility. Bindery objects are used by NDS to provide backward compatibility with bindery-based utilities. This way, users can access the resource from NetWare 3.2 workstations.

B *Bindery Queue* — Represents a print queue placed in the NDS tree by an upgrade or migration utility. This is a special type of Bindery object that points to older NetWare 3.2 print queues. Users accessing the tree through Bindery Services can print to bindery-based queues. Otherwise, you'll need to create a true NDS print queue object for everybody else.

That's all of them.

We've discussed all the interesting CNA objects offered by NetWare 5. You'll want to get to know all these leaves because future discussions center around how to organize, design, and manage these cute little network entities. Once you understand the relationships between NDS objects, you can start building your tree — that's later in Chapter 3.

TIP

As you've seen in this discussion, every leaf and container object is represented by an icon graphic that depicts its purpose. For example, printers are printers, servers are computers, and users are people. These icons are used throughout this book and in graphical NDS utilities. NetWare Administrator, for example, uses icons to provide a snapshot of the entire NDS tree in a hierarchical structure. This feature makes it easier for administrators and users to locate and use NetWare 5 resources. Cool.

How do you feel? Any twinges in your carbon-based cranium yet? So far, we've explored all the chlorophyll-based plants that make up NetWare 5's revolutionary NDS Garden. However, this is only the beginning. Your success as a CNA is defined by your ability to manage NDS objects and their properties.

EXERCISE 2.1: GETTING TO KNOW NDS (MATCHING)

Part I

Write C for container or L for leaf next to each of the following objects:

1. ___ Volume
2. ___ Country
3. ___ User
4. ___ Group
5. ___ Organizati
6. ___ NetWare ?
7. ___ Print Que
8. ___ Organiza
9. ___ Comput
10. ___ Organiz

See Appendix

PART II

Indicate wheth   below would be a container or a leaf object.
If you think it   object, indicate what type of container (that
is, Country, O   ational Unit).

1. _____ The Human Resources department
2. _____ David IV
3. _____ A database server
4. _____ The PAYCHECK print queue
5. _____ ACME, Inc.
6. _____ The Administrator Organizational Role
7. _____ UK (that is, United Kingdom)
8. _____ A dot matrix printer
9. _____ The Tokyo office
10. _____ The SYS: volume

See Appendix C for answers.

Overview of NDS Management

Now that you understand what the NDS tree is made of, we need to explore how it works. As you manage the NDS tree, pay particular attention to its structure. A well-designed tree will make resource access and management much easier. As a matter of fact, an efficient Directory tree provides all the following benefits:

▸ Make resource access easier for users

▸ Make administration easier for you (the CNA)

▸ Provide fault tolerance for the NDS database

▸ Decrease network traffic

The structure of the tree can be based on location, organization, or administration. In many cases, it's a combination of all three. Many factors influence the structure of your NDS tree. You might need to study workgroups, resource allocation, and/or learn how data flows throughout your network.

As a CNA, it is your responsibility to navigate and manage the tree, not to design or troubleshoot it — that's what CNEs are for. You can learn all there is to know about NDS design and implementation in *Novell's CNE Study Guide for NetWare 5*.

For now, let's focus on three key NDS management topics:

▸ *NDS Naming* — NDS naming defines rules for locating leaf objects. One of the most important aspects of a leaf object is its position in the NDS tree. Proper naming is required when logging in, accessing NDS utilities, printing, and for most other CNA management tasks.

▸ *NDS Partitioning* — NDS partitioning deals with database performance and reliability. Since the tree houses all your network resources, it can grow large very quickly. As with any database, size can decrease performance and reliability. For this reason, NetWare 5 has a built-in database distribution feature called *partitioning and replication*. Partitioning breaks the database tree into small pieces and replication places those pieces on multiple servers. This strategy increases database performance and provides distributed fault tolerance.

▶ *Time Synchronization* — Time synchronization is a temporal assurance scheme that forces all NetWare 5 servers to agree on what time it is. This is particularly important because all NDS background operations and security strategies rely on a time stamp. Time synchronization is accomplished through the use of four different time server types.

So, without further ado . . . let's get on with the show, starting with NDS naming.

TIP

As a CNA, you're really only responsible for understanding NDS Naming — partitioning and time synchronization are primarily CNE tasks. However, in the interest of fair play, I'm going to introduce *all* the NDS management topics in this section. Remember, as a CNA, focus on NDS Naming . . . the other two are extracurricular.

NDS Naming

Your name identifies you as a truly unique individual. Let's take NDS-Head Fred, for example. This name says, "Hi, I'm Fred, and I have an NDS tree growing out of my head!" In much the same way, an NDS object's name identifies its location in the hierarchical tree. NDS naming impacts two important NetWare 5 tasks:

▶ *Login* — You need to identify your exact location in the NDS tree in order for NetWare 5 to authenticate you during login.

▶ *Resource Access* — NDS naming exactly identifies the type and location of NetWare 5 resources, including file servers, printers, login scripts, and files.

The whole NetWare 5 NDS naming scheme is much more complicated than "Hi, I'm Fred." It requires both your name and location. For example, a proper NDS name would be "Hi, I'm Fred in the ADMIN division of ACME." As you can see in Figure 2.12, Fred's NDS name identifies who he is and where he works. This naming scheme relies on a concept called *context*.

Check it out.

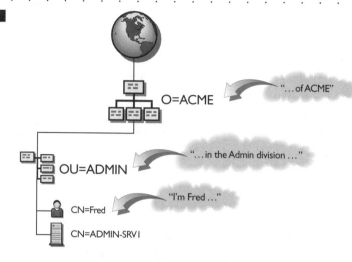

FIGURE 2.12

Getting to know the real "Fred"

O=ACME

"...of ACME"

OU=ADMIN

"...in the Admin division ..."

CN=Fred

"I'm Fred ..."

CN=ADMIN-SRV1

REAL WORLD

Novell recommends that before you implement NDS, you create a document that describes your naming standards. The NDS naming rules we're going to learn here only work if object names are consistent across the WAN. A naming standards document provides guidelines for naming key container and leaf objects, including users, printers, servers, volumes, print queues, and Organizational Units. In addition, it identifies standard properties and value formats. Consistency, especially in the naming scheme used for objects, provides several benefits:

▶ Consistent naming schemes provide a guideline for network administrators who will add, modify, or move objects within the Directory tree.

▶ A naming standard eliminates redundant planning. The standards give CNAs an efficient model to meet their needs, but leave implementation of resource objects open and flexible.

▶ Consistent naming schemes help users identify resources quickly, which maximizes users' productivity.

▶ Consistent naming allows users to identify themselves easily during login.

Context

As we learned earlier, the whole NDS naming strategy hinges on the concept of context. Context defines the position of an object within the Directory tree structure. When you request a particular network resource, you must identify the object's context so that NDS can find it.

In Figure 2.12, Fred's context is ". . . in the ADMIN division of ACME." This context identifies where Fred lives in the NDS tree structure. It identifies all container objects leading from him to the [Root]. In addition to context, Figure 2.12 identifies Fred's common name (CN). A leaf object's common name specifically identifies it within a given container. In this example, the User object's common name is "Fred."

Two objects in the same NDS tree may have the same common name — provided, however, that they have different contexts. This is why naming is so important. As you can see in Figure 2.13, our NDS tree has two "Freds," but each has a different context.

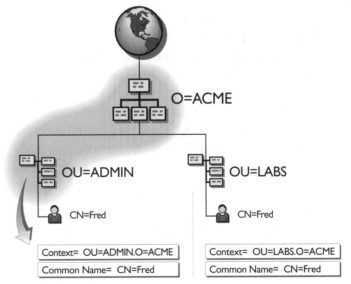

Understanding NDS context

Each NDS object has a naming type associated with it. This naming type is identified with a one- or two-character abbreviation:

▶ O=Organization container

▶ OU=Organizational Unit container

▶ CN=common name of leaf object

Also notice the syntax used to create an object's context. In Figure 2.13, Fred's context is created by identifying each of his containers in reverse order leading to the [Root]. Also note that each container is separated by a period.

In general, NDS context defines two important things:

▶ *Current context* — "where you are"

▶ *Object context* — "where you live"

Current context defines "where you are" in the NDS tree at any given time. It is not "where you live." This is a very important distinction. In Figure 2.13, for example, Fred "lives" in OU=ADMIN.O=ACME. But, at any given time, he can hang out in O=ACME or OU=LABS.O=ACME.

This is all made possible by *tree walking*. Tree walking allows users to navigate anywhere within the NDS tree structure. Fred's current context impacts the utilities he uses and the resources he can access. In technical terms, current context is a logical pointer in the Novell Client, which identifies the NDS default container for your workstation. Simply stated, it's where you are, not where you live.

A user's current context can be set in one of the following ways:

▶ During login, using the Advanced NDS tab of the GUI Novell Client Login window

▶ With the CONTEXT login script command

▶ At any time, using the CX utility

As we'll see in just a moment, current context also impacts how you approach object naming. As a matter of fact, it is the foundation of distinguished naming.

In contrast to current context, *object context* defines "where you live." In Figure 2.13 earlier, for example, Fred's object context is OU=ADMIN.O=ACME or OU=LABS .O=ACME, depending on which Fred you're talking about. Context is identified by listing all containers starting from Fred and moving back toward the [Root]. Object context is used for two important purposes:

▸ Logging in

▸ Accessing resources

When logging in, users must provide their complete object context. In Figure 2.13 earlier, for example, Fred would type the following:

```
LOGIN .CN=FRED.OU=ADMIN.O=ACME
```

In addition to logging in, you'll need a resource's object context when trying to access it. This is particularly important for Servers, Printers, Profile login scripts, Directory Map objects, Volumes, and Groups. The server in Figure 2.12, for example, has the same object context as Fred (that is, OU=ADMIN.O=ACME). Since Fred and the server have the same object context, they can refer to each other by their common names. Isn't that friendly?

You can view information about an object's context or change your own current context by using the CX command line utility. CX is the key NetWare 5 utility for dealing with NDS context. It allows you to perform two important tasks: change your workstation's current context and/or view information about any resource's object context.

CX is a relatively straightforward command with a great deal of versatility. As a matter of fact, it's similar to the file system CD command in its general approach. If you type CX by itself, the system displays your workstation's current context. This is marginally interesting, at best. CX really excels when you combine it with one or more command line switches. Here are some of the more interesting ones:

▸ **CX** — View your workstation's current context.

▸ **CX /T** — View the Directory tree structure below your current context.

▸ **CX /A /T** — View all objects in the Directory tree structure below your current context.

▸ **CX /R /A /T** — Change your current context to the [Root] and view all objects in the Directory tree.

▸ **CX /CONT** — List containers only below the current context in a vertical list with no directory structure.

▸ **CX /C** — Scroll continuously through output.

▸ **CX .OU=ADMIN.O=ACME** — Change your current context to the ADMIN container of ACME.

▸ **CX /?** — View on-line help, including various CX options.

▸ **CX /VER** — View the version number of the CX utility and the list of files it executes.

Probably the most useful CX option is

▸ **CX /R /A /T**

I'm sure there's a hidden meaning somewhere in the rodent reference. Regardless, the CX /R /A /T option displays the relative location of all objects in the NDS tree (see Figure 2.14).

FIGURE 2.14

Using CX /R /A /T in the ACME tree

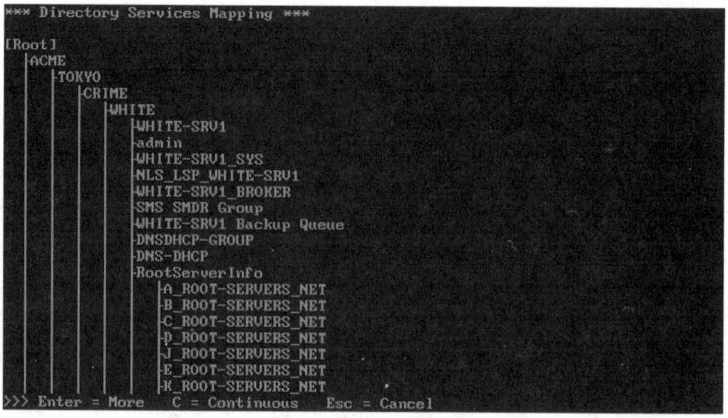

```
*** Directory Services Mapping ***

[Root]
 ACME
   TOKYO
     CRIME
       WHITE
         WHITE-SRV1
         admin
         WHITE-SRV1_SYS
         NLS_LSP_WHITE-SRV1
         WHITE-SRV1_BROKER
         SMS SMDR Group
         WHITE-SRV1 Backup Queue
         DNSDHCP-GROUP
         DNS-DHCP
         RootServerInfo
           A_ROOT-SERVERS_NET
           B_ROOT-SERVERS_NET
           C_ROOT-SERVERS_NET
           D_ROOT-SERVERS_NET
           J_ROOT-SERVERS_NET
           E_ROOT-SERVERS_NET
           K_ROOT-SERVERS_NET
>>> Enter = More    C = Continuous    Esc = Cancel
```

If you don't remember where you live, the CX utility can be your guide. You can use it before logging in to find your home context if you are in the F:\LOGIN directory. It can also be used by administrators to print out the complete NDS tree structure every Friday afternoon. Of course, this can be a valuable asset to your NetWare 5 log book. All in all, CX is a very useful utility for dealing with NDS navigation and object naming.

Now that you've discovered the importance of context, it's time to review how it impacts NDS naming rules. Knowing where you live is only half of the equation. Now we have to discover exactly who you are.

REAL WORLD

NetWare 5 includes a new WAN phone book called Catalog Services. This is a flat-file, customizable catalog of the NDS database. With Catalog Services, both developers and network administrators can easily write applications that search the NDS database and extract specific information quickly and efficiently.

One of the first applications to demonstrate the capabilities of Catalog Services is *Contextless Login*. This application allows users to log into the network from anywhere without having to specify their NDS contexts. Technically, this is known as Contextless Login, although many CNEs are now using the slang term "Blue Sky Login."

To activate Blue Sky Login, you need to run NDS Catalog Services on your NetWare 5 server and configure the Novell Client for Contextless Login. Refer to *Novell's CNE Study Guide for NetWare 5* for detailed instructions on configuring NetWare 5 Contextless Login.

To illustrate the capabilities of Blue Sky Login, imagine that user Fred tries to log into the network from a workstation outside his NDS context. Being a typical user, Fred would type **LOGIN FRED**. In the old days, NDS would parse the database and return an error message. With Blue Sky Login, however, NDS scans Catalog Services and quickly returns a list of all users in the NDS tree with the first name of "Fred." Now all he has to do is simply select his name from the list and continue into the "Cloud." Very cool!

Distinguished Names

Home is where the heart is. Similarly, your network productivity is defined by the container you live in — your context. To access resources efficiently, you must be in close proximity to them. Otherwise, security and naming gets more difficult. Context is the key.

Now that we understand how NDS context works, let's review the naming rules associated with it:

▸ Current context defines your workstation's current position in the Directory tree.

▸ An object's context defines its home container.

▸ Each object has an identifier abbreviation that defines it for naming purposes (O=Organization, OU=Organizational Unit, and CN=common name of leaf objects).

▸ Context is defined by listing all containers from the object to the [Root], in that order. Each object is separated by a period.

▸ Context is important for logging in and accessing NDS resources.

So, there you have it. That's how context works. With this in mind, it's time to explore the two main types of NDS names:

▸ Distinguished names

▸ Typeful names

An object's *distinguished name* is its complete NDS path. It is a combination of common name and object context. Each object in the NDS tree has a distinguished name that uniquely identifies it in the tree. In Figure 2.12, Fred's distinguished name would be "I'm Fred in the ADMIN division of ACME."

Notice how the distinguished name identifies Fred as an individual, as well as the context in which he lives. Similarly, in Figure 2.13, Fred's NDS distinguished name would be .CN=Fred.OU=ADMIN.O=ACME. Once again, Fred's distinguished name is a combination of his common name and his context.

Here's another example (refer to AEinstein in Figure 2.15). AEinstein's context is OU=R&D.OU=LABS.O=ACME. His common name is CN=AEinstein. Therefore, his distinguished name is a simple mathematical addition of the two:

```
.CN=AEinstein.OU=R&D.OU=LABS.O=ACME.
```

Elementary, my dear Einstein, elementary. There's no "new math" here; only simple addition. If you want complex calculations, refer to Chapter 5, "NetWare 5 Security."

FIGURE 2.15

Building AEinstein's distinguished name

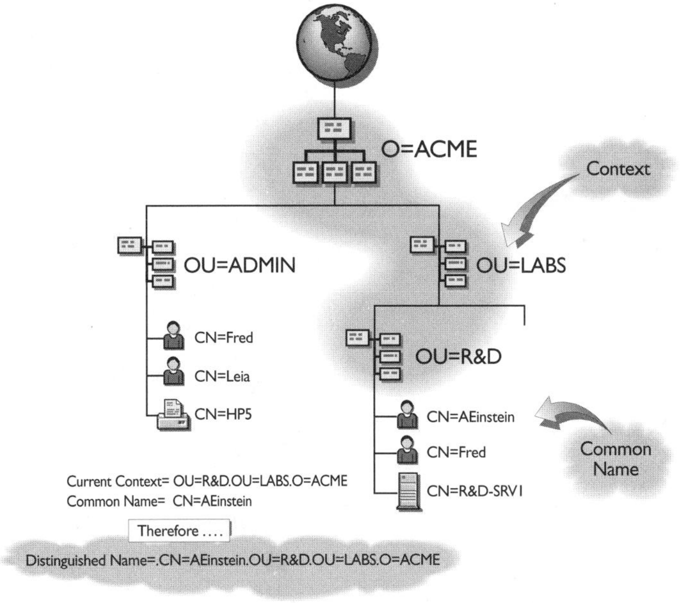

Notice the use of periods. Neither the context nor the common name started with a period, but the distinguished name did. The leading period identifies the name as a (complete) distinguished one. Otherwise, it is assumed to be an incomplete, or relative, distinguished name. A *relative distinguished name* lists an object's path from itself up to the current context—not the [Root]. The relativity part refers to how NDS builds the distinguished name. Remember, all objects must have a unique distinguished name. The relative distinguished name is simply a shortcut.

It seems appropriate to demonstrate the relative distinguished name concept with the help of Albert Einstein.

Again, refer to Figure 2.15. If AEinstein's current context was the same as his object context, OU=R&D.OU=LABS.O=ACME, then his relative distinguished name would be the same as his common name, CN=AEinstein. But life is rarely this simple. What if Albert Einstein used the CX command to change his current context to OU=LABS.O=ACME? What would his relative distinguished name be now? See Figure 2.16. Correct! His relative distinguished name would become CN=AEinstein.OU=R&D. When you add this to his current context of OU=LABS.O=ACME, you get the correct distinguished name:

```
.CN=AEinstein.OU=R&D.OU=LABS.O=ACME
```

Piece of cake. Once again, notice the use of periods. The relative distinguished name does not use a leading period. This identifies it as a relative (not complete) distinguished name.

▶ · ◀

Building AEinstein's relative distinguished name

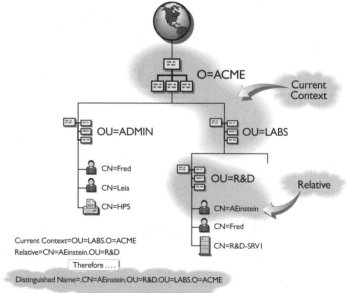

As you can see, object and current context play a very important role in distinguished and relative distinguished naming. Whether it's fair or not, you are defined by the place where you live. Of course, it can get even weirder. NDS supports trailing periods, which allow you to change the current context while using relative distinguished naming . . . as if that wasn't hard enough already. The bottom line is that each trailing period moves the current context up one container.

It seems simple at first, but it can get crazy very quickly. Let's take Leia, for example. She lives in the ADMIN container. If we were in LABS, she couldn't use a relative distinguished name to identify herself — or could she? A single trailing period would move her current context up to O=ACME. Then she could use a relative distinguished name to move down the ADMIN side of the tree (see Figure 2.17). Her current context would be OU=LABS.O=ACME, and her relative distinguished name would be:

```
CN=Leia.OU=ADMIN.
```

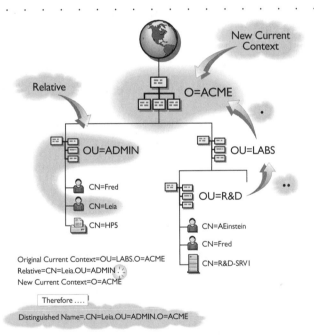

Using trailing periods

The resulting distinguished name would be Leia's relative name plus her new current context (remember, the trailing period moved the current context from OU=LABS.O=ACME up to O=ACME). That is, her distinguished name would be:

```
.CN=Leia.OU=ADMIN.O=ACME
```

Piece of cake. It gets even weirder if Leia's current context is:

`OU=R&D.OU=LABS.O=ACME`

In this case, her relative distinguished name would be:

`CN=Leia.OU=ADMIN..`

Are we having fun yet? Just like anything in life, it's very important where you place your dots. Here's a quick summary:

- ▸ All objects in the NDS name are separated by dots.

- ▸ Distinguished names are preceded by a dot. This identifies them as complete.

- ▸ Relative distinguished names are not preceded by a dot. This identifies them as incomplete.

- ▸ Trailing dots can only be used in relative distinguished names, and they modify the current context. Each dot moves the context up one container.

For a complete summary of NDS distinguished naming rules, refer to Table 2.2. Now let's step back in reality for a moment and explore the other NDS naming category — typeful names.

T A B L E   2.2

Getting to Know
Distinguished Naming

DISTINGUISHED	RELATIVE NAMES	DISTINGUISHED NAMES
What it is	Complete unique name	Incomplete name based on current context
How it works	Lists complete path	Lists relative path from from object to [Root] object to current context
Abbreviation	DN	RDN
Leading period	Leading periods required	No leading periods allowed
Trailing periods	No trailing periods allowed	Trailing periods optional

Typeful Names

Typeful names use attribute type abbreviations to distinguish between the different container types and leaf objects in NDS names. In all the examples to this point, we've used these abbreviations to help clarify context, distinguished, and relative distinguished names. The most popular abbreviations are

- ► C: Country container

- ► O: Organization container

- ► OU: Organizational Unit container

- ► CN: common name of leaf objects

These attribute types help to avoid the confusion that can occur when creating complex distinguished and relative distinguished names. I highly recommend that you use them. Of course, like most things in life — they are optional! You can imagine how crazy NDS naming gets when you choose not to use these attribute abbreviations. This insanity is known as *typeless naming*.

Typeless names operate the same as typeful names, but they don't include the object attribute type. In such cases, NDS has to "guess" what object types you're using. Take the following typeless name, for example:

```
.Admin.ACME
```

Is this the ADMIN Organizational Unit under ACME? Or is this the Admin user under ACME? In both cases, it's a valid distinguished name, except that one identifies an Organizational Unit container and the other identifies a User leaf object (see Figure 2.18). Well, here's the bottom line — which one is it? It's up to NDS.

Fortunately, NetWare 5 has some guidelines for "guessing" what the object type should be.

1. The leftmost object is a common name (leaf object).

2. The rightmost object is an Organization (container object).

3. All middle objects are Organizational Units (container objects).

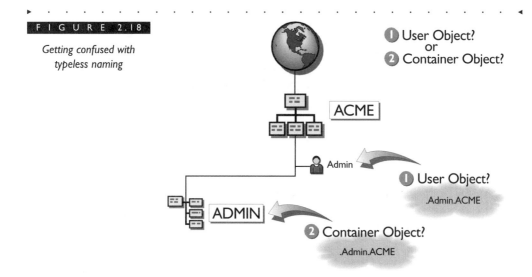

FIGURE 2.18

*Getting confused with
typeless naming*

Although this works for most cases, it's only a general guideline. Many times, typeless names are more complex. Take our example in Figure 2.18, for instance. We know now that the rightmost object is an Organization, but what about "Admin"? Is it a common name or an Organizational Unit? We still don't know. Fortunately, NetWare 5 includes a few exceptions to deal with complex typeless scenarios. Here's how it works:

▶ *Exception Rule 1: Container objects* — Many NetWare 5 utilities are intelligent enough to resolve their own typeless names depending on what they are trying to accomplish. CX, for example, is used primarily for changing context. If you apply the CX command to a typeless name, it assumes the leftmost object is an Organization or Organizational Unit. This is because you can't change context to a leaf object. Other utilities that allow you to change context include NETADMIN and NetWare Administrator. In summary, here's how our example from Figure 2.18 would look with the CX utility:

```
CX .ADMIN.ACME resolves as ".OU=ADMIN.O=ACME"
```

▶ *Exception Rule 2: Leaf objects* — Similarly, resource-based utilities recognize the leftmost object of a typeless name as a leaf object. Many of these utilities are expecting to see a common name. The most prevalent are LOGIN, MAP, and CAPTURE. Here's how it works for our example in Figure 2.18:

```
LOGIN .Admin.ACME resolves as ".CN=Admin.O=ACME"
```

▶ *Exception Rule 3: Contextless Login* — If you have Catalog Services and Contextless Login activated, NDS will resolve typeless names by offering the user a list from the NDS Catalog. See the "Real World" icon a few pages back.

There you have it. This completes our discussion of typeless names and NDS naming in general. As you can see, this is a very important topic because it impacts all aspects of NDS design, installation, and management. No matter what you do, you're going to have to use the correct name to log in or access NDS resources. As we've learned, an object's name is a combination of "who they are" (common name) and "where they live" (context).

Now, let's shift our focus from naming to partition management. NDS partitioning is the second of our three NDS management concepts. Don't forget your seat belt.

NDS Partitioning

As you will quickly come to appreciate, the NDS tree grows and grows and grows. Before you know it, you'll have a huge monstrosity on your hands — the size of Jupiter. Fortunately, NetWare 5 includes a segmentation strategy known as NDS partitioning. *Partitioning* breaks up the NDS tree into two or more pieces that can be separated and distributed, which makes dealing with NDS objects more manageable.

Since the NDS tree is stored in a database, pieces of the database can be distributed on multiple file servers. This strategy is known as *replication*. NDS replicas provide two important benefits to the "Cloud": First, replicas increase network performance by decreasing the size of database files and placing resources closest to the users who need them. Second, replicas increase fault tolerance because extra copies of the database are distributed on multiple servers throughout the WAN.

To understand partitioning, we need to review the characteristics of our NDS Cloud:

▸ It is a database that replaces the bindery.

▸ It contains data on all objects in the Directory tree, including their names, security rights, and property values. All network information except the file system comes from the Directory.

▸ It is network-centric, not server-centric, like the older bindery. This allows the Directory to track all network resources throughout the WAN.

▸ NDS uses the Directory for access control to other objects in the WAN. NDS checks the Directory to make sure that you can view, manipulate, create, or delete resource objects.

▸ NDS uses the Directory for authentication — an important part of logging in.

▸ Except for Server and Volume objects, the Directory does not contain information about the file system. NetWare 5 data is still restricted to internal server volumes.

TIP

Keep in mind, though, that size and number of partitions can significantly affect the synchronization and responsiveness of your network. Avoid creating partitions that are too large (greater than 5,000 objects) or with too many copies (more than 10) because host servers can take too long to synchronize, and managing replicas becomes more complex. On the other hand, avoid partitions that are too small (fewer than 100 objects). If a partition contains only a few objects, the access and fault-tolerance benefits may not be worth the time you invest in managing it.

NDS partitions have nothing to do with the logical disk partitions you're used to on the server disk. NDS partitions are logical pieces of the "Cloud," which can be distributed on multiple servers. Hard disk partitions are physical divisions of the internal disks that separate the NetWare 5 operating system from DOS. Although these two concepts are unrelated, they work together in an odd way — one is stored on top of the other. To really mess up your mind, note that logical NDS partitions are stored on internal disk partitions—brain drain!

As you can see in Figure 2.19, NDS partitioning simply breaks the ACME organization into two pieces:

▶ *Partition A*—Known as the *root partition* because it is the only one that contains the global [Root] object.

▶ *Partition B*—Known as the *LABS partition* because OU=LABS is the highest container object in that segment. In addition, Partition B is termed a *child* of Partition A, because LABS is a subset of the ACME Organization.

▶ · ◀

Breaking the NDS tree into two partitions

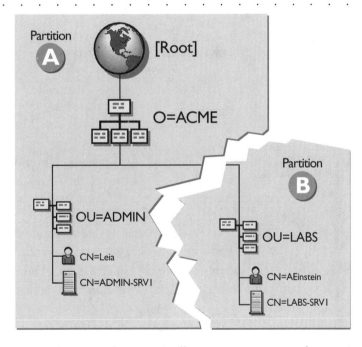

Partitioning has many advantages because it allows you to separate the tree into smaller segments. Since 90 percent of all the resources accessed by users are within their own partitions, CNEs (not CNAs) can increase efficiency by locating users near the resources they use the most. We can also increase network fault tolerance by placing copies of other partitions on local servers. This is known as replication. NetWare 5 supports four different types of NDS replicas:

► *Master* — A read/write copy of the original partition. Each partition has only one Master replica. When you first define a partition, the Master is created by default. If you would like to redefine a partition boundary or join it with another, you must be able to access the server that holds the Master replica of that partition. This is the key difference between the Master and other replica types. If the Master replica becomes unavailable for any reason, you can upgrade any Read/Write replica using NDS Manager or NetWare Administrator.

► *Read/Write* — A read/write copy of any partition. Each partition may have multiple Read/Write replica copies. When you change objects in a Read/Write replica, those changes are propagated to all other replicas of the same partition. This process, known as *replica synchronization*, creates background traffic over WAN communication lines. Both Master and Read/Write replicas generate synchronization traffic. Be careful how many of these replicas you distribute. Finally, Read/Write replicas cannot be used to redefine partition boundaries — that requires a Master.

► *Read-Only* — A read-only copy of any partition. These replicas are used for searching and viewing objects only. You cannot make any changes to a Read-Only replica. These replicas receive synchronization changes from Read/Write and Master copies, although they don't generate as much synchronization traffic.

► *Subordinate References* — A special type of replica created and maintained by NDS. A Subordinate Reference is created automatically on a server when it contains a parent replica, but not any of the children. In simpler terms, Subordinate References are created on servers "where the parent is, but children are not." Think of it as NDS baby-sitting. The key difference is that Subordinate References do not contain object data — they point to the replica that does. This facilitates tree connectivity. The good news is that if you eventually add a child replica to the server, the Subordinate Reference is removed automatically.

In general, Read/Write replicas are the most popular for CNA/CNE management. Master replicas are created automatically during partitioning, and Subordinate References flourish throughout the tree as needed. Read-Only replicas, however, can be very effective if you have many servers and few containers.

TIP

In the past, Subordinate References caused a great deal of WAN traffic during replica synchronization — which is called the "heartbeat" and occurs every 30 minutes. To solve this problem, NetWare 5 introduces a scheme known as _transitive synchronization_ (discussed later). Transitive synchronization eliminates Subordinate References from the replica synchronization process. This eliminates all traffic to and from Subordinate References, and therefore, increases synchronization efficiency. Great!!

Figure 2.20 illustrates a simple, saturated replication scheme. As you can see, each Server has a copy of each partition. This provides exceptional fault tolerance and accessibility, but synchronization may be a problem. In large environments, this scheme would not be very practical because of synchronization delays. Replica updates take place automatically at specific intervals. Some updates (such as changing a user's password) are immediate (within 10 seconds). Other updates (such as login updates) are synchronized every five minutes. Changes made to Figure 2.20, for example, would generate 27 replica updates — that's 3^3. This is manageable. But consider what background traffic would look like with 50 servers and 20 different partitions — that's 9,536,743,164,062,000,000,000,000,000,000 updates every few minutes. Wow!

All this synchronization magic is accomplished within a group of servers known as a _replica ring_. A replica ring is an internal system group that includes all servers containing replicas of a given partition. In Figure 2.20, the replica ring for Partition A includes:

- _Master:_ CN=ADMIN-SRV1.

- _R/W:_ CN=LABS-SRV1.

- _R/W:_ CN=R&D-SRV1.

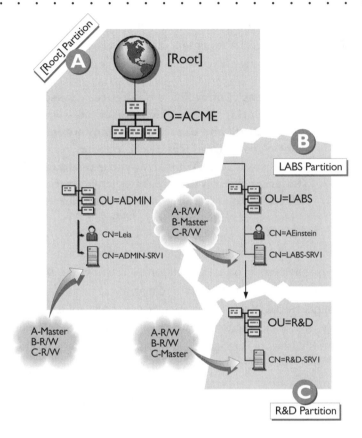

FIGURE 2.20

Saturated replication in the ACME NDS tree

If you are using NetWare 5 Pure IP, you may have a problem synchronizing between IP-Only and IPX-Only networks. This problem is further aggravated when you try to synchronize replicas directly from a Pure IP server to a Pure IPX server.

To resolve this, NetWare 5 includes *transitive synchronization*. Transitive synchronization eliminates the requirement that all servers in a replica ring must be able to communicate and synchronize with each other directly. When an NDS change is made, a source server checks each target server. If the servers can't communicate with each other because of differing protocols, the source server doesn't continue to try to communicate the changes to the target. Instead, the target receives the updates through an intermediary server that uses both IP and

IPX. Also, if the source server's replica is more recent than a target server's Replica, the source server does not need to synchronize with that target server. This reduces synchronization traffic.

TIP

Transitive synchronization is not necessary if you configure your Pure IP network with IPX Compatibility Mode. Refer to *Novell's CNE Study Guide for NetWare 5* for more information on migrating to Pure IP and dual protocol stack support.

As NDS synchronizes partition replicas, it creates network traffic. If this traffic crosses WAN links unmanaged, it can increase costs and overload slow WAN links during high-use periods. Fortunately, NetWare 5 includes the WAN Traffic Manager (WTM) to help you manage synchronization traffic across WAN links.

Here's some of the things that the WTM can do for you:

▸ WTM controls server-to-server traffic generated by NDS.

▸ WTM can restrict traffic based on cost, time of day, type of traffic, and/or a combination of these.

▸ WTM controls periodic events initiated by NDS — such as replica synchronization.

▸ WTM does *not* control events initiated by CNA/CNEs or users.

▸ WTM does *not* control non-NDS server-to-server traffic such as time synchronization. Fortunately, we have Network Time Protocol (NTP) to solve that problem.

NetWare 5 WAN Traffic Manager consists of three components: WTM.NLM, NetWare Administrator Snap-in, and WAN Traffic Policies.

Well, there you have it. That's partitioning and replication in a nutshell. Sit back, relax, and wallow in your newfound knowledge. There's time for only one more NDS management topic — time synchronization.

Time Synchronization

"Does anybody really know what time it is; does anybody really care?"

NDS does. As a matter of fact, NDS has to! Every aspect of NDS existence relies on time. Sound familiar? Time synchronization is a method of ensuring that all NDS objects report the same time stamp. Time stamps are important for

► Replica synchronization

► Messaging

► Login authentication and time-based security

► File and directory operations

Time stamps report time according to the Universal Time Coordinated (UTC) equivalent. This is a time system that adjusts to the local time zone and Daylight Savings Time. It is also equivalent to Greenwich Mean Time (GMT). UTC is calculated using three values for each time server:

► Local time

► +/– time zone offset from UTC

► – Daylight Savings Time offset

For example, in NORAD, Colorado, the time is seven hours behind GMT. Therefore, if the time in NORAD is 12:00 noon and there is no Daylight Savings Time, UTC is 19:00.

All of this fancy temporal footwork is accomplished during server installation with the GUI Time Zones and Time Synchronization worksheets (see Figure 2.21). With these worksheets, you can define your new NetWare 5 server as one of four different time servers. Time servers provide a consistent source for the time stamps that NDS and other features use. Each time you install a NetWare 5 server, you must provide it with specific time configuration parameters, including time server type and the previous three UTC values.

FIGURE 2.21

Time Configuration Parameters Worksheet in NetWare 5 Installation/Upgrade

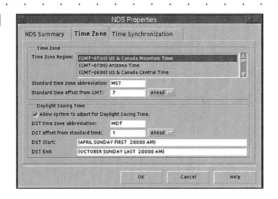

As you just learned, all NetWare 5 servers are time servers of some type. Time servers create and manage time stamps. There are two general categories of time servers: *time providers* and *time consumers*. Time providers provide time and are categorized as Primary, Reference or Single-Reference servers. Time consumer servers request their time from a provider and are categorized as Secondary servers.

Regardless, all time servers have the same fundamental responsibilities. First, they provide time to any requesting time provider, time consumer, or workstation. Second, they manage time synchronization and make sure everyone agrees what time it is. And, finally, they all adjust their internal clocks to correct discrepancies and maintain a consistent time across all NetWare 5 servers.

So, which time server are you?

▶ *Single-Reference* — A time provider. This is the default configuration for most small WANs. It provides time to Secondary servers and cannot coexist with Primary or Reference servers.

▶ *Reference* — A time provider. These servers act as a central point of time control for the entire network. They get their time from an external source such as the Internet or an atomic clock.

▶ *Primary* — A time provider or time consumer. These servers work together with other Primary servers to "vote" on the correct time. This voting procedure determines network UTC in combination with values received from Reference servers.

▶ *Secondary* — A time consumer. This is part of the default configuration. These servers do not participate in voting and are told what the time is by time providers.

Let's take a closer look.

Single-Reference Time Servers

As we learned earlier, this is the default configuration for most small WANs. If used, it stands alone as the only time provider on the entire network. Therefore, it cannot coexist with Primary or Reference time providers (see Figure 2.22). All other NetWare 5 servers in the same tree default to the Secondary time server type.

FIGURE 2.22

Default time configuration with Single-Reference and Secondary servers

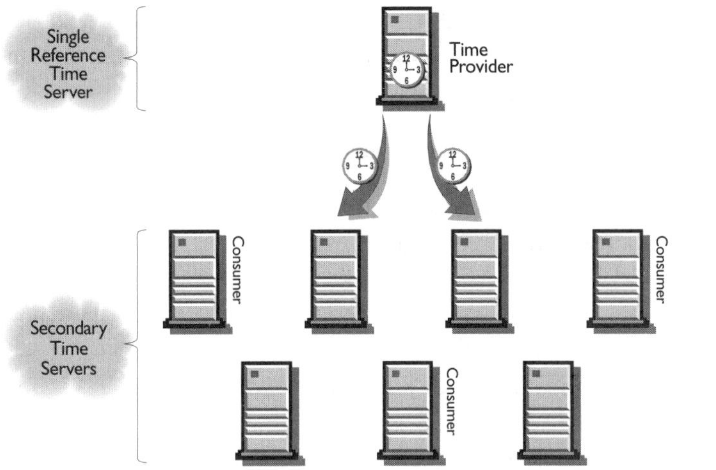

It's important to note that time servers never send out their time automatically. They must be asked to report their time. This only happens when a server's *synchronization flag* has been activated. The synchronization flag occurs when the server is confident that its internal clock is within a *synchronization radius* of accepted time. The synchronization radius defaults to 2,000 milliseconds (2 seconds). You can adjust this value through NWConfig. The key point here is that Single-Reference servers always activate their synchronization flag because they're the only ones on the network that matter.

Finally, Single-Reference time servers typically get their time from their own internal clock. You can, however, connect the server to a more reliable external time source such as the Internet, a radio clock, or atomic time provider.

▶ · ◀

REAL WORLD

It is possible for a Single-Reference time server to coexist with other time providers, although it's not recommended. The Single-Reference time server will not check with the other time providers when sending out NDS time stamps. As far as it's concerned, it's always right.

Reference Time Servers

Reference time servers are like Single-Reference servers in that they provide a central point of time control for the entire network. These time providers almost always get their time from an external source (such as the Internet, radio clocks, and/or atomic providers).

Reference time servers differ from Single-Reference servers in one important area—they can coexist with Primary servers. As you can see in Figure 2.23, Reference time servers provide time to Primary servers. Primaries then vote on what time they think it should be and eventually provide time to Secondary time consumers. Even though voting occurs with Reference time servers, it's important to note that Reference servers always win! No matter what time the primaries decide it is, they eventually agree with the Reference server. It's like saying, "Go ahead and argue about the time as long as your answer eventually matches mine." The Reference server is given higher priority because it's thought to be more reliable. This is because it typically uses an external time source. If you use the internal server clock, you're defeating the purpose of Reference and Primary voting.

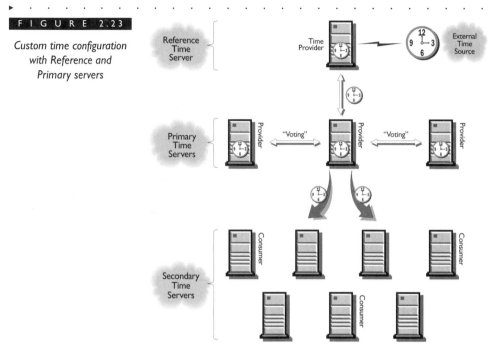

FIGURE 2.23

Custom time configuration with Reference and Primary servers

If you have a Reference server, why bother with Primaries at all? It's simple — fault tolerance. If the Reference server ever goes down, the Primaries can take over and negotiate time for all the Secondary time consumers.

Primary Time Servers

Primary time servers work together to vote on the correct time. This voting procedure can operate with or without the help of a Reference server. In either case, Primary servers vote every 5 minutes and adjust their internal time 50 percent of the time value discrepancy. They do not correct 100 percent because of oscillation errors. The 50 percent correction allows all the time servers to eventually converge on a single time stamp. This convergence is made easier with the presence of a Reference server, since it provides an ultimate goal. Without a

Reference server, multiple primaries continue to vote until two of them agree. At this point, both synchronization flags are set and Secondary servers receive the new time stamp.

There are a few important configurations in this scenario. First, there's the *polling interval*, which is the waiting period between votes. By default, it's five minutes. Next, there's the question of who votes with whom. In one configuration method, all Primaries vote with everybody, whereas in another, you can specify exactly who votes with whom. We'll explore these options a little later. Finally, there's the offset threshold — that is, by how much should a Primary be allowed to change its clock during voting? The default is 2 seconds. The offset threshold is also a configurable parameter.

Refer to Figure 2.23 above for a review of Primary and Reference server voting. Notice that Secondary consumers ultimately get their time stamp from Primary servers. Again, this increases fault tolerance by creating redundant time providers.

Secondary Time Servers

Secondary time servers are part of the default configuration. They are the ultimate time consumers. They do not participate in voting and are told exactly what time it is by any of the other three types of time providers. Remember, time providers only give time stamps when they're asked for them. This puts the responsibility on the shoulders of Secondary time servers. Every 5 minutes they poll a specific time source for the correct time. If there's a discrepancy, the Secondary server changes its internal clock by 100 percent. By default, this time polling occurs every five minutes. (Of course, this is configurable.)

Probably more than 90 percent of your NetWare 5 servers will be Secondary time consumers. In a generic configuration with 100 servers, you may have 7 Primaries, a Reference, and 92 Secondary time servers. It sure puts things in perspective.

For a summary of these four different time server types, refer to Table 2.3.

T A B L E 2.3

Getting to Know NetWare 5
Time Servers

TYPE	TIME PROVIDER	DESCRIPTION	GETS TIME FROM	ADJUSTS CLOCK	GIVES TIME TO
Single-Reference	Yes	Default configuration; only services Secondary time servers	Internal clock mostly	No	Secondary
Reference	Yes	Same as Single-Reference except it participates in Primary voting	External source mostly	No	Primary and Secondary
Primary	Yes	Participates in voting to determine correct time or stamp	Voting procedure Reference server	Yes (50 percent correction per polling interval)	Secondary
Secondary	No	Default configuration; consumes time stamp from other providers	Single-Reference, Reference, or Primary	Yes (100 percent correction per polling interval)	Clients only

Now that you're a time-server pro, you will need to choose between two different time configuration methods:

▸ *Default* — The default method assumes that only two types of time servers are necessary — Single-Reference time providers and Secondary time consumers. This method is simple and efficient, but does not provide the flexibility required by large NDS implementations.

▸ *Custom* — The custom method, on the other hand, requires administrative planning. It uses Reference, Primary, and Secondary servers to minimize a single point of failure. In addition, the custom configuration method cuts down on network traffic by minimizing unneeded synchronization chatter. This is accomplished with the help of TIMESYNC.CFG — a custom time configuration file.

That's how time synchronization works in the default NetWare 5 IPX world. However, if you're using Pure IP or a mixed protocol network, NetWare 5 servers communicate time with each other using TCP/IP. This is accomplished using two time synchronization components:

▸ *Network Time Protocol (NTP)* — This is an open IP standard that provides time stamps for time synchronization by using external Internet time sources. When NTP.NLM is loaded on an IP server, Network Time Protocol becomes the time source for both IP and IPX servers. In this configuration, IPX servers must be set to Secondary servers. By the way, NTP.NLM can be found is the SYS:ETC directory and must be loaded manually.

▸ *TIMSYNC.NLM* — This is the NetWare 5 time synchronization management tool, regardless of server protocol. TIMSYNC.NLM loads automatically when the server is installed.

NetWare 5 NTP supports two different types of time servers: *server* and *peer*. *Server* time servers allow local servers to be synchronized to remote servers but remote servers can't be synchronized to the local server. This is the typical Single Reference or Reference model from above. *Peers*, on the other hand, allow the local server to synchronize its time with a remote and vice versa. This is an ideal model for distributed time synchronization fault tolerance.

When NTP is installed, the configuration file NTP.CFG is created. This file specifies the type of time server you're working with and where it should go to find local time. By default, NTP.CFG specifies the local clock as 127.127.1.0. This means the local clock timer will kick in when all outside sources become unavailable. Following is a list of sample time sources available via the Internet:

▸ `server clock.llnl.gov` (Lawrence Livermore National Laboratory)

▸ `server ntp.nasa.com` (NASA Ames Research Center)

▸ `server ntp2.usno.navy.mil` (U.S. Naval Observatory)

▸ `server 198.93.3.1` (Sony Corporate Headquarters)

You can change the NTP.CFG configuration of any of these sources by replacing the term "server" with "peer." Also note that NTP does not negotiate time as Primary Servers used to do in the past. Instead, NTP assumes that the time it gets from an Internet time source is the correct time. Thereby, it changes its own time according to the time it receives and all Secondary Servers within its Replica Ring change their time to match that of the server running NTP.

We're all out of time! (Pun intended.)

That's everything you need to know about the "Cloud." Well, not really, but it's a very good start. Remember, every cloud has a silver lining and this chapter has been yours. Can you feel the twinge in the crown of your cranium? Has your NDS tree begun to sprout? Pretty soon, you'll be NDS-Head Fred, too!

The goal of this chapter was to make you think until it hurt — to generate enough neurokinetic energy to stimulate cranial growth. Have we succeeded? You be the judge. It all started with an NDS getting-familiar period. Once you were comfortable with the concept of a tree in a cloud, we learned about the many different objects that live there — including the [Root] and leaves. We learned that NDS objects come in two different flavors: Tupperware containers and physical leaf resources. We learned about Country objects, Users, License Certificates, and the Alias object (if that's what it's really called).

Then, we discovered a whole new garden of NDS management with three key NetWare 5 CNA technologies:

- ▶ *NDS Naming* — With NDS objects come NDS names. Names uniquely identify "who we are" and "where we live." It works much the same way in NDS. NDS naming was the first of three important management topics we covered. We learned about the common name (who) and context (where). And we learned how these two are combined to create the distinguished name.

- ▶ *NDS Partitioning* — Then we explored partitioning — the second NDS management topic. NDS partitions are small pieces of the larger NetWare 5 puzzle. We can distribute these pieces on servers throughout the WAN for increased fault tolerance and better resource access. This process is known as replication. We learned about the four different NDS replica types and how and when they can be used. By now, the [Root] should be forming around your cerebellum.

▸ *Time Synchronization* — This was the final NDS management topic. NDS has to know what time it is: Time stamps are required for logging in, NDS replication, and many other important network tasks. This is accomplished with the help of three different time providers (Single-Reference, Reference, and Primary) and one special time consumer server (Secondary). We not only learned about servers, we explored two different configuration methods (default and custom). That's just about when we ran out of time!

So, here we are — NDS-Head Fred! So far, we've explored the basics of NetWare 5 and the intricacies of NDS. That completes our discussion of NetWare 5 CNA basics. Now you're ready to start the real journey:

▸ Getting Connected (Chapter 3)

▸ NetWare 5 File System (Chapter 4)

▸ NetWare 5 Security (Chapter 5)

▸ NetWare 5 Workstation Management (Chapter 6)

▸ NetWare 5 Printing (Chapter 7)

▸ NetWare 5 Installation (Chapter 8)

Don't be scared — I'll be with you every step of the way. And we'll explore NDS many times throughout this book. This is only the beginning and pretty soon you'll become a full-fledged superhero . . . .

Speaking of superheroes, remember ACME? It's time to SAVE THE WORLD again!!! Starting with NetWare 5 Connectivity.

See ya there!!

EXERCISE 2.2: UNDERSTANDING NDS NAMING

Answer the following questions using the directory structure shown in Figure 2.24.

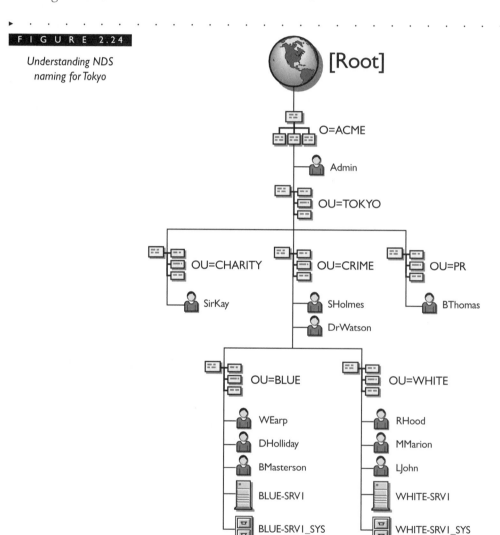

FIGURE 2.24

Understanding NDS naming for Tokyo

1. Indicate a typeless distinguished name for BMasterson.
2. Provide a typeful distinguished name for RHood.
3. List a typeless relative distinguished name for the CRIME Organizational Unit, assuming that your current context is the [Root].
4. Show a typeful relative distinguished name for the BLUE-SRV1 server object from the default current context.
5. If your current context is .CRIME.TOKYO.ACME, what is the shortest name that accurately references the SHolmes User object?
6. Assume your current context is .TOKYO.ACME. Indicate a typeless relative distinguished name for the LJohn User object.
7. If your current context is .PR.TOKYO.ACME, what would be a typeful relative distinguished name for SirKay?
8. Assume your current context is .WHITE.CRIME.TOKYO.ACME. Provide a typeless relative distinguished name for Admin.
9. If your current context is .BLUE.CRIME.TOKYO.ACME, what would be a typeful relative distinguished name for BThomas?
10. Assume your current context is .WHITE.CRIME.TOKYO.ACME. What is the longest possible typeful relative distinguished name for the SYS: volume on the BLUE-SRV1 server?
11. If DHolliday attaches to the BLUE-SRV1 server by default, what is his current context after login? Give two LOGIN commands for DHolliday.
12. How would MMarion visit SirKay?
13. How can you make sure that SirKay's workstation drops him into his home context when he attaches to the "Cloud"?
14. Provide ten LOGIN commands for SHolmes from .BLUE.CRIME.TOKYO.ACME:
15. What is the easiest way to move above ACME from the .PR.TOKYO.ACME context?

See Appendix C for answers.

EXERCISE 2.3: PLANT A TREE IN A CLOUD

Circle the 20 NDS-related terms hidden in this word search puzzle using the hints provided. No punctuation characters (such as blank spaces, hyphens, and so on) should be included. Numbers should always be spelled out.

```
O  R  G  A  N  I  Z  A  T  I  O  N  A  L  R  O  L  E  D
R  B  I  N  D  E  R  Y  L  O  C  A  L  I  T  Y  O  X  M
G  W  J  U  G  C  Z  P  B  O  W  X  E  V  K  N  J  X  G
A  S  Q  E  R  N  A  S  U  P  E  R  V  I  S  O  R  Q  B
N  G  V  D  C  L  D  N  R  O  O  G  V  X  Z  Y  Z  T  R
I  L  Z  W  I  T  T  Q  R  U  R  K  K  V  G  H  I  N  B
Z  S  U  A  T  R  A  I  L  I  N  G  P  E  R  I  O  D  X
A  M  S  N  Y  M  E  X  P  E  J  J  J  J  J  U  T  A  B
T  I  M  E  S  Y  N  C  H  R  O  N  I  Z  A  T  I  O  N
I  D  C  U  R  R  E  N  T  C  O  N  T  E  X  T  B  R  U
O  V  E  V  H  V  Z  Z  Y  O  Q  F  R  F  V  T  Y  M  T
N  U  X  Z  N  B  W  X  M  E  R  S  I  A  N  J  H  D  B
A  J  E  M  A  N  L  U  F  E  P  Y  T  L  Y  H  F  I  W
L  O  T  Y  P  E  L  E  S  S  N  A  M  E  E  S  D  V  R
U  K  Y  Z  Q  M  O  R  G  A  N  I  Z  A  T  I  O  N  X
N  K  M  W  H  D  N  R  L  F  S  B  T  J  P  I  H  B  N
I  T  G  U  D  O  I  R  E  P  G  N  I  D  A  E  L  Y  U
T  Q  I  F  V  I  H  U  S  V  N  W  L  E  B  Z  M  E  E
```

Hints:

1. Object that represents a logical NDS pointer to another object in the tree.
2. Predecessor to NDS found in pre-NetWare 4 versions of the operating system.
3. Container object that uses pre-determined two-character names.
4. The context that would be displayed if you issued the CX command with no options.
5. Command-line utility used to view or change your current context.

6. Object that represents a logical pointer to a physical directory in the NetWare 5 file system.

7. Object that represents a set of users and is used for assigning rights.

8. Identifies a name as a distinguished name.

9. Similar to a Country object, except that it can exist in a Country, Organization, or Organizational Unit container.

10. Item that represents a resource in the NDS database.

11. Container object that can be used to represent a company, university, or association.

12. Object that represents a position or role with an organization.

13. Container object that is considered as a "natural group."

14. Object that represents a login script that is used by a group of users who reside in the same or different containers.

15. Special superuser used for bindery emulation.

16. Temporal assurance scheme that forces all NetWare 5 servers to agree on what time it is.

17. Allows you to change the current context while using relative distinguished naming.

18. Name that contains object attribute abbreviations.

19. Name that does not contain object attribute abbreviations.

20. Controls server-to-server traffic generated by NDS.

See Appendix C for answers.

EXERCISE 2.4: NOVELL DIRECTORY SERVICES

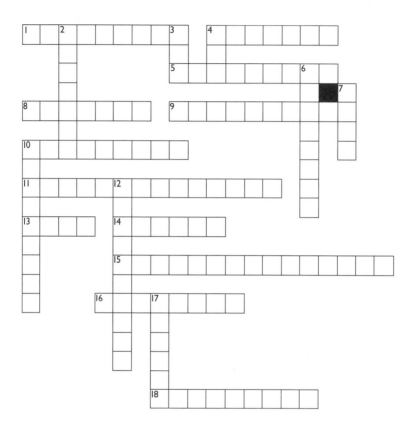

Across

1. A piece of the "Cloud"
4. Mysterious object class
5. Time consumer
8. Congenial time provider
9. Leaf object name
10. Type of writeable replica
11. Purpose of replication
13. NDS tree apex
14. Initial copy of partition

15. Solitary time provider
16. Holds object information
18. Like Tupperware

Down

2. Partition copy
3. The "Cloud"
4. Also known as GMT
6. Rarely used replica
7. Terminal object
10. Arrogant time server
12. Every server is one
17. Special trustee (in brackets)

See Appendix C for answers.

Let Me In!
NetWare 5 Connectivity

Welcome to the NetWare 5 garden!

This is the beginning of an exciting adventure for you — as the NetWare 5 Gardener. So far, you've learned all about the NDS "Cloud" and explored the myriad CNA/CNE features of NetWare 5. Now you get a chance to breathe life into your glorious NDS tree as a Gardener.

The next six chapters will prepare you for the challenge of a lifetime — NetWare 5 administration. You'll venture through the NetWare 5 file system, security, workstation management with Z.E.N.works, NDPS printing, and, finally, installation. However, the journey must start somewhere. Welcome to "Point A." The challenge begins today — connecting to the network and building ACME's NDS tree.

In the beginning, the garden is bare. You have a withering sapling (NDS tree), some soil (volumes), a greenhouse (server), and plenty of weeds. Not a promising sight. Fortunately, you have plenty of fertilizer (this Study Guide) to get you started. Once the soil has been prepared, you can start seeding. Be sure to segment your garden, because certain plants require more attention than others. Once the seeds are in place, it's time for garden management.

Garden management is the fun part. This is where the magic occurs. It's amazing how quickly your trees will bloom with the right combination of watering, love, sunshine, and weeding. The trick is determining how much is enough. Just as in life, there is such a thing as too much. Too much water, for example, could lead to overhydration, while too much sunshine could lead to dehydration. Gardening is a very tricky business — green thumb required.

This is your life as a NetWare 5 Gardener. You start with a sapling NDS tree, some default NetWare 5 files, and the Admin user. Now you must turn it into a thriving forest of communication and productivity. Good luck. To make matters worse, ACME's trying to save the world at the same time. Wow, you're going to need plenty of fertilizer!

In this chapter, we're going to discover the NetWare 5 garden and begin planting the seeds of connectivity. We'll learn about basic network components, install the Novell Client, and eventually log in to the tree. Then we'll explore login scripts, browse our new garden and eventually add some new plants (users). Here's a sneak peek at what's ahead:

▶ *Connecting to the Network* — Before you can show off your green thumb, you must gain access to the NDS garden. This is accomplished by configuring the NetWare 5 client and logging in using its built-in GUI tool.

In addition, we'll learn how user context can help make tree browsing a snap for first-time saplings.

▶ *Configuring Login Scripts* — Next, we'll learn how login scripts can help you customize users' connections and establish important login settings. Think of these as "batch files" for the network.

▶ *Welcome In!* — Once you gain access to the NetWare 5 garden, you can use a variety of Novell and third-party tools to *browse* the tree. Browsing not only acquaints you with the tree, it also aids in NDS navigation — which is required for CNA administration. However, we're not going to stop there. We'll learn how to create NDS users using a variety of tools and manage their access to advanced resources — using Alias, Directory Map, and Group objects.

So, that's life in the NetWare 5 garden. And if this isn't enough for you, you'll get a chance to build the entire ACME NDS tree at the end of the chapter. Green thumb required.

So, let's start by gaining access to this exciting new NDS garden.

▶ · ◀

Connecting to the Network

The first rule of gardening is "know your garden." Know the quality of the soil, know the angle of the sun, and definitely know the layout of the plants. The NetWare 5 garden is a haven for user connectivity. For that reason, you must understand the relationships between objects and the general layout of the tree.

Instead of flowers and tomatoes, this garden organizes network resources (such as users, groups, printers, servers, volumes, and so on). As you can see in Figure 3.1, our garden organizes these resources into a hierarchical directory tree.

NDS allows these resources to be managed in a single view. This is significant because it dramatically increases administrative flexibility, allowing you to manage the tree and its objects by using various properties and security capabilities. This contrasts with the earlier NetWare bindery which was server-centric and inflexible. The Directory is network-centric; that is, it's distributed and replicated on multiple servers throughout WAN. This increases resource availability and fault tolerance.

The ACME NDS garden

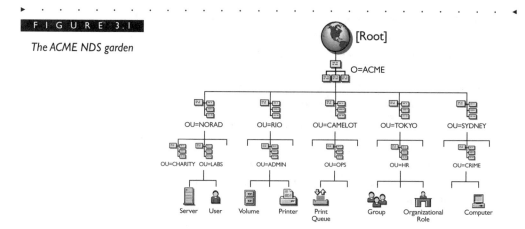

All in all, our garden is a pretty amazing place. It seems as though it's been designed for gardening from the very beginning. Management of NetWare has never been so accommodating — notice I didn't say "easy." They're not the same thing. NDS accomplishes this with three main principles:

▸ *Single Point of Login* — NetWare 5 users log into the network once — using one username and one password. Once there, they have instantaneous access to all authorized network resources. Very cool. A single user login also makes your job easier. You create each user account *once* for the entire NetWare 5 WAN. Multiple user accounts on multiple servers are no longer necessary. We'll explore this in the next section.

▸ *Easy Administration* — NetWare 5 consolidates all NDS administrative functions into a single, easy-to-use graphical utility — NetWare Administrator. This is a Windows-based tool that allows you to make changes to the Directory with the simple click of a mouse. It does virtually everything in NetWare 5 — get used to it.

▸ *Tree Walking* — NetWare 5 tree walking refers to an automatic background process that locates physically separated resources. Basically, it means that

NDS keeps track of objects even if they're scattered from here to eternity. Tree walking allows users to access resources without having to know where they live. Users simply ask NDS for the object, and tree walking goes and finds it on the nearest NetWare server. Also, this applies to your ability to *browse* the tree within a variety of GUI tools — such as NetWare Administrator, ConsoleOne, and Netscape Navigator. Speaking of browsing, we'll tour the NDS garden later in this chapter.

Of course, the NDS garden is only available to authenticated users. Remember, users don't log into NetWare servers any more — they log into the "Cloud." And, to gain access to the "Cloud," users must utilize a special set of hardware/software known as the *connectivity client*. Now let's learn more about the fundamental components of your network and learn how to access the NDS garden using a supercharged NetWare 5 client.

Overview of Network Components

In its simplest form, a *network* is a group of computers that can communicate with each other, share resources (such as hard disks and printers), and access remote hosts or other networks. In fancier terms, a network is a geographically dispersed computer system that connects intelligent workstations using high-speed protocols over a diverse collection of cabling in an attempt to balance advanced hardware components with sophisticated software applications. Cool!

As you can see in Figure 3.2, the network is composed of three main hardware components, each with its own native software and/or protocols:

▶ *Server* — This is the network boss. The server establishes the communications procedures for network workstations and allocates shared resources. In addition, the server houses the all-important network operating system — in this case, NetWare 5.

▶ *Workstations* — These are the true workhorses of a network. They handle 95 percent of the network processing load. Also, each workstation represents the user's link to the network. Workstations must be as user-friendly as they are smart. In our world, the workstations use the Novell Client for resource access and connectivity to the server.

> ▶ *Electronic Road* — This provides the network messages with the highway
> to travel upon. This electronic superhighway is made up of a variety of
> topology components (such as hubs and network interface cards) and
> cabling. Networks rely on cabling for connectivity, reliability, and speed.
> Today's electronic roads are controlled by TCP/IP or IPX protocols.

▶ · ◀

FIGURE 3.2

*Understanding network
components*

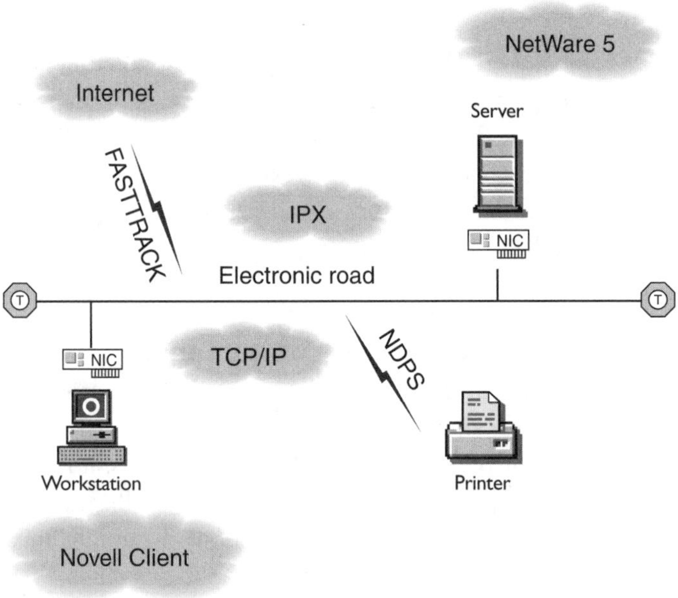

In addition to these key hardware/software components, the network offers a
variety of peripherals and remote connectivity. As you can see in Figure 3.2, we
included a shared printer as a peripheral resource and access to Internet web pages
via the FastTrack Web server. NetWare 5 includes all these features and more.

Now, let's take a closer look at each of these main components and learn how
they combine to create network "synergy." After all, the whole *is* greater than the
sum of its parts when you're talking about NetWare 5.

At the Server

The server is the "boss" of your network. As such, it has a substantial impact on
network performance. The server houses the network operating system, processes
disk requests, stores LAN applications and data, controls network security, and

provides central system fault tolerance. If there is one critical hardware component, it is the network file server. Keep in mind, though, that a network is a distributed data communications system. This means that 95 percent of the network processing occurs at the workstation, not at the server. Therefore, the server's processing capability is *not* as important as its bus throughput, disk type, or network interface card (NIC) architecture.

The importance of these components becomes clear when you analyze the primary function of your server: to process requests from the network by accepting incoming data packets and shuffling them off to internal memory. Memory acts as a holding cell until the server CPU is ready to work on the request. Typically, the network packet consists of a request for specific data located at a specific address somewhere inside the server disk. The CPU locates the data and sends the packet back to memory, where it waits until the requested data arrives. Once the reply packet arrives, it attaches the data and sends it off to the original workstation through the server NIC.

Novell servers use IBM-compatible computers with 80486 or Pentium processors. As such, they allow multi-user access and run a specialized Network Operating System (NOS) — NetWare 5. This is the true brains of your network. The NOS manages file system memory, users and groups, network applications, data, security, CPU usage, and shared resources. In NetWare 5, the NOS consists of three main components:

- *Kernel* — This forms the core of the operating system and provides basic functionality. This is analogous with the NetWare Core Protocol (NCP).

- *Server Console* — This allows you to control and manage your server. The server console displays a console prompt, which is similar to the DOS prompt. Some of the tasks you can perform at the server console include shutting down and restarting the server, executing console commands, running NLMs, running Java classes and applets, editing configuration files, setting server configuration parameters, adding namespaces to volumes, viewing network traffic, and sending messages.

- *NetWare Loadable Modules (NLMs)* — These are software programs that run on the server and provide added functionality. Most of them can be loaded and unloaded while the server is running. The four main types of NLMs are:

disk drivers with the .CDM and .HAM extensions (control communication between NetWare 5 and internal storage devices); LAN drivers with the .LAN extension (control communication between NetWare 5 and the internal NIC); namespace modules with the .NAM extension (enable files with non-DOS naming conventions to be stored on NetWare 5 volumes); and NLM utilities with the .NLM extension (management utilities or server application modules allowing you to run services that are not part of the kernel).

To learn more about the NetWare 5 server and its related components, check out the installation instructions in Chapter 8.

The Electronic Road

As we learned at the beginning of this section, communication is the goal of networking. The communications pathway shown in Figure 3.2 is the road on which all network messages travel. Servers and workstations communicate with each other using "the electronic road." This framework relies on three important concepts:

▸ *Topology* — The physical arrangements of network, servers, and workstations (such as the Ethernet 10BASE-T star)

▸ *Protocol* — The set of rules that control the topology (such as TCP/IP and IPX)

▸ *Cabling* — The physical pathway upon which electronic signals travel (such as twisted pair, fiberoptic, and coaxial)

Topology components are distributed devices that establish the network protocol and facilitate the movement of messages over cabling throughout the topology. This is the pavement of our electronic road. The key topology component in Figure 3.2 is the NIC.

NICs contain the electronic components that establish and control network communications. They are advanced modems that transmit digital packets of data over short distances at very high speeds. The NIC is the principal network hardware device that differentiates a network node (server or workstation) from a stand-alone microcomputer. As you can see from Figure 3.2, all servers and workstations must have an internal NIC. This is their connectivity point to the network.

For more information about NetWare's electronic road, see Chapter 2, "NetWare 5 IP Services" in *Novell's CNE Study Guide for NetWare 5*. Also, you'll get a chance to build, troubleshoot, and conceptualize the electronic road in Chapters 12 through 22 of *Novell's CNE Study Guide for NetWare 5*. These are the chapters that comprise the *Service and Support* (Novell Course 580) and *Networking Technologies* (Novell Course 565) requirements for NetWare 5 CNEs.

At the Workstation

Of all the places you'll go in your life, few will be as interesting as the NetWare 5 client. There you'll find fun, adventure, and LAN drivers. The client is one of the most important aspects of a NetWare 5 system because it's where the users meet the network. As a CNA, you will spend just as much time managing the workstations as you will managing the server and electronic road — probably more. In addition, managing workstations can be even more challenging because it encompasses a much more diverse collection of users, applications, and operating systems.

Someday, I guarantee you'll get the question, "Where's the ANY key?" To help you sleep at night, the interface should be as transparent as possible. To achieve transparent connectivity, NetWare 5 breaks the workstation into five key components (see Figure 3.3):

► *LAN driver and LSLC32* — The internal workstation NIC provides communications between the local Workstation Operating System (WOS) and the NetWare 5 server. This hardware device is managed by a series of workstation connectivity files: LAN driver and LSLC32.NLM. The NIC-specific LAN Driver (CNE2000.LAN, for example) is further supported by CMSM.NLM and ETHERTSM.NLM. Finally, LSLC32.NLM is a Link Support Layer driver that acts as a switchboard to route network protocol packets between the LAN driver and appropriate communications protocols.

► *Protocols* — Protocols determine (through a set of rules) the language used to move data across the network. It's imperative that the workstation, server, and electronic road all agree which protocol should be used. In NetWare 5, you have two choices: TCP/IP and IPX. Both of these protocols are implemented at the NetWare 5 client using a series of workstation connectivity files called Open Datalink Interface (ODI). Furthermore,

Windows provides its own implementation of workstation protocol—
called Windows Network Driver Interface Specification (NDIS). Regardless
of the protocol you choose, it's imperative that you configure the Novell
Client appropriately.

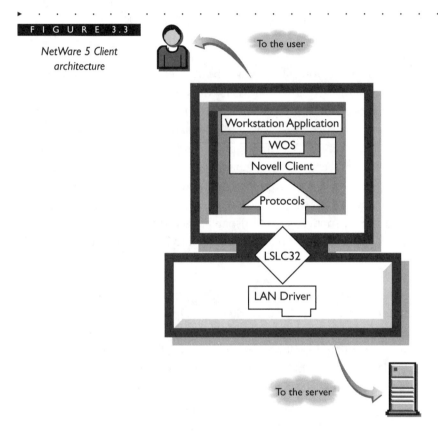

F I G U R E 3.3

*NetWare 5 Client
architecture*

To the user

Workstation Application

WOS

Novell Client

Protocols

LSLC32

LAN Driver

To the server

▶ *Novell Client*— The Novell Client is the centerpiece of transparent
workstation connectivity to a NetWare 5 WAN. It works with other
workstation software components (such as WOS and applications) to enable
the following features: access to NetWare services such as printing, browsing,
and filing; enforcement of network security to ensure that only approved
users can access the network; and management of data communications to

and from the workstation so that other network devices can understand and receive data. The Novell Client performs these tasks by running as a program on the workstation. In addition, it uses a GUI login window for user access to the network. The Novell Client software is included with the NetWare 5 CD-ROM, and we'll explore installation and setup in the next section. The good news is the Novell Client runs automatically once it's been installed, and provides an integrated portal to the native workstation operating system.

▶ *Workstation Operating System (WOS)* — The WOS (such as Windows 95/98) provides a common interface for network access and local applications. This way, users can access network resources in their own native environment. NetWare 5 supports the following workstation operating systems: DOS, Windows 95/98, Windows NT, Windows 3.x, OS/2 (using the OS/2 Client available from Novell's Web site), Macintosh (using the NetWare Client for Mac OS available from Novell's Web site), and UNIX (using NetWare NFS available from Novell's Web site). Note that DOS and Windows workstations support both TCP/IP and IPX protocols, while OS/2 and Macintosh clients only support native IPX.

Although NetWare 5 supports all the workstation operating systems listed here, you can only administer the network from Windows workstations.

TIP

▶ *Workstation Application* — Applications provide the workstation with a reason to exist. They create, request, and store user files. However, note that applications do not communicate directly with the network. They rely on the WOS and Novell Client to route requests to and from the NetWare 5 LAN. For example, when a user selects Save As in a word processor, the application asks the WOS and eventually the Novell Client to provide a list of network locations available for file storage.

The components shown in Figure 3.3 can be organized into two functional categories: workstation hardware and workstation software. *Workstation hardware* encompasses the first two components — LAN driver and protocols. The hardware is responsible for physically connecting the workstation to the network and providing a communications path to the server. This hardware is *not* responsible for the content of the data, how the data is used on the workstation, and guaranteeing network privileges to access any program or resource on the LAN. These are the responsibilities of the workstation software.

The *workstation software* encompasses the top three components in Figure 3.3 — the Novell Client, WOS, and workstation application. The primary responsibilities of this software are to create the content sent to and from the network, format the data so that all network resources can understand it, help ensure that only authorized users access the network, and control the flow of data within the workstation so that it finds the correct applications and users.

As a NetWare 5 CNA, it's important that you understand the functional responsibilities of all these network components and how the user data flows from workstation over electronic road to the NetWare 5 server. Probably the most important connectivity topic for you is Novell Client installation. This is a very complex and troublesome task because the workstation is such a diverse battleground. It's where the users plot their assaults against *your* network.

So, let's arm ourselves with some Novell Client installation knowledge.

Installing the Novell Client

As we just learned, the NetWare 5 workstation is a diverse battleground. This is where users and CNAs fight for control of network resources. However, it's not just the users that you're up against. In NetWare 5, the Novell Client is much more integrated with the workstation's native GUI environment than previous versions. For this reason, you must be intimately familiar with both the Novell Client and Windows 95/NT interface. Egad!

To install the NetWare 5 Client for Windows 95/98 or Windows NT, you'll need to run the WINSETUP.EXE file from the root directory of the *Novell Client* CD-ROM. WINSETUP.EXE automatically activates the correct workstation setup file from a platform-specific directory when you plug in the CD-ROM (it uses the *AutoRun* feature of Windows 95/98/NT). During the Client installation process, you establish specific protocol and NDS configurations. In addition, you will select from a list of various workstation components, including Novell Distributed

Print Services (NDPS), Novell Workstation Manager, a Novell NDS provider, and Z.E.N.works support.

Refer to Exercise 8.2 in Chapter 8 for detailed NetWare 5 Client installation instructions. In this exercise, you'll get hands-on experience installing the Novell Client on Windows 95/98 and Windows NT workstations. During the exercise, you'll notice some significant differences between the two platforms. Check them out in Table 3.1.

T A B L E   3.1

Novell Client installation comparison for Windows 95/98 and Windows NT

INSTALLATION TOPIC	WINDOWS 95/98	WINDOWS NT
Client installation directory	E:\PRODUCTS\WIN95\ IBM_ENU	E:\PRODUCTS\WINNT\ i386
Client setup file	SETUP.EXE	SETUPNW.EXE
Accept license agreement	Yes	N/A
Protocol preferences & NDS	Before components selection	After components selection

During and after the Novell Client installation, you must make sure that Windows and the Client are working in unison. This is accomplished by configuring three Client settings:

▸ *Communication Protocols* — Communication protocols are the common language of the network. The Novell Client for Windows 95/98 and Windows NT supports both TCP/IP and IPX protocols. TCP/IP is the protocol of the Internet while IPX supports previous versions of NetWare. For the most part, IPX support is provided solely by the Novell Client, while Windows itself helps establish TCP/IP communications. As a CNA, you must decide which protocol to use on each distributed workstation. Many organizations enable both TCP/IP and IPX protocol to ensure network compatibility. This allows each workstation to connect to previous versions of NetWare, the Internet, and/or NetWare 5 LANs utilizing *Pure IP*.

▸ *Protocol Specification* — Depending on which communications protocol you choose, Novell and Windows use different specifications for supporting workstation communication. Legacy, DOS, and Windows 3.1 workstations must use the ODI specification from Novell for IPX and TCP/IP support. Windows 95/98 and Windows NT workstations, on the other hand, use the native Microsoft Windows specification called NDIS.

▶ *LAN Driver* — As we learned earlier, the workstation LAN driver controls the internal NIC. The driver is usually provided by the board manufacturer although Windows ships with several generic drivers of its own. Whenever you have a choice, choose the manufacturer-specific driver because it's usually more current.

Once you've connected to the network using the Novell Client, there's only one task left — *logging in*. Let's get connected!

Logging In

As a NetWare 5 CNA, you've already accomplished the hard part — automating the workstation connection. Now it's the user's turn. The good news is that the Novell Client provides a friendly GUI login utility for Windows 95/98 and Windows NT users. As you can see in Figure 3.4, the GUI login window provides simple Username and Password input boxes within the native MS Windows environment. This is important because it gives the users a familiar window into which they can provide mandatory network authentication information. The good news is that NetWare 5 supports a single login for access to all network resources. Once the user logs in, the user is granted automatic access to all resources in the NDS tree — provided the user has sufficient access rights.

F I G U R E 3.4

GUI Login utility for NetWare 5

To log into a NetWare 5 tree, the user must have a workstation with the current Novell Client software installed. In addition, the user must have a "live"

connection to the network with a functioning NIC and a correctly configured protocol stack. Finally, each user must have a valid name and password. The name (also known as *login ID*) is the same as the User object name. NDS requires a valid NDS context so that it can differentiate between users with similar names.

So how do you get access to the NetWare 5 GUI login window? Good question. NetWare 5 offers numerous choices:

▸ Typically, the Novell Client login window appears when the workstation boots up. However, in Windows NT, you'll need to press Ctrl+Alt+Del keys simultaneously to activate login.

▸ You can click the Windows Start button and select the login choice from the Programs option. Typically, the NetWare 5 login utility is placed in the Novell folder.

▸ You can click the "N" icon in the Windows System tray and select Login.

▸ You can run the LOGINW95.EXE file from the C:\NOVELL\CLIENT32 subdirectory on a Windows 95/98 workstation.

In addition to the basic GUI login window, the Novell Client provides an Advanced tab for login script and NDS configuration. As you can see in Figure 3.5, this tab allows you to configure two different types of login information:

▸ *NDS* — The NDS tab shown in Figure 3.5 allows you to configure critical directory information during login. This includes the tree name, server, and, most importantly, user context. The Context field defines where the user "lives" in the NDS tree. If this field is configured correctly, the user can simply type his or her object name in the User Name field above (as shown in Figure 3.4). NetWare 5 provides three different ways of establishing a user context before or during login: using the Context field shown in Figure 3.5, using the Name Context field in the Novell Client Configuration window (found in the Network icon of Control Panel), and/or by setting the current context at the DOS prompt or in a login script using the CONTEXT command.

FIGURE 3.5

NetWare 5 Advanced GUI Login window

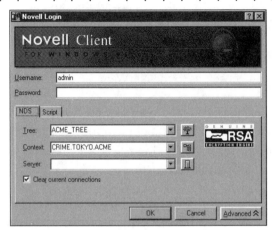

> ► *Script* — This tab allows you to establish individual login script settings within the GUI login window. This option also allows you to suspend the running of scripts and/or define specific identifier variables. We will discuss login scripts in more depth in just a moment.

Congratulations . . . you're in! I bet you didn't realize NetWare 5 connectivity could be so much fun.

Now that you've learned everything about network hardware/software and you've logged into the NetWare 5 LAN with your new Novell Client, your users are well on their way toward the NDS garden. Of course, they're not quite there yet. Before you can gain access to network resources, you must pass Phase 2 of authentication — login scripts. Login scripts are batch files for the network that provide a variety of user configurations — including drive mappings, printer redirection, and environmental variables. Let's learn more about how CNAs can use these scripts to achieve greater LAN synergy.

Green thumb required.

LAB EXERCISE 3.1: CONNECTING TO THE NETWORK WITH WINDOWS 95

In the next six chapters, we will explore many of the NetWare 5 tools you need to build a new Global Electronic Village — including NetWare 5 installation, connectivity, the NetWare 5 file system, security, Z.E.N.works, and NDPS. Periodically along the way, I'm going to need you to return to ACME and help implement key global technologies — otherwise known as "Lab Exercises."

Warning: All exercises in this book should be performed in an isolated, non-production environment.

TIP

To perform this exercise, you will need:

▸ A NetWare 5 server called CRIME-SRV1.CRIME.TOKYO.ACME (which can be installed using the directions found in Chapter 8, Exercise 8.1).

▸ A workstation running the NetWare 5 Novell Client for Windows 95/98 (which can be installed using the directions found in Chapter 8, Exercise 8.2).

Although this exercise is designed for Windows 95/98 workstations, you'll find that the login process for Windows NT workstations is similar.

TIP

In this exercise, we will walk through some very important Client 32 workstation connectivity steps: namely Connection and Login. Follow very carefully, and try this at home — if you dare!

1. On a Windows 95/98 workstation:

   a. Right-click the red "N" in the System Tray. (The System Tray is located, by default, on the right end of the Windows taskbar.)

   b. Select NetWare Login from the pop-up menu that appears.

2. When the initial Novell Login window appears:

   a. Make sure the following is listed in the Username field:

     `admin`

b. Type the following in the Password field:

ACME

(You'll notice that asterisks, rather than the actual password, are displayed for security reasons.)

c. Click Advanced.

3. When the expanded Novell Login window appears, the NDS tab should be selected by default.

a. Enter the following in the Tree field:

ACME_TREE

b. Enter the following in the Context field:

CRIME.TOKYO.ACME

c. Enter the following in the Server field:

CRIME-SRV1

d. Make sure the Clear Current Connections checkbox is marked.

4. Click the Script tab

a. This tab allows you to control the processing of login scripts. It allows you to override existing User and Profile login scripts assigned to this user, as well as to bypass all login scripts. For example, if you want to override your existing User login script (if any), you could indicate the login script name in the Login Script field. If you wanted to override your existing Profile login script (if any), you could indicate the login script name in the Profile Script field.

You'll notice that three checkboxes on this page are marked by default: Run Scripts, Display Results Window, and Close Automatically. If you leave these settings unchanged, any login scripts that have been set up for you will be executed during the login process, including any listed on this dialog box. The Results screen will then briefly appear on the screen after login is complete.

b. Click the Close Automatically checkbox to unmark it. (This will cause the Results screen to remain displayed instead of closing automatically.)

5. Click the Variables tab:

a. A Variable dialog box will appear. (If you wanted to pass on any variables to the login script processor, you would indicate them here.)

b. Click Cancel.

6. Click OK to initiate the login process.

7. A Results window should appear on the screen:

a. You will notice that it lists information such as your current context, your User object's context, your current tree, the server to which you are currently attached, and any drives that are mapped.

b. Review the contents of the window, then click Close.

Congratulations! You have successfully logged into the network.

Configuring Login Scripts

Login scripts are an expression of your LAN's vocal cords. Once your users have been authenticated with a valid username and password, NetWare 5 greets the user with login scripts. In short, login scripts are batch files for the network. They provide a simple configuration tool for user customization — drive mappings, text messages, printer redirection, and so on.

Login scripts are one of your most important configuration responsibilities. From one central location, they enable you to customize all users or just specific groups of users. Many of the configurations we've talked about are session-specific and disappear when users log out. Login scripts give you the ability to re-establish these settings every time your users log in. This is amazing stuff.

NetWare 5 supports four types of login scripts, which are executed in systematic progression. As you can see in Figure 3.6, there's a flowchart logic to how login scripts are executed. Here's a quick look:

▶ *Container login scripts* — These are properties of Organization and Organizational Unit containers. They enable you to customize settings for all users within a container.

▶ *Profile login scripts* — These are properties of the Profile object. These scripts customize environmental parameters for groups of users. This way, users who are not directly related in the NDS tree can share a common login script.

▶ *User login scripts* — These are properties of each User object. They are executed after the Container and Profile scripts and provide customization at the user level.

▶ *Default login script* — This is executed for any user who does not have an individual User script. This script contains some basic mappings for the system and a COMSPEC command that points to the appropriate network DOS directory.

▶ . . . . ◀

F I G U R E   3.6

*The flow of NetWare 5
login script execution*

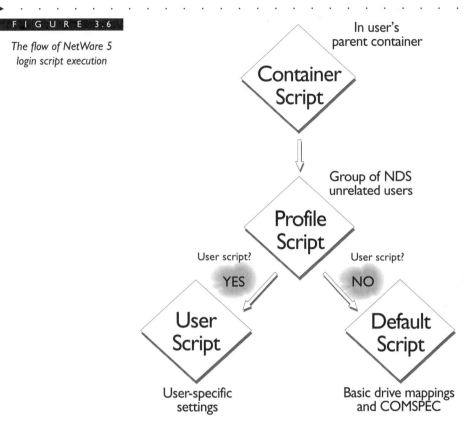

Login scripts consist of commands and identifiers, just like any other program or batch file. In addition, login script syntax must follow specific rules and conventions. Let's start our discussion with a more detailed look at the four login script types and then explore the commands that make them productive.

Login Script Types

We just saw that there are four types of NetWare 5 login scripts—Container, Profile, User, and Default. All four work in concert to provide LAN customization for containers, groups, and users. As you'll quickly learn, login scripts are an integral part of your daily CNA grind. Let's start with a description of the four different login script types.

Container Login Script

Container login scripts are properties of Organization and Organizational Unit containers. In previous versions of NetWare, there was one System login script that was executed for all users. In NetWare 5, it is possible for every container to have its own login script. As you can see in Figure 3.6, the Container is the first login script executed — Profile and User scripts follow.

There is one important difference between the NetWare 5 Container login script and earlier System login scripts. A Container script only executes for users within the container. As you can see in Figure 3.7, the Admin user executes the ACME Container login script. SHolmes, on the other hand, doesn't execute any Container login script because the CRIME Organizational Unit doesn't have a script. Similarly, RHood executes the WHITE Container login script, whereas AEinstein executes none.

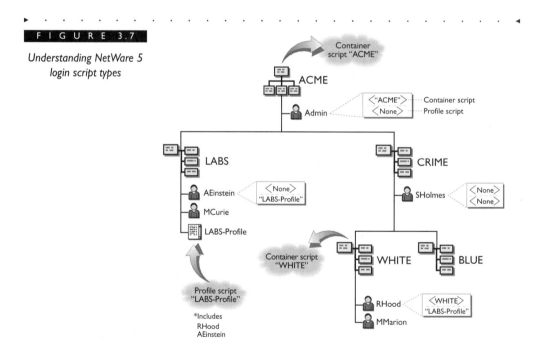

F I G U R E   3.7

Understanding NetWare 5 login script types

This is an important point because many CNAs assume that Container login scripts can be inherited by lower containers. This is not the case. If you wish to have one login script for all users to share, you have three options: (1) You can create a Profile login script and have all users point to it; (2) you can use the cut-and-paste feature within NetWare Administrator to copy one script to all containers; or (3) you can use an INCLUDE statement in each Container login script, which executes a text file containing these commands. Regardless, the moral of the story is NetWare 5 no longer provides a single script for all users.

As you plan login scripts for your network, keep in mind that at some point you'll need to maintain them. Use Container login scripts to provide access to network resources, Profile scripts for a specific group's needs, and User login scripts only in special circumstances. Following are the types of things you might do within a Container login script:

▸ Send messages to users within a container

▸ Establish the first search drive mapping to SYS:PUBLIC

▸ Establish the second search drive mapping to DOS directories

▸ Create other search drive mappings for application directories

▸ Establish a network drive mapping U: to each user's home directory

▸ Connect users within a container to appropriate network printers

▸ Use IF . . . THEN statements for access to specific resources based on times, group memberships, and other variables

▸ Transfer users to an appropriate container-based menu system and/or application

Drive mappings are logical pointers to physical network directories. We'll learn all about them in Chapter 4, "NetWare 5 File System."

TIP

Profile Login Script

The Profile login script is a property of the Profile object. This script customizes environmental parameters for groups of users. Each User object can be assigned a single Profile script — that's all. This way, users who are not directly related in the NDS tree can share a common login script. For example, Figure 3.7 shows how the AEinstein and RHood objects can share the LABS-Profile login script even though they live in different parts of the tree. Also note how the Profile login script executes after the Container script, and in Mr. Einstein's case, the Profile login script is the only script that executes.

Figure 3.8 shows an example of how the Profile login script is created in NetWare Administrator. Once the script has been defined, two things must happen so that you can use it: (1) each user must have the Browse right to the object and the Read property right to the Profile object's Login Script property (assuming the user and Profile are defined in different containers); and (2) the complete name of the Profile object must be defined in the user's Profile Login Script property.

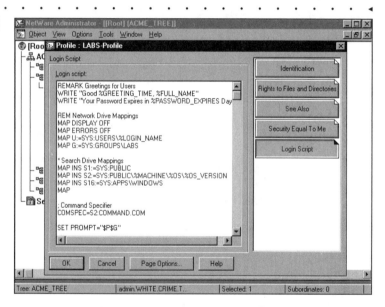

F I G U R E   3.8

Creating the LABS-Profile script in NetWare Administrator

Profile login scripts should be used to customize specific group configurations. Some tasks you can accomplish with Profile login scripts include the following:

▶ Send messages to users within a group

▶ Establish network drive mappings to special data directories, report files, or other servers that contain critical group information

▶ Establish search drive mappings to group application directories

▶ Connect to group-specific printers such as high-resolution LaserJets, plotters, or faxes

REAL WORLD

Remember, users can be assigned to only one Profile object, but other Profile login scripts can be specified at the command line. For example, the following line would allow RHood to execute the "WHITE-Profile" script in addition to his default "LABS-Profile" script:

```
LOGIN RHOOD /P.CN=WHITE-Profile.OU=WHITE.OU=CRIME.OU=TOKYO.O=ACME
```

Wasn't that fun?

User Login Script

The User login script is a property of each User object. The User script is executed after the Container and Profile scripts, and provides customization all the way down to the user level. Although User scripts are a nice feature, they can quickly become a maintenance nightmare — imagine hundreds and hundreds of User login scripts constantly screaming for attention. Nope, one baby is enough. A better strategy is to use Container and Profile scripts as much as possible and eliminate the User scripts altogether.

The primary purpose of the User login script is user-specific customization. This level of customization can be accomplished in the Container and Profile scripts by using IF . . . THEN logic commands. But, if you absolutely have to create a user-specific script, it's nice to know that it's there.

User login scripts should be created only in special circumstances. Remember, you have to maintain any scripts you create. Some instances when a User script might be justified include:

▶ Establish network drive mappings to specific user directories, provided that these directories do not correspond with the drive mappings made in the Container script

▶ Connect to commonly used printers, in addition to the ones selected in the Container and Profile scripts

▶ Send weekly messages to remind the user about time-sensitive tasks

▶ Activate a special user-specific menu system and/or application

Default Login Script

The Default login script is executed for any user who does not have an individual User script. This poses an interesting dilemma. Earlier we said it's a good idea not to have a User script. This means the Default script will automatically execute. Oops. This is a problem because the Default script typically overrides already-established drive mappings and COMSPEC settings.

Fortunately, Novell has recognized this problem and provides you with the means to disable the Default login script using the following statement:

```
NO_DEFAULT
```

This command must be placed in a Container or Profile login script.

 The Default login script cannot be edited because it is included in the SYS:LOGIN\LOGIN.EXE command code. It can, however, be disabled by including the NO_DEFAULT command in a Container or Profile script.

TIP

This completes our discussion of the different login script types. In leaving this little discussion, consider the factors that determine how you use login scripts and which types you'll need. These factors include the needs of users, their knowledge level, the size of your network, the complexity of the WAN, the type of groups, and access requirements for different containers.

Remember, login script design can go a long way toward increasing your CNA quality of life and decreasing your daily workload. This is your first shot at parenthood (system customization); don't underestimate it.

Login Script Commands

Login scripts consist of commands and identifiers just like any other program or batch file. In addition, login script syntax must follow specific rules and conventions. The syntax for login script programming is quite simple, but you must be sure to organize identifier variables and commands with appropriate grammar — much like learning to talk. For example, consider the following line:

```
MAP U:=SYS:USERS\%LOGIN_NAME
```

This line uses proper login script syntax. It starts with the login script command MAP and uses appropriate identifier variable grammar — %LOGIN_NAME. The cool thing about this line is that it changes for each user. For example, when Dr. Watson logs in, the system creates a U: drive for him, and it points to SYS:USERS\DRWATSON. On the other hand, when SHolmes logs in, his U: drive points to SYS:USERS\SHOLMES. Cool!

Another good example of login script vernacular is the WRITE command. Consider the following statement:

```
WRITE "Good %GREETING_TIME, %FULL_NAME!"
```

Depending on the time of day and user who logs in, this single statement will provide a custom message. For example, Leia gets the following message when she turns on her machine in the morning:

```
"Good Morning, Princess Leia!"
```

This can go a long way in making users feel warm and fuzzy about the LAN. As a matter of fact, some users get the perception that NetWare 5 actually cares about them and is personally wishing them a nice day. Regardless of the LAN's motivation, the point is that users feel good about using the network!

All this configuration magic is made possible because of two login script elements:

▶ Identifier Variables

▶ Login Script Commands

Let's take a closer look at how they work.

Identifier Variables

Identifier variables enable you to enter a variable (such as LAST_NAME) rather than a specific name (Watson). When the login script executes, it substitutes real values for the identifier variables. This means that you can make your login scripts more efficient and more flexible. In addition, it makes the concept of a single Container script feasible.

As we saw in earlier examples, identifier variables are preceded by a percent sign (%) and written in all uppercase. This is the ideal syntax for identifier variables because it allows you to use them anywhere in the script, including inside quotation marks (" "). Table 3.2 lists some of the most interesting identifier variables available in NetWare 5. Learn them. These cute little guys can go a long way in customizing Container and Profile scripts.

TABLE 3.2

*Login Script Identifier
Variables for NetWare 5*

CATEGORY	IDENTIFIER VARIABLE	DESCRIPTION
Date	DAY	Day number 01 through 31
	DAY_OF_WEEK	Day of week (Monday, Tuesday, and so on)
	MONTH	Month number (01 through 12)
	MONTH_NAME	Month Name (January, February, and so on)
	NDAY_OF_WEEK	Weekday number (1 through 7, where 1 equals Sunday)
	SHORT_YEAR	Last two digits of year
	YEAR	All four digits of year
Time	AM_PM	a.m. or p.m.
	GREETING_TIME	Time of day (morning, afternoon, or evening)
	HOUR	Hour of day on a 12-hour scale
	HOUR24	Hour of day on a 24-hour scale
	MINUTE	Minutes (00 through 59)
	SECOND	Seconds (00 through 59)
User	CN	User's full common name as it exists in NDS
	ALIAS_CONTEXT	Y if REQUESTER_CONTEXT is an Alias
	FULL_NAME	User's unique full name as it appears in both NDS and the bindery
	LAST_NAME	User's last name in NDS or full name in bindery-based NetWare 5
	LOGIN_CONTEXT	Context where user exists
	LOGIN_NAME	User's unique login name truncated to eight characters
	MEMBER OF "GROUP"	Group object that user is assigned to
	NOT MEMBER OF "GROUP"	Group object that the user is not assigned to
	PASSWORD_EXPIRES	Number of days before password expires
	REQUESTER_CONTEXT	Context when login started
	USER_ID	Unique hexadecimal ID assigned to each user

CATEGORY	IDENTIFIER VARIABLE	DESCRIPTION
Workstation	MACHINE	Type of computer (either IBM_PC or other name specified in NET.CFG)
	NETWARE_REQUESTER	Version of Requester being used (NetWare Requester for DOS or OS/2)
	OS	Type of operating system on the workstation (MSDOS, OS/2, and so on)
	OS_VERSION	Operating system version loaded on the workstation
	P_STATION	Workstation's 12-digit hexadecimal node ID
	SHELL_TYPE	Version of the workstation's DOS shell for NetWare 2 and 3 user
	S_MACHINE	Short machine name (IBM, and so on)
	STATION	Workstation's connection number
Miscellaneous	FILE_SERVER	NetWare 5 server name that workstation first attaches to
	NETWORK_ADDRESS	IPX external network number for the cabling system (8-digit hexadecimal number)
	ACCESS_SERVER	Shows whether the access server is functional (true or false)
	ERROR_LEVEL	An error number (0 equals no errors)
	%n	Replaced by parameters entered after the LOGIN command (starting with %0)

In addition to these identifier variables, you can use any NDS property name within a NetWare 5 login script. Just be sure to use the same syntax — that is, uppercase and preceded by a percent sign.

Login Script Commands

The identifier variables shown in Table 3.2 must be used with valid login script commands. As you can see in Figure 3.9, NetWare 5 includes a plethora of commands that can be used in various configurations. In the remainder of this section, we'll present the commands as part of a productive NetWare 5 Container login script.

In each case, refer to Figure 3.9 for appropriate syntax. Also, use the reference letter ("A", for example) as a pointer to the correct line in the example script. Here we go!

FIGURE 3.9

*A typical NetWare 5
login script*

A
```
REMARK Greetings for users
WRITE "Good %GREETING_TIME, %FULL_NAME!"
WRITE "Your Password Expires in %PASSWORD_EXPIRES Days"
```

B
```
REM Network Drive Mappings
MAP DISPLAY OFF
MAP ERRORS OFF
MAP U:=SYS:USERS\%LOGIN_NAME
MAP G:=SYS:GROUPS\"%Group Membership"
```

C
```
*Search Drive Mappings
MAP INS S1:=SYS: PUBLIC
MAP INS S2:=SYS: PUBLIC \%MACHINE\%OS\%OS_VERSION
MAP INS S16:=SYS:APPS\WINDOWS
MAP DISPLAY ON
MAP
```

D
```
; Command Specifier
COMSPEC= S2:COMMAND.COM
```

E
```
SET PROMPT= "$P$G"
SET TEMP= "U:\USERS\%LOGIN_NAME\TEMP"
```

F
```
IF DAY_OF_WEEK= "Friday" THEN BEGIN
    MAP R:=.REPORTS.LABS.NORAD.ACME
    DISPLAY R:FRIDAY.TXT
    PAUSE
END
```

G
```
IF MEMBER OF "OPS-Group" THEN #CAPTURE P=HP4S1-P1 NT TI=10
IF MEMBER OF "ADMIN-Group" THEN #CAPTURE P=HP5-P1 NFF NT
IF MEMBER OF "LABS-Group" THEN #CAPTURE P=CANONBJ-P1 NB
```

H
```
NO_DEFAULT
```

I
```
PCCOMPATIBLE
DRIVE U:
EXIT "Start"
```

A: WRITE and REMARK

Login scripts should always start with documentation. This is accomplished using the REMARK command. Any line beginning with REMARK is ignored by NetWare 5. It does, however, provide a useful tool for documenting the many different sections of your Container and Profile scripts. Besides the word REMARK, NetWare 5 supports three other variations — REM, an asterisk (*), and a semicolon (;). As you can see in Figure 3.9, all possibilities have been used. Another use of documentation is edit tracking. When multiple supervisors are maintaining the same container login script, it's a good idea to document who does what when. Finally, documentation is necessary for CNAs who follow you. After all, you do plan on winning the lottery, don't you?

REAL WORLD

Here's a list of things to think about when creating NetWare 5 login scripts. It's always a good idea to have a few guidelines in mind before you begin exploring all the possibilities:

▶ *Minimum* — None. All four login script types are optional. Of course, if no User script exists, the Default will run. So, at the absolute minimum, you must have one User script with one command — EXIT or NO DEFAULT.

▶ *Case* — Login scripts are not case sensitive, except for identifier variables in quotation marks. They must be uppercase and preceded by a percent sign (%). See the "WRITE" example later in this chapter.

▶ *Characters per line* — 150 maximum, although 78 is recommended for readability.

▶ *Commands per line* — One. Also, press Enter to mark the end of each line. Lines that automatically wrap are considered one command.

▶ *Blank lines* — Have no effect. Use them to visually separate groups of commands.

▶ *Documentation* — Use any variation of the REMARK command to thoroughly document what's going on.

One of the most popular login script commands is WRITE. With it, you can display a variety of friendly messages during login script execution. One of the friendliest is shown in Figure 3.9. Other identifier variables you can use with the WRITE command include:

```
Your password expires in %PASSWORD_EXPIRES days.

Today is %MONTH_NAME %DAY.

At the tone, the time is %HOUR:%MINUTE %AM_PM.

You're connected as workstation %STATION.

You're attached to %FILE_SERVER.
```

Don't underestimate the power of communication. Goodwill flourishes with a quick note to your users now and again.

B: Network Drive Mappings

The next section in Figure 3.9 establishes user-specific and group-specific drive mappings. Drive mapping is the single most important purpose of login scripts. Mappings are essential to NetWare 5 navigation and provide a facility for representing large directory paths as drive letters. The problem with mapping is that it's both session-specific (meaning drive pointers disappear when users log out) and user-specific (meaning they're unique for each user). The temporary nature of drive mappings makes them particularly annoying—because complex MAP commands must be entered each time a user logs in. Fortunately, this process can be automated using NetWare 5 login scripts.

In addition to standard MAP statements, NetWare 5 login scripts support MAP NEXT and MAP %1 commands. The latter will map the first network drive to a specific directory or volume. Also, the "1" can be replaced by any number from 1 to 26.

TIP

Before you get too excited about network and search drive mappings, it's a good idea to turn off the display of drive mapping and drive mapping errors. MAP DISPLAY OFF stops complex mappings from displaying during execution, and MAP ERRORS OFF avoids confusing users with mappings to directories they don't have rights to. Don't worry, we'll turn them back on later.

The MAP command is most useful when combined with identifier variables. This way, you can accomplish user-specific and group-specific mappings with only one command. Notice the second network drive mapping in Figure 3.9. Here we're using the Group Membership property from NDS. The trick is getting the quotation marks in the right place.

C: Search Drive Mappings

Once the network drive mappings have been established, it's time to shift your attention to search drive mappings. By default, the first two should always be SYS:PUBLIC and the network DOS directory structure. Notice our creative use of identifier variables in search mapping 2. This single statement intelligently maps every workstation to the appropriate version of DOS. Of course, these statements must be combined with the exact DOS structure outlined in Chapter 4.

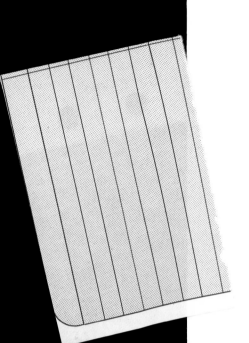

The three key identifier variables are:

▸ *%MACHINE* — This identifies the machine, such as IBM_PC, PowerBook, NEC, and so on. These values are established using the LONG MACHINE TYPE parameter in NET.CFG.

▸ *%OS* — This identifies the operating system as MSDOS, Windows NT, OS/2, PCDOS, DRDOS, and so on.

▸ *%OS_VERSION* — This identifies the specific version of DOS running on the workstation (for example, v5.00, v7.01, v6.22). This value is determined by the NetWare 5 client.

Next, you should create a search drive mapping for every application that users are likely to access. In these cases, you can use MAP INS S16 to systematically create mappings in order. In each case, S16 will drop to the next available search number. Finally, turn MAP DISPLAY back on and issue one final MAP command to show the user what he or she has available.

D: COMSPEC

The next step is to create a COMSPEC for the new DOS directory mapping. COMSPEC stands for "COMmand SPECifier," and it helps NetWare 5 find COMMAND.COM when it's lost. This happens all the time when terminate-and-stay resident programs (TSRs) and Windows applications need extra space. If COMMAND.COM cannot be found, your users will get one of these messages:

```
"Invalid COMMAND.COM"

"COMMAND.COM cannot be found"

"Insert Boot Disk in Drive A:"
```

Interestingly, this causes the hair to stand up on the back of your neck — especially if it happens all day. It must be a kinetic reaction.

COMSPEC solves the "lost DOS" problem by telling the system where to search for appropriate COMMAND.COM file. Keep in mind that each version of DOS on each of your workstations supports a different type of COMMAND.COM. You must be sure to point to the correct file. This is accomplished by using the

S2: drive mapping we created earlier. Remember, it points to the correct DOS directory structure for each workstation.

▶ · ◀

REAL WORLD

Setting COMSPEC to a network directory for COMMAND.COM has its advantages. However, many CNAs still insist on pointing to a local drive such as C:\DOS. It's your choice. Here are some reasons to use the NetWare 5 DOS directory structure:

 ▶ *Speed* (with file caching)

 ▶ *Central Management* (all workstations point to the file server)

 ▶ *Diskless Workstations* (it's required)

E: SET

The SET command enables you to configure DOS environment variables within the login script. You can use the SET command exactly the same as you would in DOS (except that you'll need to surround the values with quotation marks). Otherwise, most SET variables are configured in the user's AUTOEXEC.BAT file. In Figure 3.9, we've included two important SET variables:

```
SET PROMPT="$P$G"
```

This configures the local and network prompt to display the current directory path. We want users to feel like they're at home.

```
SET TEMP="U:\USERS\%LOGIN_NAME\TEMP"
```

This points the Windows TEMP directory to an NetWare 5 drive under the user's area. Whatever you do, don't use the SET PATH command in a Container login script; it overwrites local and network search drives.

F: IF ...THEN ... ELSE

The IF . . . THEN command enables you to use script programming logic. It checks a given condition and executes your command only if the condition is met.

In addition, you can add the ELSE statement to selectively execute another command only when the condition is not met. For example, you can have the system display a fancy message and fire phasers whenever it is the user's birthday (using MONTH and DAY identifier variables). Otherwise, display a message pointing out that it's not his/her birthday the other 364 days of the year.

The IF . . . THEN command is the most versatile login script tool. Learn it, use it, be it!

IF . . . THEN effectively enables you to execute any command based on condition, including login name, context, day of the week, or group membership. As you can see in Figure 3.9, we are executing these three commands only on Friday:

▸ *MAP* — This maps the R: drive to a Directory Map object.

▸ *DISPLAY* — This displays a text file that is stored on the R: drive.

▸ *PAUSE* — This temporarily stops execution of the login script to allow the user time to read the display. Just as with the DOS PAUSE command, execution resumes when the user presses any key.

Also notice the use of BEGIN and END. If you plan on including multiple commands within a nested IF . . . THEN statement, you must use BEGIN to start and END to mark the bottom of the nest. As a side note, IF . . . THEN statements can be nested up to ten levels.

You can do anything with an IF . . . THEN statement. Don't be shy. Before you resign yourself to creating Profile and User login scripts, explore the use of IF . . . THEN statements in Container scripts.

G: # (DOS Executable)

The DOS executable (#) command has been included by Novell to support external programs. Because NetWare 5 has a limited number of login script commands, you might run across a case where you need to run a non-login script program. The most obvious oversight that comes to mind is CAPTURE, which is an NetWare 5 printing command that redirects local ports to shared network printers. This command should be included in Container and Profile scripts for user and group automation. You can do so with the following command:

```
#CAPTURE P=.HP5-P1.CRIME.TOKYO.ACME /NT /TI=10
```

There is one problem with this scenario. While CAPTURE is running, the entire login script and LOGIN.EXE is swapped into workstation RAM. Once the # command is finished, NetWare 5 reloads the login script from memory. But what if the external program is a TSR or never returns stolen RAM to the workstation? In both of these cases, you run the risk of wasting 70K to 100K of workstation RAM. This is a bad thing. By default, NetWare 5 swaps login scripts and LOGIN.EXE into extended or expanded memory.

Fortunately, CAPTURE is not one of those misbehaving # commands. As you can see in Figure 3.9, we've combined the #CAPTURE program with IF . . . THEN statements to customize group-specific printing captures within a single Container login script. Once again, the goal is to satisfy all of your users' needs from within a single, centrally managed login script.

H: NO_DEFAULT

Here's another command that helps you avoid conflicts between a central Container script and the Default login script. As you remember from our earlier discussion, the Default login script is contained in LOGIN.EXE and cannot be edited. In addition, it conflicts with drive mappings and the COMSPEC command from Container and Profile scripts. Finally, the Default login script executes only if there is no User script, which conflicts with our goal of having one centrally managed Container login script.

Fortunately, by using the NetWare 5 NO_DEFAULT statement, you can skip the Default login script even without a User script. Simply place it toward the end of your Container or Profile script and everything will be fine. Sometimes life can be so easy.

I: EXIT

Congratulations, you've made it to the end of our mammoth Container login script. Don't forget your users — they're counting on you for a friendly menu system. As a CNA, it is your job to orchestrate a smooth transition from each user's login script to his/her menu system. Fortunately, you have the EXIT command.

EXIT terminates any login script and executes a specific network program. The program can be an .EXE, .COM, or .BAT file and must reside in the default directory. When combined with the DRIVE command (as shown in Figure 3.9), EXIT can facilitate a smooth transition from a login script to a menu system. In the case of Figure 3.9, we're exiting to a "START" batch file residing in either SYS:PUBLIC or the user's home area.

Here's what START looks like:

```
ECHO OFF
CLS
CAPTURE P=HP5-P1.CRIME.TOKYO.ACME /NFF /NT
TSA_SMS /SE=CAM-FIN-SRV1 /P=RUMPELSTILTSKIN /D=C /B=30
NMENU LEIA.DAT
```

In this scenario, the DRIVE command dumps Leia into her own home directory, where the menu system resides. Otherwise, she would be placed in the first available network drive (by default). In addition, the PCCOMPATIBLE line ensures that her clone workstation returns a %MACHINE value of "IBM_PC".

It's important to note that the EXIT command skips all other login scripts. For this reason, you'll want to be careful where you place it. Only use EXIT in a Container login script if you're convinced there are no Profile or User scripts, or if you'd rather not execute those scripts because they've been created by non-authorized managers. All in all, this is a great strategy for skipping unnecessary login scripts and making a smooth transition to user menu systems.

Before we move on to Step 3: Menu System, let's take a quick look at some other powerful login script commands.

Other Login Script Commands

In addition to the commands shown in Figure 3.9, NetWare 5 includes a potpourri of other login script commands. Here's a few more interesting system configuration tools:

▸ *BREAK*—If "BREAK ON" is included in a login script, you can press Ctrl+C or Ctrl+Break to abort the normal execution of a login script. This is not a good thing, especially in the hands of users. The default is BREAK OFF.

▸ *CLS*—Use CLS to clear the user's screen during login script execution.

▶ *CONTEXT* — This command changes the workstation's current NDS context during login script execution. It works similarly to the workstation CX and NAME CONTEXT commands (see the "Logging In" section earlier in this chapter).

▶ *FDISPLAY* — Works the same as DISPLAY, except that it filters out formatting codes before showing the file on the screen. In other words, it can be used to display the text of an ASCII file without showing all the ASCII formatting codes.

▶ *FIRE PHASERS* — "Beam me up, Scotty." FIRE PHASERS can also be combined with identifier variables to indicate the number of times the phaser sound should blare. For example, FIRE PHASERS %NDAY_OF_WEEK will fire five phasers on Thursday.

▶ *GOTO* — This command enables you to execute a portion of the login script out of regular sequence. GOTO jumps to login script labels — text followed by a colon (TOP:, for example). Do not use GOTO to enter or exit a nested IF . . . THEN statement. This will cause the keyboard to explode. You can go through a lot of users that way.

▶ *INCLUDE* — As if one login script isn't enough. The INCLUDE command branches to subscripts from anywhere in the main Container script. These subscripts can be text files with valid login script syntax, or entire login scripts that belong to different objects in the NDS tree. Once the subscript has been completed, control shifts to the next line in the original script. Now we're really getting crazy. Consider using INCLUDE subscripts with IF . . . THEN statements to ultimately customize Container login scripts. Now there's no excuse for using Profile, User, or Default scripts. As a matter of fact, everyone in the WAN can share the same Container script by distributing INCLUDE statements to all Organizational Units. Think of the synergy.

▶ *LASTLOGINTIME* — As you've probably guessed, this displays the last time the user logged in. This can be combined with WRITE statements to ensure that no one was logging in while you're on vacation. When the cat's away, the mice will play.

▸ *SWAP* — As you recall from our earlier discussion, the # command swaps 100K of stuff into workstation RAM and doesn't always give it back. The SWAP command can be used to force the 100K out of workstation RAM onto the local or network disk. Simply identify a path with the SWAP command, and LOGIN.EXE will bother you no more. When the # command is completed, LOGIN.EXE continues on its merry way. If this bothers you, NOSWAP will force LOGIN.EXE into conventional workstation RAM.

REAL WORLD

The NetWare 5 GUI Login utility provides an Advanced "Script" tab for login script management. The Script page allows users to bypass default scripts by running specified login scripts, or choosing not to run any scripts at all.

This is accomplished by entering the path and name of a text file in the Login Script box. This will run the file as a login script and bypass all other scripts assigned to you. Also, if you know the name of a Profile object that contains a login script you would like to run, you can enter the name in the Profile Script box.

To avoid running any login scripts, deselect the Run Scripts option. By doing so, no login scripts (even those entered above) will run.

This completes our discussion of NetWare 5 login scripts. I hope you've gained an appreciation for how these cute little tools help you customize user and group connections.

Once the Container and Profile scripts have been executed, NetWare 5 opens the door to a whole new world — the expansive NDS Garden.

**LAB EXERCISE 3.2: CONFIGURING
ACME'S LOGIN SCRIPTS**

Just when you think you're finally going to have a moment to get to some items on your to-do list, SHolmes comes cruising into your office. He said that he'd like to be able to have the members of a special gang-prevention inter-departmental task force share some applications, reports, and other data — and asks if you have any ideas. Of course you have ideas; after all, you are a CNA!

To perform this exercise, you will need:

▸ A NetWare 5 server called CRIME-SRV1.CRIME.TOKYO.ACME (which can be installed using the directions found in Chapter 8, Exercise 8.1).

▸ A workstation running the NetWare 5 Novell Client for Windows 95/98 (which can be installed using the directions found in Chapter 8, Exercise 8.2).

Part I: Create a Login Script

1. Construct a login script from the following notes you made for yourself:

   a. Insert a comment at the top of the login script indicating the purpose of the login script, the author (you), and the date/time the file was created.

   b. Turn off the display of drive mappings.

   c. Allow users to access files in the SYS:PUBLIC directory.

   d. Allow users to access executable files under the SYS:APPS\CRIME\ TF-GP directory. (Comment out this line for the moment.)

   e. Map the U: drive to the user's home directory.

   f. Display a greeting that is displayed each time a user logs in, including the username, day, date, and time.

   g. Display a file called SHARED\CRIME\TF-GP\MESSAGE.NEW containing the important news of the day. (Comment out this line for the moment.)

h. On Wednesdays, fire phasers and display a reminder to members of the task force that the weekly meeting is at 9:00 a.m. in Conference Room 3-D.

i. If the user is a member of the TF-GPMGR group, run the DrWatson login script. (Comment out this line for the moment.)

j. General notes:

- Whenever appropriate, don't forget to insert a PAUSE statement so that messages don't scroll off the screen before the user has a chance to read them.

- Insert appropriate remarks through the login script so that someone else who looks at it can easily understand what you have done.

Part II: Create a Temporary User Object

1. Log in as Admin, if you haven't already done so.

2. Launch the NetWare Administrator utility.

3. Set the context to the CRIME container.

a. When the main NetWare Administrator screen appears, select Set Context from the View menu.

b. When the Set Context dialog box appears:

- Make sure the following is listed in the Tree field:

  ACME_TREE

- Type the following in the Context field:

  CRIME.TOKYO.ACME

- Click OK.

- The CRIME container should now be the first icon at the top of the tree.

4. Create the TEMP1 User object.

   a. Right-click the CRIME container.

   b. Select Create from the pop-up menu that appears.

   c. When the New Object dialog box appears, double-click User to select it.

   d. When the Create User dialog box appears:

      • Type the following in the Login Name field:

      Temp1

      • Type the following in the Last Name field:

      Temp1

      • Mark the Define Additional Properties checkbox.

      • Click Create.

   e. When the User: Temp1 dialog box appears:

      • The Identification page will be displayed by default.

      • Click the Password Restrictions tab.

   f. When the Password Restrictions page appears, click Change Password.

   g. When the Change Password dialog box appears:

      • Type the following in the New Password field:

      ACME

      • Type the following in the Retype New Password field:

      ACME

      • Click OK.

   h. When the User: Temp1 dialog box reappears, click OK to save your changes.

Part III: Create a Profile Object

I. Create the TF-GP Profile object.

    a. When the main NetWare Administrator screen appears, click the CRIME container.

    b. Press Insert.

    c. When the New Object dialog box appears, highlight Profile, then press Enter.

    d. When the Create Profile dialog box appears:

      • Type the following in the Profile Name field:

        `TF-GP`

      • Mark the Define Additional Properties checkbox.

      • Click Create.

    e. When the Profile: TF-GP dialog box appears:

      • The Identification will be displayed by default.

      • In the Other Description field, type the following:

        `Gang Prevention Task Force`

      • Click the Login Script tab.

    f. When the Login Script page appears:

      • In the Login Script box, key in the login script you created in Part I of this exercise.

      • Click the Security "Equal to Me" tab.

    g. When the Security Equal to Me page appears, click Add.

    h. When the Select Object dialog box appears, double-click the Temp1 user in the Available Objects list box to select it.

    i. When the Security Equal to Me dialog box reappears, click OK to save your changes.

    j. Exit the NetWare Administrator utility.

2. Test the new Profile login script.

   a. Log into the tree as the Temp1 user to check things out.

   b. Watch the screen carefully as the Profile login script is executed.

3. Log in as Admin.

   a. If you encountered any errors, fix the TF-GP Profile login script — then log in as Temp1 to test it.

   b. Otherwise, on the main NetWare Administrator screen, click the Temp1 user object to select it, then press Delete to delete it.

Welcome In!

Welcome to the NetWare 5 Garden. Green thumb required.

What does it mean to have a green thumb? Does it mean you're a Martian? No. Does it mean you should bathe more often? Probably not. Does it mean you get along well with plants? Bingo.

The term "green thumb" implies that you understand the delicate balance of life in the garden. It means that you appreciate your chlorophyll-based friends and constantly nurture them. It means that you love the smell of fresh-cut flowers, dirt between your toes, and the hot sun beating down the back of your neck. To have a green thumb is to be blessed — and dirty.

As a NetWare 5 CNA, you need a *red* thumb. You must appreciate the delicate balance of life on the WAN. To have a red thumb means that you appreciate your users and their resources. It means that you like the smell of laser printer toner, NDS objects between your toes, and disgruntled users breathing down the back of your neck. It means that you need to get a life!

Once you've found your way into the NetWare 5 garden, it's time to learn a little bit about management. So, what is garden management all about? It involves a combination of tools, knowledge, luck, and experience. You must know when to fertilize, when to water, and when not to spray pesticides. Similarly, NDS management is a combination of CNA tools (NetWare Administrator), knowledge of NDS objects, luck, and WAN experience.

In this section, we will learn how to browse the NetWare 5 garden, create NDS users, and help these users gain access to valuable resources. In summary, we'll explore the following three areas:

- ▶ *Just Browsing* — We'll learn how to browse NDS resources using a variety of tools — including Windows 95/NT Explorer, Network Neighborhood, and Netscape Navigator.

- ▶ *Creating NDS Users* — You'll finally get an opportunity to build the ACME tree with help from NetWare Administrator, ConsoleOne, and UIMPORT.

- ▶ *Managing Resource Access* — Finally, we'll learn how to support nomadic users with Alias, Directory Map, and Group objects.

Are you ready for a tour of the NetWare 5 garden? Tour guide optional.

Just Browsing

We learned earlier in the chapter that the first rule of gardening is "know your garden." We also learned that it's important to understand the relationships between objects and the general layout of the tree. This is where *browsing* comes in.

Browsing is a technical CNA term that means "to walk around the NDS tree looking at stuff." Browsing not only acquaints you with the tree, it also aids in NDS navigation. NDS navigation is required for a myriad of management tasks (such as creating users, adding security, configuring volumes, and partitioning). If you know what your tree looks like and how to navigate it effectively, you'll be well on your way to "green thumbship."

In the world of NetWare, Novell and their friends (Microsoft and Netscape) offer a variety of tools for NDS browsing. In this section, we'll explore the three most powerful tools:

▶ *NetWare Administrator* — A Windows-based CNA tool that allows you to graphically manage all objects and properties in the NDS tree.

▶ *Windows 95/NT* — A native Windows-based workstation environment that provides resource browsing through the Network Neighborhood.

▶ *Netscape Navigator* — A Windows-based Java tool that allows you to browse web pages and GUI applications such as the NetWare 5 documentation.

Now, let's begin our tour of the NDS garden with a quick look at NetWare Administrator.

Browsing With NetWare Administrator

NetWare Administrator is a Windows-based tool that allows you to graphically manage objects and properties in the NDS tree. You can also browse the tree by clicking specific container objects and expanding their contents. Then, detailed resource information is just a double-click away. With this utility, you can view, create, move, delete, and assign rights to any object in the NDS tree. Of course, you can only mess around with the objects for which you have access rights.

Once you access the NDS Garden using the new Novell Client, you can perform a variety of management tasks with NetWare Administrator:

▶ Create and delete objects (such as users and groups)

▶ Assign rights to the NDS tree and file system

▶ Set up Novell Distributed Print Services (NDPS)

▶ Set up and manage NDS partitions and replicas

▶ Browse object and property information throughout the tree

▶ Move and rename NDS objects

▶ Set up and manage licensing services

TIP

You may restrict access to NetWare Administrator by moving it from SYS:PUBLIC into another, more restricted subdirectory (such as SYS:SYSTEM). Everyday users don't need this powerful tree-browsing utility.

NetWare Administrator runs as a multiple-document interface application. That means you can display up to nine different browsing windows at one time. The primary window is shown in Figure 3.10. It provides a background for viewing one or more secondary windows.

REAL WORLD

NetWare 5 includes two versions of NetWare Administrator: Windows 3.1 (SYS:PUBLIC\NWADMN3X) and Windows 95/98/NT (SYS:PUBLIC\WIN32\ NWADMN32). In this book, we'll focus on the 32-bit Windows 95/98/NT version.

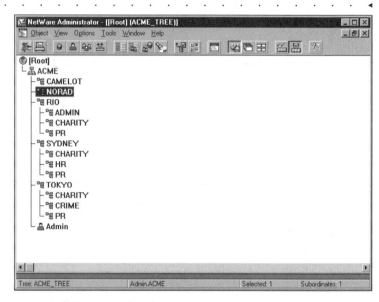

FIGURE 3.10

The main browsing window in NetWare Administrator

To open a secondary browser window in NetWare Administrator, select a container object from the primary window, and choose the Browse option from the Tools menu.

The new browser window will display all NDS objects in your new current context. You can now manage any of the objects, directories, and/or files in the window. Figure 3.11 shows a secondary browser window for the CAMELOT container of ACME. Notice all the resources (servers, users, volumes, and so on).

You can open up to nine browser windows at a time. To view multiple windows, select the Tile option from the Windows menu. Figure 3.12 shows three browser windows tiled for [Root], CAMELOT, and NORAD. Once again, notice how easy it is to view multiple ACME resources — regardless of their location. Finally, the title for each of the browser windows displays its context. This helps you track where all of your resources are — in the logical NDS world.

You can also browse the NDS tree by walking through container objects. Since they're glorified Tupperware bowls, containers can be opened and closed. Of the several ways to expand the contents of a container, here are just a few:

▶ *Double-click the container object.* When you double-click a container, it expands its contents. This also shows all subordinate container objects. If the container is expanded, you can collapse it by double-clicking it again.

FIGURE 3.11

A secondary NetWare
Administrator browsing
window

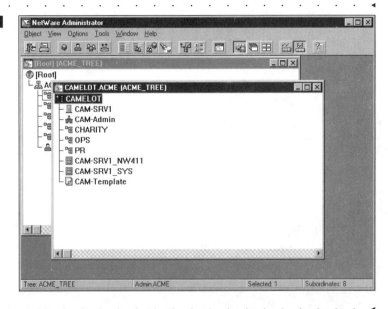

FIGURE 3.12

Three tiled NetWare
Administrator browsing
windows

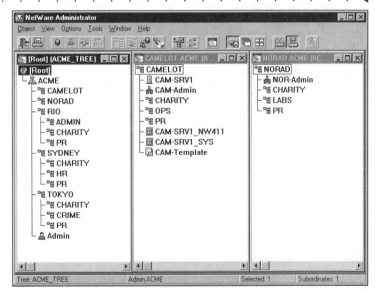

▶ *Select a container object in the tree and choose the Expand option from the View menu.* This will expand the contents of the container. You can collapse the container by using the Collapse option from the same menu.

▶ *Select a container object and press the plus (+) key on the numeric keypad of your keyboard.* The container object will expand and show its contents (sounds embarrassing). You'll find that the plus (+) key above the equal sign (=), however, doesn't work. You must use the numeric keypad. You can collapse the container by pressing the minus (−) key on the numeric keypad.

▶ *Select a container object and press the right mouse button.* Select the Browse option from the pull-down menu that appears. This launches a new browser window with the contents of the container object. Figure 3.13 shows the short menu that appears when the right mouse button is pressed. By the way, this is a great shortcut feature. In this case, "right" is right. Draw your own conclusions.

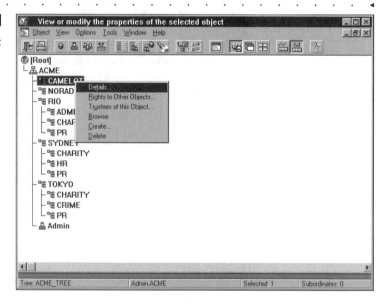

You can also browse the properties of any given object by choosing Details from the shortcut menu in Figure 3.13. Or, here are a few other ways to browse NDS properties:

▸ Double-click a leaf object. Remember, double-clicking a container object expands and/or contracts it — not so for leaf objects.

▸ Select the object and then choose the Details option from the Object menu. This works for containers as well.

▸ Select the object and press the right mouse button. Choose Details from the pull-down menu that appears. This works for containers as well.

The object dialog box is organized into pages that you can access with the buttons that run down the right side of the dialog. The Identification page always appears first and is shown in Figure 3.14. You can browse specific NDS properties by selecting the corresponding page button. Each object type has a different set of page buttons because each object type has a different set of properties. Figure 3.14 shows the page buttons for the O=ACME container object.

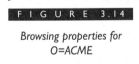

F I G U R E   3.14

Browsing properties for
O=ACME

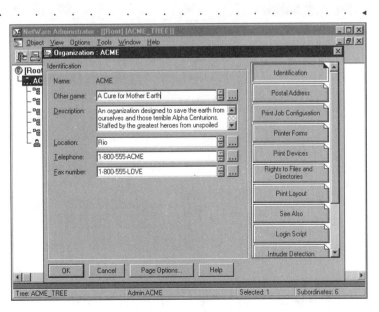

TIP

The pages in an object dialog box are all part of the same dialog. In other words, when you select a different page, you are still in the same dialog. If you press OK or Cancel on any page, you are affecting the entire dialog box, not just the individual page. For example, OK will save modifications to all of the pages and Cancel will exit the dialog box without saving changes to any page. To move between pages of the dialog box, select the desired page.

You can find object and property information in the NDS tree by using the Search feature. You can perform this function without having to expand each of the container objects. It's much easier, trust me. The search operation will browse the entire tree, unless you narrow the search criteria.

For example, in Figure 3.15, the search criteria is configured to find all of the Users in the ACME tree who have a Department property equal to "Charity." You can further narrow the search by starting at a subcontainer instead of the [Root]. Or, you can expand your searching criteria to include all Charity objects, not just Users. As you can see, the NetWare Administrator searching engine is very sophisticated. Maybe you'll find what you're looking for.

▶ . . . . ◀

FIGURE 3.15

Searching the ACME tree for CHARITY users

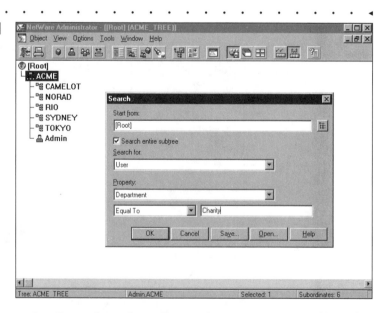

This completes our brief tour through NetWare Administrator. You will quickly come to appreciate this utility—or not. Whatever your feelings are about

Windows, you can't argue with NetWare Administrator's graceful interface and consolidated functionality. It does everything—even things its Java-based cousin (ConsoleOne) can't. Speaking of family, let's check out the native Windows 95/NT environment.

Browsing With Windows 95/NT

NetWare Administrator is great, but it's not the only game in town. Two of Novell's friends provide additional browsing tools for the NDS garden and other applications. The first such tool is Microsoft's Windows 95/NT Network Neighborhood.

As you can see in Figure 3.16, Windows' own Network Neighborhood icon allows you to explore the NetWare 5 NDS tree.

F I G U R E . 3 . 1 6

Browsing the NDS tree with Windows 95/98/NT Network Neighborhood

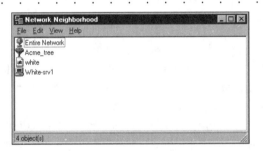

The initial Network Neighborhood screen lists all NDS trees and servers available on the wire. You can browse a particular tree by double-clicking the tree icon and navigating its subsequent container objects. In addition, you can view properties about servers and volumes by double-clicking their respective icons within the Network Neighborhood Explorer.

All this functionality is made possible because the Windows 95/NT Registry integrates very well with NetWare 5's Novell Client. Without this integration, the native Windows 95/NT desktop wouldn't recognize advanced NDS resources.

Browsing With Netscape Navigator

Novell's other browsing partner (Netscape) offers a more advanced and comprehensive garden management tool. Furthermore, Netscape Navigator extends your workstation's browsing capabilities beyond the NDS tree to Internet/intranet Web servers and Java-based NetWare 5 documentation.

Netscape Navigator (and other similar browsers) perform many of the same tasks as the Novell Client, including:

- Displaying network resources

- Logging into networks and network services

- Accessing network printing resources

- Accessing network file storage resources

- Calling and executing applications

- Providing a user interface and user utilities to access and use network resources

These more advanced browsers offer standard interfaces for access to TCP/IP networks. As such, they use built-in protocols such as FTP (for file storage), Telnet (for login access), and HTTP (for graphical access to network resources). Furthermore, the Netscape Navigator browser provides a GUI platform for Java programs. Java's a programming language that allows computer programmers to create one version of a program that can run on virtually any computer platform — from Windows to Macintosh to mainframes. This ability is particularly important on computer networks. Since networks already connect many different kinds of platforms, Java allows those platforms to support a single application without costly translation.

One excellent example of a Java program running in Netscape Navigator is Novell's own NetWare 5 documentation. As you can see in Figure 3.17, the main documentation browsing window operates within a run-time version of Netscape Navigator. Furthermore, this allows users to browse the documentation CD-ROM in a familiar HTTP environment.

Installing Netscape Navigator is similar to installing the Novell Client. Simply run the setup program from a CD-ROM or download it for free from Netscape's Internet site (www.netscape.com). Once Netscape is installed, it will create an icon on the desktop for easy access to the browser.

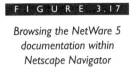

F I G U R E   3.17

*Browsing the NetWare 5
documentation within
Netscape Navigator*

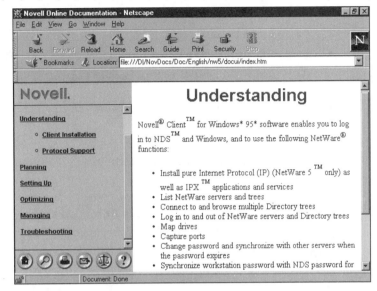

That completes our tour of the NetWare 5 garden. This was a rather nice, quiet stroll through NDS. We really should do this more often — stop to smell the roses. I especially enjoyed the browsing part. How about you?

Now that you're familiar with the garden, it's time to get down to business. To succeed in the NDS garden, you must be down to earth (literally) and focus on the NDS objects themselves. Now it's time to put on our canvas gloves and dig in.

Ready, set, garden.

Creating NDS Users

Welcome to ACME's garden. Don't step on the daffodils.

Now that you understand the fundamentals of NDS gardening, it's time to put your knowledge to the test. Did somebody say "test"? Anyway, today's the *big day*. We finally get to build ACME's tree. In Chapter 1, we learned all about ACME and their mission to save the world. Then, in Chapter 2, we learned about NDS objects and the layout of the ACME tree. Finally, in this chapter, we get to build the ACME tree, starting with NDS users.

Fortunately, NetWare 5 provides us with three different ways to create NDS users:

▸ *NetWare Administrator* — Allows you to create and manage NDS objects quickly and easily from a Windows-based workstation.

▸ *ConsoleOne* — Is a Java-based tool that allows you to create and manage NDS objects from either the workstation or NetWare 5 server.

▸ *UIMPORT* — Allows you to import users from a database application into the NDS tree.

Now let's build ACME's NDS tree starting with NetWare Administrator. Green thumb required.

Creating NDS Users with NetWare Administrator

As we learned previously, NetWare Administrator is your friend. It allows you to create and manage NDS objects quickly and easily. We have discovered NetWare Administrator's browsing capabilities. Now we're going to learn about its creating capabilities.

After enabling NetWare Administrator from your Windows workstation, the main browsing screen appears. First, select a container in which to create your User objects. In our case, we're starting with OU=CAMELOT (see Figure 3.18).

FIGURE 3.18

Creating new users in CAMELOT

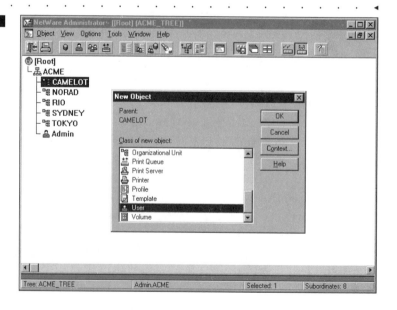

Once you have selected a container, you can choose the Create option from the Object menu (or use the shortcut menu by pressing the right mouse button). Next, you are presented with a list of objects (as shown in Figure 3.18). Select the User object and press Enter, or double-click it with the mouse.

If you want to create multiple users at once, the Intermediate Dialog window has a dialog box for this. Also, you can specify a home directory for the user at this point. Finally, if you're going to create many similar users, consider the special Template object. You'll find it in the New Object window with all the other NDS leaves.

Once you create a Template object and define its many properties, you can establish a link with User objects by marking the Copy Template box during user creation. This feature allows global changes, such as a company address or fax number, to be made in one place and passed on to all User objects. Furthermore, the Template object maintains a link with its host User objects. When a change is made to the Template object using the Details on Multiple Users option, the change is also made to the associated User object's properties automatically, and the link is dynamic. Very cool. Check out Figure 3.19 for the default Template Identification window.

FIGURE 3.19

The Template Identification page in NetWare Administrator

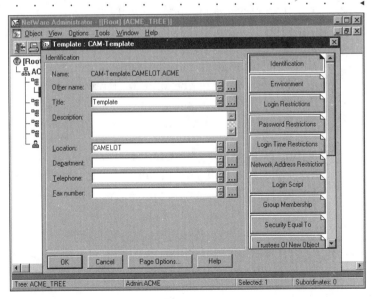

User objects represent the people who use your network, and they are the most fundamental objects in NDS. Most importantly, a User object regulates access to the network and network services because each user must have a unique object to log in. By default, the Admin object is the only default user account. It is created when NDS is installed for the first time. In addition, the Admin user is placed in the same container as the first NetWare 5 server. It's important to understand that the Admin object is a not a super-user account. When it is created, it is granted all authority within NDS and the file system. However, this authority can be reduced to that of any user *and* the object can be deleted. Keep in mind, though, you should never delete or modify the Admin object unless you know additional User objects have been given similar rights.

In addition to creating User objects, you can modify their properties using NetWare Administrator. The simplest way is to double-click the User object and pull up the identification page. You'll notice that the Login Name and Last Name property fields are already filled in and cannot be changed. These are the two required properties for creating a User object.

In addition to individual modification, you can change properties for multiple users by selecting the Details on Multiple Users option from the Object menu. For example, if you select an Organizational Unit, you can change all the User objects that are contained in the Organizational Unit in one sweeping action. This is an excellent way of modifying global properties such as address and/or fax number.

Now you can see what I meant when I said, "NetWare Administrator is your friend." However, it's not the only tool provided by NetWare 5 for NDS user creation. Now, let's take a look at a cool new server-based Java tool called ConsoleOne. This is undoubtedly the future of NetWare user management.

Creating NDS Users with ConsoleOne

ConsoleOne is a GUI Java utility that runs on the NetWare server or Novell Client workstation. It is included in NetWare 5 as a glimpse of the future direction of administrative utilities. And since ConsoleOne is written in Java, it can run on a variety of platforms — including Windows, Macintosh, and UNIX clients, and the NetWare 5 server.

Currently, only a limited number of objects can be created using ConsoleOne, including Users, Groups, Organizations, and Organizational Units. Furthermore, you can establish most properties for these objects, but any advanced NDS management tasks must be made using NetWare Administrator.

As you can see in Figure 3.20, the ConsoleOne interface resembles Windows. However, you will notice a number of Novell-specific enhancements — such as a graphic toolbar, Explorer-like navigation, and context-sensitive menu system.

FIGURE 3.20

The Novell ConsoleOne window

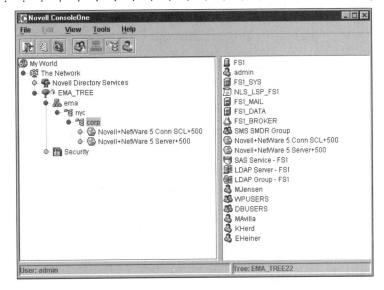

Follow these simple steps to create an NDS user with ConsoleOne:

▶ *Step 1* — First, install the Java Run-Time Environment on your workstation. Next, log in as Admin so the ConsoleOne utility will display the NDS tree and all containers you have access to. Finally, launch ConsoleOne from the Application Launcher window or the SYS:PUBLIC\MGMT directory. The application is named CONSOLE1.EXE.

REAL WORLD

The ConsoleOne utility is written in Java, and thus requires the Java RunTime Environment application. This application can be installed using the *NetWare 5 Client* CD-ROM. It is available as an option through the Windows 95/98 and Windows NT client selections. For more detailed installation information, see the "Part II: ConsoleOne" section of Exercise 3.3 later in this chapter.

▸ *Step 2* — When ConsoleOne launches, the left window will display the NDS tree you're currently using. The right window contains the leaf objects in the selected container (see Figure 3.20). In the left window, browse the NDS tree to the container which will host your new User object. Click the container to select it.

▸ *Step 3* — Next, select File from the menu bar and choose New and User. In the New User window, enter a Login Name and a Last Name. As with NetWare Administrator, these are the required fields for creating an NDS User object.

▸ *Step 4* — Finally, you'll need to indicate if you want to define additional properties or create additional users at this time. This is accomplished by marking the appropriate boxes in the New User Object Creation window. Click Create when you're finished. Finally, collapse the container and expand it again to view the User objects you just added to the NDS tree. All done!

As you can see, ConsoleOne provides an excellent GUI window for NDS user creation. However, ConsoleOne currently doesn't offer the same level of management as NetWare Administrator. I guess we'll have to wait a little while for this new Java tool to catch up.

Now, let's explore the final NDS user creation tool — UIMPORT. This is actually more of a database import tool than a GUI NDS manager. Check it out.

Creating NDS Users with UIMPORT

UIMPORT allows you to import users from a database application to Novell Directory Services. This utility can also be used to create, delete, and update User objects and their existing properties. If you are using a database that has the ability to convert records to a comma-separated ASCII file, you can use UIMPORT to migrate this data to the NDS. Here's how it works:

▸ *Step 1* — Create a data file based on your existing database.

▸ *Step 2* — Create a control file to interpret and act on the data file.

▶ *Step 3*—Just do it!

The UIMPORT utility relies on two files:

▶ *Data File (ACMEDATA)*—The creation of your data file involves generating an ASCII comma-separated file from an existing database.

▶ *Control File (ACMECTRL)*—The control file consists of some control parameters and field definitions. It defines where the information should be placed in NDS.

It all starts with ACMEDATA—this is the easy part. The data file is created by your database application when you save the information in a comma-separated ASCII file (sometimes referred to as a *comma-delimited file*). A comma in the data file indicates a separation of fields in the NDS database. When a record is read through UIMPORT, a comma indicates the transfer of a new property. An example of the structure of your database might be as follows:

```
Last Name:
First Name:
Local Address:
Street:
City:
State or Country:
Zip Code:
Description:
Job Title:
```

After you have created a data file in delimited ASCII format, it should look something like this:

```
Madison,James,"111 Calle de Carnival","Rio de Janeiro",
Brazil,57775,Facilities,Administrator
```

Next, you must create an import Control File (ACMECTRL) to control how the data information is written to NDS. The control file can be created using any ASCII text editor. You will enter a set of control parameters first, followed by a list of field definitions. Control parameters define how the information is separated in the data file. The field parameters define how the information is to be written to NDS. Table 3.3 displays a list of the control parameters, along with a brief definition of each.

TABLE 3.3 UIMPORT Control Parameters	CONTROL PARAMETER	EXPLANATION
	Separator	Defines the type of separator used in the data file (such as a comma or a semicolon).
	Quote	Defines the character used for string data in the data file.
	Name Context	Defines the NDS context where the users will be created.
	Replace Value	Enables you to overwrite or add data to multivalue fields (such as overwrite an existing telephone number in a User object).
	User Template	Specifies the use of a user template in the creation of your users.
	Import Mode	Defines how User objects will be created. C = Create, B = Create and Update, and U = Update data for existing objects.
	Delete Property	Enables you to delete a property from a User object in NDS.
	Create Home Directory	Allows the creation of a home directory for user objects.
	Home Directory Path	Required if you create a home directory for users. The volume name is not necessary in the inclusion.
	Home Directory Volume	Required if you create a home directory for users.

Next, the field definitions define which properties correlate with established user properties. These fields are listed below and can be selected based on your particular needs:

Name	Telephone	Location
Last Name	Fax Number	Group Membership
Other Name	Job Title	See Also
Postal Address	Description	Skip
E-mail Address	Department	Login Script

Using our previous Data File (ACMEDATA) as an example, this is what our import Control File (ACMECTRL) would look like:

```
Import Control
  Name Context="OU=FAC.OU=ADMIN.OU=RIO.O=ACME"
  User Template=Y
Fields
 Last Name
 Other Name
 Postal Address
 Postal Address
 Postal Address
 Postal Address
 Department
 Job Title
```

TIP

Notice the NAME CONTEXT line in the previous example. This ensures that the users are imported into the correct container. If you don't specify one in the control file, UIMPORT places them into your current context — all users in the same container.

Once you've created your data and control files, you're ready to run UIMPORT. Type the following at your workstation command line:

```
UIMPORT ACMECTRL ACMEDATA
```

Off it goes. Keep in mind, you must have Supervisor access rights to the UIMPORT container to import users. This prevents random users from overpopulating your NDS database. Also, if an error should occur during the process, it will be displayed at the workstation command line. Consider using the redirect symbol to create an error log file:

```
UIMPORT ACMECTRL ACMEDATA > UIMPORT.LOG
```

Congratulations! You've taken a very big step today toward saving the world. ACME's garden is in place. Now, all you have to do is water, fertilize, weed, and manage it. Be sure the users get enough sun and, whatever you do, don't let the snails get them.

I bet you didn't think gardening could be so much fun. It really pays off if you get to know your plants intimately. Put yourself in their roots, try to understand what makes them tick. Understand their dreams, their goals. Plants have feelings, too, you know.

Speaking of *feelings*, let's finish off this chapter with a quick look at managing resource access. After all, the NDS garden is a very big place and many times users need help getting in touch with their "resources."

Managing Resource Access

Users use resources. Their lives depend on it. A user's accessibility to resources hinges on your NDS design. Therefore, each user's life balances on the accessibility of NDS objects in the tree. But there's no pressure!

NDS accessibility is important because it defines all access points to NetWare 5 resources. NetWare 5 provides three different strategies for maintaining NDS accessibility:

▸ Use an Alias object to refer to an object in another container.

▸ Use an Application object or Directory Map object to refer to file system resources in another container.

▸ Use a Group object to refer to group members from anywhere in the NDS tree.

Let's gain access.

Creating an Alias to an Object

An Alias is an object that refers to or points to the actual object in another container of the NDS tree. This is helpful when you have a resource that must be accessed by users who are in different containers. However, users still need rights to the original object.

For example, in Figure 3.21, an Alias object in the ADMIN container points to the AEinstein User object in the LABS container. This means that AEinstein can log in from either the ADMIN or LABS context — giving him easier access to his user identity.

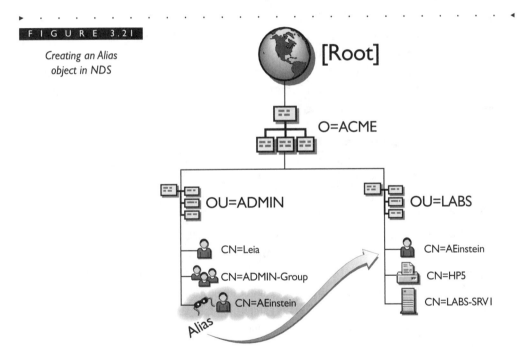

FIGURE 3.21

Creating an Alias object in NDS

To create an Alias object in NetWare Administrator, highlight the container where you will place the Alias. Next, select File and Create from the menu and choose the object Class Alias. Enter an Alias name and a Distinguished Context for its host. If you do not know the Distinguished Name of the host object, browse the NDS tree to find it.

Creating an Application or Directory Map Object

NDS provides two objects that provide accessibility to file systems in other containers:

▶ Application object

▶ Directory Map object

These objects are useful when you have an application or directory that must be accessed by users in multiple containers. Pointing an Application object to an application on a volume in another container is helpful when you don't want to install it on multiple servers. Similarly, pointing a Directory Map object to files on a remote volume allows users to access files in a central location.

Application and Directory Map objects operate very similarly to the Alias object we just learned about. However, these objects point to file system resources instead of NDS objects themselves.

Creating Group Objects with Global Membership

A Group object can contain members from anywhere in the NDS tree and can be used in any context to grant rights. Because User objects are members of a Group, rights granted to the Group pass to the Members. This allows you to create a global Group object and regulate global access to resources.

Furthermore, the Group object's location in the NDS tree is not as important as its membership. In this way, the Group differs dramatically from the Alias, Application, and Directory Map objects. Think of it more as a flat-file database of NDS users. Therefore, the Group object provides a single point of NDS management. Members can use resources (applications, directories, data files) on all volumes that the Group object has rights to. This is an ideal strategy for providing enhanced resource access to NetWare 5 nomads.

Congratulations — you made it! Together we have survived a tour through NetWare 5's expansive NDS garden. We started with a withering sapling (NDS tree), some soil (volumes), a greenhouse (server), and plenty of weeds. Through this chapter, we learned how to prepare the soil, install thick gloves, gain access to the garden, build login scripts, browse the NDS pathways, create redwood trees, and manage NetWare 5 nomads. Wow, we've been busy . . . green thumb required!

As we learned at the beginning of this chapter, garden management is the fun part. This is where the magic occurs. It's amazing how quickly your trees will bloom with the right combination of watering, love, sunshine, and weeding. In the remaining chapters of this book. we'll explore four of the most majestic realms in the garden:

- ► File system

- ► Security

- ► Z.E.N.works

- ► NDPS Printing

So, brace yourself for more fun. Red thumb required!

LAB EXERCISE 3.3: "TREE WALKING" FOR TODDLERS

In this exercise, we will explore the NDS tree structure using two different utilities: NetWare Administrator (NWADMN32.EXE) and ConsoleOne (CONSOLE1.EXE).

To perform this exercise, you will need:

▸ A NetWare 5 server called CRIME-SRV1.CRIME.TOKYO.ACME (which can be installed using the directions found in Chapter 8, Exercise 8.1).

▸ A workstation running the NetWare 5 Novell Client for Windows 95/98 or Windows NT (which can be installed using the directions found in Chapter 8, Exercise 8.2).

▸ A *NetWare 5 Novell Client Software* CD-ROM.

Part I: NetWare Administrator

The NetWare Administrator utility is undoubtedly the most versatile utility available in NetWare 5. It can be used to perform a variety of functions, including the type of network administrator tasks that are available in FILER, PARTMGR, and PCONSOLE.

1. Log into the tree as Admin, if you haven't already done so. (Use the method described in Exercise 3.1.)

2. Execute the NetWare Administrator utility.

   a. Click Start in the Windows taskbar.

   b. Select Run from the Start Menu.

   c. When the Run dialog box appears:

   • Type the following in the Open field:

   `\\WHITE-SRV1\SYS\PUBLIC\WIN32\NWADMN32.EXE`

   • Click OK.

3. Set the context for the NetWare Administrator utility to the TOKYO container.

a. Determine the context that is currently set for the NetWare Administrator utility. To do so, look to see what container icon is listed at the top of the tree. For example, if the [Root] icon is the top icon, it would mean that the context is set to the [Root].

b. Select Set Context from the View menu.

c. When the Set Context dialog box appears:

- Make sure the following is listed in the Tree field:

  ACME_TREE

- Click the Browser button to the right of the Context field.

d. When the Select Object dialog box appears:

- To navigate the tree, double-click a container in the Browse Context list box on the right side of the screen to move down one level in the tree, or double-click the up-arrow in the Browse Context list box to move up one level in the tree. The objects that are located in each container that you select will be displayed in the Available Objects list box on the left side of the screen. Practice walking up and down the tree until you feel comfortable with the procedure.

- Next, walk all the way down the tree, so that the [Root] icon is displayed at the top of the Available Objects list box on the left side of the screen.

- Click the CRIME container in the Available Objects list box.

- Click OK.

- When the Set Context dialog box appears, TOKYO.ACME should be listed in the Context field. (If you had wanted to, you could have manually typed in this context, rather than browsing the tree to find it.)

- Click OK to return to the main NetWare Administrator screen.

- When the main NetWare Administrator screen re-appears, the TOKYO container should be displayed at the top of the tree.

4. Set the context for the NetWare Administrator utility to the [Root].

   a. A quick way to move up one level in the tree is to use the Backspace key on your keyboard. Press the Backspace key twice to change the context from CRIME to the [Root].

   b. The [Root] icon should now be displayed as the top icon in the tree.

5. Explore the browser window.

   a. What is the current context set for this utility?

   b. What would the current context be if you hadn't changed it?

   c. Is it the same current context that would be displayed using the CX command at the DOS prompt?

   d. How many objects are displayed in the [Root]?

   e. What type of containers are displayed in the [Root]?

   f. What type of leaf objects are represented?

   (See Appendix C for answers.)

6. Open a container object and view its contents.

   a. There are three methods available for opening a container and viewing its contents:

      • Double-click the container's object name or icon.

      • Click the container object to select it, then select the Expand option from the View menu.

      • Press the plus sign (+) on the numeric keypad portion of your keyboard.

   b. Practice using each of these methods to view the contents of various containers. Determine the type of containers that are in each container, as well as the type of leaf objects.

7. Viewing the object dialog (object details) of a container object.

    a. The object dialog lets you display and edit information relating to an object's properties. When you open an object dialog, you'll notice that there is a column of page buttons along the right side of the screen. You can click each button, one at a time, to view the category of information on that page. There two methods available for viewing the information relating to a container object:

      • Click the container object with the left mouse button to select it, then select the Details option from the Object menu.

      • Click the container object with the right mouse button to select it, then select Details from the pull-down menu that appears on the screen.

    b. Practice using both of these methods to look at the information available for various types of container objects, including the [Root], the ACME Organization object, and the CRIME Organizational Unit object.

8. View the object dialog (object details) of a leaf object.

    a. There are three methods for viewing the information relating to a leaf object:

      • Double-click the leaf object.

      • Click the leaf object with the left mouse button to select it, then select the Details option from the Object menu.

      • Click the leaf object with the right mouse button to select it, then select Details from the menu that appears on the screen.

    b. Practice using all three of these methods to look at the information available for various types of leaf objects in the CRIME container.

9. Exit the NetWare Administrator utility.

    a. Select the Exit option from the File menu to exit the NetWare Administrator utility.

Part II: ConsoleOne (Client Component)

The ConsoleOne utility is a Java utility that can be used to manage NDS objects and their properties. It is much more limited in scope, however, than the NetWare Administrator Utility. This utility has both a server and a client component. We will be using the Client component in this exercise.

1. Install the Java Runtime Environment application.

a. The ConsoleOne utility is written in Java, and thus requires the Java Runtime Environment application. If you have already installed this application, skip to Step 2.

b. Exit any applications you are running.

c. Insert the *NetWare 5 Novell Client Software* CD-ROM in your workstation's CD-ROM drive. The WINSETUP.EXE program should execute automatically.

d. When the first "Winsetup — Novell Clients" screen appears, click the language to be used for the installation process.

e. When the second "Winsetup — Novell Clients" screen appears, click the workstation operating system for this workstation.

Although this exercise is designed for Windows 95/98 workstations, you'll find that the Java installation process for Windows NT workstations is similar.

TIP

f. When the third "Winsetup — Novell Clients" screen appears, click Install Java.

g. When the InstallShield Self-extracting EXE dialog box appears, advising that this will install the Java Runtime environment, click Yes to continue.

h. Wait while the InstallShield extracts the files required for the installation process and prepares the InstallShield Wizard.

i. When the Welcome dialog box appears, read the information on the screen about exiting any applications you are running, then click Next.

j. When the Software License Agreement screen appears, read the information on the screen, then click Yes to agree to the license terms.

k. When the Select Components dialog box appears, review the default values for components to be installed, space requirements, and destination directory, then click Next.

l. When the Start Copying dialog box appears, review the information in the Current Settings box to make sure the information listed is correct, then click Next to begin the file copy process.

m. Wait while the files are copied.

n. When the Setup Complete dialog box appears, mark the "Yes, I Want to View the README file" checkbox, then click Finish to complete the installation process.

o. When the Notepad window opens, read the README notes, then select Exit from the File menu to exit Notepad.

2. Launch ConsoleOne.

a. Click Start in the Windows taskbar.

b. Select Run from the Start Menu.

c. When the Run dialog box appears:

   • Type the following in the Open field:

   `\\WHITE-SRV1\SYS\PUBLIC\MGMT\CONSOLE1.EXE`

   • Click OK.

3. Explore the ConsoleOne browser window. Practice navigating the tree.

a. To navigate the tree:

   • In the left pane, click the dot to the left of a container object to expand (or collapse) the list of its contents below it in the left pane.

   • In the left pane, click the container object itself to display its contents in the right pane.

   • In the right-hand pane, double-click a container object to expand (or collapse) the list of its contents below it in the right pane.

b. Practice navigating the tree.

4. Change the context. (If you look at the options in the menu bar, you'll notice that this utility does not have a Set Context option.)

5. Manage objects.

    a. To view and manage objects and their properties, select the object in the right pane, then:

       • Click the icon and select Properties from the File menu, *or*

       • Right-click the icon and select Properties from the pop-up menu that appears.

    b. Practice viewing the properties of various objects.

LAB EXERCISE 3.4: BUILDING ACME'S NDS TREE

Congratulations! You're ready to start building the ACME tree. The world is in very good hands with you on the job. In this exercise, we are going to build the ACME tree using three different utilities: NetWare Administrator (a Windows-based utility), ConsoleOne (a Java utility), and UIMPORT (a batch utility).

To perform this exercise, you will need:

▶ A NetWare 5 server called CRIME-SRV1.CRIME.TOKYO.ACME (which can installed using the directions found in Chapter 8, Exercise 8.1).

▶ A workstation running the NetWare 5 Novell Client for Windows 95/98 or Windows NT (which can installed using the directions found in Chapter 8, Exercise 8.2).

In this exercise, you will create Organizational Unit, User, Printer, and Print Server objects in the CAMELOT, RIO, and SYDNEY branches of the tree. (You can't create Server objects because they are created automatically when you install or migrate to NetWare 5. You also can't create Print Queue objects because they require volume names for servers that haven't been installed.)

You will need the following additional information when building the tree:

▶ The Location property for each container or leaf object should always contain the city or Location (such as Camelot, Rio, or Sydney). The Department should always be the full name of the container (such as Administration, Financial, Marketing, and so on).

▶ The address, phone, and fax information for the CAMELOT Organizational Unit and its subcontainers is as follows:

London Road
Bracknell, Berkshire RG12 2UY
United Kingdom
Phone: (44 344) 724000
Fax: (44 344) 724001

▶ The address, phone, and fax information for the RIO Organizational Unit and its subcontainers is as follows:

Alameda Ribeirao Preto 130-12 Andar
Sao Paulo 01331-000
Brazil
Phone: (55 11) 253 4866
Fax: (55 11) 285 4847

▶ The address, phone, and fax information for the SYDNEY Organizational Unit and its subcontainers is as follows:

18 Level
201 Miller St.
North Sydney NSW 2060
Australia
Phone: (61 2) 925 3000
Fax: (61 2) 922 2113

▶ Each Organizational Unit will have the following Intruder Detection/Lockout limits:

Incorrect Login Attempts: 5

Intruder Attempt Reset Interval: 10 days

Intruder Lockout Reset Interval: 20 minutes

▶ Template objects (and User objects) should contain the following account restrictions, unless otherwise specified:

• Each user will be limited to three concurrent logins.

• Each user will be required to have a unique password consisting of 8 characters or more, and will be required to change their password every 60 days. Each user will be allowed six grace logins.

• Each user will be restricted from logging in each day between 3:00 a.m. and 4:00 a.m. (when backups and system maintenance are finished).

Now that you know the plan, let's go ahead and implement it! Ready, set, build!!

Part I: NetWare Administrator

1. Log into the network as Admin, if you haven't already done so.

2. Launch the NetWare Administrator utility.

3. Set the current context for the NetWare Administrator utility to the [Root].

    a. Use the method of your choice to set the context to the [Root].

    b. The contents of the [Root] should be displayed at this point. If not, use *one* of the following methods to do so:

- Double-click the [Root] icon to display its contents, *or*

- Click the [Root] icon and select the Expand option from the View menu, *or*

- Click the [Root] icon and press the plus sign (+) on the numeric keyboard of the keyboard.

4. Create the CAMELOT Organizational Unit.

    a. To create the Camelot Organizational Unit, use *one* of the following methods:

- Click the ACME icon and press the Insert key, *or*

- Click the ACME icon and select the Create option from the Object menu, *or*

- Click the ACME icon with the right mouse button, and choose Create from the pop-up menu that appears.

    b. When the New Object dialog box appears:

- Use the scroll bar on the right side of the dialog box to bring it into view, then highlight it. (Alternately, you could type the letter "O" (which happens to be the first letter in the term "Organizational Unit." This would highlight the Organizational Role object class, since Organizational Role is the first object in the list that begins with the letter "O." You could then press the down-arrow key once to highlight the Organizational Unit object class.)

- Once the selection is highlighted, either double-click it, click OK, or press Enter.

c. When the Create Organizational Unit dialog box appears:

- Type the following in the Organizational Unit Name field:

  CAMELOT

- Mark the Define Additional Properties checkbox.

- Click Create.

d. Because you selected the Define Additional Properties check box in Step 4c, the "Organizational Unit: CAMELOT" dialog box appears.

- You'll notice that the Identification page button is selected by default.

- Type the following in the Other Name field:

  CAMELOT

- Type the following in the Location field:

  CAMELOT

- Type the following in the Telephone field:

  44 344 724000

- Type the following in the Fax Number field:

  44 344 724001

- Click the Postal Address page button.

e. When the Postal Address page appears:

- Type the following in the Street field:

  London Road

- Type the following in the City field:

  Bracknell

- Type the following in the State or Province field:

`Berkshire, United Kingdom`

- Type the following in the Postal (Zip) Code field:

  `RG12 2UY`

- Click the Intruder Detection/Lockout page button

f. When the Intruder Detection/Lockout page appears:

- Mark the Detect Intruders checkbox.

- Type the following in the Incorrect Login Attempts field:

  `5`

- Type the following in the Intruder Attempt Reset Interval field:

  `10 days, 0 hours, 0 minutes`

- Mark the Lock Account after Detection checkbox.

- Type the following in the Intruder Lockout Reset Interval field:

  `0 days, 0 hours, 20 minutes`

- Click OK to return to the main browser window in the NetWare Administrator utility.

5. Create a Template object in the CAMELOT container.

a. To create a Template object in the CAMELOT Organizational Unit container, use *one* of the following methods:

- Click the CAMELOT icon and press the Insert key, *or*

- Click the CAMELOT icon and select the Create option from the Object menu, *or*

- Click the CAMELOT icon with the right mouse button, and choose Create from the pop-up menu that appears.

b. When the New Object dialog box appears, choose the Template object type using *one* of the following methods:

- Use the scroll bar on the right side of the dialog box to bring it into view, then highlight it. (Alternately, you could type the letter "T," which happens to be the first letter in the term "Template." This would highlight it, since it is the first object in the list that begins with the letter "T.")

- Once the selection is highlighted, double-click it, click OK, or press Enter.

c. When the Create Template dialog box appears:

- Type the following in the Template Name field:

CAM-UT

- Mark the Define Additional Properties checkbox.

- Click Create to create the new Template called CAM-UT.

d. When the "Template: CAM-UT" dialog box appears:

- You'll notice that, by default, the Identification page button has been selected, allowing you to type in property information for that category.

- Fill in the same location, telephone, fax, and address information as you did for the CAMELOT Organizational Unit in Step 4d.

- You won't be able to set any Intruder Detection parameters for this User Template, as Intruder Detection parameters are set per container, not per leaf object.

- Click the Login Restrictions page button.

e. When the Login Restrictions page appears:

- Mark the Limit Concurrent Connections checkbox.

- The Maximum Connections field should then list a maximum connection value of "1." Type the following value in the field to replace the existing one:

3

- Click Password Restrictions page button.

f. When the Password Restrictions page appears:

- Ensure that the Allow User to Change Password checkbox is marked.

- Mark the Require a Password Checkbox.

- A default value of "5" will appear in the Minimum Password Length field. Type the following value in the field to replace the existing one:

  8

- Mark the Force Periodic Password Changes checkbox.

- A default value of "40" will appear in the Days Between Forced Changes field. Type the following value in the field to replace the existing one:

  60

- Mark the Require Unique Passwords checkbox.

- Mark the Limit Grace Logins checkbox.

- A default value of "6" will appear in the Grace Logins Allowed and Remaining Grace Logins fields.

- Click Change Password.

g. When the Change Password dialog box appears:

- Type the following in the New Password field:

  ACME

- Type the following in the Retype New Password field:

  ACME

- Click OK.

- Click Login Time Restrictions page button.

h. When the Login Time Restrictions page appears:

- A grid will be displayed on the screen showing days of the week along the left edge, and time of day across the top. Each cell in the grid represents a half-hour period during the week. You'll notice that when you place the mouse cursor in a cell, the day and time represented by that cell is displayed. White (blank) cells represent times during which the user is allowed to log in. Gray cells indicate times that the user is prevented from logging in.

- Click the 3:00 and 3:30 cells for each day of the week. (Alternately, you can drag the cursor to select multiple cells.)

- When you are finished updating the Time Restrictions, click OK to accept the changes you made to this Template object and return to the main NetWare Administrator browser window.

6. Create the CHARITY Organizational Unit under the CAMELOT container.

   a. Use the same methods described in Step 3 to create a CHARITY Organizational Unit under the CAMELOT Organizational Unit.

   b. Fill in the appropriate location, phone, fax, address, and Intruder Detection information.

7. Create a Template object for the CHARITY Organizational Unit. Use the same method described in Step 4 to create a Template for the CHARITY Organizational Unit called CHARITY-UT. This time, however, we'll save time by copying the properties from the Template you created in the CHARITY Organizational Unit earlier, rather than having to key them in again. Make the following modifications to the directions in Step 4:

   a. On the Create Template dialog box, click the Use Template or User checkbox instead of the Define Additional Properties checkbox when you create the Template.

   b. Click the Browse button to the right of the Use Template or User field and either walk the tree or change the context so that the CAM-UT User Template object appears in the Available Objects pane on the Select Objects screen.

   c. Double-click the CAM-UT User Template object to select it.

8. Create the SirGalahad User object.

   a. To Create the Sir Galahad User object, use *one* of the following methods:

- Click the CHARITY Organizational Unit and press the Insert key, *or*

- Click the CHARITY Organizational Unit and select the Create option from the Object menu, *or*

- Click the CHARITY Organizational Unit with the right mouse button, and choose Create from the pop-up menu that appears.

b. When the New Object dialog box appears, choose the User object type by using *one* of the following methods:

- Use the scroll bar on the right side of the dialog box to bring it into view, then highlight it. (Alternately, you could type the letter "U," which happens to be the first letter in the word "User." This would highlight the User object class, since it is the first object in the list that begins with the letter "U.")

- Once the selection is highlighted, either double-click it, click OK, or press Enter.

c. When the Create User dialog box appears:

- Type the following in the Login Name field:

  `SirGalahad`

  (This is a required property for a User object.)

- Type the following in the Last Name field:

  `Galahad`

  (This is also a required property for a User object.)

- Mark the Use Template checkbox.

- Click the Browse button to the right of the Use Template field.

d. When the Select Object dialog box appears:

- The CAM-UT Template object should be displayed in the Available Objects pane on the left side of the screen. Double-click this object to select it.

- Normally, you would also create a home directory for this user, but you can't at this time because the CAM-CHR-SRV1 server has not been installed yet.

- Click Create to create this user using the defaults in the CHAR-UT template.

9. Create the .OPS.CAMELOT.ACME Organizational Unit, then create the following objects under it: the OPS-UT Template object and the KingArthur User Object.

10. Create the .FIN.OPS.CAMELOT.ACME Organizational Unit, then create the following objects under it: the FIN-UT Template object and the Guinevere User object.

11. Create the .DIST.OPS.CAMELOT.ACME Organizational Unit, then create the following objects under it: the DIST-UT Template object and the Merlin User object.

12. Create the .PR.CAMELOT.ACME Organizational Unit, then create the following objects under it: the PR-UT Template object and the CEttelson User object.

13. To exit the NetWare Administrator utility, choose the Exit menu option from the File menu.

Part II: ConsoleOne

1. Execute the ConsoleOne utility on your workstation.

2. Create the RIO Organizational Unit under the ACME Organization.

   a. When the main ConsoleOne window appears, click the dot to the left of The Network.

   b. Click the dot to the left of Novell Directory Services.

   c. Click ACME_TREE.

d. When the Login dialog box appears:

- Ensure that the following is listed in the Tree field:

    ACME

- Type the following in the Context field:

    CRIME.TOKYO.ACME

- Type the following in the Username field:

    admin

- Type the following in the Password field:

    ACME

- Click OK.

e. The contents of the ACME Organization will be displayed in the right pane. Use one of the following procedures:

- Right-click ACME, select New, then select Organizational Unit, *or*

- Click ACME, select New from the File menu, then select Organizational Unit.

f. When the Organizational Unit dialog box appears:

- Type the following in the Organizational Unit Name field:

    RIO

- Click Create.

- Double-click ACME to display its contents.

3. Create the ADMIN, CHARITY, and PR Organizational Units under the RIO Organizational Unit, then create the AUDIT, FAC, and MRKT Organizational Units under the ADMIN Organizational Unit.

4. Create Template objects. Only four types of objects can be created with ConsoleOne: Organization, Organizational Unit, User, and Group. ConsoleOne cannot be used to create Template objects, nor can User objects be created with ConsoleOne if a Template object is used. If you have a need for Template objects, you will probably want to use NetWare Administrator for creating User objects instead of ConsoleOne.

5. Using ConsoleOne, create the GWashington User object under the ADMIN.RIO.ACME Organizational Unit object.

    a. Navigate the tree until the ADMIN.RIO.ACME container is displayed in the right pane.

    b. Use of the following methods:

- Right-click ADMIN, select New, then select User, *or*

- Click ADMIN, select New from the File menu, then select User.

    c. When the User dialog box appears:

- Type the following in the Login Name field:

  `GWashington`

- Type the following in the Last Name field:

  `Washington`

- Click Create.

    d. When the Create Authentication Secrets dialog box appears:

- Type the following in the New Password field:

  `ACME`

- Click OK.

- Double-click ADMIN to display its contents. (Make sure the GWashington object is displayed)

6. Create the SirPercival User object under the CHARITY.RIO.ACME Organizational Unit object.

7. Create the JHughes User object under the PR.RIO.ACME Organizational Unit object.

8. Create the ALincoln User object under the AUDIT.ADMIN.RIO.ACME Organizational Unit object.

9. Create the JMadison User object under the FAC.ADMIN.RIO.ACME Organizational Unit object.

10. Create the TJefferson User object under the MRKT.ADMIN.RIO.ACME Organizational Unit object.

11. Set Intruder Detection defaults for the Organizational Unit objects that you created in Steps 2 and 3. (Sorry, this is a manual process.)

- Type the following in the Detect Intruders field:

  Yes

- Type the following in the Incorrect Login Attempts field:

  5

- Type the following in the Intruder Attempt Reset Interval field:

  10 days

- Type the following in the Lock Account After Detection field:

  Yes

- Type the following in the Intruder Lockout Reset Interval field:

  20 minutes

- Click OK to save your changes.

12. Set property values for the User objects you created in Steps 5 through 10. Unfortunately, the ConsoleOne utility has no way to automate this process. You can either make these changes manually in ConsoleOne (too much work) or use the Details on Multiple Users feature in NetWare Administrator. (Naturally, if you had created these objects using a Template object in NetWare Administrator, you would not have to worry about this step after the fact.) To make the changes in NetWare Administrator:

a. Select Exit from the File menu to exit the ConsoleOne utility.

b. Launch the NetWare Administrator utility.

c. Select the User objects to be changed:

- Hold down the Ctrl key while you click all of the User objects that you created in Steps 5 through 10.

- Select Details on Multiple Users from the Object menu. (**Note:** This feature is only available for use with Users, Groups, Templates, or containers which contain Users objects.)

d. When the Details on Multiple Users dialog box appears, the Identification page will be displayed by default. Make the following changes on that page:

- Type the following in the Other Name field:

  `Rio de Janeiro`

- Type the following in the Telephone field:

  `(55 11) 253 4866`

- Type the following in the Fax Number field:

  `(55 11) 285 4847`

e. Click Postal Address, then make the following changes on the Postal :

- Type the following in the Location field:

  `Rio`

- Type the following in the Street field:

  `Alameda Ribeirao Preto 130-12 Andar`

- Type the following in the City field:

  `Alameda Ribeirao Preto 130-12 Andar`

- Type the following in the State or Province field:

  `Brazil`

- Type the following in the Postal (Zip) Code field:

  `01331-000`

- Click OK to save your changes.

f. When the second Details on Multiple Users dialog box appear:

- Read the information on the screen, advising you that applying the changes to all of the selected users may take an extended amount of time and asking if you want to continue.

- Mark the Pause When Errors Occur checkbox.

- Click Yes.

13. Exit the NetWare Administrator utility.

Part III: UIMPORT

1. Before you can run the UIMPORT utility, you must have created two files: an ASCII control file and a comma-delimited ASCII data file. The data file is typically created by exporting user information from a database file. The control file consists of some control parameters and field definitions that define where information should be placed in the NDS. The UIMPORT utility can only be used to add users. It cannot be used to create other objects in the NDS tree. Because of this, before you run UIMPORT, you must create any Organization or Organizational Unit objects that you will need.

a. Since you don't have a database containing the information for the users in the SYDNEY subtree, you'll need to create a data file from scratch using an ASCII text editor. Let's try a very simple test case. Let's try importing the User objects for the network administrators for the HR Organizational Unit and each of its four subcontainers into the HR container. To create the data file, type in the following lines into an ASCII file you create called ACMEDATA:

```
Ghandi,Ghandi,"Human Resources"

MTeresa,Teresa,Food

ASchweitzer,Schweitzer,Medical

FNightingale,Nightingale,Shelter

Buddha,Buddha,Peace
```

You'll notice that Human Resources is enclosed in quotation marks. This is because it contains a space.

b. Next, create an import control file by typing in the following lines in an ASCII file you create called ACMECTRL:

```
Import Control
    Name Context=.OU=HR.OU=SYDNEY.O=ACME
    User Template=Y
Fields
    Name
    Last Name
    Department
```

2. Before you can import this data, you must create the NDS subtree structure using the NWADMIN or NETADMIN utilities. Use the utility of your choice (NetWare Administrator is the best choice) to create the initial SYDNEY subtree structure, including:

- A SYDNEY Organizational Unit under the ACME Organization

- CHARITY, HR, and PR Organizational Units under the SYDNEY Organizational Unit

- FOOD, MEDICAL, PEACE, and SHELTER Organizational Units under the HR Organizational Unit

When you create each of these containers, be sure to create a User Template object for each. Don't forget to update both the containers and the User Templates with the property values listed at the beginning of this chapter.

3. After you've set up the NDS subtree structure for the SYDNEY portion of the tree, you can execute the UIMPORT utility by typing UIMPORT ACMECTRL ACMEDATA at the DOS prompt and pressing Enter. To see the result of using this utility, type **CX .HR.SYDNEY.ACME /A /T**.

Part IV: SPECIAL CASES

Now that you've had an opportunity to build the basic ACME tree, let's explore some of their special conditions. Following is a list of some of ACME's more challenging NDS management requirements. Please help them out.

I. ACME needs a site administrator in each location. This will be a revolving position among each of the division heads. For example, the NORAD administrator (named NORAD-Admin), will have administrative access to all divisions of NORAD, and the position will alternate among AEinstein, DClarke, and SirGawain.

2. In addition, all of the site administrators will share a common login script. It will be a mechanism for global security, drive mappings, and special messaging.

3. The Human Rights Tracking application is constantly being updated. Can you think of an easier way to manage its search drive mappings?

4. Also, each of the Human Rights department administrators needs access to the Human Rights Tracking program. Security could be a problem.

5. All the employees in the Auditing department need easy access to all the resources in the Financial container for auditing purposes. Also, the auditors don't want to have to navigate the tree to see them.

6. In addition, the Auditing application is constantly being updated. Searching drive mapping is becoming a problem.

7. As a matter of fact, the Financial database is due for some major changes as well. I see a pattern forming here. Please help us out.

8. The following traveling users need a simpler context for accessing ACME from distributed locations: AEinstein, DHoliday, and MCurie.

9. Everyone in the Crime Fighting division needs to share a common login script.

10. Finally, Leonardo daVinci believes in empowering his scientists. After all, he's a "lab rat," not a bureaucrat. To distribute the administrative load evenly, he and his scientists take turns managing the R&D department — each scientist takes the helm for three months out of the year.

EXERCISE 3.5: CONNECTING TO THE NETWARE 5 NETWORK

Circle the 20 connectivity-related terms hidden in this word search puzzle using the hints provided. No punctuation characters (such as blank spaces, hyphens, and so on) should be included. Numbers should always be spelled out.

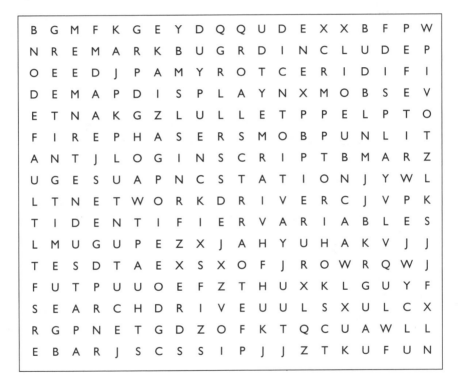

```
B  G  M  F  K  G  E  Y  D  Q  Q  U  D  E  X  X  B  F  P  W
N  R  E  M  A  R  K  B  U  G  R  D  I  N  C  L  U  D  E  P
O  E  E  D  J  P  A  M  Y  R  O  T  C  E  R  I  D  I  F  I
D  E  M  A  P  D  I  S  P  L  A  Y  N  X  M  O  B  S  E  V
E  T  N  A  K  G  Z  L  U  L  L  E  T  P  P  E  L  P  T  O
F  I  R  E  P  H  A  S  E  R  S  M  O  B  P  U  N  L  I  T
A  N  T  J  L  O  G  I  N  S  C  R  I  P  T  B  M  A  R  Z
U  G  E  S  U  A  P  N  C  S  T  A  T  I  O  N  J  Y  W  L
L  T  N  E  T  W  O  R  K  D  R  I  V  E  R  C  J  V  P  K
T  I  D  E  N  T  I  F  I  E  R  V  A  R  I  A  B  L  E  S
L  M  U  G  U  P  E  Z  X  J  A  H  Y  U  H  A  K  V  J  J
T  E  S  D  T  A  E  X  S  X  O  F  J  R  O  W  R  Q  W  J
F  U  T  P  U  U  O  E  F  Z  T  H  U  X  K  L  G  U  Y  F
S  E  A  R  C  H  D  R  I  V  E  U  U  L  S  X  U  L  C  X
R  G  P  N  E  T  G  D  Z  O  F  K  T  Q  C  U  A  W  L  L
E  B  A  R  J  S  C  S  S  I  P  J  J  Z  T  K  U  F  U  N
```

Hints:

1. Login script command that can be set to allow or disallow users from pressing Ctrl+C or Ctrl+Break to abort the normal execution of a login script.
2. NDS Object that specifies the physical path to a file system volume or directory.
3. Login script command that is similar to the DISPLAY command, except that it filters out formatting codes.

4. Login script command that uses a noisemaker to draw attention to something on the screen or a breach of security.
5. Login script identifier variable that returns a value of "morning," "afternoon," or "evening."
6. Used in a login script instead of literal values.
7. Login script command that executes a DOS file written in login script format.
8. Login-related file that may contain search mappings, drive mappings, printer connections, messages, and other commands.
9. Login script command that is used to assign drive pointers.
10. Login script that can be used to turn on or off the display of drives being mapped.
11. Mapping that associates a drive letter with a network path.
12. Login script identifier variable that prevents the execution of the Default login script.
13. Login script command that suspends operation of the login script until a key is pressed.
14. Login script command that can be used to add comments to a login script.
15. Novell Client screen that allows you to suspend the running of login scripts.
16. Network drive inserted into the DOS PATH.
17. Login script identifier variable that displays the workstation connection number.
18. Number of levels deep a login script IF . . . THEN statement can be nested.
19. Utility that allows you to import users from a database application into the NDS tree.
20. Login script command that allows you to display information listed in quotation marks.

EXERCISE 3.6: LET ME IN!

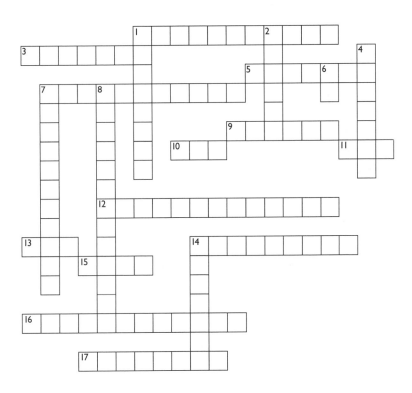

Across

1. Indicates identifier variable
3. Netscape Navigator, for example
5. Second login script executed
7. Novell Client installation program
9. Operating system core
10. Controls the workstation
11. NetWare server program
12. Protocol such as TCP/IP or IPX
13. Also known as network board
14. First login script executed
15. Last login script executed

16. Main topic of chapter
17. Physical layout of network

Down

1. Set of rules
2. Runs NetWare 5
4. Executed if no User login script
6. Conditional login script command
7. Runs the Novell Client
8. Displays the console prompt
14. Physical pathway of network signals

CHAPTER 4

File Cabinet of Life: NetWare 5 File System

Just when you think you have NetWare 5 and NDS figured out, a little voice inside your head whispers, "There is another . . ."

Another what? Listen more closely, ". . . directory structure."

Another directory structure? How could that be? You may think that there's only one NetWare 5 directory structure and it's the foundation of NDS. Well, that's where you're wrong. If you look closely at Figure 4.1, you'll see two Directory trees — one above the server and one below it.

The Directory tree above the NetWare 5 server is NDS. It organizes network resources into a logical WAN hierarchy. The Directory tree below the server is the file system. It organizes network data files into a functional application hierarchy. Pretty simple, huh? The important thing is to separate the two in your mind. NDS handles resource data and the file system handles application data. Think of it as the "File Cabinet of Life."

In the past, cave-LANs relied on "sneakernet" for file sharing. First, users copied files to a diskette, then ran down the hall to a co-worker's machine. Finally, the coworker transferred the files from the diskette to his or her own directory structure. Voilà!

With the advent of NetWare (and coaxial cabling), society experienced the dawning of a new age — the file server. The file server became the central repository of shared data and applications. Life was good.

Then, NetWare 4 came along. Once again, society experienced the dawning of a new age — NDS. The file server suddenly became a small fish in a very large, global pond. Volumes took on lives of their own. People started treating them as independent objects, free from the servers that house them. Is this progress? I'm not so sure. It under-emphasizes the importance of the file server. Let's be honest. It's still the most important resource in the WAN. And what do file servers do? They serve files. How? Through the NetWare file system.

Every NetWare 5 file server contains a hierarchical directory structure for storing shared data files and applications. It's called the file system. The file system organizes internal disks into one or more volumes. Volumes are then divided into directories that contain subdirectories or files. On the surface it looks a lot like DOS. But don't be fooled; it's a whole new world. Check out Figure 4.2!

 In earlier versions of NetWare, the "file system" was referred to as the "directory structure." In NetWare 5, it is referred to as the "file system" to distinguish it from the NDS directory structure.

TIP

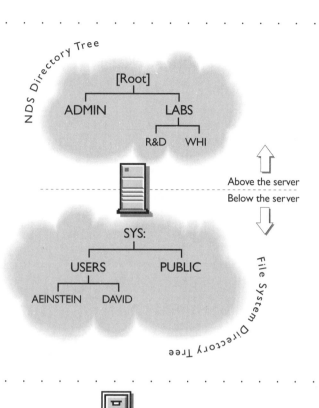

FIGURE 4.1

The two NetWare 5
Directory trees

NDS Directory Tree

[Root]

ADMIN   LABS

R&D   WHI

Above the server

Below the server

File System Directory Tree

SYS:

USERS   PUBLIC

AEINSTEIN   DAVID

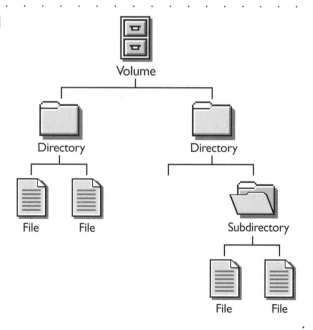

FIGURE 4.2

The NetWare 5 file system

Volume

Directory   Directory

File   File

Subdirectory

File   File

The NetWare 5 file system is the "File Cabinet of Life" (see Figure 4.3). In such an analogy, the file server is the filing cabinet and the volumes are the drawers. Also, the directories are hanging folders, the subdirectories are file folders, and the files become individual sheets of paper. Pretty nifty, huh?

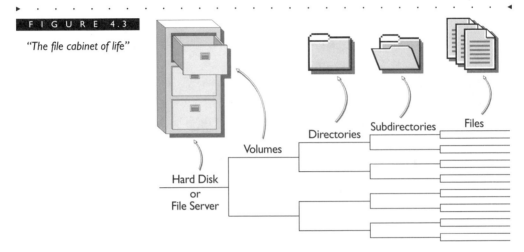

FIGURE 4.3

"The file cabinet of life"

As a NetWare 5 CNA, you are responsible for building and managing this network-wide e-Rolodex. You need to ensure that it's well organized, easily accessible to users, and large enough to handle all your users' needs.

With this analogy in mind, we're going to explore the three key components of NetWare 5's file system: volumes, directories, and files. In the first section, we will discover the NetWare *volume*, and learn about its dual personality as a logical NDS object and physical disk resource. Then, we'll focus our journey even further into the NetWare 5 file system *directory* structure—using a variety of file management tools. Finally, we'll explore the "leaf objects" of the NetWare 5 file system *files*. These are the functional chunks of data which are served to users on silver hard drive platters.

So how do we accomplish all of this great File System Management? In general, networking puts a great strain on file management. Fortunately, NetWare 5 includes a number of file system utilities that are specifically designed to work in a network environment, such as:

- *FILER*—A text-based utility that is used to manage directories and files, display volume information, and salvage and purge deleted files. This is a *pure* file system utility—that's all it does.

▸ *NetWare Administrator* (runs under Windows 95/98/NT) — NDS-based tools that can be used to perform a variety of file management tasks such as creating, deleting, renaming, copying, or moving directories and/or files. You can also use them to assign trustee rights, determine effective rights, and modify Inherited Rights Filters. In addition, they display Volume object information and, finally, allow you to purge and salvage deleted files. Wow!

▸ *NDIR* — This command-line utility allows you to view a plethora of information about volumes and directories — but you can't modify anything with it.

▸ *FLAG* — Allows you to view or modify directory and file attributes. It can also be used to modify the owner of a directory or file and to view or modify the search mode of executable files.

▸ *NCOPY* — Allows you to copy network files from one location to another.

TIP

Many of these file system utilities are DOS-based command-line utilities (such as NDIR and FLAG). If you ever need help at the DOS command prompt, type the utility name followed by "/?".

It's a good thing you have so many friends to help you out. In this chapter, we will explore these and other NetWare 5 file management tools. However, we're going to approach them in a slightly unique way. Instead of talking about each utility alone, we are going to explore how they combine to help you manage three key file-system components:

▸ Volumes

▸ Directories

▸ Files

In each area, we will explore all the file management tools that apply to that component. Also, we'll provide some examples of how they can be used to simplify your CNA life. This makes sense, because we're managing volumes, directories, and files — not utilities. So, without further ado, let's start out with NetWare 5 volumes.

Managing NetWare 5 Volumes

Volumes are cool — mostly because they're so unique. They can span multiple disks, or they can be subdivisions of a single disk. They are physical storage units within the file server, but also independent logical objects that stand alone. They are neither here nor there — they are everywhere!

The volume represents the highest level in the NetWare 5 file system. It is the root of the server directory structure. Volumes are also leaf objects in the NDS Directory tree. Because of this unique position, they act as a bridge between NDS and the file system. The first volume on each NetWare 5 server is named "SYS:". It is created automatically during NetWare 5 installation. In addition, an NDS Volume leaf object is created in the server's home container. In our example, it is called WHITE-SRV1_SYS — a logical representation of the physical SYS: volume on server WHITE-SRV1.

Volumes are at the top of the file system food chain. They also represent a bridge between physical files on server disks and logical leaf objects in the NDS tree. For your managing pleasure, NetWare 5 includes three key tools for managing volumes:

► FILER

► NetWare Administrator

► NDIR

As a NetWare 5 CNA, you must take volume space management very seriously. Remember, data is the functional core of your network. As such, you'll need to be able to easily view volume space usage information, restrict space by user and directory, and be able to locate files according to a variety of attributes (including access date, ownership, and size). In addition, NetWare 5 offers three cool volume space optimization strategies to help you in your fight against "disk hogs." They are block suballocation, file compression, and data migration.

Let's explore the challenging world of NetWare 5 volume management starting with FILER.

FILER

The DOS-based FILER menu utility can be used to display a variety of volume information, including:

► Volume statistics relating to space usage, directory entries, and compression

► Volume features such as volume type, block size, name space, and installed features (such as compression, migration, suballocation, or auditing)

► Date and time information, including creation date/time, owner, last modified date/time, last archived date/time, and archiver

To view information relating to the current volume, choose the "View volume information" option from the "Available options" menu, as shown in Figure 4.4. A Volume menu will appear that gives you the option of viewing volume statistics, features, or dates and times.

FIGURE 4.4

Available Options menu in FILER

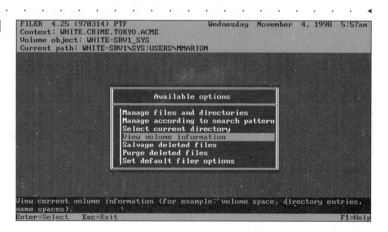

If you select the "Volume statistics" option, a screen will appear that is similar to the one in Figure 4.5. This screen lists statistics relating to volume space usage, maximum and available directory entries, and file-compression space usage.

If you select the "Volume features" option, a screen will appear that is similar to the one in Figure 4.6. This screen includes information about the volume type (that is, non-removable), the block size, the name space(s) installed, and volume optimization features (such as compression, migration, and suballocation).

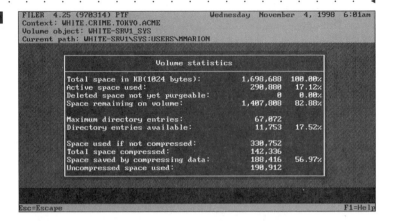

F I G U R E 4.5

Volume statistics in FILER

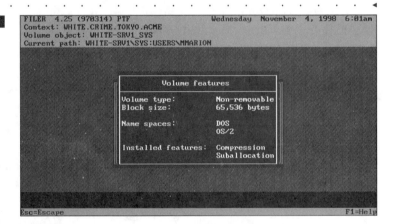

F I G U R E 4.6

Volume features in FILER

Finally, if you choose the "Dates and times" option, a Volume dates and times window will be displayed. This window displays information such as the volume creation date/time, owner, the last modified date/time, the last archived date/time, and the archiver.

FILER is the most useful non-NDS file management tool. It focuses on volumes, directories, and files as physical storage units within the NetWare 5 server — no NDS nonsense to confuse you. This is appealing to many CNAs. If you want fancy NDS footwork, however, refer to NetWare Administrator.

Hey, good idea!

NetWare Administrator

The NetWare Administrator utility treats volumes as NDS objects. It displays roughly the same information as FILER, but from a slightly different point of view:

▶ Identification

▶ Statistics

▶ Dates and Times

▶ User Space Limits

▶ Trustee Security

▶ Attributes

To display volume information using NetWare Administrator, walk the tree until you find your desired volume — in our case it's .CN=WHITE-SRV1 _SYS.OU=WHITE.OU=CRIME.OU=TOKYO.O=ACME. When you select a volume, the Identification page button activates by default. Because of this, a screen similar to the one in Figure 4.7 magically appears. It's marginally interesting, containing information on volume name, host server, NetWare 5 version, host volume, and location.

The Statistics page is the really interesting NetWare Administrator volume page (see Figure 4.8). It displays statistical information relating to the available disk space, volume type (non-removable), deleted files, compressed files, block size, name spaces, and installed volume optimization features (such as block suballocation, file compression, and data migration). Colorful pie charts are also displayed, showing the percentage of disk space and directory entries used. Very cool.

The next stunning volume page in NetWare Administrator is User Space Limits. As you can see in Figure 4.9, NetWare 5 allows you to restrict the amount of disk space each user can use on a volume. You can also use this same screen to track the amount of space any particular user has available.

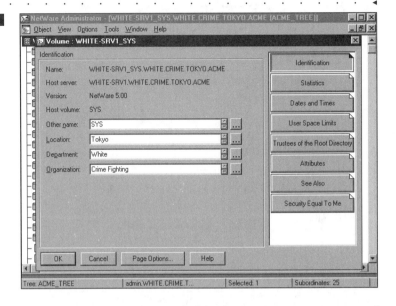

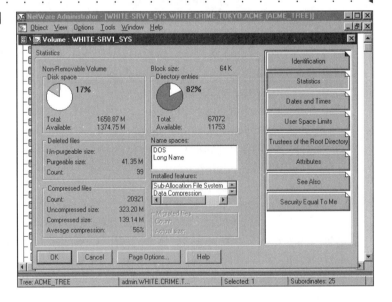

Setting User Space Limits in NetWare Administrator

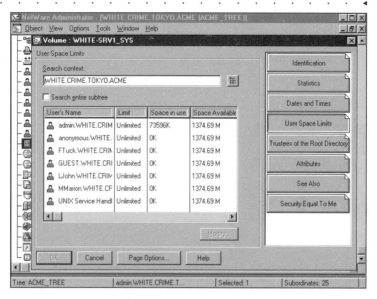

TIP

Volume space usage is tracked by file *ownership*. This means that users are charged for disk space whenever they copy or create a file for the first time on the host volume. If users are continually running out of space, they may be getting charged for ownership of files they don't actually "own." To solve this problem, consider using NetWare Administrator to change the Ownership property of certain files to Admin or some other unrestricted user.

In addition to Identification, Statistics, and User Space Limits, NetWare Administrator provides a few other volume-related page buttons:

▶ *Dates and Times* — Displays values for the volume creation date and time, owner, last modified date and time, last archived date and time, and "user last archived by." The latter options offer valuable information for managing data backup.

▶ *Trustees of the Root Directory* — Displays security information concerning the trustees of the root directory, their effective rights, and the directory's Inheritance Filter. You should be careful about who gets access rights to the root directory of any volume — especially "SYS:". We'll learn more about this in the Chapter 5.

▶ *Attributes* — Displays directory attributes for the root directory of the given volume. This is another security option offered in Chapter 5.

▶ *See Also* — Displays who and what is related to the Volume object. This is basically a manual information record for tracking special volume details.

Now let's explore the final volume management tool — NDIR. Just imagine "the forest moon of NDIR."

NDIR

NDIR, as its name implies, is mostly a directory and file utility. It does, however, offer a few statistics for NetWare 5 volumes, namely:

▶ Volume space statistics

▶ Directory entry statistics

▶ Compression space statistics

Figure 4.10 shows an example of the type of information that can be displayed by typing:

```
NDIR /VOLUME
```

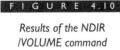

```
G:\USERS\MMARION>NDIR /VOL

Statistics for fixed volume WHITE-SRV1/SYS:
Space statistics are in KB (1024 bytes).

Total volume space:                      1,698,688   100.00%
Space used by 55,319 entries:              290,800    17.12%
Deleted space not yet purgeable:                 0     0.00%
                                        ----------
Space remaining on volume:               1,407,808    82.88%
Space available to ADMIN:                1,407,808    82.88%

Maximum directory entries:                  67,072
Available directory entries:                11,753    17.52%

Space used if files were not compressed:   330,752
Space used by compressed files:            142,336
                                        ----------
Space saved by compressing files:          188,416    56.97%

Uncompressed space used:                   190,912

Name spaces loaded: OS/2

G:\USERS\MMARION>
```

You'll notice that "NDIR /VOLUME" lists a variety of volume information, including space used, space remaining, deleted space not yet purgable, space available for use by you, maximum and available directory entries, as well as compression statistics. It's amazing that all this information can be viewed from such a small utility!

Now that you're a NetWare 5 volume management pro, let's take a moment to learn more about volume optimization with block suballocation, file compression, and data migration. Now we're cooking with steam!

Optimizing NetWare 5 Volumes

One of NetWare's key benefits is enhanced filing security and control through centralized disk storage. Along these lines, NetWare 5 offers three impressive volume optimization strategies aimed at solving your serious disk space shortage problems:

- ▸ Block Suballocation

- ▸ File Compression

- ▸ Data Migration

Block Suballocation solves the problem of wasted space with medium to large block sizes. *Data Migration* solves the problem of disk cram by providing an efficient method for near-line storage. *File Compression* eases the pain of purchasing expensive on-line disks by automatically compressing inactive files.

Let's take a closer look at how you can become a CNA hero by optimizing NetWare 5 volume space.

Block Suballocation

Technically speaking, a "block" is a discrete allocation unit of disk space. In less technical terms, it's a chunk of hard disk. A file is made up of one or more chunks of data, as needed. Each NetWare 5 volume has a predefined block size. These blocks range in size from 4K all the way up to 64K. A disk-inefficiency problem can arise when you use medium to large block sizes and store numerous small files. As you can see in Figure 4.11, a 64K block is fully occupied by a 5K or 63K file—it can't tell the difference. The problem is that the 5K file results in 59K of unusable wasted disk space. A couple thousand 5K files later, and you've wasted more than 100MB of internal server disk space — not a good thing.

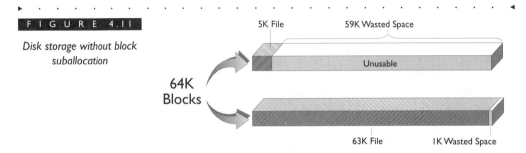

FIGURE 4.11

Disk storage without block suballocation

Block suballocation solves this problem of wasted disk space by dividing partially used disk blocks into 512-byte suballocation blocks. These suballocation blocks can be used by multiple files.

For example, a 5K file would still take the first 5K of a 64K block — as shown in Figure 4.12. But the remaining 59K becomes available for leftovers from other full blocks. A second 100K file, for example, would take up another 64K block and send the remaining 36K over to the first block (as shown in Figure 4.12). Without block suballocation, the remaining 36K would occupy another entire 64K block — therefore wasting another 28K of space in addition to the 59K already wasted from the 5K file.

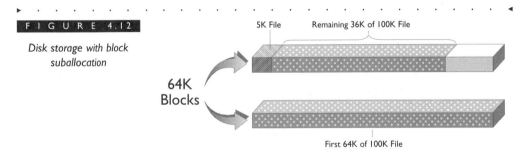

FIGURE 4.12

Disk storage with block suballocation

Bottom line:

▶ *Without block suballocation* — The two files totaling 105K would occupy three 64K blocks and waste 87K of server disk space.

▶ *With block suballocation* — The two files totaling 105K would occupy two suballocated blocks, leaving 23K of server disk space to be used by a third file.

The most important thing to remember about block suballocation is that it only works when files exceed the block size. Files always start at the beginning of a new block. You cannot start a new file within an already-occupied suballocation block. You can, however, store the remainder of large files within the suballocation area.

Finally, block suballocation is activated at the volume level within NetWare 5. When it's installed, you can view suballocation statistics in NetWare Administrator.

File Compression

The second volume optimization feature offered by NetWare 5 is file compression. As I'm sure you can imagine, this is a very popular feature for CNAs because they can relate to the idea of more than doubling the server disk space without spending more money.

File compression enables NetWare 5 volumes to hold more on-line data by automatically compressing inactive files. Users can save up to 63 percent of the server's disk space by activating file compression — that's 1GB of files in 370MB of space. File compression is activated in one of two ways:

▶ By flagging directories and files as Immediate Compress (IC)

▶ By using the MONITOR utility or SET command at the server console to configure various inactivity delay parameters

By default, file compression is turned ON (during NetWare 5 server installation) and the inactivity delay is set to 14 days. This means that if a file is not accessed within 14 days, it will automatically be compressed. Users can avoid having their files compressed by flagging specific files as Don't Compress (DC). Finally, files are automatically decompressed when users access them. Decompression occurs much faster than compression, at a rate of 100K per second.

Compressing files on a NetWare 5 server occurs in five steps:

▶ *Step 1* — A timer goes off and file compression begins. By default, a file is eligible to be compressed beginning at midnight on the day at which the inactivity delay expires. Once file compression is activated, NetWare automatically reads and analyzes each file.

▶ *Step 2* — NetWare 5 builds a temporary file describing the original file. This feature ensures that the original file is not at risk if data is corrupted during the compression process. In addition, if a disk error or power failure occurs during compression, the original, uncompressed file is retained.

▶ *Step 3* — NetWare 5 determines whether any disk sectors can be saved by compressing the file. A gain of at least 20 percent (by default) is required before a file is compressed. This parameter is configurable using the MONITOR utility or SET console command.

▶ *Step 4* — NetWare 5 begins creation of the compressed file.

▶ *Step 5* — NetWare 5 replaces the original with the compressed file after an error-free compressed version has been created.

There are several SET parameters for managing file compression. In addition, you can use the IC and DC attributes to activate and deactivate compression on specific files. This is accomplished using NetWare Administrator or FLAG. And since compression is activated at the volume level, you can use any of the volume management tools discussed previously for viewing compression statistics. Be forewarned, however, that compression is not easily turned OFF. As a matter of fact, the only way to deactivate compression at the volume level is to destroy and re-create the physical server volume . . . ouch!

TIP

Wouldn't it be cool if you could activate file compression on this book before shoving it into your brain? That way, you could only decompress the topics you needed at appropriate times. The only danger with this scenario is the chance of filling up your brain with uncompressed knowledge, thereby eliminating important childhood memories such as swimming in rivers, *Gilligan's Island*, summer break, and your first kiss.

Data Migration

Data migration solves the problem of disk cram by providing an efficient method for "near-line" storage. *"What is near-line?"* you ask. Near-line storage is somewhere between on-line (hard disks) and off-line (tape backup)—I know you probably saw that coming.

As you can see in Figure 4.13, on-line storage is provided by fast, internal server disks. The problem with on-line storage is that it's finite in capacity. On the other extreme, we have off-line storage in the form of tape backups and rewritable CD-ROMs. This type of storage is infinite in size because multiple tapes/CDs can be used. In addition, off-line storage media can be placed off-site for disaster recovery and better system fault tolerance. The problem with off-line storage is it requires human intervention—someone must stroll over to the backup device and place the tape in the correct drive, which takes time and effort—two luxuries CNAs don't have in abundance.

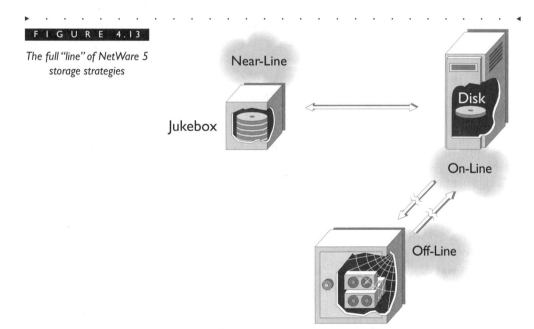

FIGURE 4.13

The full "line" of NetWare 5 storage strategies

So, what are our options? Fortunately, NetWare 5 includes a form of "near-line" storage that solves both problems. Near-line storage is much faster than off-line tape but has the potential for infinite storage capacities, which can be very useful.

Data migration provides near-line storage by automatically transferring inactive data to a tape drive or optical disk (jukebox) without actually removing the data's entries from the server volume's Directory Entry Table (DET) or File Allocation Table (FAT). The data still appears to be on the volume. This means that users can transparently access the data without having to worry about which tape it's on or where the file exists.

Data migration is part of NetWare 5's High-Capacity Storage System (HCSS). HCSS extends the storage capacity of a NetWare server by integrating an optical disk library or jukebox. HCSS uses rewritable optical disks to move files between faster low-capacity storage devices (the server's hard disk) and slower high-capacity storage devices (jukebox). HCSS is fully integrated into NetWare 5 and activated using special drivers on the server.

Once HCSS has been activated, migration is performed on a file-by-file basis, according to two criteria:

▶ *Capacity threshold* — The percentage of the server's hard disk that can be used before HCSS starts migrating files from the hard disk to the jukebox.

▶ *Least Recently Used (LRU)* — A series of guidelines that determines which files are moved from the server's hard disk to the jukebox. These guidelines move the least-active files first.

TIP

Near-line data migration is still much slower than on-line disks, so the system must have a way of informing users that the file is on its way. Many near-line tape manufacturers provide terminate-and-stay-resident programs (TSRs) that display a message while NetWare is searching for the near-line file, something like, "Hold your horses, we're working over here!"

Similar to file compression, there are several SET parameters for managing data migration. In addition, you can use the Don't Migrate (DM) attributes to deactivate migration on a file-by-file basis. This is accomplished using NetWare Administrator or FLAG. And since migration is activated at the volume level, you can use any of the volume management tools discussed previously for viewing migration statistics. Be forewarned, however, that there are performance sacrifices for installing HCSS. You should only consider data migration if you need real-time access to archived files. Some sample implementations include law libraries, financial information, and medical records.

There you go. That's everything you wanted to know about volume management but were afraid to ask! Now that you've gotten cozy with some of NetWare 5's finest file system tools, let's see what they can do with directories and files. Who knows, you might even meet some new tools along the way.

Managing NetWare 5 Directories

NetWare 5 volumes are further organized into directories and files. Directories are logical volume subdivisions that provide an administrative hierarchy to network applications and data files. They allow you to further organize your data into content-specific file folders. Directories can contain other directories (called *subdirectories*) or files.

Volumes are important, but directories win the prize. These are the true organizational containers of the NetWare 5 file system. A logical directory design can save hours of security and file management. In this section, we will explore many of the same utilities we just discussed, but from a totally different point of view:

▶ FILER

▶ NetWare Administrator

▶ NDIR

▶ NCOPY

So, let's get started.

FILER

FILER is NetWare 5's most comprehensive directory and file management tool. Earlier we learned about its volume savvy, but you ain't seen nothing yet. In its natural element, FILER can perform the following magic:

▶ Create, delete, and rename directories

▸ Copy and move entire subdirectory structures

▸ View or change directory information such as owner, directory creation date/time, directory attributes, trustees, Inherited Rights Filter, and space restrictions

▸ View your effective rights for directories

▸ Set up search and view filters (include and exclude options)

The first step is to select the default directory. If you look at the top of the screen, you'll notice that it lists the current path. To choose a different directory, choose the "Select current directory" option from the "Available options" menu, as shown in Figure 4.14. You can either modify the path manually or walk the tree by pressing Insert. If you walk the tree, don't forget to press Esc when you're finished selecting directories. When the correct directory is selected, press Enter to return to the "Available options" menu.

▸ · ◂

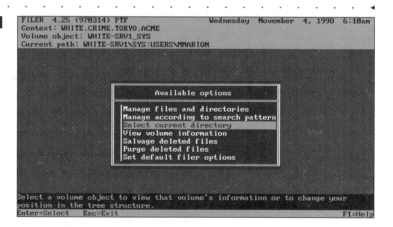

F I G U R E   4.14

"Available options"
menu in FILER

The next step is to determine if you want to use any search or view filters to limit the directories that are displayed. If so, select the "Manage according to search pattern" option from the "Available options" menu. As you can see in Figure 4.15, a screen appears that lists the directory include and exclude patterns. You can also specify Hidden and/or System directories. After you've made your selections, press F10 to return to the "Available options" menu.

► · ◄

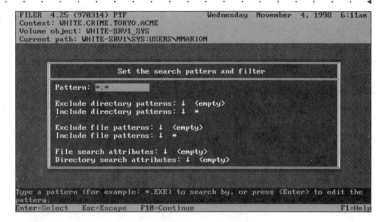

FIGURE 4.15

"Set the search pattern and filter" menu in FILER

Now you're ready to go exploring—inside the selected directory. Select the "Manage files and directories" choice from the "Available options" menu. You'll notice that the subdirectories and files in the current directory appear. In addition, you'll see a double-dot ".." (representing the parent directory) and a dot "." (representing the current directory).

You can do a number of different things with this screen. For example,

► If you want to make another directory the current directory, you can walk the tree again.

► If you want to create a new subdirectory, highlight the parent directory, press Insert, and type in the name.

► If you want to delete a subdirectory, highlight it and press Delete. If you want to delete multiple directories at once, mark them all using F5 before pressing Delete.

► If you want to rename a subdirectory, highlight it and press F3, then enter the new name.

To display information about the current directory, highlight the period "." and press F10. The "Subdirectory options" menu will be displayed. Press Enter to select the "View/Set directory information" option. A directory information screen will pop up, similar to the one in Figure 4.16. This screen lists information about the directory, such as the owner, the creation date/time, the directory attributes, the Inherited Rights Filter, the trustees of the directory, the directory space limitations, and your effective rights for this directory.

▶ · ◀

FIGURE 4.16

Directory information
in FILER

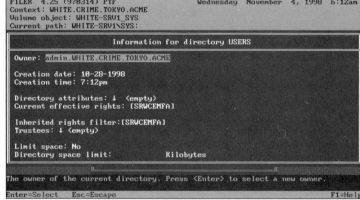

If you have the appropriate rights, you can change any parameter listed, except for effective rights, which are calculated by NetWare 5 (as you'll see in painstaking detail in Chapter 5). Go ahead and press Esc twice to return to the "Directory contents" screen.

If you highlight a subdirectory and press F10, a "Subdirectory options" screen will be displayed, as shown in Figure 4.17. Two of the most interesting options allow you to move or copy an entire branch of the tree at one time. Cool.

▶ · ◀

FIGURE 4.17

Subdirectory options
in FILER

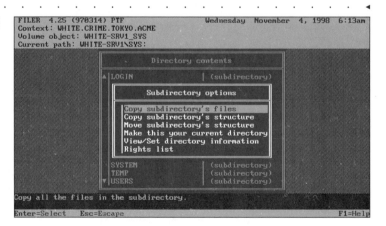

That does it for FILER. Now, let's see what NetWare Administrator can do for NetWare 5 directories.

NetWare Administrator

NetWare Administrator is primarily an NDS-management tool. However, it also offers a few directory-related functions, such as:

► Create, move, delete, and rename directories

► Copy, move, and delete entire subdirectory structures

► View or change directory information, such as owner, attributes, trustees, Inherited Rights Filter, or space limitations

► Set up search and view filters (include and exclude options)

First of all, walk the tree until the directory with which you want to work is in view. Click the directory, then click the Object menu. If you look at the options in the Object menu, you'll notice that you can perform the following file management tasks: create a directory; delete a directory; rename, copy, and/or move a directory. You can also select the Details option to view information about your directory.

If you select Details, the "Identification" page button is activated by default. As you can see in Figure 4.18, this page includes two important pieces of information: the directory name and the name spaces available on the volume.

If you select the "Facts" page button, as shown in Figure 4.19, another screen appears with more detailed directory information, including the owner, the directory creation date/time, the last modified date/time, the last archived date/time, and the archiver. It also lists the volume space available on this directory and the disk space restrictions — if any.

As you recall from our volume management discussion, disk space can be a valuable commodity on your network. As such, you may consider restricting space by directory instead of by user. This is accomplished using the Restrict Size field in Figure 4.19. Keep in mind that this feature tracks space usage by all network users for the highlighted directory and all subdirectories. I suggest that you use the volume-based restriction . . . it's a lot safer.

▶ . . . . ◀

FIGURE 4.18

Identification page for directories in NetWare Administrator

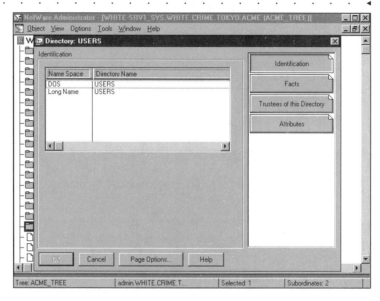

▶ . . . . ◀

FIGURE 4.19

Facts page for directories in NetWare Administrator

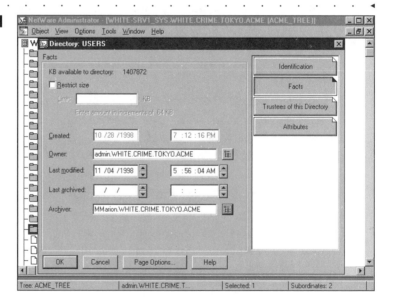

That's enough of NetWare Administrator for now. As you can see, it augments the FILER functions in a prettier Windows-based user interface. Now, for something completely different. Let's go back to the command line — starting with the forest moon of NDIR.

NDIR

In the previous section, NDIR offered us limited functionality at the volume level, because it's not a volume utility — it's a directory/file utility. As you'll see in this section, NDIR opens a whole new world of directory/file information to you, including:

- ▸ Owner, creation date, attributes, and archive information

- ▸ Subdirectories/files

- ▸ Inherited Rights Filter

- ▸ Effective rights

In addition, directory information can be sorted according to almost any criteria (owner, creation date, attributes, and so on). If you don't specify any formatting options, NDIR lists the following information about each directory: the directory name, Inherited Rights Filter, your effective rights, the creation date/time, and the owner.

By default, NDIR lists all subdirectories and files in the specified directory (unless otherwise noted). You can display directory information selectively by using wildcards and/or display options. For example, use /C to scroll continuously or /SUB to include subdirectories and their files. You can also list directories that contain (or do not contain) a specific directory attribute.

The beauty of NDIR is its logic-searching capabilities. Check them out:

- ▸ *Date options* — such as AFT (after), BEF (before), and EQ (equals)

▸ *Size options* — such as LE (less than), EQ (equal to), and GR (greater than)

▸ *Sorting options* — such as /REV SORT (reverse order), /SORT CR (creation date), /SORT OW (owner), and /SORT UN (unsorted).

Table 4.1 lists some of the more common NDIR directory commands.

TABLE 4.1 *Common NDIR Directory Commands*	COMMAND	RESULT
	NDIR	Displays subdirectories and files in the current directory
	NDIR /DO	Displays directories only
	NDIR /DO /SUB	Displays directories and subdirectories only
	NDIR /SPA	Displays space limitations for this directory
	NDIR /DO /C	Displays directories only — scrolls continuously when displaying information
	NDIR /DO CR AFT 10/01/99	Displays directories only — those created after 10/01/99
	NDIR /DO /REV SORT CR	Displays directories only — sorts by directory creation date, with newest listed first

Figure 4.20 shows an example of output from the NDIR /DO command. Use it or lose it.

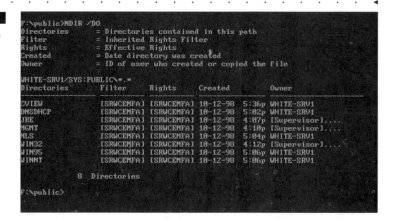

FIGURE 4.20

The NDIR /DO command

NCOPY

NCOPY is the NetWare 5 version of COPY. Can you guess what it does? Very good—it copies stuff. NCOPY is similar in function to the DOS XCOPY command and allows the use of the same wildcards. Benefits of using NCOPY include:

▸ Directory/file attributes and name space information are automatically preserved.

▸ Read-after-write verification feature is ON by default. (You must use the /V switch to use verification if you're copying files on local drives.) (DOS only.)

▸ NetWare 5 physical or object volume names can be specified in a path.

TIP

Because NCOPY is a NetWare 5 utility, it accesses the NetWare 5 File Allocation Table (FAT) and Directory Entry Table (DET) more efficiently than the DOS COPY or XCOPY commands. It is faster than COPY and XCOPY if the files are being copied from one directory to another on the server, because it works within server RAM rather than copying the directories and/or files to and from workstation RAM. It is also a safer method because it uses the NetWare 5 read-after-write verification fault tolerance feature by default.

Table 4.2 lists some of the more common NCOPY commands.

TABLE 4.2	COMMAND	RESULT
Common NCOPY Commands	NCOPY G:REPORTS C:REPORTS	Copies the REPORTS directory from the G: drive on the server to the default directory on your workstation C: drive
	NCOPY F:DATA C:DATA /S	Copies the DATA directory from the F: drive to the C: drive, including subdirectories

(continued)

T A B L E 4.2	COMMAND	RESULT
Common NCOPY Commands (continued)	NCOPY G:2000 ..\ARCHIVE /S /E	Copies the 2000 directory on the G: drive (as well as its subdirectories and their files, including empty subdirectories) to an ARCHIVE directory under the current directory's parent directory
	NCOPY .TEMP /V	Copies the current directory to the TEMP directory and verifies that the procedure was accurate (only needed if copying files on a local drive)

That completes our discussion of directory management. Wasn't that fun? There's only one more file system component left — and we've saved the best for last. Hold on to your hats; we're entering the file management zone.

Managing NetWare 5 Files

Files are individual items of data. They represent the bottom level of the file-server food chain. Files can contain valuable user data or network applications. It doesn't matter. What does matter is their location. Files should be stored in logical subdirectories according to their purpose and security level. That's the ultimate goal of the NetWare 5 file system — organize the user's data so that it's secure and easy to find.

Earlier, I said that directories win the prize — I fibbed. Files are really the most important components. After all, *what's the ultimate goal of the NetWare 5 file system?* File sharing. *What do users ask for when they log into the "Cloud"?* Files. *Why are we here?*

Anyway, file management looks a little like directory management, and it uses most of the same tools. However, that's where the similarities end. Directories are for organization; files are for productivity. And what's more important? Here's a list of the tools we'll explore in this section:

▸ FILER

- ▸ NetWare Administrator

- ▸ Windows 95/98

- ▸ NDIR

- ▸ NCOPY

Don't just sit there; get moving. There are only a few utilities left. Ready, set, go.

FILER

Let's visit our old friend FILER just one last time. Now we're focusing on real file management, including:

- ▸ Creating, deleting, renaming, copying, and moving files

- ▸ Managing file attributes

- ▸ Setting up search and view filters (include and exclude options)

- ▸ Salvaging and purging deleted files

As before, the first FILER step is to select the default directory. Refer to the "Managing NetWare 5 Directories" section earlier in this chapter for more details. Once you're there, you can alter the include and exclude filters for specific files, or even check out Hidden and/or System documents. After you've made your selections, you can press F10 to return to the "Available options" menu.

In addition to the search/view filters, FILER presents Copy and Delete options when working with files. First, select the "Set default filer options" choice from the "Available options" menu. A "Filer settings" screen will appear, as shown in Figure 4.21. You can set a number of defaults for copying and deleting files, including confirmations and messaging help. When all of file management settings are correct, press Esc to return to the "Available options" menu.

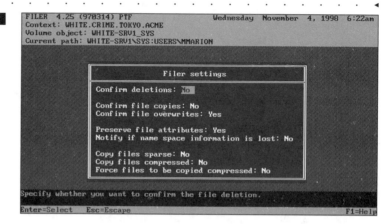

"FILER settings" screen

Now you're ready to display your files. Select the "Manage files and directories" option from the "Available options" menu. You'll notice a plethora of subdirectories and files in the current directory—as well as a double-dot (..) for the parent directory and a dot (.) for the current directory. Now, you're ready to get busy:

▸ Walk the tree to select another directory as the current directory.

▸ Delete a file by highlighting it and pressing Delete. If you want to delete multiple files at once, mark them all with the F5 key before pressing Delete.

▸ Rename a file by highlighting it and pressing F3.

Next, select a particular file to work with by highlighting it and pressing F10. The "File options" menu appears. This menu gives you the option of copying, viewing, or moving the file; displaying trustees of the file; or viewing/modifying file information. If you select the "View/Set file information" option from the "File options" menu, a file information screen pops up, similar to the one in Figure 4.22. This screen lists information about the file, such as the owner; access, archive, creation, and modification dates; file attributes; the Inherited Rights Filter; the trustees of the file; the owning name space; and the file size and EA size; as well as your effective rights.

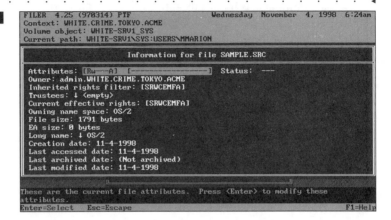

F I G U R E   4.22

"File information"
screen in FILER

```
FILER  4.25 (970314) PTF              Wednesday  November  4, 1998  6:24am
Context: WHITE.CRIME.TOKYO.ACME
Volume object: WHITE-SRV1_SYS
Current path: WHITE-SRV1\SYS:USERS\MMARION
┌──────────────────────────────────────────────────────────────────────┐
│                   Information for file SAMPLE.SRC                       │
├────────────────────────────────────────────────────────────────────────┤
│ Attributes: [Rw----A] [-------------------] Status:  ---                │
│ Owner: admin.WHITE.CRIME.TOKYO.ACME                                     │
│ Inherited rights filter: [SRWCEMFA]                                     │
│ Trustees: ↓ <empty>                                                     │
│ Current effective rights: [SRWCEMFA]                                    │
│ Owning name space: OS/2                                                 │
│ File size: 1791 bytes                                                   │
│ EA size: 0 bytes                                                        │
│ Long name: ↓ OS/2                                                       │
│ Creation date: 11-4-1998                                               │
│ Last accessed date: 11-4-1998                                          │
│ Last archived date: (Not archived)                                    │
│ Last modified date: 11-4-1998                                          │
└────────────────────────────────────────────────────────────────────────┘
These are the current file attributes.  Press <Enter> to modify these
attributes.
Enter=Select    Esc=Escape                                      F1=Help
```

If you have appropriate rights, you can change most of the parameters listed, except for effective rights, owning name space, file size, and EA size. Press Esc three times to return to the "Available options" menu.

There are two more choices in the "Available options" menu that relate to files, namely "Salvage deleted files" and "Purge deleted files." Salvage allows you to recover deleted files that have not yet been purged. (*Purging* is the process of permanently removing deleted files from the system.)

If you choose "Salvage deleted files," you will be given three options:

▸ Salvage files from an existing directory

▸ Salvage files from DELETED.SAV (because the parent directory has been deleted)

▸ Set salvage options (that is, indicate whether to sort the list by filename, file size, deletion date, or deletor)

If you choose "Purge deleted files" from the "Available options" menu, you can specify the filename pattern to be used when selecting purged files. It will also allow you to choose whether to purge files in the current subdirectory only, or to purge the files in the entire subdirectory tree structure. Be very careful when purging files: You can never recover these files.

This completes our discussion of FILER altogether. It's been a wondrous journey, and I hope you have learned to appreciate how helpful it can be for volume, directory, and file management. Now, let's visit NetWare Administrator one last time.

NetWare Administrator

NetWare Administrator is another important file management tool. It allows us to perform any of the following filing functions from a friendly Windows-based interface:

- Create, delete, and rename files

- Copy and move files

- View or change file information such as owner, attributes, trustees, and Inherited Rights Filter

- Set up search and view filters (include and exclude options)

- Salvage and purge deleted files

First of all, walk the tree until the desired file is in view. Click the file, then click the Object menu. If you look at the options in the Object menu, you'll notice file management options that allow you to delete the file, rename it, copy it, or move it. The same options can be accessed from the Details menu as well.

If you select the "Facts" page button, a screen appears with the file's owner, size, file creation date/time, last modified date/time, last archived date/time, and archiver (see Figure 4.23). If you have the appropriate rights, you can modify all of these parameters except for the size and creation date.

If you select the "Trustees of this File" page button, you will be allowed to view, add, or modify trustees and display their effective rights, as well as view or change the Inherited Rights Filter for the file. Similarly, if you select the "Attributes" page button, you can view the attributes that have been set for this file, and you can change them if you have the appropriate access rights (see Chapter 5).

F I G U R E   4 . 2 3

Facts page for files in NetWare Administrator

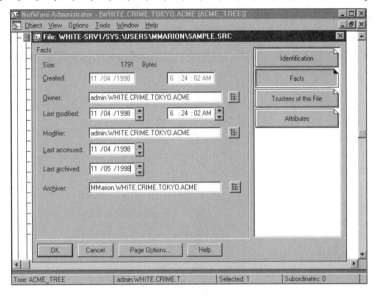

In addition to the usual file management stuff, NetWare Administrator allows you to salvage or purge deleted files. Interestingly, both of these functions are handled by the same menu option: Choose Salvage from the Tools menu (see Figure 4.24).

The Salvage menu (shown in Figure 4.24) provides three choices:

▸ Include pattern using wildcards or filenames

▸ Sort options (deletion date, deletor, filename, file size, or file type)

▸ Source (current directory or deleted directories)

When all the options are set correctly, click the List button to list the files indicated. As with any Windows 95/98 utility, you have a variety of options for selecting a desired object. First, you can select a single file by clicking on it. Or, you can select sequentially listed files by clicking on the first file, holding down the Shift key, then clicking on the last file in the range. And finally, you can select non-sequentially listed files by holding down the Ctrl key while selecting files.

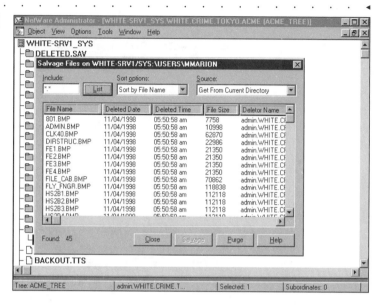

When you have selected all the desired files, you can click either the Salvage or Purge button at the bottom of the screen to salvage or purge the selected file(s). If salvaged, the NetWare 5 files will be restored with their original trustee rights and extended attributes intact. If you choose to purge the files, they will not be available for salvaging at a later date. However, if you leave the files alone, NetWare will purge them by itself when the volume gets low on space — on first-in, first-out priority.

To salvage a file, a user must have Read and File Scan rights to the file and the Create right to its parent directory. In addition, you need the Supervisor right to universally purge files from all users. Otherwise, purging only deletes the files that you own. This is described in more detail in Chapter 5.

TIP

Windows 95/98

Both Windows 95/98 and Windows NT provide built-in file management functions — called the Windows Explorer. In addition, the Novell Client allows you to use Explorer's native Windows environment for managing NetWare 5 volumes, directories, and files. This gives you the ability to manage the network file system just like you would your local drives.

As you can see in Figure 4.25, the Novell Client allows you to manage the NetWare 5 file system from within the Windows 95 Network Neighborhood. Each of the GUI tabs provides similar information from a different perspective: Volume Statistics, NetWare Info, Volume Information, and NetWare Rights. The Windows 95/98 Network Neighborhood supports the following file management information:

- Name

- Owner

- Creation date

- Available space

- Directory entries

- File attributes

- Archive dates

- Size

- Effective rights

- Trustees

To view information about a specific NetWare 5 file object in Windows 95/98, simply highlight a volume, directory, or file, and click the right mouse button. Then choose "Properties" from the abbreviated menu. You should get a screen similar to the one in Figure 4.25.

Well, that does it for Windows. You can bid the GUI environment a fond farewell as we move to the NetWare 5 command line. NDIR awaits!

► · ◄

F I G U R E   4 . 2 5

*NetWare 5
file management in
Windows 95/98 Network
Neighborhood*

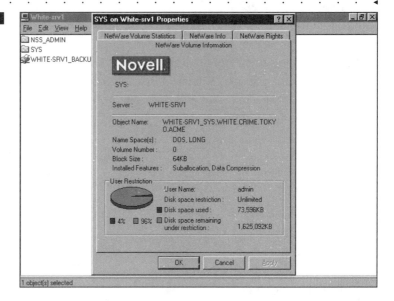

NDIR

As we discussed earlier, NDIR is a very versatile command-line utility that allows you to selectively list a large variety of directory and file information, sorted by a number of different parameters. From a file management standpoint, NDIR displays: Filename, Owner, creation date and time, last modified date and time, size, file attributes, access rights, Macintosh filing structures, version information for application files, and extended details.

If you don't specify any formatting options, NDIR lists the following information about each file: the filename, size, last update (modified) date, and owner. You can customize the output by specifying one of the following formatting options:

- ► /COMP (compression statistics)

- ► /DA (Dates)

- ► /D (detail)

- ► /L (long names)

▸ /M (Macintosh)

▸ /R (rights)

By default, NDIR lists all subdirectories and files in the current directory, unless otherwise noted. You can selectively list the information by specifying a particular file, using wildcards, or by indicating a display option such as /C (scroll continuously), /FI (list every occurrence within your current directory and path), /FO (list files only), and /SUB (include subdirectories and their files). You can also list files that contain (or do not contain) a specific file attribute.

NDIR also lets you restrict files by specifying date options such as AFT (after), BEF (before), and EQ (equals); size options such as LE (less than), EQ (equal to), and GR (greater than); and NOT (all except).

NDIR lists files in alphabetical order by default. You can change the order files are sorted in by specifying one of the following options: /REV SORT (reverse order), /SORT AC (access date), /SORT AR (archive date), /SORT CR (creation date), /SORT UP (update date), /SORT OW (owner), /SORT SI (size), or /SORT UN (unsorted).

If you really want to get to know NDIR, check out Table 4.3.

T A B L E 4.3	COMMAND	RESULT
Common NDIR Commands	NDIR /FO	Displays files only — those in the current directory
	NDIR /FO /C	Displays files only — scrolls continuously
	NDIR /FO /SUB	Displays files only — those in the current directory and its subdirectories
	NDIR /FO /REV SORT SI	Displays files only — sorts by size, starting with the largest file
	NDIR /FO /SORT UP	Displays files only — sorts by last modified date
	NDIR /FO /SORT OW	Displays files only — sorts by owner

(continued)

T A B L E 4.3	COMMAND	RESULT
Common NDIR Commands (continued)	NDIR /FO OW EQ DAVID	Displays files only — where the owner is David
	NDIR R*.* /SIZE GR 500000	Displays files and directories whose names begin with "R," and that exceed 500K in size
	NDIR *.BAT /FO	Displays files only — those in the current directory with an extension of .BAT
	NDIR /FO /AC BEF 06-01-99	Displays files only — those not accessed since 06/01/99
	NDIR \WHOAMI.EXE /SUB /FO	Displays files only — lists all occurrences of the WHOAMI.EXE file, starting the search at the root of the volume
	NDIR Z:*.EXE /VER	Displays the version number for those files on the Z: drive with an .EXE extension
	NDIR *.* /R /FO	Displays files only — lists your effective rights for each file
	NDIR Z:NW ADMIN.EXE /D	Displays detailed file information for the Z:NetWare Administrator file
	NDIR SYS: SHARED*.* /RO	Displays those files in the SYS:SHARED directory that have the Read Only attribute set
	NDIR *.* /FO /NOT RO	Displays files only — those that do not have the Read Only attribute set
	NDIR F:*.* /FO /REV SORT AC	Displays files only — sorts by access date, listing the file with the most recent access date first
	NDIR /FO DA	Displays files only — lists access, archive, creation, and update dates

Output from the NDIR /FO command is shown in Figure 4.26. And that does it for NDIR. Now, let's explore the final NetWare 5 file management tool — NCOPY.

FIGURE 4.26

The NDIR /FO command

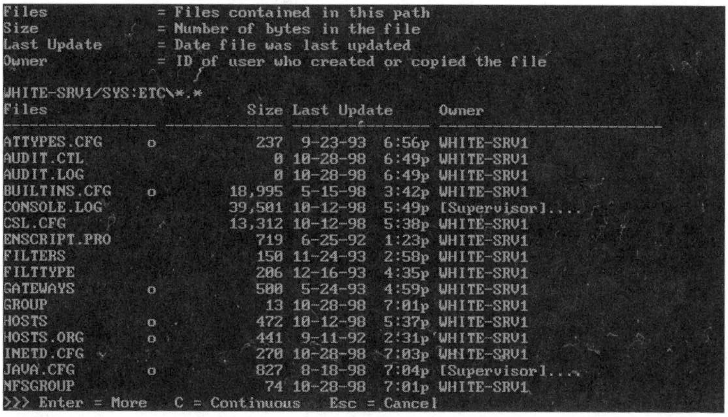

```
Files              = Files contained in this path
Size               = Number of bytes in the file
Last Update        = Date file was last updated
Owner              = ID of user who created or copied the file

WHITE-SRV1/SYS:ETC\*.*
Files                       Size  Last Update      Owner
-----------------------     ----  -----------      -----
ATTYPES.CFG        o         237   9-23-93   6:56p  WHITE-SRV1
AUDIT.CTL                      0  10-28-98   6:49p  WHITE-SRV1
AUDIT.LOG                      0  10-28-98   6:49p  WHITE-SRV1
BUILTINS.CFG       o      18,995   5-15-98   3:42p  WHITE-SRV1
CONSOLE.LOG               39,501  10-12-98   5:49p  [Supervisor]....
CSL.CFG                   13,312  10-12-98   5:38p  WHITE-SRV1
ENSCRIPT.PRO                 719   6-25-92   1:23p  WHITE-SRV1
FILTERS                      150  11-24-93   2:58p  WHITE-SRV1
FILTTYPE                     206  12-16-93   4:35p  WHITE-SRV1
GATEWAYS           o         500   5-24-93   4:59p  WHITE-SRV1
GROUP                         13  10-28-98   7:01p  WHITE-SRV1
HOSTS              o         472  10-12-98   5:37p  WHITE-SRV1
HOSTS.ORG          o         441   9-11-92   2:31p  WHITE-SRV1
INETD.CFG                    270  10-28-98   7:03p  WHITE-SRV1
JAVA.CFG           o         827   8-18-98   7:04p  [Supervisor]...
NFSGROUP                      74  10-28-98   7:01p  WHITE-SRV1
>>> Enter = More    C = Continuous    Esc = Cancel
```

NCOPY

NCOPY can be used to copy files as well as directories. What a surprise. As we discussed earlier, NCOPY is similar in function to the DOS XCOPY command, except that it automatically preserves directory attributes and name space information. In addition, NCOPY supports logical volume names and always performs a copy verification.

Refer to Table 4.4 for an exploration of NCOPY from a file management point of view.

TABLE 4.4

Common NCOPY Commands

COMMAND	RESULT
NCOPY JULY.RPT F:	Copies a file in the default directory called JULY.RPT to the F: drive.
NCOPY F:PHONE.NUM C:	Copies the PHONE.NUM file from the F: drive to the C: drive.
NCOPY F:*.RPT A: /A	Copies files with a *.RPT extension that have the archive bit set (and thus, need to be backed up) from F: to A:.

(continued)

TABLE 4.4	COMMAND	RESULT
Common NCOPY Commands (continued)	NCOPY DOC1.WP TEMP1.* /C	Copies the DOC1.WP file and renames the new version TEMP1.WP, without preserving extended attributes and name space information.
	NCOPY F:R*. G: /F	Copies files beginning with the letter "R" from the F: drive to the G: drive, forcing the copying of sparse files.
	NCOPY *.DOC A: /I	Copies files with a .DOC extension from the current directory to the A: drive and notifies you when extended attributes or name space information cannot be copied because the target volume doesn't support these features.
	NCOPY F:*.DOC A: /M	Copies files with the *.DOC extension that have the archive bit set (and thus need to be backed up) from F: to A:, then turns off the archive bit of the source files. (This allows NCOPY to be used for backup purposes.)
	NCOPY C:FRED.LST C:TOM.LST /V	Copies FRED.LST to TOM.LST on the C: drive using the verify option.
	NCOPY /?	Displays on-line help for the NCOPY utility.

Well, there you have it—the wonderful world of NetWare 5 file system management. Aren't you a lucky camper? Now you are an expert in gardening NDS and non-NDS trees. In this section, we focused on the three main components of the NetWare 5 file system—volumes, directories, and files. We discovered a variety of tools and learned how they help us manage each of these components. See Table 4.5 for a complete summary. The important thing is to focus on the file system, not the tool—a unique, but effective approach.

T A B L E   4 . 5

NetWare 5 File Management
Utilities Summary

MANAGEMENT OBJECT	MANAGEMENT TASK	MANAGEMENT UTILITY
Managing volumes	Displaying volume space usage	NetWare Administrator, Windows 95/98/NT, FILER, NDIR
	Modify user space limits	NetWare Administrator
	Manage file compression	NetWare Administrator, FILER, NDIR
	Manage data-migration attributes	NetWare Administrator, FLAG
Managing Directories	View directory information such as creation date, last access date, owner, and attributes	NetWare Administrator, Windows 95/98/NT, FILER, NDIR
	Modify directory information such as last access date, owner, and attributes	NetWare Administrator, Windows 95/98/NT, FILER
	Create a directory	NetWare Administrator, Windows 95/98/NT, FILER
	Rename a directory	NetWare Administrator, Windows 95/98/NT, FILER
	Delete the contents of a directory	NetWare Administrator, Windows 95/98/NT, FILER
	Remove a directory and its contents, including subdirectories	NetWare Administrator, Windows 95/98/NT, FILER
	Remove multiple directories simultaneously	NetWare Administrator, Windows 95/98/NT, FILER

(continued)

TABLE 4.5

NetWare 5 File Management Utilities Summary (continued)

MANAGEMENT OBJECT	MANAGEMENT TASK	MANAGEMENT UTILITY
Managing Directories	Copy a directory structure (while maintaining all NetWare 5 information)	NetWare Administrator, Windows 95/98/NT, FILER, NCOPY
	Move a directory structure	NetWare Administrator, Windows 95/98/NT, FILER
Managing files	View file information such as creation date, last access date, owner, and attributes	NetWare Administrator, Windows 95/98/NT, FILER, NDIR
	Modify file information such as creation date, last access date, owner, and attributes	NetWare Administrator, Windows 95/98/NT, FILER
	Copy files	NetWare Administrator, Windows 95/98/NT, FILER, NCOPY
	Copy files while preserving NetWare 5 attributes	NetWare Administrator, FILER, NCOPY
	Salvage deleted files	NetWare Administrator, FILER
	Purge deleted files	NetWare Administrator, FILER
	Set a file or directory to purge upon deletion	NetWare Administrator, FILER, FLAG

I guess we're done then, huh? Wrong! We haven't journeyed into the mysterious land of drive mapping yet. I'm sure you'd rather not go there, but buck up, soldier, you're a CNA — you can handle it.

But can your users?

LAB EXERCISE 4.1: NETWARE 5 FILE SYSTEM

In this exercise, we will use the Windows-based graphical NetWare Administrator utility to manage NetWare 5 directories and files. First, we will create a SHARED directory under the SYS: volume. Next, we will create an ADMIN directory under the SHARED directory. Then, we will create subdirectories and files under the ADMIN directory. Finally, we will manipulate the files and directories we have created under the ADMIN directory.

To perform this exercise, you will need:

▶ A NetWare 5 server called CRIME-SRV1.CRIME.TOKYO.ACME (which can be installed using the directions found in Chapter 8, Exercise 8.1).

▶ A workstation running the NetWare 5 Novell Client for Windows 95/98 or Windows NT (which can be installed using the directions found in Chapter 8, Exercise 8.2).

Follow these simple steps very carefully:

1. Log in as Admin, if you haven't already done so.

2. Launch the NetWare Administrator utility.

3. Open an independent browse window for the SYS: volume.

    a. Navigate the tree to locate the SYS: volume. (In other words, the CRIME-SRV1_SYS object in the CRIME container.)

    b. Click the SYS: volume icon.

    c. Select NDS Browser from the Tools menu.

    d. When the Set Context dialog box appears:

        • Ensure that the following is listed in the Tree field:

        `ACME_TREE`

        • Confirm that the following is listed in the Context field:

        `CRIME-SRV1_SYS.CRIME.TOKYO.ACME`

- Click OK.

- The current context for this browse window will be set to the SYS: volume.

- Click the Maximum button in the upper-right corner of the window to make it take up the full screen.

4. Create a SHARED directory under the SYS: volume.

   a. Click the SYS: volume.

   b. Select Create from the Object menu.

   c. When the Create Directory dialog box appears:

   - Type the following in the Directory name field:

     SHARED

   - Click Create to create the directory.

   - The new directory will appear under the SYS: volume.

5. Create an ADMIN directory under the SYS: volume.

   a. Right-click the SHARED directory.

   b. Select Create from the pop-up menu that appears.

   c. When the Create Directory dialog box appears:

   - Type the following in the Directory name field:

     ADMIN

   - Click Create to create the directory.

   - Double-click the SHARED directory to display its contents.

6. Create the following three directories under the SHARED directory: PROJECT1, PROJECT2, and PROJECT3.

   a. Click the SHARED directory.

   b. Press Insert.

c. When the Create Directory dialog box appears:

- Type the following in the Directory name field:

  PROJECT1

- Mark the Create Another Directory checkbox.

- Click Create to create the directory.

d. When the Create Directory dialog box appears:

- Type the following in the Directory name field:

  PROJECT2

- Click Create to create the directory.

e. When the Create Directory dialog box appears:

- Type the following in the Directory name field:

  PROJECT3

- Unmark the Create Another Directory checkbox.

- Click Create to create the directory.

- Double-click the SHARED directory to display its contents.

7. Open a second browse window for the SYS: volume.

a. Click the SYS: volume icon.

b. Select NDS Browser from the Tools menu.

c. When the Set Context dialog box appears:

- Ensure that the following is listed in the Tree field:

  ACME_TREE

- Confirm that the following is listed in the Context field:

  CRIME-SRV1_SYS.CRIME.TOKYO.ACME

- Click OK.

- The current context for this browse window will be set to the SYS: volume.

   d. Select the Tile option under the Window menu to reshape the browse windows and view the contents of all three windows at the same time.

8. Display the contents of the ETC directory in the second browse window. In other words, double-click the ETC directory to open the directory and see its contents.

9. Copy each of the following files in the ETC directory to the corresponding directory you created in Step 4:

   ▸ ATTYPES.CFG to the PROJECT1 directory

   ▸ BUILTINS.CFG to the PROJECT2 directory

   ▸ TRAPTARG.CFG to the PROJECT3 directory

   a. To select the files, drag the ATTYPES.CFG file from the ETC directory in the source browser window to the PROJECT1 directory in the target browser window.

   b. When the Move/Copy dialog box appears:

   - You'll notice that the Copy button is selected by default.

   - Ensure that the correct source and destination paths are listed in the From and Destination fields.

   - Click OK to copy the file. Repeat this same procedure for the remaining two files — making sure to drop each one in the appropriate directory.

   c. Confirm the files were copied. Double-click each destination directory to confirm that the files were copied successfully.

   d. Close the source browser window. To do so, click the Close button in the upper right of the browser window that shows the contents of the ETC directory.

10. Move the BUILTINS.CFG and TRAPTARG.CFG files from the PROJECT2 and PROJECT3 directories to the PROJECT1 directory.

    a. To select the files:

- Click the BUILTINS.CFG file.

- Hold down the Ctrl key and click the TRAPTARG.CFG file.

- Continue to hold down the Ctrl key and drag the files on top of the PROJECT1 directory.

    b. When the Move/Copy dialog box appears:

- You'll notice that the Move button is automatically activated.

- Ensure that the correct source and destination paths are listed in the From and Destination fields.

- Click OK to move the designated files to the PROJECT1 directory.

11. Rename the PROJECT1 directory to DONE1.

    a. Click the PROJECT1 directory.

    b. Select Rename from the Object menu.

    c. When the Rename dialog box appears:

- Type the following in the New Name field:

    DONE1

- Click OK to rename the directory.

- You'll notice that the PROJECT1 directory has been renamed to DONE1.

12. Copy the DONE1 directory and its contents to the PROJECT2 directory.

    a. Drag the DONE1 directory onto the PROJECT2 directory.

    b. When the Move/Copy dialog box appears:

- You'll notice that the Copy button is automatically activated.

- Ensure that the correct source and destination paths are listed in the From and Destination fields.

- Click OK to confirm the copy.

13. Move the new DONE1 directory and its contents from the PROJECT2 directory to the PROJECT3 directory.

   a. To select the directory:

   - Double-click the PROJECT2 directory to open the directory and view its contents.

   - Click the DONE1 directory under the PROJECT2 directory. and hold down the mouse button.

   - While holding down the Ctrl key, drag the DONE1 directory from the PROJECT2 directory to the PROJECT3 directory

   b. When the Move/Copy dialog box appears:

   - You'll notice that the Move button is automatically activated.

   - Ensure that the correct source and destination paths are listed in the From and Destination fields.

   - Click OK to confirm the move.

14. Set the Purge attribute for the TRAPTARG file under the PROJECT3\DONE1 directory.

   a. Double-click the PROJECT3 directory and the DONE1 subdirectory to open them and see their contents.

   b. Double-click the TRAPTARG.TXT file under the PROJECT3/DONE1 directory.

   c. When the Details page dialog box for this file appears, click the Attributes page button.

   d. When the Attributes page button appears:

   - Click the Purge Immediate attribute.

   - Click OK to save your changes.

15. Simultaneously delete the three files in the PROJECT3/DONE1 directory.

   a. To select the files:

   - Click the first filename listed.

   - While holding down the Shift key, click the last filename listed.

   - Press the Delete key.

   b. When the Delete dialog box appears, select Yes to confirm the deletion.

16. Salvage the files you deleted in Step 15.

   a. Click the DONE1 directory under the PROJECT3 directory.

   b. Select Salvage from the Tools menu.

   c. When the Salvage dialog box appears:

   - Click the List button near the top left of the window. You'll notice that the TRAPTARG.CFG file is not listed because you set it as "immediate purge" before deleting it.

   - Click the first filename listed.

   - While holding down the Shift key, click the second name.

   - Click the Salvage button.

   - Click the Close button to close the Salvage window.

   d. Confirm the salvage process. Double-click the DONE1 directory to confirm that the two files have been salvaged.

17. Limit the Temp1 user to 2048K of disk storage space on the SYS: volume.

   a. In the CRIME.TOKYO.ACME container, create a TEMP1 User object with a password of ACME.

   b. On the main NetWare Administrator screen:

   - Click the CRIME-SRV1_SYS volume.

   - Select Details from the Object menu.

   - Click the User Space Limits page button.

c. When the Users Space Limits page appears, click the Browse button to the right of the Search Context field.

d. When the Select Object dialog box appears:

- Navigate the tree until the CRIME container object appears in the Available Objects pane.

- Click the CRIME container object in the Available Objects pane.

- Click OK.

e. When the User Space Limits page reappears:

- Click the Temp1 User object.

- Click Modify.

f. When the Volume Space Restriction dialog box appears:

- Mark the Limited Volume Space checkbox.

- Type the following in the "Volume Space Limit (KB)" field:

  2048

- Click OK to save your changes and return to the User Space Limits page.

- Click OK to return to the main NetWare Administrator screen.

18. Limit the maximum size of the PROJECT3 directory.

a. On the main NetWare Administrator screen:

- Right-click the PROJECT3 directory you created earlier in this exercise.

- Select Details from the pop-up menu that appears.

b. When the DIRECTORY: PROJECT3 dialog box appears, click the Facts page tab.

c. When the Facts page appears:

- Mark the Restrict Size checkbox.

- Type the following in the Limit field:

  2048

- Click OK to save your changes and return to the main NetWare Administrator screen.

19. Exit the NetWare Administrator utility.

Drive Mapping

Drive mapping is one of the great mysteries of life. Forget about the pyramids, alien cornfields, or quarks—drive mapping has them all beat.

It doesn't have to be this way. As a matter of fact, drive mapping is really pretty simple. The problem is that it requires you to unlearn the fundamentals of DOS. Let me explain. In the DOS world, drive letters point to physical devices. In Figure 4.27, the A: and B: letters point to floppy drives, C: and D: point to hard drives, and the E: drive is a CD-ROM. Pretty simple, huh? Well, it works fine on workstations, because they typically use multiple storage devices.

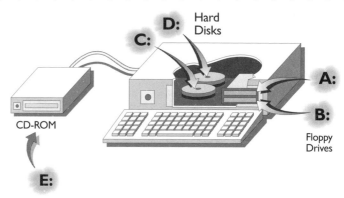

FIGURE 4.27

Drive mapping to physical local devices

So, how does this theory apply to NetWare 5 drives? If we extrapolate from the local theory, we would use 21 different drive letters (F-Z) to point to 21 physical devices—not very likely. So, Novell returned to the proverbial drawing board and came up with a slightly different approach—just different enough to confuse you, me, CNAs, and especially users. Here's how it works:

NetWare 5 drive letters point to logical *directories instead of* physical *drives.*

This is also pretty simple; a little too simple. As a matter of fact, users treat the NetWare 5 drives just like local drives—mistake. The first time they use the CD command, all heck breaks loose. Let me tell you a little story—ironically, about Little John.

One seemingly innocent summer day in August, Little John was working on his financial files in the SYS:SHARED\FIN directory. For his convenience, you have mapped this directory to drive letter G: (see Figure 4.28). He suddenly realizes that his report templates are at home, that is, SYS:USERS\LJOHN (drive map U:). Any other time he would simply type U: and press Enter to get home, but not today. Today he confuses his network and local drives. Today is a bad day for Little John.

F I G U R E   4.28

Drive mapping to logical network directories

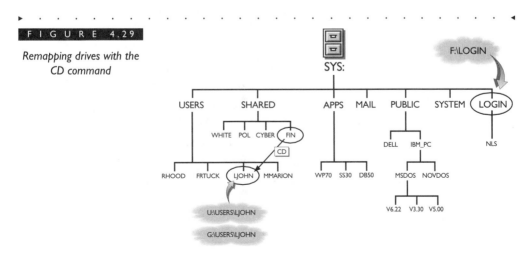

Instead of using the existing U: drive mapping, Little John types **CD\USERS\LJOHN** from the G: drive. This would work fine in the DOS world, but it's unforgivable in the NetWare 5 world. What has he done? Correct. Little John has inadvertently remapped his G: drive to SYS:USERS\LJOHN. Remember, NetWare 5 drive letters are logical pointers to NetWare 5 directories, not physical devices. As you can see in Figure 4.29, Little John now has two letters mapped to his home directory. Of course, he doesn't realize this. Let's return to the story.

F I G U R E   4.29

Remapping drives with the CD command

Oblivious to the changes in his world, Little John searches the G:\USERS\LJOHN directory for his report templates. He can't find them. "Ah," he thinks. "They're in my home directory. That's drive U:." He quickly switches over to U:\USERS\LJOHN, unaware that this is the same directory. Remember, he thinks the G: and U: drives are different hard disks. He searches in vain and doesn't find the report templates on the U: drive either — he wouldn't. This is where it gets interesting.

Disgruntled, Little John decides to return to his financial directory and continue work without the missing templates. Naturally, he types G: and presses Enter to return to the G:\SHARED\FIN directory — it doesn't work. "That's odd," he thinks. "It's always worked before." Much to his dismay, all of the financial files seem to have been removed from the G: drive and replaced by a duplicate copy of his home files. At least that's how it appears to Little John. Remember, he thinks the G: and U: drives are different hard disks. In actuality, Little John has remapped the G: drive to G:\USERS\LJOHN with the CD command. Oops.

In a panic, Little John deletes the duplicate copy of his home files — hoping it will clear enough space for his financial files to return. Of course, he has inadvertently deleted all his home files, because they are not duplicates. It's simply a duplicate drive mapping. He comes rumbling down the hall to your office, screaming at the top of his lungs, "Somebody has deleted my financial files!" Incidentally, Little John is not a little man. After picking yourself off the floor, you proceed to explain to him that the NetWare 5 CD command doesn't change directories as it does in DOS. Instead, it cancels data. Of course, this is a lie, but it stops him from using the CD command in the future. Fortunately, you're a CNA and you can save the day! Use SALVAGE to undelete his files and MAP to return G: back to G:\SHARED\FIN where it belongs.

Just another day in the life of a NetWare 5 CNA. (Hey that rhymes!)

This story has been brought to you by NetWare 5 and your local neighborhood DMV (Drive Mapping Vehicle). It's a great example of what can happen when users get local and network drive mappings confused. For this reason, you have a choice to make: Do you perpetuate the myth or tell your users the truth? If you perpetuate the myth that NetWare 5 drives point to physical disks, you'll need to use the MAP ROOT command to make them appear as such. This will also nullify the effects of CD. If you decide to tell your users the truth, consider that knowledge is power.

Also consider that they may not want to know the truth. Either way, NetWare 5 provides you with three different approaches to drive mapping:

▸ Network Drive Mapping

▸ Search Drive Mapping

▸ Directory Map Objects

Network drives use a single letter to point to logical directory paths. The previous example uses network drives. *Search drives*, on the other hand, provide additional functionality by building a search list for network applications. Finally, *Directory Map objects* are centralized NDS resources that point to logical directory paths. They help ease the transition from one application version to another. Let's take a closer look.

Network Drive Mappings

Network drive mappings have a singular purpose—convenience. They provide simple directory navigation for accessing data files. As we learned earlier, NetWare 5 supports 21 network drives by default: F–Z. In Figure 4.28, the F: drive points to SYS:LOGIN and the U: drive points to SYS:USERS\LJOHN. These mappings make it easy for users to find their stuff—as long as they don't use the dreaded CD command. Little John simply types U: followed by Enter to get home to U:\USERS\ LJOHN. Without drive mappings, movement throughout the Directory tree would be cumbersome and time-consuming. It would involve long path names and confusing directory searches. Yuck!

Network drive mappings are user-specific, temporary environment variables. Each user has a different set of drive mappings within his or her workstation RAM. These mappings are created each time the user logs in. When the user logs out or turns off the machine, these mappings are lost. For this reason, you'll want to automate the creation of drive mappings in Container and Profile login scripts (see the "Configuring Login Scripts" section in the Chapter 3). Also, you can place your mappings in the Windows 95/98 Registry and make them permanent. This way, they'll always be available when you access the network.

Network drive mappings are created using the MAP command. We'll explore this command in depth later in this chapter. For now, consider creating any or all of the following drive mappings for your users:

▸ *U:* — each user's home directory (for example, SYS:USERS\LJOHN)

▸ *F:* — SYS:LOGIN

▸ *G:* — group-specific data directories (for example, SYS:SHARED\FINAN)

▸ *H:* — global shared directory (for example, SYS:SHARED)

Now, let's expand our understanding of NetWare 5 drive mapping with search drives. They help us build an internal search list for network applications.

Search Drive Mappings

Search drive mappings extend one step beyond network mappings by helping users search for network applications. When a user executes an application, NetWare 5 searches two places for the program file:

1. The current directory.

2. The internal NetWare 5 search list. Search drive mappings build the internal search list. They are the NetWare 5 equivalent of local PATH statements.

TIP

Most DOS applications cannot access NetWare 5 volumes by their volume name. Instead, they typically rely on network and search drive mappings.

The beauty of the NetWare 5 search list is that it allows you to prioritize application directories. NetWare 5 searches for programs in the order in which they are listed. The list can be a combination of local and network directories. For example, the following search list would find Windows on the local drive first; otherwise, it would use the network version in SYS:APPS\WINDOWS:

```
S1:=SYS:PUBLIC

S2:=SYS:PUBLIC\IBM_PC\MSDOS\V6.22

S3:=C:\WINDOWS

S4:=SYS:APPS\WINDOWS

S5:=SYS:APPS\SS30
```

Because search drive mappings are primarily used to build search lists, you should be more concerned with the order of the list than with the letter assigned to each directory. As you can see from this list, NetWare 5 assigns search drive mappings in search order—and each is preceded by the letter "S." As a matter of convenience, NetWare 5 also automatically assigns a drive letter to each search directory—in reverse order (to avoid using network drive letters).

For example, the first search drive (S1:) inherits the letter Z:, the second mapping (S2:) gets the letter Y:, and so on (see Figure 4.30). This allows you to navigate through search directories if necessary, although I don't recommend it. You are limited to a total of 16 search drives that inherit network drive letters. That is, you can have more than 16 search drives, but the extra ones will have to point to already-existing drive letters—such as C:.

Because the NetWare 5 search list and DOS PATH statements accomplish the same thing, there's a little conflict of interest. As a matter of fact, the NetWare 5 search list systematically eliminates directories in the DOS path. To avoid this problem, consider incorporating your DOS path into the NetWare 5 search list. This is accomplished using the MAP INSERT command (see the "Drive Mapping" section later in this chapter).

TIP

If a search drive encounters an existing network drive letter, the drive skips the letter and inherits the next one. For this reason, you should always assign network drive mappings first.

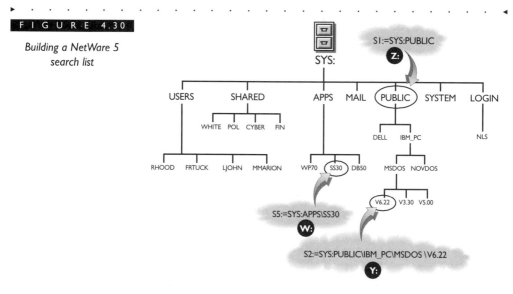

Building a NetWare 5
search list

This completes our discussion of network and search drive mappings. Refer to Table 4.6 for a summary of how they work.

		NETWORK DRIVE	SEARCH DRIVE
	FUNCTION	MAPPING	MAPPING
	Purpose	Movement	Searching
	Assignment Method	As the letter	In search order
	Letter Assignment	By you	By NetWare 5
	First Letter	F:	Z:
	Directory Types	Data	Applications

T A B L E   4.6

Comparing Network and
Search Drive Mappings

Now, let's take a moment to explore Directory Map objects before we dive into the MAP command.

Directory Map Objects

In earlier chapters, we learned about a special NDS leaf object that helped us deal with drive mapping in the NetWare 5 file system — the Directory Map object. This special-purpose object allows us to map to a central logical resource instead of to the physical directory itself, mainly because physical directories change and logical objects don't have to.

This level of independence is very useful. Let's say, for example, that you have a central application server in the TOKYO container that everybody points to. On the server is an older copy of WordPerfect (WP5). You have two options for adding this application to your internal search lists:

1. *Search drive mapping* — Use a traditional search drive mapping in each container's login script (five of them). This mapping would point to the physical directory itself — TOKYO-SRV1\SYS:APPS\WP5.

2. *Directory Map object* — Create a central Directory Map object in TOKYO called WPAPP. Then, each of the five search drive MAP commands can point to the logical object instead of the physical APPS\WP directory. Finally, here the WPAPP object points to the physical directory as TOKYO-SRV1\SYS:APPS\WP5.

Both of these scenarios accomplish the same thing: They create a search drive mapping to WordPerfect 5 for all users in the Tokyo location. But, once you upgrade WordPerfect, you'll find the second option is much more attractive. In the first scenario, you'll need to change five different search drive statements in five distributed login scripts on five different servers. This is a lot of work!

In the second scenario, however, you'll only need to change the one Directory Map object reference, and all the other MAP statements will automatically point to the right place. Amazing! In the next section, we'll explore the MAP command and learn how it can be used to reference Directory Map objects.

Mapping Drives with MAP

So, now that you know everything there is to know about network, search, and NDS drive mappings, the next logical question is, "How?" It's simple — the MAP command. The NetWare 5 MAP command allows you to

▸ View drive mappings

▸ Create or modify network or search drive mappings

▸ Point to Directory Map objects

▸ Map drives to a fake root — to fool users or install special applications

▸ Change mappings from one type to another

▸ Integrate the network and local search lists

▸ All sorts of other stuff

TIP

The DOS CD command will change the MAP assignment in the DOS window, but not in the current Windows applications. Also, the MAP command is faster than CD because it has drive letters. Finally, the NetWare 5 MAP command is most like the DOS SUBST command.

As I'm sure you've probably guessed, the MAP command is the heart and soul of NetWare 5 drive mapping. Now, let's take a closer look at some fun and exciting MAP commands — starting with plain old MAP. Also, there's a MAP summary table at the end of this section for your review. Ready, set, MAP!

MAP

You can use the MAP command without any options to display a list of your current drive mappings. As you can see in Figure 4.31, the local drives (A: through E:) are listed first, followed by the network drives, and finally, the search drives. Also, note the cool dashes in the middle. They separate the network drives from the search drives.

TIP

NetWare 5 does not track information on local drive assignments. Even though a map list will show that drives A: through E: are assigned to local drives, that doesn't necessarily mean they point to real devices. If you really want to mess with your users, map network drives to local devices. Or, even better, map local drives to network directories.

▶ . . . . ◀

FIGURE 4.31	

The plain old MAP command

```
G:\SHARED\FIN>MAP

Drives A,B,C,D,E map to a local disk.
Drive F: = WHITE-SRV1_SYS: \PUBLIC
Drive G: = WHITE-SRV1_SYS: \SHARED\FIN
Drive U: = WHITE-SRV1_SYS: \USERS\MMARION
----------- Search Drives -----------
S1: = Z:. [WHITE-SRV1_SYS: \PUBLIC]
S2: = C:\NOVELL\CLIENT32
S3: = C:\WINDOWS
S4: = C:\WINDOWS\COMMAND
S5: = C:\DOS

G:\SHARED\FIN>
```

MAP G:=WHITE-SRV1\SYSSHARED\FINAN

You can use the MAP command followed by a drive letter (A: through Z:) to create network drive mappings. In this case, the G: drive is assigned to the SYS:SHARED\FIN directory on the WHITE-SRV1 file server.

We also could have used the relative distinguished name or distinguished name for the volume instead of using the physical volume name. For example, we could have typed:

```
MAP G:=WHITE-SRV1_SYS:SHARED\FIN
```

or

```
MAP G:=.WHITE-SRV1_SYS.WHITE.CRIME.TOKYO.ACME:SHARED\FIN
```

If the G: drive already exists, it will replace the existing assignment without displaying a warning. However, if you attempt to re-map a local drive (that is, Drive A: through Drive E:), you will receive a warning that the drive is currently assigned to a local device. NetWare 5 is polite and asks you if you want to assign it to a network drive anyway.

MAP NP E:=SYSMAIL

Using the NP parameter allows you to overwrite local or search drives without being prompted. It must be listed first or second. In this example, the E: drive would be re-mapped without the usual warning:

```
Warning: You are attempting to re-map a local drive.
```

MAP S3:=SYS:APPS\WP70

You can use the MAP SEARCH command followed by a search drive number (S1: through S16:) to map a directory to a specific search drive. The number in the search drive defines the pointer's place in the search list (that is, its priority).

TIP

Search drive mappings share the same environment space as the DOS path. As a result, if you assign a NetWare 5 search drive number using the MAP SEARCH command, it will overwrite the corresponding pointer in the DOS path. (For example, if you use the MAP S1: command, it will overwrite the first pointer in the DOS path.) The only way to retain existing pointers in the DOS path is to use the MAP INS or MAP S16: commands (listed later in this section), which insert new search drives into the DOS path rather than replacing existing ones.

In this example, the SYS:APPS\WP70 directory will be assigned as search drive S3:, which is the third item in the search list. It will also map the directory to the next available drive letter, starting with Z: and moving backward. Review the "Search Drive Mappings" section earlier in this chapter.

TIP

There is a way to specify which network drive letter is assigned when creating a search drive. In the previous example, if you want to assign network drive letter W: to the S3: search drive, you can use the following command:

```
MAP S3:=W:=APPS\WP70
```

A very interesting thing happens if you remap an existing search drive number. NetWare 5 assigns the new directory, as specified, without warning you that an existing search drive with the same number already exists. It does not, however, overwrite the network drive letter that was originally associated with the search drive number. Instead, it assigns a new network drive letter to the new directory and converts the old network drive letter into a full-fledged network drive mapping — thus stripping away its searching ability. Conversely, if you attempt to re-map the network drive associated with a search drive, you will receive a warning that the drive is already in use as a search drive and will be asked if you want to overwrite it. If you say "Yes," both the network drive and its associated search drive will be mapped to the new directory. Weird, huh?

MAP INS S1:=SYS:PUBLIC

The MAP INSERT command can be used to insert a new search drive into the search list, at the number specified, without overwriting an existing drive mapping. All existing search drives below the new pointer are then bumped up one level in the list and renumbered accordingly.

In this example, we are inserting a new drive as S1:. Therefore, NetWare 5 bumps up and renumbers all other search drives in the list. Then, it inserts the new drive at the top of the list as search drive S1:.

The interesting thing about this scenario is that it has no effect on existing network drives. All previous drives retain their original drive letters, even though they change positions in the search list.

Earlier, we learned that both the MAP INSERT and MAP S16: commands could be used to preserve the DOS path. This way, when you log off the network, your NetWare 5 search drives will be deleted, but your local PATH statements will remain intact. Remember, DOS PATH drives don't count toward your limit of 16 network search drives.

TIP

So, what happens when you mix the **MAP INSERT** and **MAP S16:** statements? You create a strange "genetic" breed. The resulting command, **"MAP INSERT S16:"** places your search drives in the NetWare 5 search list, but after the **DOS PATH** directories. Weird.

MAP DEL G:

The MAP DEL command deletes an existing drive mapping. This command can be used with both network and search drive pointers. The MAP REM command performs the same function. Remember, network drive mappings and search drive mappings are deleted automatically if you log off the network or turn off your workstation.

MAP ROOT H:=SYS:ACCT\REPORTS

You can use the MAP ROOT command to create a false root. This command solves user problems like the one we had with Little John. The user sees this drive as if it were the root directory; therefore, he can't wander off too far with the dreaded CD command.

MAP ROOT can also be used for application programs that need to be installed in the root directory. For security reasons and administrative purposes, you should never install applications in the actual root, so here's a great compromise. The

Install program thinks it's installing WordPerfect, for example, in the root directory, when it's actually a false root pointing to SYS:APPS.

To determine if a drive mapping is actually a false root, use the MAP command alone. As you can see in Figure 4.32, the H: drive is shown differently than are the other network drives. Instead of showing a blank space between the volume name and the directory name, it shows a blank space followed by a backslash following the directory name. This clues you in that we're dealing with a different breed — a false root.

▶ · ◀

F I G U R E   4.32

The MAP ROOT command

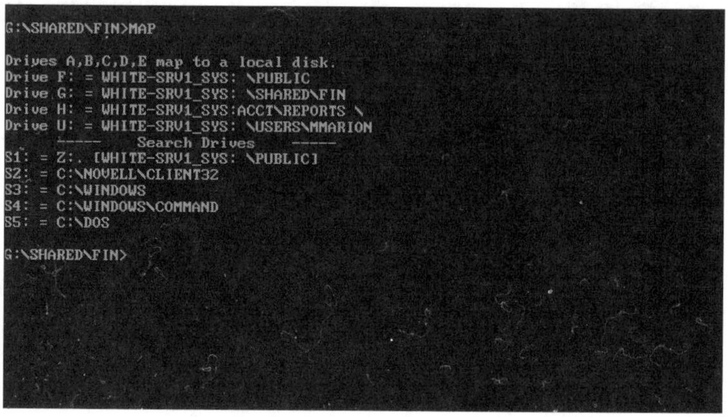

```
G:\SHARED\FIN>MAP

Drives A,B,C,D,E map to a local disk.
Drive F: = WHITE-SRV1_SYS: \PUBLIC
Drive G: = WHITE-SRV1_SYS: \SHARED\FIN
Drive H: = WHITE-SRV1_SYS:ACCT\REPORTS \
Drive U: = WHITE-SRV1_SYS: \USERS\MMARION
            ------    Search Drives    ------
S1: = Z:. [WHITE-SRV1_SYS: \PUBLIC]
S2: = C:\NOVELL\CLIENT32
S3: = C:\WINDOWS
S4: = C:\WINDOWS\COMMAND
S5: = C:\DOS

G:\SHARED\FIN>
```

MAP N SYS:DATA

You can use the MAP NEXT (N) command to assign the next available drive letter as a network drive mapping. It doesn't work, however, with search drive pointers.

MAP C I:

The MAP CHANGE (C) command can be used to change a regular NetWare 5 drive to a search drive, or vice versa. In this example, Drive I: will still point to the same directory to which it was originally assigned, but it would also be added to the end of the NetWare 5 search list. Conversely, if you use the MAP CHANGE command with a search drive, the search drive number is deleted from the search list, but the network drive letter originally associated with it is retained as a network drive mapping.

TIP Although the **MAP NEXT** command doesn't work with search drives, there is another technique that you can use to achieve the same effect, namely the **MAP S16:** command. The **MAP S16:** command assigns the next available search drive number to the specified directory. Because search drives update the **DOS Path**, NetWare 5 does not allow you to assign search drive numbers that would cause holes to exist in the DOS path. For instance, if only search drives **S1:** through **S4:** exist, NetWare 5 would not let you create search drive **S7:**. Instead, it would just assign the next search drive number in the list (**S5:**, in this example).

MAP S5:=.WPAPP.TOKYO.ACME

You can also map a drive to a Directory Map object (WPAPP) instead of to the directory itself. This is especially useful if the directory name changes from time to time — such as every time you upgrade WordPerfect or Microsoft Word — and you don't want to change every MAP statement in every login script.

In this case, you only need to change the reference in the central Directory Map object. All other drive mapping commands will reflect that change instantly. It's fun at parties. But whatever you do, don't place a colon (:) at the end of the Directory Map object.

TIP Directory Map objects appear as folders in the Windows 95/98 Network Neighborhood. You can activate them with the Map Network Drive option from the File menu. Also, you can access Directory Map objects on the Resource side of the NetWare User Tools for Windows.

MAP /?

The MAP /? command displays on-line help for all variations of the MAP command.

MAP /VER

The MAP /VER command lists the version of the MAP utility that you are using as well as the files the utility needs to execute. If you use the /VER option, all other parameters will be ignored.

Table 4.7 provides a quick summary of all the really amazing MAP commands you've learned today.

	COMMAND	RESULT
T A B L E 4.7 *Getting to Know the MAP Commands*	MAP	Displays a list of current drive mappings.
	MAP G:=WHITE-SRV1\SYS:SHARED\FINAN	Maps the G: drive as a network drive that points to the SHARED\FINAN directory on the SYS: volume of the WHITE-SRV1 server (using the physical volume name).
	MAP G:=.WHITE-SRV1_SYS. WHITE.CRIME.TOKYO. ACME:SHARED\FINAN	Maps the G: drive as a network drive that points to the SHARED\FINAN directory on the SYS: volume of the WHITE-SRV1 server (using the Volume object name).
	MAP NP E:=SYS:HR\EVAL	Maps the E: drive to the HR\EVAL directory, suppressing the warning that you are about to remap a local drive.
	MAP S3:=SYS:APPS\WP70	Maps the S3: search drive to the SYS:APSS\WP70 directory and assigns the next available drive letter in reverse alphabetical order as a network drive.
	MAP S3:=W:= SYS:APPS\WP70	Maps the S3: search drive to the SYS:APPS\WP70 directory and assigns W: as the associated network drive.
	MAP INS S1:=SYS:PUBLIC	Inserts a new S1: search drive at the beginning of the search list, renumbering all existing search drives accordingly. Also assigns the next available drive letter in reverse alphabetical order as a network drive.
	MAP DEL G:	Deletes the G: network drive (see MAP REM command).

TABLE 4.7	COMMAND	RESULT
Getting to Know the MAP Commands (continued)	MAP REM G:	Deletes the G: network drive (see MAP DEL command).
	MAP ROOT H:=SYS:ACCT\REPORTS	Maps the H: drive as a false root pointing to the SYS:ACCT\REPORTS directory.
	MAP N SYS:DATA	Maps the next available network drive letter to the SYS:DATA directory.
	MAP C I:	Changes the I: network drive to the next available search drive number.
	MAP C S4:	Changes the S4: search drive to a network drive.
	MAP S5:=WPAPP	Maps the S5: search drive to a Directory Map object called WPAPP in the current container.
	MAP /?	Displays on-line help information for the MAP command.
	MAP /VER	Displays version information about the MAP utility, including the files it needs to execute.

Mapping Drives with Windows 95/98

In addition to the MAP command, NetWare 5 allows you to create network and search drive mappings using Windows 95/98. In Windows 95/98, you can use the Network Neighborhood to map network drives to volumes and directories. This facility does not allow you to create search drive mappings. To map a network drive in the Windows 95/98 Network Neighborhood, consult Figure 4.33 and follow these steps:

1. Select the volume or directory you want to map.

2. From the File menu, choose "Map Network Drive." The Map Network Drive window appears, showing the path you have selected.

3. Choose a drive letter.

4. Select the "Reconnect at Logon" option so that this drive will be available the next time you log in. Incidentally, these permanent settings are stored in the Windows 95/98 Registry.

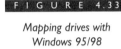

Mapping drives with Windows 95/98

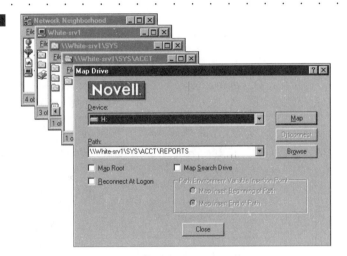

It's important to note that all drive mappings are viewed globally by the Novell Client. Therefore, any time a drive is mapped within Windows 95/98, the drive is accessible and visible everywhere else in Windows. In addition, whenever a drive is changed to a different directory, the directory change affects only that specific instance of the drive. For example, if the drive is changed to the SHARED directory at the MS-DOS prompt, no other MS-DOS prompt or Windows application will display this change. For this reason, you want to be sure to use the Network Neighborhood.

In the beginning . . . there was the NDS Directory tree. We discovered the [Root], leaf objects, proper naming, and Read/Write replicas. We learned how to name it, partition it, browse it, manage it, and groom it. Just when we thought we understood the true meaning of NetWare 5 life, another tree appeared — the non-NDS Directory tree.

This strange new tree is very different. Instead of a [Root], it has a *root*; instead of leaves, it has *files*; and instead of replicas, it has *duplexing*. But once you get past its rough exterior, you'll see that the non-NDS tree shares the same look and feel as the NDS one. And they approach life together with a similar purpose — to logically organize user resources, except this time the resources are files, not printers.

In this chapter, we have learned everything there is to know about our non-NDS friend. We learned how to name it, partition it, browse it, manage it, and groom it. All in a day's work.

So, what does the future hold? Well, now that we've learned everything about NDS and non-NDS trees, we can expand our minds to the rest of NetWare 5 management. We will combine our "treeologist" skills and forge ahead into the great CNA abyss:

► NetWare 5 Security — Chapter 5

► NetWare 5 Workstation Management — Chapter 6

► NetWare 5 Printing — Chapter 7

► NetWare 5 Installation — Chapter 8

During your journey through the rest of this book, look back to the fun times you had in gardening class. Count on your NDS and non-NDS gardening skills — because you will need them. Oh yes, you will.

Good luck, and by the way . . . thanks for saving the world.

LAB EXERCISE 4.2: MAPPING DRIVES WITH MAP

Follow the steps listed below to create sample drive mappings for the directory structure that was created in Exercise 4.1, "Creating a Directory Structure for ACME."

Determine which commands you would use to perform the following tasks:

1. Display on-line help information for the MAP command.

2. Display your current drive mappings.

3. Map drive F: to the USERS directory. (Normally, it would point to each user's individual home directory, but they have not been created yet.)

4. Map drive G: to the POL subdirectory under the SHARED directory, using the physical name of the volume.

5. Map the J: drive to the same directory as the F: drive.

6. Map drive S: to the SHARED directory, using the Volume object name.

7. Map the S1: search drive to the SYS:PUBLIC directory without overwriting the existing pointers in the DOS path.

8. Map the S2: search drive to the V6.22 directory without overwriting the existing pointers in the DOS path.

9. Map the S3: search drive to the SS30 subdirectory.

10. Map the S4: search drive as a false root to the DB50 subdirectory.

11. Display your current drive mappings again. How does the system indicate a false root?

12. Map the S5: search drive to the WP70 subdirectory, specifying that W: be assigned as the associated network drive. Did it work?

13. To view the effect of the CD command on search drive mappings, switch to the Z: drive. Type **CD ..** and press Enter to switch to the root directory. Type the **MAP** command to list your current drive mappings. What happened? What should be done to fix the problem? Fix the problem.

14. Delete the J: drive.

15. Delete the S3: search drive using a different command than you did in Step 14. What happened to your other search drive mappings? What happened to the network drive associated with those search drives?

16. Change the S4: drive from a search drive to a network drive. What happened to the search drive itself? What happened to the network drive associated with it?

See Appendix C for answers.

LAB EXERCISE 4.3: MAPPING DRIVES WITH WINDOWS

In addition to the MAP command, NetWare 5 allows you to create network and search drive mappings using Network Neighborhood in Windows 95/98/NT. To perform this exercise, you will need:

► A NetWare 5 server called CRIME-SRV1.CRIME.TOKYO.ACME (which can be installed using the directions found in Chapter 8, Exercise 8.1).

► A workstation running the NetWare 5 Novell Client for Windows 95/98 or Windows NT (which can be installed using the directions found in Chapter 8, Exercise 8.2).

Complete the following steps on your client workstation.

1. Launch Network Neighborhood. To do so, double-click the Network Neighborhood icon on your Windows 95/98/NT desktop.

2. Select the directory to be mapped.

   a. Double-click the CRIME-SRV1 server icon.

   b. Double-click the SYS: volume icon.

   c. Click PUBLIC directory icon.

3. Map the drive.

   a. Select the Novell Map Network Drive option from the File menu.

   b. When the Map Drive dialog box appears:

     • The next available drive letter will be listed in the Device field. Select the drive letter you want to assign from the pulldown menu.

     • The path to the directory you have selected will be listed in the Path field.

- Mark the "Reconnect at logon" checkbox so that this drive will be available the next time you log in.

- Click MAP to map the drive.

4. Exit the Network Neighborhood utility. (Back out of this utility by clicking the Close button in the upper-right corner of each of the open windows relating to this utility.)

LAB EXERCISE 4.4: FILE CABINET OF LIFE

Circle the 20 file system-related terms hidden in this word search puzzle using the hints provided. No punctuation characters (such as blank spaces, hyphens, and so on) should be included. Numbers should always be spelled out.

```
N  E  T  W  O  R  K  D  R  I  V  E  Q  F  X  J  P  U
D  I  R  E  C  T  O  R  Y  X  M  J  M  K  S  R  R  P
I  R  E  X  S  E  A  R  C  H  D  R  I  V  E  B  S  F
R  E  A  D  G  O  E  D  B  Z  P  Y  E  V  B  T  S
Y  L  D  A  T  A  M  I  G  R  A  T  I  O  N  R  I  X
W  I  L  N  F  Q  H  H  L  Q  J  T  Y  G  I  B  B  T
T  F  I  L  E  C  O  M  P  R  E  S  S  I  O  N  T  T
X  I  N  D  C  Y  P  P  W  G  I  N  E  J  K  T  X  S
B  L  O  C  K  S  U  B  A  L  L  O  C  A  T  I  O  N
T  E  Q  P  Z  I  F  V  Q  F  Y  M  H  W  L  F  F  K
I  S  N  P  H  Y  L  G  M  B  G  W  N  L  U  F  R  N
B  C  C  U  I  A  Y  E  U  F  J  H  B  Z  L  U  K  K
G  A  O  R  S  N  E  A  K  E  R  N  E  T  M  H  G  J
K  N  P  G  E  E  W  L  E  G  X  A  M  H  Y  Q  L  D
V  G  Y  E  J  A  R  I  H  U  J  P  Y  O  S  U  S  L
V  Q  Y  P  N  E  T  A  D  M  I  N  E  M  H  L  R  F
O  P  K  N  S  U  P  E  R  V  I  S  O  R  D  M  H  P
```

Hints:

1. Process that allows several files to share the last part of a single disk block.
2. Directory right required for salvaging files you own.
3. Transfer of inactive or infrequently used data to near-term storage.
4. File system component on which you can impose a disk space limitation.
5. File storage method used to save disk space.
6. File right required for salvaging files you own.
7. NetWare 5 menu utility used for salvaging and purging files.
8. NetWare 5 command-line utility used for assigning directory/file attributes.

9. NetWare 5 command-line utility used for copying files.
10. NetWare 5 command-line utility used for viewing file information.
11. Legacy menu utility that just can't compete with NetWare Administrator.
12. Drive mapping to server directory.
13. Process used to prevent deleted files from being recovered.
14. Another file right required for salvaging files you own.
15. Process used to recover deleted files.
16. Type of drive mapping that modifies the DOS path.
17. Console command that can be used to configure file compression parameters.
18. File-sharing procedure used before the advent of LANs.
19. File system right required for salvaging files you don't own.
20. Object whose disk space usage can be limited.

LAB EXERCISE 4.5: NETWARE 5 FILE SYSTEM

Across

1. Purpose of MAP command
7. Home of deleted files
11. Windows file management utility
13. Data migration storage system
14. Analogous to file cabinet
16. Unit of disk space
17. Data migration hardware
18. DOS directory creation utility
19. Analogous to folder contents

Down

1. Letter assigned to device
2. Immediate purge attribute
3. Mapping command-line utility

4. Immediate compression attribute
5. Analogous to a file folder
6. NetWare directory renaming utility
8. Don't migrate attribute
9. Main topic of this chapter
10. DOS directory deletion utility
12. Required NetWare volume
15. Highest level in the file system

Keep the Bad Guys Out: NetWare 5 Security

Security is an interesting thing. Everyone wants it, but how much are you willing to pay? On the one extreme, you could live in a titanium vault — secure, but very uncomfortable. On the other extreme, you could live in a 1960s Woodstock fantasy — fun, but way too risky. My guess is that you live somewhere in between. Whether you know it or not, your security requirements fall in a spectrum between a titanium vault and the 1960s. The key to security is gauging the range of your boundaries.

Goal: *Let the good guys in and keep the bad guys out!*

Security in the Information Age poses an even more interesting challenge. Computers and communications have made it possible to collect volumes of data about you and me — from our last purchase at the five-and-dime to our detailed medical records. Privacy has become a commodity to be exchanged on the open market. Information is no longer the fodder of afternoon talk shows. It has become the unit of exchange for the 21st Century, more valuable than money.

A recent study has shown that 92 percent of the Fortune 500 companies think security is important enough to do something about. Even the government is getting involved with the "clipper chip" and other antitheft policies. I bet you thought you left "cops and robbers" behind in childhood. Well, this is a variation on the game, and the stakes are very high.

As a CNA, it is your responsibility to design, install, and manage the NetWare 5 network. But, most importantly, you must protect it. You need a brain filled with sophisticated security strategies and a utility belt full of advanced protection tools. Think of this chapter as your impenetrable network armor.

NetWare 5 security is, in general, fairly good. But for many of today's WANs, it's not good enough. As a matter of fact, most of NetWare's security features need to be "turned on." It's not secure right out of the box. A truly secure network protects more than just user data — it protects everything!

So, what is "everything"?

The definition of "everything" has changed in NetWare 5. Now the world exists in a nebulous cloud full of Tupperware containers and User objects. As the NetWare 5 universe becomes more open and interconnected, security becomes more and more important.

So, what is "security"?

Simply stated, security is freedom from risk. Therefore, network security can be considered as any effort you take to protect your network from risk. Of course, it's difficult to protect your network from things you cannot see or understand. So, the first thing you need to do in developing a security model is to learn about risks.

So, what is "risk"?

Risk is a combination of value and threat. The value you determine is the cost of your network resources if you were to lose them. Value extends well beyond monetary value — it encompasses data integrity, confidentiality, and the value of data to competitors. Threats are more difficult to define. They come from a variety of different sources, including people, technology, and the environment. The very nature of computer networks puts them at continual risk. In summary, sharing data makes it harder to protect data. Of course, you don't have a choice. The first step toward true network security is risk analysis.

The goal of risk analysis is to define your network security principles and identify the threats against them. A "threat" is a person, place, or thing that poses some danger to a network asset. Threats can be physical (file servers and workstations), topology-related (wiretapping), network-related (back/trapdoors, impersonation, and piggybacking), data (logic bombs and Trojan horses), and people (intentional sabotage or unintentional bumbling).

The goal of your threat-based security model is to determine how likely your network is to experience any of these threats. What are the chances, for example, that your system has a back/trapdoor in place? Is wiretapping a possibility? How about impersonation or, even worse, logic bombs? The best approach is to make a realistic judgment of each threat's probability in relation to your WAN. This becomes the foundation of your network's risk index. You can then use this index to develop a successful system of security countermeasures.

So, what are "countermeasures"?

Countermeasures are actions that create a protective barrier against network threats. In many cases, countermeasures can reduce the probability of serious threats. The good news is that vulnerability decreases as countermeasures increase. There is, however, never a vulnerability level of zero because countermeasures themselves have vulnerabilities built in. The bad news is that countermeasures cost money. As a matter of fact, the more serious the threat, the higher the cost of the countermeasure. Because it's difficult to quantify the decrease in threat probability as a result of countermeasures, cost justification becomes a challenge. But all in all, countermeasures are necessary to keep your network running, and, therefore, money must be spent on them. After all, money makes the world go 'round.

As a CNA, it's your job to identify network threats and implement appropriate countermeasures to eliminate them. This isn't easy. You have many factors working against you—including money, office politics, and user productivity. But there are some quick and easy countermeasures that can dramatically improve your network security:

▸ Restrict physical access to file servers.

▸ Remember that one of your network's most insecure entry points is through virtual links.

▸ Consider using dial-back systems with multi-layered password protection. Remember, anyone with a modem and phone line can gain access to your network.

▸ Background authentication and NCP packet signing protect data packets as they travel over topology lines. In addition, data encryption offers further protection.

▸ Many advanced routers allow you to filter Service Access Protocols (SAPs), Routing Information Protocols (RIPs), and specific frame types. Consider filtering non-essential packets to increase performance and keep the bad guys out.

▸ Don't use the Supervisor or Admin accounts—use an equivalent instead. Also, don't delete the original Admin account once you have made yourself equivalent. There's some existentialist ramifications in there somewhere.

▸ Always create a backdoor. Consider using one or more null characters (Alt+255) in usernames and passwords. It's hard to track. The beauty of a null character is that it appears as an underscore or space, depending on the utility being used. For instance, if an intruder sees a username with a space or underline, he or she may never guess that it's a null character. Also, many times you can't tell how many null characters are involved— especially when they're sequentially added to the end of a username.

▶ NetWare 5 includes an extensive auditing system that allows you to audit login events as well as file/directory events. Use it!

▶ Classify people into security levels, identify the highest security risks, then implement countermeasures against these people, including training sessions, tracking, or extensive auditing.

▶ Track rights carefully and make sure you know what you're doing before you get started. Calculating effective rights can be very tricky, especially if you use an Inherited Rights Filter (IRF). Many times, users inadvertently end up with access rights they shouldn't have.

▶ Consider restricting the following file system access rights: Supervisor, Access Control, and Modify [SAM].

▶ Be careful when assigning distributed administrative responsibility. Remember, power corrupts and absolute power corrupts absolutely!

Well, there you go. Risk analysis and countermeasures. These are key factors in protecting your NetWare 5 WAN. Sometimes, however, NetWare 5 security just isn't good enough. You need to develop appropriate countermeasures for all network threats, not just a few. After all, the '60s was a great decade, but welcome to the '90s. This is the Information Age and your data is a valuable commodity.

Fortunately, NetWare 5 uses a dramatically improved security model for creating and maintaining your impenetrable network armor. This model allows you to perform risk analysis at five different levels. It also includes numerous countermeasures for dealing with "bad guys." Whatever you do, don't let this information fall into the wrong hands.

As you can see in Figure 5.1, the NetWare 5 security model consists of five different barriers. Each layer creates an increasingly strong barrier against user access. Each time you pass through a door, you are greeted with an even stronger barrier. Here's a quick preview:

▶ · ◀

FIGURE 5.1

The NetWare 5 security model

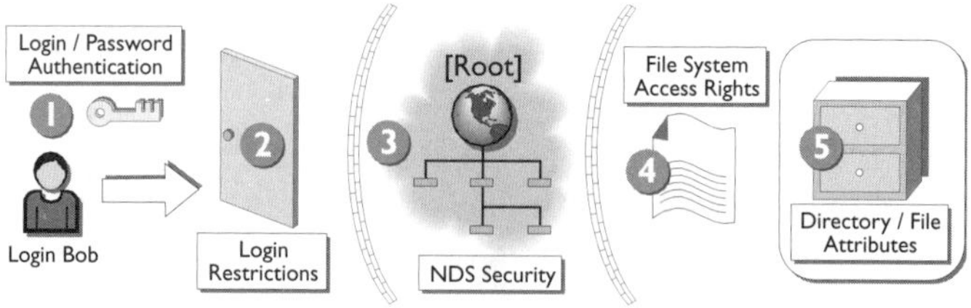

▶ *Layer 1: Login/Password Authentication* — It all starts with Login/Password Authentication. Remember, users don't log into NetWare servers any more — they log into the "Cloud." When a user requests login via a Novell Client login screen (or the LOGIN command-line utility), the authentication process begins automatically. There are two types of authentication: *initial authentication* (which occurs during the login process) and *background* (or *continuing*) *authentication* (which occurs whenever the user needs access to additional services after initial authentication is complete). If a user supplies the correct parameters during the login process (such as tree name, context, username, and password) — the user moves on to Layer 2 of the security model.

▶ *Layer 2: Login Restrictions* — At Layer 2, the user is presented with a number of account restrictions that must be met, including login restrictions, password restrictions, station restrictions, time restrictions, and Intruder Detection/Lockout restrictions. If a user successfully meets all of these restrictions, he or she is allowed to continue on to Layer 3.

▶ *Layer 3: NDS Security* — Once you enter the "Cloud," your ability to access leaf and container objects is determined by a sophisticated NDS security structure. At the heart of NDS security is the Access Control List (ACL). The ACL is a property of every NDS object. It defines who can access the object (trustees) and what each trustee can do (rights). The ACL is divided into two types of rights: object rights and property rights. These rights are designed to provide efficient access to NDS objects without making it an administrative nightmare. You be the judge.

▸ *Layer 4: File System Access Rights* — Well, here we are. Congratulations! You've finally made it to NetWare 5 Nirvana. You've passed through three very difficult barriers of network armor. The search is over — your files await you. Ah, but not so fast! Before you can access any files on the NetWare 5 server, you must have the appropriate file system access rights. Once again, another barrier pops up to bite you. Following is a list of the eight rights that control access to NetWare 5 files: Supervisor, Read, Write, Create, Erase, Modify, File Scan, Access Control.

▸ *Layer 5: Directory/File Attributes* — Directory and file attributes provide the final and most sophisticated layer of the NetWare 5 security model. These attributes are rarely used, but provide a powerful tool for specific security solutions. If all else fails, you can always turn to attribute security to save the day. NetWare 5 supports three different types of attributes: Security attributes, Feature attributes, and Disk Management attributes. Because attribute security affects all users, including Admin, it can be used to override file system access that file system trustee assignments would otherwise allow. Naturally, however, if a user has been granted the right to modify file and directory attributes, he or she can change or remove an attribute, and thus remove the restriction.

Well, there you have it. That's a brief snapshot of NetWare 5's five-layered security model. For a more in-depth introduction, check out the "NetWare 5 Security" section in Chapter 1.

Now we'll take a much closer look at each of these layers and learn how they can be used to create your impenetrable network armor. Of course, if someone should get lucky enough and break through your network armor, it would be nice to know what they're doing there. That's where NetWare 5 auditing comes in. And, yes, we'll discuss it, too. But not yet. Now it's time to attack the first layer of NetWare 5 security — Login/Password Authentication.

REAL WORLD

In October 1967, a task force was assembled by the Department of Defense (DoD) to address computer security safeguards that would protect classified information and computer networks. The task force was formed primarily because networks were just beginning to make an impact on all the world's computers. Of course, they had no idea what they were in for during the next 30 years. The DoD now explores security alternatives through the National Computer Security Center (NCSC). In December 1985, the DoD published a document affectionately known as "The Orange Book." Yes, I've seen it — it is orange.

In addition to the "Orange Book," the DoD has a related security specification called "The Red Book" — you get the idea! The Red Book defines a very high level of security within and between computer networks. This is where NetWare 5 shines! For example, Windows NT is C-2 secure according to the "Orange" book, but only NetWare 5 is C-2 secure according to both the "Orange" and "Red" books.

These documents are entitled "The Department of Defense Trusted Computer System Evaluation Criteria (TCSEC)." The Orange Book was designed to provide security guidelines for both developers and administrators. The major goal of the document is "to encourage the computer industry to develop trusted computer systems and products; making them widely available in the commercial marketplace." The book basically consists of a spectrum of evaluation criteria for differing levels of security. It lists basic requirements for very low and very high levels of security.

To be truly secure, your system must satisfy six fundamental requirements:

1. It must have a clear and well-defined security policy enforced.

2. All system elements must be associated with access control labels.

3. All individuals accessing the system must be identified.

4. Audit information must be selectively kept and protected so that all security actions can be traced.

5. The computer system must contain hardware/software mechanisms that can be independently evaluated.

6. The countermeasures that enforce these basic requirements must be continuously protected against tampering and/or unauthorized changes.

So, there you have it. Is your system truly secure? Well, in addition to these six requirements, the Orange Book includes evaluation criteria for four different divisions of security—A through D. Just like in school, A is good and D is bad. Working your way from the bottom, Division D is simply the bottom of the totem pole. This classification is reserved for those systems that have been evaluated, but have failed to meet the requirements for a higher evaluation class.

Division C, on the other hand, provides security on a "need to know" basis. Division C security includes auditing and accountability. The Orange Book further classifies Division C into two classes—C-1 and C-2. Most of today's network operating systems, including NetWare 5 and NT, vow to meet C-2 requirements at the very minimum (the government requires it). Class C-2 is entitled "Controlled Access Protection." Systems in this class enforce a more finely grained discretionary control than C-1 systems. C-2 users are individually accountable for their actions through login procedures, auditing of security-related events, and resource isolation. The idea here is to permit or refuse access to any file.

The bottom line is that NetWare 5 satisfies Class C-2 security through an integrated trust suite called NetWare Enhanced Security (NES). NetWare Enhanced Security is a distributed network operating system made up of three types of network components: servers, workstations, and network media.

The server component of NES contains a Network Trusted Computing Base (NTCB) partition, which is used to enforce the security policies and protect data stored on the server. The Trusted Network Interpretation (TNI) describes an NTCB as "the totality of protection mechanisms within a network system—including hardware, firmware, and software—the combination of which is responsible for enforcing a security policy."

For NES, the NTCB is distributed among multiple heterogeneous server and workstation NTCB partitions. The server NTCB partition contains the trusted hardware, firmware, and software that implement the security policies enforced by the server component. Because untrusted software is not permitted on the server, the entire server is included in the server NTCB partition.

Now that you understand the importance of NTCB, let's review the requirements for each of the three NES components:

> ▸ *Servers*—The server is evaluated as a Class C-2 IAD component, which means that it provides Identification and Authentication (I), Audit (A), and Discretionary Access Control (D) functions within the enhanced security architecture. The architecture allows you to connect an arbitrary number

(continued)

(continued)

of servers within your network. These servers must be evaluated as Class C-2 or higher security with respect to architecture, and may provide one or more of the IAD security functions. The architecture does not permit use of unevaluated servers such as NetWare 3.11 or NetWare 4.01.

▸ *Workstations* — The architecture permits an arbitrary number of single-user client workstations, potentially from different vendors. These products must be evaluated as Class C-2 or higher security with respect to architecture, and may provide none, some, or all of the IAD security functions. In particular, a diskless workstation might be evaluated as a Class C-2 "nil" component. This means that the workstation does not provide local enforcement of Identification and Authentication, Direct Access Control, or Auditing, but is capable of being securely used within the enhanced security network.

▸ *NetWork media* — Network media components are usually "nil" components, such as passive cabling.

You can compose a trusted Class C-2 network system by interconnecting an arbitrary number of NetWare 5 servers, other servers, client workstations, and passive network cabling. To determine the ratings of server and client workstation components, ask the vendor for the Evaluated Products List (EPL) entry for the product.

Layer One — Login/Password Authentication

When you log into a NetWare 5 server, the world changes. Suddenly you have access to a plethora of resources that weren't available before — printers, files, users, and e-mail. Whatever you do, don't take the login process for granted. It's a complex series of sophisticated communication steps between your client and the server.

Obviously, logging in involves supplying the correct information to the Novell Client — such as tree name, context, username, and password (see Chapter 3 for more details). But the real goal of logging in is *security*. After all, it's the only way to differentiate between real users and "bad guys." Now let's take a closer look at how hard it is to get access to a NetWare 5 server.

Getting In

The first two layers of the NetWare 5 security model are concerned with gaining access to the network — that is, "getting in." Once you're in, the bottom three layers take over. They control what you can do once you get there — access to NDS resources and the file system. As you can see in Figure 5.2, there's a lot going on during the login process. Also, notice that there are three ways to be denied, and only two ways to be granted access to the NetWare 5 Cloud. This is because of authentication. Let's take a closer look at the flowchart in Figure 5.2.

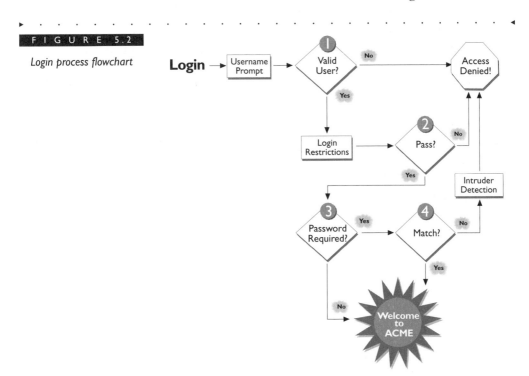

FIGURE 5.2

Login process flowchart

Unless you're using the new NetWare 5 contextless login feature, when you log in you'll need to provide, at a minimum, your distinguished (complete) login name including NDS context as well as your password. (If you click on the Advanced button on the login screen, you'll also be allowed to specify the preferred tree, context, preferred server, and so on). NetWare 5 then goes to the nearest writeable (that is, Master or Read/Write) replica of your parent partition and attempts to match the information you supplied against specific user properties in the NDS database. In other words, to verify that your User object exists. If your username does not exist in the context specified, you'll be denied access.

If you do provide a valid username and context, the system continues to decision two — account restrictions. Using the information provided by the writeable (Master or Read/Write) replica, NetWare 5 checks all your major account restrictions including login restrictions, time restrictions, station restrictions, network address restrictions, accounting balance, and account lockout. If you try to log in from an unauthorized workstation or during the wrong time of day, for example, access will be denied.

If you pass login restrictions, NetWare 5 moves on to the final two decisions — passwords. First, it uses your NDS information to determine whether a password is required. If a password is not required, you are authenticated automatically and access is granted. Bad idea. If a password is required, you are prompted for it. Good idea. That brings us to the final login decision: Does the password you provided match the one in the NDS database? If not, access is denied and Intruder Detection is incremented.

If you provide the correct password, NetWare 5 uses it to decrypt the private authentication key. This completes the initialization phase of login authentication and access is granted. We'll discuss the two phases of authentication in just a moment.

In summary, the NetWare 5 login process consists of four decisions:

1. Are you using a valid username (including context)?

2. Do you pass login restrictions?

3. Is a password required?

4. Does your password match?

If all of these conditions are met, access is granted. As you can see in Figure 5.2, there are three ways to be denied access — you type an invalid username, you don't pass login restrictions, or you provide the incorrect password. Now you should have a new appreciation for all the work that's involved when you log into the tree.

Initial Authentication

From a security standpoint, the entire login process points to one goal—authentication. This is the only way you can gain access to a NetWare 5 network. Authentication involves the username, the password, the client, NDS, and the NetWare 5 server. There sure are a lot of cooks in the kitchen. Once you've been initially authenticated, NetWare 5 activates a secondary authentication scheme—background authentication. Background authentication keeps the user validated throughout the current session. An additional feature, called NCP packet signing, validates every user packet as it's sent from the workstation to the server. This also applies to the active session only. We'll take a look at background authentication and NCP packet signing in just a moment.

In both cases, NetWare 5 authentication guarantees the following:

▸ Only the purported sender built the message.

▸ The message came from the workstation where the authentication data was created.

▸ The message pertains to the current session.

▸ The message contains no information counterfeited from another session.

▸ The message has not been tampered with or corrupted.

▸ You are who you say you are.

▸ You're doing what you say you're doing.

NetWare 5 authentication is based on the Rivest, Shamir, and Adleman (RSA) scheme. This is a public key encryption algorithm that is extremely difficult to break. In addition to RSA, authentication uses a independent private key algorithm as well. One key is public (which means that all users on the network can have access to it), while the other is kept private (which means only a designated user knows about it). If a message is encrypted with a private key, it can be decrypted with a public key and vice versa. As you can see in Figure 5.3, initial authentication consists of four sophisticated steps. Let's take a closer look.

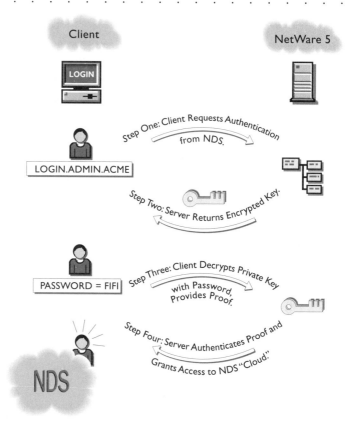

FIGURE 5.3

NetWare 5 initial authentication

TIP

Initial and Background Authentication are critical aspects of NetWare 5 login security — after all, they encompass Layer One! However, they are not emphasized in the NetWare 5 CNA/CNE courseware. As such, you may want to "stroll" through these next two sections without losing too many brain cells. Don't get me wrong, this is fascinating stuff (that's why I'm talking about it), it's just not a critical portion of the curriculum.

Step One: Client Requests Authentication

NetWare 5 authentication requires the Novell Client to run. It uses a special workstation module to control the encryption and decryption of public and private keys — RSA.NLM. In Step One, Admin logs in by providing his or her full NDS context. The client requests authentication from the NetWare 5 server. The request is then handled by a special program within the core OS — Authentication Services.

Step Two: Server Returns Encrypted Key

Once the authentication request has been accepted, NetWare 5 matches the user information with an encrypted private key. This private key can only be decrypted by the user password. That's Step Three.

Step Three: Client Decrypts Private Key

In Step Three, the user provides a valid password to decrypt the private key. The password is then erased from memory to prevent a hacker from obtaining it illegally. This is where the fun begins. With the private key, the client creates an authenticator. This credential contains information identifying the user's complete name, the workstation's address, and a validity period (the duration of time the authenticator is valid). In addition, there are other undocumented values that make up the authenticator.

The client then creates an encryption called a *signature* using the authenticator and private key. The private key is then removed from memory while the authenticator and signature remain in workstation RAM throughout the login session. The signature is used for background authentication and validates all packets sent during this session.

Finally, the client requests authentication using a proof. The proof is constructed from the signature, the request for authentication, and a random-generated number. It is further encrypted by the user's private key. The proof is sent across the WAN instead of the signature to prevent anyone from illegally obtaining the valuable signature. An internal client random-number generator ensures that each message sent from this workstation includes a different proof. The proof also assures NetWare 5 that the message has not been modified. This is the goal of background authentication and NCP packet signing.

Step Four: The User Is Authenticated

During the final step, authentication services validates the proof as an authentic construct of the authenticator, the private key, and the message (request for authentication). Once the proof has been validated, the user is granted conditional access to the NDS Cloud. Permanent access is granted once you successfully pass Layer Two of the NetWare 5 security model — login restrictions.

Table 5.1 summarizes the key concepts in initial authentication. Here's a madcap recap: Admin logs in by providing his or her complete name. The client (RSA.NLM) requests authentication from the server (Authentication Services). The server returns an encrypted private key. Admin enters a valid password and the private key is decrypted. The client then creates an authenticator with the private key, which includes Admin's complete name, the workstation address, a validity period, and other undocumented values. Next, the client creates a signature by encrypting the authenticator with the private key. Finally, a proof is constructed from the signature, private key, and a random number for traveling over the WAN. The proof is sent to Authentication Services, which validate it and grant Admin access to the NDS Cloud. All of this magic occurs in less than a second. Wow!

TABLE 5.1 *Understanding NetWare 5 Authentication*	AUTHENTICATION ELEMENT	DESCRIPTION
	Client	Participates in initial authentication on behalf of the user. Controlled by a special RSA NLM.
	Authentication Services	Participates in initial authentication on behalf of the server. Consists of features built into the core NetWare 5 OS.
	Username	Initiates initial authentication through login request. Also is used by the server in combination with the user password to create an encrypted private key.
	Encrypted Private Key	A specific key for each user, which can be decrypted only with the valid password.
	RSA Public Key	Used by Authentication Services to validate user information.
	Password	Entered by the user to decrypt the private key. Once this occurs, the password is removed from workstation RAM for security purposes.
	Authenticator	A special credential created by the client with user- and session-specific information including the user's complete name, the workstation address, a validity period, and other undocumented values.

TABLE 5.1	AUTHENTICATION ELEMENT	DESCRIPTION
Understanding NetWare 5 Authentication (continued)	Signature	A background authentication credential created by a combination of the authenticator and encrypted private key. The signature is used to validate all packets sent during this session. It is also the foundation of the proof.
	Proof	A temporary encryption created for traveling over the WAN. It is constructed from the signature, a message, the user's private key, and a randomly generated number. The random-number generator ensures that each message contains a unique proof.

Once you have been initially authenticated, the second phase begins — background authentication. In this phase, the signature and proof are used to continually authenticate all packets during the current session. Let's take a closer look.

Background Authentication

Welcome to the second phase of NetWare 5 incognito. Background authentication and NCP packet signing are designed to protect the WAN from experienced hackers who forge data packets or pose as unauthenticated clients.

In earlier versions of NetWare, hackers could use protocol analyzers to capture server requests and forge their own instructions. For example, I could request something simple like "log in as Guest," then capture the packet and add something harmful like, "While you're at it, please make me Supervisor Equivalent." This is a bad thing. NCP packet signing solved this problem by requiring a unique signature on all messages. The signature is represented as a unique proof, which is the combination of the workstation signature and a random number. If a message doesn't have the correct proof attached, it is discarded. When this occurs, an error message is sent to the error log, the affected workstation, and the server console. The alert message contains the login name and the station address of the invalid client.

NCP packet signing occurs at both the workstation and the server. NetWare 5 contains a default level of packet signing — the client signs only if the server requests it and the server signs only if the client requests it. Therefore, signing doesn't occur. You can customize NCP packet signing by using the SET server console command and Novell Client configuration parameters.

In both cases, the packet-signing level ranges from zero to three: 0 deactivates NCP packet signing and 3 creates the highest level of protection available. Table 5.2 shows some common client-server combinations (this is not an exhaustive list). Notice what happens when either the client or server uses packet signing levels of 0 and 3. This can cause havoc on the WAN. Consider activating minimal packet signing—client (1) and server (2).

TABLE 5.2 *Understanding NCP Packet Signing Options*	CLIENT LEVEL	SERVER LEVEL	DESCRIPTION
	0	3	The client does not sign packets and the server requires it; therefore, the workstation cannot log into this server.
	3	0	Packet signing is required by the workstation, but the server does not support it. Workstations with this level will not communicate with unsigning servers because they consider them to be unsecure.
	1	1	This is the default. The client signs only if the server requests it, and the server signs if the client requests it. Therefore, signing doesn't occur.
	1	2	Client signs only if the server requests it and the server does request packet signing. This is the minimal setting for activating background authentication and packet signing.
	3	3	Client always signs and requires server to sign. Server always signs and requires clients to sign. Therefore, everyone signs and all is well. This is the maximum level of packet signature protection.

Finally, packet signing does have a cost. This background protection scheme causes a slight decrease in server performance because of the overhead involved. Not only is the header of each packet marginally larger, but the workstations perform additional processing for each packet transmitted. The server must also perform processing to validate each signed packet. That's OK; your security is worth it.

You've been authenticated. How does it feel? Isn't it nice to know that your life has a purpose? We all need a little validation. But we're not finished yet. Remember, we just have conditional access to the WAN. To become a permanent resident of the NDS Cloud, we must successfully pass through the second layer of the NetWare 5 security model — login restrictions. Login restrictions offer much more administrative flexibility because you can limit users according to a large number of criteria including time of day, workstation, intruder detection, and so on. Let's get restricted.

REAL WORLD

NCP packet signing and background authentication became necessary because of the overzealous activities of a group of students at Lieden University in the Netherlands. These mischievous students are considered "the Netherlands hackers." This means they expose security loopholes as a means of plugging them. A few years ago, they discovered a simple piggyback intrusion mechanism for NetWare 2.2 and 3.11 servers. The NCP packet signing feature was implemented in NetWare 3.12 and all future versions as a way of slamming this backdoor. Way to go, team.

Layer Two — Login Restrictions

Login restrictions further scrutinize WAN access by matching the login name with a variety of NDS qualifications:

- ► Is this user authorized to log in on this date?

- ► Is this user authorized to log in during this time period?

- ► Is this user authorized to log in from this workstation?

- ► Will this user ever get the password right?

> ▸ What is the meaning of life?

The first layer of NetWare 5 security (login authentication) restricts invalid users. Login restrictions, on the other hand, restrict valid users. If you look at the page tabs along the right side of Figure 5.4, you'll notice that several obvious account restrictions, such as Login Restrictions, Password Restrictions, Time Restrictions, Network Address Restrictions, and Account Balance restrictions. In addition, NetWare 5 supports a password-tracking feature called Intruder Detection/Lockout. This security feature can be configured to track unauthorized login attempts and automatically lock an account when the number of unsuccessful attempts exceeds the maximum allowed. If an account is locked by this feature, the user has two choices: wait until the Intruder Lockout Reset Interval has occurred or have an administrator unlock the account.

FIGURE 5.4

Account restrictions for Maid Marion

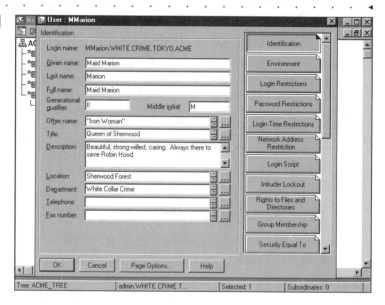

In summary, NetWare 5 account restrictions fall into six different categories:

- ▸ Login Restrictions

- ▸ Password Restrictions

- ▸ Time Restrictions

► Station Restrictions (Network Address Restrictions)

► Account Balance Restrictions

► Intruder Detection/Lockout

As with most types of account restrictions, *login restrictions* are set for each user. Maid Marion, for example, can have her account disabled by the network administrator, her account access automatically expire at a predetermined date/time, or have a limit placed on the number of concurrent connections she is allowed to have.

Password restrictions impact login authentication. On this screen, we can define a variety of Maid Marion's password settings, including requiring her to have a password, requiring a minimum password length, allowing her to change her password, forcing periodic password changes, requiring a unique password, and limiting grace logins. Remember, the password is used by the client to decrypt the authentication private key.

The next option is *time restrictions*. These limitations determine when a user can be connected to the NDS tree. Time restrictions are not login restrictions per se — but rather, connection restrictions. This means users cannot log in or be connected to the tree during prohibited time periods.

Similarly, *station restrictions* do not allow users to log in or attach from unauthorized workstations. NetWare Administrator calls these *network address restrictions* because they allow you to limit user access to a specific protocol, LAN address, or node ID.

In addition, NetWare 5 includes an Accounting feature that allows you to manage *Account Balance Restrictions* for user access to network resources. Users are charged for a variety of NetWare 5 activities, including connection time, processor utilization, and disk space usage.

Finally, there's *Intruder Detection/Lockout*. Unlike the other types of account restrictions, Intruder Detection/Lockout is a global feature that is activated at the container level. Options that can be set include:

► Whether to track unsuccessful login attempts

▶ The maximum number of unsuccessful login attempts allowed before intruder detection is activated

▶ The time span during which unsuccessful login attempts must occur to count toward the limit

▶ Whether the user account should be locked if the maximum number of unsuccessful login attempts is reached

▶ The amount of time an account remains locked due to intruder detection

Although the parameters for tracking intruder attempts are set at the container level, the results of such tracking are recorded with each User object, including Incorrect Login Count, Account Reset Time, and Last Intruder Address. If, for example, the Incorrect Login Attempts parameter in the WHITE container is set to three, and Maid Marion attempts to log in with the incorrect password four times in a row, intruder detection will be activated. If the Lock Account After Detection parameter has been set in the WHITE container, her account will be locked as well. Once her account has been locked, she has two options — wait until the Intruder Lockout Reset Interval has occurred, or have an administrator unlock her account. This feature allows you to sleep better at night, knowing that NetWare 5 is doing all it can to keep intruders out of your WAN.

As we said earlier, all of these account restrictions (except Intruder Detection/ Lockout) are activated at the user level. This means you have to set them for each individual user — too much work. Fortunately, NetWare 5 includes a Template object for global configurations. If, for example, you'd like to set a minimum password length for all users in the WHITE container, you could create a Template object with the correct settings. Then, all User objects associated with WHITE-UT would dynamically inherit those settings. Figure 5.5 shows the WHITE-UT Template in the WHITE container. Notice all the page buttons listed on the right-hand side. I'm a big believer in the theory, "Less work and more play makes life worth living." And the Template object is right up my alley. Use it or lose it.

Now let's take a much closer look at each of the five NetWare 5 login restrictions, starting with login restrictions.

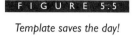

F I G U R E 5.5

Template saves the day!

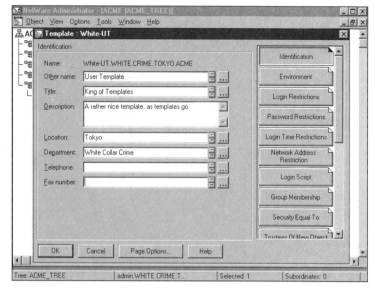

Login Restrictions

NetWare 5 login restrictions provide a method for controlling and restricting user access to the NDS tree. They can be found on the Login Restrictions page in NetWare Administrator (see Figure 5.6). As you can see, there are three main options:

▶ Account Disabled

▶ Account Has Expiration Date

▶ Limit Concurrent Connections

There is also a Last Login field that lists the last date/time this user logged into the tree.

▶ · ◀

F I G U R E   5.6

Login restrictions in
NetWare Administrator

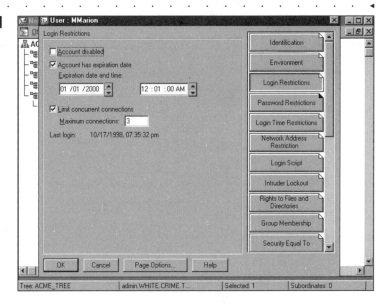

Account Disabled

This option is self-explanatory. The account is either disabled or not. This option is not related to the Intruder Detection/Lockout feature. It is possible, for example, for an account to be locked but not disabled. In both cases, however, the effect is the same—the user can't log in. To disable an account, you have two choices:

▶ *Manually*—By marking the Account Disabled checkbox.

▶ *Automatically*—By marking the Account Has Expiration Date checkbox and supplying a date and time in the Expiration Date and Time section. Also, the user account will become disabled whenever Grace Login rules are broken.

Account Has Expiration Date

This option is a useful tool for temporary employees or students in an academic environment. It allows you to automatically lock an account as of a specific date/time. The way this feature works is that the account expires automatically the first time the user logs in after the specified date/time. This checkbox is unmarked by default. In Figure 5.6, you'll notice that Maid Marion's account is set to expire just after midnight on January 1, 2000.

Limit Concurrent Connections

Let's face it, users are nomadic. They like to migrate throughout the WAN and log in from multiple workstations. As you can see in Figure 5.6, you can limit the number of workstations a user can be logged into at one time by marking the Limit Concurrent Connections checkbox and typing a value in the Maximum Connections field. An ideal setting might be three concurrent connections. This means that Maid Marion can only log in from three workstations simultaneously. That's probably plenty. You can enhance the effects of this restriction by combining it with one or more station restrictions.

Last Login

The Last Login parameter allows users to track activity on their login account. You should train users to periodically check this parameter for intruder logins. For example, if Maid Marion was gone for a week, but saw that the last login was three days ago, she would have reason to believe an intruder had used her account.

That does it for login restrictions. Now let's take a closer look at password restrictions.

Password Restrictions

The next set of login restrictions properties deal with passwords. As you can see in Figure 5.7, there are six main options:

▸ Allow User to Change Password

▶ Require a Password

▶ Force Periodic Password Changes

▶ Require Unique Passwords

▶ Limit Grace Logins

▶ Change Password

Password restrictions in
NetWare Administrator

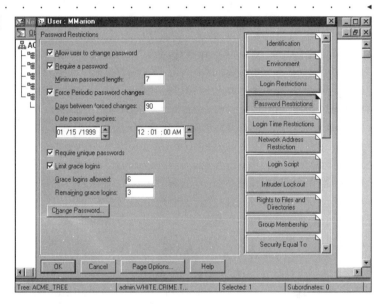

Password restrictions directly impact login authentication. As we saw in Figure 5.2, NetWare 5 access can be granted in one of two ways—by providing the correct password (if one is needed) or automatically (if no password is required). Although NetWare 5 does not require each User object to have a password, you should make it mandatory within your organization. Otherwise, authentication is crippled. Once you require a password, the question remains, "Who manages it?" If you place the burden of password management on the user, the other four password restriction parameters become important. Let's take a closer look

Allow User to Change Password

If you allow users to change their passwords, you're opening a can of worms. On the one hand, it shifts the burden of password management from you to them — this is a good thing. On the other hand, it allows them to mess around with an important authentication parameter — this is a bad thing. You'll probably find that most annoying user complaints deal with password management and printing. Well, one out of two isn't bad. If you don't allow users to change their passwords, all the work falls on you. It's your call. You'll need to balance security concerns versus practicality.

Require a Password

As we discussed earlier, by default, NetWare 5 does not require a password — which is bad. This should be the very first parameter that you change when creating user accounts. If you activate Require a Password and Force Periodic Password Changes, the system will ask for a password the first time users log in. Once you activate the Required Password parameter, it's a good idea to set a minimum password length to some number greater than five characters (the default). There are many password-hacking routines that can guess a five-character password in less than 20 minutes.

On the other hand, you want a password length that doesn't intimidate fragile users. Consider that most users can't easily remember strings in excess of seven to ten characters. The last thing you want to do is force large passwords — thereby causing users to write them down on a piece of paper and tape them to the front of their monitors. NetWare 5 supports minimum password lengths from 1 to 128 characters in length. It also supports most alphanumeric and ASCII characters.

One strategy to consider when creating passwords is to join two unrelated words with a punctuation mark such as:

- DOOR!GROUND

- SHOE;QUARK

- LATCH_PURPLE

Don't forget that you can use one or more null characters (Alt+255) to deter hackers. It's even trickier when used in succession at the end of a password. I bet you can't tell there are seven successive null characters at the end of the second example.

Force Periodic Password Changes

Once a password has been required and a minimum password length of seven characters has been set, you should explore using the Force Periodic Password Changes restriction. This parameter forces users to change their passwords at periodic intervals. If you activate the option, NetWare 5 asks you to input the days between forced changes. The default is 40 days. This is a little short and can become a nuisance very quickly. Remember, users love to complain about password problems. A periodic password interval of 90 days seems to be optimal.

Password expiration seems to be a touchy topic for users and administrators alike. Administrators want the interval to be short for better security, and users want the interval to be long for less interference. Either way, someone has to track it.

As a matter of fact, you can train your users to check Password properties periodically by right-clicking on the NetWare Services icon (the red "N" in the system tray) and choosing User Administration/Novell Password Administration from the pull-down menu. This will tell them exactly when their password will expire. Once the password interval has expired, the user is required to change his or her password. This is where grace logins come in. We'll talk about them in just a moment.

Also, if you're going to impose the effort of forcing periodic password changes, do yourself a favor and make them unique. It doesn't make sense to have users change their passwords every 90 days if they're going to use the same one over and over again.

Require Unique Passwords

The Require Unique Passwords feature prevents a user from reusing previous passwords. NetWare 5 tracks only the last eight passwords for each user. Don't let your users learn this. Otherwise, they'll create sequential passwords such as FIFI1, FIFI2, FIFI3, and so on. In fact, I've seen users change their passwords eight times in succession so they can reuse the original one. To solve this problem, NetWare 5 requires at least 24 hours between password changes. Do yourself a favor and perpetuate the myth that NetWare 5 keeps track of all passwords forever.

REAL WORLD

Many times password expiration and grace logins cause unneeded friction between CNAs and users, especially when users abuse the privilege and CNAs ultimately have to change the passwords anyway. Consider making password expiration a big "event." In container login scripts, use the PASSWORD_EXPIRES login script identifier variable to count down the number of days until password expiration (see Chapter 3). Then when the day arrives, throw a party, bring in balloons and cake, and have everyone change their passwords at once. Turning this event into a party makes password transition every 90 days fun and unobtrusive. It's also a great excuse to have four parties a year.

Limit Grace Logins

As we discussed earlier, if you force periodic password changes, users have to change their passwords when the periodic password interval has expired. When this occurs, NetWare 5 notifies the user that the password has expired, advises how many grace logins will be left (if you don't change it this time), and asks if they'd like to change it.

This provides users with an opportunity to change their passwords right away. If they don't, the system will lock their accounts. The problem with this message is the words "Would you like." It should say something like, "You better change your password now or your computer will explode." Unfortunately, this message is not configurable. This means that many users see it as a choice and decide to retain their existing passwords. This is where grace logins come in. Grace logins allows users to log in without changing their passwords. This is a temporary situation, because even grace logins expire.

As you can see in Figure 5.7 earlier, we've given Maid Marion six grace logins. This means she can log in six times without changing her password when it expires. If she does so a seventh time, however, her account will be locked. Once again, encourage your users not to rely on grace logins. If you need to change a user's password, you'll find that there's a convenient Change Password button on the Password Restrictions page in NetWare Administrator. Users can also change their password using the SETPASS command at the DOS prompt.

That completes our discussion of password restrictions. Aren't they fun? As you can see, there's much more to NetWare 5 passwords than meets the eye. Remember, this is the foundation of our login authentication strategy. Don't underestimate the importance of passwords. Use them — or suffer the consequences.

Time Restrictions

The next two account restrictions deal with when and where you get to log in. Time restrictions determine *When*.

How many of you have suffered from the curious custodial syndrome (CCS)? Let's see a show of hands. Ah, just as I thought — almost all of you. CCS is a problem that afflicts many of today's modern businesses. It's caused by the simple fact that the network stays up 24 hours a day and you don't. Since nighttime janitors often have access to your equipment, they can easily hack into your networks. One simple solution is to set time restrictions. In other words, restrict network after 9:00 at night and before 6:00 in the morning (see Figure 5.8).

F I G U R E   5.8

Time restrictions in NetWare Administrator

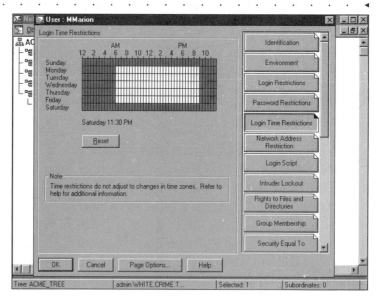

Each square in Figure 5.8 represents a 30-minute interval. The shaded area represents inactive time periods. The white area shows that users can log in any time between 6:00 a.m. and 9:00 p.m. Time restrictions go beyond login restrictions and become connection restrictions. Not only can they not log in — they can't even be connected. If a user fails to heed a time restriction warning, the user connection will be cleared without saving any open files. This is a very serious problem. Clearing Maid Marion's connection could result in hardware failure, data corruption, or data loss. Make sure users understand that when they receive such a message, they need to immediately save their work and log out.

Here are some common time restriction strategies:

▶ *Restrict After Hours* — ACME doesn't expect employees to work between the hours of 9:00 p.m. and 6:00 a.m. This is to avoid burnout. Setting a time restriction during this period helps protect the network against curious custodians.

▶ *Restrict Weekends* — ACME restricts most employees from accessing the network on weekends. Remember, all work and no play . . . .

▶ *Activate Backup Periods* — One down side of time restrictions is that they don't allow a window of opportunity for performing backups. If you're backing up the system late at night, you'll have to activate a backup time window. Test your backup to determine how long it takes and give the system a large enough window — let's say from 11:00 p.m. till 1:00 a.m. for the account involved. Check the documentation that is included with your backup software for additional guidelines for handling this potential security problem.

▶ *Restrict Specific Users* — Remember, time restrictions are set for each User object. If temporary or part-time workers, for example, work only on Tuesdays and Thursdays, consider deactivating their accounts on other days.

Don't go crazy with time restrictions. Intelligent time restrictions increase network security, but careless time restrictions can significantly hinder user productivity. (It also causes angry users to call you in the middle of the night when they're trying to meet a contract deadline.) In other words, you want to give users time to work, but not leave the network susceptible to CCS.

Station Restrictions

Station restrictions are the other half of the when/where dynamic duo. They deal with where. Now that we've solved our CCS problem, another one pops up — Nomadic User Syndrome (NUS), which hinders network security for a variety of reasons. First, nomadic users take up multiple network connections and block access for other users. Secondly, NUS implies that users are often logging in from workstations other than their own. And, finally, NUS impairs your ability to limit intruders from accessing physical workstations.

Station restrictions help solve NUS. They allow you to virtually chain users to specific machines. Instead of restricting them with passwords, disk restrictions, or time slots, you physically restricting the workstation(s) from which they can log in. As you can see in Figure 5.9, NetWare 5 station restrictions go a few steps farther:

- ▶ Protocol Restrictions

- ▶ Network Address Restrictions

- ▶ Node Restrictions

▶ · ◀

FIGURE 5.9

*Getting to know station
restrictions*

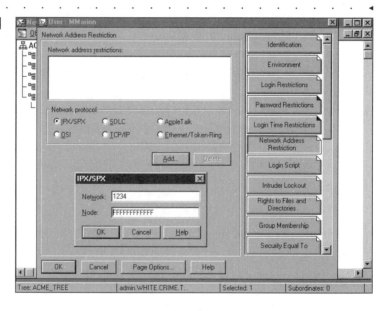

First pick a protocol. The default is IPX/SPX. Other options include OSI, SDLC, TCP/IP, AppleTalk, and Ethernet/Token Ring. Each protocol treats network address restrictions differently. The IPX/SPX address format consists of an 8-digit external network address and 12-digit hexadecimal node ID. The network address identifies an external LAN segment, while the node ID identifies a specific workstation. Maid Marion, for example, is restricted to any workstation (FFFFFFFFFFFF) on the 1234 network segment. We could further refine her restriction by listing one or more physical node IDs on the 1234 segment.

The TCP/IP address format expresses logical and physical IDs in the traditional dotted-decimal notation. In this case, you can also restrict all workstations on a logical network or a specific physical machine. Finally, the Ethernet/Token Ring address format uses a SAP address, block ID, and PU ID (physical unit). Once again, these values specify all stations on a LAN segment or a specific workstation.

Unfortunately, NetWare Administrator doesn't dynamically interrogate the LAN to determine addresses for you. You must use other NetWare 5 or third-party utilities to gain network and node ID information. As a word of warning, don't go hog wild with station restrictions. Use it only if you suffer from NUS. Like other login restrictions, if it's abused or mishandled, station restrictions can significantly impede user productivity. What happens, for example, when Maid Marion travels to another location? Or, what if we restrict her to one workstation and the machine goes down? These are all important considerations. Although station restrictions are a useful security tool, they can also be detrimental to user relationships.

Account Balance Restrictions

NetWare 5 includes an Accounting feature that can be turned on in NetWare Administrator by right-clicking a Server object, choosing Details, then choosing Accounting. If you haven't created users yet, you can set up Accounting balances and limits using a Template object. If you've already created your users, you can set up Accounting balances and limits using the Accounting Balance tab for each User object in NetWare Administrator. If you click on the Accounting Balance tab, you'll notice that you can set:

▶ *Account Balance* — This field specifies the amount of credit granted to a user for purchasing network services, such as connection time. This is a dynamic value. As the user utilizes network services, this value is reduced.

▶ *Allow Unlimited Credit* — If this checkbox is marked, it prevents a credit balance from being imposed on the user.

▶ *Low Balance Limit* — This field specifies the minimum account balance that must be maintained for the user to access the network. If the user's Account Balance value falls below this value, the user will be automatically logged out of the server within 30 minutes.

This completes our discussion of what, when, and where. Now only one question remains: "Who?"

Intruder Detection/Lockout

Welcome to Whoville. This is not so much a restriction as it is a security tracking feature. Intruder Detection/Lockout tracks invalid login attempts by monitoring users who try to log in without correct passwords. As you recall from Figure 5.2, this feature increments every time a valid user provides an incorrect password. It also leads directly to Access Denied! Once Intruder Detection has reached a threshold number of attempts, the account is locked completely.

There's one very important thing you need to know about this final login restriction — it's a container-based configuration. All the previous restrictions have been user-based. As you can see in Figure 5.10, intruder detection is activated at the Organization or Organizational Unit level. Once an account has been locked, it must be reactivated at the user level. There are two main configuration elements:

▶ Intruder Detection Limits

▶ Lock Account after Detection

Once Intruder Detection/Lockout has been activated at the container level, all users in that container are tracked. Let's take a closer look.

F I G U R E   5.10

Intruder Detection for the WHITE container

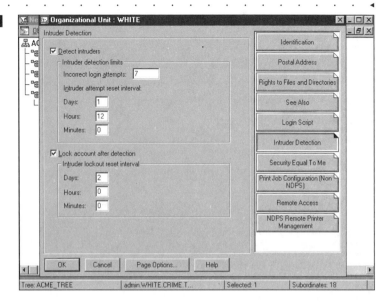

Intruder Detection Limits

Intruder Detection is turned off by default. To activate it, you simply click the Detect Intruders checkbox. Once you activate Intruder Detection, it begins tracking incorrect login attempts. This parameter is set to seven by default. As soon as the incrementing number exceeds the threshold, account lockout occurs (if this feature has been specified). Finally, the Intruder Attempt Reset Interval is a window of opportunity, so to speak. The system uses it to increment the incorrect login attempts. It is set to 30 minutes by default.

Here's how it works. Assume the Incorrect Login Attempts parameter is set to 7 and Intruder Attempt Reset Interval is set to 1 day, 12 hours (see Figure 5.10). The system will track all incorrect login activity and lock the user account if the number of incorrect login attempts exceeds 7 in the 36-hour window. Pretty simple, huh? Now let's take a look at what happens once Intruder Detection is activated.

Lock Account After Detection

This is the second half of Intruder Detection/Lockout. After all, the feature wouldn't be much good if you didn't punish the intruder for entering the wrong password. When you activate the Lock Account After Detection parameter, NetWare 5 asks for an Intruder Lockout Reset Interval. By default, this value is set to 15 minutes. Doesn't make much sense, does it? This invites the hacker to come back 15 minutes later and try all over again. Typically, a value equal to or exceeding the Intruder Attempt Reset Interval is adequate. As you can see in Figure 5.10, we're locking the account for two days, giving you enough time to track down the intruder.

So, what happens to the user when the account is locked? As you can see in Figure 5.11, NetWare 5 tracks account lockout at the user level. The Intruder Lockout screen provides three important pieces of information:

> *Incorrect Login Count* — A dynamic parameter that tells the user how many incorrect login attempts have been detected during this reset interval. If the account is locked, the incorrect login count should equal the lockout threshold.

> *Account Reset Time* — Informs the user how much time is remaining before the account is unlocked automatically.

> *Last Intruder Address* — Shows the network and node address of the workstation that attempted the last incorrect login. This parameter provides you with valuable information, regardless of whether the account is locked. This is pretty undeniable evidence that someone tried to hack this account from a specific workstation. You don't have to worry about disputed evidence or planted gloves.

So, who's going to unlock Maid Marion's account? You! Only Admin or distributed administrators can unlock accounts that have been locked by the Intruder Detection feature (in other words, someone with the Supervisor right to the User object). But what about Admin? After all, Admin is the most commonly hacked account — with good reason. If you don't have an Admin-like user to unlock the Admin account, consider using the ENABLE LOGIN command at the file server console. It's always nice to have a back door.

There you have it. This completes our discussion of Intruder Detection/Lockout and login restrictions in general.

Intruder Lockout for
MMarion

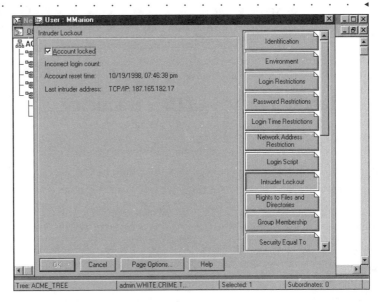

Congratulations, you are in! You've successfully navigated the first two layers of the NetWare 5 security model—login/password authentication and login restrictions.

In login/password authentication, we discussed the first two phases of WAN access—initial authentication and background authentication/packet signing. Initial authentication is a sophisticated four-step process that develops a user-specific, session-specific signature and proof. This signature is then used by background authentication and packet signing to validate incoming workstation packets. Once you've been authenticated, NetWare 5 grants you conditional access to the WAN. Permanent access relies on login restrictions.

Login restrictions are the second layer of the NetWare 5 security model. They define what, when, where, and who gets access to the system. "What" is account and password restrictions, "when" is time restrictions, "where" is station restrictions, and "who" is Intruder Detection/Lockout.

NetWare 5 has never been more secure. And we haven't even accessed any resources yet. The first two layers get us in, but what we can do inside the "Cloud" relies on NDS and file system security. How secure do you feel now?

For some great hands-on experience with NetWare 5 Login Restrictions, check out Lab Exercise 5.3 at the end of the chapter.

TIP

Layer Three — NDS Security

Welcome to the "Cloud"!

The NDS park is a great place to hang out. It has trees, swings for the kiddies, a bike trail, and external entities. Feel free to look around. Browse all day if you'd like. But don't touch anything. You haven't been secured yet.

Access to the tree is one thing; being able to do anything there is another. Until you've been granted sufficient NDS access rights, all the pretty objects are useless to you. No trees, no swings, no bike paths. Once you enter the NDS park, your ability to access leaf and container objects is determined by a sophisticated NDS security structure. At the heart of NDS security is the ACL, which is a property of every NDS object. It defines who can access the object (trustees) and what each trustee can do with it (access rights).

This strategy poses two important questions:

▸ What rights do I need to do stuff?

▸ How do I get these rights?

These are good questions. Fortunately, I have some simple answers. First, NDS supports two types of access rights — object and property. Object rights define an object's trustees and control what they can do with the object. Property rights, on the other hand, further refine NDS security by limiting access to only specific properties of the object. Fortunately, these rights are fairly self-explanatory. Browse, for instance, allows you to see an object. Hmmmm, no "brain drain" there.

So, that leaves us with an answer to the second question: "How do I get these rights?" It's a simple three-step process:

▸ *Step One: Assigning Trustee Rights* — Someone gives you specific rights to specific objects through trustee assignments, inheritance, and/or security equivalence.

▸ *Step Two: Filtering IRF Rights* — Someone else can filter certain rights if they want to.

▸ *Step Three: Calculating Effective Rights* — The result is effective rights, which define what you can actually do to the object.

As easy as 1-2-3. And you thought NDS security was going to be hard — nope. It can get weird, though. As I'm sure you can imagine, the potential combination of object/property rights can be staggering — almost infinite. So, you're going to want to try to keep it under control. In this section, we'll talk about default NDS rights and how you can use the simple three-step method for limiting potential loopholes. Finally, we'll talk about NDS administration and explore Admin, distributed administrators, and "special" cases. So, without any further ado, let's get on with the show — starting with NDS access rights.

Understanding NDS Access Rights

Access to NDS objects is controlled by 12 different NDS access rights — sounds reasonable. These 12 rights are organized into two functional groups:

▸ Object rights

▸ Property rights

Let's use the famous "box analogy" to understand the difference between these two different sets of NDS access rights. Think of an NDS object as a box. Like any other three-dimensional rectangloid, the box has external characteristics. You can look at the box and describe its color, size, and shape. By describing the outside of the box, you have a good idea of the type of box it is. But you don't know anything else about it, especially what's inside the box. With object rights, you can look at the box, destroy the box, relabel the box, or create a new one. But you can't get specific information about what's inside the box — that requires property rights.

The contents of the box are similar to what's inside an NDS object — in other words, properties. In most cases, the contents of different boxes will vary. One box may contain caviar, while another contains video games. To see what's inside the box, you need permission to open it and look inside. With the proper rights, you can compare properties in this box with properties in other boxes, you can read the packing list, or you can change the contents of the box altogether. It all depends on which property rights you have.

If you're feeling a little boxed in, that's okay. We'll try to take it slow. But before we can move on to the three-step NDS security model, we must explore each of these 12 rights in depth. You'll need to have a firm understanding of default NDS rights before you start changing things around. The default rights in NetWare 5 are very sophisticated. In many cases, they're good enough. Let's start with a closer look at object and property rights.

Object Rights

Object rights control what a trustee can do with any object. As you can see in Figure 5.12, the object rights spell a company name — BCDRSI (that is, B.C. Doctors, Inc.). So, what do NDS object rights have to do with dinosaurs? Absolutely nothing, but it's an easy way to remember these rights. Just visualize *Jurassic Park* and all the sick dinosaurs. What would they do without dinosaur doctors?

FIGURE 5.12

A Jurassic set of object rights

Object Rights

B	Browse
C	Create
D	Delete
R	Rename
S	Supervisor
I	Inheritable

Following is a description of the six object rights and their functions:

- ▶ *Browse* — Grants the right to see objects in the Directory tree. With this right, you can see the outside of the box.

- ▶ *Create* — Grants the right to create new objects within this container. Obviously, the Create right is only available for container objects. With this right, you can create a new box.

▶ *Delete* — Grants the right to delete the object from the NDS tree. With this right, you can throw away the box.

▶ *Rename* — Grants the right to change the name of the object, in effect changing the Object Name property. This is the only object right that has any impact on properties, except Supervisor. With this right, you can relabel the box.

▶ *Supervisor* — Grants all access privileges. Anyone with Supervisor rights to an object also has access to all its properties. In the NDS tree, the Supervisor right can be blocked with the Inherited Rights Filter (IRF). In effect, anyone with Supervisor rights owns the box.

▶ *Inheritable* — Activates NDS container "inheritance." As we'll learn in just a moment, inheritance allows CNEs to assign sweeping sets of object and All Properties rights to a large number of objects. This is accomplished by assigning rights to a given container and activating the Inheritable right ("I"). With "I", all objects in the home container and all subcontainers will inherit the rights. It's important to note that this right is granted by default for object rights and All Properties rights, and that "I" can only be assigned to container objects.

TIP

Later, in Step One of the **NDS** security model, we're going to learn about a concept called *inheritance*. Inheritance is based on the fact that object and property rights flow down the **NDS** tree from container to container, and from a container to leaf objects within the container. They do not, however, flow from a leaf object to any other object. It's a fairly simple concept, but there's one exception you need to be aware of. By default, object rights and **All Properties** rights are inherited, but **Selected Properties** rights are not. This means that rights you assign to selected properties apply to the specific object only and do not flow down the tree, unless, of course, the Inheritable property right is explicitly granted. Keep this in the back of your mind when we get to inheritance later on.

Except for a few minor exceptions, object rights have no impact on properties. Remember, we're dealing with the outside of the box at this point. If you want to have control over the contents of the box, you'll need to be granted property rights.

Property Rights

Property rights control access to the information stored within an NDS object. They allow users to see, search for, and change the contents of the box. At a minimum, you must be a trustee of an object in order to be granted rights to its properties. As you can see in Figure 5.13, the property rights almost spell a word — SCRAW(L)I(NG). To cure the dinosaur, you'll have to write a pretty big prescription. This involves that unique medical skill known as SCRAWlIng. (Wait 'til you see my signature at the end of Chapter 8.)

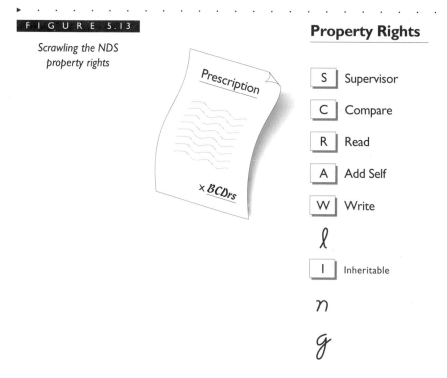

FIGURE 5.13

Scrawling the NDS property rights

Property Rights

S — Supervisor

C — Compare

R — Read

A — Add Self

W — Write

I — Inheritable

Here's a description of the six NetWare 5 NDS property rights:

▶ *Supervisor (S)* — Grants all rights to the property. In the NDS tree, the Supervisor right can be blocked by an object's Inherited Rights Filter (IRF).

▶ *Compare (C)* — Allows you to compare any given value to the value within the property. This is analogous to saying, "I'm not going to tell you what my phone number is, but I'll let you guess it." With the Compare right, an operation can return True or False, but will not give the value of the property. Compare is automatically granted when users are assigned the Read property right.

▶ *Read (R)* — Grants the right to see the value(s) of the property. This is better than Compare because it actually allows you to view the value(s).

▶ *Add Self (A)* — Allows you to add or remove yourself as a value of the object property. This right is only meaningful for properties that contain object names as values, such as group membership lists and mailing lists. This right is automatically granted with the Write right.

▶ *Write (W)* — Grants the right to add, change, or remove any values of the property. This is better than Add Self because it allows you to change any value, not just yourself.

▶ *(L)* — This is not a property right but is needed to spell a word.

▶ *Inheritable (I)* — Enables an object trustee of a container to inherit the assigned property rights to objects within a container. Without this right, the remaining property rights assigned to the trustee apply only the container object's properties and not to the properties of the objects in the container. This right is granted by default when the All Properties option is selected, and removed by default when the Selected Properties option is selected. This right is only available for container objects.

▶ *(N)* — This is not a property right but is needed to spell a word.

▶ *(G)* — This is not a property right but is needed to spell a word.

One of the most notable object/property exceptions involves the Supervisor [S] object right. Be careful. It gives the user Supervisor [S] property rights to All Properties.

TIP

Property rights can be assigned in one of two ways — via All Properties and/or Selected Properties. As you can see in Figure 5.14, NetWare Administrator provides two choices. The All Properties option assigns the rights you indicate to all properties of the object. A list of these properties is displayed in the Selected Properties window. If the All Properties radio button was marked along with the Read checkbox, for example, it would allow you to view the values of all the properties for the given object.

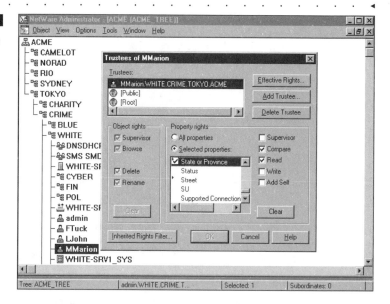

F I G U R E 5.14

Assigning selected property rights in NetWare Administrator

The Selected Properties option, on the other hand, allows you to fine-tune NDS security for specific properties. Simply mark the Selected Properties radio button, highlight one or more properties from the Selected Properties window, then mark the right(s) you want to assign. It's important to note that the list of properties available will be different for each type of object. For instance, you'll notice that a Group object has far fewer properties than a User object. Finally, granting rights to selected properties overwrites any rights granted through the All Properties option. This is very powerful, because it allows you to get very specific with certain properties even though a general assignment already exists.

TIP

Trustees of an NDS container can be granted the Inheritable property right. By default, the Inheritable property right is granted to an object trustee when container rights are assigned through the All Properties option. However, the Inheritable right must be manually assigned to an object trustee when container property rights are assigned through the Selected Properties option. If you then need to block the inheritance of selected property rights lower in the tree, you can create a new trustee assignment which revokes the Inheritable right.

Now that you understand the 12 different NDS access rights, it's time to start our three-step model. Here's a quick preview:

▶ *Step One:* Assign trustee rights

▶ *Step Two:* Filter IRF rights

▶ *Step Three:* Calculate effective rights

Let's get started.

Step One: Assign Trustee Rights

I keep talking about how simple the NDS security model is—easy as 1-2-3. Well, now I get a chance to prove it. A lot has been written about NDS security and most of it is intimidating. Granted, there are a lot of complexities involved, but if you approach it with an open mind, everything falls into place. So far, we've talked about object and property rights. Understanding these rights is a prerequisite to building an NDS security model. But it's certainly not enough. Now you have to learn how to implement these rights in the ACME NDS tree.

Step One deals with assigning these rights. In many cases, this is enough. You only need Steps Two and Three under special circumstances. NDS rights can be assigned in one of three ways:

▶ Trustee assignments

▶ Inheritance

▶ Security equivalence

Trustee assignments involve work — this is bad, of course, since our goal is to minimize the amount of work we do. But you have to start somewhere. Trustee assignments are granted using NetWare Administrator, FILER, and/or RIGHTS. Inheritance, on the other hand, doesn't involve work — this is good. Inheritance normally happens automatically when you assign trustee rights at the container level and include the Inheritable (I) right. Just like water flowing down a mountain, trustee rights flow down the NDS tree — from top to bottom. The beauty of this feature is that you can assign sweeping rights for large groups of users with a single trustee assignment.

Finally, security equivalence gives us the added flexibility we need in today's modern world. There are a variety of security equivalence strategies, including ancestral inheritance (AI), Organizational Roles, Groups, Directory Map objects, and so on. You'll learn that security equivalence is a way of augmenting the other two trustee assignment strategies. Let's take a closer look at Step One, starting with trustee assignments.

Trustee Assignments

You have to start somewhere and Step One starts with work. A trustee is any NDS object with rights to any other object. Trustees are tracked through the ACL (Access Control List) property. Every object has an ACL property, and the ACL lists the trustees of that object and the rights they have. NetWare 5 supports a variety of trustees, including:

User — A leaf object in the NDS tree. It represents a person with access to network resources. Individual users can be assigned specific NDS rights through the User trustee type.

Group — A leaf object with a membership list. The membership list includes users from anywhere in the NDS tree. This is a great option to use if NDS rights need to be assigned to users in different containers. Rights granted to a Group object are passed on to all members of the group.

Container — All container objects are considered "natural groups" and can be used to assign NDS rights to multiple trustees. If you make any container object a trustee of any other object, all users and subcontainers of the container inherit those same rights. The ultimate rights to all objects in the tree are granted using the [Root] object.

Organizational Role — A leaf object, similar to a groups, except that users are identified as occupants. This object is used to specify a particular role in the organization rather than just a group of users.

[Root] — When NetWare 5 is installed on the first server in your tree, the [Root] is created at the highest level of the tree. Since all users who successfully log into the tree are essentially equivalent to the [Root], assigning the [Root] as trustee of another object gives all users the same rights granted to the [Root]. This means that you need to be very careful when assigning rights to this trustee. Unlike the [Public] trustee, however, users must be authenticated to receive rights that have been granted to the [Root].

[Public] — A special system-owned trustee. Rights granted to [Public] are passed to every object connected to the network. This means users do not have to be logged in in order to inherit [Public] rights. Therefore, you need to be very careful when assigning rights to the [Public] trustee. Don't forget that when NetWare 5 is installed, [Public] is made a trustee of the [Root] and is assigned the Browse right to the [Root]. This means that anyone that is connected to the tree (whether or not they are logged in) can view every object in the tree!

Once you identify who is going to get the rights, you have to determine what rights you're going to give them and where the rights will be assigned. *What* consists of any of the twelve object and property rights — simple. *Where* can be any object in the NDS tree — also simple. Take Figure 5.15, for example. As you can see, Sherlock Holmes is granted all object rights to the .OU=TOKYO.O=ACME container. In the figure, we have satisfied all three of the trustee assignment elements — who, what, and where.

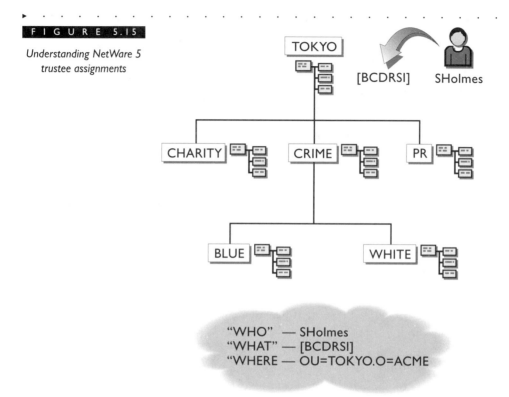

FIGURE 5.15

Understanding NetWare 5 trustee assignments

So, how is this accomplished in NetWare Administrator? It depends on your point of view. You have two choices:

▸ *Rights to Other Objects* — This is from Sherlock Holmes' point of view.

▸ *Trustees of this Object* — This is from OU=TOKYO's point of view.

It really doesn't matter which option you choose. You can either assign rights from the user's point of view or the object's point of view. In the first example, we assign security from Sherlock Holmes' point of view. In NetWare Administrator, highlight the SHolmes object and click the right mouse button. An abbreviated dialog box appears. As you can see in Figure 5.16, there are two security options. In this case, we're interested in "Rights to Other Objects".

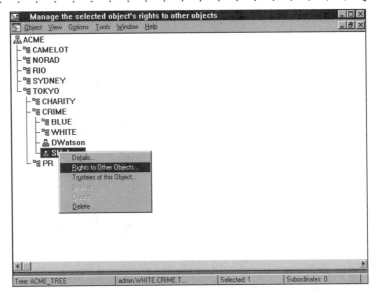

TIP

You can also make an object a trustee of another object in NetWare Administrator by dragging the object over another object. Naturally, any trustee rights indicated are not actually assigned until you click the **OK** button on the dialog box that appears.

The "Rights to Other Objects" dialog box is shown in Figure 5.17. This displays the NDS security window from Sherlock Holmes' point of view. As you can see, he has been granted all object rights to the TOKYO Organizational Unit. Specifically, the Supervisor object right implies the Supervisor property rights to All Properties. This was accomplished using the Add Assignment button.

The second option allows you to assign NDS rights from TOKYO's point of view. In this case, you would select OU=TOKYO.O=ACME from the Browse window and click using the right mouse button. The same abbreviated menu will appear (as shown earlier in Figure 5.16). This time, though, choose Trustees of This Object. Figure 5.18 shows the NDS security window from TOKYO's point of view. Notice the default trustee. In addition, SHolmes has been added with all object and property rights. This was accomplished using the Add Trustee button.

FIGURE 5.17

Assigning NDS rights from the user's point of view

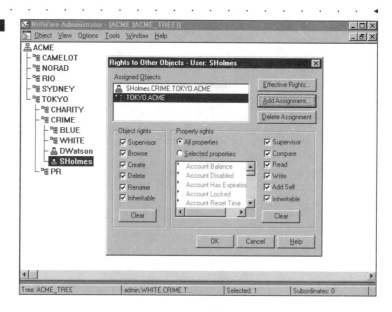

FIGURE 5.18

Assigning NDS rights from the object's point of view

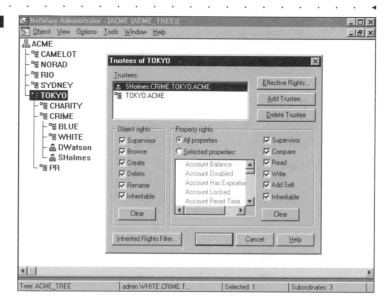

There you have it. As you can see, it doesn't matter how we assign trustee rights. Both methods accomplish the same thing—Sherlock Holmes (who) is granted [BCDRSI] object rights (*what*) to .OU=TOKYO.O=ACME (*where*). I told you trustee assignments would be simple. Now that we've explored the "work" part, let's take a closer look at inheritance — the "no work" part.

> **REAL WORLD**
>
> All of this fancy trustee assignment footwork is accomplished using a special NDS property called the Access Control List (ACL). It controls who can access objects and what they can do with them. Some important ACL objects include applications, printers, and users.

Inheritance

NDS rights can also be assigned through inheritance. This is an automatic side effect of trustee assignments. As you can see in Figure 5.19, Sherlock Holmes got a lot more than he bargained for. When you assigned him the [BCDRSI] object rights to .OU=TOKYO.O=ACME, he actually inherited these rights for all containers and objects underneath TOKYO as well. Now he has all object rights to all containers and all objects in that portion of the tree — this might not be a good thing.

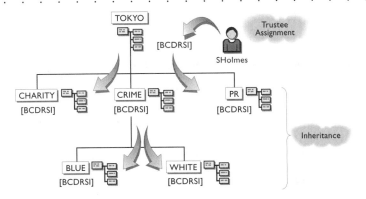

FIGURE 5.19

NDS inheritance for Sherlock Holmes

As you recall from our ACME overview in Chapter 1, Sherlock Holmes heads up the Crime Fighting division. He probably shouldn't have Supervisor object rights to Charity and PR. Fortunately, we can rectify the situation. NetWare 5 provides two methods for overriding inheritance:

▶ *New trustee assignment* — Trustee assignments override inherited rights for that trustee. For instance, if we assign SHolmes Browse [B   ] rights to CHARITY and PR, he would lose his inheritance for these containers. The new trustee assignment would become his effective rights and inheritance within these containers would reflect the changes. Creating a new trustee assignment is particularly useful for overwriting property rights granted with the All Properties option.

▶ *Inherited Rights Filter (IRF)* — The IRF is much more serious. It can be used to block the inheritance of object rights, All Properties rights, or Selected Property rights. A [B   ] IRF on CHARITY and PR, for instance, wouldn't allow anybody to inherit [CDRSI], including SHolmes. So, who manages these containers? What about SirKay and BThomas? Stay tuned for the answer.

Inheritance is a great thing. It allows you to assign sweeping NDS object rights with minimal effort. Remember, as a CNA, "work" is a bad word. As far as property rights go, only one type can be inherited. Remember, there are two ways of assigning property rights — All Properties or Selected Properties. By default, the rights assigned using the All Properties option are inherited. Rights assigned to Selected Properties are not (unless, of course, the Inheritable right is specifically granted). Combine this with what we learned about trustee assignments and we could have an effective strategy for property customization.

▶ · ◀

REAL WORLD

In addition to the two options listed here, you can stop NDS inheritance by simply removing the Inheritable (I) object right. NDS rights don't flow down the tree unless they are accompanied by the Inheritable (I) right. Without the Inheritable (I) right, assignments apply to the current container only.

Of course, this option wouldn't work for SHolmes, because we do want his rights to flow down the CRIME portion of the tree. Unfortunately, we can't selectively remove the Inheritable (I) right from CHARITY and PR without granting a new trustee assignment — option 1.

TIP **In previous version of NetWare, rights granted to selected properties could not be inherited. In NetWare 5, selected property rights can be inherited if the Inheritable (I) right is explicitly granted. (By default, the Inheritable right is not granted when the Selected Properties option is selected.)**

Here's an example:

Let's assume that Maid Marion is shy. She's a user in the .OU=WHITE. OU=CRIME.OU=TOKYO.O=ACME container. She doesn't want Sherlock Holmes to see any of her properties except Telephone and E-mail Address. This can be a problem since he inherits all rights from his [BCDRSI] assignment to the TOKYO container. Fortunately, as a CNA, you have a solution. You simply assign SHolmes the Read [R] property right to Maid Marion's Selected Properties — Telephone and E-mail Address. This trustee assignment overrides his inheritance through All Properties. Voilà, Maid Marion is safe (see Figure 5.20).

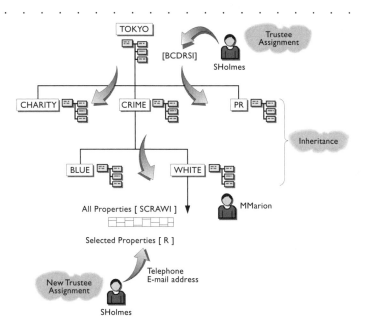

FIGURE 5.20

Protecting Maid Marion with a new trustee assignment

Trustee assignments and inheritance are the two main strategies of Step One. But special situations may arise when you need something more. This is where security equivalence comes in. Let's take a closer look.

▶ . . . . ◀

REAL WORLD

If you attempt to use NetWare Administrator to assign rights to specific properties, you'll notice that the utility automatically assigned deafult object and All Properties rights at the same time. Make sure you modify the default assignments to reflect the appropriate rights.

Security Equivalence

If trustee assignments or inheritance aren't quite getting the job done, security equivalence may be the answer. Security equivalence simply states, "One object is equivalent to another with respect to NDS rights." Users, for example, are security equivalent to their parent container. Security equivalence is different from inheritance in that it operates at the trustee assignment level. Don't confuse the two. Security equivalence applies when an object is made equivalent to another object's explicit trustee assignments.

NetWare 5 provides five strategies for security equivalences:

▶ Ancestral Inheritance (AI)

▶ Organizational Role object

▶ Group object

▶ Directory Map object

▶ Other Leaf objects

Ancestral Inheritance (AI)   Ancestral inheritance (AI) is a very cool term. But, before you get too caught up in it, you should know a little secret — it doesn't really mean anything. AI simply implies that an object is security equivalent to its ancestor (parent container). This means any rights you assign to an NDS container are typically absorbed by all the objects in the container. This is not inheritance; this is security equivalence. Therefore, AI can get very strange. Earlier we learned that containers can be trustees and they're thought of as "natural groups." This is true. But, remember, any rights that you assign to a container are implicitly assigned to all objects within the container. For example, suppose we assigned OU=CRIME [BCDRSI] rights to TOKYO instead of SHolmes (see Figure 5.19 earlier). Now, both users in OU=CRIME—Sherlock Holmes and Dr. Watson—gain the same trustee assignments and inheritance shown in Figure 5.19 earlier. Pretty simple.

Well, that's not all. Not only do the objects in OU=CRIME absorb its trustee assignments, but all objects underneath CRIME as well! This means Maid Marion, Robin Hood, and all their friends would get the same trustee assignments as Sherlock Holmes and Dr. Watson. Wow. This concept is also called *implied security equivalence*. However tempting it is, avoid AI unless you know what you're doing.

Organizational Role (OR)   Organizational Roles are another type of security equivalence. These special NDS objects are designed as task identifiers. Jobs that require multiple temporary users are excellent candidates for Organizational Roles. Postmaster, for example, is a job that can be assigned to multiple users on a rotating basis. When a user is performing the Postmaster duties, he or she will need special NDS and file system rights. Let's say the White-Collar Crime Dept. has a Postmaster OR that changes occupants every three months. This person needs special NDS security to e-mail objects and the file system. Instead of continually moving trustee assignments around, you can define security once for the Organizational Role, then switch occupants. Let's say it's Little John's turn, for example. When you remove Maid Marion from the Postmaster OR and replace her with LJohn, he immediately absorbs the NDS security of that object. Suddenly, Little John has all the security he needs to perform Postmaster duties—an elegant solution. Later, we'll explore the Organizational Role as one solution for creating distributed administrators. For now, let's move on to the next security equivalence option—Groups.

REAL WORLD

AI allows you to make broad trustee assignments at high levels in the tree. For example, you could place a mail server at O=ACME and grant the container rights to it. Because of AI, all objects in the ACME organization will have immediate access to the mail server. This also applies to file system rights. You could place all the CRIME files on a single server in the OU=CRIME container, then assign appropriate file system rights to OU=CRIME. Because of AI, all users in the CRIME division would have immediate access to the central server.

Groups As we learned earlier, groups are another trustee type for assigning NDS rights. They allow you to distribute rights to users that are in different containers (or a subset of the users in a single container). First, create a Group object, then assign it rights, and finally, add members. This is similar to the Organizational Role object, in that it works using the security equivalence concept. Members of any group absorb (not inherit) rights assigned to the host Group object. Groups also differ from AI containers in that they don't involve "implied inheritance." Rights assigned to groups only apply to specific members of the group. And, as we all know, users can be easily removed from a group.

Directory Map Objects In very special circumstances, security equivalence can be used to facilitate Directory Map objects. These objects allow you to map directory paths to a centralized object instead of to a physical location. To accomplish this, you must first create a Directory Map object that points to a physical location in the file system, then create a logical drive pointer to the Directory Map object using the MAP command. There's one problem with this scenario: The drive mapping doesn't work until the user is assigned explicit or inherited file system rights to the physical directory. This involves a lot of planning, a lot of work, and some careful tracking. An easier solution would involve assigning the file system rights to the Directory Map object itself, then making each user a security equivalent of the NDS object. This makes security assignments much clearer.

In summary, when you create a Directory Map object, be sure to assign adequate file system rights to its physical directory. Then when you use the MAP command to create logical pointers, be sure to assign the host user security equivalence to the Directory Map object. Believe me, this will make drive mapping and security much easier to manage. Really!

REAL WORLD

Don't forget about NDS rights when dealing with Directory Map objects. If the Directory Map is outside your container, you'll need at least Read [R] property rights to the object's PATH property to access the host directory or application.

Other Leaf Objects   A user can be explicitly granted security equivalence to any other object (typically a User object). This gives the User object the same rights as the object it has been made security equivalent to. This strategy can be dangerous, and thus should only be used as a temporary measure.

There you have it—Step One. Don't get discouraged—this is the tricky part. Once you assign NDS rights, the rest more or less takes care of itself. In Step One, we learned there are three different ways of assigning rights to NDS trustees—trustee assignments, inheritance, and security equivalence. We also learned there are a variety of different trustee types as well as the concept of ancestral inheritance (implied security equivalence). The good news is, most of your work stops here. Only in special cases will you need to go on to Steps Two and Three. Of course, you remember Murphy's Law Number 342—special cases will appear just when you least expect them. So, in honor of Murphy, and to decrease your stress level, let's take a quick look at Steps Two and Three.

Step Two: Filtering IRF Rights

Earlier we learned there are two ways of blocking unwanted inherited rights:

▸ New trustee assignments

▸ Inherited Rights Filter (IRF)

If you want to block rights for a particular user, create a new trustee assignment for that user at the level in the tree at which the rights should be restricted. If you want to block inheritance from virtually all users, modify the object's IRF.

As it turns out, there's a problem with Sherlock Holmes' inheritance. Since he's been assigned [BCDRSI] object rights to .OU=TOKYO.O=ACME, he becomes distributed administrator of that entire section of the tree—this is bad. Sherlock Holmes is responsible for the Crime Fighting division. He has no authority over CHARITY or PR. However, his inheritance model shows [BCDRSI] object rights to both OU=CHARITY and OU=PR (see Figure 5.19 earlier). We're obviously going to have to do something about this right away.

Welcome to planet IRF. NetWare 5 includes an Inherited Rights Filter that blocks inherited rights at any point in the tree. Right off the bat, you'll need to understand five very important points about how the IRF works:

▶ It's an inclusive filter, which means the rights that are in the filter are the ones that are allowed to pass through.

▶ An IRF can only block rights that have been inherited from trustee assignments higher in the tree — also known as the *Inherited* Rights Filter. As you recall from our earlier discussion, inheritance requires the Inheritable (I) object and/or property right. Therefore, IRFs only work on rights inherited in conjunction with (I).

▶ The IRF does not apply to trustee assignments themselves. In other words, if your User object is assigned rights to an object via a trustee assignment, that assignment would be unaffected by the object's IRF.

▶ An IRF applies to everyone in the tree. Once you've modified an object's IRF, everyone is affected, including Admin (unless, of course, they have an explicit trustee assignment to that object).

▶ IRFs are typically used to protected servers and block NDS administrative access from other system users. They can be dangerous if used improperly, and thus, great care should be taken if you choose to modify them.

TIP

The NDS Supervisor object right can be blocked by an IRF in the NDS tree. It cannot be blocked, however, by an IRF in the file system. If you attempt to block the Supervisor [S] right in the NDS tree with an IRF, NetWare Administrator will first require you to make an explicit Supervisor [S] trustee assignment to someone else (assuming, of course, that one does not already exist). This is so that access to that portion of the tree is not permanently blocked. Imagine how much fun it would be if the Supervisor object right was filtered for everybody. Does the term "reinstall" mean anything to you?

The IRF can be used to block inheritance of either object rights or property rights assigned through the All Properties option. Remember, Selected Properties aren't inherited (unless, of course, the Inheritable (I) right is explicitly granted). Figure 5.21 shows how the IRF can be used to solve our Sherlock Holmes problem. We create an inclusive IRF of [B   ] to block everything under CHARITY and PR except the Browse right. His inheritance in OU=CRIME, however, remains unaffected.

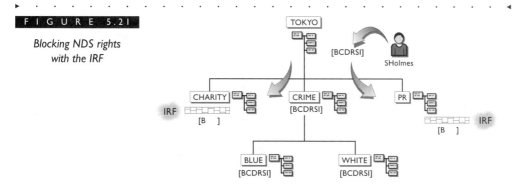

F I G U R E   5.21

*Blocking NDS rights
with the IRF*

So, how do we assign an IRF? Once again, NetWare Administrator is our friend. Earlier we learned that trustee assignments can be assigned in one of two ways — "Rights to Other Objects" and "Trustees of This Object." IRFs are accomplished using only one of these two choices. Can you figure out which one? Correct — it's "Trustees of This Object." Remember, IRFs are host-object specific. They work from the host's point of view and apply to every object in the NDS tree.

Figure 5.22 shows the IRF input screen for OU=PR. Notice the downward arrows that appear next to each option checkbox. These differentiate IRF rights from trustee assignments. Anywhere you see a downward arrow, you can assume it's an IRF. Also notice that the IRF window doesn't include the Inheritable (I) right. This is logical since the Inheritable right *allows* inheritance, not blocks it!

If the IRF applies to all objects in the tree, who is going to administer the OU=CHARITY and OU=PR containers? As you can see in Figure 5.22, no one can have the [CDRS] object rights. Fortunately, trustee assignments override the IRF. Remember, the "I" in IRF stands for *"Inherited."* It only works on inherited rights. Figure 5.23 introduces two new players — SirKay (the administrator of OU=CHARITY) and BThomas (the administrator of OU=PR). We will simply assign BThomas the [BCDRSI] object rights to OU=PR. Now he is the container administrator for this section of the tree and everyone else, including Sherlock Holmes and Admin, has been locked out. The same holds true for SirKay and OU=CHARITY.

NOVELL'S CNA STUDY GUIDE FOR NETWARE 5

F I G U R E 5.22

Filtering NDS rights in NetWare Administrator

F I G U R E 5.23

Covering the IRF with new trustee assignments

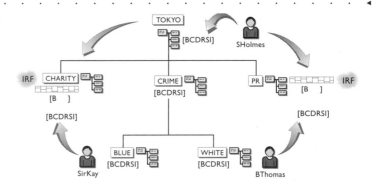

So, let me ask you — which activity occurs first? The IRF or the new trustee assignment? Correct . . . the new trustee assignment. Remember, NetWare Administrator will not allow us to set an IRF for OU=PR until someone else has explicitly been granted Supervisor privileges. So, first we assign BThomas [BCDRSI] privileges, then we set the IRF to [B   ].

Good work.

So, what's the bottom line? What can Sherlock Holmes really do in the TOKYO portion of the tree? "It's elementary, my dear Watson, elementary." More accurately, it's Step Three: Calculating Effective Rights.

Step Three: Calculating Effective Rights

Effective rights are the bottom line. This is the culmination of our three-step process. In Step One, we assign the rights. In Step Two, we filter the rights. In Step Three, we calculate exactly what the rights are.

Calculating effective rights is about as simple as modern math. Any object's effective rights are the combination of NDS privileges received through any of the following:

▸ Trustee assignments made to a User object

▸ Inheritance minus rights blocked by an IRF

▸ Rights granted to the [Root]

▸ Rights granted to the special [Public] trustee

▸ Security equivalences to parent containers, Groups, Organizational Roles, and so on.

TIP

Some of the NetWare utilities that display effective rights include NetWare Administrator, NDIR, and FILER.

I don't know if you've ever done modern math, but it's ugly. It would be easy if any of the assignments shown here canceled out the others. But, unfortunately, life isn't easy. These assignments work in combination with each other. Consider it modern math in the 7th Dimension.

Let's start with a simple example. Refer to Figure 5.24. In this first example, Sherlock Holmes gets a trustee assignment (TA) of [BCDRSI] to OU=CRIME. On the right side of the figure, we've created an effective rights calculation worksheet.

This is an *effective* (pun intended) tool for helping you get through modern math. You can create one at home with paper, a pencil, and a ruler.

▶ · ◀

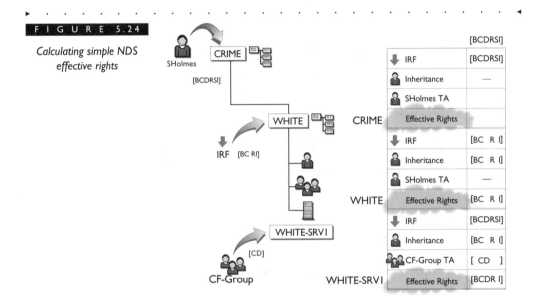

FIGURE 5.24

Calculating simple NDS effective rights

CRIME	
	[BCDRSI]
⬇ IRF	[BCDRSI]
👤 Inheritance	—
👤 SHolmes TA	
Effective Rights	

WHITE	
⬇ IRF	[BC R I]
👤 Inheritance	[BC R I]
👤 SHolmes TA	—
Effective Rights	[BC R I]

WHITE-SRV1	
⬇ IRF	[BCDRSI]
👤 Inheritance	[BC R I]
👥 CF-Group TA	[CD]
Effective Rights	[BCDR I]

It starts with SHolmes' trustee assignment (TA) to OU=CRIME. Since there's no inheritance or IRF involved, his effective rights in this container are the same. Those effective rights become inherited rights in all subcontainers—one of which is OU=WHITE. To further complicate things, there's an IRF of [BC R I] on the WHITE container. Since the IRF blocks [D S], Sherlock Holmes' inherited rights become [BC R I]. With no other trustee assignments, his effective rights in OU=WHITE are the same—[BC R I].

Finally, we arrive at the WHITE-SRV1 Server object. No rights are blocked by the IRF, so SHolmes' inherited rights are equal to the effective rights of the WHITE container—[BC R I]. In addition, one of Sherlock Holmes' groups (the "CF-Group") is assigned [CD] object rights to the WHITE-SRV1 server. These rights combine with his inherited rights to create ultimate effective rights of [BCDR I] for the server object. Remember, inherited rights and new trustee assignments *combine* when they come from two different sources—in this case the User SHolmes and his group (CF-Group).

TIP

One of the trickiest aspects of NDS effective rights is deciding when trustee assignment (TA) rights override inherited rights (IR), and when they are combined. It's simple: If the trustee is the same, then TA overrides IR; if trustees are different, then TA combines with IR. In summary:

Same = override; Different = combine!

You see . . . that wasn't so hard. In this simple example, we had a limited number of different elements — one user trustee assignment, one group trustee assignment, and one IRF. Of course, the world is not always this simple. Now let's take a look at a more complex example.

Just when you think you understand it, they throw something like this at you. In this example (see Figure 5.25), there's one user assignment, one group trustee, an Organizational Role equivalent, AI, and three IRFs. Hold on to your hat!

Once again, we're going to use the effective rights calculation worksheet in Figure 5.25. As before, it begins with Sherlock Holmes at the OU=CRIME container — trustee assignment of [R I]. In addition, the container is granted [CD   ] rights to itself. Since Sherlock Holmes lives in this context, he gains an ancestral inheritance of [CD   ]. This, combined with his user assignment, gives the effective rights [CDR I]. In this case, the IRF is useless — simple window dressing. Remember, trustee assignments override the IRF in the same container.

Sherlock Holmes' effective rights in OU=CRIME flow down to become his inherited rights in the OU=WHITE subcontainer. The IRF, however, blocks [CD SI] so his inheritance becomes [R   ]. This combines with a CF-Group trustee assignment of [CD   ] to give the effective rights [CDR   ].

Now, here's the tricky part. The OU=WHITE effective rights would normally flow down to the WHITE-SRV1 object. However, we restricted the Inheritable right at the OU=WHITE container. Therefore, the [CDR   ] effective rights stay in OU=WHITE and there is no inheritance at the WHITE-SRV1 level.

So what's the bottom line? Let me tell you — the effective rights for WHITE-SRV1 are equivalent to any trustee assignments (TA) to the object. So, WHITE-SRV1 gets [BC   ] from the CF-Role Organizational Role and that's the effective rights. No sweat!!

FIGURE 5.25

Calculating complex NDS rights

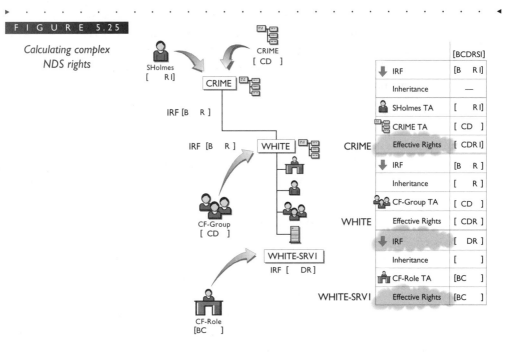

As you can see, effective rights get very hairy very quickly — just like modern math in the 7th Dimension. This is probably because there're so many forces at work. Remember, effective rights are the combination of trustee assignments, inheritance, [Public], and security equivalence. The default NDS rights are looking better and better all the time.

There you have it. The simple three-step NDS security model:

▸ *Step One: Assigning NDS Rights* — Through trustee assignments, inheritance, and/or security equivalence.

▸ *Step Two: Filtering IRF Rights* — The inclusive filter allows you to block inherited rights. Remember to avoid isolating sections of the tree by using new trustee assignments with IRFs.

▸ *Step Three: Calculating Effective Rights* — Just like modern math in the 7th Dimension.

After you determine a user's effective rights, you may need to discover where those rights came from to ensure proper inheritance and trustee assignments. Be forewarned . . . NDS security can quickly become a maze of uncertainty if you don't constantly monitor it.

Along those lines, here's a quick list of the places you should look for object trustee assignments:

- ▸ User object

- ▸ Groups the user is a member of

- ▸ Organizational roles the user is an occupant of

- ▸ Security equivalences the user may have

- ▸ Containers the user is in up the tree to the [Root]

- ▸ Rights granted to the [Public] trustee

- ▸ Rights granted to the [Root]

These assignments will show up in the Trustees of this Object window of NetWare Administrator. In addition, you can view an object's effective rights by pressing the Effective Rights button in the Trustees screen of NetWare Administrator (shown earlier in Figure 5.22). Finally, if your users are having problems gaining access rights to NDS containers, consider checking some of the following trustees: Group/Organizational Role membership, security equivalences, and explicit container/user rights. And, if all else fails, you should always check the IRF — it has a way of messing everything up.

Now, I bet you're glad you made it through the simple steps of NDS security. Fortunately, there's a sophisticated foundation of NDS default rights to start from. And Steps Two and Three are optional. Your security system doesn't need to be this complex, but in case it is, you have *Novell's CNA Study Guide for NetWare 5* to fall back on.

NDS Security Guidelines

The goal of network security is to keep your network services and resources secure ("keep the bad guys out"), while giving your network users the access they require ("let the good guys in"). For example, most users typically have no need to create and delete NDS objects or modify property values. With this in mind, check out the following guidelines for implementing NDS security:

1. *Start with default assignments* — The purpose of default assignments is to give users access to the resources they need without giving them access to resources or information they don't. When creating network access, you can start with default assignments, then make additional assignments to network or container administrators.

2. *Don't forget that assigning the Supervisor object right implies granting the Supervisor right to All Properties* — In some cases, you may want to grant container administrators all object rights except the Supervisor right, then assign property rights using the Selected Properties option.

3. *Exercise caution when granting the Supervisor object right to a Server object* — Remember that granting the Supervisor object right to a Server object gives that user Supervisor file system rights to all volumes associated with the server. This is the one instance where NDS object rights are inherited in the file system. One way to avoid this problem is to assign all object rights except for Supervisor, then do not assign the Supervisor or Write property right to the Object Trustees (ACL) property.

4. *Avoid assigning rights using the All Properties option* — Although this may seem like the simplest way to assign rights, it's actually very dangerous. Using this option, it's very easy to inadvertently give users or perhaps even container administrators access to resources or information they do not need. It's very important, for example, to avoid accidentally granting users access to the Object Trustees (ACL) property of various objects.

5. *Assign property rights using the Selected Properties option* — This option is much safer than the All Properties option, in that it allows you to be more selective in the rights that are granted.

6. *Avoid assigning the Write property right to the Object Trustees (ACL) property of any object* — If a user has this right, he or she can grant anyone, including himself or herself, all rights, including the Supervisor right. This is another reason for exercising caution when granting rights via the All Properties option.

7. *Exercise caution when filtering Supervisor rights with an IRF* — You should never have only one user that has Supervisor rights to a container. If that user is inadvertently (or deliberately) deleted, you will then lose control of that portion of the tree.

This completes all the "special" and "not-so-special" aspects of NetWare 5 NDS Administration. As you can see, it's a tricky, critical piece of your life as a CNA. To help, Table 5.3 outlines all the rights necessary to create and manage daily NDS resources. Just think of it as a blueprint for NDS success. Hey, that rhymes.

TABLE 5.3

Summary of NDS Resource
Access Rights

NDS RESOURCE	ADMINISTRATIVE ACTION	NECESSARY RIGHTS
Alias	Grant users appropriate NDS rights to the Alias Host object	Authority to grant NDS rights to objects in other containers (that is, Write [W] privileges to the object's ACL property)
Application	1) Grant users appropriate file system rights to the application referred to by the Application object.	To perform Step 1, you must have Supervisory or Access Control file system rights to the directory or file.
	2) Associate users with Application objects.	To perform Step 2, you must have the Write [W] property right to the ACL property of the Application and User objects.

(continued)

TABLE 5.3

*Summary of NDS Resource
Access Rights (continued)*

NDS RESOURCE	ADMINISTRATIVE ACTION	NECESSARY RIGHTS
Directory Map	1) Grant users appropriate file system rights to the directory referred to by the Directory Map object.	To perform Step 1, you must have Supervisory or Access Control file system rights to the directory or file.
	2) Grant users the Read [R] property right to the Path property of the Directory Map object.	To perform Step 2, you must have the Write [W] property right to ACL property of the Directory Map object.
Group	Add users to the Group Membership list of the Group object.	Write [W] property right to the ACL property (that is, Member and Object Trustees) of the Group object.
Organizational Role	Add users to the Occupant list of the Organizational Role object.	Write [W] property right to the ACL property (that is, Occupant and Object Trustees) of the Organizational Role object.
NDPS Printer	Add users to the User Role list of the NDPS Printer object.	Write [W] property right to the Users and Object Trustees ACL properties.
Profile	1) Add the Profile object to each User object's Profile property. 2) Grant users the Read [R] property right to the Login Script property of the Profile object.	To perform both Steps 1 and 2, you must have the Write [W] property right to the ACL (that is, Object Trustees) property of the Profile object.
Volume/ directory	Grant users the appropriate file system rights to the directory or file you want to target in the Volume object. (By default: Read and File Scan rights to SYS:PUBLIC)	Supervisory or Access Control file system rights to the directory or file you want to target in the Volume object.

Wow. That's NDS security! In this section, we've explored the simple three-step model for configuring NDS access rights. We've learned about trustee assignments, inheritance, and security equivalence. The IRF came along to help us lock inherited rights, and quickly became the foundation of "modern math" in the 7th Dimension—calculating effective rights. We also discussed guidelines for implementing NDS security as well as identifying where rights come from. That's all there is to it.

At the beginning of the chapter, we learned that security is "freedom from risk." At this point, you're probably thinking NDS security is freedom from sanity. Don't worry — it's not as crazy as you think. We've provided a detailed exploratorium at the end of the chapter for your enjoyment. And in the next section — file system access rights — you'll get a chance to review the three-step approach. Here's the good news. File system security is very similar to NDS security. Let's check it out.

For some great hands-on experience with NetWare 5 NDS security, check out Lab Exercise 5.3 later in this chapter.

TIP

LAB EXERCISE 5.1: CALCULATING NDS EFFECTIVE RIGHTS

OK, now that you're a pro with NetWare 5 NDS security, let's experiment with "modern math." In this section, we explored NetWare's version of calculus — calculating effective rights. We learned that effective rights are calculated according to the following formula:

Effective Rights = trustee assignments + inheritance − IRF (Inherited Rights Filter)

In this exercise, we'll begin Calculus 101 with NDS access rights. Then, in Lab Exercise 5.2 (later in the chapter), you'll get an opportunity to explore file system access rights. Also, we've included some beautiful graphic worksheets to help you follow along. You can create your own at home with a pencil, some paper, and a ruler.

So, without any further ado, let's get on with CASE #1.

Case #1

In this case, we are helping Sherlock Holmes gain administrative rights to the Crime Fighting division of ACME. Refer to Figure 5.26. It all starts at .CRIME.TOKYO.ACME, where he is granted [CD I] NDS privileges. There is no IRF (meaning all rights are allowed to flow) and no inheritance in CRIME.

In the next container, WHITE, SHolmes gets [SI] from his CF-Group. Also, there's an IRF of [D I]. Finally, these privileges flow down to the WHITE-SRV1 Server object and become inherited rights. But the server's IRF is set to [B R], so some of them are blocked. Also, SHolmes has an explicit trustee assignment of [D] to the WHITE-SRV1 server. Finally, Sherlock's home container, .OU=WHITE, is granted [C] privileges to the Server object.

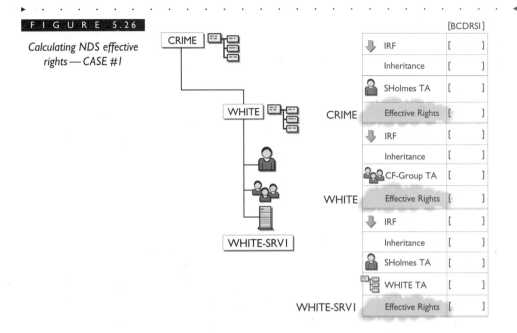

F I G U R E 5.26

Calculating NDS effective rights — CASE #1

Case #2

After careful consideration, you decide that these rights are inadequate for Sherlock and his administrative needs. So, let's try it one more time. But, in this case, we're going to use the "CF-Role" Organizational Role instead of the CF-Group. This gives us more administrative flexibility and narrows the scope of rights assignments. For this case, refer to Figure 5.27.

▶ · ◀

Calculating NDS effective rights — CASE #2

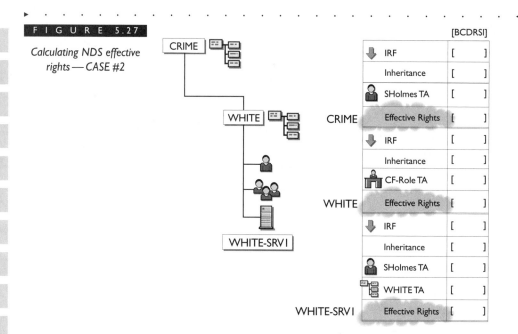

		[BCDRSI]
⬇	IRF	[ ]
	Inheritance	[ ]
👤	SHolmes TA	[ ]
CRIME	Effective Rights	[ ]
⬇	IRF	[ ]
	Inheritance	[ ]
	CF-Role TA	[ ]
WHITE	Effective Rights	[ ]
⬇	IRF	[ ]
	Inheritance	[ ]
👤	SHolmes TA	[ ]
	WHITE TA	[ ]
WHITE-SRV1	Effective Rights	[ ]

As before, it starts in the .CRIME.TOKYO.ACME container. Sherlock Holmes is granted the [B R I] rights to the container. Also, there is no inheritance in CRIME, but the IRF has been set to [CD   ] anyway.

In the next container, WHITE, SHolmes gets [BCD   ] through his CF-Role Organizational Role. Also, there's an IRF of [CDRS]. Finally, the WHITE-SRV1 Server's IRF is set to [B   R   ]. In addition, SHolmes has an explicit trustee assignment of [CD   ] to the WHITE-SRV1 server. Finally, Sherlock's home container, WHITE, is granted [C   ] privileges to the Server object. Now, let's see what he ends up with.

Case #3

In this final case, let's bounce over to the .BLUE.CRIME.TOKYO.ACME container and help out Wyatt Earp — their administrator. Refer to Figure 5.28. As with most NDS trees, it actually starts much higher up — above TOKYO. Wyatt Earp inherits [BCDR I] to .TOKYO.ACME through his User object. The IRF is wide open, so all rights are allowed to flow through. In addition, he's granted Rename privileges as a user and Browse privileges through his home container—BLUE.

FIGURE 5.28

Calculating NDS effective rights — CASE #3

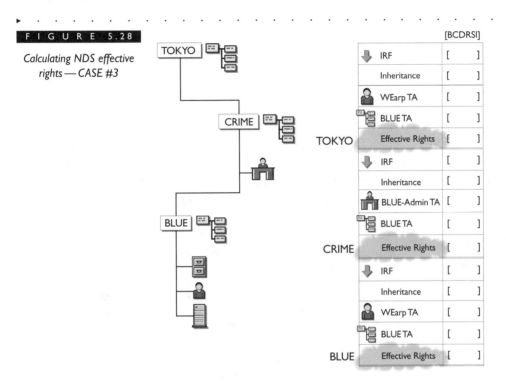

		[BCDRSI]
⬇ IRF		[ ]
Inheritance		[ ]
🧍 WEarp TA		[ ]
🗄 BLUE TA		[ ]
TOKYO	Effective Rights	[ ]
⬇ IRF		[ ]
Inheritance		[ ]
🏛 BLUE-Admin TA		[ ]
🗄 BLUE TA		[ ]
CRIME	Effective Rights	[ ]
⬇ IRF		[ ]
Inheritance		[ ]
🧍 WEarp TA		[ ]
🗄 BLUE TA		[ ]
BLUE	Effective Rights	[ ]

In the next container, CRIME, WEarp gets all object rights through his BLUE-Admin Organization Role. This overshadows the Browse privileges he ancestrally inherits from BLUE. Also, don't forget the CRIME IRF of [BCD I]. Finally, all rights flow down to the BLUE container and become inherited. But the Organizational Unit's IRF is set to [DR], so most of them are blocked. In addition, WEarp has an explicit trustee assignment of [C] to BLUE. This assignment is enhanced by the Browse privilege he inherits from BLUE. Good luck.

See Appendix C for the answers.

Well, there you have it. Great work. Now that you're an NDS security guru, let's rustle on over to Layer Four—File System Access Rights.

Layer Four — File System Access Rights

NetWare 5 security exists on two functional planes:

▶ Above the server

▶ Within the server

To understand the two functional planes of NetWare 5 security, use the server as a midpoint (see Figure 5.29). NDS security occurs above the server — the "Cloud." In this plane, the server is at the bottom of the tree. It is treated as any other leaf object, just like users, printers, and groups. NDS security applied above the server ends when it gets to a leaf object. There's no transition into the file system.

FIGURE 5.29

The two functional planes of NetWare 5 security

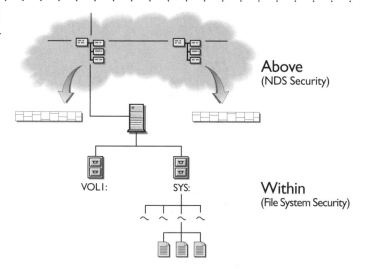

Above
(NDS Security)

Within
(File System Security)

VOL1:   SYS:

File system security, on the other hand, occurs within the server. In this case, the server is the top of the file system tree. The server contains the volumes that contain the directories that house the files. A user can't access a directory or file unless the proper rights have been assigned. Again, file system security ends once it gets to the server. There's no transition into the NDS security structure. Understanding the server's point of view will help you understand NDS and file system security.

The good news is NDS and file system security have a lot in common. You don't have to learn a whole new model. The same simple three-step approach applies. There're trustee assignments, inheritance, and security equivalence. The file system uses an IRF, and calculating effective rights is still ugly. There are, however, a few minor differences between NDS and file system security:

▸ NDS has 12 access rights broken into two groups — object and property. The file system uses eight access rights.

▸ Rights do not flow from NDS into the file system except in one special instance — Supervisor [S] object right to the Server object, which grants the trustee Supervisor file rights to the [Root] of all the server's volumes. Or, to be more specific, you need Write [W] privileges to the ACL property of the Server.

▸ The NDS Supervisor object and property rights can be blocked by an IRF. The Supervisor file system right, on the other hand, cannot be blocked by an IRF.

That does it. As you can see, the file system and NDS have much more in common than you think. Let's start our discussion of security within the server by describing the eight file system access rights.

Understanding File System Access Rights

Welcome inside the server. It's kind of dark and cold in here, but very secure. Before you can access any files, though, you must have appropriate file system access rights. As you can see in Figure 5.30, they also spell a word — WoRMFACES (the "O" is implied). Holy anatomical nematodes, Batman! It's not a pretty sight, but certainly a name you will not forget. Let's check them out.

▸ W (Write) — Grants the right to open and change the contents of files and directories.

▸ (O) — Doesn't exist but is needed to spell a word.

▸ R (Read) — Grants the right to open files in the directory and read their contents or run applications.

▸ M (Modify) — Grants the right to change the attributes or name of a file or directory. As we'll learn in just a second, the Modify right has a dual personality.

▸ F (File Scan) — Grants the right to see files and directories.

▸ A (Access Control) — Grants the right to change trustee assignments and the IRF.

▸ C (Create) — Grants the right to create new subdirectories and files.

▸ E (Erase) — Grants the right to delete a directory, its files, and subdirectories.

▸ S (Supervisor) — Grants all rights to a directory and its subdirectories and files. This right cannot be blocked by the IRF (unlike NDS security).

FIGURE 5.30

WoRMFACES

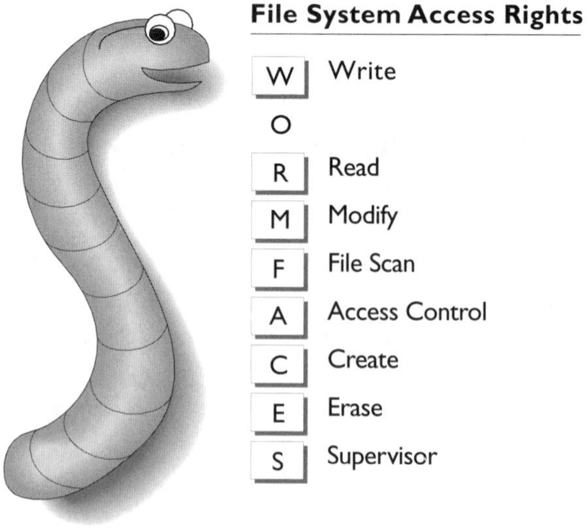

File System Access Rights

W	Write
O	
R	Read
M	Modify
F	File Scan
A	Access Control
C	Create
E	Erase
S	Supervisor

In this list, there are three rights you may want to steer clear of — [SAM]. (They're easy to remember because they spell a word). The Supervisor right grants all privileges to directories and files and it can't be filtered. Users with the Supervisor right can make trustee assignments and grant all rights to other users. Access Control also allows users to make trustee assignments, but they can only grant the Supervisor right if they already possess it. In addition, these users can modify the IRF. Finally, the Modify right has a split personality — Dr. Jekyll and Mr. Hyde. As Dr. Jekyll, Modify allows users to rename files and directories. Many applications require this. As Mr. Hyde, Modify allows users to change file and directory attributes. As we'll see a little later, attributes constitute the fifth layer of the NetWare 5 security model. I don't think you want users messing around with it.

REAL WORLD

The Supervisor access right is just as dangerous in the file system as it is in NDS. The tricky part is that it can leak its way into the file system without you knowing it. Any user with the Write [W] property right to a server's ACL will implicitly receive Supervisor file system rights to the [Root] of all volumes on the server. And to make things worse, the user will not appear on any file or directory trustee list. There's a variety of ways to get the Write [W] property right to a server's ACL, including Supervisor object rights, Supervisor All Properties rights, and security equivalence. You may consider blocking these rights with a Server object IRF.

Recognizing the eight file system access rights is only the beginning. To effectively configure and manage file system security, you must understand what they do. Individually, the rights are somewhat useless. But in combination, they become valuable security tools. Table 5.4 summarizes the file system rights requirements for common network tasks. Believe me, this will be an invaluable aid when it comes time to configure application and data security. Use it or lose it.

TABLE 5.4	FILE SYSTEM TASK	RIGHTS REQUIREMENTS
Rights Requirements for Common File System Tasks	Open and read a file	Read
	See a filename	File Scan
	Search a directory for files	File Scan
	Open and write to an existing file	Write, Create, Erase, and (sometimes) Modify
	Execute an .EXE file	Read and File Scan
	Create and write to a file	Create
	Copy files from a directory	Read and File Scan
	Copy files to a directory	Write, Create, and File Scan
	Make a new directory	Create
	Delete a file	Erase
	Salvage deleted files	Read and File Scan for the file and Create for the directory
	Change directory or file attributes	Modify (Mr. Hyde)
	Rename a file or directory	Modify (Dr. Jekyll)
	Change the IRF	Access Control
	Change trustee assignments	Access Control
	Modify a directory's disk space restrictions	Access Control

So, where do you begin? As with NDS, file system security starts with the defaults. NetWare 5 provides a sophisticated set of default file system access rights. These rights should become the foundation of your application and data security strategies. They aren't, however, as comprehensive as NDS defaults. You'll need to assign security whenever you create new application and data directories. Let's take a quick look at the NetWare 5 defaults:

▶ *User* — A unique user directory can be created during User object conception. By default, the user gets all file system rights except Supervisor to their home directory — [RWCEMF]. The directory name will match the User object name unless otherwise specified. Its location is also configurable.

▸ *Supervisor* — The Bindery Services Supervisor object is granted Supervisor [S] file rights to the [Root] of all volumes. This user performs special bindery functions using the Admin password.

▸ *Creator* — Whoever creates the File Server object (usually Admin) automatically gets Supervisor [S] file system rights to all volumes on the server. This can be blocked by filtering the Supervisor [S] object right with a Server object IRF.

▸ *Container* — The server's parent container is granted Read and File Scan [RF] access rights to SYS:PUBLIC. This way, all users and objects in the server's home container can access NetWare 5 public utilities.

This completes our discussion of file system access rights. As you can see, there's a lot more than meets the eye. Be sure to use Table 5.4 when assigning rights to new application and data directories. Also, test these rights before you let the users loose. Many times, applications have strange unobvious requirements. Now that you know what to do, let's learn how to do it. Remember, the NetWare 5 file system behaves exactly the same as NDS:

▸ *Step One*: Assigning trustee rights

▸ *Step Two*: Filtering IRF rights

▸ *Step Three*: Calculating effective rights

Ready. Set. Go!

File System Three-Step Shuffle

This gives us an opportunity to review the three-step NDS security model. Fortunately, file system security imitates it to the letter. Remember, NetWare 5 security starts with two simple questions:

▸ What rights do I need to do stuff?

▸ How do I get these rights?

Well, so far we've learned about the eight file system access rights and what rights are needed for common network tasks. Now we get to answer the question, "How do I get these rights?" As with NDS, file system security is as easy as 1-2-3:

▶ *Step One: Assigning Trustee Rights* — You assign the access rights through trustee assignments, inheritance, and/or security equivalence.

▶ *Step Two: Filtering IRF Rights* — In special circumstances, you can filter inherited rights at the directory or file level.

▶ *Step Three: Calculating Effective Rights* — The result is effective rights (that is, what users can actually do to directories and files).

Once again, it's as easy as 1-2-3. Except in this case, we're assigning access rights to files and directories, not NDS objects. Let's take a closer look at this simple three-step model from the file system's point of view.

Step One: Assigning Trustee Rights

You have to start somewhere, and Step One starts with work. A trustee is any NDS object with rights to directories or files. Trustees are tracked through the DET (directory table). The file system supports the same trustee types as NDS — users, groups, containers, Organizational Roles, and [Public]. Once you identify "who" is going to get the rights, you have to determine "what" rights you're going to give them and "where" the rights will be assigned. This is shown in Figure 5.31. MMarion is granted all rights except [SAM] to the SYS:SHARED directory. These rights are then inherited for all subdirectories underneath. As you can see, the "who" is MMarion, the "what" is [RWCEF], and the "where" is SYS:SHARED. This is an explicit trustee assignment.

File system trustee rights can be assigned using the NetWare Administrator, RIGHTS, or FILER utilities. So, how is this accomplished in NetWare Administrator? Once again, it depends on your point of view, and you have two choices:

▶ *Rights to Files and Directories* — This is from Maid Marion's point of view.

▶ *Trustees of this Directory* — This is from SYS:SHARED's point of view.

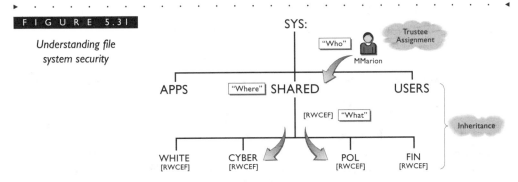

*Understanding file
system security*

It really doesn't matter which option you choose. You can either assign rights from the user's point of view or the directory's point of view. In the first example, we assign security from Maid Marion's point of view. In NetWare Administrator, double-click Maid Marion and her User Information window appears. Choose Rights to Files and Directories tab from the right-hand list and voilà — Figure 5.32 appears.

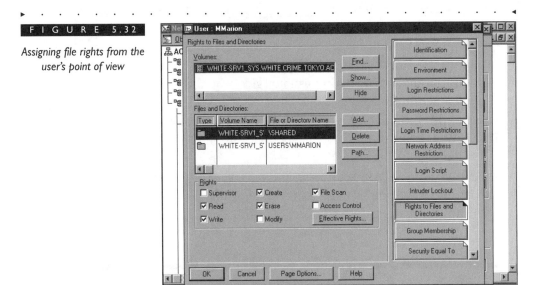

*Assigning file rights from the
user's point of view*

Figure 5.32 shows the security window from Maid Marion's point of view. As you can see, she has been granted [RWCEF] access rights to SYS:SHARED. In addition, she's also a trustee of SYS:\USERS\POLIT\MMARION — by default. You can create trustee assignments by using the Add button.

REAL WORLD

The Security Information window shown in Figure 5.32 only displays trustee assignments for a single volume at a time. By its very nature, NDS allows you to view information about multiple volumes throughout the WAN. To bring up the trustee assignments for a different volume, use the Show button. You can also browse for other volumes using the Find button. In Figure 5.32, we're only looking at Maid Marion's trustee assignments for WHITE-SRV1_SYS.

The second option allows you to assign access rights from SYS:SHARED's point of view. In this case, you would double-click WHITE-SRV1_SYS from the Browse window of NetWare Administrator. All of its directories should appear. Then, highlight SHARED and click the right mouse button. A pull-down menu will appear — choose Details. Once the SYS:SHARED Details window appears, choose Trustees of this Directory from the right-hand list (see Figure 5.33).

In this screen, NetWare Administrator gives you the choice of adding trustees or setting the IRF (Inherited Rights Filter). Notice that MMarion has been added with the [RWCEF] access rights. You can create other trustee assignments for SYS:SHARED using the Add Trustee button. Also, notice the IRF allows all rights to flow through — this is the default.

There you have it. As you can see, it doesn't matter how we assign access rights. Both methods accomplish the same thing — Maid Marion (who) is granted [RWCEF] trustee rights (what) to SYS:SHARED (where).

REAL WORLD

In addition to NetWare Administrator, you can use FILER and RIGHTS (command-line utility) to assign file system access rights.

▶ · ◀

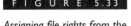

F I G U R E   5 . 3 3

Assigning file rights from the directory's point of view

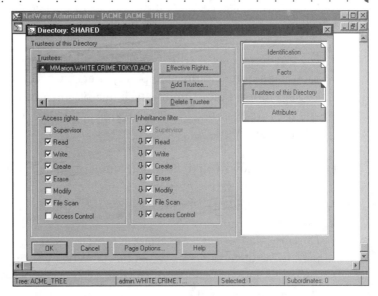

Now that we've explored the "work part," let's take a closer look at inheritance — "no work."

As we learned earlier, access rights are also assigned through inheritance. This is an automatic side effect of trustee assignments. As you can see in Figure 5.28, Maid Marion inherits [RWCEF] access rights in all subdirectories of SYS:SHARED. Inheritance is a great thing. It allows you to assign sweeping file system access rights with minimal effort. Remember, as a CNA, work is bad.

But many times, inheritance gets out of hand. Fortunately, NetWare 5 allows you to override inheritance using a new trustee assignment or an IRF. We'll explore these topics in just a moment.

If trustee assignments or inheritance aren't quite getting the job done, security equivalence may be the answer. Security equivalence simply states, "One object is equivalent to another with respect to file system access rights."

As we learned earlier, users, for example, are security equivalent to their parent container. We also learned that security equivalence operates at the trustee assignment level — this is not inheritance.

NetWare 5 provides five strategies for security equivalence:

▶ *Ancestral Inheritance (AI)* — Typically, any object is security equivalent to its ancestors (parent containers). This means any rights you assign to an NDS container are absorbed by all the objects in the container. This is not inheritance — this is security equivalence.

▶ *Organizational Role* — Our special NDS objects designed as task identifiers. Jobs that require multiple temporary users are excellent candidates for Organizational Roles. Simply assign file system access rights to the Role and they are absorbed by all occupants of the Role. Once again, this is not inheritance.

▶ *Groups* — Allows you to distribute similar rights to either users in different containers or a subset of users in a single container. Members of any group absorb (not inherit) rights assigned to the host Group object.

▶ *Directory Map* — In very special circumstances, security equivalence can be used to facilitate Directory Map objects. When you create a Directory Map object, be sure to assign adequate file system rights to its physical location. Then when you use the MAP command to create logical pointers, be sure to assign the host user security equivalence to the Directory Map object. This way, the appropriate file system access rights follow the Directory Map object all the way to the target user.

▶ *Other objects* — A user can be explicitly granted security equivalence to any other object (typically a User object). This gives the User object the same rights as the object it has been made security equivalent to. This strategy can be dangerous, and thus, should only be used as a temporary measure.

This completes Step One of the file system security model. Remember, this is the hard part. Step Two and Step Three are optional. Step Two allows us to filter inherited rights and Step Three combines all rights assignments into a single mathematical formula — math in the 7th Dimension. Let's keep rolling!

Step Two: Filtering IRF Rights
Earlier we learned there are two ways of blocking unwanted inherited rights:

▶ New trustee assignments

▶ Inherited Rights Filter (IRF)

If you want to block rights for a particular user, create a new trustee assignment for that user at the level in the tree in which the rights should be restricted. As we discussed earlier, the rights that are inherited by an object are overwritten when the same object is granted a new trustee assignment lower in the tree — unless, of course, the assignment above the new one includes the Supervisor file system right. (In the file system, the Supervisor right cannot be blocked using a new trustee assignment lower in the tree.)

If you want to block inheritance from virtually all users, modify the object's IRF. The IRF blocks inherited rights at any point in the tree. There are, however, four very important points you must understand about how the IRF works:

▶ It's an inclusive filter, which means the rights that are in the filter are the ones that are allowed to pass through.

▶ An IRF can only block rights that have been inherited from object trustee assignments higher in the tree. (That's why it's called an *Inherited* Rights Filter.) It does not apply to trustee assignments themselves. In other words, if your User object is assigned rights to an object via a trustee assignment, that assignment would be unaffected by the object's IRF.

▶ An IRF applies to everyone in the tree *except* Admin or anyone else with the Supervisor file system right.

▶ They can be dangerous if used improperly, and thus, great care should be taken if you choose to modify them.

This is the only place where file system and NDS security differs. The NDS IRF can be used to block the Supervisor right. The file system IRF, on the other hand, cannot block the Supervisor right. As you can see in Figure 5.30, the IRF is assigned using the Trustees of this Directory option. Also, notice that the Supervisor right has been grayed out. This means it cannot be removed. Also notice the downward arrows that appear next to each option checkbox. These differentiate IRF rights from trustee assignments. Anywhere you see a downward arrow, you can assume it's an IRF.

When you assign an IRF, all sorts of crazy things happen. My word of advice is, "Avoid them at all cost." But if you can't, you'll need to deal with Step Three — calculating effective rights.

Step Three: Calculating Effective Rights

As we learned earlier, effective rights are the bottom line. This is the culmination of our three-step process. In Step One, we assign the rights. In Step Two, we filter the rights. In Step Three, we calculate exactly what the rights are. We also learned that calculating effective rights is as simple as modern math — in the 7th Dimension! Any object's effective rights are the combination of file system privileges received through any of the following:

▸ Trustee assignments made to the User object

▸ Objects the user receives rights through such as parent containers, groups, or Organizational Roles

▸ Rights granted to the special [Public] trustee

▸ Security equivalences

▸ Inheritance minus rights blocked by the IRF

As we learned earlier, calculating effective rights for NDS can be mind-boggling and fun. The file system is no different. Let's use Maid Marion as an example. Suppose we're concerned about users making changes to our political database. To protect it, we assign an [RF] filter to SYS:SHARED\POL. This will block MMarion's inherited rights of [RWCEF]. Therefore, her effective rights should be Read and File Scan [RF]. But as you can see in Figure 5.34, her effective rights in SYS:SHARED\POL are, in fact, [RWF]. How did this happen? She must be getting the [W] right from somewhere else. Ah, I remember. She's a member of the POL-Group and they've been granted Write privileges to SYS:SHARED\POL. Therefore, her effective rights become inherited rights minus the IRF plus group trustee assignments.

FIGURE 5.34

Calculating effective rights for Maid Marion

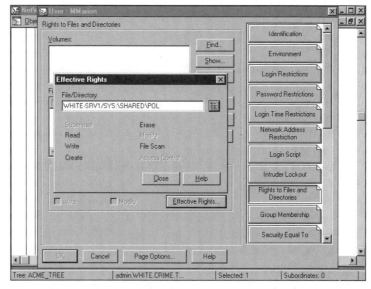

NetWare Administrator provides an excellent tool for viewing effective rights — check out Figure 5.34. All you have to do is identify the user (MMarion) and the directory (SYS:SHARED\POL) — NetWare Administrator does all the rest.

There you have it. The simple three-step file system security model:

▶ *Step One: Assigning NDS Rights* — Through trustee assignments, inheritance, and/or security equivalence.

▶ *Step Two: Filtering IRF Rights* — The inclusive filter allows you to block inherited rights.

▶ *Step Three: Calculating Effective Rights* — Just like modern math in the 7th Dimension.

That was a fun review. It's fortunate for us that NetWare 5 basically uses the same model for both NDS and file system security. Even though these two layers apply to dramatically different network elements, they approach security in a similar way. Hopefully, now you have a firm handle on access rights, default assignments, trustees, inheritance, the IRF, and effective rights. They all work together as a synergistic solution for risk management. Of course, there's always that isolated exception when four layers of security aren't quite enough. You never know when a hacker will show up with armor-piercing bullets. Fortunately, NetWare 5 has one more layer for just these emergencies — file/directory attributes. Let's check it out.

For some great hands-on experience with NetWare 5 file system access rights, check out Lab Exercise 5.3 at the end of the chapter.

TIP

▶ · ◀

Layer Five — Directory/File Attributes

Welcome to the final layer. I bet you never thought you'd get here. Directory and file attributes provide the final and most sophisticated layer of the NetWare 5 security model. These attributes are rarely used, but provide a powerful tool for specific security solutions. If all else fails, you can always turn to attribute security to save the day.

Attributes are special assignments or properties that are assigned to individual directories or files. Attribute security overrides all previous trustee assignments and effective rights. Attributes can be used to prevent deleting a file, copying a file, viewing a file, and so on. Attributes also control whether files can be shared, mark files for backup purposes, or protect them from data corruption using the Transactional Tracking System (TTS). Directory and file attributes can be set using the NetWare Administrator, FLAG, or FILER utilities. They can also be viewed using the NDIR utility. Some NetWare 5 attributes are unavailable from DOS utilities.

Attributes allow you to manage what users can do with files once they have access to them. Attributes are global security elements that affect all users, regardless of their rights, and they override all previous levels of security. Let's say, for example, Maid Marion has all rights except [SAM] to the SYS:APPS\WP directory — [RWCEF]. You can still restrict her from deleting a specific file by assigning it the Read-Only attribute. Therefore, the true effective rights for Maid Marion in this directory are the combination of her effective file system rights and file attributes.

NetWare 5 supports two types of attributes: directory and file. Directory attributes apply to directories only, whereas file attributes can be assigned to files. In both of these cases, attributes fall into one of three categories:

▶ Security Attributes

▸ Feature Attributes

▸ Disk Management Attributes

Security attributes affect users' security access—what they can do with files. Feature attributes, on the other hand, affect how the system interacts with files. That is, whether the files can be archived, purged, or transactionally tracked. Finally, disk management attributes apply to file compression, data migration, and block suballocation.

Let's take a closer look at NetWare 5 attribute security, starting with security attributes.

Security Attributes

Security attributes protect information at the file and directory level by controlling two kinds of file access—file sharing and file alteration. File access security controls not so much who can access the files, but what kind of access they have. Once users have been given the proper trustee assignments to a given directory, they're in the door. Security attributes tell users what they can do with the files once they're there. Here's a list of NetWare 5's security attributes and a brief description. An asterisk (*) indicates an attribute that applies to both directories and files.

▸ *Copy Inhibit (Ci)* — Only valid on Macintosh workstations. Prevents users from copying the file. Even if users have been granted the Read and File Scan [RF] rights, they still can't copy this specific file. Macintosh users can, however, remove the Copy Inhibit attribute if they have been granted the Modify [M] access right.

▸ *Delete Inhibit (Di)* * — Prevents users from erasing the directory or file.

▸ *Execute Only (X)* — This is an extremely sensitive attribute and provides a very high level of NetWare 5 security. Once set, it cannot be cleared. The only way to remove the Execute Only attribute is to delete the file. The Execute Only attribute can be assigned to .EXE and .COM files. Files that have this attribute assigned cannot be copied or backed up—just executed or deleted. Note that some applications don't work properly if flagged with the Execute Only attribute — so test them carefully before granting access to your users.

▸ *Hidden (H)** — Valid on both DOS and OS/2 machines. Hidden is reserved for special files or directories that should not be seen, used, deleted, or copied over. However, the NDIR command will display the directory if the user has File Scan [F] access rights.

▸ *Normal (N)** — No directory or file attributes have been set. This is the default. Normal files are typically flagged non-sharable, Read/Write automatically.

▸ *Read-Only (Ro)* — No one can write to the file. When Read Only is set or cleared, NetWare 5 also sets or clears the Delete Inhibit and Rename Inhibit attributes. Consequently, a user can't write to, erase, or rename a file when Read Only is set. A user with the Modify access right can remove the Delete Inhibit and Rename Inhibit attributes without removing Ro. In this case, the file can be deleted or renamed, but not written to.

▸ *Read/Write (Rw)* — Allows users to change the contents of the file. This attribute is automatically assigned using the Normal (N) switch.

▸ *Rename Inhibit (Ri)** — Prevents a user from renaming the file or directory.

▸ *Sharable (Sh)* — Allows the file to be accessed by more than one user at a time. This attribute is usually used in combination with Read-Only for application files. The default "Normal" setting is non-sharable.

▸ *System (Sy)** — Applies to DOS and OS/2 workstations. The NetWare 5 OS assigns this attribute to system-owned files and directories. System files are hidden and cannot be deleted, renamed, or copied. However, the NetWare 5 NDIR command will display the file if the user has File Scan access rights.

That does it for security attributes. Now let's take a closer look at feature attributes.

Feature Attributes

Feature attributes provide access to special NetWare 5 functions or features. These features include backup, purging, and transactional tracking. As a matter of fact, there are only three feature attributes in NetWare 5, and one of them applies to both directories and files (P). Here's how they work:

▸ *Archive Needed (A)* — A status flag set by NetWare 5 which indicates that the file has been changed since the last time it was backed up. NetWare 5 sets this attribute when a file is created or modified and clears it during SBACKUP full and incremental sessions.

▸ *Purge (P)* * — Tells NetWare 5 to purge the file when it is deleted. The file then cannot be salvaged with the FILER utility. Purge at the directory level clears all files and directories from the salvage table once they're deleted. This attribute is best used on sensitive data.

▸ *Transactional (T)* — Indicates that the file is protected by NetWare 5's internal TTS, which prevents data corruption by ensuring that either all changes are made, or no changes are made when a file is being modified. The Transactional attribute should be assigned to TTS-tracked databases and accounting files.

That does it for NetWare 5 feature attributes. Now let's take a quick look at disk management.

Disk Management Attributes

The remaining seven file and directory attributes apply to NetWare 5 disk management — file compression, data migration, and block suballocation. File compression allows more data to be stored on a volume by compressing files that are not being used. Once you enable this disk management feature, volume capacity increases up to 63 percent. Data migration is the transfer of inactive data from a NetWare 5 volume to an external optical disk storage device — such as a jukebox. This process is transparent to the user because files appear to be stored on the volume. Data migration is made possible through NetWare 5's internal High-Capacity Storage System (HCSS) — as seen in the previous chapter. Finally, block suballocation increases disk storage efficiency by segmenting disk allocation blocks. Suballocation is turned on by default when you install NetWare 5. You can turn it off using one of the following seven attributes. Here's a quick look at NetWare 5's disk management attributes:

▶ *Can't Compress (Cc)* — A status flag set by NetWare 5. Indicates that the file can't be compressed because of insignificant space savings. To avoid the overhead of uncompressing files that do not compress well, the system calculates the compressed size of a file before actually compressing it. If no disk space will be saved by compression, or if the size difference does not meet the value specified by the "Minimum Percentage Compression Gain" parameter, the file is not compressed. This attribute is shown on attribute lists, but cannot be set by the user or CNAs.

▶ *Compressed (Co)* — A status flag set by NetWare 5. Indicates that the file has been compressed by the system. Once again, this attribute is shown on attribute lists but cannot be set by the user or CNAs.

▶ *Don't Compress (Dc)* * — Marks a file or directory so that it is never compressed. It is a way of managing file compression.

▶ *Don't Migrate (Dm)* * — Marks a file or directory so that it is never migrated to a secondary storage device. This is the only way you can directly manage data migration. Otherwise, all files are automatically migrated once they exceed the timeout threshold (assuming, of course, that the Migration feature is turned on — which is the default).

▶ *Don't Suballocate (Ds)* — Prevents an individual file from being suballocated even if suballocation is enabled on the volume. This is typically used for files that are huge or appended to frequently, such as databases. This attribute is your only tool for managing suballocation once it's been activated.

▶ *Immediate Compress (Ic)* * — Marks a file or directory for immediate compression. NetWare 5 will compress the file as soon as it can without waiting for a specific event to initiate compression — such as a time delay. As a CNA, you can use Immediate Compress to turn on compression and Don't Compress to turn it off. Both attributes operate at the file and directory level.

▸ *Migrated (M)* — A status flag set by NetWare 5. Indicates that the file has been migrated. This attribute is shown on an attribute list, but can't be set by the user or CNAs.

Any of these attributes can be modified using the FLAG command-line utility or the NetWare Administrator graphical utility. In addition to these tools, attributes can be viewed using NDIR.

These file and directory attributes, when used in combination, can create effective security tools to control who has access to do what with specialized NetWare 5 files. The default attribute combination for all files is Normal — nonsharable Read/Write. There are special instances, however, when you can justify customizing these attributes, such as the following

▸ Standalone applications that are not to be shared should be flagged nonsharable Read-Only.

▸ Data files that are shared but not written to simultaneously should be flagged nonsharable Read/Write.

▸ Data files that are part of larger multi-user applications can be flagged Sharable Read/Write only if the application supports internal record locking.

▸ Application files that are accessed by simultaneous users should be flagged Sharable Read-Only.

▸ Large important database files should always be flagged with the Transactional (T) attribute, but be sure the application supports TTS.

▸ Sensitive archive files should be flagged with the attribute Hidden. These include records that are only accessed once a month.

▶ All System files owned by NetWare 5 should be flagged System. This is an attribute assigned by NetWare 5, not you.

▶ Sensitive application files that cost a significant amount of money should be flagged Execute Only by the network administrator. However, be careful, because not all applications will run when flagged "X."

For some great hands-on experience with NetWare 5 directory/file attributes, check out Lab Exercise 5.3 later in this chapter.

TIP

Congratulations! You've completed the NetWare 5's five-layered security model. Wow, what a wild ride. It all started with risk analysis and countermeasures. We learned the absolute goal of NetWare 5 security:

Let the good guys in and keep the bad guys out.

We also learned that NetWare 5's five-layered security model is an increasingly more secure series of barriers against network threats — users. In Layer One, they log into the "Cloud" with initial and background authentication. Then login restrictions take over. This barrier controls the user's conditional access through five different types of restrictions — login, password, station, time, and Intruder Detection/Lockout. Once users pass through the first two barriers, their ability to access leaf and container objects is determined by a sophisticated NDS security structure. At the heart of NDS security is a simple three-step process — trustee assignments, IRF, and effective rights.

But what about security within the server? NDS security isn't enough. Now we must protect the file system. File system security operates in much the same way as NDS object rights. They're granted with the help of trustee assignments, inheritance, and security equivalence. We learned how the eight different access rights can be used to protect NetWare 5 files and directories. But sometimes this isn't enough. That's where attributes come in. The final barrier allows you to override previous security with three different attribute types — security, feature, and disk management.

As a CNA, it is your responsibility to manage the NetWare 5 network. But most importantly, you must protect it. Hopefully now you've gained a new appreciation for the value of an impenetrable network armor. We've filled your brain with sophisticated security strategies and given you a utility belt full of advanced protection tools — like NetWare Administrator and effective rights worksheets.

So, where do you go from here? The world is your oyster. It's amazing what a little security can do for your fragile psyche. Once all your risks are in check, there's no limit to what you can do.

So far, you can manage NDS, connect to the network, map drives, and secure the WAN. I'd say you're becoming a full-fledged "NetWare 5 Superhero"! But what about the big picture? Now I think you're ready to journey into the three realms of Z.E.N.works.

Go grasshopper . . .

REAL WORLD

Now you're a NetWare 5 security expert—a real Sherlock Holmes of the WAN. But before you can move on to NetWare 5 Z.E.N.works and Printing, you should take a moment to explore a few final tips concerning NetWare Enhanced Security. Remember, information is valuable and many of today's advanced networks require Class C-2 security configurations.

Here's a few "Dos" and "Don'ts."

Do List

- ▶ Do read the online manuals before installing the server software.

- ▶ Do physically restrict the server console to prevent access by anyone other than network administrators.

- ▶ Do make and securely store frequent backups of NTCB configuration files. Your computer system can be replaced, but it may not be possible to replace the data stored on your system.

- ▶ Do set the console parameter to disable use of audit passwords (as required for the NetWare Enhanced Security configuration).

- ▶ Do configure your audit trails properly: only trusted users as Audit Administrators and Audit Viewers; only workstation NTCBs as Audit Sources.

- ▶ Do provide sufficient space for audit data collection.

- ▶ Do archive audit files on a regular basis.

(continued)

(continued)

▶ Do keep a manual record of per-user and per-file audit configuration flags, since they are not backed up by SBACKUP.

▶ Do file reports (User Comment Forms) with Novell if you find any problems with the server programs or documentation.

▶ Do create a separate account (for example, BBAILEY-ADM) for administrative work.

▶ Do set up a separate administrative account for each administrator. (Don't share administrator accounts.)

▶ Do use a strong password for your administrative accounts.

▶ Do change the password frequently for your administrative accounts.

▶ Do set up a separate administrative account for each administrator (that is, do not share the Admin account).

▶ Do configure the server to remove DOS (either UNLOAD DOS or SECURE CONSOLE) after NetWare 5 has booted.

▶ Do configure the IPX restriction on all Printer objects so that print servers will accept connections only from valid printer drivers.

▶ Do protect SYS:PUBLIC, SYS:SYSTEM, and SYS:MAIL by defining the appropriate file system rights settings.

▶ Do set up print queues, print servers, and printers such that only trusted users are on the list of operators, only evaluated print servers are on the list of servers, and all users are on the list of users.

▶ Do modify the "Template" settings before creating any users: set minimum password length to at least eight characters, password required to "yes," and account disabled to "true."

▶ Do use the Template object when creating new users.

▶ Do develop a site policy for password changes, and enforce it.

▶ Do configure the Template and all NDS User objects so that each user can change his or her own password.

▶ Do enable password expiration.

- ▶ Do configure audit trails to shut off operations when audit trails fill, to avoid audit loss.

- ▶ Do physically protect the licensing diskette.

- ▶ Do protect printed output and instruct users to do likewise.

- ▶ Do protect removable media (such as tapes and floppy disks) and instruct users to do likewise.

Don't List

- ▶ Don't allow general (nonadministrative) users to have access to the server console.

- ▶ Don't type your administrative password at any time other than (a) when running INSTALL to set up the server, (b) at the server console SBACKUP prompt, or (c) to the NTCB of an evaluated client component.

- ▶ Don't specify the optional parameters (-s, -na, -ns) when you boot the server for normal operation. This is because the STARTUP.NCF, AUTOEXEC.NCF, and INITSYS.NCF files help initialize the server's secure state.

- ▶ Don't install arbitrary untrusted NLM executables.

- ▶ Don't give the [Public] object any additional rights beyond those available in the standard distribution (that is, "out of the box"). Rights given to the [Public] object are available to all users on the network.

- ▶ Don't give sensitive names to what is public information (such as usernames, container names, server names, e-mail addresses, or people's names).

- ▶ Don't add unevaluated peripherals to the server hardware configuration.

- ▶ Don't use workstations as queue servers or queue operators, unless the queue server is an evaluated part of a workstation component.

- ▶ Don't install name space NLM programs that are not part of the NetWare Enhanced Security configuration. Consequently, only the DOS namespace is supported on the server.

- ▶ Don't use undocumented console operations, as they may place the server into an unevaluated configuration.

(continued)

(continued)

▶ Don't load NLM programs associated with the AppleTalk Filing Protocol (ATFP) or TCP/IP protocol suite.

▶ Don't use undocumented console operations, as they violate the server's NetWare Enhanced Security configuration.

▶ Don't believe all telephone calls or e-mail messages you receive. For example, the Computer Emergency Response Team (CERT) has documented cases of messages telling users to temporarily change their passwords to a certain value "for debugging purposes."

**LAB EXERCISE 5.2: CALCULATING
FILE SYSTEM EFFECTIVE RIGHTS**

Here you are. In case you're lost, this is modern math — Part 2. In this exercise, we're going to explore the wonderful world of file system effective rights. Now that you've helped "administrate" Sherlock Holmes and Wyatt Earp, it's time to "liberate" the rest of the crime-fighting team, namely Robin Hood, Maid Marion, Dr. Watson, Little John, and Friar Tuck.

Ah, a CNA's job is never done.

Case #1

FrTuck has been made a trustee of the SYS:SHARED directory and granted Read, Write, Create, and File Scan rights. The IRF for the SYS:SHARED directory contains all rights; the IRF for the SYS:SHARED\CYBER directory contains Supervisor, Read, and File Scan; and the IRF for the CYBER.DOC file contains Read, Write, Create, and File Scan. Calculate FrTuck's effective rights in the SYS:SHARED directory, the SYS:SHARED\CYBER directory, and the CYBER.DOC file, using the worksheet in Figure 5.35.

► · ◄

F I G U R E 5.35

Calculating file system effective rights — Case #1

SYS: SHARED	S	R	W	C	E	M	F	A
Inherited Rights Filter								
Inherited Rights — User								
Inherited Rights — Group								
Trustee Assignment — User								
Trustee Assignment — Group								
Effective Rights								

SYS: SHARED\CYBER	S	R	W	C	E	M	F	A
Inherited Rights Filter								
Inherited Rights — User								
Inherited Rights — Group								
Trustee Assignment — User								
Trustee Assignment — Group								
Effective Rights								

CYBER.DOC	S	R	W	C	E	M	F	A
Inherited Rights Filter								
Inherited Rights — User								
Inherited Rights — Group								
Trustee Assignment — User								
Trustee Assignment — Group								
Effective Rights								

Case #2

DrWatson was granted the Read, Write, Create, and File Scan rights to the SYS:SHARED directory. The CRIME Group, of which he is a member, was granted Read, Write, Create, Erase, Modify, and File Scan rights to the SYS:CRIME directory. The CRIME Group was also granted Read and File Scan rights to the CRIME.DB file. The IRF for the SYS:SHARED directory is all rights; the IRF for the SYS:SHARED\CRIME directory is Supervisor and Access Control; and the IRF for the CRIME.DB file is Supervisor, Read, Write, Create, and File Scan. Calculate DrWatson's effective rights in the SYS:SHARED directory, the SYS:SHARED\CRIME directory, and the CRIME.DB file, using the worksheet in Figure 5.36.

F I G U R E 5.36

Calculating file system effective rights — Case #2

SYS: SHARED	S	R	W	C	E	M	F	A
Inherited Rights Filter								
Inherited Rights — User								
Inherited Rights — Group								
Trustee Assignment — User								
Trustee Assignment — Group								
Effective Rights								

SYS: SHARED\CRIME	S	R	W	C	E	M	F	A
Inherited Rights Filter								
Inherited Rights — User								
Inherited Rights — Group								
Trustee Assignment — User								
Trustee Assignment — Group								
Effective Rights								

CRIME.DB	S	R	W	C	E	M	F	A
Inherited Rights Filter								
Inherited Rights — User								
Inherited Rights — Group								
Trustee Assignment — User								
Trustee Assignment — Group								
Effective Rights								

Case #3

MMarion was granted the Modify and Access Control rights to the SYS:SHARED\
POL directory. In addition, the POL Group, of which she is a member, was granted
the Read, Write, Create, Erase, and File Scan rights to both the SYS:SHARED and
SYS:SHARED\POL directories. The IRF for the SYS:SHARED directory contains all
rights; the IRF for the SYS:SHARED\POL directory contains the Supervisor right; and
the IRF for the CRIME.RPT file contains all rights. Calculate MMarion's effective rights
to the SYS:SHARED directory, the SYS:SHARED\POL directory, and the CRIMEP.RPT
file, using the worksheet in Figure 5.37.

F I G U R E 5.37

Calculating file system effective rights — Case #3

SYS: SHARED	S	R	W	C	E	M	F	A
Inherited Rights Filter								
Inherited Rights — User								
Inherited Rights — Group								
Trustee Assignment — User								
Trustee Assignment — Group								
Effective Rights								

SYS: SHARED\POL	S	R	W	C	E	M	F	A
Inherited Rights Filter								
Inherited Rights — User								
Inherited Rights — Group								
Trustee Assignment — User								
Trustee Assignment — Group								
Effective Rights								

CRIME.RPT	S	R	W	C	E	M	F	A
Inherited Rights Filter								
Inherited Rights — User								
Inherited Rights — Group								
Trustee Assignment — User								
Trustee Assignment — Group								
Effective Rights								

Case #4

SHolmes was granted all rights to the SYS:SHARED directory. The CRIME Group, of which he is a member, was granted Read, Write, Create, and File Scan rights to the SYS:SHARED\CRIME directory. The CRIME Group was also granted Read and File Scan rights to the CRIME.DB file. The IRF for the SYS:SHARED directory contains all rights; the IRF for the SYS:SHARED\CRIME directory contains the Supervisor right; and the IRF for the CRIME.DB file contains Supervisor, Read, and File Scan rights. Calculate SHolmes' effective rights to the SYS:SHARED directory, the SYS:SHARED\CRIME directory, and the CRIME.DB file, using the worksheet in Figure 5.38.

Calculating file system effective rights — Case #4

SYS: SHARED	S	R	W	C	E	M	F	A
Inherited Rights Filter								
Inherited Rights — User								
Inherited Rights — Group								
Trustee Assignment — User								
Trustee Assignment — Group								
Effective Rights								

SYS: SHARED\CRIME	S	R	W	C	E	M	F	A
Inherited Rights Filter								
Inherited Rights — User								
Inherited Rights — Group								
Trustee Assignment — User								
Trustee Assignment — Group								
Effective Rights								

CYBER.DB	S	R	W	C	E	M	F	A
Inherited Rights Filter								
Inherited Rights — User								
Inherited Rights — Group								
Trustee Assignment — User								
Trustee Assignment — Group								
Effective Rights								

The answers to all of these cases are in Appendix C.

LAB EXERCISE 5.3: ACME SECURITY

In this exercise, we are going to explore the exciting world of NetWare 5 NDS and file system security.

To perform this exercise, you will need:

- A NetWare 5 server called CRIME-SRV1.CRIME.TOKYO.ACME (which can be installed using the directions found in Chapter 8, Exercise 8.1).

- A workstation running the NetWare 5 Novell Client for Windows 95/98 or Windows NT (which can be installed using the directions found in Chapter 8, Exercise 8.2).

Initially, the Crime division, the White-Collar Crime department, and the three White-Collar Crime units (Cyber Crime, Financial Crime, and Political Crime) will all be sharing the same server (.CRIME-SRV1.CRIME.TOKYO.ACME)—but not the same data. The Users in the Crime division office will be located in a container called CRIME.TOKYO.ACME. The users in the White-Collar Crime department will be located in a container under CRIME called WHITE. The users in WHITE's three Crime units will be located in subcontainers under WHITE called CYBER, FINAN, and POL, respectively. You will need to create Group objects for each of these workgroups (namely, CRIME-Group, WHITE-Group, CYBER-Group, FIN-Group, and POL-Group) in their respective containers.

Temporarily, the manager of each workgroup will act as a network administrator for his or her respective workgroup. Because these administrator assignments are temporary, you will need to create an Organizational Role for each in their container (called CRIME-Admin, WHITE-Admin, CYBER-Admin, FIN-Admin, and POL-Admin, respectively).

Each workgroup will be given rights to the SYS:SHARED directory as well as to its own subdirectory under the SYS:SHARED directory (namely, SYS:SHARED\CRIME, SYS:SHARED\WHITE, SYS:SHARED\CYBER, SYS:SHARED\FIN, and SYS:SHARED\ POL). The SHARED directory will contain those files that are shared by the entire division, whereas the individual subdirectories will contain those files that are shared by each workgroup. An Inherited Rights Filter (IRF) will be placed on each of the subdirectories under SHARED, so that users from one department cannot see the files from another.

Everyone in these five workgroups will have access to the word processing program (stored in SYS:APPS\WP70). In addition, the Financial Crime unit will have access to the spreadsheet program (stored in SYS:APPS\SS30) and the Cyber Crime unit will have access to the database program (stored in SYS:APPS\DB50). Each workgroup is currently generating a list of other applications that they'd like on the server.

Template objects will be used for consistency in creating User objects and will contain the following account restrictions:

▸ Each user will be assigned a home directory under the appropriate subdirectory of the USERS directory (SYS:USERS\CRIME, SYS:USERS\WHITE, SYS:USERS\CYBER, SYS:USERS\FIN, or SYS:USERS\ POL).

▸ Each User will be limited to three concurrent logins.

▸ Each User will be required to have a unique password consisting of 7 characters or more and will be required to change their password every 90 days. Each User will be allowed 6 grace logins.

▸ Because employees in this division work long hours, there will be no time restrictions on anyone's account except between 3:00 a.m. to 4:00 a.m. daily (when system backups and network maintenance are performed).

▸ Intruder detection will be set to lock for 24 hours after 6 incorrect attempts in 24 hours. Intruder detection statistics will be kept for 30 days.

Now that you know the plan, let's go ahead and implement it!

1. Log into the tree as Admin, if you haven't already done so.

2. Execute the NetWare Administrator utility.

3. Create the basic file system directory structure.

    a. Create the USERS directory under the CRIME-SRV1_SYS volume object.

b. You should have already created the SHARED directory under the CRIME-SRV1_SYS volume in an earlier exercise.

d. Create the CRIME, WHITE, CYBER, FIN, and POL subdirectories under the SHARED directory.

e. Create the APPS directory under CRIME-SRV1_SYS, then create the following directories under it: DB50, SS30, and WP70.

4. Set the following Intruder Detection/Lockout defaults for the CRIME, WHITE, CYBER, FIN, and POL containers:

Incorrect Login Attempts: **6**

Intruder Attempt Reset Interval: **1 days, 0 hours, 0 minutes**

Lock Account After Detection: **On**

Intruder Lockout Reset Interval: **30 days, 0 hours, 0 minutes**

5. Create a Template object for the TOKYO container called TOKYO-UT with the following property values:

a. Identification page. Type the following information in the appropriate fields:

Location: **Tokyo, Japan**

Telephone: **813-5481-1141**

Fax Number: **813-5481-855**

b. Environment page button. Select the following home directory information:

Volume: **CRIME-SRV1_SYS.CRIME.TOKYO.ACME**

Path: **USERS\TOKYO**

c. Login Restrictions page button. Limit users to three concurrent connections.

d. Password Restrictions. Set the following restrictions:

- Allow users to change their own password.

- Require each user to have a password.

- Indicate a Minimum Password Length of **7**.

- Require Forced Periodic Password Changes every **90** days.

- Require Unique Passwords.

- Allow 6 Grace Logins Allowed.

- Use an initial password of ACME for each user.

e. Login Time Restrictions page button. Restrict login privileges between 3:00 a.m. and 4:00 a.m. every day.

f. Postal Address page button. Enter the following information in the appropriate fields:

Street: **Toei Mishuku Building; 1-13-1, Mishuku**

City: **Setagaya-ku, Tokyo 154**

State or Province: **Japan**

6. Copy the TOKYO-UT Template to the CRIME, WHITE, CYBER, FIN, and POL containers. The name of each new template should be the container name followed by "-UT" (as in "CRIME-UT"). Also, change the Home Directory Path in each template to correspond to the correct subdirectory under the USERS directory for that container (namely SYS:USERS\CRIME, SYS:USERS\WHITE, SYS:USERS\CYBER, SYS:USERS\FIN, or SYS:USERS\ POL).

7. Create Group objects. Before you can create users, you will need to create the Group objects that they will be members of. Create a Group object in the CRIME, WHITE, CYBER, FIN, and POL containers using the container name followed by "-Group" (as in "CRIME-Group"). Type the following information in the appropriate fields:

Location: **Tokyo, Japan**

Department: **Crime-Fighting**

Organization: **ACME**

8. Create User objects. Next, create the following users in the designated containers using the Template object in each container: SHolmes (CRIME), RHood (WHITE-Admin), FrTuck (CYBER-Admin), LJohn (FIN-Admin), and MMarion (POL-Admin). Assign each person as a member of the Group object in their container.

9. Create Organizational Role objects. Your next task will be to create an Organizational Role object for each workgroup manager. The naming scheme to use is the container name followed by "-Admin" (as in "CRIME-Admin"). Assign the following occupants to the organizational roles you create: SHolmes (CRIME), RHood (WHITE-Admin), FrTuck (CYBER-Admin), LJohn (FIN-Admin), and MMarion (POL-Admin).

10. Now that you've created the Organizational Roles for container administration, let's give them the rights they need. In this section, we will create an exclusive container administrator for CRIME (SHolmes) and WHITE (RHood). As you know, an exclusive administrator has all NDS rights to a container and blocks most rights (especially [S]) from everyone else. To start, assign SHolmes as the administrator for .CRIME.TOKYO.ACME.

a. Right-click the CRIME container.

b. Select Trustees of this Object from the pop-up menu that appears.

c. When the Trustees of CRIME dialog box appears, click Add Trustee.

d. When the Select Object dialog box appears, double-click the SHolmes object in the Available Objects list box to select it.

e. When the Trustees of CRIME dialog box appears, assign SHomes all object rights and all property rights to All Properties.

- In the Objects Rights section, make sure all of the following checkboxes are marked (that is, mark any that aren't marked yet): Supervisor, Browse, Create, Delete, Rename, and Inheritable.

- In the Property Rights section, ensure that the All Properties radio button is selected.

- In the Property Rights section, ensure that all the following checkboxes are marked (that is, mark any that aren't marked yet): Supervisor, Compare, Read, Write, and Add Self.

- Click OK to save your changes.

f. Finally, click the OK button at the bottom of the screen. Good work.

11. You have successfully made SHolmes an administrator of the .CRIME.TOKYO.ACME container. He currently shares this role with Admin. Now comes the "exclusive" part. We need to create an IRF of [B] for the CRIME container. This will block Admin, but not SHolmes.

a. Right-click the CRIME container.

b. Select Trustees of this Object from the pop-up menu that appears.

c. When the Trustees of CRIME dialog box appears, click Inherited Rights Filter.

d. When the Inherited Rights dialog box appears:

- You'll notice that currently, the defaults are selected — that is, all five object rights [SBCDR] and all five property rights [SCRWA].

- To make SHolmes an exclusive administrator, unmark all rights except Browse in the Object Rights section (namely [SCDR]).

- In the Property Rights section, unmark the checkboxes for all five rights (namely, [SCRWA]).

- Click OK twice to return to the main NetWare Administrator browser window.

e. Very good work. Now, repeat these steps (10 and 11) to make each of the following exclusive container administrators of their container: RHood (WHITE), FrTuck (CYBER), LJohn (FIN), and MMarion (POL).

12. Assign file system rights to the file system. You are now ready to start assigning rights to the file system. First, assign rights to the SHARED directory. Because all five workgroups will have the same level of access to the SHARED directory, you can grant these rights at the container level rather than at the Group level.

a. Right-click the SHARED folder.

b. Select Details from the pop-up menu that appears.

c. When the Directory: SHARED dialog box appears, click the Trustees of this Directory page button.

d. When the Trustees of This Directory dialog box appears, click Add Trustee.

e. When the Select Object dialog box appears, walk the tree until the CRIME container is displayed in the Available Objects list box on the left side of the screen, then double-click it.

f. When the Directory: SHARED dialog box re-appears:

- You'll notice that the CRIME container has automatically been granted the Read and File Scan rights.

- Mark the Write, Create, and Erase checkboxes.

- Click the OK button to accept this trustee assignment.

13. Assign the rights listed in Step 11 to the following containers for the designated subdirectories. (Remember, that rights are not flowing down because of IRFs that were assigned earlier in this exercise.)

a. Grant CRIME rights to the SHARED\CRIME directory.

b. Grant WHITE rights to the SHARED and SHARED\WHITE directories.

c. Grant CYBER rights to the SHARED and SHARED\CYBER directories.

d. Grant FIN rights to the SHARED and SHARED\FIN directories.

e. Grant POL rights to the SHARED and SHARED\POL directories.

14. Assign trustee rights for the APPS subdirectories. Now that you know how to grant trustee rights for directories to containers and Group objects, use the same techniques to make the trustee assignments. If you'd really like a challenge, see if you can make these assignments from the trustee's perspective (that is, container or group), rather than the directory's perspective. (**Hint:** You can use the Rights to Other Objects . . . option in the Object menu.)

a. Grant the CRIME container [RF] rights to the SYS:APPS\WP70 directory (since all five workgroups will have access to the word processing application).

b. Grant the FIN-Group [RF] rights to the SYS:APP\SS30 directory.

c. Grant the CYBER-Group [RF] rights to the SYS:APPS\DB50 subdirectory.

15. Assign trustee rights to Organizational Role objects. Grant the trustee rights listed here to the Organizational Roles indicated.

a. All five Organizational Roles should be granted all rights to the SHARED directory.

b. Each Organizational Role should be granted all rights to their corresponding workgroup's subdirectory under the SHARED directory.

c. Each Organizational Role should be granted all rights to the home directories of each user in their workgroup.

16. Verify effective rights. You can verify an object's effective rights to a directory from the object's perspective or the directory's perspective. Verify an object's effective rights from the directory's perspective.

a. Right-click the directory.

b. Select Details from the pop-up menu that appears.

c. When the directory's property page appears, click the Trustees of this Directory page button.

d. When the Trustees of This Directory page appears, click Effective rights.

e. When the Effective Rights dialog box appears, click the Browser button to the right of the Trustee field.

f. When the Select Object dialog box appears, walk the tree until the desired object is displayed in the Available Object list box on the left side of the screen, then double-click the object to select it.

g. When the Effective Rights dialog box reappears, the effective rights for this object will be displayed in black. (The rights that are not effective will be displayed in gray.)

h. Practice verifying the effective rights of different objects for various directories that we worked with in this exercise from the directory's point of view.

i. Practice verifying the effective rights of different objects for various directories that we have worked with in this exercise from the object's point of view. (**Hint:** Use the Rights to Other Objects menu option.)

LAB EXERCISE 5.4: KEEP THE BAD GUYS OUT!

Circle the 20 security-related terms hidden in this word search puzzle using the hints provided. No punctuation characters (such as blank spaces, hyphens, and so on) should be included. Numbers should always be spelled out.

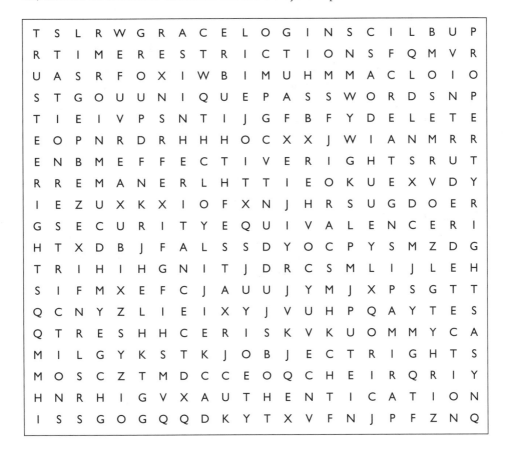

```
T  S  L  R  W  G  R  A  C  E  L  O  G  I  N  S  C  I  L  B  U  P
R  T  I  M  E  R  E  S  T  R  I  C  T  I  O  N  S  F  Q  M  V  R
U  A  S  R  F  O  X  I  W  B  I  M  U  H  M  M  A  C  L  O  I  O
S  T  G  O  U  U  N  I  Q  U  E  P  A  S  S  W  O  R  D  S  N  P
T  I  E  I  V  P  S  N  T  I  J  G  F  B  F  Y  D  E  L  E  T  E
E  O  P  N  R  D  R  H  H  H  O  C  X  X  J  W  I  A  N  M  R  R
E  N  B  M  E  F  F  E  C  T  I  V  E  R  I  G  H  T  S  R  U  T
R  R  E  M  A  N  E  R  L  H  T  T  I  E  O  K  U  E  X  V  D  Y
I  E  Z  U  X  K  X  I  O  F  X  N  J  H  R  S  U  G  D  O  E  R
G  S  E  C  U  R  I  T  Y  E  Q  U  I  V  A  L  E  N  C  E  R  I
H  T  X  D  B  J  F  A  L  S  S  D  Y  O  C  P  Y  S  M  Z  D  G
T  R  I  H  I  H  G  N  I  T  J  D  R  C  S  M  L  I  J  L  E  H
S  I  F  M  X  E  F  C  J  A  U  U  J  Y  M  J  X  P  S  G  T  T
Q  C  N  Y  Z  L  I  E  I  X  Y  J  V  U  H  P  Q  A  Y  T  E  S
Q  T  R  E  S  H  H  C  E  R  I  S  K  V  K  U  O  M  M  Y  C  A
M  I  L  G  Y  K  S  T  K  J  O  B  J  E  C  T  R  I  G  H  T  S
M  O  S  C  Z  T  M  D  C  C  E  O  Q  C  H  E  I  R  Q  R  I  Y
H  N  R  H  I  G  V  X  A  U  T  H  E  N  T  I  C  A  T  I  O  N
I  S  S  G  O  G  Q  Q  D  K  Y  T  X  V  F  N  J  P  F  Z  N  Q
```

Hints:

1. Property of an object that lists trustees of the object.
2. Making sure you are who you say you are.
3. Object right that is only valid for containers.
4. Object right that allows you to remove an object from the NDS tree.
5. The rights that an object can actually exercise for an object, directory, or file.
6. The number of times a user can log in with an expired password.

7. Object used for assigning rights to multiple users.
8. Flowing down of money or trustee rights.
9. Feature that tracks invalid login attempts.
10. Controls the rights that can be inherited from a parent container or directory.
11. Privileges assigned to an object that control its access to other objects, directories, or files.
12. Privileges required to view or modify the property of an object.
13. Special trustee which is somewhat similar to the EVERYONE Group found in earlier versions of NetWare.
14. Object right that allows you to change the object's name.
15. Method of granting an object the same rights as another object.
16. Account restrictions that limit a user to specific workstation node IDs.
17. Account restrictions that limit the hours during which a user can log in.
18. Privileges granted to an object that determine its access to another object, directory, or file.
19. System Fault Tolerance feature that protects database applications from corruption by backing out incomplete transactions.
20. Account restriction that requires a User to supply a new password that is different from previous passwords.

See Appendix C for answers.

LAB EXERCISE 5.5: NETWORK 5 SECURITY

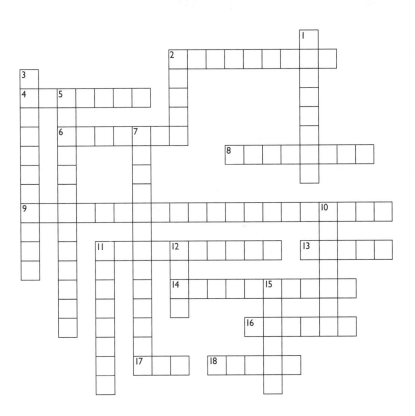

Across

2. What is the "O" for?
4. Graphical administrator tool
6. Automatically granted with the Read property right
8. Tracking important network events
9. Object is security equivalent to parent
11. Can be blocked by an NDS IRF
13. Is initially granted access to entire tree
14. Restricts access to directories and files
16. Required for changing file attributes

17. File system rights to consider restricting
18. Required for deleting a directory or file

Down

1. Handy for creating multiple users
2. Required for changing file contents
3. New object/property right
5. Required for changing file system IRF
7. Property rights that can be inherited
10. Automatically granted with Write property right
11. Keeping the bad guys out
12. Required for looking at file contents
15. Required for viewing objects in the NDS tree

See Appendix C for answers.

CHAPTER 6

The Zen of NetWare 5: NetWare 5 Workstation Management

So, you're cruising down the information superhighway minding your own business, and wham — it hits you — a large pink and aquamarine neon sign saying: *"Z.E.N.works . . . 7 miles"*

Of all the places you'll go in your cyber-life, few will be as interesting as Z.E.N.works. In this virtual cyber-city, you'll find fun, adventure, and the Novell Application Launcher (NAL). The Z.E.N.works Client is one of the most important aspects of your WAN because it's where the users meet the cyber-road.

I call it the *"Infobahn Access Site for Virtual Villagers."* Someday, I guarantee you'll get the question, "Where's the ANY key?" This is your life as a NetWare 5 CNA.

To help you sleep at night, we're going to try to keep the client interface as transparent as possible — avoiding confusion and unnecessary support calls. In the Z.E.N.works client world, transparent connectivity is accomplished by two key workstation components (see Figure 6.1):

▸ *NIC* — The internal Network Interface Card (NIC) provides communications between the local workstation operating system (WOS) and the NetWare 5 server. This hardware device is managed by a series of workstation connectivity files built into the Novell Client.

▸ *Workstation Operating System (WOS)* — The WOS manages all local workstation services. It coordinates among local applications (word processing, spreadsheets, and databases) and local devices (file storage, screens, and printers). All these local activities must be somehow orchestrated with network services. Once again, this is accomplished using the Novell Client.

Z.E.N.works is a desktop management tool that integrates with the Novell Client and orchestrates all NetWare 5 workstation activity. In effect, it's a whole new cyber-world . . . where users behave and CNAs have the upper hand. It sounds like paradise to me!

In this chapter, we're going to explore every corner of the Z.E.N.works cyber-kingdom. You will learn how to install this great tool and take full advantage of its three separate realms: Workstation Maintenance, Desktop Management, and Application Management. Let's start with a quick introduction, and then learn what it takes to become king or queen of your Z.E.N.works world.

▶ • ◀

FIGURE 6.1

*The two main components
of workstation connectivity*

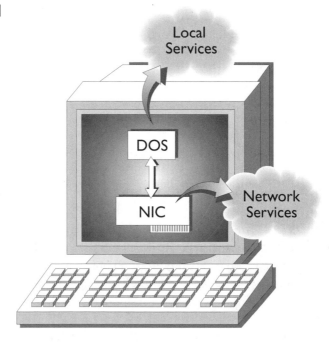

▶ • ◀

Zero Effort Networks

Unlike its name implies, Z.E.N.works has little to do with ancient meditation and/or wisdom. In actuality, it's a clever acronym for "Zero Effort Networks." While it's impossible to achieve "zero effort" networking, Z.E.N.works does greatly improve the manageability of user access to the Infobahn. Think of it as a highly evolved on-ramp to the information superhighway.

Z.E.N.works is a desktop management tool that reduces the hassle of connecting PCs to small, medium, and large networks. Z.E.N.works leverages NDS to help CNAs manage Windows-based desktops by providing policy-enabled software distribution, desktop management, and workstation maintenance. The beauty of Z.E.N.works is that it allows you to achieve all these things without having to visit the user's workstation—no more late night flights to Timbuktu. Darn!

Here's a sample Q&A dialog between a Z.E.N.works CNA and his or her users:

▸ User Question: "I need access to that software right now!"

> ► CNA Answer: "Here ya go. Press F5, and you'll see the application."

> ► User Question: "I log into a different workstation every day."

> ► CNA Answer: "No problem. You'll see your own desktop configuration wherever you are."

> ► User Question: "My workstation is broken."

> ► CNA Answer: "No sweat. I'll fix it from here."

So, how does it do it? Z.E.N.works extends the NDS schema to include Workstation objects. These objects allow you to configure and control workstations from within the NDS tree. Then, each time a user logs into the network, Z.E.N.works registers the workstation with NDS. Once a workstation has been registered, you can configure and control it remotely. This includes tasks such as upgrading software, repairing workstation problems, and gathering inventory information. Check it out in Figure 6.2.

TIP

To take full advantage of the NDS integration features of Z.E.N.works, you must use the 32-bit version of NetWare Administrator. By default, NetWare Administrator 32 is copied to the SYS:PUBLIC\WIN32 directory during Z.E.N.works installation.

NetWare 5 ships with a "Z.E.N.works Starter Pack." This includes a subset of the Z.E.N.works functionality. You can install the Z.E.N.works Starter Pack using the steps provided later in this chapter. The full Z.E.N.works product must be purchased separately. To use Z.E.N.works, you must accomplish two tasks: first, install Z.E.N.works components on the server; second, upgrade the Novell Client on each workstation.

Once the kingdom of Z.E.N.works has been installed, you can take full advantage of its three separate realms:

> ► *Realm 1*: Workstation Maintenance

> ► *Realm 2*: Desktop Management

> ► *Realm 3*: Application Management

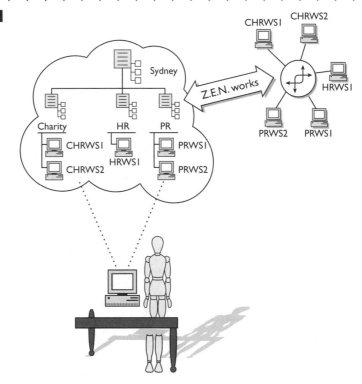

FIGURE 6.2

Remote network management through NDS

Let's take a quick look at the benefits of Z.E.N.works and then explore the features provided by each of these three realms. Remember, you're the king/queen of your own cyber-kingdom.

Benefits of Z.E.N.works

Z.E.N.works makes use of NDS and NetWare Administrator to provide you with the ability to manage your workstations from a central location. This architecture provides numerous benefits to CNAs and users.

As a CNA, Z.E.N.works provides the following administrative benefits:

▸ Integrated installation of Z.E.N.works components

▸ Application management and distribution

▸ Desktop configuration, management, and maintenance

▸ Workstation maintenance using a Remote Control utility

▸ Workstation management via a single Workstation object or workstation Group objects in the NDS tree

▸ A scheduler utility to run programs automatically on Windows 95/98/NT clients

As a user, Z.E.N.works provides the following productivity benefits:

▸ Send help requests to a designated support contact

▸ Install, run, and repair applications automatically

▸ Retain customized desktop configurations, access rights, application access, and printer associations when using any Windows computer on the network

All those benefits in a single package—no wonder it's called "Z.E.N."-works. Now let's learn more about the architecture of Z.E.N.works with a brief tour through its three realms. Don't forget your camera.

Realm 1: Workstation Maintenance

The first realm of Z.E.N.works is the largest. Workstation Maintenance encompasses all the CNA tasks associated with daily user productivity. In this realm, you'll use three NetWare 5 workstation tools: Novell Workstation Manager, NetWare Administrator, and the Novell Help Requester.

Here's what you have to look forward to in the realm of Z.E.N.works Workstation Maintenance:

▸ *Policies*—Z.E.N.works includes various *Policy Packages,* which are NDS objects you create to help you maintain Workstation objects in the NDS tree. Each package is a collection of *policies* that allow you to set up parameters for managing workstations, users, groups or containers. For example, the policies found in the Workstation Package help you set up controls that apply to Windows workstations on your network—including printers, systems, Remote Access Server (RAS), remote control, and login restrictions. Refer to Figure 6.3 for a list of the policies found in the WIN95 Workstation Package object.

FIGURE 6.3

WIN95 Workstation Policy
Package in NetWare
Administrator

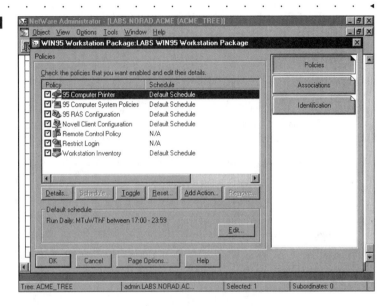

▶ *NDS registration* — Workstations must be registered with NDS before they can be imported into the tree and managed as other NDS objects. Z.E.N.works includes a Workstation Registration Agent that automatically registers workstations as long as two conditions have been met: the workstation has been updated to the Novell Client for Z.E.N.works and the workstation has been used to log into the network at least once. Once this happens, the agent sends the workstation's address to NDS and places it in a holding tank — NDS Registration List. Once a workstation appears in the list, it can then be imported into the NDS tree. As a CNA, you can use one of three methods for invoking the Workstation Registration Agent: NAL, Z.E.N.works Scheduler, or a customized login script.

▶ *Remote control* — Once Z.E.N.works has been installed and workstations have been registered with NDS, you can establish remote-control access to them by distributing the appropriate User Agents. User Agents allow you to connect and manage workstations using the remote-control facility within NetWare Administrator. As a CNA, you have two options for automatically distributing User Agents to Windows 3.*x*, Windows 95, and/or Windows NT workstations: TSR applications or Application objects via NAL. Regardless of the distribution scheme you choose, be sure that users have the appropriate NDS and file system rights to accept remote-control instructions.

▶ *Novell Help Requester* — The Novell Help Requester utility allows users to notify the Help Desk or network administrator of workstation problems via e-mail or phone. This tool provides pertinent information about the user and workstation involved, such as the user's context and the workstation ID. Using NAL, you can push the Help Requester application to all user workstations. When the Application Launcher Window opens on a user's desktop, the Help Requester icon appears as a selection. Users can then be instructed to use this utility whenever a problem occurs.

As you can see, Z.E.N.works offers myriad benefits for workstation maintenance in the virtual age. Now let's cruise over to the user desktop and see what it does for them.

Realm 2: Desktop Management

In addition to CNA maintenance, Z.E.N.works offers numerous benefits to the user. This desktop management functionality falls into three different areas:

▶ *Customizing applications* — You can customize the user desktop by enabling two specific Z.E.N.works policies: the User System Policy (in the User Policy Package) and the Computer System Policy (in the Workstation Policy Package). The User System Policy allows you to customize the desktop functions available to specific users. For example, hiding applications such as NetWare Neighborhood, Run, and Find can help reduce access problems and server traffic. Similarly the Computer System Policy allows you to customize the Windows properties of a specific workstation. For example, you can use the Properties button to launch a utility that allows you to identify applications that should run when the workstation connects to the network.

▶ *Printing configuration* — One of the most costly and time-consuming aspects of CNA management is printing configuration. Fortunately, Z.E.N.works provides a solution that allows you to configure a user's printing environment through NDS. You can even autoload the correct print driver for a user when he or she logs in.

▶ *User profiles* — Desktop settings such as Wallpaper, Screen Saver, and Sounds can be standardized and deployed to every user in the enterprise. These settings can even be configured so that users cannot modify them. As a matter of fact, most of the normal user-defined preferences set in the Windows Control Panel can be configured using the Desktop Preference Policy in the User Policy Package. Very cool!

If you get the feeling from this discussion that "Big Brother" is watching . . . you're not far off. Z.E.N.works Desktop Management allows Big Brother to tightly control user access and productivity. The good news is *you* are Big Brother!

Now, let's complete our brief journey through the kingdom of Z.E.N.works by exploring the final realm — Application Management.

Realm 3: Application Management

Installing shared network applications is easier, but the process still has many drawbacks. For example, you must install an icon on each user's desktop, you might have to visit each geographically-separated workstation, you may assume more complex support responsibilities, and you must continually maintain desktop settings — including icons, drive mappings, and so on.

Z.E.N.works solves all these problems with the Novell Application Launcher (NAL). This special workstation management tool enables you to distribute network-based applications to users' workstations and to manage the applications as objects in the NDS tree. Users then access the applications assigned to them using the Application Launcher Window or Application Explorer.

In addition, NAL implements solutions such as fault tolerance and load-balancing to guarantee that users always have access to the applications they need. Furthermore, if the user deletes application .DLL files from his or her hard disk, NAL automatically detects the missing files and restores them when the user attempts to launch the application.

So, what can NAL do for you? Here's a list:

▸ NAL provides multilevel folders to hierarchically order Application objects in the NDS tree.

▸ NAL automatically grants file rights to users so that they can access the applications assigned to them.

▸ NAL automatically grants NT Supervisor rights to the Admin user so that Admin can handle advanced Registry settings in Windows NT. This is accomplished by using the Windows NT Service Control Manager, which allows CNAs to make changes to secure NT servers/workstations.

▸ NAL provides an application-suspension configuration to allow you to schedule a time when application access will terminate.

▸ NAL provides the snAppShot utility — which can be used to capture a workstation's configuration before and after an application is installed.

NAL is your friend. It increases user productivity and decreases CNA headaches. Whatever you do, don't miss the benefits offered by Z.E.N.works Realm 3.

That completes our brief tour through the Z.E.N.works cyber-kingdom. As you can see, this is a powerful, comprehensive tool for workstation maintenance, management, and control. As a CNA, you should quickly become the king or queen of your Z.E.N.works world. Remember, workstation connectivity is typically a war between user desires and centralized standardization. Whatever you do, don't let your virtual villagers run amok.

Now, let's begin our new "Z.E.N." training with a comprehensive lesson in Z.E.N.works construction — also known as installation. To progress, you must become *one* with the workstation.

LAB EXERCISE 6.1: UNDERSTANDING Z.E.N.WORKS

Match the following terms with their descriptions:

a. Realm 1: Workstation Maintenance

b. Realm 2: Desktop Management

c. Realm 3: Application Management

Category	Item
____	Autoloading print drivers
____	Remote Access Server (RAS)
____	NAL Scheduler
____	Help Desk Policy
____	Customizing applications
____	SnAppShot
____	Remote Control
____	Application Explorer
____	Customizing desktop settings
____	WIN95 Workstation Package object
____	Automatic granting of rights to Windows NT Registry
____	Balancing user access and standardization
____	Workstation Registration Agent
____	WIN NT policies
____	Automatic restoration of .dll files
____	Workstation IDs
____	User preferences in Windows Control Panel
____	NDS Registration List
____	Application Launcher window
____	Hiding Network Neighborhood
____	Mandatory user profiles
____	Novell Help Requester

Z.E.N.works Installation

Repeat after me:

"I *am* the workstation."

"I *am* the user."

"I *am* Z.E.N.works."

To fully understand the workstation, you must *become* the workstation . . . this is Z.E.N.works. As we mentioned earlier, NetWare 5 ships with a *Z.E.N.works Starter Pack* CD-ROM. The Z.E.N.works Starter Pack consists of NAL and the Workstation Manager. The Remote Control utility, Help Requester application, and Hardware Inventory are not included. To install the full Z.E.N.works product, you must use the "real" Z.E.N.works CD — which must be purchased separately.

Before we tackle the detailed steps of Z.E.N.works construction, let's take a closer look at some installation requirements.

Before You Begin

To install Z.E.N.works, you must ensure that your server and workstations meet the minimum requirements discussed here. In addition, you must have appropriate NDS and file system rights. Remember, Z.E.N.works is a fully network-integrated client connectivity solution. Don't take the installation lightly.

Server Requirements

Z.E.N.works relies on a high level of synergy between the NetWare 5 server and Novell Client. Let's begin with the server. Following is a checklist of minimum hardware and software requirements for Z.E.N.works installation:

▸ A Novell NetWare 4.11 (or later) server

▸ NDS-integration (bindery emulation not supported)

▸ 70MB of available server memory

▸ 205MB of available server disk space

▸ The NetWare server must also have the 32-bit version of NetWare Administrator (NWADMN32.EXE) installed in the SYS:PUBLIC\WIN32 subdirectory

REAL WORLD

A full Z.E.N.works implementation is a fairly sophisticated and complex project. In general, it consists of five phases rolled out over a five-day period. Here's a quick preview:

▸ *Phase 1: Planning* — First, you should determine how many workstations will be added to your NDS tree. Then, you should plan the distribution of policy objects and redesign the NDS tree as needed.

▸ *Phase 2: Installation* — Next, you should install Z.E.N.works on all the servers and workstations that require it. Also, be sure that you update your existing NetWare 5 Client with full Z.E.N.works functionality. Finally, consider creating a Workstation Import Policy.

▸ *Phase 3: Initial NDS Registration* — Once Z.E.N.works has been installed, the new and improved workstations must send NDS registration information to the Workstation Registration property of select NDS containers. Don't worry, this is accomplished automatically when users log in.

▸ *Phase 4: Import Workstations* — Next, you must import all your new Z.E.N.works workstations into the NDS tree using NetWare Administrator 32.

▸ *Phase 5: Final NDS Registration* — Finally, your NDS-enhanced workstations will automatically register themselves with their own logical NDS objects the next time users log in. All done!

In this chapter, we will explore all of these Z.E.N.works implementation activities — and more! Sit back, relax, and enjoy the show.

Client Requirements

Next, you must ensure that the Novell Clients meet Z.E.N.works minimum installation requirements. Here's a quick checklist:

▸ Windows 95 and Windows NT clients can use all the Z.E.N.works features.

▸ Windows 3.1 and DOS clients use a subset of the Z.E.N.works features.

▸ Workstations must support the latest Novell Client software.

▸ A network connection via NDS. Bindery connections do not support Z.E.N.works.

▸ An Intel 486/33 processor or better.

▸ 16MB of RAM for Windows 95 and Windows 3.1 workstations, or 24MB of RAM for Windows NT workstations.

▸ 24MB of available hard disk space.

TIP

Windows 3.1 cannot use all the Z.E.N.works features because the Registry (found only in Windows 95 and Windows NT) is needed to store some of the advanced configuration information created by Z.E.N.works.

Rights Requirements

To install Z.E.N.works, you must have a minimum set of NDS and file system rights. In addition, users need special file system rights to access NAL-delivered applications. How secure do you feel?

▸ *NDS Rights* — To install Z.E.N.works, you must have Supervisor object rights to the [Root] of the NDS tree. In addition, users need Read and Compare property rights to All Properties for any Container, Group, or User object associated with a NAL application. Fortunately, these NDS rights are assigned automatically when you associate a user with an Application object.

▶ *File System Rights* — To use the Z.E.N.works application-management features, users need certain file system rights to the directory in which NAL is installed and the directories containing NAL applications. Fortunately, Z.E.N.works automatically assigns users Read and File Scan file system rights to the default NAL directory (SYS:PUBLIC). The second rights assignment occurs when users are associated with NAL-delivered Application objects. And here's the cool part — these rights are then revoked when the user is disassociated from the Application object. Very cool.

That's all there is to it . . . no sweat. Now that your NetWare server and clients are ready, it's time for Z.E.N.works construction. Take three deep breaths, assume the lotus position, and continue.

Z.E.N.works Server Installation

The Z.E.N.works cyber-kingdom relies on synergy between the NetWare server and Novell client. As such, Z.E.N.works construction involves two main tasks:

▶ *Z.E.N.works server installation* — First, you must copy the Z.E.N.works tools to the NetWare server and activate a customized list of features.

▶ *Z.E.N.works Client installation* — Next, you must install the Novell Client at each Z.E.N.works workstation and perform some local configurations.

Once you've synergized the Z.E.N.works server and client, life is good. Your virtual villagers have enhanced access to the Infobahn and you can control them more easily. Let's start with Z.E.N.works server installation . . . here's how it works:

▶ *Step 1*: Getting Started

▶ *Step 2*: Z.E.N.works Installation Type

▶ *Step 3*: Choose Z.E.N.works Components

▶ *Step 4*: Choose Z.E.N.works Parts

> *Step 5*: Choose the Z.E.N.works Servers

> *Step 6*: Workstation Registration Rights

> *Step 7*: The End

That's all there is to it. Now let's install Z.E.N.works on one of ACME's SYDNEY servers.

Step 1: Getting Started

You must install Z.E.N.works separately on each Z.E.N.-based server. To start off, you must log into the server as an Administrator with Supervisor object rights to the [Root] of the NDS tree. Next, close all applications on your administrative workstation and insert the Z.E.N.works 1.0 CD-ROM into the appropriate drive.

The Z.E.N.works installation CD is designed with an auto-run feature that automatically launches the first screen when you insert the CD-ROM. Otherwise, you can run "WINSETUP.EXE" from the root directory of the CD. Now you're in!

The first Z.E.N.works server installation screen is a language query — that is, what's your native language? If none of the words on the screen looks familiar, you're in trouble. However, if you speak English, choose the first language and continue. By the way, English is the only language available in Z.E.N.works' initial release.

The next screen (shown in Figure 6.4) allows you to select from a number of installation options:

> *Install Z.E.N.works* — Installs the Z.E.N.works desktop tool on selected servers, but you must be currently logged into each.

> *View Quick Start* — Takes you to the Z.E.N.works Quick Start online documentation.

> *Windows 95* — Installs the Novell Client for Windows 95.

> *Windows NT* — Installs the Novell Client for Windows NT.

> *Windows 3.x* — Installs the Novell Client for Windows 3.x.

> *Browse CD-ROM* — Allows you to view the contents of the Z.E.N.works installation CD-ROM.

When you click "Install Z.E.N.works," an Installation Wizard guides you through the process of installing the Z.E.N.works desktop tool on one or more NetWare servers. Follow the on-screen prompts to read the introductory information and accept the license agreement. Now we're rocking.

FIGURE 6.4

The opening Z.E.N.works Server Installation screen

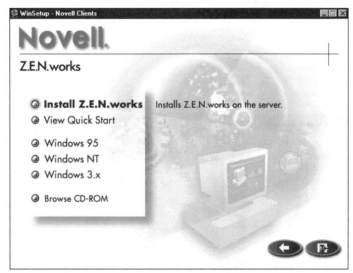

REAL WORLD

The installation instructions are based on Z.E.N.works Version 1.0. Subsequent versions might behave slightly differently. Stay on your toes!

Step 2: Z.E.N.works Installation Type

Once you've activated the Z.E.N.works server Installation Wizard, you should find your way to the "Z.E.N.works Setup Type" screen shown in Figure 6.5. At this point, you must choose among three types of Z.E.N.works installation:

▸ *Typical* — A Typical installation copies all the server-based components of Z.E.N.works to the server you're logged into. This includes application management, workstation maintenance, desktop management, and the

NetWare Administrator 32. However, copies of the Novell Client software for Windows are *not* copied to the network.

▶ *Compact* — A Compact installation copies only the minimum program options. This is a subset of the typical installation type. Choose this option only if your server is short on disk space.

▶ *Custom* — The Custom installation type allows you to choose the options you want to install, including the Novell Z.E.N.works clients. In addition, this advanced Wizard allows you to specify multiple target servers.

F I G U R E 6.5

The Z.E.N.works Setup Type
installation screen

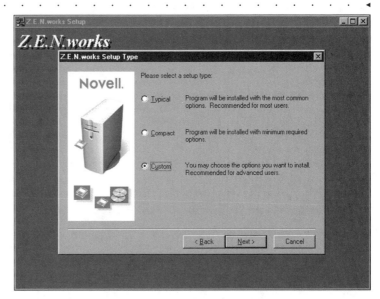

In this section, we're going to explore the Custom installation type. Why not? We're CNAs, we can handle it. Make the appropriate choice and click Next to continue.

Step 3: Choose Z.E.N.works Components

If you choose the Custom option, the Installation Wizard will respond with a list of Z.E.N.works components. As you can see in Figure 6.6, the first three components correspond to the three realms of the Z.E.N.works kingdom. The final two options are administrative.

F I G U R E   6.6

The Z.E.N.works
Select Components
installation screen

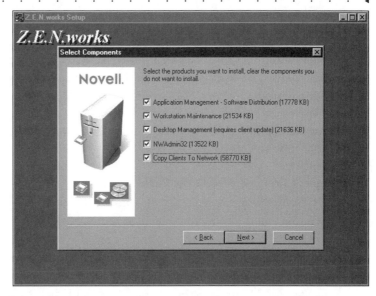

Here's a quick list:

▸ *Application Management/Software Distribution* — This is the NAL piece.
Choosing this component will allow you to distribute network-based
applications to users' workstations and manage the applications as objects
in the NDS tree.

▸ *Workstation Maintenance* — This represents the first and largest realm in
the Z.E.N.works kingdom. Workstation Maintenance encompasses all the
CNA tasks associated with daily user productivity, including policies, NDS
registration, hardware inventory, remote control, and the Novell Help
Requester. Go for it!

▸ *Desktop Management* — Choosing this option allows you to customize three
important aspects of the user desktop: application interface, printing
configuration, and user profiles.

▸ *NWAdmin 32* — Choosing this component copies a Z.E.N.works-enhanced
version of NetWare Administrator to the target server(s). This is a good idea.

▶ *Copy Clients to Network* — This final option copies the Novell Client Installation Wizard to each target server. This allows you to execute the Z.E.N.works Client installation from a central network repository. It saves time shuffling CD-ROMs all around the WAN. However, keep in mind, the Z.E.N.works Client is older than the currently shipping NetWare 5 Client. Be careful!

If you want a fully functional Z.E.N.works kingdom, choose all the components and click Next to continue.

Step 4: Choose Z.E.N.works Parts

Once you've selected the Z.E.N.works installation components, you must further refine your focus to include *Parts*. Z.E.N.works installation Parts are logical network entities that allow you to implement the components you just selected. As you can see in Figure 6.7, Z.E.N.works installation Parts include Files, Schema Extensions, Application Objects, and Workstation Registry Entities.

Select all the Z.E.N.works installation Parts and click Next to continue.

Step 5: Choose the Z.E.N.works Servers

Next, you must select the Z.E.N.works target servers. At this point, the Wizard will automatically list all servers to which you've been authenticated. By default, your initial login server will be selected. Check it out in Figure 6.8.

To install Z.E.N.works on multiple servers, you must be authenticated to each server, have rights to NDS, and be mapped to each SYS: volume *before* launching the Z.E.N.works installation program. As you can see in Figure 6.8, only one server is selected. To install Z.E.N.works on multiple servers on the list, click the Select All button. Then, all configurations made during the remainder of the installation process will apply to all servers selected.

Once you've selected the Z.E.N.works target servers, click Next to continue. At this point, you must confirm the language you selected in Step 1 and acknowledge the Z.E.N.works summary information. At this point, the Installation Wizard begins copying files to your target Z.E.N.works servers.

FIGURE 6.7

The Z.E.N.works Select
Parts installation screen

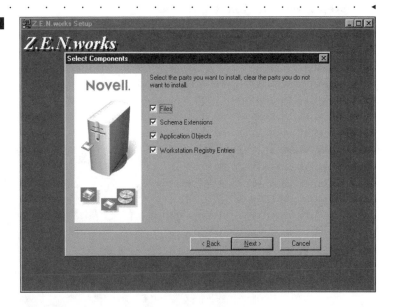

FIGURE 6.8

The Z.E.N.works List
of Tree/Servers
installation screen

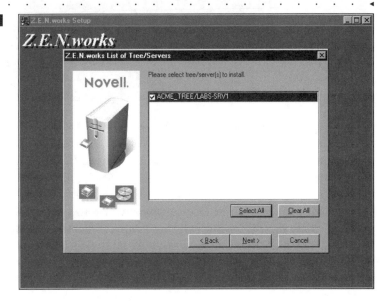

Step 6: Workstation Registration Rights

After the files have been copied to the server, a Workstation Registration Rights screen appears, allowing you to define an NDS rights scope for workstation registration. Before Z.E.N.works can create Workstation objects in NDS, users of those workstations must be granted appropriate rights. Check out the Workstation Registration Rights Assignment screen in Figure 6.9.

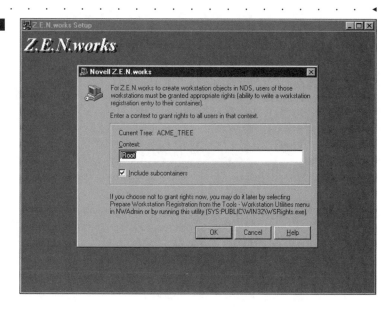

FIGURE 6.9

The Z.E.N.works
Workstation Registration
Rights Assignment screen

Granting rights at the [Root] level facilitates registration throughout the tree. If you restrict the workstation registration context, you will limit your own ability to manage workstations outside that context. Input **[Root]** in the Context field and mark the Include Subcontainers checkbox. Click OK to continue.

> **If you choose not to grant workstation registration rights now, you may do it later by selecting Prepare Workstation Registration from the Tools menu of NetWare Administrator. Also, you can accomplish the same task by running the WSRIGHTS.EXE program in SYS: PUBLIC\WIN32.**

TIP

Step 7: The End

By default, the README file and Setup Log should be opened in the Windows WordPad utility. If you're not interested in viewing these files, simply remove the checkmarks from the Readme and Setup Log boxes before you click OK.

Once the necessary files have been installed on your target Z.E.N.works servers, it's time for Stage Two — Z.E.N.works Client installation. At this point, the server is ready to accept Z.E.N.works instructions, but the workstation doesn't know what to do. Stretch your legs, open your mind, and attack the Z.E.N.works Client.

REAL WORLD

The special Z.E.N.works 1.0 version of NetWare Administrator (NWADMN32 .EXE) is placed in the SYS:PUBLIC directory of your target Z.E.N.works server. The extended NDS utility allows you to manage all the Z.E.N.works components for your workstation. Unfortunately, it is not the same NWADMN32.EXE file that all other NetWare 5 servers extend. Features such as DNS/DHCP and FastTrack use the NetWare Administrator utility found in SYS:\PUBLIC\WIN32. This means you'll have to be careful to use the correct utility when managing various NetWare 5 features. This also means that DNS/DHCP and FastTrack objects will appear as "unknown" icons in the Z.E.N.works version of NetWare Administrator. Try not to let this freak you out!

Z.E.N.works Client Installation

Once you've activated the Z.E.N.works servers, it's time to attack the front line . . . where the users live . . . the Client! Z.E.N.works Client installation is the trickiest of the two stages because it involves hundreds of diverse workstations, and even worse, hundreds of diverse user opinions. As you know, users can be very protective of their desktop environment. When they get wind of the powerful management capabilities of Z.E.N.works, they might not like the "Big Brother" implications — play it low-key.

Fortunately, NetWare 5 offers a variety of options for installing the Z.E.N.works Novell Client. Follow along in Figure 6.10:

▸ *Local Installation* — You can meander from workstation to workstation with the Z.E.N.works CD-ROM in tow. This option allows you to install this special Novell Client directly to the local workstation. *Admin on the Go!*

▸ *Network Installation* — This also involves traveling to every workstation, but this time you don't have to bring the CD-ROM with you. The Network Installation option allows you to set up the Novell Client from files located on a centralized NetWare server. *Admin on the Go!*

▸ *Multiple Workstation Installation* — This is the good one! Z.E.N.works includes two methods for automatically updating Novell Client workstations from a single point of administration. This option involves no meandering and no CD-ROM. You're going to be thrilled to learn about the Z.E.N.works Automatic Client Upgrade (ACU) and Unattended Install. *Admin @ Home!*

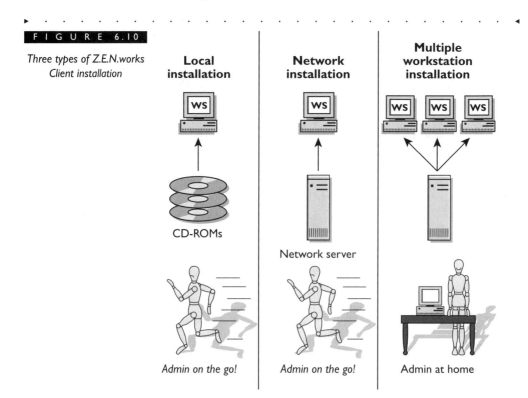

F I G U R E   6.10

Three types of Z.E.N.works Client installation

| **Local installation** | **Network installation** | **Multiple workstation installation** |

CD-ROMs

Network server

Admin on the go!   *Admin on the go!*   *Admin at home*

REAL WORLD

In addition to the three client installation options discussed previously, Z.E.N.works offers a supplemental client installation automation tool called NCIMAN.EXE. This utility allows you to specify information such as Preferred Server, Name Context, Advanced Settings, and License Agreement acceptance. NCIMAN.EXE is located in the following directories on your Z.E.N.works or NetWare Client CD-ROMS:

- *Windows 95* — PRODUCTS\WIN95\IBM_ENU\ADMIN\NCIMAN.EXE

- *Windows NT* — PRODUCTS\WINNT\i386\ADMIN\NCIMAN.EXE

So, let's learn how to install the Z.E.N.works Novell Client the hard, medium, and easy ways. Just remember to send the users to lunch when you do so.

Local Installation

This is the *hard* option.

The Local Installation option is the most difficult to execute because you must drag the Z.E.N.works CD-ROM to every workstation. If you can get beyond that nomadic necessity, the Local Installation is actually fairly easy. Simply insert the Z.E.N.works CD-ROM into the local workstation and run WINSETUP.EXE. Once you choose an installation language, the opening Client Installation screen appears. Look familiar? Check it out in Figure 6.4.

This time we're going to select one of the middle three installation options— Windows 95, Windows NT, or Windows 3.*x*. To install the Novell Client locally, simply click the appropriate workstation platform and follow the bouncing ball. Once you're finished, reboot the workstation and the NetWare Login screen appears.

That's all there is to it. Now, hop over to the next 4,000 workstations and repeat this process.

Network Installation

This is the *medium* option.

You can simplify the Client installation process a little bit by eliminating the need for a CD-ROM. Instead you can execute the Z.E.N.works Client installation from files located on a central NetWare 5 server.

First, authenticate to one of your Z.E.N.works servers and run one of the following programs:

- *Windows 95* — SETUP.EXE located in the SYS:PUBLIC\CLIENT\WIN95\ IBM_ENU directory

- *Windows NT* — SETUPNW.EXE located in the SYS:PUBLIC\CLIENT\ WINNT\i386 directory

- *Windows 3.x* — INSTALL.EXE located in the SYS:PUBLIC\CLIENT\ DOSWIN32 directory

Once you've activated the appropriate installation program, follow the bouncing ball and reboot the computer. Once you've done so, the NetWare Login screen appears.

That's all there is to it. Now, hop over to the next 4,000 workstations and repeat this process.

SETUPNW.EXE only works from Windows NT clients that have been logged in to the Power Users or Administrators group.

TIP

Multiple Workstation Installation

This is the *easy* option.

If you don't have nomadic tendencies, or you don't want to spend the time and effort visiting every workstation, Z.E.N.works has an option for you. The Automatic Client Upgrade (ACU) and Unattended Install provide a method for automatically updating the Novell Client for Windows on every workstation in the network from a single point of administration.

So, how does it work? When a user logs into the NetWare 5 server, ACU checks the version stamp of that client and automatically updates the workstation if the version is not current. Unfortunately, users can interrupt the automatic upgrade at any time. To solve this problem, you can add the Unattended Install parameter to force the Novell Client upgrade. At the end of the Unattended Install, the workstation reboots and the user is able to log in.

To install the Z.E.N.works Client on multiple workstations, follow these simple steps:

▶ *Step 1: Getting Started* — First, jot down the Z.E.N.works Client installation programs discussed earlier in the "Network Installation" section. Next, be sure to grant users Read and File Scan rights to the appropriate directories. Finally, determine which workstations should be updated, and then modify Container or Profile login scripts to launch the programs on appropriate workstations. That's the next step.

▶ *Step 2: ACU Login Scripting* — To enable the ACU for a Windows 95 workstation, add the following command to appropriate login scripts:

```
#LABS-SRV1\PUBLIC\CLIENT\WIN95\IBM_ENU\SETUP.EXE /ACU
```

In this case, the Client will execute the Windows 95 Z.E.N.works installation program automatically when users log in. Also note, we've used the "LABS-SRV1" sample ACME server. Modify this command as needed for Windows NT and/or Windows 3.*x* workstations.

▶ *Step 3: Adding the Unattended Installation Parameter* — The user can cancel the ACU process at any time, and if Murphy was right, the user will. If this happens, the workstation continues using the older Client software and Z.E.N.works functionality is severely limited. To solve this problem, simply add the "/U" parameter (for Unattended Install) after the "/ACU" option in the login script command shown in Step 2. This will force the workstation to accept the Novell Client upgrade without user intervention. I highly recommend the use of Novell's Unattended Installation parameter.

Congratulations — you're finished! You've successfully constructed your own Z.E.N.works cyber-kingdom. First, we activated the Z.E.N.works server(s) with the help of an administrative workstation, Z.E.N.works CD-ROM, and seven simple steps. Then we ventured into the jungle of user workstations with the help of three different installation options: local, network, or automatic. I prefer the latter because it forces a Z.E.N.works Novell Client upgrade without visiting every workstation. Don't get me wrong, I like to travel, but just not that much.

Now that the kingdom of Z.E.N.works has been installed, you can take full advantage of its three separate realms:

▸ *Realm 1*: Workstation Maintenance

▸ *Realm 2*: Desktop Management

▸ *Realm 3*: Application Management

Now, let's take a comprehensive tour through each of these three realms and learn what it takes to become king or queen of your own Z.E.N.works cyber-kingdom.

REAL WORLD

The Novell Client integrated into Z.E.N.works is older (and less feature-rich) than the currently available Client (Version 3.0 and above). If you follow the earlier instructions to install the Z.E.N.works Client, you will probably overwrite your newer Client with older (less feature-rich) software.

To solve this problem, we suggest that you keep your updated Client programming and modify it for full Z.E.N.works functionality. This is accomplished using the steps outlined in the section, "Stage 2: Z.E.N.works Client Installation," in Exercise 6.1.

Bottom Line: Don't install Z.E.N.works Client. Instead, update your existing Client to support Z.E.N.works features.

LAB EXERCISE 6.2: INSTALLING Z.E.N.WORKS IN THE CRIME-FIGHTING DIVISION OF ACME

Welcome back to ACME!

Now it's time to bring some "Zen" into ACME's cyber-kingdom. As you learned in this section, Z.E.N.works relies on synergy between the NetWare server and Novell client. As such, this exercise involves two main tasks:

▸ *Stage 1: Z.E.N.works Server Installation* — First, you must copy the Z.E.N.works tools to the NetWare server and activate a customized list of features.

▸ *Stage 2: Updating the NetWare 5 Client for Z.E.N.works* — Next, you must upgrade the appropriate NetWare 5 Client on each workstation to be used with Z.E.N.works and perform some local configurations.

Once you've synergized the Crime Fighting Z.E.N.works server and client, life is good. The ACME heroes can control their enhanced Infobahn roadsters a little more easily.

The following hardware is required for this exercise:

▸ A NetWare 5 server that meets the minimum hardware requirements for installing Z.E.N.works.

▸ A workstation that is running the NetWare 5 Windows 95/98 or Windows NT Client.

▸ (Optional) A second workstation running the same Windows operating system as the first workstation.

The *Novell Z.E.N.works 1.0 with Online Documentation* CD-ROM and the *NetWare 5 Novell Client Software* CD-ROM are required for this exercise.

To perform this exercise, you will need the following NDS rights (which is why you will be logging into the tree as Admin):

▸ Supervisor object rights to the NetWare 5 server where you will install Z.E.N.works.

▶ Supervisor object rights to the NDS container where you will install Z.E.N.works.

▶ Rights to modify the schema of the NDS tree into which you are installing Z.E.N.works.

TIP

The CD-ROM used in this exercise is not included with NetWare 5 and must be purchased separately. It contains the full Z.E.N.works 1.0 product and should not be confused with the Z.E.N.works Starter Pack that is included with NetWare 5.

Let's start at the NetWare 5 server.

Stage 1: Z.E.N.works Server Installation

As we learned in this section, the Z.E.N.works server installation consists of seven simple steps. Follow the bouncing ball:

1. Perform the Z.E.N.works installation:

a. Log into your tree as Admin, if you have not already done so.

b. Exit any other applications that are running.

c. Insert the *Novell Z.E.N.works 1.0 with Online Documentation* CD-ROM in your workstation's CD-ROM drive. The WINSETUP.EXE file should launch automatically.

d. When the first "WinSetup — Novell Clients" screen appears, click the language to be used during the Z.E.N.works installation process.

e. When the second "WinSetup — Novell Clients" screen appears, click Install Z.E.N.works to install Z.E.N.works on the server.

f. When the "Welcome to Z.E.N.works!" window appears:

• Read the information on the screen. Note that it strongly recommends that all programs using files in SYS:PUBLIC and its subdirectories be terminated prior to running this Setup program. It also strongly recommends that you exit all Windows programs before running this Setup program. (You should have done the latter in Step 1b.)

• Click Next.

g. When the Software License Agreement window appears, read the agreement, then click Yes to accept its terms.

h. When the Z.E.N.works Setup Type window appears, click Custom to indicate that you'd like to perform a custom installation, then click Next.

TIP

You must select the Custom installation method to be allowed to specify which Z.E.N.works components you want to install. For example, the Typical and Compact methods do not allow you to copy the Novell client software for Windows 95, Windows NT, and DOS/WIN clients to the server.

i. When the first Select Components window appears, ensure that the first four checkboxes are marked, then click Next.

j. When the second Select Components window appears, verify that all boxes are checked, then click Next.

k. When the Z.E.N.works List of Tree/Servers window appears, confirm that only the ACME_TREE/CRIME-SRV1 checkbox is marked, then click Next.

l. When the Z.E.N.works Language Selection window appears, ensure that the language you want to use for installation is checked, then click Next.

m. When the Start Copying Files window appears, review the summary of components to be installed in the Current Settings list box. If everything is correct, click Next.

n. Wait while the Z.E.N.works files are copied to the server. (This may take a while.)

o. Z.E.N.works Workstation Auto-Registration requires that users have the rights to write a registration request to their container in order to register their workstations with NDS and to keep the workstations synchronized with NDS. Because object rights flow down through the NDS tree unless modified or blocked lower in the tree, you will undoubtedly find that assigning the rights at the [Root] level facilitates workstation registration throughout the tree. When the Novell Z.E.N.works window appears:

- Read the information on the screen.

- Verify that the following context is listed in the Context field:

  [Root]

- Confirm that the Include Subcontainers checkbox is marked.

- Click OK.

p. When the Novell Z.E.N.works Workstation Auto-Registration Rights Utility window appears:

- Read the information on the screen indicating that the Novell Z.E.N.works Workstation Auto-Registration rights were successfully set up.

- Click OK to acknowledge the message.

q. When the Setup Complete window appears:

- Ensure that the Launch Read Me File checkbox is marked.

- Confirm that the Launch Setup Log File checkbox is marked.

- Click Finish.

r. When the "Readme.txt — Notepad" window appears, read the Z.E.N.works Release Notes, then click Close (X) to exit the Notepad utility.

s. When the "Setuplog.txt — Notepad" window appears, read the information in the Setup Log, then click Close (X) to exit the Notepad utility.

t. When the Z.E.N.works window appears, click the Exit icon located in the lower-right corner of the screen.

2. Using the NetWare Administrator utility, view the NDS objects that were created by the Z.E.N.works installation process:

a. Click Start on the Windows taskbar, then click Run.

b. When the RUN dialog box appears, type the following in the Open field, and then click OK:

```
Z:\PUBLIC\WIN32\NWADMN32
```

c. View the objects that Z.E.N.works has added to your NDS tree.

d. Exit the NetWare Administrator utility.

Once the necessary files have been installed on your target Z.E.N.works servers, it's time for Stage Two — Z.E.N.works Client installation. At this point, the server is ready to accept Z.E.N.works instructions, but the workstation doesn't know what to do. Stretch your legs, open your mind, and attack the Client upgrade.

TIP

If you use the NetWare Administrator shortcut from the Windows 95/NT desktop, the additional Z.E.N.works objects may not appear within the Create menu. This is because the shortcut doesn't point to the new Registry keys created by the Z.E.N.works installation. To solve this problem, use File/Run or re-create the NetWare Administrator shortcut and point to Z:\PUBLIC\WIN32.

Stage 2: Updating the NetWare 5 Client for Z.E.N.works

Once you've activated the Z.E.N.works servers, it's time to attack the front line . . . where the users live . . . the Client! Z.E.N.works Client installation is the trickiest of the two stages because it involves hundreds of diverse workstations, and even worse, hundreds of diverse user opinions. As you know, users can be very protective of their desktop environments.

Now that you've successfully installed Z.E.N.works on your server, it's time to shift our focus to the distributed workstations. After all, the server won't have anyone to serve if the clients can't speak Z.E.N.works.

In the next two sections, we'll explore the detailed upgrade steps for two prominent workstation platforms:

▶ Windows 95/98

▶ Windows NT

Choose the section that relates to you . . . and we're off!

NetWare 5 Windows 95/98 Client Installation

To upgrade the NetWare 5 client on a Windows 95/98 workstation, you will need the following components:

- ▸ A NetWare 5 server with enough free space to install the NetWare 5 Novell Client for Windows 95/98 installation files. (You cannot upgrade your workstation directly from CD-ROM because you need to modify the NWSETUP.INI file.)

- ▸ A workstation with the NetWare 5 Novell Client for Windows 95/98 installed.

- ▸ (Optional) A second workstation with the NetWare 5 Novell Client for Windows 95/98 installed.

- ▸ The *NetWare 5 Novell Client Software* CD-ROM.

Complete the following steps to perform a local upgrade of the NetWare 5 Novell Client for Windows 95/98 on your workstation. (This procedure installs the Z.E.N.works Remote Control Agent on the workstation.)

TIP

The instructions listed here are designed for manually upgrading the NetWare 5 Novell Client for Windows 95/98 on a workstation that is logged into the network as Admin. To upgrade the remaining client workstations on your network, consult the NetWare 5 *Online Documentation* **CD-ROM regarding the use of the Automatic Client Upgrade (ACU) and Unattended Install features.**

1. Log in to the tree as Admin if you haven't already done so.

2. Exit any applications that may be running.

3. Copy the NetWare 5 Novell Client for Windows 95/98 installation files to the server.

　a. Using the method of your choice, create the following folder on your server:

```
SYS:\PUBLIC\CLIENT\WIN95-98
```

b. Using the method of your choice, copy the appropriate Novell Client files from the *NetWare 5 Novell Client Software* CD-ROM to the folder you created. They are located in the \PRODUCTS\WIN95*language* folder and its subdirectories. (For example, if you are an English-speaking person in the United States, you would copy files from the \PRODUCTS\WIN95\IBM_ENU directory and its subdirectories.)

4. Update the NWSETUP.INI file on the server.

   a. Using the Windows Explorer utility, browse to the directory where you copied the NetWare 5 Client files (that is, SYS:\PUBLIC\CLIENT\ WIN95-98) and right-click the NWSETUP.INI file.

   b. Select Properties from the pop-up menu that appears.

   c. When the NWSETUP.INI Properties dialog box appears, unmark the box designating the file as read-only (if it's marked), then click OK.

   d. When the Windows Explorer screen re-appears, double-click the NWSETUP.INI file to edit it.

     • Scroll down to the [PossibleInstallList] section near the end of the file and delete the semi-colon (;) in front of option 10.

     • Scroll down to the bottom of the file and delete the semi-colon (;) in front of the line that has the label [NWRCA] and the option below it.

     • Delete the semi-colon (;) in front of the line that has the label [NWRCA.key] and the option below it.

     • Click File to display the File menu, then click Exit.

     • When prompted, click Yes to save the file before exiting.

     • Exit the Windows Explorer utility.

5. Upgrade the existing NetWare 5 Novell Client for Windows 95/98 on your workstation.

   a. Launch the SETUP.EXE file:

     • Click Start in the Windows taskbar.

- Click Run.

- When the Run dialog box appears, type the following path in the Open field:

  ```
  Z:\PUBLIC\CLIENT\WIN95-98\SETUP.EXE
  ```

- Click OK.

b. When the Novell Client for Windows 95/98 License Agreement window appears:

- Read the agreement.

- Click Yes to accept its terms and conditions.

c. When the Welcome to the Novell Client for Windows 95/98 Install window appears:

- Click Custom to indicate that you'd like to perform a Custom installation.

- Click Next.

d. When the Protocol Preference window appears:

- Ensure that the IP and IPX radio button is selected.

- Click Next.

e. When the Login Authenticator window appears:

- Verify that the "NDS (NetWare 4.x or Higher)" radio button is selected.

- Click Next.

f. When the "Novell Client for Windows 95/98 Custom Options" window appears:

- Ensure that the following checkboxes are marked:

  ```
  Novell Workstation Manager

  Novell Distributed Print Services

  Novell NDS Provider @ ADSI

  Novell Remote Control Agent
  ```

- Click Install.

g. Wait while the NetWare 5 Client software is installed.

h. When the Novell Client for Windows 95/98 Installation window appears, click Reboot to reboot the computer.

i. When the Novell Login dialog box appears, log into your tree as the Admin user.

6. Verify that the Z.E.N.works Remote Control Agent was installed on your workstation.

a. Click Start in the Windows taskbar.

b. Click Programs.

c. Click Novell.

d. Click Remote Control.

e. Remote Control Agent should appear as a menu option.

7. (optional.) If you have a second Windows 95/98 workstation available:

a. Upgrade the NetWare 5 Novell Client for Windows 95/98 on it, using the instructions in Steps 1, 2, 5, and 6 above.

b. Log in as the SHolmes user. (The password is ACME.)

NetWare 5 Windows NT Client Upgrade

To upgrade the NetWare 5 client on a Windows NT workstation, you will need the following components:

▶ A workstation with the NetWare 5 Novell Client for Windows NT installed.

▶ (Optional) A second workstation with the NetWare 5 Novell Client for Windows NT installed.

▶ The *NetWare 5 Novell Client Software* CD-ROM.

Complete the following steps to perform a local upgrade of the NetWare 5 Windows NT client on your workstation. (This procedure installs the Z.E.N.works Remote Control Agent on the workstation.)

TIP

The instructions listed here are designed for manually upgrading the NetWare 5 Novell Client on a workstation. To upgrade the remaining network workstations on your network, consult the NetWare 5 Online Documentation regarding the use of the NetWare 5 Automatic Client Upgrade (ACU) and Unattended Install features.

1. Exit any applications that may be running.

2. Modify the Network dialog box.

    a. Right-click Network Neighborhood.

    b. Click Properties in the pop-up menu that appears.

    c. When the Network dialog box appears:

        • Click the Services tab.

        • Click Add.

        • Scroll down to the bottom of the Network Service list box and choose Z.E.N.works Remote Control, then click OK.

    d. Insert the *NetWare 5 Novell Client Software* CD-ROM in your workstation's CD-ROM drive. If the WINSETUP.EXE program is automatically launched, click the Exit button in the lower-right corner of the screen.

    e. When the Windows NT Setup dialog box appears:

        • Type the following path to the NetWare 5 client files (assuming that your CD-ROM is assigned as drive D:):

        `D:\PRODUCTS\WINNT\i386`

        • Click Continue.

    f. When the Network dialog box re-appears, click Close.

    g. When the Network Settings change dialog box appears, click Yes to restart your computer.

3. Verify that the Z.E.N.works Remote Control Agent was installed on your workstation.

    a. Click Start in the Windows taskbar.

    b. Click Programs.

    c. Click Novell.

    d. Click Remote Control.

    e. Remote Control Agent should appear as a menu option.

4. (Optional.) If you have a second Windows NT workstation available:

    a. Install the NetWare 5 Novell Client for Windows NT on it using the instructions in Steps 1, 2, and 3.

    b. Log in as the SHolmes user. (The password is ACME.)

Congratulations . . . you've created ACME's first Z.E.N.works cyber-kingdom — and Sherlock Holmes thanks you. Now it's time to attack the three realms of this new kingdom. Ready, set, *charge!*

Z.E.N.works Realm 1: Workstation Maintenance

The art of Zen is a method of enhancing your senses. Our senses link us to the outside world. They allow us to react to our environment both intellectually and instinctively. Even more important, our senses provide vital information about our internal environment.

Technically speaking, sensation is accomplished with the help of specialized organs dispersed throughout the body. These *sense organs* react to stimuli by sending neural impulses to the brain. General sensory receptors distributed in most major organs provide us with information about a variety of bodily needs, including hunger, thirst, fatigue, and pain. Ouch!

Extrasensory perception (ESP) is the least understood and probably the most valuable of your senses. ESP allows you to make unconscious decisions about external stimuli that you can't see, hear, taste, smell, or touch. ESP also allows you to react to environments that would otherwise be out of your reach — spatially or temporally. Everyone has ESP, but some people use it more than others. The true art of Zen is to get in "touch" with your ESP.

So, what about Z.E.N.works? Your network relies on sensory input from workstations for external and internal data. Without this data, there would be nothing for the server to do. In some strange way, workstations give the network a reason to live. Z.E.N.works is a way of allowing your workstation to get in "touch" with its own ESP power.

There's a lot more to the NetWare 5 workstation than meets the eye. It's a complex collection of sensory organs and connectivity hardware that makes Workstation Maintenance an incredible challenge. Furthermore, workstations and users provide an even greater challenge — *diversity*. Diversity in workstation software and hardware is almost as varied as eye color and nose size. Understanding the impact of the many different types of local software on your WAN is no small feat! It's going to take all your senses and a great deal of effort to control this chaos.

Fortunately, Z.E.N.works offers Realm 1 — Workstation Maintenance. This is the largest of the Z.E.N.works realms and encompasses all CNA tasks associated with daily user productivity. In this realm, we'll be introduced to three NetWare 5 workstation tools: Novell Workstation Manager, NetWare Administrator, and the Novell Help Requester.

In this first Z.E.N.works realm, we'll explore four different methods of accessing our workstation's ESP:

▸ *Z.E.N.works policies* — This allow you to set up parameters for managing workstations, users, groups, and/or containers in *Policy Packages*.

▸ *NDS registration* — This allows you to import workstations into the NDS tree and manage them as centralized leaf objects.

▸ *Z.E.N.works Remote Control* — This allows you to connect and manage remote workstations from the central GUI interface of NetWare Administrator.

▸ *Novell Help Requester* — This allows users to notify the Help Desk or LAN administrator of workstation problems via e-mail or phone. This tool provides pertinent user/workstation information that can help you solve problems quickly and remotely.

If you can learn to get in touch with the Zen of Workstation Maintenance, you may be able to control the chaos of user diversity. Whatever you do, don't underestimate the importance of Workstation Maintenance. In addition to being the brains of the LAN, the workstation is also the user's point of contact. The network is only successful if the users are productive and happy.

So, take a deep breath, achieve internal peace, and tap the power of workstation ESP . . . starting with policies.

Z.E.N.works Policies

Z.E.N.works includes various *Policy Packages* — which are NDS leaves that help you maintain Workstation objects in the NDS tree. Each package is a collection of *policies* that allow you to set up parameters for managing Workstation, User, Group, or Container objects.

Each Policy Package object can be associated with other resources in the NDS tree. Z.E.N.works provides seven separate Policy Package objects to choose from, in three different categories:

▶ *Container Policy Package* — Includes one Package only — the Container Package.

▶ *Workstation Policy Packages* — Includes three Package objects: Windows 95 Workstation Package, Windows NT Workstation Package, and Windows 3.1 Workstation Package.

▶ *User Policy Packages* — Also includes three Package objects: Windows 95 User Package, Windows NT User Package, and Windows 3.1 User Package.

Except for the Container Policy Package, all objects are organized according to the workstation's OS platform. Once you configure a Policy Package, you can associate it with other NDS objects — like Users and Workstations. This way, distributed users can experience changes in their desktop configurations, printer availability, and application privileges immediately — provided that the workstation has been upgraded to the Z.E.N.works Novell Client.

Furthermore, when you associate Packages with a Container object, the policies you enable in the Package apply to all Workstation and User objects in the container. This is an easy way of implementing sweeping changes throughout the network.

Let's learn more about Z.E.N.works policies by exploring each of these three Package categories.

REAL WORLD

Z.E.N.works eases the complexity of using policies by allowing you to create policy NDS objects through NetWare Administrator. Storing Policy objects in NDS eliminates the need to manually copy policy files to the SYS:PUBLIC directory of multiple servers. In addition, NDS automatically replicates policies throughout the tree and provides fault tolerance through replication.

Even though Z.E.N.works policies are NDS objects, they will not appear in the NDS tree browser of NetWare Administrator. Instead, Policy objects must be accessed through their parent Package. Finally, policy configurations allow you to customize numerous policies within a Package.

Container Policy Package

The Container Policy Package is singular and simple. In this category, you will only find one Policy Package object (Container), which includes one Z.E.N.works policy (Search).

Figure 6.11 shows the Container Policy Package Configuration screen in NetWare Administrator. It shows the single Search policy contained within the single Container Policy package. This policy helps you determine which Policy Packages are in effect for resources in a specific container. In addition, the Search policy improves security by identifying NDS objects which shouldn't have policies (and do), and it avoids unnecessary traffic by limiting the search to a specific container.

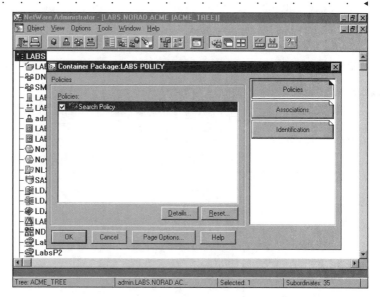

FIGURE 6.11

The Container Policy Package screen in NetWare Administrator

Workstation Policy Packages

The Workstation category includes three different Policy Package objects. The policies found in these Packages help you set up controls that apply to Windows workstations throughout the WAN. This way, you can apply specific policy controls to specific Windows platforms. The three platforms included in this category are

▸ WIN95 Workstation Package

▶ WIN NT Workstation Package

▶ WIN 3x Workstation Package

These Workstation Package controls apply to workstations only—regardless of the user who logs into the network. Once you configure these controls, you can associate the Package with Container objects, workstation Groups, or individual Workstation NDS objects. It's important to note that Workstation Policy Packages can be created before Workstation objects are registered in the NDS tree. If you do this, you'll need to associate the Package with the specific objects once they've been registered.

Check out Figure 6.12 for an illustration of the policies found in the WIN95 Workstation Policy Package. For a more detailed description of these Workstation policies, check out Table 6.1.

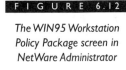

F I G U R E   6.12

The WIN95 Workstation Policy Package screen in NetWare Administrator

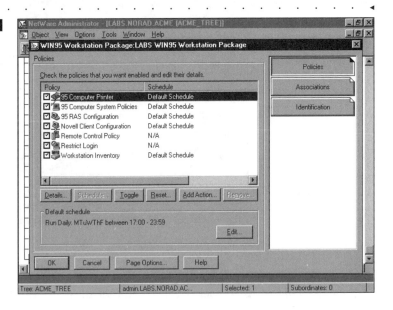

TABLE 6.1

*Z.E.N.works Policies in the
Workstation Packages*

WORKSTATION POLICY PACKAGE	POLICY	DESCRIPTION
WIN95 Workstation Package	95 Computer Printer	Assigns printers and printer drivers to Windows 95 workstations. Through this policy, the Printer object appears in the Printer Control Panel and the printer driver is automatically installed on the workstation.
	95 Computer System Policies	Used to define applications that are automatically delivered to Windows 95 desktops regardless of the user who authenticates to the network.
	95 RAS Configuration	Used to configure dial-up network settings for the Windows 95 workstation.
	Novell Client Configuration	Used to set Client configuration parameters for Novell Client protocols and services. Novell Client settings include client LOGIN and default CAPTURE parameters. Protocol settings include IPX 32-bit protocols and NetWare/IP configurations. Service settings include host resource Management Information Base (MIB), SNMP, IP Gateway, and Target Service Agent (TSA) configurations.
	Remote Control Policy	Used to specify whether or not Remote Controlling is allowed for workstations associated with this policy. You can specify other settings regarding Remote Control as well — including audible warnings before starting a remote session.
	Restrict Login	Used to set rules regarding login times and occurrences for workstations associated with this policy.
	Workstation Inventory	Populates NDS with an asset inventory representing the hardware present in this workstation.

(continued)

TABLE 6.1

Z.E.N.works Policies in the
Workstation Packages (continued)

WORKSTATION POLICY PACKAGE	POLICY	DESCRIPTION
WIN NT Workstation Package	NT Computer Printer	Identical to the 95 Computer Printer Policy, except this policy assigns printers and print drivers to Windows NT workstations.
	NT Computer System Policies	Used to define applications that are automatically delivered to Windows NT desktops, regardless of the user who authenticates to the network.
	Novell Client Configuration	Same as WIN95 Workstation Package.
	Remote Control Policy	Same as WIN95 Workstation Package.
	Restrict Login	Same as WIN95 Workstation Package.
	Workstation Inventory	Same as WIN95 Workstation Package.
WIN 3x Workstation Package	3x Computer System Policies	Used to specify files to download from the network to one or more workstations. The types of files you can manage using this policy are ASCII text (such as .BAT, .INI, or .CFG) or binary (such as .EXE, .COM, or .DLL).
	Remote Control Policy	Same as WIN95 Workstation Package.

TIP

The Windows 3.x Policy Packages contain fewer policies than the Windows 95 and Windows NT Packages. This is simple because Windows 3.x doesn't support the Registry; therefore, any policies that require access to the Windows 95/NT Registry are unavailable to Windows 3.x workstations.

User Policy Packages

The User Policy category includes three Package objects that mirror the Workstation Policy functions. However, User Policy Packages apply to the users themselves, and not to their workstations.

Interestingly, User Policies apply to users who access the network from specific Windows platforms. In this way, they act similarly to the Workstation Policies. Here's a quick list of three NDS objects included in the User category:

▶ WIN95 User Package

▶ WIN NT User Package

▶ WIN 3x User Package

The parameters configured in these User Packages apply to associated users, regardless of the workstation they use to log in. However, the parameters will only take effect when they match the platform the user is using. Also, keep in mind that any user can only be associated with one platform-specific User Package. For example, the Admin User object can only be associated with one WIN95 User Package. Fortunately, Z.E.N.works will notify you when Package conflicts occur.

Check out Figure 6.13 for an illustration of the policies found in the WIN95 User Package. For a more detailed description of these User Policies, check out Table 6.2.

▶ ·◀

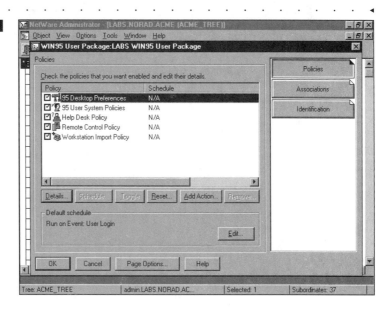

F I G U R E   6.13

The WIN95 User Package screen in NetWare Administrator

TABLE 6.2

Z.E.N.works Policies in the
User Packages

USER POLICY PACKAGES	POLICY	DESCRIPTION
WIN95 User Package	95 Desktop Preferences	Used to set up a default desktop configuration through Control Panel for users who access this policy from a Windows 95 workstation.
	95 User System Policies	Used to define restrictions to desktop applications for Windows 95 users associated with this Package.
	Help Desk Policy	This policy must be used to enable the Novell Help Requester application. This policy requires a current name and phone number or e-mail address for the support contact. Use this policy to establish communication rules between users and the Help Desk.
	Remote Control Policy	Used to specify whether or not Remote Controlling is allowed on workstations being used by objects associated with this policy. You can also specify other settings regarding Remote Control, such as visible or audible warnings.
	Workstation Import Policy	This policy is used to set rules about how workstations are named and where the Workstation objects should appear in the NDS tree once they are imported.
WIN NT User Package	Dynamic Local User	Used to manage user access to Windows NT workstations using NDS.
	NT Desktop Preferences	Used to set up a default desktop configuration through Control Panel for users who access this policy from Windows NT workstations.

USER POLICY PACKAGES	POLICY	DESCRIPTION
WIN NT User Package (continued)	NT User Printer	This policy assigns printers and printer drivers to users of Windows NT workstations who are associated with this policy.
	NT User System Policies	Used to define restrictions to desktop applications for Windows NT users who are associated with this policy.
	Help Desk Policy	Same as WIN95 User Package.
	Remote Control Policy	Same as WIN95 User Package.
	Workstation Import Policy	Same as WIN95 User Package.
WIN 3x User Package	Help Desk Policy	Same as WIN95 User Package.
	Remote Control Policy	Same as WIN95 User Package.
	Workstation Import Policy	Same as WIN95 User Package.

That completes our journey through the seven different Z.E.N.works Policy Packages. Wasn't that fun? Now, let's complete our discussion of Z.E.N.works policies by learning a thing or two about policy planning. Remember, an ounce of prevention is worth a ton of cure . . . especially if the cure comes in a red-and-black medicine bottle.

Policy Planning

Z.E.N.works policies can be very powerful workstation maintenance tools. However, they can also get out of hand very quickly. To curb the complexity of Z.E.N.works policy construction, follow these four valuable planning tips:

▶ *When to create Policy Packages* — Consider the following criteria when creating Policy Packages: the size of the network, the platforms present on the network, and the need for multiple Packages of the same type in a single container. Sometimes it's necessary to create multiple Policy Packages of the same type in a single container because workstations and users might have differing managing needs. For example, you may want to enable Remote Control for the users in your container but disallow anyone from remote-controlling yours. In this case, you would create two Windows 95 User Packages — one enabling Remote Control for them and one disabling Remote Control for you.

▶ *Where to place Policy Packages* — Create Container Packages at the highest level of the tree without exceeding the location or site container. In contrast, place User and Workstation Packages in the lower container, that houses the workstations and users. Sometimes you may want to create a single-purpose container for workstations. If so, place the Workstation Packages in that container.

▶ *Who to associate Policy Packages with* — By default, policies are applied to leaf objects just as NDS rights are applied. This means policies associated directly with the User or Workstation object take precedent over policies associated with home containers. This means you should associate policies with containers whenever possible.

▶ *Policy Configuration* — As I mentioned earlier, policies can get out of hand very quickly. As a matter of fact, some policies can affect the structure of the NDS tree, or impact network performance and bandwidth. Too many policies can reduce network access speed, limit the scaleability of the NDS tree, create a need for future partitioning, or clutter user searching capabilities. Be sure to configure the policies so that each partition still has fewer than 1,500 objects per partition after the workstations are added to the tree. Also, be sure to place Workstation objects in the same container as their associated users. Finally, try to avoid single-purpose containers whenever possible. They are bad news.

That completes our discussion of Z.E.N.works policies. Wow, they are complex little buggers. However, they can be powerful allies if configured and distributed intelligently. To become a Z.E.N.works Policy Pro, follow these two simple guidelines: "planning" and "less is more."

Now, let's continue tapping the power of workstation ESP by exploring NDS registration.

Workstation NDS Registration

To fully tap the Zen of a workstation, you must integrate it with the NDS Cloud. In effect, workstations must be registered with NDS before they can be imported into the tree and fully maintained. Fortunately, Z.E.N.works includes a Workstation Registration Agent that automatically registers workstations as long as two conditions have been met:

▶ *Condition 1* — The workstation has been updated to the Novell Client for Z.E.N.works.

▶ *Condition 2* — The workstation has been used to log into the NDS tree at least once.

Once these two conditions have been met, the agent sends the workstation's address to NDS and places it in a "holding tank" — NDS Registration List. Once a workstation appears on the list, it can then be imported into the tree.

In short, Z.E.N.works workstation NDS registration is accomplished in two steps:

▶ *Step 1*: Registering Workstations with NDS

▶ *Step 2*: Importing Workstations into the NDS tree

Ready, set, "registrate."

Step 1: Registering Workstations with NDS

Before you can import a workstation into the NDS tree, it must appear in the NDS Registration List. The Registration List is a property of each Container housing workstations. Z.E.N.works provides three different methods for activating the Workstation Registration Agent:

▶ *Z.E.N.works Scheduler* — This relies on the Workstation Manager component of Z.E.N.works and only supports the Windows 95 and Windows NT platforms. If your workstations have been upgraded using the Z.E.N.works

Novell Client, workstation registration happens automatically. This occurs the first time a user logs into the network using the new client. In case you care, all of this magic is accomplished using the WSREG32.DLL file.

▶ *Novell Application Launcher (NAL)* — You can use NAL to automatically run the Workstation Registration Agent if the Z.E.N.works Workstation Manager hasn't been installed. First, you'll need to create an Application object for each agent program — WSREG32.EXE for Windows 95/NT workstations and WSREG16.EXE for Windows 3.*x* and DOS workstations. Next, associate each Application object with the appropriate Container, Group, or User objects. Finally, the Workstation Registration Agent will run when the user logs in.

▶ *Login Script* — If NAL and Workstation Manager are not installed, you can always resort to login script registration. This is accomplished by executing the appropriate Agent program within Container or Profile login scripts. *Hint:* Use the "#" command to run external programs. In addition, you may want to use the "% PLATFORM" identifier variable to specify Windows NT (WNT), Windows 95 (W95), and/or Windows 3.*x* (WIN) workstations.

So, how do you know if it worked? Good question.

REAL WORLD

You should prepare to import registered workstations into the NDS tree by configuring a Workstation Import Policy. First, begin by creating a Workstation Policy Package for each workstation platform on your network — such as Windows 95, Windows NT, and Windows 3.*x*. Then, configure the Workstation Import Policy to create Workstation objects in the desired container and with the desired naming features. This way, you can associate the Package with appropriate workstations and importing will be a breeze.

There are two ways to verify that your workstations have been registered with NDS. First, check the appropriate log file at the root of each workstation's local hard drive. In the Windows 95/NT environment, the file is called WSREG32.LOG. In the Windows 3.*x* world, it's called WSREG16.LOG. These log files record information about the success and/or failure of the NDS Registration process.

If you don't like log files, or just don't want to travel to every workstation in the WAN, consider using NetWare Administrator. This magic GUI tool can be used to verify NDS Registration by checking out the Registered Workstations page for each workstation Container — it lists all registered workstations in a graphical window. Check out Figure 6.14.

F I G U R E   6.14

The Registered Workstations page in NetWare Administrator

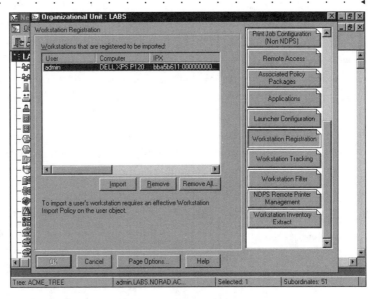

Once your workstations appear in the NDS Registration List, they can be imported into the NDS tree. That's Step 2.

Step 2: Importing Workstations into the NDS Tree

Registered workstations do not become NDS objects until you import them into the tree — welcome to Step 2. Even after you import workstations, you must periodically re-import them to keep the network addresses updated. This ensures that NIC replacement, re-assigned network addresses, or changes in a workstation's location do not affect your ability to access the NDS object.

Follow these four steps to import a workstation from the NDS Registration List:

▶ *Step 1: Create a User Policy Package* — Start by opening NetWare Administrator and browsing to the Workstation's home container. Highlight the Container and click Object and Create to build a new User Policy Package. Match the platform of the Package to the workstations you want to import — such as WIN95 or WIN NT. Click Create to continue.

▶ *Step 2: Configure the Workstation Import Policy* — First, you'll need to enable the Workstation Import Policy of your new User Policy Package and click the Details button. Next, you should configure the host location for the Workstation object by clicking the Workstation Location button. Then, you'll need to configure a naming convention for the Workstation objects by accessing the Workstation Naming button. By default, the Computer Name and workstation's network MAC address are used as naming attributes. You can also choose to use the workstation's IP or IPX network address to identify it. Refer to Figure 6.15 for more information. Finally, you should associate the new User Policy Package with the workstation's home Container and click OK to continue.

F I G U R E   6.15

Configuring the Workstation Import Policy

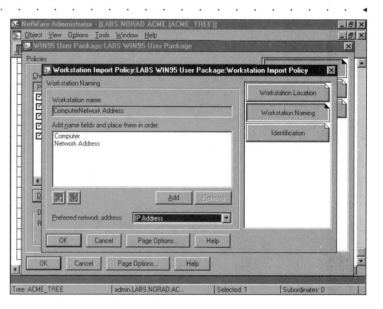

▶ *Step 3: Import the Workstations* — With the home Container still highlighted in NetWare Administrator, select the Import Workstations command from the Tools menu. Check it out in Figure 6.16. Next, specify the full Distinguished Name of the home container in the Import From tab and click OK to begin the import process.

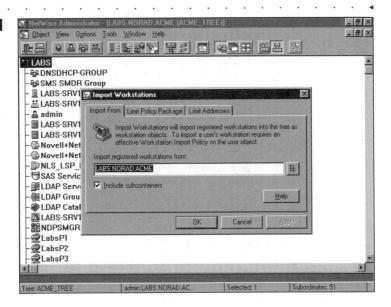

FIGURE 6.16

The Import Workstations option in NetWare Administrator

▶ *Step 4: The End* — Once you've activated the Import Workstations utility, NDS will begin building Workstation objects. At the end of this process, a verification screen will appear and list the total number of workstation entries created. You can further verify the import procedure by reviewing the Success Log in Notepad — it's called NSUCCESS.LOG. Finally, you should ensure that the Workstation objects were placed in the right container by collapsing and expanding the NetWare Administrator browser. As you can see in Figure 6.17, our Workstations have found their way into the correct ACME container.

▸ · ◂

FIGURE 6.17

*New Workstation
objects in the NetWare
Administrator browser*

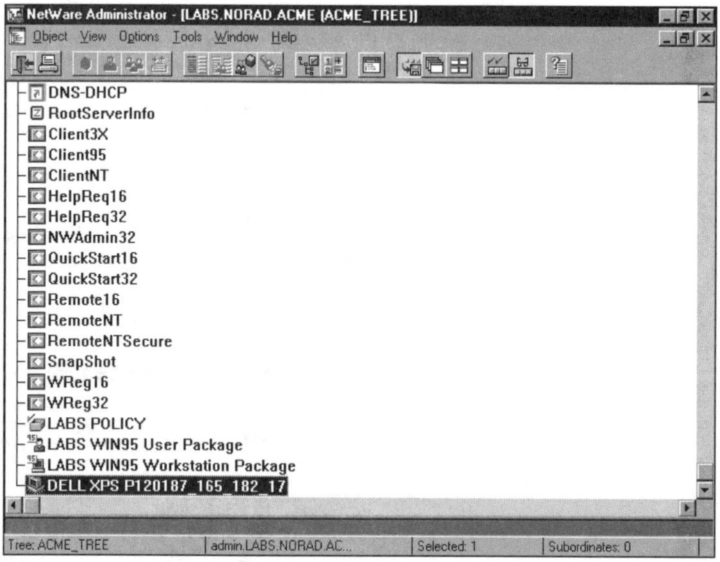

NetWare Administrator - [LABS.NORAD.ACME [ACME_TREE]]

Object View Options Tools Window Help

- DNS-DHCP
- RootServerInfo
- Client3X
- Client95
- ClientNT
- HelpReq16
- HelpReq32
- NWAdmin32
- QuickStart16
- QuickStart32
- Remote16
- RemoteNT
- RemoteNTSecure
- SnapShot
- WReg16
- WReg32
- LABS POLICY
- LABS WIN95 User Package
- LABS WIN95 Workstation Package
- DELL XPS P120187_165_182_17

Tree: ACME_TREE   admin.LABS.NORAD.AC...   Selected: 1   Subordinates: 0

That does it . . . mission accomplished. Your Z.E.N.works clients are now part of the global NDS Cloud. This level of synergy will provide you with centralized access to critical workstation maintenance duties. As a matter of fact, the final two aspects of Realm 1 rely on NDS integration:

▸ Z.E.N.works Remote Control

▸ Novell Help Requester

It's all downhill from here.

▸ · ◂

REAL WORLD

You can also configure the Import Workstations utility to update Workstation objects automatically. Simply associate the application with NAL or the Z.E.N.works Scheduler. This way, you can ensure that the latest workstation address information finds it way to the central NDS database.

LAB EXERCISE 6.3: EXPLORING Z.E.N.WORKS REALM 1 — POLICIES AND NDS REGISTRATION

To fully tap the Zen of our ACME workstations, you must integrate them with the NDS Cloud. In effect, workstations must be registered with NDS before they can be imported into the tree and fully maintained. The actual process of registering NetWare 5 clients involves both NDS and NetWare 5 policies. Here's a quick preview:

- ▶ *Stage 1:* Prepare the CRIME container for registration

- ▶ *Stage 2:* Create a Workstation Import Policy

- ▶ *Stage 3:* Register the workstation(s)

- ▶ *Stage 4:* Import the registered workstation(s)

The following hardware is required for this exercise:

- ▶ A NetWare 5 server with Z.E.N.works 1.0 installed

- ▶ A workstation running the updated NetWare 5 Client for Windows 95/98 or Windows NT

- ▶ (Optional) A second workstation running the same NetWare 5 Client as the first workstation

Let's help our friends in Tokyo with some Crime Fighting workstation registration. Check it out!

Stage 1: Prepare the CRIME Container for Registration

Before Z.E.N.works can create Workstation objects in the NDS tree, it is necessary to grant users the rights to write a workstation registration entry to their container. In this first step, we will grant the User objects located in the CRIME container the rights to write a workstation registration entry to the CRIME container.

Perform the following tasks on your first workstation.

1. Log into the tree as the Admin User, if you haven't already done so.

2. Launch the NetWare Administrator utility. To do so, click Start on the Windows taskbar, then click Run. When the Run dialog box appears, type the following in the Open field, and then click OK:

```
Z:\PUBLIC\WIN32\NWADMN32
```

3. At this point, you must prepare the container for registration, if you haven't already done so. This involves granting users the rights they need to write a workstation registration entry to the container. In our case, we did this during the Z.E.N.works server installation process by granting these rights at the [Root] level (which gives you more flexibility). Because we have not done anything to modify these rights since that time, you're finished with this step.

Stage 2: Create a Workstation Import Policy

Before you can import a workstation into the NDS tree, you must create a Workstation Import Policy and associate it with the CRIME container. Perform the following steps on Workstation #1.

1. Create a WIN95 or WIN NT User Policy package:

a. In NetWare Administrator, right-click the CRIME container, then click Create.

b. When the New Object dialog box appears, type the following to select Policy Package, and then press Enter:

P

c. When the Create Policy Package dialog box appears:

- Open the pull-down menu in the Select Policy Package Type field and click the User Package that matches your workstation's platform. For instance, if you are a Windows 95 user, you would select WIN95 User Package.

- In the Name field, type:

  Platform User Package

  where *Platform* is the type of platform (such as WIN95).

- Mark the Define Additional Properties checkbox.

- Click Create.

2. Configure the Workstation Import policy.

   a. When the User Package dialog box appears:

   - In the Policies window, mark the Workstation Import Policy checkbox.

   - Click Details.

   b. When the Workstation Import Policy dialog box appears:

   - You'll notice that the Workstation Location page is displayed by default.

   - Verify that the "Allow Importing of Workstations" checkbox is marked.

   - Open the pull-down menu in the Create Workstation Objects In field, and choose Selected Container.

   - Ensure that the Path field contains the following path:

     CRIME.TOKYO.ACME

   - Click the Workstation Naming tab.

   c. When the Workstation Naming page appears, click Add to be allowed to add another attribute to the workstation naming convention.

   d. When the Add Name Field dialog box appears, double-click User.

   e. When the Workstation Naming page reappears, note that User now appears in the "Add Name Fields and Place Them in Order" field.

   f. Next, reorder the names in the "Add Name Fields and Place Them in Order" field:

- Click User.

- Ensure that the following is listed in the Preferred Network Address field:

  IPX Address

- Click the up-arrow twice to move User above Computer. (Workstation objects in your container will now be listed by username, followed by computer name and IPX address.)

- Click OK to close the Workstation Import Policy dialog box.

3. Associate the User Package with your container.

  a. When the User Package dialog box re-appears, click the Associations tab.

  b. When the Associations page appears, click Add.

  c. When the Select Object dialog box appears:

  - In the right pane, double-click the arrow to move the context up one level in the tree and display the CRIME container.

  - In the left pane, double-click the CRIME container. The CRIME container should now be listed in the Associations list box on the Associations page.

  - Click OK to save your changes.

Stage 3: Register the Workstation(s)

Once the users and containers have been prepared, we can begin the registration process. There are three methods for registering a Z.E.N.works workstation:

▶ Use the Z.E.N.works Scheduler to automatically perform workstation registration for workstations that have the NetWare 5 Client installed. This occurs the first time a user logs in from such a workstation.

▶ Run WSREG32.EXE manually or from a login script for Windows 95 and NT workstations (or WSREG16.EXE for Windows 3.1x workstations).

▶ Run the WSREG Application object using the Application Launcher (NAL).

Since you just updated the NetWare 5 Client for Z.E.N.works, your workstation(s) should have automatically been registered when you logged into the tree at the end of the installation process.

1. Verify workstation registration through the log file. Perform the following steps on your first workstation.

   a. Launch the Window Explorer utility.

      • Click Start in the Windows taskbar.

      • Click Programs.

      • Click Windows Explorer.

   b. When the main Windows Explorer window appears:

      • The contents of the root directory of the C: drive is displayed by default.

      • In the right pane, find the WSREG32.LOG file, then double-click it to view it.

      • If the Open With dialog box appears, scroll down and click Notepad to associate the Notepad utility with this file, then click OK.

      • View the contents of the log file. (You'll notice that it says that the workstation has been successfully registered for importation.)

TIP

If the log file is empty, close it, then wait a few minutes and open it again.

   c. Click Close (X) to close the log file.

   d. Click Close (X) to Exit the Windows Explorer utility.

2. (Optional.) Verify workstation registration for your second workstation by performing Steps 1a through Step 1d.

3. Verify workstation registration in NDS. Perform the following tasks on your first workstation.

    a. In NetWare Administrator, right-click the CRIME container.

    b. Click Details in the pop-up menu that appears.

    c. The Identification page appears by default. Use the scroll bar to locate the Workstation Registration tab, then click it.

    d. When the Workstation Registration page appears:

        • View the information that is shown for the registered workstation(s). (Use the scroll bar to show the fields that not shown.)

        • Click Cancel.

Stage 4: Import the Registered Workstation(s)

Now that the Workstation Import policy exists and everyone's been prepared, we can get on with the real work — importing the Crime Fighting workstations.

A registered workstation does not become an NDS object until it is imported into the NDS tree. When you import registered workstations into the tree:

    ▸ Each existing Workstation object is updated with the network address of the workstation to which it corresponds.

    ▸ A Workstation object is created for each registered workstation that does not already have one.

There are several methods that you can use to import registered workstations into the NDS tree. You can schedule workstation importation to occur automatically using the Novell Workstation Manager Scheduler feature or the Application Launcher. You can also import workstations manually using the Import Workstations option in the NetWare Administrator Tools menu or from the command line using the WSIMPORT.EXE utility.

In this final step, we will import workstations manually using the Import Workstations utility in the NetWare Administrator Tools menu. Are you ready?!

    1. Import registered workstations.

        a. In NetWare Administrator:

           • Click the CRIME container to select it.

- Click Tools in the menu bar to display the Tools menu.

- Click Import Workstations.

b. When the Import Workstations dialog box appears, the Import From page should be displayed by default.

- Ensure that the following container is listed in the Import Registered Workstations From field:

    `CRIME.TOKYO.ACME`

- Verify that the Include Subcontainers checkbox is marked.

- Click OK.

c. When the Import Workstations dialog box appears, note the number of workstations created, then click Close.

If workstation importation does not occur, wait a few minutes, then try Step 1b again.

TIP

2. To view your Workstation object(s) in NetWare Administrator:

a. Double-click the CRIME container to collapse it.

b. Double-click the CRIME container again to expand it.

c. Scroll down and find the new Workstation object(s). Note that the naming convention used is: Username+Computer Name+IPX address.

d. Exit NetWare Administrator.

That does it . . . mission accomplished. Our Crime Fighting ACME clients are now part of the global NDS Cloud. This level of synergy will provide you with centralized access to critical workstation maintenance duties. As a matter of fact, the final two aspects of Realm 1 rely on NDS integration:

▸ Z.E.N.works Remote Control

▸ Novell Help Requester

It's all downhill from here.

Z.E.N.works Remote Control

Now that you've established a Zen-like synergy between yourself and NetWare 5 workstations, it's time to take a vacation to Tahiti. Tahiti can be quite beautiful this time of year—clear aqua oceans, sparkling sunshine, and incredibly exotic umbrella-laden drinks. Unfortunately, two days into your vacation the cellular phone rings. It's the poor CNA you left in charge of the WAN while you were gone. It seems as though he (or she) is having a horrible time configuring the Windows NT Workstation Registry. Oops!

So, what do you do? Well, you have two choices:

▸ Hop on a plane and fly back to the office, cutting your vacation short and fixing the problem in person.

▸ Implement the built-in Remote Control facility of Z.E.N.works. This enables you to hook up your notebook modem to the cellular phone and access the troubled Windows NT Workstation object from Tahiti.

Life is good. Once Z.E.N.works has been installed and workstations have been registered with NDS, you can establish remote-control access to them by distributing the appropriate *User Agents*.

The User Agent application allows you to connect to and manage a workstation using the Remote Control utility in NetWare Administrator. The following User Agent applications must be running on Windows workstations before you can access them remotely:

▸ *Windows 95 or Windows 3.x workstations*—These require the WUSER.EXE application. This User Agent is supported by the REMOTE16 Application object.

▸ *Windows NT workstations*—These require the WUSER32.EXE application. This User Agent is supported by either the REMOTENT or REMOTESECURE (secure) Application objects.

TIP

The Windows NT Remote Control Agents are services installed on Windows NT workstations. As such, they only need to be loaded once—after that, they load automatically when the workstation is started.

The Windows 3.*x* and Windows 95 Agents, on the other hand, must be executed each time the workstation is booted. This is accomplished by using either the Application Launcher, Desktop Management Scheduler, or NDS login script.

I'm sure you're with me when I say Z.E.N.works Remote Control can be a CNA's best friend. This facility not only saves you a trip back from Tahiti, but it helps make daily workstation maintenance much easier. In this section, we're going to learn how to distribute User Agents, establish remote-control security, and use the Remote Control facility within NetWare Administrator. But first, let's explore the minimum requirements for using Z.E.N.works Remote Control.

The future's so bright, you have to wear shades.

Remote Control Requirements

To use Z.E.N.works Remote Control, you and your users must satisfy a minimum level of NDS and file system rights. In addition, your server and work-stations must also exceed a certain level of functionality. Paradise has its price.

Following is a list of the minimum requirements for Z.E.N.works Remote Control:

▸ *NDS rights* — To view and control workstations remotely, you must have the Read NDS right to All Properties in target Workstation objects. In addition, you must have the Write NDS right to the DM Remote Verification property of each target Workstation object.

▸ *File system rights* — For your users to accept the User Agent automatically (using NAL), you must give them Read and File Scan rights to the NAL directory and the directory containing the User Agent application. Fortunately, by default, both of these tools are stored in the SYS:PUBLIC directory — and users have appropriate rights automatically.

▸ *Server requirements* — To support Z.E.N.works Remote Control, your network must have a server running NetWare 5 or NetWare 4.11.

▸ *Client requirements* — All target workstations that will be remote-controlled must be connected to the network using the Z.E.N.works version of the Novell Client. In addition, they must be authenticated to NDS and have a Workstation object registered and imported into the tree. Finally, your administrative workstation must use the updated NetWare Administrator 32 utility provided by Z.E.N.works — NWADMN32.EXE.

Once you've satisfied these minimum requirements, it's time to distribute the Remote Control User Agent. Let's check it out.

Distributing the Remote Control User Agent

To remotely control a distributed workstation, the target device must be running a platform-specific User Agent. Before you go to Tahiti, be sure that all your workstations are automatically accepting User Agents. This can be accomplished in one of two ways:

▶ *NAL Distribution* — When you install Z.E.N.works, User Agent Application objects are automatically created in the NDS tree. These objects can then be associated with Containers, Users, or Groups to ensure Remote Control activation at each workstation. In addition, you can use the Application Explorer and Force-Run option to ensure that the User Agent applications are pushed to distributed workstations each time users log in. On Windows 95 and Windows 3.x workstations, the WUSER.EXE application runs from the SYS:PUBLIC directory via REMOTE16. This must happen every time the workstation is booted. On Windows NT workstations, the NTSTACFG.EXE application runs from the SYS:PUBLIC directory. This installation program registers the Novell REMOTENT or REMOTESECURE Agent services with Windows NT the first time it's run. Following this initial installation, each service runs automatically each time Windows NT starts.

▶ *Login Script Distribution* — If you don't like the NAL alternative, you can always distribute User Agents automatically by embedding commands in login scripts. This works much the same way as registering NDS Workstation objects via login scripts. Once again, use the "%PLATFORM" identifier variable to distinguish between Windows 95 (W95), Windows NT (WNT), and Windows 3.x (WIN) platforms. You can then automatically activate User Agents when workstations connect to the network. Keep in mind, Windows NT Agents only must be run once. You may consider removing the NTSTACFG.EXE application from the login script once all the NT workstations have been activated.

Once the Z.E.N.works User Agents have been distributed, your workstations are ready to accept remote commands. This is accomplished using the Remote Control feature within NetWare Administrator 32.

Wait a minute . . . I have one question. Who gets access to your workstation? And what can they do there? Actually, I had two questions.

Security becomes a very important issue when you activate Remote Control throughout the WAN. You must determine a way of opening distributed workstations to CNAs (that's you), but closing it to everyone else (that's users). Let's learn.

Establishing Remote Control Security

Theoretically, any user can access the desktop of any workstation using the Remote Control tool in NetWare Administrator. This level of data sharing and openness is not recommended in today's capitalistic climate — information is more valuable than money!!

So, it's up to you, as the NetWare 5 CNA, to impose security restrictions on Z.E.N.works Remote Control. If Remote Control security is necessary for only a few users or workstations, you can set it up by using their individual NDS objects. However, if you must secure a large number of users or workstations, you can configure the Remote Control Policy in User or Workstation Packages. Interestingly, Remote Control access is enabled by default for all new Workstation objects. Ouch.

So, how does Remote Control security work? Well, it actually occurs from two different perspectives. First, when you attempt to remote-control a workstation, the User Agent checks the security parameters in the Workstation object. Next, it checks the Workstation Policy Package (if one exists) for security access restrictions. If you pass both workstation-oriented security parameters, the User Agent shifts to the user point of view.

Next, the User Agent checks to see if your User object has any security restrictions associated with Remote Control. Finally, it checks any User Policy Packages you've been associated with. If access is not restricted from the user point of view, the Remote Control session begins.

Table 6.3 lists the parameters you can set as security controls for remote access. You can configure these parameters through the Remote Control page of the Workstation/User object or the Remote Control Policy in a Workstation/User Package. Check them out.

TABLE 6.3	SECURITY PARAMETER	DESCRIPTION
Z.E.N.works Remote Control Security Parameters	Disable Remote Control	Disallows control of the workstation
	Prompt on Remote Control	Enables confirmation from the user before anyone can remotely access the workstation.
	Audible Signal	Enables an alert sound when the workstation is accessed.
	Visible Signal	Enables the display of an icon on the user's desktop while the workstation is being accessed remotely.

As I mentioned earlier, Z.E.N.works supports two different points of view with respect to Remote Control security: from the Workstation/User Object POV or Workstation/User Policy Package POV. Let's see how they work:

▶ *Workstation/User Object* — You can activate or restrict Remote Control access to a specific workstation using a Workstation or User object. Simply access the Remote Control page button in NetWare Administrator (see Figure 6.18). To set security parameters, mark the "Use these settings and ignore workstation Remote Control policy" box. When you do so, a list of security configurations appears. If you want to completely disallow remote-control access to the workstation or user, unmark the "Enable remote control" box. Configurations set for Workstation objects will limit access to that specific machine. On the other hand, User configurations limit what specific users can do in any remote-control scenario.

▶ *Workstation/User Policy Packages* — To set up Remote Control security for multiple users or workstations, try the Remote Control Policy. First, create a platform-specific Policy Package object and find your way to the Remote Control Policy details page (shown in Figure 6.19). As you can see from the figure, this configuration screen closely resembles the Remote Control page just discussed. Finally, remember Workstation Policy Packages apply to target workstations and User Policy Packages apply to administrators (or anyone interested in remote-controlling a workstation).

FIGURE 6.18

The Remote Control page in
NetWare Administrator

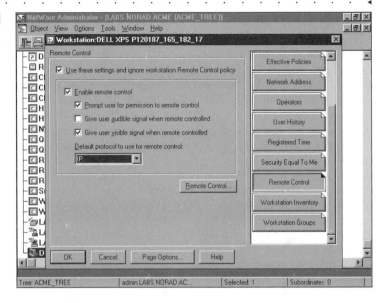

FIGURE 6.19

Remote Control Policy
details in NetWare
Administrator

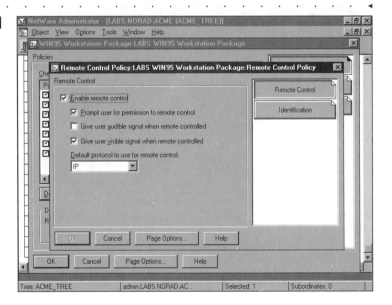

How secure do you feel? Well, it's nice to know that Z.E.N.works supports sophisticated configurations for remote-control security. Now that we've met the minimum requirements, distributed User Agents, and established remote-control security, it's time to go to Tahiti.

Well, maybe we should review the ins and outs of Z.E.N.works Remote Control before we get on the plane. Ready, set, learn.

Using Z.E.N.works Remote Control

Now it's time to get down to business and let the electrons fly. We've played around long enough—enabling and preparing the remote-control workstations. Now, let's pull all the pieces together.

NetWare Administrator is your friend. To activate a Remote Control session, simply find a target Workstation object in the NDS tree and select the Remote Control Workstation option from the Tools menu of NetWare Administrator. When the connection is made, the target workstation's desktop appears on your workstation in a special Viewing Window. Check it out in Figure 6.20.

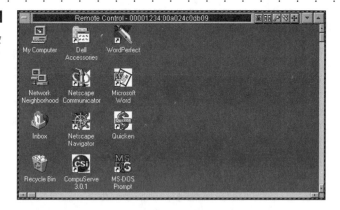

The Remote Control Viewing Window in NetWare Administrator

The Remote Control Viewing Window functions like any other Windows-based desktop. You can resize it, minimize the desktop, or access any target workstation application. In addition, the Remote Control Viewing Window contains a group of toolbar buttons in the upper-right corner of the screen. Check them out in Figure 6.20. These buttons allow you to navigate and control the target workstation as if you were there. Fortunately, from Tahiti's perspective, you're not.

REAL WORLD

To support a Remote Control session, the target workstation must be powered on and have IPX and the Novell Client for Z.E.N.works loaded. In addition, some Remote Control Policies require user permission for administrative access. In this case, a Remote Control pop-up window will appear on the user workstation as soon as a remote-control connection is attempted. The user must respond within five seconds to the prompt or the connection ends. If this occurs, you will receive a message explaining that the user did not respond to the prompt in time. Keep on trying; they're bound to say "Yes" sooner or later.

Here's a quick description of the four most useful Remote Control Viewing Window toolbar buttons:

- ▶ *Start*— When you click the Viewing Window's Start button, a Ctrl+Esc key sequence is sent to the target workstation. Use this button to open the Start menu (Windows NT 4.0 and Windows 95 workstations) or task list (Windows NT 3.5 and Windows 3.x workstations). As you can see in Figure 6.21, the remote Start button behaves exactly the same as the native one. Except in this case, you're making configurations and accessing programs on a remote machine.

F I G U R E · 6 . 2 1

Using the Remote Control Start button

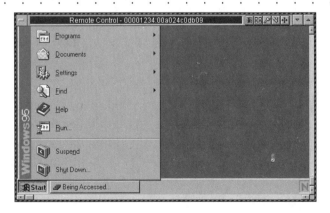

▶ *Application Switcher* — When you click the Viewing Window's Application Switcher button, you send an Alt+Tab key sequence to the target workstation. This button lets you select an application that is open on the target machine. After you click this button, press Tab on your own workstation to select an open application.

▶ *System Key Pass-Through* — The Viewing Window's System Key Pass-Through button allows you to "pass through" system keys (such as Alt and Ctrl) from your machine to the target workstation. By default, you cannot send Alt and Ctrl keystrokes from your keyboard because the target machine's keyboard is still active. When you want to use keyboard commands such as Alt+Enter to view item properties on the target desktop, you must click the System Key Pass-Through button before pressing Alt+Enter. This button is a toggle so all keys you send from this point forward are passed through until you deactivate the feature by clicking the button again.

▶ *Navigation* — When you click the Viewing Window's Navigation button, a minimized desktop of the target workstation is displayed in a small window on your machine. Then you can use a red frame in the Minimized Area window to change the framing of your target desktop. This feature helps you navigate the target machine without having to maximize the Viewing Window.

In addition to the Viewing Window toolbar buttons, you can use hot keys to control how the target desktop appears on your own workstation. Table 6.4 contains a list of the preconfigured hot keys you can use to customize the Remote Control Viewing Window.

If you'd like to change any of these hot-key assignments, click the Hot Keys option in the Viewing Window's pull-down menu. This pull-down menu is displayed when you click the upper-left corner of the window's title bar.

TABLE 6.4

Default Viewing
Window Hot Keys

HOT KEY SEQUENCE	FUNCTION	DESCRIPTION
Ctrl+Alt+M	Full screen toggle	Maximizes the Viewing Window to the size of your screen without window borders.
Ctrl+Alt+R	Refresh screen	Refreshes the target workstation's screen.
Ctrl+Alt+T	Restart viewer	Restarts your connection to the target machine and refreshes the Viewing Window.
Ctrl+Alt+S	System key routing toggle	Passes Windows-reserved keystrokes (such as Alt+Tab) to the target workstation. When this option is enabled, all system keystrokes affect only the target workstation.
Ctrl+Alt+H	Hot key enable	Enables the Control Option's hot keys on the target workstation.
Ctrl+Alt+A	Accelerated mode	Increases the refresh rate of the Viewing Window (on your machine) without changing the refresh rate on the target workstation's monitor.
Left-Shift+Esc	Stop viewing	Releases control of the target workstation and ends the Remote Control connection.

Okay, let's return to our Tahiti fantasy for just a moment. Imagine that you've successfully accessed the troublesome workstation and solved the Registry problem. Now it's time to return to your umbrella-filled exotic drink. But first, you must end the Remote Control session.

To end a Z.E.N.works Remote Control session, you can open the pull-down menu in the Viewing Window and click Close. You can also activate the System Key Pass-Through feature and press Alt+F4. Or, if you really want to be cool, you can use the keystroke sequence assigned to the Stop Viewing hot key option — Left-Shift+Esc by default.

Congratulations! You get to stay in Tahiti. Don't ever say Z.E.N.works didn't do you any favors. Speaking of favors, let's explore the final corner of Realm 1 — the Novell Help Requester. This is a great way of opening the lines of communication between your users and the Help Desk. This is a good thing, right?

LAB EXERCISE 6.4: USING Z.E.N.WORKS REMOTE CONTROL IN THE CRIME FIGHTING DIVISION OF ACME

Once Z.E.N.works has been installed and workstations have been registered with NDS, you can establish remote-control access to them by distributing the appropriate *User Agents*.

In this exercise, we're going to help the ACME Crime Fighting division access several remote Z.E.N.works clients scattered throughout the ACME globe. Here's a quick preview:

▶ *Stage 1:* Prevent Remote Control Access of Your Workstation

▶ *Stage 2:* Configure Remote Control Access to Other Workstations

▶ *Stage 3:* Activate a Remote Control Session

The following hardware is required for this exercise:

▶ A NetWare 5 server with Z.E.N.works installed.

▶ A workstation running the NetWare 5 Client for Windows 95/98 or Windows NT.

▶ (Optional) A second workstation with the same NetWare Client as the first workstation.

Keep in mind, Sherlock Holmes is counting on you. So get busy!

Stage 1: Prevent Remote Control Access of Your Workstation

Since you're the ACME CNA, you want to protect your own workstation first. To build your own Z.E.N.works firewall *against* remote access, follow these simple steps:

1. Create a Workstation Policy Package object for the Admin user. (Although you could have alternately created a User Policy Package, you'll find that a Workstation Policy Package affords greater protection, because it pertains to the workstation itself — which is what you want to control.)

a. On your first workstation, log into the tree as Admin if you haven't already done so.

b. Launch NetWare Administrator. To do so, click Start on the Windows taskbar, then click Run. When the Run dialog box appears, type the following in the Open field, and then click OK:

```
Z:\PUBLIC\WIN32\NWADMN32
```

c. When the main NetWare Administrator screen appears, right-click the CRIME container, then click Create.

d. When the New Object dialog box appears, type the following to select Policy Package, and then press Enter:

```
P
```

e. When the Create Policy Package dialog box appears:

- Open the pull-down menu in the Select Policy Package Type field and click the Workstation Policy Package that matches your workstation's platform. For example, if you are a Windows 95 user, you would select WIN95 Workstation Package.

- In the Name field, type the following:

  ```
  Adminws
  ```

- Mark the Define Additional Properties checkbox.

- Click Create.

2. Configure the Remote Control Policy.

a. When the Workstation Package dialog box appears:

- In the Policies window, mark the Remote Control Policy checkbox.

- Click Details.

b. When the Workstation Import Policy dialog box appears:

- You'll notice that the Remote Control page is displayed by default.

- Unmark the Enable Remote Control checkbox:

- Click OK.

3. Associate the Workstation Package with the Workstation object corresponding to the Admin user.

   a. When the Workstation Package dialog box reappears, click the Associations tab.

   b. When the Associations page appears, click Add.

   c. When the Select Object dialog box appears:

   • In the left pane, double-click the Workstation object associated with the Admin user. The Workstation object should then appear in the Associations list box on the Associations page.

   • Click OK to save your changes.

Stage 2: Configure Remote Control Access to Other Workstations

Now that you've protected yourself, you can get busy *unprotecting* everyone else. To configure remote control access for the other Workstation objects in the CRIME container, perform the following tasks at your client workstation. (If you don't have a second workstation, you can just read through the remainder of the exercise.)

1. Create a Group object called Managerws.

   a. In NetWare Administrator, right-click the CRIME container, then click Create.

   b. When the New Object dialog box appears, double-click Workstation Group.

   c. When the Create Workstation Group dialog box appears:

   • Type the following in the Name field:

   Managerws

   • Mark the Define Additional Properties checkbox.

   • Click Create.

   d. When the Workstation Group dialog box appears:

   • You'll notice that the Identification page is displayed by default.

- Click the Members tab.

e. When the Members page appears, click Add.

f. When the Select Object dialog box appears:

- In the left pane, double-click the Workstation object corresponding to your second workstation (if you have one).

- The Workstation object you selected should appear in the Workstations field.

- Click OK to save your changes.

2. Create a Workstation Policy Package named *Platform* Remote Control.

a. In NetWare Administrator, right-click the CRIME container, then click Create.

b. When the New Object dialog box appears, double-click Policy Package.

c. When the Create Policy Package dialog box appears:

- Open the pull-down menu in the Select Policy Package Type field and click the Workstation package that matches your second workstation's platform. For example, if it is a Windows 95 workstation, you would select WIN95 Workstation Package.

- In the Name field, type:

  `Platform WS Remote Control`

  where *Platform* is the type of platform (such as WIN95).

- Mark the Define Additional Properties checkbox.

- Click Create.

3. Enable and configure the Remote Control policy.

a. When the User Package dialog box appears:

- In the Policies window, mark the Remote Control Policy checkbox.

- Click Details.

b. When the Remote Control Policy property sheet appears:

- You'll notice that the Remote Control page is displayed by default.

- Verify that the following checkboxes are marked:

  `Enable Remote Control`

  `Prompt User for Permission to Remote Control`

  `Give User Visible Signal When Remote Controlled`

- Verify that the following value is listed in "Default Protocol to Use for Remote Control":

  `IPX`

  (**Note:** Only the IPX protocol was supported by the Z.E.N.works 1.0 Remote Control product at the time this book was written.)

- Click Cancel.

4. Associate the Workstation Package with the Managerws Group object.

a. When the Workstation Package property sheet re-appears, click the Associations tab.

b. When the Associations page appears, click Add.

c. When the Select Object dialog box appears:

- Double-click the Managerws Workstation Group object in the left pane. The object should then appear in the Associations list box on the Associations page.

- Click OK to save your changes.

Stage 3: Activate a Remote Control Session

Finally, it's time to actually start remote controlling. If you have a second workstation available, perform the following steps on it.

1. (Optional.) On your second workstation, run the appropriate User Agent application:

a. Log into the tree as the SHolmes user, if you haven't already done so. (The password is ACME.)

b. Run the Z.E.N.works Remote Control User Agent.

- Click Start on the Windows taskbar.

- Click Programs.

- Click Novell.

- Click Remote Control.

- Click Remote Control Agent.

c. The Remote Control Icon should appear in your Windows taskbar.

2. On the first workstation, initiate a remote workstation session.

a. In NetWare Administrator, click the Workstation object that you want to control remotely (that is, the one corresponding to your second workstation).

b. Click Tools in the menu bar to display the Tools menu, then click Remote Control Workstation. (Be sure that you don't accidentally select Remote Control instead.)

c. A Z.E.N.works Remote Control window will appear, indicating that it is asking the remote workstation's user for permission to access the workstation.

3. On the second workstation, a Z.E.N.works Remote Control Agent window will appear asking if you want to allow admin.CRIME.TOKYO.ACME to remotely access your workstation. Click Yes. (You must do this very quickly, or the request will time out. If it does, perform Step 4b, Step 4c, and Step 5 again.)

> **REAL WORLD**
>
> If an error message occurs indicating that the utility can't find the IPX Remote Management Agent:
>
> ▸ Confirm that the Remote Control Agent is actually loaded on the second workstation (that is, that Remote Control Agent is listed in the Windows taskbar on the second workstation).
>
> ▸ Verify that the second workstation is not waiting for some type of user input unrelated to the Workstation Remote Control feature (that is, that some type of message or dialog box is not displayed on the screen).
>
> ▸ Wait a few minutes, then perform Step 4b again.

4. On the first workstation, a Remote Control window should appear showing the screen from the second workstation.

    a. In the Remote Desktop window, display available RAM information for the second workstation.

- Click Start (which is one of the buttons that is located to the right of the title bar in the Remote Desktop window).

- Click Settings.

- Click Control Panel.

- Double-click System.

- When the System Properties dialog box appears, click the Performance tab.

- Note the value in the System Resources field.

- Click Close (X) to close the System Properties dialog box.

- Click Close (X) to close the Control Panel in the Remote Desktop window.

REAL WORLD

If the inside of the Remote Control window is blank (that is, white), it probably means that the second workstation is using a display adapter that is not supported by Z.E.N.works 1.0. If this is the case, you'll need to switch the second workstation to a Standard VGA display driver. The steps you need to perform will probably be somewhat similar to those that follow, depending on your operating system and display adapter:

▸ Close any applications that are open.

▸ Click Start in the Windows taskbar.

▸ Click Settings.

▸ Click Control Panel.

▸ Double-click Display.

▸ When the Display Properties dialog box appears, click the Settings tab.

▸ When the Settings page appears, click the Advanced Properties tab.

▸ When the Advanced Display Properties page appears, click Change.

▸ When the Select Device dialog box appears, write down the name and date of the display adapter the workstation is currently using.

▸ Click the Show All Devices radio button.

▸ In the Manufacturer's list box, click Standard Display Types.

▸ In the Models list box, click Standard Display Adapter (VGA).

▸ Click OK.

▸ When the Advanced Display Properties dialog box appears, click OK.

(continued)

(continued)

▸ When the Display Properties dialog box appears, click Close.

▸ When the System Settings Change dialog box appears, click Yes to restart the computer.

▸ After the workstation reboots, continue with Stage 3, Step 1.

b. In the Remote Desktop window, display connection information for the second workstation.

- Click Navigate (which is one of the buttons that is located to the right of the title bar in the Remote Desktop window).

- A small window will appear. Drag the rectangle in the small window to the bottom right of the small window, so that the remote workstation's system tray is visible in the Remote Desktop window.

- Right-click the Novell Workstation Manager icon in the remote workstation's system tray and click NetWare Connections. Drag the rectangle in the small window to the upper left of the small window, so that you can view the Remote Connections dialog box in the Remote Desktop window. Note which communications protocol the second workstation is using. (It should be IPX.)

- Drag the rectangle in the small window to the bottom right of the small window.

- Click OK in the Remote Desktop window to close the NetWare Connections dialog box.

- Click Close (X) in the smaller window to close it.

- For an alternate viewing technique, press Ctrl+Alt+M to view the remote screen as a full-sized screen without window borders. When you're done, press Ctrl+Alt+M to toggle to the original size screen.

    c. To end the remote control session, open the pull-down menu in the upper-left corner of the Remote Desktop window and click Close.

    d. Exit the NetWare Administrator utility.

5. (Optional.) On your first workstation, load the Remote Control Agent.

    a. Run the Z.E.N.works Remote Control User Agent.

      • Click Start on the Windows taskbar.

      • Click Programs.

      • Click Novell.

      • Click Remote Control.

      • Click Remote Control Agent.

    b. The Remote Control Icon should appear in your Windows taskbar.

6. On the second workstation, initiate a remote workstation session.

    a. On your second workstation, log into the tree as Admin.

    b. In NetWare Administrator, highlight the Workstation object that you want to control remotely (that is, the one corresponding to your first workstation).

    c. Click Tools in the menu bar to display the Tools menu, then click Remote Control Workstation. (Be sure that you don't accidentally select Remote Control instead.)

    d. A Z.E.N.works Remote Control dialog box should appear, indicating that it is unable to establish security context with the Agent. Click Close to acknowledge the message. (The reason you cannot establish a remote workstation session with the first workstation is because it is protected by the Adminws Workstation Policy that you created specifically for that purpose.)

    e. Exit the NetWare Administrator utility.

Congratulations! ACME thanks you profusely. Not to mention, you've made your own management life a lot easier — that is, no more red-eye flights across the world to fix a broken window.

Speaking of good news, let's explore the final corner of Realm 1 — the Novell Help Requester. This is a great way of opening the lines of communication between your users and the Help Desk. This is a good thing, right?

Novell Help Requester

The CNA is a brave soul whose single task it is to keep peace in the NetWare 5 Global Electronic Village. System administration, installation, and troubleshooting are typically three full-time jobs smashed into one part-time job description. In the past, the CNAs were chosen by default—a dubious distinction. Nobody fully understood the time and effort it required to manage and troubleshoot a NetWare WAN. So, the job was often given to the first employee who showed proficiency in using the copy machine or office microwave.

Fortunately, we have left the Dark Ages. Employers are beginning to appreciate the knowledge and skill it takes to correctly manage a NetWare 5 WAN. The CNA certification is gaining respect and — in many cases — becoming a requirement for system manager careers.

The responsibilities of a NetWare 5 CNA can be overwhelming at times. Fortunately, you have the comprehensive training of Novell's CNA program to guide you. This book and its affiliated courses will prepare you for 95 percent of the pitfalls of system management and troubleshooting. Unfortunately, it's the other 5 percent that always seem to jump up and bite you. This task is further complicated by two four-letter words:

▶ USER

▶ HELP

One of the most challenging aspects about helping users is the simple fact that most of the time they don't know why they need your help. Furthermore, they're sure they know what the problem is, but can't tell you how it occurred. All of this misinformation creates a wall between users and the network Help Desk.

Novell to the rescue!

NetWare 5 includes a powerful Novell Help Requester that allows users to notify you (and the Help Desk) of workstation problems via e-mail or phone. The application provides pertinent information about the user and workstation — such as the user's context and the workstation ID. Furthermore, using NAL, you can push the Help Requester application to all user workstations automatically. When the Application Launcher Window opens on a user's desktop, the Help Requester icon appears as a selection. Users can then be instructed to use this tool whenever a problem occurs. Check out Figure 6.22.

F I G U R E   6.22

*The Help Requester
icon in NAL*

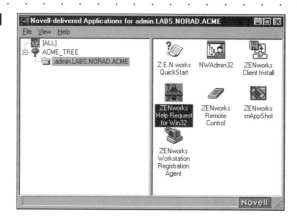

The following Help Requester applications must be running on Windows workstations before users can contact you:

▸ *Windows 95 or Windows NT workstations* — These require the HLPREQ32 .EXE application. This Requester is supported by the HLPREQ32 Application object.

▸ *Windows 3.x workstations* — These require the HLPREQ16.EXE application. This Requester is supported by the HLPREQ16 Application object.

The Novell Help Requester can dramatically improve your CNA life. Remember, you're not alone — we're all here to help. So, let's band together and figure out how to streamline communications between user problems and CNA solutions . . . starting with a minimum set of user and workstation requirements.

Help Requester Requirements

To use the Novell Help Requester, you and your users must satisfy a minimum level of NDS and file system rights. In addition, your servers and workstations must also exceed a specific level of functionality. Help has its price.

Following is a list of minimum requirements for the Novell Help Requester:

▸ *NDS rights* — To use NAL to distribute the Help Requester application, you must have Supervisor object rights to the [Root] of the NDS tree. As far as users are concerned, you don't have to worry about manually adding any NDS rights. The Read and Compare rights to "All Properties" are automatically assigned to any Container, Group, or User when you associate the Application object.

▸ *File system rights* — For your users to accept the Help Requester automatically (using NAL), you must give them Read and File Scan rights to the NAL directory and the directory containing the Help Requester application. Fortunately, by default, both of these tools are stored in the SYS:PUBLIC directory — and users have appropriate rights automatically.

▸ *Server requirements* — To support the Novell Help Requester, your network must have a server running NetWare 5 or NetWare 4.11. In addition, e-mail requests require a network-wide messaging service such as Messaging Application Program Interface (MAPI) or GroupWise.

▸ *Client requirements* — All target workstations that will be accessing the Help Requester must be connected to the network using the Z.E.N.works Novell Client. In addition, they must be authenticated to NDS and have a Workstation object registered and imported into the tree. Finally, your administrative workstation must use the updated NetWare Administrator 32 utility provided by Z.E.N.works — NWADMN32.EXE.

Once you've satisfied these minimum requirements, it's time to distribute and configure the Novell Help Requester. Let's get busy.

Configuring the Help Requester

For users to take full advantage of the Novell Help Requester, the target workstation must be running a platform-specific application. This can be accomplished automatically using the NAL. By the way, we'll explore NAL in much greater depth later in Realm 3.

When you install Z.E.N.works, Help Requester Application objects are automatically created in the NDS tree. These objects can then be associated with containers, users, or groups to ensure Help Requester functionality at each workstation. In addition, you can use the Application Explorer and Force-Run option to make sure the Help Requester applications are pushed to distributed workstations each time users log in.

On Windows 95 and Windows NT workstations, the HLPREQ32.EXE application runs from the SYS:PUBLIC directory. This must happen every time the workstation is booted. On Windows 3.x workstations, the HLPREQ16.EXE application runs from the SYS:PUBLIC directory. In either case, NAL will ensure that the Help Requester application appears on the user desktop each time he or she logs in. Check it out in Figure 6.22.

Once the Novell Help Requester has been distributed, your users are ready to send you all their problems. Well . . . not quite yet. To ensure proper communications between the Help Requester and Help Desk, you must perform some additional policy configurations.

Using NetWare Administrator, you'll need to configure the Help Desk Policy in a User Policy Package to provide the Help Requester with critical NDS information. This Help Desk Policy configuration performs a variety of important tasks:

▶ It determines if the Mail button appears in the application — enabling users to send e-mail requests.

▶ It defines MAPI or GroupWise as the messaging service.

▶ It provides default Subject line topics for Help Requester messages.

▶ It identifies the help contact's name, phone number, and e-mail address.

Help Desk Policies only apply to users and, therefore, appear in the User Policy Packages only. To set up a Help Desk Policy in a new or existing User Policy Package, complete these simple steps:

▶ *Step 1: Create a User Policy Package* — In NetWare Administrator, create a User Policy Package object that matches your workstation platform — such as WIN95 or WIN NT. In the new User Policy Package, mark the Help Desk Policy box. Click Details. The Help Desk Policy Configuration window appears.

▶ *Step 2: Help Desk Policy Information* — Enter the Help Requester contact details in the Information page button of Figure 6.23. This information identifies the primary support CNA or mailbox that users should reference when reporting workstation problems.

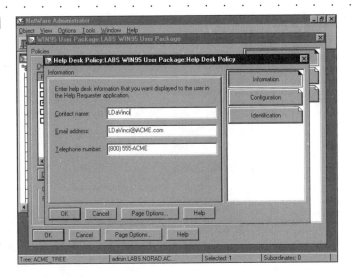

*Help Desk Policy
Information page in
NetWare Administrator*

▶ *Step 3: Help Desk Policy Configuration* — Next, you can use the Configuration page of Figure 6.24 to customize user-based Help Requester operations. These configurations include a delivery mode for the messaging service, a default Subject line for help requests, and details for automatically launching the Help Requester.

▶ *Step 4: Help Desk Policy Association* — Once you've created and configured the Help Desk Policy in a new User Policy Package, it's time to associate the Package with target containers, users, or groups. This association enhances the way NAL and the Help Requester work together. This is a good thing.

Do you need any help yet? If so, it's nice to know that Z.E.N.works supports sophisticated help configurations for NetWare 5 users. Now that we've met the minimum requirements, distributed the Help Requester application, and created a Help Desk Policy, it's time to open the floodgates.

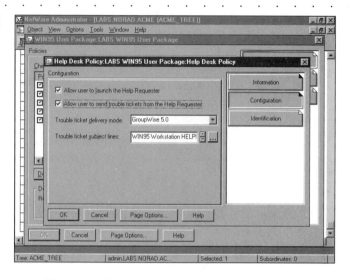

FIGURE 6.24

*Help Desk Policy
Configuration page in
NetWare Administrator*

Well, maybe we should review the ins and outs of the Novell Help Requester
before we start solving problems. Ready, set, learn.

Using the Novell Help Requester

Now it's time to get down to business and begin solving users' problems. We've
spent long enough enabling and preparing the Novell Help Requester. Now let's
show the users how it's done.

Once you have distributed the Help Requester to users with NAL, and
configured and associated a Help Desk Policy, users will be greeted with the Help
Requester Application Window. Check it out in Figure 6.25.

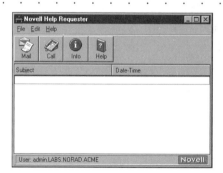

FIGURE 6.25

*The Help Requester
Application Window*

REAL WORLD

The Mail button will not appear in the Help Requester Application Window if you have not marked the "Allow user to send trouble ticket" box in the Help Desk Policy's Configuration page. If users are allowed to e-mail report problems to you, be sure that GroupWise (or a similar messaging platform) is running in the background. You may also consider activating Z.E.N.works Remote Control so that you can solve their problems remotely. Remember our Tahiti scenario in the previous section.

As you can see in Figure 6.25, the Help Requester Application Window offers the user four problem-solving buttons. Here's how they work:

▶ *Mail* — The Help Requester allows users to report problems via e-mail. For this functionality to work, you must configure a network-wide messaging system — such as MAPI or GroupWise. If a user clicks this button, the "Mail for help" window will appear. This window automatically registers the user's name, workstation ID, and offers a pull-down menu of acceptable Subjects. In addition, users can enter a message in the Message field and click Send. Once a user sends a help request, the Subject appears in the lower half of the Help Requester Application Window (shown in Figure 6.25).

▶ *Call* — If you don't want to allow e-mail help requests, users can always contact you the old fashioned way — using the phone. The Call button displays a contact name and phone number specifically applied to this user. Remember, we can customize user-based Help Desk Policies. In addition, the "Call for help" window displays basic problem background data — such as user context, workstation ID, location, and network tree.

▶ *Info* — When users click the Info button, the User and Help Desk tabs are displayed. The User tab includes the same user-specific information found in the "Call for help" window. This information helps users identify their workstation when reporting problems. Similarly, the Help Desk tab provides the contact information that is shown at the top of the "Call for help" window. The Help Desk tab also provides the e-mail address of the assigned contact person and the Help Desk Policy associated with this user.

▸ *Help* — When users click the Help button, they can review instructions for using the Help Requester features.

Now repeat after me . . . "Can I help you?" It's a good idea to get in the habit of asking this question because you're just about to be inundated with user problems. Think of this as the cyber-couch of Realm 1 and you're Dr. Freud.

Speaking of psychoanalysis . . . let's return to the true meaning of Realm 1. As you remember from our very first introduction, the Art of Zen is a method of enhancing your senses. In this realm, we've learned how the network relies on sensory input from workstations for external and internal data. Z.E.N.works is a way of allowing your workstations to get in "touch" with their own ESP powers. Hopefully, now you have a better appreciation for exactly how challenging and complex NetWare 5 Workstation Maintenance really is. User diversity unravels the fabric of network standardization. As a NetWare 5 CNA, this is one of your toughest hurdles.

Fortunately, Z.E.N.works offers another realm where Big Brother demands standardization and offers various tools for battling user diversity. Sound like paradise? Not really . . . it's just Z.E.N.works Realm 2 — Desktop Management.

Z.E.N.works Realm 2: Desktop Management

The second Z.E.N.works realm is the smallest of the three. In this corner of our cyber-kingdom, you'll learn how to tap the power of *"Mystical Management."* Hmmm.

The *Mystical* element of Realm 2 applies to how you magically transform the user desktop into an "enhanced productivity tool." Z.E.N.works Desktop Management involves user-specific and workstation-specific configurations — including desktop applications, printing, and user profiles.

Mystical Management applies to three different desktop transformations:

▶ *Customizing Desktop Applications* — You can customize the user desktop by enabling User and Computer Policies. For example, you can hide sensitive utilities and/or Force-Run applications.

▶ *Configuring Printing Environments* — You can build custom configurations for user printing environments through NDS.

▶ *Mandatory User Profiles* — You can standardize desktop settings such as Wallpaper, Screen Saver, and Sounds.

The trick to Z.E.N.works Mystical Management is to control the user desktop without him or her noticing. If you get the feeling from this preview that "Big Brother" is watching . . . you're not far off. The good news is *you* are Big Brother! Now here's the trick — don't let the users find out.

Let's explore Z.E.N.works Realm 2 — starting with desktop Applications.

Customizing Desktop Applications

Let's begin our lesson in Mystical Management by customizing desktop applications. As a Z.E.N.works CNA, you can customize the user desktop by configuring two specific policies:

▶ User System Policy

▶ Computer System Policy

Check them out.

User System Policy

The User System Policy allows you to control the desktop for specific users. The first thing you should do in this arena is consider hiding applications from users. This is accomplished using the User System Policies Page button in NetWare Administrator (see Figure 6.26).

Hiding applications (such as Network Neighborhood, Run, and Find) can help reduce network access problems and improve server performance. Remember: Big Brother knows best.

F I G U R E   6.26

Hiding desktop applications with a User System Policy

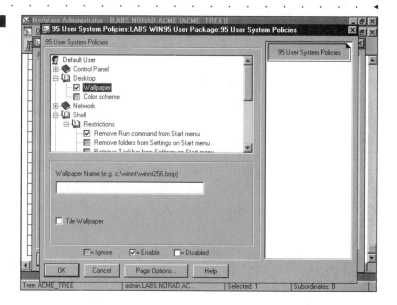

Computer System Policy

The Computer System Policy in a Workstation Policy Package allows you to control the desktop for specific workstations. For example, you can use the Properties button in Figure 6.27 to launch a utility that Force-Runs desktop applications when the workstation connects to the network. One such application you should consider force-feeding to users is the Remote Control User Agent. Remember: Big Brother needs access to your workstation.

Any changes you make to either the User System Policy or the Computer System Policy affects only the users and workstations that have been associated with the host Packages. However, if you configure both policies, they will combine to create the standardized desktop the user sees at login. Nothing like cooperation.

Now, let's see how Mystical Management can help us in the printing world.

TIP

Desktop applications that you've hidden from users through the User System Policy take effect as soon as the policy is enabled. However, applications that you set to launch automatically on a workstation through the Computer System Policy won't launch until the workstation logs back into the network.

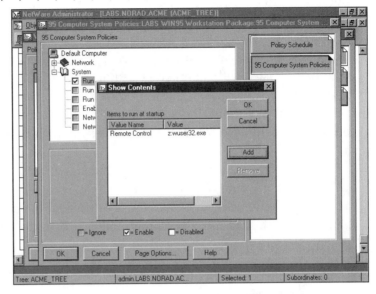

FIGURE 6.27

Configuring Force-Run
applications with a
Computer System Policy

Configuring Printing Environments

The next Z.E.N.works Mystical Management task deals with printing—you know, the greatest mystery of life (see Chapter 7, "NetWare 5 Printing with NDPS").

As you'll soon discover, one of the most costly and time-consuming aspects of network management is printing. As user demands increase and printer diversity widens, you can spend most of your day bouncing from client to client, installing print drivers and troubleshooting Printer Agents.

Fortunately, Realm 2 offers a solution that allows you to configure a user's printing environment without leaving your desk. All this magic is accomplished using two important Z.E.N.works policies:

▶ User Printer Policy

▶ Computer Printer Policy

You can customize user-specific printing configurations using the User Printer Policy. This way users can always have access to their favorite printers because printing information is stored in NDS. When they authenticate to the network, the Printer object is automatically created on their workstation desktop and the appropriate printer driver is installed. This is a great feature for nomadic users who demand access to their home printers from any location.

Similarly, you can configure workstation-specific printers using the Computer Printer Policy in the Workstation Package. For example, a group of workstations could be associated with a printer located in a nearby office. Then any user who logs in using the workstations in the group would automatically access proximity-friendly printers. Because the workstations have identities in NDS, the printer configuration associated with them is delivered to the client when they connect to the network.

User printing management can be a nightmare . . . and Z.E.N.works Mystical Management is the cure. Whatever you do, try to use policies as much as you can to ease user-specific configurations. Now, let's complete our quick journey through Realm 2 with a look at mandatory user profiles. This is the fun part.

Mandatory User Profiles

The user desktop presents a very interesting dilemma. On the one hand, it's a personal space where network users demand individuality. On the other hand, it's a network-owned environment where CNAs demand standardization. Who wins? Answer: Big Brother.

Using Z.E.N.works Mystical Management, you can standardize and deploy a Mandatory Desktop Profile to every user in the network. Once these settings have been configured, the users cannot change them. This is accomplished using the following user-specific policy:

Desktop Preferences Policy

As you can see in Figure 6.28, the Desktop Preferences Policy allows you to lock most of the user-defined preferences set in the Windows Control Panel. These include Wallpaper, Screen Saver, and Sounds. Once a user has been associated with the customized Policy Package, his or her desktop will take on a standard company-wide look-and-feel. Big Brother wins again.

TIP

If your users revolt against a standardized desktop, you can spoon-feed them a dose of individuality. The Desktop Preferences configuration in Figure 6.28 allows you to choose which settings will be mandatory. I suggest you let your users choose their own Wallpaper . . . it keeps them happy.

FIGURE 6.28

Standardizing the
user desktop with a
Desktop Preferences Policy

FIGURE 6.28

Standardizing the
user desktop with a
Desktop Preferences Policy

Do you feel mystical? You should—we've just completed our journey through Z.E.N.works Realm 2. In this corner of our cyber-kingdom, we ventured beyond workstation maintenance into the realm of Mystical Management. We learned how to transform the user desktop by customizing applications, automating printer configurations, and standardizing the workstation's look and feel. As a Z.E.N.works CNA, it's important to keep tight control over user desktop management. I hate to say it, but diversity and individuality is bad . . . Big Brother likes standardization.

Now let's complete our exhaustive journey through the kingdom of Z.E.N.works by exploring the final realm—Application Management.

Z.E.N.works Realm 3:
Application Management

In the previous realm, we talked a lot about "Big Brother." As a matter of fact, there has been a lot of hyperactivity lately surrounding the Big Brother syndrome. As a result, many people are becoming LAN-phobic. They feel that becoming part of a larger electronic system will cost them their individuality. Can you blame them?

One of the most important cures for LAN-phobia is user customization and individuality. Even though users are part of a larger whole, they need to feel as if they are vital cogs in the system's overall virtual machine. As such, users will be much more productive. Productivity is the key!

Network productivity is a tenuous balance between user individuality and standardization. It's your responsibility to set up and continually maintain a productive software environment for each user. Then users can perform their tasks in synergy with other LAN users while maintaining some unique job specialization. This strategy is accomplished by intelligently pushing application software to each client. Software, then, is not only shared by everyone on the LAN, but also customized for each user's needs.

So, how do you accomplish such a tough balancing act? The answer: *Marketing*. The marketing world would have you believe that "image is everything!" Well, they're not far off. The media onslaught of products during this century has opened our eyes and emptied our pocketbooks. The goal of marketing is to associate products with positive feelings: a car with the open road, sneakers with athletic ability, and a soft drink with beauty.

As a Z.E.N.works CNA, you must market the LAN to your users. Help them associate their workstations with productivity and general peace of mind. The trick is to make your users *want* to be on the LAN. Welcome to Z.E.N.works Realm 3.

Realm 3 includes a special version of the Novell Application Launcher (NAL) that enables you to distribute network-based applications to user workstations and manage them as objects in the NDS tree. This feature allows you to maintain network standardization while pushing individuality to each user. Very cool! Let's start our lesson in network marketing with a closer look at Z.E.N.works NAL.

Novell Application Launcher (NAL)

Z.E.N.works includes the NAL version 2.5. NAL gives you control over applications before and after they have been distributed to workstations. Your users don't need to be concerned about workstation configurations, drives, application source directories, or upgrades. You, as the NetWare 5 CNA, can manage these parameters easily and centrally from NetWare Administrator.

NAL 2.5 consists of four product components broken into two different categories:

▶ *Administrator components* — NAL Snap-In extends NetWare Administrator for Application object management, and snAppShot allows you to capture workstation configurations and generate an Application Object Template (AOT).

▶ *User components* — the Application Launcher Window displays NAL-delivered applications on the user desktop, and the Application Explorer offers more sophisticated access to NAL-delivered applications.

Let's learn more about how these four magical pieces fit together to complete the Realm 3 puzzle.

Administrator Components of NAL

Increased user productivity begins with you — the NetWare 5 Administrator. NAL 2.5 offers two powerful utilities for Application object management. They are

▶ NAL Snap-In for NetWare Administrator

▶ snAppShot

NAL Snap-In is a Windows .DLL file that extends NetWare Administrator into the realm of enhanced application management. Here are some of the great things that NAL does for CNAs:

▶ It allows you to create and properly display Application objects in the NetWare Administrator browser.

▶ It supports a number of property pages for the new Application object — including drive mappings, printer port capturing, Registry entries, program files, and UNC path settings.

▶ It allows you to create custom Windows program groups for each user on the network, granting or restricting the groups' access to applications.

▶ It provides centralized application maintenance and control. For example, the Application Launcher will automatically restore deleted configuration files (such as .DLL and .INI) when the application is launched.

▶ It gives you the option of pulling or pushing software to workstations. *Pull Distribution* places application icons on the user's desktop and runs remote installation programs when the user requests them. *Push Distribution* does the same thing—only automatically.

▶ It adds the Application object to the NDS tree. By default, it supports Windows 3.1x, Windows 95, and Windows NT workstations.

▶ It provides a Property page for Container, Group, and User objects. It also provides an Application page for Container and User objects.

▶ It adds the Export Application Object item, the Show All Inherited Applications item, and the Migrate Application Objects item to the Tools menu in NetWare Administrator.

▶ It adds a variety of other NAL functions to the Tools menu of NetWare Administrator, including Search and Replace, Synch Distribution GUIDs, Generate New GUIDs, and AOT/AXT File tools.

▶ It allows you to make Registry changes to Windows 95/NT machines without visiting users.

SnAppShot works in conjunction with the enhanced NetWare Administrator to distribute applications throughout the network. Here's how it works:

▶ First, snAppShot captures the current configuration of your workstation.

▶ Next, you install the application you're interested in distributing on your machine.

▶ Then, snAppShot captures a delta configuration to discover the changes made by your application's install.

▶ Finally, snAppShot generates an AOT that identifies the changes between the two captures. You can use the AOT to create an Application object in NetWare Administrator. Then, you distribute the Application object to workstations and all the new application dependencies follow — including Registry settings, .INI file entries, text files, .DLLs, and application programs.

That's how Realm 3 works from the CNA's point of view. Now, let's discover what the user needs.

User Components of NAL

Once you have implemented the Administrator components of NAL and created an AOT file, it's time to distribute applications to the user desktop. At this point, users can access NAL-distributed applications using one of two interfaces: *Application Launcher Window* and *Application Explorer*.

Application Launcher provides the following benefits to users:

▶ *Location-independent access to applications* — You have access to network applications on distributed servers and automated drive mappings and local configurations.

▶ *Application fault tolerance* — Primary applications are replicated to backup servers and local configurations are automatically restored if they are deleted.

▶ *Application load balancing* — Applications are stored on multiple servers where they can be distributed to users intelligently and efficiently. Application Launcher will send you an alternate copy of an application when the primary server is overworked.

▶ *Roaming profile support* — Application Launcher supports roaming profiles by detecting your current setup and pushing the components you need to the desktop.

The Application Launcher Window, shown in Figure 6.29, is an automated desktop for NAL-delivered application icons. This window runs on Windows 3.1x, Windows 95, or Windows NT workstations.

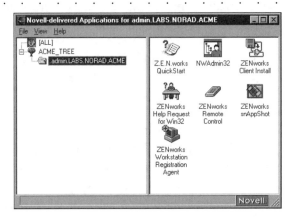

The Z.E.N.works Application
Launcher Window

The Application Launcher Window uses a *"wrapper"* technology, which means it "wraps" itself around the Windows desktop and enhances functionality. The NAL wrapper is executed as SYS:PUBLIC\NAL.EXE. Here's what the NAL.EXE wrapper does for your users' desktops:

▸ The NAL.EXE wrapper determines the proper launching executable for platform-specific clients. In the Windows 3.1x environment, it launches NALW31.EXE. In the Windows 95/NT environment, it launches NALWIN32.EXE.

▸ The NAL.EXE wrapper then launches the executable and terminates itself once the correct Application Launcher Window program has started.

▸ The NAL.EXE wrapper allows you to add a single command to a login script without being concerned about the client platform. For example, if a user moves from one operating system platform to another, the wrapper automatically adjusts to the workstation.

▸ The NAL.EXE wrapper updates appropriate files on the local workstation prior to activating the Application Launcher Window. This means the NAL wrapper can update files in the local WINDOWS\SYSTEM directory.

> **REAL WORLD**
>
> Ideally, you should set up a dedicated "clean" workstation for capturing the snAppShot AOT file because "dirty" machines may already contain delta .DLLs and Registry changes—in this case, snAppShot wouldn't capture them. In addition, you should thoroughly test this process in a lab environment before you actually implement it across the network. Finally, it would be beneficial to have a quick way to revert back to the original configuration if anything should go wrong.

The Application Explorer is an enhanced version of the Application Launcher Window that takes advantage of the Windows 95/NT Registry. The Application Explorer can deliver distributed applications to a variety of locations—beyond the simple Application Launcher Window. Here are some of the workstation-specific places you can distribute applications using the Application Explorer:

- ▸ Application Explorer Window

- ▸ Windows Explorer

- ▸ Start Menu

- ▸ System Tray

- ▸ Desktop

NAL is your friend. And by now you should have a general understanding of its basic architecture. The four NAL components we've discussed work together to ensure a balance between user productivity and global application synergy.

So, how do they work? Good question. Let's learn how to use these tools to distribute network-based applications. Oh, and look out for LAN marketeers—you never know what they're selling!

Distributing Applications Using NAL

As you learned earlier, the focus of Z.E.N.works Realm 3 is user productivity — that is, a balance between individuality and standardization. This is accomplished using a four-step model for application distribution:

▸ *Step 1:* Capture Workstation Configurations with snAppShot

▸ *Step 2:* Create Application Objects from the AOT Template

▸ *Step 3:* Associate the Application Object

▸ *Step 4:* Launch Applications with NAL.EXE

For the most part, these four steps will help you foster synergy between user productivity and shared application software. If you combine NAL distribution with desktop management policies, you can create a very powerful network-based client environment. Power is good, as long as you don't abuse it.

Let's take a closer look at distributing applications using NAL. Ready, set, distribute.

Step 1: Capture Workstation Configurations With snAppShot

SnAppShot starts the NAL distribution process by taking "before" and "after" pictures of your workstation environment. In the middle, you install the NAL application you want to distribute. At the end of this fancy process, you'll be left with an AOT file, which identifies the changes between the two snAppShot pictures. You can then use the AOT to distribute applications throughout the network and ensure all desktops are appropriately customized.

Follow along as we explore the tasks involved in Step 1:

▸ *Run snAppShot* — From your Windows workstation, run SNAPSHOT.EXE from the SYS:PUBLIC\SNAPSHOT network directory. The snAppShot Wizard appears. At the introduction screen, choose the Standard snAppShot Process.

▸ *Application Names* — Next, you'll need to define a unique name for the distributed application and NAL icon. In the NDS Application Object Name field, enter the full name of your target application. Then, click the

Application Icon Title field and type in a shorter icon caption. This is the title users will see in the Application Launcher Window or Application Explorer. Remember: NDS will use this name as the host Application object. As such, you'll need to follow NDS naming guidelines — avoiding periods (.), equals signs (=), or plus signs (+). Check out Figure 6.30. To accept the object name and icon title, click Next.

▶ *Directories* — Next, you must define directories for the application files and AOT. First, specify where snAppShot should store the application source files. This directory will contain the .FIL files that NAL uses to distribute your application. Additionally, snAppShot will create a FILEDEF.TXT log file that will soon become part of the AOT. Next, snAppShot will ask you to confirm the filename and directory for your AOT file. By default, snAppShot uses the Application object name for the file and places it in the source application directory. To accept these values, click Next.

TIP

At this point, jot down the directory and filename path for both the source files and AOT file. You will be asked to enter this information at the end of the snAppShot Wizard. Just to make things interesting, you won't be able to browse to the directory and identify it at that time. By the way, the application source file and AOT file should reside in the same directory, preferrably not in the SYS: volume — they get very big!

▶ *"Before" Picture* — Now it's time to scan your local workstation and take a "before" picture. First, identify the drives you'd like to scan in the Scan These Drives field. By default, snAppShot only scans the C: drive for installation changes. If you want to distribute a network-based application, you must include the central volume in this field. Next, snAppShot takes a "before" picture of your workstation's folders, files, Windows shortcuts, .INI files, system configurations, and Registry settings (for Windows 95/NT). When this process is complete, the Wizard will return a snAppShot Process Summary. Check it out in Figure 6.31.

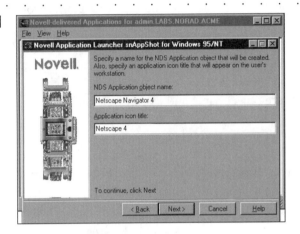

FIGURE 6.30

Naming your applications
in the snAppShot Wizard

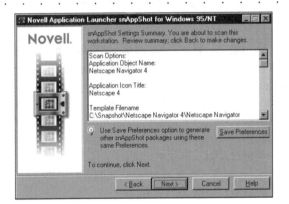

FIGURE 6.31

SnAppShot Process
Summary screen

▶ *Install Application* — Finally, you're ready to install the NAL-distributed
application. Click the Run Application Install button. Browse to the
Application Installation Wizard. SnAppShot will monitor the application
install and indicate when it's complete by displaying the "Wait for setup to
finish" screen. Once the application has been properly installed, snAppShot
will take an "after" picture and generate the AOT file.

▶ *"After" Picture* — Once your NAL-distributed application has been installed
correctly, snAppShot will take an "after" picture to determine which
workstation changes were made during setup. SnAppShot then stores this
information in the AOT Template file. To complete Step 1, click Finish.

Once snAppShot has discovered the configuration changes made by your application's setup program, you must embed this information in an NDS-based Application object. You then associate the Application object with users, and NAL takes care of the rest. Let's continue our journey through Realm 3 with Step 2 — Create Application Objects from the AOT.

Step 2: Create Application Objects from the AOT Template

The next step in the NAL distribution process involves NDS. At this point, you must take the delta information in your AOT file and assign it to an NDS-based Application object. This Application object will serve as a central source for application distribution.

To create an Application object in NDS, launch NetWare Administrator. Highlight the container where you want the Application object to reside and click the Object and Create buttons. In the Object list, choose Application.

At this point, the Object Creation Wizard will venture off into unknown territory. Since you've chosen to create an Application object, NetWare Administrator will give you the option to use an AOT. Click the "Create an Application object with an .AOT/.AXT file" option to embed AOT data into NDS.

Refer to Figure 6.32 and follow the bouncing ball. NetWare Administrator will supply the source and target paths based on information it extracts from the AOT file. Verify that these paths are correct and click Finish to complete the Application Object Creation Wizard.

Once you've created the new data-rich NDS Application object, you need to find it a friend. Specifically, you need to associate the object with User or Group objects to distribute applications. That's Step 3.

Step 3: Associate the Application Object

Once you've created an AOT-based Application object, you must associate it with users or groups. This way, NAL can custom-deliver standard applications to the user desktop. Remember, we're trying to achieve a delicate balance between individuality and standardization. NAL is your friend.

We're going to use NetWare Administrator to associate our new Application object with specific User and/or Group objects. Browse the NetWare Administrator tree until you find your new Application object. Double-click the object to open its Details window. Next, click the Associations page button and refer to Figure 6.33. Simply click the Add button to associate users/groups with this Application object.

You can also add Container objects to the application Association window for larger-scale distributions. This way, any existing or new User created below the container will automatically receive the application in their Application Launcher window or Application Explorer.

FIGURE 6.32

Creating an AOT-based Application object in NetWare Administrator

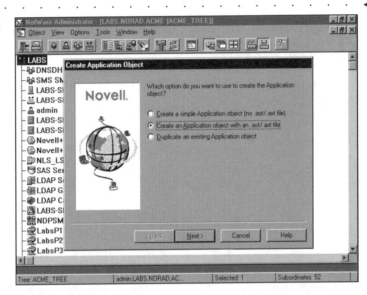

FIGURE 6.33

The Application object Associations page in NetWare Administrator

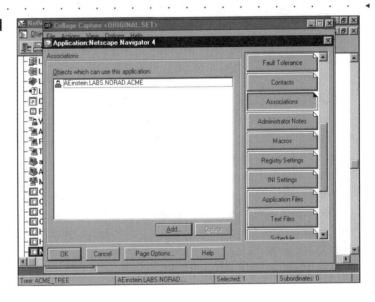

In addition, you'll need to define the application program's source location in the "Path to Executable File" page. Finally, NDS doesn't automatically assign file system rights when you associate Application objects with users, groups, or containers. Typically, the default Read and File Scan rights to SYS:PUBLIC are sufficient, since NAL resides in that directory. However, some applications store user-specific information on the server, and additional rights may be needed.

Congratulations! You've completed all the hard work through snAppShot, Application objects, and User object associations. Now it's time to let NAL do its thing — check out Step 4!

Step 4: Launch Applications with NAL.EXE

Now that we've created AOT-based Application objects and associated them with users, it's time to distribute some desktop pixie dust.

First, we must ensure that users execute the NAL.EXE file each time they log in. This can be accomplished by placing the following command in a Container login script:

```
#LABS-SRV1\SYS:PUBLIC\NAL.EXE
```

In this example, "LABS-SRV1" can be replaced by your own specific server name. Also note that the "#" command requires that NAL.EXE be completed before executing the next line of the script. In many cases, this is not a good idea. Instead, consider using the "@" symbol command — which allows the login script to continue processing while NAL.EXE is run.

When a user logs in from any workstation, the platform-specific version of NAL is launched automatically. At this point, the Application Launcher Window or Application Explorer appears on his/her desktop. Check it out in Figure 6.29. The Application Launcher Window will be populated by all applications that have been associated with this User, Group, or Container object. The user simply double-clicks the application's icon to run the program.

The first time a user double-clicks a NAL icon, the application is installed on the local workstation using the AOT created with snAppShot. When the user logs in subsequently, NAL detects that the application has been previously installed and simply launches it from the local drive. This way, users can migrate from workstation to workstation and always have access to their individual desktop environments.

Now, let's take the NAL experience one step further and learn how to manage Application objects using NetWare Administrator and the Application Launcher. It's time to earn the "A" in CNA.

Managing Applications Using NAL

Once you've created your new Application objects and your users are happily launching programs throughout the LAN, it's time to shift your focus toward management. Z.E.N.works and NetWare 5 offer a great GUI tool for application management — NetWare Administrator.

As a matter of fact, you've been using NetWare Administrator all along. Now, we're going to explore a few more Property pages from Figure 6.33. Here's a brief peek:

- ▸ Identification

- ▸ Environment

- ▸ System Requirements

- ▸ Schedules

- ▸ Fault Tolerance

Let's take a closer look.

Identification

Application Launcher doesn't use separate icons to designate Windows 3.1, Windows 95/98, or Windows NT applications. Instead, you can use the Identification property page in NetWare Administrator to specify a preferred operating system.

In addition, you can use the Identification page to supply an executable path, designate the application for install only, specify that Application Launcher run the application only once, or create custom icons.

Environment

You can use the Application object's Environment page to specify how the application should run. First, you can define command-line parameters for the application and identify a working directory. You can specify whether the application should run minimized or maximized. You can enable error logging for installation programs. You can even ask NAL to clean up drive mappings and print captures after the application has quit.

Finally, the Environment page allows you to enable 16-bit Windows-On-Windows (WOW) support. This features allows you to protect all your 32-bit applications from a crash in 16-bit space. I highly recommend it!

System Requirements

One of the most useful features offered by NAL is system-tailored launching. You can use the System Requirements page in NetWare Administrator to filter applications against a broad range of criteria:

▶ *Operating System* — This only offers application icons that match the local operating system. In addition, you can specify multiple operating systems, such as Windows 95/98 and Windows NT. However, you must select at least one Windows platform, or the Application object will be hidden from *all* Windows users.

▶ *RAM* — You can disallow applications if the local machine doesn't have enough RAM installed. This field is only valid for Windows 95/98 and Windows NT machines.

▶ *Processor* — You can disallow applications if the local machine doesn't have a fast enough processor. The choices are 386, 486, and Pentium.

▶ *Free Disk Space* — you can demand a minimum amount of free disk space on three different drives: Windows drive, TEMP drive, and D: drive.

Schedules

You can use the Schedule property page in NetWare Administrator to control when users get NAL-delivered applications. For example, you may want to distribute a large service pack to all users next week. You may also want to stagger the delivery times. This can all be accomplished using the Schedule page.

Fault Tolerance

Finally, the Fault Tolerance page in NetWare Administrator allows you to configure Application objects for load balancing and fault tolerance.

Load balancing allows you to store applications on multiple servers and then intelligently distribute them according to load. When you load-balance your applications, be sure to note that Application Launcher does not distribute applications according to server CPU use. Instead, it uses a random number to decide who gets which application. Also, be sure to enable load balancing on the same sides of a WAN link, and to give users the security rights they need to access applications on multiple servers.

Fault tolerance allows you to set up primary and alternate sources for application delivery. This protects you in case the primary server goes down, or the network link is lost.

That's all there is . . . there isn't any more.

That completes our tour of Z.E.N.works Realm 3 — Application Management. In this Realm, we've struggled to find a balance between user individuality and network-wide standardization. Fortunately, the NAL offers a powerful strategy for warding off LAN-phobia. In addition, Desktop Management Policies allow you to customize user desktops from a central standardized pool. However, just for the record, I have found that the most effective strategy for warding off LAN-phobia is a warm touch and kind heart. No one said Big Brother had to be a bully.

That completes our comprehensive journey through the Z.E.N.works cyber-kingdom. In this chapter, we've learned how to install the great Z.E.N.works desktop tool and take full advantage of its three separate realms: Workstation Maintenance, Desktop Management, and Application Management. Of all the places you'll go in your cyber-life, few will be as interesting as Z.E.N.works. This client environment is one of the most important aspects of your WAN because it's where the users meet the Infobahn. Hopefully now you have a greater appreciation for what it means to be the king or queen of your Z.E.N.works cyber-kingdom.

In addition, I hope I expanded your understanding of the unknown universe a little bit today. After all, NetWare 5 Zen is a journey . . . not a destination. Along those lines, I would like to leave you with a few intriguing thoughts:

▶ *A one-wing butterfly spins in circles — achieve balance!*

▶ *When the only choices are left and right — go straight ahead!*

► *In battle, surprise them with your decency!*

► *In tranquillity find light — in light find truth — in truth find peace — in peace find soul — in soul find tranquillity!*

► *Time opens doors to infinite possibilities — make it your friend!*

► *Be what you wish to dream — now!*

► *The end is only the beginning — good luck!*

LAB EXERCISE 6.5: DISTRIBUTING ACME APPLICATIONS USING NAL

As an ACME CNE, you must market the worldwide LAN to your users. Help them associate their workstations with productivity and general peace of mind. The trick is to make your users *want* to be on the LAN. Welcome to Z.E.N.works Realm 3.

Realm 3 includes a special version of the Novell Application Launcher (NAL) that enables you to distribute network-based applications to user workstations and manage them as objects in the NDS tree. This feature allows you to maintain network standardization while pushing individuality to each user. Very cool!

In this exercise, we're going to explore NAL from the CNE's point of view. This way, we can maintain enterprise standardization while helping each time-traveling hero unlock his or her own individuality. Here's a quick preview:

▶ *Stage 1* — Create and associate an Application object

▶ *Stage 2* — Add Application Launcher to a Container login script

▶ *Stage 3* — Launch an application from the Application Launcher window and Application Explorer

▶ *Stage 4* — Create an AOT Template file using snAppShot

▶ *Stage 5* — Create an Application object from the AOT Template file

▶ *Stage 6* — Removing Z.E.N.works

The following hardware is required for this exercise:

▶ A NetWare 5 server with Z.E.N.works 1.0 installed.

▶ A workstation running the NetWare 5 Novell Client for Windows 95/98 or Windows NT that has been updated for Z.E.N.works.

The following CD-ROMs are required for this exercise:

▶ *Novell Z.E.N.works 1.0 with Online Documentation*

▸ *NetWare 5 Novell Client Software*

Remember: NAL is your friend. Treat it nice!

Stage 1: Create and Associate an Application Object

First, let's begin by creating a simple NDS Application object with NetWare Administrator. Then, we'll associate the object with Crime Fighting heroes in the CRIME division of ACME.

Here's how it works:

1. Log in as Admin, if you haven't already done so.

2. Create an Application Object.

   a. Launch NetWare Administrator.

   b. When the main NetWare Administrator screen appears, right-click the CRIME container.

   c. Click Create in the pop-up menu that appears.

   d. When the New Object dialog box appears, double-click Application.

   e. When the first Create Application object dialog box appears:

     • Ensure that the "Create a Simple Application Object (No .aot/.axt File)" radio button is marked.

     • Click Next.

   f. When the second Create Application object dialog box appears:

     • In the Object Name field, type the following:

      `Calculator`

     • Type the following in the Path to Executable field:

      `C:\WINDOWS\CALC.EXE`

     • Click Finish.

Stage 2: Add Application Launcher to a Container Login Script

Once you've created the simple Calculator object, you can automatically distribute it throughout the CRIME organization using an NDS Container login script.

Check it out!

1. Add the Application Launcher Window and Application Explorer to the CRIME Container login script.

   a. When the main NetWare Administrator screen reappears, right-click the CRIME container.

   b. Click Details in the pop-up menu that appears.

   c. When the Organizational Unit: Crime property sheet appears, click the Login Script tab.

   d. When the Login Script property page appears, type the following lines in the Login Script list box:

      ```
      @CRIME-SRV1\SYS:\PUBLIC\NAL.EXE

      @CRIME-SRV1\SYS:\PUBLIC\NALEXPLD.EXE
      ```

2. Make Application Launcher icons available in the Start Menu, on the Desktop, and in the System Tray.

   a. Scroll down and click the Applications tab.

   b. When the Applications property page appears, click Add.

   c. When the Select Object dialog box appears, navigate to the Calculator Application object, then double-click it in the left pane.

   d. When the "Organizational Unit: Crime" dialog box reappears, do the following in the list box:

      • Ensure that the Calculator object is listed.

      • Leave the Force Run checkbox blank.

      • Verify that the App Launcher checkbox is marked.

      • Mark the Start Menu, Desktop, and System Tray checkboxes.

* Click OK.

e. Exit the NetWare Administrator utility.

Stage 3: Launch an Application from the Application Launcher Window and Application Explorer

Well done! Now it's time to reap the rewards of our hard work — that is, we must use the NetWare 5 Application Launcher Window and Application Explorer to access the new Calculator application. I'm so excited . . . how about you? Go!

1. Log in to the tree as Admin.

2. Launch the Calculator application from the Application Launcher.

a. When the "Novell-Delivered Applications for Admin.CRIME.TOKYO .ACME" dialog box appears, double-click the Calculator in the right pane to launch it.

b. When the Calculator window appears, click Close (X) to close the Calculator application.

c. When the "Novell-Delivered Applications for Admin.CRIME.TOKYO .ACME" dialog box re-appears, click Close (X) to close the window:

3. Launch the Calculator application from the System Tray.

a. You'll notice that there is now a Calculator icon in the System Tray. (The System Tray is located at the right end of the Windows taskbar.) Click the Calculator icon to launch it.

b. When the Calculator window appears, click Close (X) to close the Calculator window.

4. Launch the Calculator from the Windows Start Menu.

a. Click Start in the Windows taskbar.

b. Click CRIME.TOKYO.ACME.

c. Click Calculator.

d. When the Calculator window appears, click Close (X) to close the Calculator window.

5. Launch the Calculator from Desktop.

a. Double-click the Calculator icon on your Windows Desktop.

b. When the Calculator window appears, click Close (X) to close the Calculator window.

6. Launch the Calculator application from Application Explorer.

a. Double-click the Application Explorer icon on your Windows Desktop.

b. When the Application Explorer window appears, double-click the ACME_TREE icon.

c. When the ACME_TREE (in tree ACME_TREE) window appears, double-click CRIME.TOKYO.ACME.

d. When the CRIME.TOKYO.ACME (in tree ACME_TREE) window appears, double-click the Calculator icon to launch the Calculator program.

e. When the Calculator window appears, click Close (X) to close the Calculator window.

f. When the CRIME.TOKYO.ACME (in tree ACME_TREE) window re-appears:

- Click File to display the File menu.

- Click Exit Application Explorer.

g. When the Application Explorer dialog box appears asking if you want to close the Application Explorer, click Yes.

Stage 4: Create an AOT Template File Using snAppShot

Now that you've mastered the *simple* realm of NAL application management, I think you're ready for snAppShot! SnAppShot works in conjunction with the enhanced NetWare Administrator 32 to distribute applications throughout the network. Here's how it works:

▸ First, snAppShot captures the current configuration of your workstation.

▸ Next, you install the application you're interested in distributing on your machine.

▸ Then, snAppShot captures a delta configuration to discover the changes made by your application's install.

▸ Finally, snAppShot generates an AOT Template file that identifies the changes between the two captures. You can use the AOT to create an Application object in NetWare Administrator. Then, you distribute the Application object to workstations and all the new application dependencies follow — including Registry settings, .INI file entries, text files, .DLLs, and application programs.

In Part IV, we're going to use snAppShot to create an AOT Template file for Netscape Communicator. Then, in Part V, we're going to use the AOT Template to create a Netscape Application object.

Check it out!

1. Uninstall Netscape Navigator.

  a. Click Start in the Windows taskbar.

  b. Click Settings.

  c. Click Control Panel.

  d. Double-click Add/Remove Programs.

  e. When the Add/Remove Programs dialog box appears, click Netscape Navigator 4.04.

  f. Click Add/Remove.

  g. When the Confirm File Deletion dialog box appears, asking if you're sure you want to deinstall Netscape Navigator 4.04 and all of its components, click Yes to acknowledge the message.

  h. Wait while the Netscape Navigator 4.04 program is deinstalled.

i. When the Remove Programs From Your Computer dialog box reappears, saying that the uninstall was completed successfully, click OK to acknowledge the message.

j. Close the Control Panel folder.

2. Launch the snAppShot Utility.

a. Click Start, then Run.

b. When the Run dialog box appears:

- Browse to the Z:\PUBLIC\SNAPSHOT\SNAPSHOT.EXE directory.

- Click OK.

c. When the Z.E.N.works snAppShot introduction screen appears, click Standard.

d. When the Novell Application Launcher snAppShot for Windows 95/NT window appears:

- Type the following in the NDS Application Object Name field:

  `Netscape Navigator 404`

- Replace the text in the Application Object Title field with the following:

  `Netscape Navigator 4`

- Click Next.

e. When the next Novell Application Launcher snAppShot for Windows 95/NT screen appears:

- Type the following in the Application File(s) Location field:

  `Z:\AOTFILES\WIN95\NETSCAPE`

- Click Next.

f. When the snAppShot dialog box appears, informing you that the directory does not exist and asking if you want snAppShot to create it for you, click Yes.

g. When the next Novell Application Launcher snAppShot for Windows 95/NT screen appears:

- Verify that the following is listed in the "Application Object Template (AOT) Filename and Location" field:

    `Z:\PUBLIC\APPS\NETSCAPE\NETSCAPE NAVIGATOR 404.AOT`

- Click Next.

TIP

The application source file and the AOT file should reside in the same directory.

h. When the next Novell Application Launcher snAppShot for Windows 95/NT screen appears:

- Ensure that the following is listed in the Scan These Drives field:

    `C:`

- Click Next.

i. When the next Novell Application Launcher snAppShot for Windows 95/NT screen appears:

- Review the settings listed.

- Click Next.

j. Wait while snAppShot scans your C: drive (that is, takes the "before" snapshot). This may take a while.

3. Install Netscape Navigator.

a. When the next Novell Application Launcher snAppShot for Windows 95/NT screen appears:

- Insert the *Z.E.N.works 1.0 with Online Documentation* CD-ROM in your workstation's CD-ROM drive.

- The WINSETUP.EXE program will launch automatically. Click the Exit button in the lower-right corner to exit the utility.

- When the Novell Application Launcher snAppShot for Windows 95/NT screen re-appears, click Run Application Install.

b. When the Select Setup Program dialog box appears:

- Browse to the E:\PRODUCTS\NETSCAPE\WIN32\ENGLISH directory.

- Double-click N32E404.EXE.

c. When the Install Shield Self-Extracting EXE dialog box appears, asking if you want to install Netscape Navigator 4.04, click Yes.

d. Wait while the Install Shield extracts the files needed to install the application.

e. When the Netscape Navigator 4.04 Setup dialog box appears, read the information on the screen, then click Next.

f. When the Software License Agreement screen appears, read the agreement, then click Yes.

g. When the Select Type dialog box appears:

- Ensure that the Typical radio button is marked.

- Ensure that the Destination Directory field contains the following directory:

  `C:\Program Files\Netscape\Communicator`

- Click Next.

h. If a Question dialog box appears, asking if you want the directory to be created, click Yes.

i. If the Select Program Folder dialog box appears:

- Ensure that the following is listed in the Program Folder field:

  `Netscape Navigator`

- Click Next.

j. When the Start Copying Files dialog box appears:

- Review the settings listed in the Current Settings field.

- Click Install.

k. Wait while the setup program installs Netscape Navigator.

l. When the Question dialog box appears, asking if you would like to read the README file now, click No.

m. When the Information dialog box appears, indicating that the Setup is complete, click OK.

n. Click Close (X) to close the Netscape Navigator folder.

4. Take the "after" snapshot.

a. When the Novell Application Launcher snAppShot with Windows 95/NT dialog box appears, click Next to indicate that the application process (for Netscape) is complete.

b. When the next screen appears:

- Type the following in the Application's Install Directory field:

  `C:\Program Files\Netscape\Communicator`

- Click Next.

c. Wait while the rescanning process (that is, the "after" snapshot occurs). This may take a while.

d. When the Snapshot Completion Summary appears:

- Review the information on the screen, then click Finish.

- Click Next.

Stage 5: Create an Application Object from the AOT Template File

Congratulations on creating a wonderful Netscape AOT Template file. Now, let's put it to good use by building a Netscape Application object in the AOT foundation. Are we having fun yet?

1. Create a Netscape Application object.

a. Launch NetWare Administrator.

b. Right-click the CRIME container, then click Create from the pop-up menu that appears.

c. When the New Object dialog box appears, double-click Application.

d. When the Create Application Object dialog box appears:

- Click "Create an Application Object with an .AOT/.AXT File."

- Click Next.

e. When the next screen appears:

- Type the following in the Path to .AOT/.AXT Files:

  `Z:\AOTFILES\WIN95\NETSCAPE404.AOT`

- Click Next.

f. When the settings for the Application object appear:

- Review the settings listed.

- Click Finish.

g. When the next screen appears:

- Ensure that the following is listed in the Object Name field:

  `Netscape Navigator 404`

- Ensure that the following is listed in the Source Path (Location of Installation Files (.Fil)):

  `Z:\AOTFILES\WIN95\NETSCAPE404`

- Confirm that the following is listed in the Target Path (Client Workstation Directory Path):

  `C:\Program Files\Netscape\Communicator`

- Click Finish.

2. Associate the CRIME container with the Netscape Application object.

a. Right-click the Netscape Application object.

b. Click Details in the pop-up menu that appears.

c. When the Application: Netscape Navigator 404 appears:

- Ensure that the following is listed in the Application Title Icon field:

  `Netscape Navigator 404`

- Click the Path to Executable File radio button.

- Enter the following in the Path to Executable File field:

  C:\Program Files\Netscape\Communicator\Program\Netscape.exe

d. Click the Associations tab.

e. When the Association page appears, click Add.

f. When the Select Object dialog box appears:

- In the right pane, double-click the up arrow to move up one level in the tree.

- In the left pane, double-click the CRIME container.

- The CRIME.TOKYO.ACME container will appear in the "Objects Which Can Use This Application" list box on the Associations page.

- Click OK to save your changes.

g. Click the System Requirements tab.

- In the Operating System section, mark the checkbox of the operating system running on your workstation.

- Click OK.

3. Log in again as Admin.

a. Click Start in the Windows taskbar.

b. When the Shut Down Windows dialog box appears:

- Click the "Close All Programs and Log On as a Different User" radio button.

- Click OK.

c. Log into the tree as Admin.

4. When the NAL window appears:

    a. Double-click the Netscape Navigator 404 icon in the right pane.

    b. Wait while the application is distributed.

5. When the Systems Settings Change dialog box appears, advising you that you must reboot your computer for the new settings to take effect, click Yes to acknowledge the message.

6. After the workstation boots, log into the tree as Admin.

7. When the NAL window appears, double-click the Netscape Navigator 404 icon in the right pane to launch the utility.

8. Exit the Netscape Navigator utility.

Stage 6: Removing Z.E.N.works

1. Remove Z.E.N.works-related lines from the CRIME container login script.

    a. Right-click the CRIME container.

    b. Select Details from the pop-up menu that appears.

    c. Click the Login Script tab.

    d. Delete the following lines from the Login Script box:

```
@CRIME-SRV1\SYS:\PUBLIC\NAL.EXE

@CRIME-SRV1\SYS:\PUBLIC\NALEXPLD.EXE
```

    e. Click OK to save your changes.

    f. Exit the NetWare Administrator utility.

2. Uninstall Z.E.N.works.

    a. Click Start in the Windows taskbar.

    b. Click Settings.

    c. Click Control Panel.

d. Double-click Add/Remove Programs.

e. When the Add/Remove Programs dialog box appears:

- The Uninstall tab will be selected by default.

- Click Z.E.N.works.

- Click Add/Remove

f. When the Confirm File Deletion dialog box appears asking if you're sure you want to uninstall Z.E.N.works and all of its components, click Yes to acknowledge the message.

g. Wait while the Z.E.N.works program is uninstalled.

h. When the Remove Programs From Your Computer dialog box reappears saying that the uninstall was completed successfully, click OK to acknowledge the message.

i. When the Install/Uninstall page reappears:

- Click Novell Remote Control Agent.

- Click Add/Remove

- Click OK.

j. Close the Control Panel folder.

k. Remove the Z.E.N.works 1.0 CD-ROM from your CD-ROM drive.

Hooray!

That completes our tour of Z.E.N.works Realm 3 — Application Management. In this Realm, we've struggled to find a balance between hero individuality and network-wide ACME standardization. I think we achieved an excellent balance with NAL.

Are you having fun yet?!

LAB EXERCISE 6.6: THE ZEN OF NETWARE 5

Circle the 20 Z.E.N.works-related terms hidden in this word search puzzle using the hints provided. No punctuation characters (such as blank spaces, hyphens, and so on) should be included. Numbers should always be spelled out.

```
I  E  H  J  D  I  U  S  E  R  P  R  O  F  I  L  E  S  V  R
M  A  I  L  C  S  C  W  B  S  Y  S  P  U  B  L  I  C  W  L
P  C  J  D  L  Z  Q  R  O  I  P  B  D  F  R  F  B  H  R  O
O  U  S  E  R  S  Y  S  T  E  M  P  O  L  I  C  Y  E  A  M
R  N  K  S  N  A  P  P  S  H  O  T  Q  J  S  S  O  D  P  C
T  A  U  T  O  A  P  X  U  T  P  S  U  W  R  L  O  U  P  X
W  T  Z  U  T  O  L  N  Z  D  X  U  E  C  W  S  S  L  E  Q
O  T  C  E  W  P  O  L  I  C  Y  P  A  C  K  A  G  E  R  F
R  E  I  M  Q  U  S  E  R  A  G  E  N  T  Q  W  N  R  T  X
K  N  O  V  E  L  L  H  E  L  P  R  E  Q  U  E  S  T  E  R
S  D  E  Q  R  H  V  T  Y  Y  P  V  G  M  L  Y  A  A  C  U
T  E  L  W  O  R  K  S  T  A  T  I  O  N  Q  E  H  P  H  B
A  D  I  D  Z  E  N  W  O  R  K  S  I  O  K  I  N  Q  N  B
T  I  U  Y  R  E  M  O  T  E  C  O  N  T  R  O  L  C  O  A
I  N  L  S  V  N  N  W  N  I  A  R  H  D  P  F  U  I  L  P
O  S  N  D  Z  E  N  E  T  O  L  H  C  T  N  M  M  R  O  W
N  T  C  T  Y  V  E  A  T  W  X  K  Y  M  R  J  M  Y  G  P
S  A  D  Z  H  H  J  T  S  W  E  W  F  J  G  L  G  Y  Y  J
N  L  B  A  D  R  R  Z  T  K  V  Q  M  J  Q  P  X  C  M  F
U  L  U  T  K  T  R  B  A  U  D  E  J  P  L  H  X  F  T  C
```

Hints:

1. Automated method for installing the Novell Client on multiple workstations.
2. Can be used to create an Application object in NetWare Administrator.
3. A type of client that can only use a subset of Z.E.N.works features.

4. Utility that is used to create a Workstation object for your workstation in your container.
5. Button that will not appear in the Help Requester Application Window if you have not marked the "Allow user to send trouble ticket" box in the Help Desk Policies Configuration page.
6. Lets you distribute network-based applications to workstations and manage them as objects in the NDS tree.
7. Z.E.N.works components that allow users to notify the Help Desk or network administrator of workstation problems via e-mail or phone.
8. Collection of policies that allow you to set up parameters for managing workstations, users, groups, or containers.
9. By default, Workstation objects are created with this feature enabled.
10. Z.E.N.works feature that allows you to run programs automatically on Windows 95 and Windows NT clients.
11. Utility that can be used to capture a workstation's configuration before and after an application is installed.
12. To install Z.E.N.works, you must have these object rights to the [Root] of the NDS tree.
13. Default directory for NAL installation.
14. Method for automatically updating the Novell Client for Windows on every workstation in the network from a single point of administration.
15. Type of application that allows you to connect to and manage a workstation using the Remote Control utility in NetWare Administrator.
16. Can be created and configured using the Novell Workstation Manager component of Z.E.N.works.
17. Allows you to customize the desktop functions available to specific users.
18. Z.E.N.works extends the NDS schema to include this type of objects.
19. "Wraps" itself around the Windows desktop and enhances functionality.
20. Directory that contains SETUP.EXE file for installing Z.E.N.works Starter Pack.

**LAB EXERCISE 6.7: NETWARE 5
WORKSTATION MANAGEMENT**

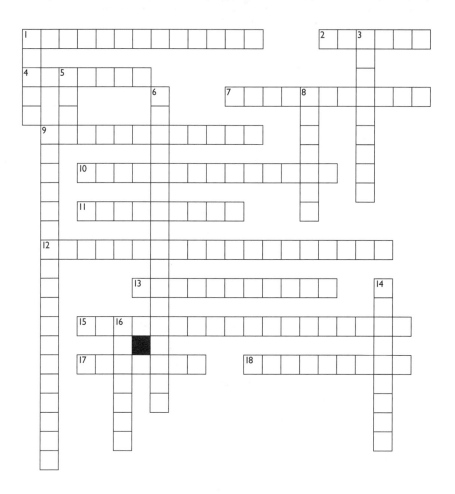

Across

1. NAL benefit
2. Most flexible Z.E.N.works installation method
4. Most limited Z.E.N.works installation method
7. Used to install a subset of Z.E.N.works
9. Type of workstations managed using Z.E.N.works
10. Another NAL benefit

11. Messaging service supported by Novell Help Requester
12. "Z.E.N.works Starter Pack" component
13. Alternative to the Application Launcher Window
15. NetWare 5 access not supported by Z.E.N.works
17. Preconfigured keystroke sequences
18. Automated desktop for NAL-delivered application icons

Down

1. Non-remote installation method
3. Parent of ZENWORKS directory
5. Another Novell Help Requester supported messaging service
6. Z.E.N.works is this type of tool
8. Most common Z.E.N.works installation method
9. "Z.E.N.works Starter Pack" component
14. Zero Effort Networking
16. Server-to-server installation method

CHAPTER 7

The Great Puzzle:
NetWare 5 Printing

The last stop on our tour down the NetWare 5 Information Superhighway is printing. I always like to save the best for last. Now that you've lived through all the administrative responsibilities of Novell's Global Electronic Village, I think you're ready to discover one of the greatest mysteries of life — NDPS.

The meaning of life? Nah. The Great Pyramids? Nope. The Sphinx? No chance. Printing has them all beat. More brain cells have been lost pondering NetWare printing than any other philosophical question.

It's not that printing itself is so puzzling. As a matter of fact, the concept of printing is fairly easy to comprehend — you click a button on your workstation and a piece of paper comes out of the printer down the hall. No rocket science here. It's true. The fundamental architecture of NetWare printing is solid — rock solid.

So, why is it such a mystery? One word — *users*! It's the users' fault. They introduce so much complexity to printing, it's a wonder paper finds its way anywhere, let alone to the correct printer. And to make matters worse, users expect too much: They want the page to be formatted correctly every time, they want their print jobs to arrive at the "correct" printer (when they don't even know what that means) and they always want their jobs to come out first.

So, how do you possibly satisfy the lofty expectations of your users while maintaining a rock-solid NetWare printing architecture? That's the greatest mystery of all. Fortunately, NetWare 5 includes a revolution in NetWare printing — Novell Distributed Print Services (NDPS). This is the next-generation printing architecture that replaces the older queue-based system.

NDPS is the result of a joint development effort by Novell, Hewlett-Packard, and Xerox. With NDPS, network-based printers are independent of servers, and printing attributes (such as forms and banners) are available to every defined printer and user on the network. It sounds better already. Bottom line: easier setup, better management, more flexibility, and happy users. Novell certainly hasn't solved your mystery entirely, but they've given you some great tools to help you crack the case — and we're going to learn all about them.

In this chapter, we're going to explore this great printing mystery and discover some startling answers. You're going to learn about NDPS architecture, how to create printing objects, and finally, what it takes to become a NetWare 5 NDPS CNA. First, however, we need to spend a few moments meditating on the true essence of printing. You must become *one* with the printer. It works . . . trust me.

▶ · ◀

The Essence of NDPS

Now repeat after me:

I *am* a printer.

I *am* a printer.

The best way to handle NDPS printing is to *become* NDPS printing. This is the essence of NDPS.

Actually, the essence of NDPS is a little more technical than that. It is a wondrous journey from the user's workstation to the network printer down the hall. And, with NetWare 5 printing, you get numerous benefits: improved overall network performance, reduced printing problems, and reduced administration costs and management time.

We already know what a great job NetWare 5 does with its file services, but printing is just as important to users. Initially, all users need access to file storage and shared print services to get the most out of NetWare. Let's begin by taking a close look at the theoretical realm of NDPS:

- ▶ NDPS Features

- ▶ NDPS Versus Queue-Based Printing

- ▶ NDPS Printer Types

Remember . . . I *am* NDPS, I *am* NDPS.

NDPS Features

NDPS was designed to handle the increasing complexity of today's large networks — specifically, to help CNAs manage printing devices in any type of network environment ranging in size from small workgroups to enterprise-wide systems. In addition, NDPS was designed with Novell Directory Services (NDS) in mind — that is to say, it's fully network-centric. This design allows administrators to create, configure, and automatically install and initialize printers without having to physically leave their desks. This fits in very well with the Z.E.N.works mindset of *"mystical management."* Today's CNA should be able to hover above the NDS cloud and control network resources like puppets at the end of a string.

· · · · · ·

To this end, NDPS offers a myriad of business solutions and features. Here's a quick list:

- ▶ Plug and Print

- ▶ Automatic Print Driver Download and Installation

- ▶ Greater Print Control

- ▶ Ease of Use

- ▶ Bidirectional Feedback

- ▶ NDS Integration

- ▶ Configurable Event Notification

- ▶ Multiple Printer Configurations

- ▶ Network Traffic Reduction

- ▶ Print Job Scheduling

- ▶ Enhanced Client Support

- ▶ Backward Compatibility

Let's take a look.

Plug and Print
Once you set up NDPS, you can plug a printer into the network and it becomes immediately available to all users. This is accomplished using automatic hardware detection.

Automatic Print Driver Download and Installation
NDPS allows you to select common printer drivers you want to automatically download and install to each workstation (see Figure 7.1). Keep in mind that

NDPS ships with English-only printing drivers. You will have to manually add non-English drivers as needed.

FIGURE 7.1

Automatic print driver download with NDPS

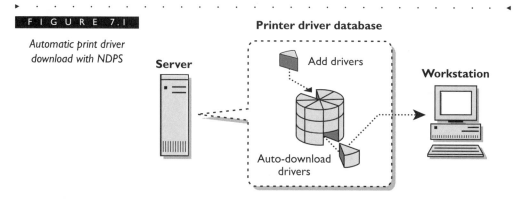

Greater Print Control

NDPS allows clients and printers to exchange real-time information about printers and print jobs. This interchange allows users and CNAs to access all sorts of information about printers—such as availability status, configuration properties, and features. As you can see in Figure 7.2, all these print control features are available from a single NetWare Administrator Printer Control page.

FIGURE 7.2

Greater print control offered by NetWare 5 NDPS

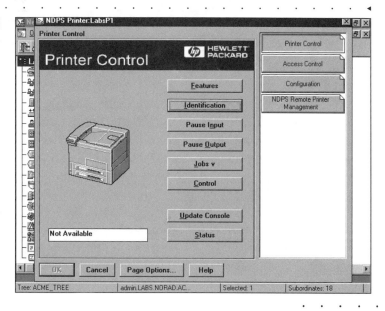

Ease of Use

Not only does NDPS make printer management easier for CNAs, it also makes printing easier for end users. Using the Novell Print Manager utility (included with the NDPS client), users can install additional printers, and are not limited to using only the printers selected by the CNA. This utility allows users to search for printers with specific characteristics. Finally, the NDPS client also allows users to easily modify printer configurations. In previous versions of NetWare, these features were "rocket science."

Bidirectional Feedback

Clients and administrators can obtain real-time information such as printer availability, print job properties, the number of jobs being printed, job hold, and job completion notification, as illustrated in Figure 7.3. All of this information is displayed using graphical pop-up windows.

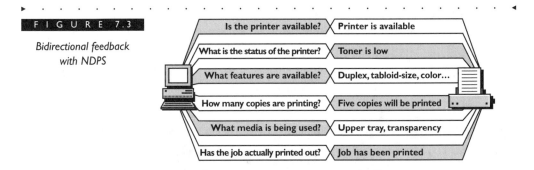

F I G U R E   7.3

Bidirectional feedback
with NDPS

Is the printer available? — Printer is available

What is the status of the printer? — Toner is low

What features are available? — Duplex, tabloid-size, color...

How many copies are printing? — Five copies will be printed

What media is being used? — Upper tray, transparency

Has the job actually printed out? — Job has been printed

NDS Integration

NDPS offers increased security and easier management via Novell Directory Services (NDS; see Figure 7.4). In the NDS tree, printers can be conveniently grouped by department, location, workgroup, and so on. This allows CNAs to create a single NDS object — an NDPS Printer object — to represent each printer on the network. Bottom line: CNAs can administer all printing devices from a single location using NetWare Administrator.

Configurable Event Notification

NDPS allows you to specify which users, operators, and administrators receive which types of notification (see Figure 7.5).

FIGURE 7.4

NDS integration with NDPS

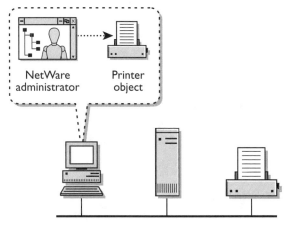

NDPS technology allows you to configure the
printer as a Directory object and access it
through NetWare Administrator

FIGURE 7.5

*Configurable event
notification with NDPS*

Multiple Printer Configurations

You can set up a printer with two specific configurations. For example, you might allow all users in a department to print to a color printer using only the black-and-white capabilities, but allow two or three individuals to use the color capabilities. This increases the efficiency and productivity of network printing.

Network Traffic Reduction

NDPS turns off Service Advertising Protocol (SAP) and communicates directly with printers. This decreases unnecessary network traffic and increases LAN/WAN bandwidth.

Print Job Scheduling

NDPS offers much more flexibility in the area of configuring print job scheduling options. For example, you can schedule a job based on the time of day or job size.

Enhanced Client Support

NDPS offers improved functionality for Windows 3.x, Windows 95, and Windows NT workstations.

Backward-Compatibility

NDPS is fully compatible with all types of printers, whether or not they have been configured to take advantage of the advanced features that NDPS offers. NDPS can be configured to work with NPRINTER and queue-based technology in conjunction with NetWare 4.11. The backward compatibility and cross-platform support offered by NDPS ensures that all of your current Queue Management Services (QMS) printers will work just as they always have, even if you do not convert them to NDPS. Finally, backward compatibility allows NDPS clients to access queue-based printers and queue-based clients to access basic NDPS features. Check out Figure 7.6.

As you can see, NDPS offers an exhaustive list of features and benefits. Probably one of the most critical to existing networks is "backward compatibility." Along these lines, let's take a closer look at how NDPS differs from legacy queue-based printing systems.

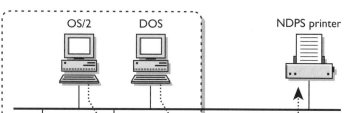

FIGURE 7.6

*Queue-based clients
printing to NDPS*

Non-enhanced clients

NDPS Versus Queue-Based Printing

The architecture of Novell legacy queue-based print services was based on the creation and linking of three components: printers, print queues, and print servers. As you can see in Figure 7.7, this placed a great burden on the NetWare file server.

Setting up queue-based printing was often a complex task. To print, user data had to follow a wondrous journey from the workstation to the network printer. First, there was *capturing*. This process redirected the print job from a local workstation to the centralized server hard drive. Next, the print job waited in a *queue* until the print server was ready for it. Finally, the *print server* grabbed the job from the queue and sent it along the wire to the correct printer. All the while, the user was holding his or her breath.

With NDPS, printer, print queue, and print server functions are combined into a single entity called a *Printer Agent*. The need to create print queues has been eliminated because users send print jobs directly to network printers. As you can see in Figure 7.8, the queue-based redirection complexity has been eliminated and Printer Agents transparently manage the entire printing journey for happy, naïve users.

FIGURE 7.7

Understanding queue-based printing architecture

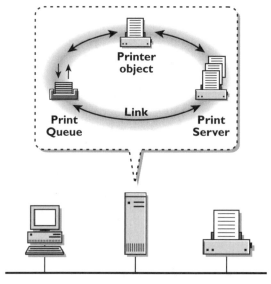

Queue-based technology requires you to create Print Queue, Printer, and Print Server objects, and link them together.

FIGURE 7.8

Understanding NDPS printing architecture

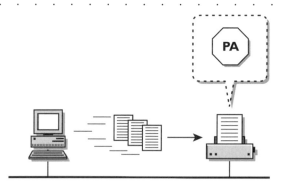

NDPS allows users to print directly to network printers using a single component: the Printer Agent.

Now, let's take a quick look at some of the most obvious differences between queue-based printing and NDPS. Follow along in Table 7.1.

▸ *Setup* — In queue-based printing systems, CNAs must create and link Print Queues, Printers, and Print Server objects. With NDPS, all you have to do is create Printer Agents and NetWare takes care of the rest.

▸ *User Printing* — In queue-based printing systems, users must capture the printer port and then redirect the data to a server-based queue file. Then the file waits in line until the print server electronically carries it to the correct printer. With NDPS, users simply print directly to printers and the Printer Agents take care of the rest.

▸ *Communications* — In queue-based printing systems, all printing communications are unidirectional. In this case, feedback consists of pop-up windows reporting a non-configurable set of events. With NDPS, communications are bidirectional. CNAs can configure event notification, including e-mail, pop-up windows, event logs, and third-party products such as beepers and faxes. As a matter of fact, event notification is limited only by the printer's capability. This provides a framework for more intelligent printers in the future.

▸ *Snap-Ins* — Queue-based printing systems don't support add-ons or extensions from third-party companies. With NDPS, you can greatly customize the capabilities of your printing system. In addition, Novell and other third-party manufacturers offer multiple snap-in interfaces for enhanced printing.

▸ *Plug-and-Print* — Queue-based printing systems don't support automatic hardware detection or plug-and-print technology. CNAs must create and configure printer objects manually. With NDPS, you can plug a printer into a network and it becomes immediately available to all users. In addition, NDPS allows you to select common printer drivers and have them automatically download and install to each workstation.

	FEATURE	QUEUE-BASED PRINTING	NDPS
T A B L E 7.1	Setup	Queues, printers, and print servers	Printer Agents
NDPS Versus Queue-Based Printing	User Printing	Capture redirection	Directly to printers
	Communications	Unidirectional	Bidirectional
	Snap-ins	None	Supported
	Plug-and-Print	None	Supported

Now that you have a handle on exactly how cool NDPS printing is, let's take a quick look at the types of printers it supports. After all, printers are the ultimate destination of our virtual journey. Without them, user files would be lost in the ether of cyber-space . . . and you don't want that.

NDPS Printer Types

Now repeat after me—I *am* a printer, I *am* a printer. Remember this is the essence of printing.

NetWare 5 NDPS printers can be configured in a variety of different ways:

▸ Network printers attached directly to the LAN/WAN and enabled through a Novell (or Third-Party) Gateway. (For example, "HPGATE.NLM" is a Hewlett-Packard Gateway included with NetWare 5.)

▸ Remote printers attached to a workstation (or remote file server) using special software provided by NDPS.

▸ Local printers attached directly to the NDPS server.

Regardless of the way you configure your NDS printer, it must be defined as one of two types: *Public Access* or *Controlled Access*. A Public Access printer is available without restriction to everyone on the network. A Controlled Access printer, on the other hand, has an associated NDS object and provides a tighter degree of administrative control and security. Let's take a closer look.

▶ · ◀

> **REAL WORLD**
>
> Public Access printers cannot be viewed using the Directory tree browser in NetWare Administrator. Instead, you must view and manage them through the Tools menu of NetWare Administrator. Just select the NDPS Public Access Printers option.

Public Access Printers

A Public Access printer is exactly what its name implies: Anyone can use the printer without being authenticated to the NDS tree. Public Access printers are still manageable through NetWare Administrator, but they are not represented as NDS objects.

To create a Public Access printer, CNAs only must ensure that a Printer Agent exists for that printer and that it has been configured and activated. Public Access printers are convenient to use, but they do not offer the security benefits of a Controlled Access printer.

For a complete comparison of Public Access and Controlled Access printers, refer to Table 7.2.

TIP

Controlled Access Printers

A Controlled Access printer provides printing security as an NDS object by validating the service requests of each client. This provides you with control over who can use the printer and what the user can do with it. Also, Controlled Access printers are the only ones that can take full advantage of NDPS—including features such as customizable event notification, multiple configurations, automatic client install, and NDS integration.

To create a Controlled Access printer, you must first create an NDPS Printer object in the NDS tree. Then, associate the printer with its own Printer Agent and voilà . . . you're ready to go.

Following is a list of the most important differences between Public Access and Controlled Access printers. Follow along with Table 7.2.

- *NDS Object* — Controlled Access printers provide tight NDS integration. They are represented as Printer objects in the NDS tree. Public Access printers are not.

- *Security* — Because of their tight NDS integration, Controlled Access printers offer a full range of network security options. Public Access printers, on the other hand, offer little or no security.

- *Configuration* — Controlled Access printers support a full range of printer configuration options. In addition, multiple configurations can be added to a single printer. On the other hand, Public Access printers allow little administrative configuration.

- *NetWare Administrator Support* — Controlled Access printers provide full NDS management using NetWare Administrator. Public Access printers also allow management through NetWare Administrator, but you cannot use the directory browser. Instead Public Access printers must be managed using the "NDPS Public Access Printers" option under the Tools menu in NetWare Administrator.

- *Event Notification* — Controlled Access printers offer a full range of event and status notification options. On the other hand, Public Access printers provide very basic job event notification.

- *Plug-and-Print* — Both Controlled Access and Public Access printers support plug-and-print automatic hardware detection. However, Controlled Access printers expand functionality with automatic client installation.

- *Automatic Client Installation* — Controlled Access printers can be automatically installed on client workstations, whereas Public Access printers cannot.

REAL WORLD

When you create a Controlled Access printer, NDS rights are automatically granted to all users in the printer's context. Other users do not have access until appropriate NDS rights are granted by you — the network administrator.

TABLE 7.2			
Comparing Controlled Access and Public Access Printers in NDPS	FEATURE	CONTROLLED ACCESS PRINTERS	PUBLIC ACCESS PRINTERS
	NDS Object	Yes	No
	Security	High	Low
	Configuration	Full range	Limited
	NetWare Administrator Support	As an NDS object	In the "Tools" menu
	Event Notification	Full range	Limited
	Plug-and-Print	Yes	Yes
	Automatic Client Installation	Yes	No

So, that's the essence of printing. It's not so bad. As a matter of fact, NDPS offers a very simplified journey from the user workstation to the printer down the hall. They say, "A well-traveled person is an enlightened person." Do you feel well-traveled? Do you feel enlightened? You should feel *something* right about now.

Let's continue our exploration of NetWare 5's NDPS mystery by gathering some clues about its basic architecture. Look out, Sherlock Holmes, here we come.

NDPS Printing Architecture

So, how does all this fancy printing work?

Now that you understand the essence of printing, it's time to do something about it. This is where the mystery begins to unfold. This is where the clues appear. Welcome to *Sherlock Holmes 101.*

As we just learned, NDPS offers important improvements over the Novell legacy queue-based printing architecture. First of all, the functions of printer, print queue, and print server have been combined into a single logical entity called the Printer Agent. This architecture ensures the scalability of NetWare 5 printing and allows you to print in any type of LAN/WAN environment. The NDPS scalability architecture also allows you to print to a variety of devices — ranging from simple dot-matrix printers to laser printers and large-scale production devices.

Figure 7.9 illustrates the major components of the NDPS architecture. As you can see, NetWare 5 printing consists of three support components surrounding the heart of NDPS (the Printer Agent):

F I G U R E 7.9

NetWare 5 NDPS printing architecture

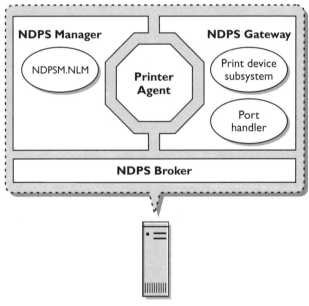

NetWare 5 server

▶ *Printer Agent* — This is the heart of NetWare 5 NDPS printing. The Printer Agent combines the functions previously performed by a printer, print queue, print server, and spooler into one intelligent, simplified entity.

▶ *NDPS Manager* — The NDPS Manager is a logical entity used to create and manage Printer Agents. It is represented as an object in the NDS tree. The NDPS Manager object stores information used by NDPS.NLM.

► *NDPS Gateway* — NDPS gateways allow you to support *"unusual"* printing environments. "Unusual" printing environments include non-NDPS-aware printers and print systems that require jobs to be placed in queues. NDPS currently supports two gateways: the Novell Gateway and third-party gateways. Furthermore, the Novell Gateway consists of a Print Device Subsystem (PDS) and a Port Handler (PH) component.

► *NDPS Broker* — When NDPS is installed, the installation utility ensures that a Broker object is loaded on your network and provides three network support services not previously available in NetWare. Although these services are invisible, you must be aware of them in case the Broker decides to take a vacation. The three NDPS support services are: Service Registry Services (SRS), Event Notification Services (ENS), and Resource Management Services (RMS).

Now, let's take a closer look at each of these four NDPS components and learn how they can be used to solve NetWare's greatest mystery . . . printing.

NDPS Printer Agent

The Printer Agent is the heart of NetWare 5 NDPS printing. Before a printer can be incorporated into NDPS, it must be represented by a Printer Agent. For simplicity's sake, the Printer Agent has a one-to-one relationship with the printer. This means no Printer Agent can represent more than one printer, and no printer can be represented by more than one Printer Agent.

REAL WORLD

The NDPS architecture is designed to operate independently of any single operating system. As such, it is fully portable to different environments and based on the International Standards Organization (ISO) 10175 Document Printing Application (DPA) Standard and Internet Engineering Task Force (IETF) RFC 1759. Most printer manufacturers follow these specifications, making NDPS fully compatible with existing and future printer environments.

The NDPS Printer Agent is a single intelligent entity that combines the functions previously performed by queue-based printer, print queue, print server, and spooler objects. This "intelligent entity" can exist in one of three different forms:

▶ *Server-based/computer-attached* — The NDPS Printer Agent can exist as a software entity running on the NetWare 5 server representing printers attached either directly to the server or a workstation. In this scenario, the Printer Agent must run on the file server and must control printers attached to servers or workstations. Check it out in Figure 7.10.

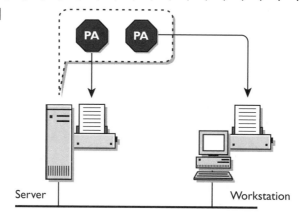

FIGURE 7.10

The server-based NDPS Printer Agents

Server   Workstation

▶ *Server-based/network-attached* — The NDPS Printer Agent can also exist as a software entity running on the NetWare 5 server representing printers attached directly to the network. In this scenario, the NDPS printer must have built-in intelligence and IP or IPX connectivity capabilities. For example, NetWare 5 includes a Hewlett-Packard Gateway that supports network-attached HP LaserJet printers. Check it out in Figure 7.11.

▶ *Network-attached embedded* — Some third-party network-attached printers are so intelligent that the NDPS Printer Agent functionality can be embedded directly into the printer. This level of firmware control eliminates the need for an NDPS server. Most CNAs will welcome the simplicity of embedding the Printer Agent functionality directly into the network-attached printer. Check it out in Figure 7.12.

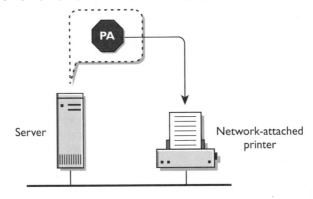

F I G U R E   7.11

*The server-based/
network-attached NDPS
Printer Agent*

Server

Network-attached
printer

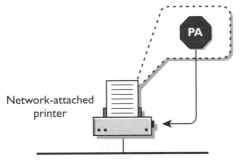

F I G U R E   7.12

*The network-attached
embedded NDPS
Printer Agent*

Network-attached
printer

As we just saw, NDPS Printer Agents can exist as NetWare Loadable Modules (NLMs) running on a NetWare 5 server, or they can be embedded directly into the printer. As printer manufacturers create NDPS gateways for their devices, server-based Printer Agents will become obsolete. Clearly, the simplicity of Option Three (network-attached embedded) appeals to CNAs everywhere.

So, what's so great about the NDPS Printer Agent? Good question. Figure 7.13 illustrates the management capabilities handled by NDPS Printer Agents. At its most fundamental level, the Printer Agent manages the processing of print jobs and many operations performed by the printer itself. As you know, NDPS supports a bidirectional communications path. With this feature, the Printer Agent can expand its functionality into the areas of event notification and client interactivity. As such, the NDPS Printer Agent can also answer queries from network clients and generate event notifications so that interested parties can be aware of job completion, printing problems, errors, or changes in job status. That's all there is to it.

▶ · ◀

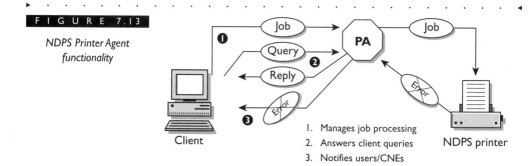

F I G U R E 7.13

*NDPS Printer Agent
functionality*

1. Manages job processing
2. Answers client queries
3. Notifies users/CNEs

It all starts with the NDPS Printer Agent. But you can't stop there. After all, Sherlock Holmes' famous magnifying glass wouldn't provide many clues without an experienced set of eyes.

NDPS Manager

The NDPS Manager object provides a platform for server-based Printer Agents. This logical NDS entity is used to create and manage printer objects. Simply stated: You must create an NDPS Manager object before creating Printer Agents. The good news is a single manager can control an unlimited number of agents. The best rule of thumb is to create an NDPS Manager object for each server that will host NDPS printers. Also make sure that each server-based local printer sits on the same server as its host NDPS Manager.

NDPS Manager runs on the NetWare 5 server as NDPSM.NLM. This NLM carries out instructions provided by the NDPS Manager object. As you can see in Figure 7.14, NDPSM.NLM can be loaded in one of two ways:

▸ *Manually* — You can manually load NDPSM.NLM at the server console by typing

```
LOAD NDPSM.NLM <NDPS Manager distinguished name>
```

▸ *Automatically* — NDPSM.NLM will automatically load when you create a Printer Agent object within NetWare Administrator.

While you can perform some configuration and management tasks directly through the NDPS Manager console interface, NetWare Administrator is a much better tool for performing these tasks. Refer to Figure 7.15 for a quick look at configuring the NDPS Manager with NetWare Administrator.

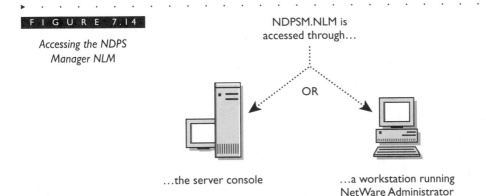

FIGURE 7.14

Accessing the NDPS Manager NLM

NDPSM.NLM is accessed through...

OR

...the server console

...a workstation running NetWare Administrator

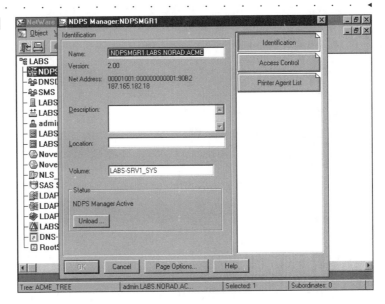

FIGURE 7.15

Configuring the NDPS Manager in NetWare Administrator

Life is full of surprises and NDPS sleuthing is no exception. Now that we understand the core functionality of NetWare 5 printing, let's take a closer look at gateway support for *"unusual suspects."* The truth is out there.

NDPS Gateways

NDPS Gateways allow you to support *"unusual"* printing environments. "Unusual" printing environments included non-NDPS-aware printers (such as UNIX, Macintosh, queue-based, and/or mainframe systems) and print systems that require jobs to be placed in queues. In addition, a gateway is necessary when you try to print to network-attached devices that don't support embedded NDPS controllers.

In short, the NDPS Gateway is a software bridge that directly links Printer Agents to NDPS printers. They accomplish this by translating NDPS commands into device-specific language that the physical printer can understand. This is possible because gateways are configured to know the specific type (make and model) of the printer being used.

NDPS currently supports two different types of gateways:

▸ *Novell Gateway* — This gateway consists of a Print Device Subsystem (PDS) and a Port Handler (PH) component. It supports local and remote printers including those using NPRINTER or queues.

▸ *Third-Party Gateways* — These alternative gateways perform the same types of tasks as the Novell Gateway, but are customized by printer manufacturers to support their own network-attached devices.

Let's cross the bridge into NDPS Gateway-land.

Novell Gateway

The Novell Gateway is built into NetWare 5 NDPS. It provides a software bridge between NDPS and legacy local and remote printers — including those using NPRINTER or queue-based technology. In addition, the Novell Gateway provides support for RP mode-enabled IPX printers and/or LPR mode-enabled IP printers.

Check out the Novell Gateway shown in Figure 7.16.

FIGURE 7.16

Understanding the Novell NDPS Gateway

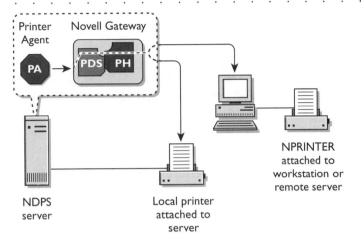

All of this fancy Novell Gateway-ing is accomplished using two key components:

▸ *Print Device Subsystem (PDS)* — The PDS is an NLM that loads automatically when a Printer Agent is created using the PDS configuration utility. The PDS retrieves printer-specific information (such as the make and model of the printer) and stores this information in an NDPS database. As a CNA, you'll need to use the Novell PDS when you create a Printer Agent for any of the following scenarios: a printer that is not connected directly to the network (including local and/or remote printers), *or* a network-attached printer without a manufacturer-specific Third-Party Gateway, *or* a printer running in PSERVER mode.

▸ *Port Handler (PH)* — The PH ensures that the PDS can communicate with the physical printer regardless of what type of interface is used. The Novell PH supports the following printer interfaces: parallel ports, serial ports, the QMS protocol, and/or remote printing (RP mode for IPX printers, and LPR mode for IP printers).

REAL WORLD

RP printers are those that support Novell's legacy Remote Printer protocol. This system is used by most network-attached printers in the IPX environment. LPR printers use a UNIX-based printing protocol in IP environments.

Third-Party Gateway

Third-Party gateways perform the same functions as the Novell Gateway, but are customized by printer manufacturers to support their own network-attached equipment. Many of the most sophisticated Third-Party Gateways (including Hewlett-Packard and Xerox systems) support plug-and-print functionality. These Third-Party Gateways can be configured to automatically create Printer Agents when an associated printer is attached to the network. This eliminates the need for manually creating Printer Agents and using the Novell PDS and PH architecture. Figure 7.17 illustrates the relationship between a typical Third-Party Gateway and the Novell Printer Agent.

FIGURE 7.17

Understanding Third-Party NDPS Gateways

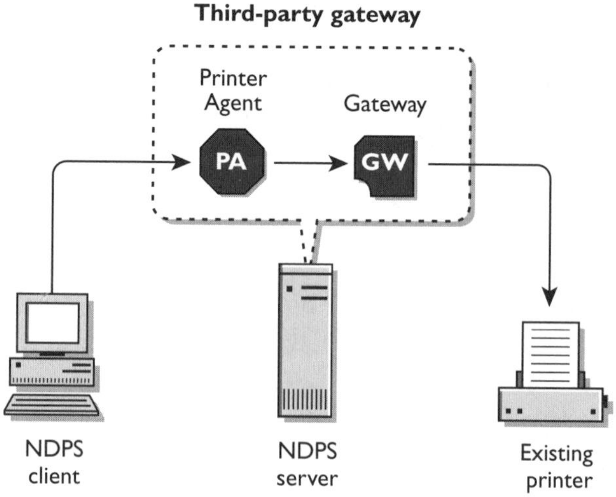

Third-party gateway

Printer Agent   Gateway

PA → GW

NDPS client   NDPS server   Existing printer

Because Third-Party Gateways are developed to interact with specific proprietary printers, they can provide a wider array of information and offer options that are not available with the generic Novell Gateway. The Hewlett-Packard (HP) Gateway, for example, enables you to view statistics, configure gateway settings, and configure printing options for HP printers using HP JetDirect print services. Furthermore, you can use the HP Gateway to create Public Access and Controlled Access printers within the realm of NDPS.

One of the most popular Third-Party Gateways (HP Gateway) is included with NetWare 5. You can activate the gateway by typing the following line at the NetWare 5 server console:

```
LOAD HPGATE.NLM
```

Once the HP Gateway has been activated, you can use NetWare Administrator to manage network-attached HP printers.

NDPS Gateways are our friends. They provide a critical link between Printer Agents and the rest of the world. Now that we've learned all there is to know about the foundation of NDPS, let's explore one last component — NDPS Broker. This Broker expands the capabilities of NDPS into the realm of service registry, event notification, and resource management.

REAL WORLD

While most current JetDirect cards are supported by NDPS, some of the older cards must be upgraded or replaced:

- If the model number of the JetDirect card is between J2337A and J2550A, the flash memory must be upgraded by installing new SIMMs.

- Any card with the model number before J2337A must be replaced.

- If the model number is greater than J2550A, the firmware revision should be greater than A.03.0. If it is not, the flash memory must be upgraded.

Check the Hewlett-Packard Web site for more information.

NDPS Broker

The NDPS Broker is a special management component that provides three important services to the NetWare 5 print architecture. The NDPS Broker comprises two complementary parts: an NDS leaf object (NDPS Broker) and a server-based NLM (BROKER.NLM). The NDPS Broker is your friend.

The good news is you don't have to worry about creating your own Broker. When NDPS is installed, the setup tool ensures that a Broker object is created and BROKER.NLM is loaded on the server. If you install NDPS on a different server, the setup tool checks to see if another Broker is needed. An additional Broker is created if NDPS is installed on a server more than three hops away from the nearest existing Broker.

Furthermore, you don't have to worry about activating the NDPS Broker, because it's loaded automatically when NDPS is initialized. To do its job, the NDPS Broker must log into the NDS tree and authenticate itself to the server. Once it's allowed access to the "Cloud," the Broker can get busy.

So, what is the NDPS Broker's job? Good question. The NDPS Broker actually has three jobs:

▸ Service Registry Services (SRS)

▸ Event Notification Services (ENS)

▸ Resource Management Services (RMS)

The NDPS Broker provides three network support services not previously available in NetWare. Although these services are invisible, you must be aware of them in case the Broker decides to take a vacation. Let's learn.

Service Registry Services (SRS)

NDPS Service Registry Services (SRS) allow Public Access printers to advertise themselves so that CNAs and users can find them. This service maintains information about device type, device name, device address, and device-specific data—such as the printer manufacturer and model number. Check it out in Figure 7.18.

Before NDPS, each printer had to periodically advertise its availability using Novell's Service Advertising Protocol (SAP). As we know, SAP generates a great deal of management overhead and bandwidth traffic. SRS helps minimize these problems by communicating directly with Public Access printers. There's no more need for SAP.

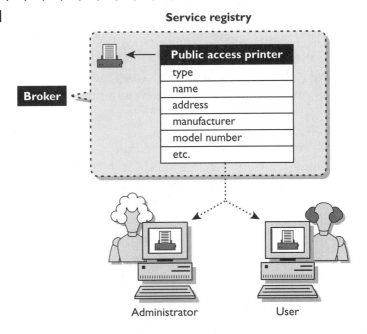

FIGURE 7.18

Understanding NDPS Service Registry Services (SRS)

Service registry

Public access printer

| type |
| name |
| address |
| manufacturer |
| model number |
| etc. |

Broker

Administrator   User

So, how is this accomplished? When you attach a Public Access printer to the network, it registers with the SRS. When an application or user wants to use it, it contacts SRS and retrieves a list of all registered printers on the network. In addition, SRS supports Multiple Service Registries with autosynchronization. This allows users to find Public Access printers anywhere on the WAN. Finally, SRS maintains a database of other services including the Registry—such as Event Notification Services and Resource Management Services. Let's check them out.

REAL WORLD

SRS uses different communication methods that depend on the network's native protocol:

▶ For IPX networks, SRS uses SAP Type 8202.

▶ For IP networks, SRS uses Multicast.

Event Notification Services (ENS)

NDPS Event Notification Services (ENS) is a *middleman* between event consumers (users) and event suppliers (printers). Users register with ENS by identifying the types of events about which they want to be notified. Similarly, printers register with ENS by identifying the kinds of events they're capable of reporting.

You can configure ENS to send event notifications to two different types of people:

▶ *Operators* — ENS can send notifications to non-job owners through Interested-Party Notification. This allows you to specify who should be notified when a specific printer or server completes a job or returns an error. To do so, use NetWare Administrator.

▶ *Users* — ENS can also be configured to notify job owners through Job-Owner Notification. This way, individual users can use the Novell Printer Manager at their workstation to specify feedback about their own print jobs only.

So, how does ENS communicate with users and operators? In a variety of ways:

▶ *Pop-Up Notification* — Messages pop up on the screens of individuals designated to receive them.

▶ *GroupWise Notification* — Messages are sent to designated recipients through GroupWise, the Novell scheduling and messaging system.

▶ *MHS Notification* — Messages are sent to recipients using Novell's Message Handling Service (MHS).

▶ *Log File Notification* — Messages are written directly to a log file on a designated NetWare server file system.

▶ *Programmatic Notification* — Two Programmatic Notification delivery methods (SPX and RPC) are shipped with NDS.

Check out Figure 7.19 for an illustration of the different ENS delivery methods. Remember, this is a built-in *middleman* for event notification between NDPS users and printers.

REAL WORLD

The open architecture of NDPS allows third parties to develop additional ENS delivery methods. By default, NDPS is enabled to work with the industry-standard Simple Network Management Protocol (SNMP). This way, developers can build NDPS Event Notification directly into their network management systems.

F I G U R E   7 . 1 9

Understanding NDPS Event Notification Services (ENS)

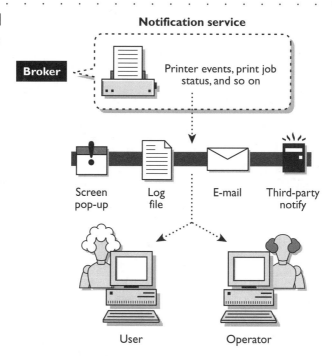

Resource Management Services (RMS)

NDPS Resource Management Services (RMS) is a central repository for printing resources. RMS allows you to install NDPS drivers, banners, and definition files in a central location, and then automatically download them to clients, printers, and anyone else who needs them. As you can see in Figure 7.20, RMS supports adding, listing, and replacing NDPS resources — including Windows-based printer drivers, Novell Printer Definition (NPD) files, banners, and fonts.

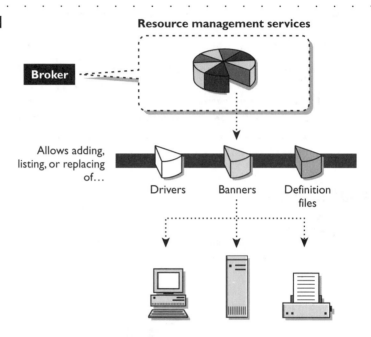

FIGURE 7.20

Understanding NDPS Resource Management Services (RMS)

RMS offers a number of brokering benefits, including improved resource sharing, more manageable resource distribution and updating, plug-and-print support, and centralized print driver downloading. In short, RMS greatly simplifies your life as a NetWare 5 CNA.

Are you an NDPS Sherlock Holmes yet?

In this chapter, we've been unraveling one of the greatest mysteries of NetWare 5 — NDPS printing. So far, you've honed your sleuthing skills by uncovering the fundamental architecture of NDPS. Congratulations, you've earned your crystal magnifying glass. However, you can't stop now. The mystery is still unsolved.

Now it's time to put all your newly acquired sleuthing skills to the test. It's time to leave the realm of NDPS theory and take *action*! Let's start at the beginning . . . NDPS construction.

Ready, set, build.

LAB EXERCISE 7.1: UNDERSTANDING NDPS

Match the following terms with their descriptions.

a. NDPS Broker

b. NDPS Manager

c. Printer Agent

d. Printer driver

e. Printer gateway

f. Public Access printer

g. Controlled Access printer

Item   *Definition*

____   Logical entity used to create and manage printer agents.

____   Converts print job into printer-specific format.

____   Provides the following support services: event notification, resource management, and service registration.

____   Has no corresponding NDS object.

____   Combines the functionality previously performed by Print Queue, Printer, and Print Server objects.

____   Can be configured with a full range of printer configuration and security options.

____   Provides a bridge between NDPS clients and legacy printers.

▶ · ◀

NDPS Printing Setup

Welcome to NDPS Printing setup. Now that you understand the fundamental architecture of NetWare 5 printing, I think you'll agree with me when I say, *"Elementary, my dear Watson."*

NDPS printing gets a bad rap. It's not very mysterious — you click a button on the workstation and your document comes out of the printer down the hall . . . assuming, of course, that you set it up correctly. And now is a good time to explore that aspect of NetWare 5 printing.

As you recall, there are three main elements within NDPS. They are:

▶ *NDPS Broker* — Provides support services from the NetWare 5 server

▶ *NDPS Manager* — Creates and manages Printer Agents

▶ *NDPS Printer Agent* — Combines the functions previously performed by a printer, print queue, print server, and spooler into one intelligent, simplified entity

Believe it or not, NDPS Printing Setup is as simple as 1-2-3. First, you must establish NDPS Services on your NetWare 5 file server with the LOAD BROKER console command. This authenticates the NDPS Broker and activates NetWare 5 printing.

Once the Broker is in place, you must create an NDPS Manager. The NDPS Manager provides a platform for Printer Agents that reside on your server. This is all accomplished using NDPSM.NLM. Once the Manager is in place, it's time to begin creating NDPS printers — using Printer Agents. NDPS supports either Public Access or Controlled Access printers. It's up to you, as the NetWare 5 CNA, to determine when you need the advanced services and security provided by Controlled Access printers. Otherwise, Public Access provides *elementary* functionality.

It's that simple . . . 1-2-3. No sweat.

Unfortunately, life is rarely that simple. There's always a Step 4. In this case, it involves workstations and users. Before you can use your new NDPS printing system, you must install printers on each workstation. Fortunately, NetWare 5 supports both automatic and manual installation processes.

Here's a quick preview of the NetWare 5 NDPS Printing Setup process:

▸ *Step 1*: Install NDPS on the server.

▸ *Step 2*: Create an NDPS Manager.

▸ *Step 3*: Create NDPS Printer Agents.

▸ *Step 4*: Install NDPS printers on workstations.

There you have it — four simple steps. No mystery here. Of course, all this techno-wizardry requires a little bit of planning. So, before we get all wrapped up in the excitement of NetWare 5 printing, let's take a moment to plan our move to NDPS . . . .

Don't forget your crystal NDPS magnifying glass.

Planning the Move to NDPS

So, you're thinking about moving to NDPS . . . good move. The key to a successful printing system is *quality construction*. And the key to quality construction is a *quality blueprint*. Planning your NDPS setup is a critical (and often overlooked) part of NDPS sleuthing. Any time you spend preparing the migration saves you hours once the users arrive.

You should consider a number of important things when moving to NDPS. Here's a quick checklist for CNAs:

▸ Develop a deployment strategy.

▸ Determine printer types.

▸ Assess your protocol needs.

▸ Exceed the minimum requirements.

Take a moment to review these important NDPS planning tips. Believe me, it'll save you many painful hours down the road.

Develop a Deployment Strategy

You can use two approaches to set up NetWare 5 NDPS: create a new system or upgrade from an existing printing environment. Regardless of which system you use, be sure to begin with a list of the new printing resources. This record helps ensure that you cover all your bases before you start to create NDPS printing objects in Step 3.

We also recommend that you create a diagram of the printing layout to help simplify object reorganization. This diagram can take a variety of forms:

▶ A tree diagram of the new NDS directory

▶ A simple list of all objects in the NDS directory

▶ An organizational chart with responsibilities and resources listed by name

This NDPS diagram should be centered around the printers and the NDPS Manager. Although many other printing items could be included, the printer and NDPS Manager objects are all that is necessary during setup. As you can see in Figure 7.21, we've expanded the LABS.NORAD.ACME container with printers and an NDPS Manager.

FIGURE 7.21

NDPS printing in the LABS Organizational Unit of NORAD

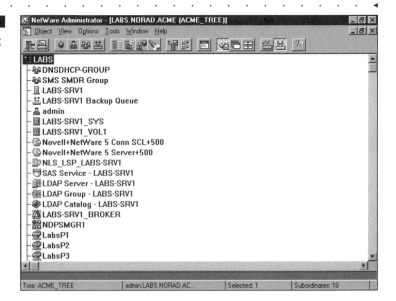

Determine Printer Types

Once you've developed your list of new printing resources, you'll need to choose between two different printer types:

▸ Public Access printers

▸ Controlled Access printers

Earlier in Table 7.2, we outlined the fundamental differences between Public Access and Controlled Access printers. Please review the list now . . . .

Welcome back. In summary, Controlled Access printers provide much better NDS integration and network printing security. In addition, they are highly configurable. For many CNAs, this will be the NDPS printer of choice.

However, there are times when Public Access printers satisfy your needs. First of all, they are immediately available to everyone on the network and require minimal administrative action. In addition, they are automatically created by Third-Party gateways or embedded printing solutions.

So, be sure to determine which printers will be controlled and which printers will be public as you develop your NDPS plan.

Assess Your Protocol Needs

NetWare 5 offers you a choice of which protocol to use with your new NDPS solution. Because of the momentum of Pure IP, you may choose to implement NDPS printing over TCP/IP — but you don't have to.

Following is a list of the five different protocol options Novell offers with NetWare 5:

▸ *NDPS Printing Over IP* — This option provides both NDPS client and NDPS server support for TCP/IP. In this configuration, NDPS provides a Port Handler using LPR/LPD, which is an IP printing protocol already installed on most network printers in use today. Fortunately, every major printer manufacturer supports this protocol.

▸ *Queue-Based Printing Over IP* — This option allows you to continue using queue-based printing on your new TCP/IP network. You will not install or use NDPS in any way. Instead, you'll use UNIX print servers to provide an IP gateway from your print queues.

▸ *NDPS Printing Over IPX* — In this environment, CNAs are able to print with NDPS using the native IPX/SPX protocol.

▸ *Queue-Based Printing Over IPX* — You may not wish to move directly to NDPS or force your clients to communicate via Pure IP. In this case, you can use the old legacy system: queue-based printing with the IPX/SPX protocol.

▸ *NDPS On Server Without Changing Client* — This option is useful if you want to upgrade from queue-based printing to NDPS without upgrading all your client workstations at the same time. This option is available for both IPX and IP environments through the Novell Upgrade Wizard.

Now you are well on your way to NDPS blueprinting. Let's review. You've developed a deployment strategy, determined which devices will be Public Access and which will need to be controlled, and you've chosen one of many protocol options. Now there's only one task left — exceed the minimum requirements. Go for the gold.

Exceed the Minimum Requirements

Just like any CNA task, NDPS Printing Setup involves minimum requirements. To support NDPS, your NetWare 5 servers and workstations must exceed the following minimum requirements:

▸ *NDPS Server* — Your NDPS server must first meet the minimum requirements for NetWare 5 (see Chapter 2). In addition, it must have 80 MB of available disk space on volume SYS: and at least 4 MB of RAM above the NetWare 5 requirements. Finally, the server must have CD-ROM capability to read the NDPS installation media.

▸ *NDPS Workstations* — The NDPS workstation must support Windows 95, Windows NT or Windows 3.1. In addition, it must be running the latest Novell Client — or, at the very least, Novell Client v 2.2. In addition, the workstation must support Windows 95 or Windows NT for access to the NDPS Administrative utilities.

That completes the NDPS Setup blueprint. Consider yourself a NetWare 5 architect. Now it's time to tie on our construction boots and build the NDPS printing system. Remember, this consists of four simple steps:

▸ *Step 1:* Install NDPS on the server.

▸ *Step 2:* Create an NDPS Manager.

▸ *Step 3:* Create NDPS Printer Agents.

▸ *Step 4:* Install NDPS printers on workstations.

If you build it, they will come . . . and print!

Step 1: Install **NDPS** on the Server

Before you can use NetWare 5 NDPS, you must determine which setup strategy you want to use. You can either upgrade your current queue-based printing resources to NDPS, or create a completely new NDPS printing system from the ground up. If you want to upgrade your existing printing environment with all its current printing objects and users intact, you'll need to use the Novell Upgrade Wizard. On the other hand, it's safer and cleaner to create a new NDPS printing system from the ground up. Regardless of the strategy you use, NDPS will not disable your current printing setup. The good news is your users can continue to print just as they always have, until you decide to disable queue-based printing. This can be done gradually, or all at once.

In this book, we're going to explore the "ground up" methodology. That means we're going to start with a fresh slate and build the NDPS objects from scratch.

In Step 1, we're going to start at the NDPS server. During server installation, you can choose between a Typical or Custom installation method. It's important to understand that whichever installation you use for the NetWare 5 server, it will have significant consequences on NDPS Printing Setup. In addition, you should understand the rights required for configuring NDPS and when and where NDPS Brokers are created.

Here are some important aspects of NDPS Printing Setup — Step 1:

▸ Typical Versus Custom Install

▸ Rights Requirements

▸ Creating the NDPS Broker

The NDPS setup process begins with an NDPS Broker. This is a key service provider for NetWare 5 file servers. Let's learn more about how, when, and where NDPS Brokers are created.

Typical Versus Custom Install

If you select the Typical server installation method, NetWare 5 automatically installs NDPS and copies the RMS resource database to the SYS:NDPS/RESDIR directory. RMS is a central repository for network resources and services. It contains printer drivers, banners, printer definition (NPD) files, and fonts.

If you select the Custom server installation method, NetWare 5 offers you the option of placing the RMS resource database on this server. In general, you'll want a resource database enabled for each NDPS Broker that you create. If disk space is an issue on a specific server and you do not intend to create a Broker object on that server, be sure the option to copy these database files is not checked.

 TIP   **On average, the RMS resource database occupies approximately 60 MB of server disk space. Of course, this number varies depending on the variety of platforms and languages your server is capable of. Check disk space capacity calculations for more information.**

Rights Requirements

To install NetWare 5 and NDPS on a given server, you must have certain NDS and file system rights. Here's a quick summary:

▸ *To install NDPS on the server* — You must have Supervisor rights at the [Root] of the NDS tree because the schema will be modified.

▸ *To install the RMS resource database* — You must have Read, Write, Modify, Create, and File Scan file system rights to SYS:NDPS/RESDIR.

▸ *To install another NDPS Broker* — You will need Browse and Create NDS rights to the container in which the Broker will be created.

Creating the NDPS Broker

The first time NDPS is installed in a Directory tree, an NDPS Broker object is created automatically in the container where the Server object resides. This is fairly simple and straightforward. However, you have much less control over when and where subsequent Brokers are created.

When NDPS is subsequently installed on other servers in the same Directory tree, certain conditions affect where, and whether or not, additional Brokers are created. In a Typical install, the NDPS utility checks every active Service Registry Service (SRS) to find a Broker that meets any of the following requirements:

▸ The Broker is running on the current server.

▸ The Broker is configured in the AUTOEXEC.NCF file to run on the current server. By the way, this happens automatically during initial NDPS installation.

▸ The Broker is running within three hops of the current server and the installing user has Supervisor NDS rights to it. (Check out Figure 7.22.)

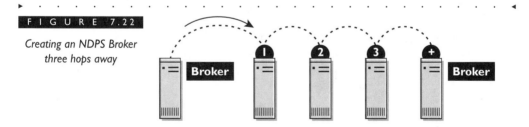

FIGURE 7.22

Creating an NDPS Broker three hops away

If an NDPS Broker is found that meets these requirements, a new Broker object is not created. Similarly, if no existing Broker meets these requirements, a new NDPS Broker object is created. Pretty simple, huh?

But where in the NDS tree is the new Broker object created? Ah, that's a more interesting question. At this point, the installation utility will search for an NDPS Broker object in the current context. If it doesn't find one, it will continue searching up the Directory tree until it reaches the highest-level container to which the installing user has Supervisor NDS object rights. If a Broker object is found and is already loaded on the local server (using the LOAD BROKER command), all services are automatically enabled. However, if a Broker object is *not* found, one is created in that context and loaded with all servers enabled.

Wow, I bet you never knew Broker-ing could be so much fun. Regardless of how it happens, the important point is — an NDPS Broker object has been created in the Directory tree and loaded on your server.

Now it's time to move on to Step 2.

Step 2: Create an NDPS Manager

Once your NDPS Broker is in place, you must create a centralized NDPS Manager. The NDPS Manager is used to control server-based Printer Agents similar to the way PSERVER was used to manage printing resources on queue-based servers. In short, you must create an NDPS Manager on each server that directly supports NDPS printers.

The good news is that a single NDPS Manager can control an unlimited number of Printer Agents. The best rule of thumb is to create an NDPS Manager object for each server that will host NDPS printers. Also, be sure that each server-based local printer sits on the same server as its host NDPS Manager.

To create an NDPS Manager in NetWare Administrator, perform the following four tasks:

▶ *Home Container* — In NetWare Administrator, select the container where you want the NDPS Manager object to reside. From the Object menu, select Create. Next highlight NDPS Manager from the New Object dialog box. Finally, type a name of your choice in the NDPS Manager Name field (see Figure 7.23).

▶ *Host Server* — Next, Browse for the host server where you want this NDPS Manager to reside. This can be any server in the current Directory tree on which you have installed an NDPS Broker. Keep in mind that any printer you designate as a Local Printer must be attached directly to this host server. Finally, the NDPS Manager will store its database on a volume on this server (see Figure 7.23).

Creating an NDPS Manager
in NetWare Administrator

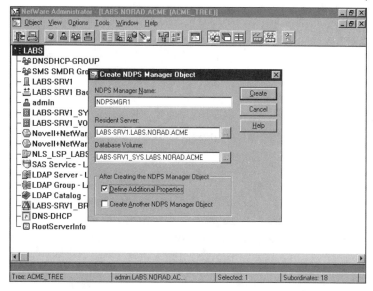

▶ *Database Volume* — Next, you'll need to identify a volume for hosting the NDPS Manager database. This is where the spooling files will be created, and it can be any volume residing on the host server (see Figure 7.23).

▶ *Administrator* — Once you've identified the Manager's host server and database volume, mark Define Additional Properties, then click Create. At this point, the NDPS Manager Details dialog appears. Specify a name for this NDPS Manager object, and click Create (see Figure 7.23).

REAL WORLD

If you move the NDPS Manager to a different server, its database will migrate automatically. As a result, local printers assigned to the NDPS Manager will no longer work. To solve this problem, you can use NetWare Administrator to reassign the NDPS Manager's database volume.

NDPS Manager runs on the NetWare 5 server as NDPSM.NLM. This NetWare Loadable Module carries out instructions provided by the NDPS Manager object. Once this object has been created using the tasks just discussed, it's time to load it. This is accomplished using a simple server console command:

```
LOAD NDPSM.NLM <NDPS Manager Distinguished Name>
```

For example, you might try the following line:

```
LOAD NDPSM.NLM NDPSMANAGER1.LABS.NORAD.ACME
```

You can type this line manually at the NetWare 5 server console, or automate the process using AUTOEXEC.NCF. Either way, you must activate the NDPS Manager before its Printer Agents can be created. If you forget this final task, and move on to Step 3 in haste, NetWare 5 will automatically prompt you to load the NDPS Manager. Isn't it nice to have Novell looking after you?

Speaking of printing guardians, let's move on to the heart of NDPS — Printer Agents. These are the workhorses of your new paper-filled office. Whatever you do, be sure to recycle their output . . . it's good for the soul.

Step 3: Create NDPS Printer Agents

The Printer Agent is the heart of NetWare 5 NDPS printing. Before a printer can be incorporated into NDPS, it must be represented by a Printer Agent. For simplicity's sake, a Printer Agent has a one-to-one relationship with each printer. This means no Printer Agent can represent more than one printer, and no printer can be represented by more than one Printer Agent. In short, it's the NDPS printer guardian.

Once you've activated your NDPS Manager, you can create NDPS Printer Agents in a variety of ways:

- *NetWare 5 Administrator* — This NDS-aware tool allows you to create Public Access printers from the Manager object or Controlled Access printers as separate printer objects. We'll explore these two activities in just a moment.

- *Novell Upgrade Wizard* — You can upgrade your queue-based printers to NDPS using this upgrade utility.

- *NDPSM.NLM* — You can create NDPS printers at the server console using the NDPS Manager NLM. Simply load the NDPSM menu utility, and press

Insert to create a new Printer Agent. This server-based tool even includes a Printer Configuration screen.

▶ *Third-Party Gateways* — Some Third-Party Gateways will automatically create Printer Agents when they find manufacturer-specific printers on the WAN. For example, HP Printer Agents are created automatically when you load the Hewlett-Packard Gateway.

In this section, we're going to focus on the first tool (NetWare Administrator), and learn how to create Public Access and Controlled Access printers. Then when you think you have it all figured out, we'll learn how to upgrade a Public Access printer to Controlled Access status.

So, without any further ado, let's create some printers.

Creating Public Access Printers

A Public Access printer is exactly what its name implies: Anyone can use the printer without being authenticated to the NDS tree. Public Access printers are still manageable through NetWare Administrator, but they are not represented as an NDS object. To create a Public Access printer, you must ensure that it has a guardian Printer Agent. Ironically, the Printer Agent is created and identified during the process of printer creation. Here's how it works:

▶ *NDPS Manager* — From NetWare Administrator, browse to the home container of this Agent's NDPS Manager. Double-click the NDPS Manager object. Next, activate the Identification page, and click Printer Agent List. Click New. Finally, specify a name for this Printer Agent. You may want to use a standard naming scheme that links the Printer Agent and Public Access printer. Remember, it's a one-to-one relationship.

▶ *Gateway* — Next, you'll need to identify the Gateway Type you want to use for this Printer Agent. Gateways allow NDPS Clients to send jobs to printers that are not NDPS-aware. In NetWare 5, you have two gateway choices by default: HP or Novell. Use the gateway that corresponds with the manufacturer of this Public Access printer. If you can't find a proprietary Third-Party Gateway to match, use Novell.

▶ *Printer/Port Type* — Next, you'll be asked to define the Connection Type and Port Type associated with your new Printer Agent. The options within the Connection Type dialog will vary depending on the Gateway you choose. Choose Local and move on to the Port Type definition. Local ports send print jobs to printers attached directly to the NDPS server. Remote ports, on the other hand, send print jobs to printers attached directly to the network or to remote computers — workstations or servers. Choose the correct Port Type and move on (see Figure 7.24).

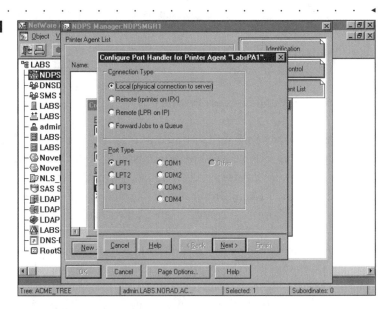

▶ *Printer Driver* — Finally, you'll need to select the printer driver that should be automatically downloaded to each Client operating system. This way, users can automatically download centralized printer drivers during Step 4. Since the list of printer drivers shipped with NetWare 5 is limited, you should probably add updated drivers to the Resource Management Services (RMS) database periodically. If you want to make the users do the work, you can choose [None] from the top of each list, and users will be prompted to provide a disk when they install the printer on their workstations.

Once you click Continue, the new Printer Agent will appear in the Host Manager's Printer Agent List window. Voilà, you're finished!

Remember, Public Access printers don't appear as objects in the NDS tree. They are simply NDPS resources available to *all* users. If you want better security and/or enhanced services, consider creating a Controlled Access printer.

Creating Controlled Access Printers

A Controlled Access printer expands the functionality of Public Access printers with NDS integration, user authentication, better event notification, and multiple configurations.

To create a Controlled Access printer, you must first create an NDPS Printer object in the Directory tree. Then, associate the printer with its own Printer Agent, and identify a host NDPS Manager. As a matter of fact, the steps for creating a Controlled Access printer are very similar to those we just went through to create a Public Access printer. They differ only in the beginning. Let's take a closer look:

▶ *Prerequisites* — To create a Controlled Access printer object in the Directory tree, you must have at least Browse and Create NDS rights for the printer's home container. You must also be designated as a Manager of the NDPS Manager object that controls this Agent. Finally, an NDPS Broker must be running on this server as BROKER.NLM.

▶ *NDPS Object* — To create a Controlled Access Printer, you must first define an NDPS Printer object in the Directory tree. In NetWare Administrator, browse to the appropriate home container, and choose Create from the Object menu. Next, select NDPS Printer from the New Object dialog box. Finally, select a printer name and you're off to the races. Check out Figure 7.25.

▶ *Printer Agent* — Next, you'll need to identify a Printer Agent for the new NDPS Printer object. In the Printer Agent Source field, select Create a New Printer Agent and then Create. Next, confirm the Printer Agent name as the name of the new NDPS Printer object you just created. This solidifies the one-to-one relationship between printers and Printer Agents.

▶ *NDPS Manager* — Finally, you'll need to associate the new Printer Agent to an existing NDPS Manager object. Simply browse and select the Manager you created in Step 2 and you're ready for the second half of Controlled Access printer creation.

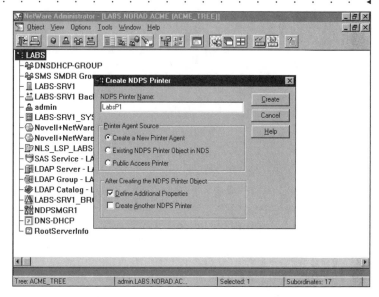

F I G U R E   7.25

Creating a Controlled Access
printer in NetWare
Administrator

The rest of the tasks necessary to create a Controlled Access printer mirror the Public Access printer steps exactly. Next, you'll select the NDPS Gateway type and click OK. Then, you'll define a Printer Type and Port Type for the new Controlled Access printer. Finally, you will select the printer driver that should be automatically downloaded to each client operating system. Click Continue and you're finished.

Now that wasn't so bad, was it? Clearly, Controlled Access printers provide many more benefits to CNAs in the areas of security and NDS management. For this reason, most of your NDPS printers should be of the Controlled Access variety. As a matter of fact, you'll come across many situations when it makes sense to convert an existing Public Access printer into a Controlled Access device. Here's how it works.

Converting Public Access Printers to Controlled Access Printers

The NDPS "plug-and-print" functionality encourages manufacturers to develop gateways through which their network-attached printers can be automatically configured as NDPS Public Access printers and made immediately available to users. In the future, a new generation of printers will have NDPS technology embedded in the printer's hardware — making NDPS even more convenient to use and administer.

In many situations, you will want to convert these Public Access printers to Controlled Access devices to take full advantage of the security and management features offered by Novell Directory Services (NDS). To convert a Public Access printer into a Controlled Access device, you'll need to follow the same basic steps as if you were creating a Controlled Access printer from scratch. There's only one major difference:

▶ *Printer Agent* — When you create a Controlled Access printer from scratch, the Printer Agent is created along with it. However, when you convert from a Public Access printer, you must specify an existing Printer Agent. At the Printer Agent field, click Browse (instead of Create). The Select Printer Agent Source dialog appears. It contains a list of available Public Access printers. Highlight the one you want to convert and click OK. At this point, the Create NDPS Printer dialog reappears with the Printer Name and Printer Agent fields filled in. Finally, select Create and the main browser window appears with your new Controlled Access printer displayed proudly.

Once you make this new Controlled Access printer available to your users, it'll become painfully clear why you need its increased security and flexible configuration. As NDS objects, Controlled Access printers provide greater configurability for CNAs. Here's a quick list of some of the Controlled Access printer features you may consider exploring:

▶ *Access Control* — Printer security is ensured through the assignment of three Access Control roles: Manager, Operator, and User. A Manager configures and troubleshoots the printer. This person adds and deletes users from the printer, configures notification profiles, and creates, modifies, or deletes printer configurations. An Operator, on the other hand, strictly maintains the printer on a day-to-day basis by pausing, restarting, reinitializing, aborting, and reordering jobs. Finally, Users can simply send, reconfigure, or remove their own print jobs only. Check out Figure 7.26 for an illustration of the NDPS Access Control configuration screen and the current Labs P1 mangers.

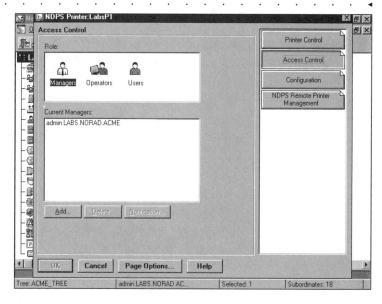

▶ *Event Notification* — In addition to Access Control, you can customize an
NDPS printer's Event Notification features. NetWare Administrator supports
two types of Event Notification: Job-Only Notification (job owners only)
and Interested-Party Notification (for Managers and Operators).

▶ *Print Job Spooling* — Finally, NetWare Administrator allows you to
customize the way a Controlled Access printer spools its jobs. By default,
the spooling area for an NDPS printer is located on the same volume as
the database for the NDPS Manager. However, the Spooling Configuration
option allows you to spool jobs to a different location for disk-management
or security purposes. In addition, you can specify the maximum amount of
disk space allowed for spooling or change its scheduling algorithm. Check
out print job spooling configuration in Figure 7.27.

That completes the core steps of NDPS Printing Setup. Let's review. First, we
activated server-based NDPS printing with the creation of an NDPS Broker. This was
accomplished automatically using the server installation procedure. Second, we
created an NDPS Manager object to support multiple Printer Agents within a
functional area of the Directory tree. Third, we created Public Access and Controlled
Access printers using the Printer Agent facility within NetWare Administrator.

FIGURE 7.27

*Configuring NDPS print job
spooling in NetWare
Administrator*

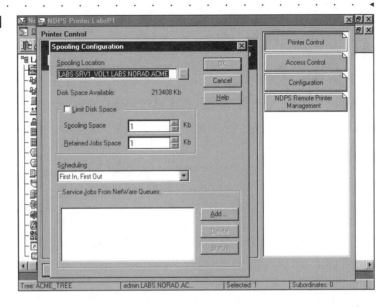

Congratulations, you are printing . . . sort of. Actually, the server is printing, but the users aren't! To open up NDPS printing to all your users (and make it truly productive), you'll need to install printing services on each workstation. Fortunately, NDPS allows you to do this automatically. Let's cruise over to the NetWare 5 workstation and check it out.

Step 4: Install NDPS Printers on Workstations

Welcome to the final frontier of NDPS Printing Setup. This is the trickiest, and most challenging, step in the whole process. Why? Simple — users!

Users present all sorts of diversity and chaos to your pristine printing system. As a CNA, you must try to standardize and control the workstation as much as possible. Don't live with the delusion, however, that you can standardize or control users . . . it'll never happen. Just try to do the best you can at simplifying their printing interface. This, in turn, will greatly simplify your life.

This section explores three important aspects of NDPS workstation installation:

► *Preparing Novell Workstations for NDPS Printing* — First, you must prepare the printing workstation as best you can. This involves Novell Client software, NDPS activation, adding printers, and the CAPTURE statement.

▶ *Automatic NDPS Workstation Installation* — NDPS offers an automatic NDPS workstation installation option. This encourages enterprise-wide standardization and saves you frequent-flyer miles.

▶ *Manual NDPS Workstation Installation* — Of course, if the automatic installation doesn't work, there's always the "old-fashioned way."

Let's improve your CNA life by controlling NDPS workstations . . . a little.

Preparing Novell Workstations for NDPS Printing

Before your users can take full advantage of NDPS, each workstation must be using the Novell Client that ships with NetWare 5. The Novell Client supports Windows 95, Windows NT, and Windows 3.1 workstations.

The NDPS components of the Novell Client require approximately 800K of RAM. If you select the Custom install option, be sure you have enabled NDPS.

If you have previously installed the new Novell Client on one or more Windows 95 or Windows NT workstations without enabling NDPS, you'll need to activate it now. Here's how it works:

▶ *Step 1:* At the Windows 95/Windows NT desktop, right-click the Network Neighborhood icon. Select Properties. The Network Properties screen appears.

▶ *Step 2:* Next, click the Add button on the Configuration page (see Figure 7.28). The Select Network Component Type screen appears. Select Service and click the Add button. The Select Network Service screen appears.

▶ *Step 3:* Next, select manufacturer Novell and network service Novell Distributed Print Services. Click the Have Disk button. The "Install from Disk" dialog appears.

▶ *Step 4:* Finally, browse to the Novell Client CD-ROM or network-loaded files and run the INSTALL.EXE program. Follow the bouncing ball.

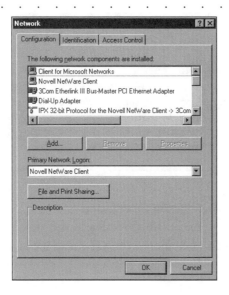

FIGURE 7.28

Enabling an NDPS printer at the workstation

Once you have enabled NDPS at the workstation, it's time to add printers. This can be accomplished automatically (good) or manually (work) — as we'll see in just a moment. As you're reading, keep in mind that Windows NT supports all the NDPS printer-management functions in its native Printer Management interface. And, finally, be sure to remove all CAPTURE statements from NDPS workstations. CAPTURE interferes with the full functionality of NDPS.

Now, let's take a closer look at automatic and manual NDPS workstation installation.

REAL WORLD

Whatever you do, be sure to run the SETUP or WINSETUP client installation utilities. NDPS doesn't support a client using the DOS INSTALL program.

> **REAL WORLD**
>
> NDPS is very sensitive to the version of Z.E.N.works and/or Novell Client you are running. If you are using the Novell Client native to Z.E.N.works, it will be version 2.5. This client does not support the TCP/IP connectivity, nor NDPS. Therefore, you'll need to upgrade to the NetWare 5 Client (version 3.0 and above). This Client ships with NetWare 5 and supports IP/IPX connectivity, Z.E.N.works, and, most importantly, NDPS.

Automatic NDPS Workstation Installation

While NDPS allows users to download and install printers on their workstations manually, it also allows you (as the NetWare 5 CNA) to designate certain printers to be downloaded and installed automatically. Very cool! Check out Figure 7.29.

FIGURE 7.29

Automatic NDPS workstation installation

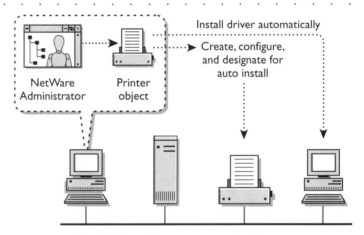

From NetWare Administrator, an administrator can create and configure Printer objects and designate printers to be automatically installed on user workstations.

You can designate a printer to be installed automatically by using the Remote Printer Management (RPM) feature in NetWare Administrator. Once you have designated a printer for automatic installation, it magically appears on the workstation's Installed Printers list next time the user logs in. We'll discuss this NDPS management tool in the next section.

Manual NDPS Workstation Installation

If you want to live dangerously, you can choose to *manually* install NDPS printers on user workstations. This is accomplished using the Novell Printer Manager tool. Also keep in mind that you can use the Windows Add Printers Wizard in the Windows Printers folder to install NDPS printers on Windows 95 and Windows NT workstations.

Here's how the Novell Printer Manager works:

▶ *Novell Printer Manager* — First, run the Novell Printer Manager from Windows. Make sure you have a search drive (Z:, for example) mapped to the SYS:PUBLIC directory on the NDPS server. If you are running Windows 3.1, execute Z:\PUBLIC\NWPMW16.EXE. If you are running Windows 95 or Windows NT, execute Z:\PUBLIC\NWPMW32.EXE.

▶ *Installed Printers* — Next, cruise to the Printer Manager's pull-down menu and select New. The Novell Printers dialog appears, displaying a list of installed printers (if any printers were previously installed on the workstation). Click Add.

▶ *Available Printers* — Once you click Add, a list of available printers appears (see Figure 7.30). You may browse for additional printers in other containers of the Directory tree. The list of available printers shows the NDPS Public Access printers on the network and the NDPS Controlled Access printers in your current NDS context. To see Controlled Access printers in different NDS contexts to which you have rights, click the Browse button and select a different context.

▶ *Select the Printer* — Once you find the printer you want, select it and click Install. The Novell Printers Install dialog appears. You may modify the printer name that appears and select a predefined configuration. Click OK. The default driver for that printer is then automatically downloaded.

F I G U R E 7.30

Manual NDPS
workstation installation

▶ *You're Done* — Finally, the Novell Printers dialog appears with the new printer appearing in the installed list. Click Close. The printer appears in the main Printer Manager window and is available for print jobs. Yeah!

Congratulations! You've passed the first test. You successfully built a NetWare 5 NDPS Printing system. Life is good.

So, everything's working fine and your users are happily printing along . . .

. . . *then zowie* — *the printer breaks!*

Oops, now what?

REAL WORLD

When an NDPS printer is installed on a Windows 3.1x workstation, the descriptive NDPS name for the printer appears in the main Novell Printer Manager window, but does not appear in the native Windows Print Manager window. Instead, the Windows Print Manager identifies the printer with driver and port information, rather than by its NDPS name. This may cause some confusion for Windows 3.1x users.

Now comes the fun part — keeping it running. This is the real mystery of life. Printing Management is your life. More than any other network resource, printing services requires constant attention. You'll need to learn how to manage Brokers, Managers, Printer Agents, and Printers. Fortunately, NetWare 5 provides a variety of powerful tools for just this type of emergency.

Check it out.

LAB EXERCISE 7.2: SETTING UP NDPS PRINTING IN THE CRIME FIGHTING DIVISION OF ACME

Welcome back to ACME! In this final ACME exercise, we will build an NDPS printing system for the Crime Fighting division of ACME. Specifically, we will create three NDPS printing components on the CRIME-SRV1 server in the CRIME.TOKYO.ACME Organizational Unit.

First, we will activate server-based NDPS printing with the creation of an NDPS Broker. Fortunately, this step occurs automatically during NetWare 5 server installation (see Exercise 2-3 in Chapter 2). Second, we will create an NDPS Manager to support multiple Printer Agents. And third, we will create a Public Access Printer and convert it to a Controlled Access Printer object using NetWare Administrator.

Here's a quick preview:

▶ *Step 1:* Verify NDPS Broker activation.

▶ *Step 2:* Create and Load an NDPS Manager.

▶ *Step 3:* Create an NDPS Printer Agent and Public Access printer.

▶ *Step 4:* Configure the workstations in the CRIME container to use the CrimePA1 Public Access printer.

▶ *Step 5:* Test the CrimePA1 printer configuration on your workstation.

▶ *Step 6:* Convert the Public Access printer to a Controlled Access Printer object.

▶ *Step 7:* Configure Admin's workstation to use the CrimeP1 Controlled Access printer.

▶ *Step 8:* Test the CrimeP1 printer configuration on Admin's workstation.

▶ *Step 9:* Configure the new Controlled Access Printer object.

Those are all the detailed steps of NDPS setup and configuration. In order to accomplish this ACME exercise, you need the following network hardware:

▸ A NetWare 5 server

▸ A workstation running either the NetWare 5 Client for Windows 95 or NetWare 5 Client for Windows NT

▸ A Printer physically attached to your server (not your workstation). Also, you'll need to determine the following information for your printer: Printer Type, Gateway Type, and Printer Driver.

In this exercise, you will need the *NetWare 5 Client* CD-ROM if you don't have the NetWare 5 NDPS client software installed on your workstation. (**Note:** You cannot use the Novell client found on the Z.E.N.works 1.0 CD-ROM for this exercise.):

Let's get started.

TIP
The Z.E.N.works 1.0 product was written to work with NetWare 4.11. Therefore, it does not support NDPS. If you still have Z.E.N.works on your server and/or workstation, follow the steps in Exercise 6-5 to remove it.

1. Verify NDPS Broker activation.

   a. Make sure your printer is powered on. If not:

     • Do a normal shutdown/poweroff of your NetWare 5 server.

     • Ensure that the printer has paper.

     • Turn the printer on and ensure that it's online.

     • Power on your server. Wait until the NetWare 5 operating system is finished loading on your server.

   b. You'll need to verify that an NDPS Broker was created and activated when you built the CRIME-SRV1 server in Exercise 8.1 (see Chapter 8). On your CRIME-SRV1 server console, press Alt+Esc until the NDPS Broker screen appears.

   c. Verify that the following three services are running:

     • Service Registry Service (SRS)

- Event Notification Service (ENS)

- Resource Management Service (RMS)

d. If the NDPS Broker is not running, use Alt+Esc to find the server console prompt. Once there, type the following and press Enter:

LOAD BROKER.NLM

2. Create and Load an NDPS Manager.

a. On your workstation, log into the tree as Admin, if you haven't already done so.

b. Launch the NetWare Administrator utility.

c. Right-click the CRIME container, then choose Create from the pop-up menu that appears.

d. When the New Object dialog box appears, scroll down and select NDPS Manager, then click OK.

TIP

If NDPS Manager is not listed as an option, it probably means that the NDPS client function is not installed on your workstation. If so, you'll need to do a custom re-install of the NetWare 5 client using the *NetWare 5 Client* CD-ROM. (Do not install the Novell client that is included on the *Z.E.N.works 1.0* CD-ROM.) During the installation, don't forget to configure both the IP and IPX protocols. Also, ensure that you mark the Novell Distributed Print Services checkbox on the "Novell Client for Windows 95/98 Custom Options" screen.

e. When the Create NDPS Manager Object dialog box appears:

- Enter the following in the NDPS Manager Name field:

NDPSMGR1

- Click the Browse button to the right of the Resident Server field. Select CRIME-SRV1 and click OK.

- Click the Browse button to the right of the Database Volume field. Click CRIME-SRV1_SYS.CRIME.TOKYO.ACME and click OK.

- Click Create to create the NDPS Manager object.

f. Once the NDPSMGR1object has been created, you must activate it at the server. I recommend that you add the LOAD statement to the server's AUTOEXEC.NCF file so that it will automatically load each time the server is booted. Here's how it works:

- At the server console, press Alt+Esc until you get to a console prompt.

- At the console prompt, type the following and press Enter:

  ```
  EDIT AUTOEXEC.NCF
  ```

- Insert the following command at the bottom of the file:

  ```
  LOAD NDPSM.NLM .NDPSMGR1.CRIME.TOKYO.ACME
  ```

- Press Esc to save the file.

- Select Yes and press Enter when asked if you want to save SYS:SYSTEM\AUTOEXEC.NCF.

- Press Esc to exit the screen that gives you the opportunity to edit another file.

- Select Yes and press Enter when asked whether to exit the EDIT utility.

g. Next, you'll need to load the NDPS Manager manually on the server (so that you don't have to reboot the server to execute the command you just added to the AUTOEXEC.NCF file). To do so, type the following at the server console prompt and press Enter:

```
LOAD NDPSM.NLM .NDPSMGR1.CRIME.TOKYO.ACME
```

The server responds with a blank Printer Agent List screen. Now it's time to fill it in.

3. Create an NDPS Printer Agent and Public Access printer.

a. Return to your workstation. In NetWare Administrator, double-click the NDPSMGR1 object you just created.

b. The Identification page for the NDPS Manager object appears by default:

- Verify that the Version field has a version number in it.

- Confirm that the Net Address field lists the network address for your server.

- Verify that the Status section indicates that the NDPS Manager is active.

- Click the Printer Agent List tab.

c. When the Printer Agent List page appears, click New.

d. When the Create Printer Agent dialog box appears:

- Type the following in the Printer Agent (PA) Name field:

  `CrimePA1`

- Ensure that the NDPS Manager you created earlier is listed in the NDPS Manager Name field.

- Select the appropriate gateway in the Gateway Type field. (In most cases, you should select the Novell Printer Gateway, even if your printer manufacturer is listed. For more details, refer to the documentation that comes with NetWare 5.)

- Click OK.

e. When the Configure Novell PDS for Printer Agent "CrimePA1" dialog box appears:

- In the Printer Type list box, select the appropriate printer driver for your printer.

- In the Port Handler Type field, ensure that Novell Port Handler is selected.

- Click OK.

f. When the first Configure Port Handler for Printer Agent "CrimePA1" dialog box appears:

- In the Connection Type section, mark the Local (Physical Connection to Server) radio button.

- In the Port Type section, ensure that the LPT1 radio box is marked (assuming that your printer is attached to the LPT1: port on your server).

- Click Next.

g. When the second Configure Port Handler for Printer Agent "CrimePA1" dialog box appears, do the following:

- In the Controller Type field, make sure Auto Select is listed.

- In the Interrupts section, verify that the None (Polled Mode) radio button is marked.

- Click Finish.

h. Wait for the Printer Agent to load.

i. When the Select Printer Drivers dialog box appears:

- Click the tab corresponding to your workstation platform.

- Select the appropriate printer driver for your printer.

- Click Continue.

j. When the Information dialog box appears:

- Review the print drivers to be installed.

- Click OK.

k. When the Printer Agent List page re-appears:

- Verify that the status of the CrimePA1 printer agent is listed as Idle.

- Click Cancel.

4. Configure the workstations in the CRIME container to use the CrimePA1 Public Access printer.

a. Click Tools in the menu bar to display the Tools menu, then select NDPS Remote Printer Management.

b. When the NDPS Remote Printer Management dialog box appears:

- Mark the "Show the Results Window on Windows Workstations" checkbox.

- Click the Add button under the "Printers to Install to Workstations" field.

c. When the Available Printers Options dialog box appears:

- Click CrimePA1.

- Click OK.

d. When the NDPS Remote Printer Management dialog box re-appears, click OK to save your changes.

5. Test the CrimePA1 printer configuration on your workstation.

a. Log back into the tree as Admin:

- Click Start in the Windows taskbar.

- Click Shutdown.

- When the Shut Down Windows dialog box appears, ensure that the "Close All Programs and Log on as a Different User" radio button is marked, then click Yes.

- Log into the tree as the Admin user.

- Wait while NDPS modifies your printer setup. Eventually, the NDPS Remote Printer Management dialog box will display a message advising you that Printer CrimePA1 is installed. Click Close to acknowledge the message.

b. Launch NetWare Administrator.

c. Click Object in the menu bar to display the Object menu, then click Print Setup.

d. When the Print Setup dialog box appears:

- In the Printer section, open the pull-down box in the Name field and select CrimePA1.

- Click OK.

e. Click the Printer icon in the toolbar.

f. When the Print dialog box appears:

- Verify that CrimePA1 is listed in the Printer field.

- Click OK.

g. A printout of your NDS tree should appear on your printer. If this happens, congratulations — you are now the proud owner of a new Public Access Printer.

6. Convert the Public Access Printer to a Controlled Access Printer object.

a. Click Tools in the menu bar to display the Tools menu, then select NDPS Remote Printer Management.

b. When the NDPS Remote Printer Management dialog box appears, click the Add button under the Printers to Remove From Workstations field.

c. When the Available Printers Options dialog box appears:

- Click CrimePA1

- Click OK.

d. When the NDPS Remote Printer Management dialog box re-appears:

- You'll notice that CrimePA1 has disappeared from the Printers to Install to Workstations field and has appeared in the Printers to Remove from Workstations field.

- Click OK to save your changes.

e. Next, we will convert the Public Access Printer into a more secure Controlled Access device. This is accomplished at your client workstation. In NetWare Administrator, right-click the CRIME.TOKYO .ACME container and select Create from the pop-up menu that appears.

f. When the New Object dialog box appears, double-click NDPS Printer.

g. When the Create NDPS Printer dialog box appears:

- Type CrimeP1 in the NDPS Printer Name field.

- In the Printer Agent Source section, click the Public Access Printer radio button.

- Click Create.

h. A Warning dialog box appears, advising you that converting a Public Access Printer to an NDPS Printer object will require every client installation of this printer to be re-installed. Click OK to acknowledge the warning.

i. When the Select Printer Agent dialog box appears, ensure that CrimePA1 is selected, and then click OK.

j. Wait while NDPS creates the NDPS Printer object.

k. The new Controlled Access Printer object will magically appear in ACME's NDS tree. Yeah!!!

7. Configure your workstation to use the CrimeP1 Controlled Access printer.

a. Click Tools in the menubar to display the Tools menu, then select NDPS Remote Printer Management.

b. When the NDPS Remote Printer Management dialog box appears, click the Add button under the Printers to Install to Workstations field.

c. When the Available Printers Options dialog box appears:

- Click CrimeP1.CRIME.TOKYO.ACME

- Click OK.

d. When the NDPS Remote Printer Management dialog box re-appears:

- CrimeP1.CRIME.TOKYO.ACME should be listed in the Printers to Install on Workstations field.

- CrimePA1 should be listed in the Printers to Remove From Workstations field. (You configured this field in an earlier step.)

- Click OK to save your changes.

8. Test the CrimeP1 printer configuration on your workstation.

   a. Log back into the tree as Admin:

- Click Start in the Windows taskbar.

- Click Shutdown.

- When the Shut Down Windows dialog box appears, ensure that the "Close All Programs and Log on as a Different User" radio button is marked, then click Yes.

- Log into the tree as the Admin user.

- Wait while NDPS modifies your printer setup. Eventually, the NDPS Remote Printer Management dialog box will display a message advising you that Printer CrimeP1.CRIME.TOKYO.ACME is installed and CrimePA1 is removed. Click Close to acknowledge the message.

   b. Launch NetWare Administrator.

   c. Click Object in the menu bar to display the Object menu, then click Print Setup.

   d. When the Print Setup dialog box appears:

- In the Printer section, open the pull-down box in the Name field and select CrimeP1.CRIME.TOKYO.ACME.

- Click OK.

   e. Click the Printer icon in the toolbar.

   f. When the Print dialog box appears:

- Verify that CrimeP1.CRIME.TOKYO.ACME is listed in the Printer field.

- Click OK.

   g. A printout of your NDS tree should appear on your printer. If this happens, you're almost finished.

9. Configure the new Controlled Access Printer object.

a. Finally, you should configure the new CrimeP1 object with additional security restrictions and pop-up notification. First, double-click the CrimeP1 NDPS Printer object in NetWare Administrator.

b. When the "NDPS Printer: CrimeP1" dialog box appears, click the Access Control tab.

c. When the Access Control page appears:

- By default, Admin is assigned as a Manager, Operator, and Print User. Also, the printer's home container (CRIME.TOKYO.ACME) is designated as a Printer User. This means that everyone in the CRIME container can use the new printer. Let's restrict access to the Admin user.

- In the Role field, click Users.

- In the Current Users field, click CRIME.TOKYO.ACME.

- Click Delete.

d. In case something goes wrong with the new Controlled Access printer, you may want to notify the CrimeP1 Manager with a pop-up notification message. To activate this NetWare 5 feature:

- Click Managers in the Role field.

- Click Admin.CRIME.TOKYO.ACME in the Current Managers field.

- Click Notification.

- If your printer driver allows you to (some may not), set up notification parameters.

e. Click OK to save your changes.

Congratulations! You are printing! You've passed the final ACME test by building an NDPS printing system. Life is good!

Now, let's continue with NDPS Printing by exploring Printing Management. This is the tough part — keeping it running. More than any other network resource, printing services require constant attention. Ready, set, manage!

NDPS Printing Management

NetWare 5 NDPS Printing Setup was a breeze. And now the system is working flawlessly. You've tested a few documents, and they printed fine. You're probably getting a little overconfident right about now. Be careful, it happens to the best of us.

Now for the real test — letting the users loose on your new, clean, "working" printing system. You know it can print in a vacuum, but what about in a war zone?

Welcome to NDPS Printing Management. In this final section, we will explore a number of key management responsibilities and learn about three key printing management tools:

- NDPS Object Management with NetWare Administrator

- NDPS Server Management with NDPSM.NLM

- NDPS User Management with the Novell Printer Manager

Most basic NDPS CNA management tasks can be performed from the NDS object point of view — using NetWare Administrator. This tool allows you to configure a multitude of NDPS Printer properties, including priority, notification, banners, and medium. NetWare Administrator also includes a Remote Printer Management (RPM) feature that allows you to add or remove workstation printers from a central GUI database.

In addition, the NDPS Manager (NDPSM.NLM) offers a variety of printing management functions through a server-based menu interface. Some of the functions you can perform at the NDPS server include status display, printer control, port tracking, printer configuration details, scheduling, and form management.

Finally, the Novell Printer Manager allows workstation users to manage all their NDPS printing tasks through an easy-to-use graphical interface. These tasks include printer installation, customized printer configuration, and print job management.

Now let's explore these three key NDPS printing management tools from your point of view — as the NetWare 5 CNA.

NDPS Object Management with NetWare Administrator

Windows-based printer management is one of the easiest ways to track print jobs and control printer objects remotely. NetWare Administrator is your friend. As you can see in Figure 7.31, this GUI tool presents NDPS Printers as leaf objects in the NDS tree. Simply double-click the printer icon and you'll open a whole new world of NDPS management:

- ▸ *Printer Control* — from the Details page

- ▸ *Print Job Configuration* — from the Job Status window

- ▸ *Remote Printer Management* — from the Tools or Details page

Let's take a closer look.

FIGURE 7.31

NDPS Printer objects in NetWare Administrator

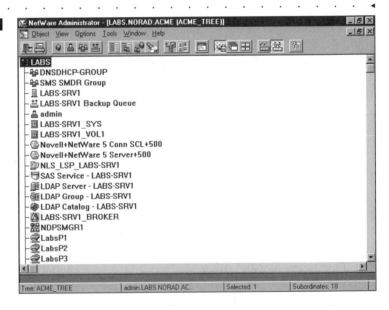

Printer Control

NetWare Administrator allows you to manage most NDPS Printer functions as properties of an NDS object. Simply double-click the Printer icon in Figure 7.31 and the Details page appears. Check out Figure 7.32.

F I G U R E   7.32

Details page of an NDPS Printer object in NetWare Administrator

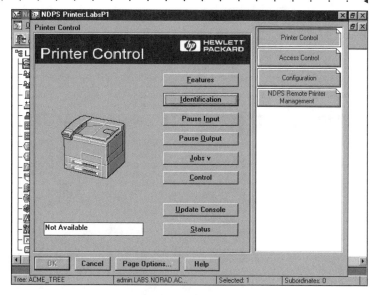

The NDPS Details page provides numerous printing control options to CNAs. Here's a quick summary:

- *Features* — Displays the services and attributes associated with this printer.

- *Jobs* — Allows you to modify the job list and spooling configuration of this printer.

- *Pause Output* — Pauses (or resumes) the printing of jobs from this printer. While the printer is "paused," users can still send jobs to it. They will simply be placed in the spool.

- *Pause Input* — This option is the inverse of Pause Output. In this case, CNAs can pause (or resume) the input of jobs to a printer's spool. While the printer is "paused," jobs will still be printed from the spool, but users can't send any new jobs to the printer.

- *Identification* — Allows you to modify the Identification properties of this printer. This information is used by users for NDS printer searching.

▸ *Control* — This is the main NDPS printer control button (see Figure 7.33). In this page, you can reset the printer, manage form feeding, mount different media, view statistics, and configure printer defaults. Very cool.

▸ *Status* — Displays the status of this printer.

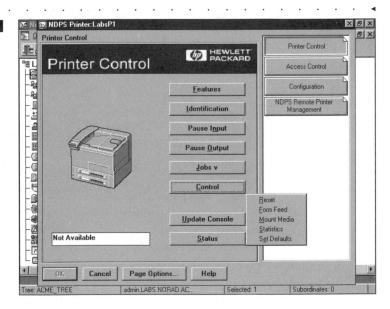

F I G U R E   7.33

NDPS Printer Control in NetWare Administrator

Print Job Configuration

NetWare Administrator also allows you to configure the way NDPS print jobs appear at the printer. Access to these print job configurations is reserved for NDPS Managers and Operators. NDPS Users can only modify the properties of their own jobs.

The NDPS Print Job Configuration window (shown in Figure 7.34) is available through the Configuration tab of a printer's Details page in NetWare Administrator. This window supports a variety of configurations, including:

▸ *Copies* — The number of copies that will be printed for this configuration. The default value is 1.

▸ *Max Copies* — The maximum number of copies that a user can print using this printer. The default value is 255.

▶ *Priority* — The priority assigned to jobs using this configuration. The default value is Medium.

▶ *Max Priority* — The maximum priority (Low, Medium, High) set by the administrator for jobs using this printer. This setting determines when the job will print in relation to other jobs with different priorities sent to this printer. The default value is Medium.

▶ *Banner* — A list of banner pages users can select from. Banner pages will be printed at the beginning of print jobs using this configuration. (If multiple copies of a document are printed, the banner page will only be printed at the beginning of the first copy). The default value is None.

▶ *Medium* — The medium (form) on which jobs can be printed without stopping the printer to mount a different medium (form). The default on the printer is Any Medium, which allows jobs to be printed using the currently mounted medium, regardless of media specified in the job data. If a medium is specified for this configuration, and a different medium (anything other than Any Medium) is mounted on the printer, this condition will cause the printer to pause for the given amount of time (default is 15 minutes) or until the new media is mounted. If this Job Wait Time expires, the job is placed on hold and returned to the spooling area.

TIP

Media are mounted by the NDPS Manager or Operator using the Printer Control/Control pull-down menu of NetWare Administrator.

▶ *Job Hold* — A variety of configurations that control how and when the job is printed. Here's a quick list of your options: Operator Hold (jobs do not print until the operator releases them), User Hold (jobs do not print until the user who submitted the job releases it), Delay Printing Until (jobs do not begin printing until the time and date specified), Pause Printer on Job Start (forces the printer to pause at the beginning of a job's submission), Pause Printer on Job End (forces the printer to pause after printing a specific job), Retain Job No Longer Than (the maximum amount of time that the job can be retained after it's been printed), and finally, Retain Job For (the amount of time that a job should be retained).

▶ *Event Notification* — By specifying event notification for a printer
configuration, you allow job owners to receive notification of printer or
job events that occur during the processing and printing of the specific job.
Notification configured in this way is sent by pop-up message box only.

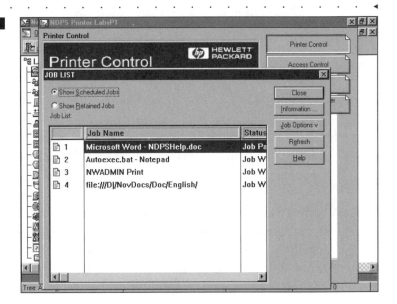

Remote Printer Management

The Remote Printer Management (RPM) feature of NDPS allows you to install
workstation printers remotely. In addition, you can use this feature to remove
printers or assign a printer to be the default printer.

RPM can be accessed in any of the following ways. Somewhat different
functionality is available at each site:

▶ *From the Tools menu of the NDS main browser in NetWare Administrator* —
By selecting the NDPS Remote Printer Management option from this
menu, you can manage printers in all containers to which you have
sufficient rights (see Figure 7.35).

▶ *From the Details page of an NDS container object* — By pressing the NDPS
Remote Printer Management button from this page, you can manage
printers for this container only.

▸ *From the Details page for a specific NDPS printer* — By pressing the NDPS Remote Printer Management button from this page, you can remotely manage a specific printer only.

▸ *From the Public Access Printer's view under the Tools menu* — By highlighting a printer and selecting the Object/Details option, you can access the Printer Control page for that printer. Then, by pressing the NDPS Remote Printer Management button from this page, you can remotely manage that specific Public Access Printer.

F I G U R E   7 . 3 5

Remote printer management in NetWare Administrator

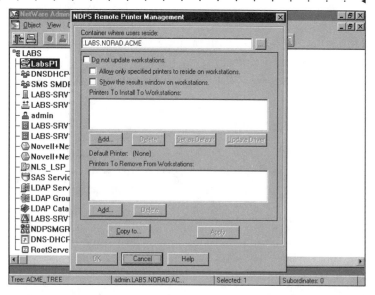

Once a printer has been designated for automatic installation, the Remote Printer configuration is stored within the object's NDS container. When a user logs in, the workstation's client software checks the user's home container for a Remote Printer Management configuration. The client then compares "time stamps" stored on the workstation and in NDS to determine whether any changes have occurred.

If the list is different, action is taken and the printer list on the client is automatically updated to match the printer list maintained by RPM in NDS. If the client finds a printer designated for installation that has not yet been installed, it is automatically installed. If a currently installed printer is added to the "Printers to Remove" list, that printer will be uninstalled automatically. If you designate a different printer to be the default in the RPM list, the change will be automatically made on each client when it logs in. If the "Do not update workstations" control is checked, you can update the Remote Printer Management configuration, but no changes will occur on the workstation.

That completes our brief romp through the GUI world of NDSP object management with NetWare Administrator. Now, let's cruise over to the NDPS server . . . it's a happening place!

NDPS Server Management with NDPSM.NLM

As we learned in Chapter 3, "NetWare 5 Java Console," the NetWare 5 server is a whole new frontier for CNA management. Fortunately, NDPS follows this theme in offering a variety of printing management tasks from NDPSM.NLM — the NDPS Manager console.

To access the NDPS Manager console, begin with the following server command:

```
LOAD NDPSM.NLM
```

A C-worthy text screen appears with the contents of the current NDPS context. Browse to the NDPS Manager object that you want and press Enter. At this point, the NDPS Manager you selected is immediately authenticated to Directory Services and the Printer Agent List is displayed. To manage a specific Printer Agent, choose that Printer Agent from the list and check out the status screen in Figure 7.36.

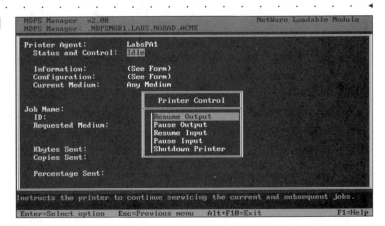

FIGURE 7.36

Printer Agent Status screen in NDPSM.NLM

As you can see, NDPSM offers some interesting management options:

▸ Status and Control Options

▸ Information Options

▸ Configuration Options

▸ Current Medium Options

Let's check them out.

Status and Control Options

The Status and Control field in Figure 7.36 enables you to control the operation of the printer. You can perform the following actions:

▸ *Pause Output/Resume Output* — Pausing output causes the printer to stop processing jobs, but allows new jobs to be submitted and held in the spooling area until output is resumed.

▸ *Pause Input/Resume Input* — Pausing input stops jobs from being submitted to the spooling area, but existing jobs will continue to print.

▸ *Shut Down Printer/Start Printer* — Shutting down the printer pauses output and input, and unloads the gateway. Currently, printing jobs are not completed. They are returned to the spooling area until the printer is started up again.

Hopefully, these functions look familiar. They are the same ones that we configured in the previous section using the NDPS Details page in NetWare Administrator. It's nice to have choices.

Information Options

The Information field provides additional data about the current Printer Agent. Selecting this field opens the Printer Information screen. The fields on the Printer Information screen provide such information as number of Active and Scheduled jobs, Notification and Resource Agents, Port Handler and Print Device System status, Printer Manufacturer and Model, and all the Directory Services Printer Objects associated with this Printer Agent. You can also see what print queues are being serviced from the NDS Printer Objects view. Cool.

Configuration Options

The Configuration field provides information about job scheduling, storage locations, and space requirements. Selecting the Configuration field displays a Printer Configuration screen, as shown in Figure 7.37.

FIGURE 7.37

Printer Configuration screen in NDPSM.NLM

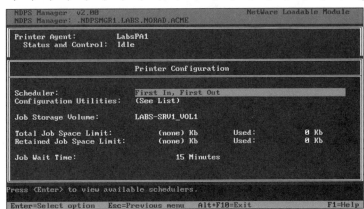

The Printer Configuration screen contains the following fields:

- ▶ *Scheduler* — Determines the order in which print jobs are serviced. Valid scheduling options are as follows: "First in, first out," "Media changes minimized," and "Print smallest job first." Third parties can add additional scheduler options for more fun.

- ▶ *Configuration Utilities* — Configures NDPS Printers and Port Handlers. Use this option if you want to change Port Handler options for this Printer Agent.

- ▶ *Job Storage* Volume — Displays the server volume that stores waiting print jobs. Press Enter in this field to display the volume name, total space in kilobytes, and total free space in kilobytes. If more than one volume exists on the server, you may change volumes here.

▶ *Total Job Space Limit*—Controls the maximum amount of space allocated to store jobs waiting to be printed. A zero allows this space to grow dynamically. If you specify a limit and that limit is reached, no more print jobs are accepted until there is room.

▶ *Retained Job Space Limit*—NDPS allows print jobs to be retained after they have been printed. This option controls the maximum amount of job space that can be used for retained print jobs. A zero allows this space to grow dynamically.

▶ *Job Wait Time*—Controls the maximum length of time that the Printer Agent will pause output while attempting to resolve a condition before moving on to the next job. (The default is 15 minutes.) For example, a job that was sent that requires a media change will cause the printer to pause for the given Job Wait Time or until the new media is mounted. If time expires, the job is placed on hold and returned to the spooling area.

Current Medium Options

The Current Medium option in Figure 7.36 allows you to control the media (forms) on which jobs can be printed without stopping to mount a different medium (form). The default on an NDPS Printer is Any Medium—which allows jobs to be printed using the currently mounted medium, regardless of media specified in the job data.

If a medium is specified for this configuration, and a different medium (anything other than Any Medium) is mounted on the printer, this condition will cause the printer to pause for the given amount of time (default is 15 minutes), or until the new media is mounted. If this Job Wait Time expires, the job is placed on hold and returned to the spooling area.

Once again, this function is also available using the NDPS Details page in NetWare Administrator. It's nice to have choices.

Speaking of choices, let's jet over to the NDPS workstation and see what the users are up to. They have printing management choices, too—thanks to the Novell Printer Manager.

NDPS User Management with the Novell Printer Manager

The Novell Printer Manager allows users to manage all their NDPS printing tasks from a GUI-based workstation. Some of the things they can do include printer installation, customized printer configuration, and print job management. In addition to the Novell Printer Manager, users can use the Printers folder in Windows 95 and Windows NT to add NDPS printers and perform certain basic printer management tasks.

As you can see in Figure 7.38, Novell Printer Manager offers an easy-to-use graphical porthole for NDPS user management. In this screen, users can view real-time status and configuration information about their printers and print jobs, and receive a variety of event notifications. Feedback includes:

▶ A printer's status

▶ A printer's characteristics and properties

▶ A printer's features

▶ Printer events that require operator intervention (such as low toner, empty paper tray, or jammed feed mechanism)

▶ A print job's status

▶ A print job's characteristics and properties

F I G U R E   7.38

User printer management in the Novell Printer Manager

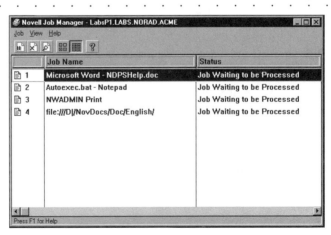

Users can also use the Novell Printer Manager to move, copy, reorder, and delete their own print jobs. Wow . . . that's a lot of power for users to handle. Be careful!

Here's a quick summary of some of the powerful things that users can do with the Novell Printer Manager:

▶ *Designate a Default Printer*—When you use the Remote Printer Management (RPM) feature to designate a printer for automatic installation on each user workstation, you can also designate that printer to be the default for users in the same context (container). This way, the user never has to install or configure that printer or designate it as the default. Instead, a configured default printer is installed automatically on each workstation when the user logs in.

▶ *Manage Access to the Novell Printer Manager*—Several options are available to help administrators manage user access to the Novell Printer Manager. This is a good idea. Depending on the particular environment you are working in, you may want to allow clients full access to the Printer Manager, or you may not want them to have any access at all. (I opt for the latter.) You can restrict access by moving the program files to a secure location or customize the Novell Application Launcher (NAL). Either way, use discretion when opening the NDPS management doors to users.

▶ *NDPS Filtering*—The Filtering feature available in the Novell Printer Manager provides a convenient method for locating NDPS printers with specific characteristics. This feature allows users to search for Controlled Access and Public Access printers within their selected context or anywhere in the tree.

▶ *Manage Installed Printers at User Workstations*—Novell Printer Manager also allows users to manage installed printers from their Windows 95, Windows NT, and Windows 3.1 workstations. Some of the tasks they can perform include customizing printing configurations, viewing printer information, changing drivers, and removing installed printers. These tasks are dangerous in the hands of inexperienced users. *Be careful!*

▶ *Printer and Job Configuration Options* — Novell Printer Manager provides CNA configuration options to users. These printer and job configurations are accomplished in exactly the same way as discussed previously — namely the Configuration tab of the Details page of NetWare Administrator and the Configuration field of NDPSM.NLM. Once again, these tasks are dangerous in the hands of mortal users!

That completes our discussion of NetWare 5 NDPS Printing Management. Printing has always been and will continue to be one of your greatest challenges as a next-generation CNA. Fortunately, the revolution is upon us. I hope you're as impressed as I am about the improved management tools NetWare 5 offers.

CONGRATULATIONS!

Mystery solved. I enjoy a good mystery, how about you? NetWare 5 Printing is a great place to start. We discovered a lot of interesting things about it today, and I think you're definitely ready to attack it on your own. If you're still feeling a little skittish, however, here's a quick review.

It all started with the Essence of Printing. In the old days, we used to print by ourselves. Now, we get to share this honor with hundreds of strangers. Network printing has probably had a major impact on the social fabric of humanity — we just don't notice it. We went on a little journey through the life of a print job — starting with the NDPS Broker and Manager, then moving to the Printer Agent, and ending at the Public or Controlled Access printer. Wasn't that fun?

Then, we learned all the steps involved in NDPS Printing Setup. It's not so bad. There are only four steps and they're not very hard. First, you install the NDPS Broker, then create an NDPS Manager, and finally, configure Printer Agents and Printers. Then, to top it all off, you must activate the NDPS workstation. No sweat.

Once it's up and running, the fun part starts — keeping it running. NDPS Printing Management focused on three CNA and user tools: NetWare Administrator, NDPSM.NLM, and Novell Printer Manager. We learned how to configure, manage, and customize the NetWare 5 printing system. I bet you didn't realize how much help there is out there! Don't worry — you're not alone.

LAB EXERCISE 7.3: THE GREAT PUZZLE

Circle the 20 NDPS-related terms hidden in this word search puzzle using the hints provided. No punctuation characters (such as blank spaces, hyphens, and so on) should be included. Numbers should always be spelled out.

```
S A S U I U S E R U R A H I H A K U N V P M
N X G Q T F N N C L I E N T S U P P O R T T
O V C R Z F S A A R E M O T E P R I N T E R
V T H E W O P G O P E R A T O R K W M T G M
E R K S Z T M I H U I A Z N H I D X B L V X
L X N T U T O I F C D N T I A K G N N S O B
L Z T R N D C U P M L O S E B G L Y B A O W
U B I D I R E C T I O N A L F E E D B A C K
P N D S I N T E G R A T I O N V B R H O P Q
G B A C K W A R D C O M P A T I B I L I T Y
R P R I N T E R D R I V E R E C P E G H W X
A R O O M C F T P Y V L J S W Q Q L P G C W
D I H R W K A W Y N M F Y X O N V C V P T Y
E N N Y T S T S E P O O F W M V P Z O P M I
W T G A G H E G U J C G O G J A V W L D O S
I Q Y R Y M A W K N E J U B L H X H J P S P
Z U G O M X T N O V E L L G A T E W A Y D W
A E U I C L C T D X L N H H X Q L L V D R D
R U R B N O V E L L P R I N T M A N A G E R
D E X T E T J O T N E G A R E T N I R P I U
W H S C B B X H D G L R P R C O U Y A Q F D
```

Hints:

1. Feature that allows NDPS clients to access queue-based printers and queue-based clients to access basic NDPS features.
2. Enhancement over unidirectional communications found in earlier versions of NetWare.

3. One of the minimum rights needed for the destination container where the NDPS Printer object will reside.

4. Legacy process for redirecting print jobs from a local workstation port to a network printer.

5. Enhanced in NetWare 5 to provide improved NDPS-related functionality for Windows 3.x, Windows 95, and Windows NT workstations.

6. Another minimum right needed for the destination container where the NDPS Printer object will reside.

7. Type of user responsible for adding and deleting users from the printer; configuring notification profiles; and creating, modifying, and deleting printer configurations.

8. NDPS feature that allows network administrators to administer all printing devices from a single location using NetWare Administrator.

9. Provides a software bridge between NDPS and legacy local and remote printers, including those using NPRINTER or queue-based technology.

10. Utility that allows users to manage all NDPS printing tasks from their workstations.

11. Utility that can be used to upgrade queue-based printers to NDPS.

12. Type of user who maintains a printer on a day-to-day basis by managing print jobs and setting configuration defaults.

13. Printing component that ensures that the PDS can communicate with a physical printer, regardless of what type of interface is used.

14. Legacy printing object required in earlier versions of NetWare.

15. Printing component that combines the functions previously performed by a printer, print queue, print server, and spooler into one intelligent, simplified entity.

16. Can be downloaded automatically after NDPS is installed.

17. Printer that is attached to a workstation, a remote file server, or the network cable.

18. Protocol that is turned off by NDPS to decrease unnecessary network traffic and increase LAN/WAN bandwidth.

19. Third-party add-ins or extensions that weren't available in earlier versions of NetWare.

20. Designation that allows someone to send, reconfigure, or remove their own print jobs.

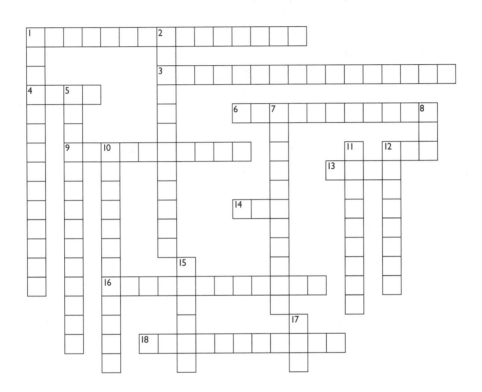

Across

1. Used for communicating with a printer
3. More secure than Public Access printers
4. New NetWare 5 printing architecture
6. Manages Printer Agents
9. Provides SRS, ENS, and RMS support services
12. Queries a printer in its native language
13. Minimum megabytes of RAM required for NDPS
14. Allows Public Access printers to advertise themselves
16. Less secure than Controlled Access printers
18. Server boot file used to load NDPSM.NLM

Down

1. Bridge between NDPS clients and legacy printers
2. Is attached directly to an NDPS server
5. Workstation utility for managing NDPS printing tasks
7. Legacy printing object
8. Central repository for printing resources
10. Relies on automatic hardware detection
11. LPT or COM port
12. Rock-solid until you add users
15. Minimum MB of available disk space required for NDPS
17. Middleman between users and printers

CHAPTER 8

Start Your Engines: NetWare 5 Installation

If you build it, they will come!

In Chapter 1, we learned all about ACME's mission — to save the world — and discovered Novell's high-stakes solution — NetWare 5 Global Electronic Village. In addition, we discovered ten features that make up the Global Electronic Village and learned how to connect them using the Information Superhighway.

While the world seems to be concentrating on the highway itself (intranetworks and the Internet), it's your job to pay attention to the electronic vehicle — NetWare 5 supercar. Your server is the vehicle of the Information Superhighway. It provides a platform for the protons and photons as they bounce along in the fast lane at the speed of light. If you're going to help ACME save the world, you need to learn how to build the NetWare 5 supercar and ensure that it remains in peak condition. As a NetWare 5 CNA, you become an Infobahn Mechanic.

With all its incredible looks and legendary power, the NetWare 5 supercar consists of four basic components:

▸ *Braking System* — This provides connectivity and reliability. Your server braking system is made of topology components that connect workstations, file servers, and other network devices.

▸ *Engine* — This provides power and movement. Your server engine is constructed of network storage devices — the fundamental shared data resources of the LAN/WAN.

▸ *Interior* — This provides comfort, functionality, and safety. Your server interior consists of numerous workstations: a dashboard for user interface.

▸ *Transmission/Tires* — This lays the rubber to the road and carries out the engine's instructions. Your server's transmission is handled by NetWare 5 NDPS printing — ultimately moving data from shared storage to a user's hands.

Welcome to *Auto Shop 101*. In this chapter, you'll learn what it takes to become a CNA Mechanic and build a NetWare 5 supercar. We're going to skip hardware assembly (that's the easy part) and jump straight into software installation. This is where you breathe life into an otherwise useless heap of silicon. NetWare 5 is the brains that navigates your Infobahn supercar.

Although the main focus of this chapter is the NetWare 5 installation process, we'll briefly explore three different ways of building the NetWare 5 supercar:

▶ *Installation* — You can use the NetWare 5 Installation program to create a fresh new Novell server from scratch. NetWare 5 supports both IPX and IP protocols, and automatically detects a variety of hardware devices including hard disk drives and network boards. During the latter stages of the installation process, you will use a Java-based GUI interface — the NetWare 5 Installation Wizard.

▶ *Upgrade* — You can also install NetWare 5 on an existing NetWare 3.1*x*, NetWare 4.*x*, intraNetWare, or intraNetWare for Small Business server without losing any existing data files. This type of upgrade is called an *in-place upgrade*. To begin the upgrade process, simply execute INSTALL.BAT at the server console and choose "Upgrade from NetWare 3.1x or 4.1x" instead of "New Server" on the "Welcome to the NetWare Server Installation" screen.

▶ *Migration* — NetWare 5 also includes an elaborate migration utility, ironically called the *Novell Upgrade Wizard* (see Figure 8.1). This GUI migration tool allows you to upgrade the bindery and data from a NetWare 3 server across the wire to an existing NetWare 5 server. The Wizard migrates NetWare 3 printers and queues, pinpoints potential conflicts or errors that may occur, and provides options for resolving problems before the migration begins. This is all accomplished using a simple drag-and-drop modeling interface. Your life as a NetWare 5 Mechanic just got a whole lot easier.

REAL WORLD

If you would like to migrate a NetWare 2 server to NetWare 5, you'll need to upgrade it to NetWare 3 first. This is accomplished using older NetWare 3 utilities, or the REXXWARE Migration Toolkit.

FIGURE 8.1

Novell Upgrade Wizard

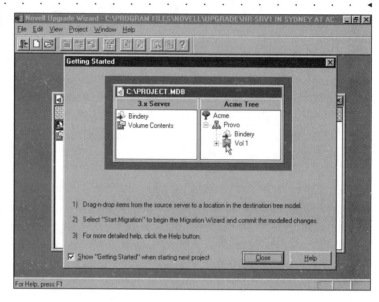

So, which NetWare 5 installation option is for you? Your choice depends on a number of factors—such as the operating system you're currently running, the hardware you have, and which NetWare 5 features you plan to use (such as block size, block suballocation, file compression, and so on). The *Installation* process, for example, assumes that you're starting with a "neoteric" server—no users, no files, no communications.

The *Upgrade* and *Migration* methods, on the other hand, jump in midstream. Using these options, you will upgrade or migrate an existing server from NetWare 3 or NetWare 4—all the way to NetWare 5. Keep in mind that the NetWare 5 Upgrade and Migration processes are not "upgrades" in the traditional sense. From coach to first class is an upgrade; Windows 98 is an upgrade; better carpeting is an upgrade. NetWare 5 is a "New Frontier."

Here's a few scenarios that might help you determine which installation option is best for you:

▸ If you want to start from scratch and use predetermined defaults for most parameters, use the *Installation* method to perform a Basic installation.

▸ If you want to start from scratch but supply customized information for some or all configurable parameters, use the *Installation* method to perform a Basic installation, then select "Customize" at the end of the process to configure the desired parameters.

▸ If you have an existing Novell server and want to upgrade to NetWare 5 using the same hardware, you should perform an *in-place upgrade* via NetWare 5's Installation program Upgrade choice.

▸ If you are running NetWare 3.1*x* on a server, but would like to convert the file system and bindery to a new NetWare 5 server, use the Novell Upgrade Wizard to perform an *across-the-wire migration*. This method is particularly useful if you need to upgrade your server to newer, more powerful hardware, and/or you want to consolidate multiple servers to one machine.

Now it's time to pull out our cyber-wrenches and begin building the NetWare 5 supercar. The NetWare 5 Installation process is dominated by SERVER.EXE, Java-based screens, and TCP/IP. It can be a little intimidating at first, especially if you've never installed NetWare before. But have no fear, Mechanic David is here.

In this chapter, we will traverse the various steps of the NetWare 5 Installation process together—all 14 of them. We'll learn about disk partitions, regional settings, network protocols, Novell Licensing Services (NLS), and Novell Directory Service (NDS) context. Finally, we'll walk through the server and client installation lab exercises near the end of the chapter.

Before we explore the detailed steps of the NetWare 5 Installation process, let's take a quick look at the advantages and disadvantages of the NetWare 5 Installation method (which is covered in this course) and the NetWare 5 Upgrade and Migration methods (which are beyond the scope of this course). Study this material carefully. The choice you make today can irrevocably alter the path of your destiny—*or not!*

Advantages and Disadvantages of Each Installation Method

Don't jump the gun. I know you're excited about diving into the ACME Upgrade, but hold on for a second. We need to make a rational decision about which installation option is best for you. After all, it's only first period and we have all day to get through *Auto Shop 101*.

As mentioned previously, there are three different NetWare 5 installation options:

- ▶ *Installation* — Start from scratch and create a new NetWare 5 server using Basic or Custom configurations.

- ▶ *Upgrade* — Upgrade an existing Novell server to NetWare 5 using the In-Place Upgrade option.

- ▶ *Migration* — Migrate bindery and file information from an existing Novell server to a destination NetWare 5 server using the Novell Upgrade Wizard.

Let's take a closer look at the advantages and disadvantages of each of these three options. Choose *carefully*!

NetWare 5 Installation

If you're starting from scratch, the NetWare 5 *Installation* option (INSTALL.BAT) is best for you — assuming that you have sufficient hardware and the know-how to pull it off. During the Basic installation, you'll rely on the Installation Wizard to make most of the tough decisions. At the end of the Basic installation, you're given a chance to customize your server settings. This may be too much control for you — don't let it go to your head.

Advantages

The NetWare Installation method requires only one computer — the server. Following is a list of key advantages associated with the NetWare 5 Installation method:

▶ You can design your NDS database and file system structure from scratch, for maximum efficiency.

▶ If you want, you can retain your existing NetWare 3 or NetWare 4 server while setting up and testing the new NetWare 5 server.

Disadvantages

Unfortunately, the NetWare 5 Installation method is not all "sugar and cream." It does have disadvantages, including:

▶ It's more time-consuming than other methods, because you must create all network objects, security, and configurations from scratch.

▶ It requires additional hardware if you're upgrading from an existing server — namely, the new server. This allows you to retain your old server while installing NetWare 5.

It's always a good idea to set up a pilot system whenever you migrate to a new frontier. For this reason, you may consider starting out with a few installations that are done from scratch. Then, when you have it all figured out, you can upgrade or migrate the remainder of your production servers using the NetWare 5 Upgrade or Migration methods. Let's take a look.

NetWare 5 Upgrade

The NetWare 5 Upgrade method can be used to upgrade an existing server running any of the following NetWare versions:

▶ NetWare 3.1x or NetWare 3.2

▶ NetWare 4.x

▶ intraNetWare

▶ intraNetWare for Small Business

This method, like the NetWare 5 Installation method, uses INSTALL.BAT. With this method, however, you choose "Upgrade from NetWare 3.1x or 4.1x" instead of "New Server" on the "Welcome to the NetWare Server Installation"

The beauty of this type of upgrade is that it's *in place*. This means that you only need one computer — the server.

Advantages

The NetWare 5 Upgrade method has a number of advantages, including:

▸ You can use your existing hardware if it meets the minimum requirements for NetWare 5.

▸ It's probably the most convenient method of upgrading your network to today's standards.

▸ It allows you to use block suballocation and disk compression on server volumes.

Disadvantages

Unfortunately, the Upgrade advantages don't outweigh the single most harmful disadvantage — no "escape pod." Check it out:

▸ There is a small risk of data loss. For example, if a power outage occurs during the upgrade, and both your backups are defective, you might lose data (that is, no "escape pod").

▸ This option cannot be used to upgrade NetWare 2 servers and non-NetWare servers to NetWare 5. (You would first need to upgrade such servers to NetWare 3 or NetWare 4.)

NetWare 5 Migration

You can use the Novell Upgrade Wizard to migrate a NetWare 3.x server to NetWare 5. This method is considered a *migration* rather than an upgrade, because information is copied across the network during the process. Using this method, you can move your NetWare 3.*x* bindery, passwords, security rights, and data "across the wire" to a location in an existing NetWare 5 NDS tree.

You'll need three computers for the Across-the-Wire migration method:

▸ Source (existing) server

▸ Destination (NetWare 5) server

▸ Workstation running an appropriate version of the Windows 95/98 or Windows NT client

Advantages

The NetWare 5 Migration option has so many advantages, I just don't know where to start. How about at the beginning:

▸ The Novell Upgrade Wizard provides graphical modeling capabilities that allow you to organize the new server structure off-line prior to the migration. Using this feature, you can drag network objects and file volumes from the NetWare 3 server to the new NDS tree.

▸ This is the safest method, because the source server remains intact. This could prove to be especially useful if a power outage or connection loss occurs during the migration (finally, an "escape pod"). This is probably the single most important advantage in the entire Upgrade/Migration process.

▸ You are given the option of determining whether to migrate all or selected information — volumes only.

▸ Multiple servers can be migrated to a single destination server. This enables you to consolidate the data from older servers to newer, more powerful computers. Great idea!

▸ The Novell Upgrade Wizard pinpoints potential conflicts or other problems between the NetWare 3 server and the NDS tree (such as NDS security, object name conflicts, and disk space limitations) and provides you with various options for resolving such problems.

Disadvantages

The NetWare 5 Migration is so great, it's difficult to find any faults at all. However, in the interest of fair play, here are a few:

▶ More hardware is needed for this method than with other methods.

▶ The Novell Upgrade Wizard cannot be used to migrate a NetWare 4 server to NetWare 5.

Well, there you have it—the advantages and disadvantages of NetWare 5's three installation options: Installation, Upgrade, and Migration. Remember, we're not talking simple upgrade here—this is serious business. We're building a NetWare 5 supercar.

In this chapter, we're going to explore the detailed steps of the NetWare 5 Installation process. Before we do, however, we must take a quick look at some important installation setup tasks—namely pre-installation checklists, hardware requirements, protocols, and additional products.

It's time to begin . . . .

▶ · ◀

Before You Begin

NetWare 5 construction can be very tricky and requires careful planning to avoid gremlins. In order to make this process as painless as possible, you'll need to satisfy a variety of pre-installation requirements before you begin. Here's a quick preview:

▶ *Pre-installation Checklist* — First, you'll need to perform a variety of tasks before you start the NetWare 5 Installation process. For instance, you'll need to create the appropriate "computer room" environment for your equipment, verify that your computers meet the minimum NetWare 5 hardware requirements, and make sure that you have the appropriate software available. In addition, you'll need to ensure that you have a plethora of supercar-related information handy prior to installation — including a detailed NDS design, the Admin username and password, and much more.

▶ *Understanding the NetWare 5 Server* — The server's main purpose is to handle requests from network clients such as workstations and printers. Its main components are the kernel (which provides core services), the system console (which allows you to perform a variety of tasks), and NetWare Loadable Modules (which are software programs that can be loaded and unloaded while the server is running).

▶ *Choosing a Protocol* — Before you attack the NetWare 5 server, you must determine which communications protocol(s) you want to use. Your choices include Pure *Internet Protocol* (IP) and/or *Internet Packet Exchange* (IPX).

▶ *Additional Products and Services* — Finally, you'll want to determine which additional NetWare 5 products and services you want to install *before* you get started. Some of these products are bundled with NetWare 5, while others are available at an additional cost. Some of the more popular NetWare 5 enhancements include Novell Distributed Print Services (NDPS), NDS Catalog Services, Secure Authorization Services, and Z.E.N.works.

Now, let's prepare ourselves for the onslaught of NetWare 5 supercar construction. *Grease-covered jumpsuit required.*

Pre-Installation Checklist

Before you attack the NetWare 5 server, you must prepare, prepare, prepare. In this section, we will explore three different Pre-installation checklists:

▶ *Hardware* — First, you must create a clean "computer room" environment for your new electronic supercar. This includes a secure environment and clean power.

▶ *Software* — Next, you'll need to make sure that you have the appropriate CD-ROMs, diskettes, and documentation necessary for any software you plan to install including DOS, NetWare 5, and applications.

▶ *Planning* — Finally, you will have to endure an infinite (not quite) list of pre-installation planning tasks before attempting supercar surgery. In this section, we'll discuss numerous planning tips — everything from startup directory name to mouse type. Knock yourself out.

So, without any further ado, let's get prepared.

Hardware Pre-Installation Checklist

Following is your hardware pre-installation checklist:

▶ Determine whether your "computer room" meets recommended power and operating environment requirements. Consult your hardware documentation to determine applicable temperature, humidity, heat-dissipation, and power requirements. You'll also want to make sure that you provide appropriate uninterruptible power supply (UPS) protection for your servers (as well as critical network workstations and other peripherals).

▶ Verify that the server meets the minimum hardware requirements for NetWare 5. (See the section titled "Minimum Hardware Requirements" later in this chapter.)

▶ Install any required hardware (such as network interface cards, hubs, cabling, uninterruptible power supplies, and so on).

TIP

For access to a detailed list of Novell-certified network hardware, click the "Yes, Tested and Approved" link at `http://developer. novell.com/`.

Software Pre-Installation Checklist

Following is your software pre-installation checklist:

▶ DOS 3.3 or higher. (DOS 7 is included on the NetWare 5 License diskette. Do *not* use the version of DOS that ships with the Windows 95, Windows 98, or Windows NT operating systems.)

▶ DOS CD-ROM drivers.

▶ NetWare 5 Operating System CD-ROM.

▸ NetWare 5 License diskette.

▸ NetWare 5 Novell Client Software CD-ROM.

▸ (Optional) Application CD-ROMs, diskettes, and documentation. (Before you purchase any applications for use on the server, make sure they are certified for use with NetWare 5.)

TIP

For access to a detailed list of Novell-certified applications, click the "Yes, Tested and Approved" link at `http://developer.novell.com/.`

Planning Pre-Installation Checklist

For your planning pre-installation checklist, determine the following:

▸ The amount of hard disk space to allocate to the DOS partition. (The DOS partition should be at least 50MB.). You must ensure that your DOS partition is large enough to support disk drivers, LAN drivers, namespace modules, the SERVER.EXE boot file, and repair utilities. You'll need even more space if you plan to store additional utilities on the DOS partition (such as diagnostic software, mouse drivers, SCSI drivers, and antivirus software).

▸ The type of NetWare 5 installation media to use (CD-ROM, network, batch file, and so on).

▸ The language to use during the installation process if you're installing an International version of NetWare 5. (The initial release of NetWare 5 supports English, French, German, Italian, Spanish, and Portuguese.)

▸ The name of the directory to use for NetWare 5 startup files. (The default is C:\NWSERVER.)

▸ Whether to use DOS CD-ROM drivers for the entire installation process, or switch to NetWare drivers mid-stream.

▸ The Server ID Number to use. This number is similar to the Internal IPX Number used in earlier versions of NetWare. You will only need to create one if you don't want to use the one that is randomly generated by the Installation process. Don't forget that it must be a unique number.

▶ Whether you want the server's AUTOEXEC.BAT file to automatically load SERVER.EXE (and thus, load the NetWare 5 operating system) every time the server is booted. If so, be sure to track the AUTOEXEC.00X backup file.

▶ Whether to add any special SET parameters and/or commands to the server's AUTOEXEC.NCF or STARTUP.NCF files.

▶ The appropriate regional settings (that is, country, code page, and keyboard).

▶ The required NetWare 5 drivers (and configuration information) for any devices that cannot be autodetected by the Installation Wizard, such as mouse type and video mode. For the record, NetWare 5 attempts to detect the following types of hardware devices and select the appropriate drivers:

- Platform support module

- Hot Plug PCI support module

- Storage adapters

- Storage devices (such as hard disks, CD-ROMs, and tape drivers)

- LAN adapters

▶ The size of the NetWare partition on each hard disk (if you don't want to use the defaults).

▶ The size of the SYS: volume (if you don't want to use the defaults).

▶ The name and size of any additional volumes.

▶ A server name that must consist of 2 to 47 characters (including letters, numbers, hyphens, and/or underscores—but no spaces). Don't forget that the first character cannot be a period. Since this is a new server, you'll need to make one up.

▸ Which communication protocol(s) to use. The server can be configured to use IP or IPX only — or to run both protocols concurrently.

▸ The server IP address, subnet mask, and optionally, the router (gateway) address. These are only required if you plan to configure the IP protocol on this server.

▸ The time zone the server lives in.

▸ The detailed NDS design for the NDS tree.

▸ Whether you will be installing this server into an existing NDS tree, or creating a new NDS tree.

▸ The Directory tree name. Since this is a new tree, you'll need to make one up.

▸ The detailed Directory context for this server (that is, its location in the NDS tree).

▸ The time server designation (for example, Single Reference, Reference, Primary, or Secondary). If this is the only server in a tree, the server should be designated as a Single Reference time server.

▸ The Admin username and full NDS context. Since this is a new tree, you'll need to make one up.

▸ The Admin password. Since this is a new tree, you'll need to make one up.

▸ What additional NetWare 5 products and services to install. See the section titled "Selecting Additional Products and Services" later in this chapter for further information.

▸ Which NetWare 5 components to customize.

Wow! That's quite a list. If you can fulfill *all* these prerequisites, you're ready for *advanced* Auto Shop!

Now, let's continue our preparation odyssey with a quick look at the minimum hardware requirements. Did somebody say "blowtorch"?

Minimum Hardware Requirements

Before you can install NetWare 5, you must ensure that your server satisfies a minimum set of requirements. Keep in mind, these are just minimum requirements — the *recommended* values are considerably higher.

The *minimum* hardware requirements for a NetWare 5 server include the following:

▸ A server-class PC with a Pentium or higher processor

▸ A VGA or higher-resolution display adapter (SVGA recommended)

▸ 64MB of RAM (128MB recommended to run Java-based applications)

▸ 50MB DOS partition (256MB recommended)

▸ 500MB free disk space for the SYS: volume (1GB of volume space recommended for additional products)

▸ One or more network boards

▸ The appropriate network cabling (Ethernet, Token Ring, FDDI, ARCnet, baseband, and so on) and related components (hubs, UPS units, and so on)

▸ A CD-ROM drive that can read ISO 9660-formatted CD-ROM disks (if NetWare 5 is being installed from CD-ROM).

▸ (Optional) PS/2 or serial mouse

**This list shows the *minimum* hardware required for NetWare 5,
not the recommended configuration. You can optimize server
performance by increasing the amount of server memory, disk
space, and processor speed.**

**For example, you'll want to ensure that you have sufficient additional
server RAM and hard disk space for any optional NetWare 5
products and services you want to install, as well as applications,
online documentation, and the file system. You'll also want to make
sure that your server has sufficient RAM and hard disk space to
provide the optimum level of server performance required by your
organization. For instance, consider creating a DOS partition that is
twice as big as server RAM (for example, 256MB on a server that has
128MB of RAM). This allows support for a DEBUG core dump as well
as additional room for DOS and NetWare drivers.**

Choosing a Protocol

Before you perform a NetWare 5 Installation, you must determine which
communications protocol(s) you want to use: Pure Internet Protocol (IP) and/or
Internet Packet Exchange (IPX). Check them out.

Pure IP

IP is designed to allow your network to share data with other IP networks,
including the Internet. If you want to configure your NetWare 5 server for IP, you
must know the appropriate IP address, subnet mask, and (optionally) the router
(gateway) address. If you select this option, Compatibility Mode will be enabled
by default. Compatibility Mode provides passive support for IPX. In other words,
if the server receives an IPX request, NetWare 5 will process it.

**If desired, Compatibility Mode can be disabled either during the
Customization part of the NetWare 5 Installation process or after
installation by removing the LOAD SCMD command from the
server's AUTOEXEC.NCF file.**

IPX

You can configure your NetWare 5 server for IPX (Novell's traditional communications protocol) to facilitate legacy NetWare IPX applications. NetWare 5 automatically loads and binds all detected IPX frame types for your network board.

TIP

If no frame types are detected, the Installation Wizard sets default frame types of Ethernet 802.2 for IPX/SPX and Ethernet_II for TCP/IP. If you want, you can remove unwanted frame types during the Customize step at the end of the Installation process. For further information on frame types, consult the Networking Technologies section in my *Novell's CNE Study Guide for NetWare 5* book.

One advantage of NetWare 5 is that you can bind both the IP and IPX protocols to a single network board. Now, let's complete our NetWare 5 preparation tasks with a quick preview of additional products and services. Remember — more is better!

Selecting Additional Products and Services

Before you begin the NetWare 5 construction process, you must settle on which additional NetWare 5 products and services (if any) you want to install. These products and services provide added functionality for the operating system. Some of them are bundled with NetWare 5, while others are available at additional cost.

Here's a quick list of the additional products and services that are available in NetWare 5:

- Novell Distributed Print Services (NDPS)

- LDAP Services

- NDS Catalog Services

- WAN Traffic Manager Services

- Secure Authentication Services (including SSL)

- Novell PKI Services

▸ Novell Internet Access Server

▸ Storage Management Services

▸ Novell DNS/DHCP Services

Well, there you have it! We've installed the LAN components, followed the pre-installation checklist, built an NDS design, and found our *NetWare 5 Operating System* CD-ROM. Now can we get started?!

Yes!

Now that you've satisfied all the NetWare 5 construction requirements, it's time to begin building the NetWare 5 supercar. In the remainder of this chapter, we're going to explore the NetWare 5 Installation process itself.

If you're interested in finding out more about the NetWare 5 Upgrade and Migration procedures, check out my *Novell's CNE Update to NetWare 5* book.

TIP

There's nothing like building an Infobahn roadster from the ground up.

▸ · ◂

NetWare 5 Installation

I know how you feel. It's been a lo-o-o-o-o-o-ng day already. I feel your pain — because I care. Together we can get through this thing. Together we can conquer NetWare 5 Installation.

Depending on how much control you like, NetWare 5 Installation offers *Basic* and *Custom* options. Fortunately, the NetWare 5 Basic Installation is essentially a subset of the Customized method — it's just simpler and faster because the program asks a minimum of questions and uses defaults for most configurable parameters.

On the other hand, if you're a control freak and need total input over all 14 steps, you can use the Custom Installation option. But, be forewarned. In order to make it through the Custom steps, you must know what you're doing — there's no one there to hold your hand.

So, in the spirit of goodwill and to increase your chances of building a functional NetWare 5 supercar, we will walk through all the NetWare 5 Installation steps in depth. Of course, if this discussion isn't enough for you, there's a detailed step-by-step ACME walk-through at the end of this chapter (see "Lab Exercise 8.1: Installing the CRIME-SRV1 Server in TOKYO").

TIP

Historically, each Novell product has had its own installation program. In NetWare 5, Novell introduces a standardized installation process called Novell Installation Services (NIS). This standard Installation Wizard can be used for all Novell products as well as third-party products which conform to Novell specifications.

So what's new in NetWare 5 Installation? Check it out:

▶ *Standardized installation architecture* — Novell uses Novell Installation Services (NIS) to standardize the server construction steps (see the previous Tip).

▶ *The Novell Installation Wizard* — This program uses a Java-based GUI during the later stages of the server installation process. (The earlier stages of the process still use a text-mode interface.)

▶ *Automatic hardware detection and selection of drivers* — NIS auto-detects platform support modules, PCI HotPlug Support modules, storage adapters, storage devices (such as hard disks, CD-ROMs, and tape units), and LAN adapters.

▶ *Batch support* — This feature allows you to install one server, then use the same profile to install other servers.

▶ *Concurrent support* — This feature provides concurrent support for Internetwork Packet Exchange Protocol (IPX) and pure Internet Protocol (IP).

▶ *Version checking* — This feature ensures that only the latest files are copied to the server.

REAL WORLD

The *Network* installation method consists of two basic steps. First, in Step 1, you must ensure that the existing server has a CD-ROM drive mounted as a NetWare device (with the NetWare 5 Operating System CD-ROM inserted). Or, you can copy the installation program files from the NetWare 5 Operating System CD-ROM to the existing server's volume. Then, in Step 2, you will temporarily install the appropriate NetWare 5 client files on the DOS partition of the new server. Finally, you will use the new server as a client to log into the existing server and run the NetWare 5 Installation program.

There are a few tricks to keep in mind when you're accessing NetWare 5 Installation files from a notebook CD-ROM or volume:

- ▸ **CD-ROM** — If you are installing from a shared CD-ROM, use CDINST.NLM instead of CDROM.NLM.

- ▸ **NSS** — NetWare 5 cannot be installed from a NSS volume.

- ▸ **Batch** — This method allows you to install multiple servers with the same configuration. This method also involves two steps. First, you install NetWare 5 on a host server. Second, you install additional servers using the same profile. Piece of cake.

In addition, NetWare 5 offers three fundamental methods for building a server from scratch:

- ▸ *Local CD-ROM* — This is the easiest way to install NetWare 5 because it uses the server's local CD-ROM drive.

- ▸ *Network* — This is the best choice if your server doesn't have a CD-ROM drive, or you want to install multiple servers at once. This is also referred to as the "Server-to-Server" or "Remote Network Installation Area" method. To use the Network method, you will need two computers: an existing server (that acts as a source for all program files) and a new server (the target).

▶ . . . . ◀

> ### REAL WORLD
>
> Unlike earlier versions of NetWare, you no longer have to decide whether to perform a Simple or Custom install. Instead, you simply install the NetWare 5 operating system, then choose whether or not to customize certain parameters at the end of the process. So what can we customize? All sorts of things, such as the core operating system, file system, protocols, Directory Services, and additional products and services. Cool.

In this chapter, we'll use the local CD-ROM method for all Installation options. It's the most common.

TIP

Now it's time to don our grease-covered overalls and attack the NetWare 5 supercar. Let's start with a quick preview of the four stages of server construction:

▶ *Stage 1*: Getting started

▶ *Stage 2*: C-Worthy input screens

▶ *Stage 3*: GUI input screens

▶ *Stage 4*: Customization

It all starts in Stage 1, where you perform pre-installation tasks and run INSTALL.BAT. Then, in Stage 2, you get to attack the text-mode portion of the installation process, including choosing the type of installation, selecting regional settings, modifying selected drivers, creating the NetWare partition and SYS: volume, and mounting the SYS: volume.

Once you've built the foundation frame of your supercar, it's time to plug in the key functional components. In Stage 3, you will perform the GUI-based portion of the installation process including naming the server, selecting networking protocols, choosing the server time zone, installing Novell Directory Services (NDS), and installing Novell Licensing Services (NLS). Finally, in Stage 4, you will finish the installation by selecting additional products and services and customizing server parameters — but only if you want to!

That's all there is to it. Let's not waste another moment. It's finally time to build your first NetWare 5 server — a sleek, Infobahn roadster.

Stage 1: Getting Started

The NetWare 5 core operating system (OS) consists of a single file called SERVER.EXE. In order to load NetWare 5, you must first boot the server using DOS, and then execute this file. Once you do, SERVER.EXE transfers operating control from DOS to NetWare.

To accomplish all this magic, you must perform some pre-Installation preparatory tasks, including: pre-planning, configuring the DOS partition, and installing the NetWare 5 CD-ROM. Here's how Stage 1 plays out:

▸ *Step 1*: Complete pre-installation tasks

▸ *Step 2*: Run INSTALL.BAT

Let's take a closer look.

Step 1: Complete Pre-Installation Tasks

There are a number of tasks you'll need to perform before you can install your NetWare 5 server, such as:

▸ Determine if your "computer room" meets recommended power and operating environment requirements. (See the "Hardware Pre-Installation Checklist" section earlier in this chapter.)

▸ Verify that your server meets the minimum NetWare 5 hardware requirements — and that all hardware is compatible. (See the "Minimum Hardware Requirements" section earlier in this chapter.) Be sure that you install and configure any hardware that is necessary (such as network interface cards, hubs, cabling, uninterruptible power supplies, and so on) Refer to the manufacturer's documentation provided with each device for configuration instructions.

▶ Confirm that you have all of the appropriate DOS, NetWare 5, and application software and documentation that you will need. (See the "Software Pre-Installation Checklist" section earlier in this chapter.)

▶ Be sure you that you have done all of the planning required and have the required information handy. (See the "Planning Pre-Installation Checklist" section earlier in this chapter.)

▶ Back up your existing system. Create at least two full server backups on tape or other storage media. Remember that all data on the server will be destroyed during the pre-installation process. If your computer is currently being used as a server, be sure to back up the network security information (such as NDS or the bindery), as well as the file system.

▶ Boot the server using the DOS version supplied by your computer manufacturer. (NetWare requires DOS 3.3 or higher.) DOS 7 is included on the NetWare 5 License diskette. Do *not* use the version of DOS that ships with the Windows 95, Windows 98, or Windows NT operating systems.

▶ Create a boot diskette. To format a diskette and make it bootable, insert the diskette in the floppy drive and type the following:

FORMAT A: /S

After the disk is formatted, you'll need to use the DOS COPY command to copy two important utilities to the diskette: FDISK.EXE and FORMAT.COM. You may also want to include copies of your AUTOEXEC.BAT and CONFIG.SYS files, DOS CD-ROM drivers, and utilities such as EDIT.COM (to edit ASCII files), XCOPY.EXE (to copy files) and MEM.EXE (to display information about available RAM).

▶ Create the DOS partition. Use the DOS FDISK utility to delete existing partitions and create a new, active DOS partition of 50MB or more — leaving the rest of the hard disk space free. (Unlike other operating systems such as OS/2 and UNIX, NetWare 5 does not have its own cold-boot loader. To start the server, you must boot from a DOS prompt.)

TIP

You'll need to ensure that your DOS partition is large enough to support disk drivers, LAN drivers, namespace modules, the SERVER.EXE boot file, and repair utilities. You'll need even more space if you plan to store additional utilities on the DOS partition, such as diagnostic software, mouse drivers, SCSI drivers, and antivirus software.

▶ Format the DOS partition. Use the DOS FORMAT utility on the boot diskette you made to format the new partition and make it bootable. In other words, type the following:

```
FORMAT C: /S
```

TIP

Be sure to copy all DOS CD-ROM drivers from your computer *before* you run FDISK or FORMAT. Doing so afterward won't help, because you will have wiped out the files. Also, be sure that the logical name of the CD-ROM driver in your AUTOEXEC.BAT file does not conflict with any INSTALL utility filenames (such as "INSTALL").

▶ Install the CD-ROM drive as a DOS device, following the instructions provided by the drive manufacturer.

▶ Use the DOS DATE and TIME commands to verify the computer's date and time, then modify them if necessary.

Consider the NetWare 5 server *prepared*. Now, we can start the installation process by loading INSTALL.BAT. Check it out.

Step 2: Run **INSTALL.BAT**

At the server console, insert the *NetWare 5 Operating System* CD-ROM into the server's CD-ROM drive. At the server's DOS prompt, switch to the drive letter assigned to the CD-ROM drive, and type **INSTALL**.

TIP

If you have a bootable CD-ROM that meets the El Torito standards, the Installation program will boot when the CD-ROM is inserted in the CD-ROM drive. The installation program will detect existing partitions and allow you to retain an existing DOS partition or create a new one. To determine if your computer meets the El Torito CD-ROM standards, contact your computer manufacturer.

That completes Stage 1. The infant server has been prepared and we have the ball rolling with INSTALL.BAT. At this point, you'll be greeted by the text-mode portion of the installation. Check it out in Stage 2.

Stage 2: C-Worthy Input Screens

Once the server has been prepared, it's time to begin supercar construction. In Stage 2, we'll build the foundation of the server using a "C-Worthy" text-based interface. This early server foundation consists of regional configurations, disk/LAN drivers, one or more NetWare 5 partitions, and the SYS: volume.

TIP

You can typically abort the installation process at nearly any point by pressing Alt + F10. Most screens also allow you to press Esc to return to the previous screen.

Here's where we go from here:

▸ *Step 3*: Choose the type of installation

▸ *Step 4*: Select regional settings

▸ *Step 5*: Modify selected drivers

▸ *Step 6*: Create the NetWare partition and mount the SYS: volume

Ready, set, rivet!

Step 3: Choose the Type of Installation

As the Installation program begins to load, a NetWare title screen appears. Wait for a few minutes until the next screen appears. If you have an International version of the program, a NetWare Installation screen appears, giving you the opportunity to select the language to be used during the installation process. Available languages include English, French, German, Italian, Spanish, and Portuguese. Next, the "NetWare 5 Software License and Limited Warranty" screen appears. Press F10 to accept the terms of the License Agreement.

When the "Welcome to the NetWare Server Installation" screen appears, indicate the type of installation and the startup directory (that is, the destination for the NetWare 5 server boot files). Check it out in Figure 8.2. You'll notice that the defaults are New Server (for the type of installation desired) and C:\NWSERVER (for the startup directory). Although default settings work fine for most configurations, you can press F2 to gain access to the Advanced Settings menu.

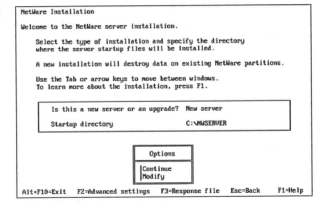

FIGURE 8.2

*Selecting the
NetWare 5 Server
Installation type in Step 3*

```
NetWare Installation

Welcome to the NetWare server installation.

    Select the type of installation and specify the directory
    where the server startup files will be installed.

    A new installation will destroy data on existing NetWare partitions.

    Use the Tab or arrow keys to move between windows.
    To learn more about the installation, press F1.

        Is this a new server or an upgrade?  New server

        Startup directory                    C:\NWSERVER

                            Options

                            Continue
                            Modify

    Alt+F10=Exit   F2=Advanced settings   F3=Response file   Esc=Back   F1=Help
```

TIP

During a new server installation, the installation program will not delete system partitions or other partitions such as DOS, Windows, or UNIX. It will, however, delete a NetWare partition containing a SYS: volume as well as any other volumes that are part of that partition. If you want to keep such volumes, you should perform a NetWare 5 Upgrade instead of an Installation.

If you press F2, you'll notice that you can use the Advanced Settings screen to configure a number of cool server parameters including:

▸ *CD-ROM Driver to Access Install* — Choices include DOS and NetWare (the default). Select DOS if you want to continue using the DOS CD-ROM driver during the installation process.

▶ *Server ID Number* — The Server ID number is a hexadecimal number of up to eight digits in length, which uniquely identifies the server on the network. You can replace the randomly generated number with a custom number if the server exists in a filtered environment (where routers between network segments are configured to forward data only from specific computer addresses) and/or you want to use a pre-determined numbering scheme to identify servers in a particular department or location.

▶ *Load Server at Reboot* — Choices include Yes (the default) and No. Select Yes if you want the server's AUTOEXEC.BAT file to automatically load the NetWare 5 operating system whenever the system is rebooted. If you chose Yes, the old AUTOEXEC.BAT and CONFIG.SYS files are renamed and saved with a .00X extension.

▶ *Server Set Parameters* — Indicate any SET parameter commands that you want to add to the STARTUP.NCF file.

Review the default settings and modify them if necessary. Then, press F10 to save the values on the Advanced Settings screen and return to the "Welcome to the NetWare Server Installation" screen.

Server ID Numbers are similar to Internal IPX Numbers used in earlier versions of NetWare.

TIP

Step 4: Select Regional Settings

After you have configured your NetWare 5 Installation parameters, the Regional Settings screen appears, as shown in Figure 8.3. Regional settings are used to customize server language and keyboard settings. If you are located in the United States, the default values are:

▶ Country: 001 (USA)

▶ Code Page: 437 (United States English)

▶ Keyboard: United States

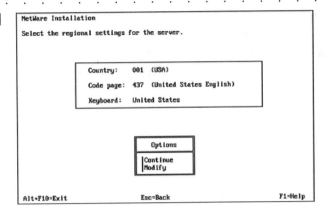

FIGURE 8.3

Regional Settings screen in Server Installation Step 4

```
NetWare Installation

Select the regional settings for the server.


        Country:    001  (USA)

        Code page:  437  (United States English)

        Keyboard:   United States




                 Options

                 Continue
                 Modify



Alt+F10=Exit            Esc=Back                F1=Help
```

Review the default settings and modify them if necessary. Nah, just leave them alone and continue.

Step 5: Modify Selected Drivers

During Step 5, the Installation Wizard attempts to automatically detect certain types of hardware and determine the appropriate drivers. Other drivers must be selected manually. Drivers that may be auto-detected include platform support, PCI HotPlug support, storage adapters, storage devices (such as hard disks, CD-ROMs, and tape drives), and LAN adapters. Drivers that are not auto-detected, and thus must be selected manually, include mouse type and display adapter. The drivers to be selected/confirmed appear on a series of three screens.

As you can see in Figure 8.4, the first NetWare 5 driver screen lists mouse type and video mode parameters. Since these devices are not auto-detected by the installation program, you will need to select the appropriate settings manually.

- ▶ *Mouse type* — Although the installation program supports PS/2 and serial mouse types, a mouse is not required. If you really want to, you can use the keyboard's arrow-keys to control pointer movement. Yuck!

- ▶ *Video mode* — The installation program is optimized to use Super VGA resolution and work with display hardware that is VESA 2 complaint. You should only choose Standard VGA if your video card does not support 256 colors.

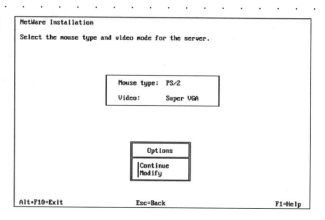

F I G U R E 8.4

*Driver detection screen #1
in Server Installation Step 5*

Review the values listed on this screen and modify them if necessary.

The system then automatically copies a number of server boot files from the CD-ROM to your startup directory. These include files such as SERVER.EXE, disk drivers, LAN drivers, NWCONFIG.NLM, NWSNUT.NLM, VREPAIR.NLM, and other NLMs. These files allow you to activate the NetWare operating system from the DOS partition and get things started.

As you can see in Figure 8.5, the second NetWare 5 driver screen lists the following types of auto-detected drivers:

- ▶ *Platform Support Module* — The performance of servers with multiple processors and other configurations can be optimized by loading a platform support module driver. If no platform support module driver is detected, the server probably doesn't need one. (Platform support modules have a .PSM filename extension.)

- ▶ *PCI HotPlug Support Module* — Computers that provide support for PCI HotPlug technology allow storage adapters and network boards to be inserted and removed while the computer is powered on. If no PCI HotPlug support driver is detected, your computer probably does not support PCI HotPlug technology. (HotPlug modules have an .NLM extension.)

- ▶ *Storage adapters* — A storage adapter is a hardware device that provides a link between the computer and one or more storage devices. Storage adapters require a software driver called a host adapter module (HAM) to communicate with the computer (host). Because a single storage adapter can control more than one type of storage device, only one HAM may be required. Various types of storage adapters (such as IDE and SCSI) may be auto-detected. If a particular storage adapter is not detected, choose the appropriate driver from the list or load it from a manufacturer-specific diskette. Make sure that any storage adapters are installed and configured properly, and that their settings do not conflict with other hardware devices in the same computer. For more information on configuring a particular storage adapter, contact the storage adapter manufacturer.

FIGURE 8.5

Driver detection screen #2 in Server Installation Step 5

```
NetWare Installation

The following device drivers were detected for this server.  Add, change, or
delete device drivers as needed.


 ┌─ Device types ──────── Driver names ──────────────────────────┐
 │                                                                │
 │  Platform Support Module:    (optional)                        │
 │                                                                │
 │  HotPlug Support Module:     (optional)                        │
 │                                                                │
 │  Storage adapters:           AHA2940                           │
 │                                                                │
 └────────────────────────────────────────────────────────────────┘
                         ┌──────────────────┐
                         │     Options      │
                         ├──────────────────┤
                         │Continue          │
                         │Modify            │
                         └──────────────────┘

 Alt+F10=Exit  Esc=Back                                    F1=Help
```

Review the values listed on this screen and modify them if necessary.

TIP

Earlier versions of NetWare (such as NetWare 3.12) employed a type of architecture known as *Monolithic Architecture*. This architecture used a single disk driver with a .DSK extension as the interface between NetWare and the disk controller. NetWare 5 does not support these drivers.

Instead, NetWare 5 uses a newer architecture, called NetWare Peripheral Architecture (NWPA), in which two drivers share this responsibility: a Host Adapter Module (with — what else — a .HAM filename extension) and a Custom Device Module (with a .CDM filename extension). HAM drivers control the host adapter hardware. CDM drivers control storage devices (such as hard disks, CD-ROMs, and tape drives) or autochangers attached to a host adapter bus.

As you can see in Figure 8.6, the third NetWare 5 driver screen lists the following types of drivers:

▶ *Storage devices* — Storage devices require a software driver, called a Custom Device Module (CDM) to communicate with the storage adapter that controls it. Each type of storage device requires a separate CDM. The Installation Wizard auto-detects many types of storage devices such as SCSI drives, IDE drives, CD-ROM drives, and tape drives. If a particular storage device is not detected, choose the appropriate driver from the list provided or load it from a manufacturer-specific diskette.

▶ *Network boards* — A network board is used to facilitate communication between the computer and the network. Network boards require a software driver called a *LAN driver* to communicate with the network. The installation program auto-detects many types of network boards. If a particular network board is not detected, choose the appropriate driver from the list provided, or load it from a manufacturer-specific diskette. Make sure that any network boards are installed and configured properly, and that their settings do not conflict with other hardware devices in the same computer. For more information on configuring a particular network board, contact the network board manufacturer.

▶ *NetWare Loadable Modules* — Some servers and network configurations require that you load a NetWare Loadable Module (NLM) before completing the server installation. For instance, if you are installing the server in a Token Ring environment, you may need to load ROUTE.NLM. If so, add it to the NetWare Loadable Modules field.

Review the values listed on this screen and modify them if necessary.

Step 6: Create the NetWare Partition and Mount the SYS: Volume

To complete the NetWare 5 server foundation, we'll need to create internal disk partitions and volumes. In Step 6, the "Volume SYS and Partition Properties" screen appears. This text-mode screen displays the default parameters for creating NetWare partitions and the SYS: volume. These parameters include device name, NetWare partition size, Hot Fix size, and SYS: volume size. Follow along in Figure 8.7.

F I G U R E   8.6

*Driver detection screen #3
in Server Installation Step 5*

```
NetWare Installation

The following device drivers were detected for this server.  Add, change, or
delete device drivers as needed.


┌─ Device types ───────── Driver names ─────────
│  Storage devices:        SCSIHD

   Network boards:         3C90X

   NetWare Loadable Modules:  (optional)



                    ┌──────────────┐
                    │   Options    │
                    ├──────────────┤
                    │Continue      │
                    │Modify        │
                    └──────────────┘

Alt+F10=Exit  Esc=Back                              F1=Help
```

F I G U R E   8.7

*Modifying partition
properties in Server
Installation Step 6*

```
NetWare Installation

Create a NetWare partition and volume SYS.

       ┌─── Volume SYS and Partition Properties ───┐
       │ Device:       SEAGATE ST32550N rev:0019 [V312-A0-D0:0]
       │
       │ NetWare Partition Size (MB):      1019.8
       │
       │ Hot Fix Size (MB):                   3.8
       │
       │ Volume SYS Size (MB):             1015.9
       │
       │ NOTE: Press F1 for size recommendations.
       │       For NSS partitions, leave unpartitioned space on a device.
       └───────────────────────────────────────────┘

                    ┌──────────────┐
                    │   Options    │
                    ├──────────────┤
                    │Continue      │
                    │Modify        │
                    └──────────────┘

Alt+F10=Exit                                        F1=Help
```

Partitions are associated with operating systems such as DOS, Windows, UNIX, or NetWare, and are used to divide a large storage area into smaller, more manageable portions. With NetWare 5, up to four partitions can exist on a single storage device. Each NetWare partition can contain up to eight volumes and each volume can include up to 32 volume segments. The NetWare 5 Installation Wizard uses the following defaults for creating NetWare partitions:

▶ *Single hard disk per server* — If the server contains only one hard disk, the INSTALL utility will create a single NetWare 5 partition consisting of all free disk space beyond the DOS partition.

▶ *Multiple hard disks per server* — On the first hard disk, the INSTALL utility will create a single NetWare 5 partition consisting of all free disk space beyond the DOS partition. On the remaining hard disks, INSTALL utility will create one NetWare 5 partition per hard disk, where each partition consists of all of the available space on that disk.

TIP

Don't forget that if you plan to use NSS, you will need to leave additional free space on each hard disk that will contain an NSS partition, rather than using all of the free space on each disk for a NetWare partition.

Partition Size The size of a NetWare partition can range from 2MB up to the full size of the storage device. Typically, you will not want a partition to span storage devices unless you are using RAID technology.

Hot Fix Size NetWare 5 uses the Hot Fix fault tolerance feature along with read-after-write verification to ensure that data is successfully written to the server's hard disk. If this cannot be accomplished after several attempts, NetWare marks the block as bad and redirects the data to the Hot Fix Redirection Area. Because Hot Fix is automatically optimized for your server storage device, you can usually just use the default. If your storage devices includes hardware redirection, you can turn off this feature by setting the Hot Fix size to zero (0).

SYS:Volume To display configuration parameters for the SYS: volume, select Modify from the Options menu, then press F3 (see Figure 8.8). Here's a quick list:

▶ Volume Name: SYS

▶ Volume Block Size: 64KB Blocks

▶ Status: New, Not Mounted

▶ File Compression: On

▶ Block Suballocation: On

▶ Data Migration: Off

FIGURE 8.8

Modifying volume parameters in Server Installation Step 6

```
NetWare Installation
Create a Net┌──────────────────────Volume Information──────────────────────┐
          │                                                            │
    ┌─────┤   Volume Name:            SYS                             │
    Devic │                                                            │
    NetWa │   Volume Block Size:      32 KB Blocks                    │
    Hot F │   Status:                 New, Not Mounted               │
    Volun │   File Compression:       On                             │
    Unpar │   Block Suballocation:    On                             │
          │   Data Migration:         Off                            │
          └────────────────────────────────────────────────────────┘
                    ┌──────────────────┐
                    │ Options          │
                    ├──────────────────┤
                    │ Continue         │
                    │ Modify           │
                    └──────────────────┘
   Alt+F10=Exit    F10=Save    Esc=Cancel    F3=Volume Properties    F1=Help
```

If you plan to have additional volumes on this partition, you will need to decrease the size of the SYS: volume, to leave room for the other volume(s). It's probably a good idea to create one or more additional volumes for your data, to keep it separate from your NetWare operating system files. It also makes it easier to restrict access to specific directories or files. (For example, you may want to store payroll information on a separate volume from other data.)

Volume Block Size The default volume block size is a function of volume size and is automatically calculated by the Installation program. In earlier versions of NetWare, a large block size could result in large amounts of wasted space. In NetWare 5, the file compression and block suballocation features are set to ON by default, thus optimizing hard disk space. In other words, the default should probably work just fine.

TIP

Novell recommends the minimum SYS: volume sizes listed in Table 8.1. Although the basic NetWare operating system requires only about 350MB, it's important to make sure that the SYS: volume is large enough to handle any additional NetWare products and services, online documentation, and applications that may be installed. For optimal performance, the SYS: volume should also have sufficient space available for system operations.

T A B L E 8 . 1	NETWARE 5 PRODUCTS	MINIMUM SYS:VOLUME SIZE
Recommended Minimum SYS:Volume Size	NetWare 5 operating system	350MB
	NetWare 5 with default products	450MB
	NetWare 5 with all products	550MB
	NetWare 5 with all products and documentation	700MB
	Additional space required (Add to each of the sizes in column 2.)	100MB

TIP

You can create additional partitions and volumes after installation by loading NWCONFIG.NLM at the server console.

That's it—you've successfully built the foundation frame of our NetWare 5 supercar. You've established a number of installation parameters, selected drivers, and configured the internal server hard drive. All in a day's work.

Now it's time to add function to the frame with protocols, NDS, and licensing. It's time to get GUI!

Stage 3: GUI Input Screens

In Stage 2, the Installation Wizard loaded the core server OS and built an internal NetWare partition and SYS: volume. At this point, the server is alive— but barely breathing! In order to pump life into our supercar, we must establish networking protocols, an NDS context, and licensing authentication. Welcome to Stage 3.

Stage 3 jump-starts the server by adding function to its minimal foundation. Here's what it takes:

▸ *Step 7*: Name the NetWare 5 server

▸ *Step 8*: Select networking protocols

▸ *Step 9*: Choose the server time zone

▸ *Step 10*: Install NDS

▸ *Step 11*: Install Novell Licensing Services (NLS)

And I have more good news. In this stage, we will leave the ugly text-mode world and enter the kingdom of Java. The rest of the NetWare 5 installation process is presented using a GUI user interface. I'm feeling "warm-and-fuzzy" already. Check it out! (Speaking of fuzzy, you've probably noticed that the screen shots in this chapter showing the NetWare 5 installation procedure appear fuzzy. This was unavoidable.)

Although a mouse is recommended, you can use the keystrokes listed in Table 8.2 to navigate through the Installation program. If necessary, you can use the arrow keys on the numeric keypad for cursor movements. If you do, don't forget that the NumLock (number lock) button must be on for cursor movements to be enabled on the keypad.

T A B L E 8.2	KEYSTROKE	ACTION
Using a Keyboard Instead of a Mouse for GUI Screens	Tab	Move to next element
	Shift+Tab	Move to previous element
	Alt+F7	Move to next window
	Alt+F8	Move to previous window
	Up-arrow (keypad 8)	Move cursor up
	Down-arrow (keypad 2)	Move cursor down
	Left-arrow (keypad 4)	Move cursor to the left
	Right-arrow (keypad 6)	Move cursor to the right
	Hold Shift while pressing keypad	Accelerate cursor movement
	Enter	Select
	Keypad 5	Select or click an object
	Keypad 0	Lock a selected object (to drag)
	Keypad . (period)	Unlock a selected object (to drop)
	Keypad + (plus)	Double-click an object

Step 7: Name the NetWare 5 Server

At this point, the Installation Wizard copies a number of files to the server hard drive (called the "preparatory file copy" process). A Java Virtual Machine is then created on the server and the GUI portion of the Installation Wizard is loaded. Welcome to the "warm-and-fuzzy" kingdom. This step may take a while.

When the Server Properties dialog box appears, type the server name in the Server Name field (see Figure 8.9). Don't forget that a server name must be unique among servers in your NDS tree. The name should consist of 2 to 47 characters (including letters, numbers, hyphens, and/or underscores—but no spaces). The first character cannot be a period.

FIGURE 8.9

Naming your server in Server Installation Step 7

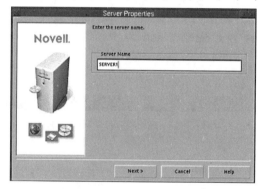

When the Configure File System dialog appears, review the information listed. If you modified the size of the SYS volume in an earlier step, you can create additional volumes using available free space, as shown in Figure 8.10. To do so, click the Free Space icon, then click Create.

When the New Volume dialog box appears, type the name of the new volume in the Volume Name field and click OK. Check it out in Figure 8.11. The new volume should then be listed on the Configure File System screen.

When the Mount Volumes dialog box appears, you are asked whether to mount all volumes when the server reboots, or to mount them now. Ensure that Yes is selected to mount all volumes when the server reboots.

Step 8: Select Networking Protocols

Once you've named the new NetWare 5 server, it's time to begin speaking to the cyber-world. At this point, the Protocols dialog box should appear. It asks you to specify the network protocols for each internal server NIC (Network Interface Card). Follow along in Figure 8.12.

F I G U R E   8.10

Configuring the file system in Server Installation Step 7

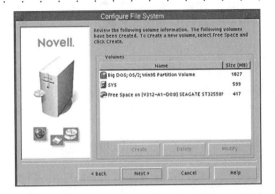

F I G U R E   8.11

Creating a new volume in Server Installation Step 7

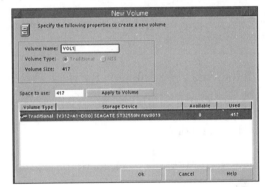

F I G U R E   8.12

Selecting networking protocols in Server Installation Step 8

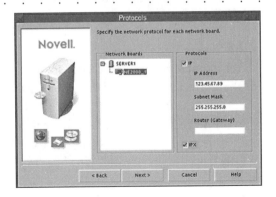

TIP

If your server is connected to the Internet, you will need to register with the Internet Network Information Center (InterNIC) and obtain a unique IP address. For information on receiving an IP address, contact your Internet Service Provider (ISP) or the Internetwork InterNIC directly at hostmaster@internic.net**.**

To configure the IP protocol, follow these simple steps:

▶ In the Network Boards pane on the left, click the icon for your network board.

▶ In the Protocols section on the right, mark the IP checkbox.

▶ In the Protocols section on the right, enter the IP address in the IP Address field.

▶ In the Protocols section on the right, enter the subnet mask in the Subnet Mask field.

▶ (Optional) In the Protocols section on the right, enter the router (gateway) address in the Router (Gateway) field.

To configure the IP protocol:

▶ In the Protocols section on the right, mark the IPX checkbox.

Now you're talking to the world. So, what time is it in Turkey? No idea . . . check out Step 9.

Step 9: Choose the Server Time Zone

Every NetWare 5 server must be a time server of some type. As such, the server must keep track of the correct time at all times (*funny, huh?*). At this point, the Time Zone dialog box appears, as shown in Figure 8.13. Choose the correct time zone for your server and make sure that the "Allow system to adjust for Daylight Saving Time" checkbox is marked. — unless, of course, Daylight Savings time doesn't exist for you. In this case, ignore it!

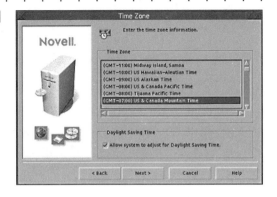

FIGURE 8.13

Choosing a time zone in Server Installation Step 9

Step 10: Install Novell Directory Services (NDS)

Now it's *time* to install Novell Directory Services (NDS) on your new NetWare 5 server. I knew this day would finally come!

This is probably one of the most important steps in the installation process. At this point, your NetWare 5 supercar is alive and well, but it needs an internal navigation system to find its way around. Welcome to the NDS "Cloud."

At the beginning of Step 10, the NDS Install dialog will appear. If this is the first NetWare server in your NDS tree, select "Create a new NDS Tree," as seen in Figure 8.14. Take note of the fact that the resources available in the new tree will not be available to users that are logged into a different tree. Sorry, only one tree at a time.

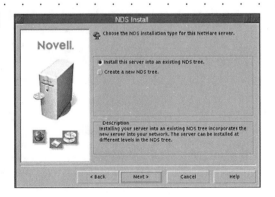

FIGURE 8.14

Creating a new NDS tree in Server Installation Step 10

Next, the Installation Wizard will ask some important NDS configuration questions. Follow along in Figure 8.15:

▶ Enter the tree name in the Tree Name field. This is usually the [Root] name of your tree followed by the term "TREE". (For example, ACME_TREE.) Consult your NDS Design document for tree-naming rules.

▶ Enter the location for the server in the Context for Server Object field (for example, OU=LABS.OU=NORAD.O=ACME). Once again, this information can be found in your NDS Design document. You do have one, don't you?

▶ Enter the leaf name of the Admin User object in the Admin Name field if you want it to be something other than "Admin." Keep it as Admin — it will make your life easier.

▶ Enter the context for the Admin User object in the Admin Context field if you want it to be different than the context of the Server object.

▶ Enter the password for the Admin User object in the "Password" and "Retype Password" fields. Keep track of this information for future reference. If you lose any of the Admin configuration details, your life will get much more complicated.

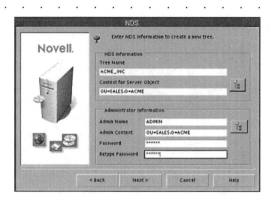

F I G U R E   8.15

NDS Server Context dialog box in Server Installation Step 10

TIP

Interestingly, you may find that some NetWare and/or third-party utilities will require you to enter the original Admin password even if you have subsequently changed it. Be forewarned!

At this point, the Installation Wizard will check for duplicate tree names and install NDS. When the NDS Summary screen appears, as shown in Figure 8.16, write down the following information and store it in a safe place for future reference:

- ▶ NDS tree name

- ▶ Server context

- ▶ Administrator name

- ▶ (Password you entered on previous screen)

F I G U R E   8.16

NDS Installation Summary screen in Server Installation Step 10

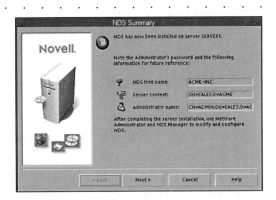

Congratulations . . . you've successfully integrated your Infobahn hot rod with the global NDS tree. This is a great feeling. And believe me, it's all downhill from here.

Step 11: Install Novell Licensing Services (NLS)

Now it's time to license the NetWare 5 server. To do so, Novell has created a whole new licensing engine called Novell Licensing Services (NLS). NLS helps you monitor and control the use of licensed software on your network.

NetWare 5 itself is a *licensed application*. It requires the number of users connecting to the network to remain within the number of licenses provided by the NetWare software. Typically, NetWare is installed with 250 or 500 user licenses. When NetWare is installed, the following NetWare License objects are added to the NDS tree:

▶ *License Container Objects* — NetWare 5 supports two different types of License container objects: a *User* license container and a *Server* license container. These objects are added to the NDS tree when NetWare 5 is installed. They appear as leaf objects in the container that includes the Server object. License container objects can contain multiple license Certificate objects. To manage licenses for users, you use the "Novell + NetWare 5 Conn SCL+500" license container. This is where the initial user license certificates are placed by default. This name is a compound fragment made up of the Publisher, Product, and version attributes. In addition, the number at the end of the license container object's name indicates the number of users the license certificate accommodates.

▶ *License Certificate Objects* — License Certificate objects are also created in NDS when the NetWare 5 server is installed. All License Certificate objects are installed into a license container. These objects contain information about the product such as the Publisher, Product name, version, how many licenses the certificate allows, and whether additional licenses are available. Each license included in the certificate allows a *licensed connection* to be made. A licensed connection is initiated when a user requests a network connection by logging in. When the server receives the request, it checks to make sure a licensed unit is available in the license certificate stored in NDS. If a license unit is available, the server allows the client to complete the network connection.

TIP

Most general NLS licenses use the server/connection methodology. However, NetWare MLA-type licenses use the container/tree methodology. This means you do not have to assign the license to an individual server. Instead, you assign it to a container or NDS tree. It applies to all servers and users in that logical realm.

NLS license management is based on the concept of ownership. The user object that installs the license becomes the owner. Regardless of NDS rights, only the owner of a license can change the properties of a license object. By default, the Admin user is assigned as the owner of the license certificate. As the owner, Admin always has access to a NetWare user license to connect to the network. Unfortunately, some people delete Admin. If so, you will lose access to NLS license management. Make sure to assign ownership to permanent users in the NDS tree.

At this point, we're ready to create a legal NetWare 5 supercar. First, insert your NetWare license diskette in the floppy drive and select the appropriate license file — as shown in Figure 8.17. Be sure to use the unique license diskette. NetWare 5 is kind of picky about such things. However, if you are upgrading the server for practice purposes only, you can mark the "Install without licenses" box. This will give you a two-user server.

REAL WORLD

Once the server has been upgraded or installed, you can use NetWare Administrator, NLS Manager (SYS:PUBLIC\WIN32\NLSMAN32.EXE), or NWCONFIG .NLM to install and create additional license certificates. NetWare Administrator and NLS Manager can be used to monitor and manage license usage. NLS Manager allows you to create reports to see how licenses are used over a period of time.

To install additional licenses from NetWare Administrator, do the following:

▶ **Step 1** — Select Tools, Install License, Install License Certificate.

▶ **Step 2** — Browse to and select the .NLF certificate file found on the diskette.

▶ **Step 3** — Finally, you'll need to supply the NDS context for the License Certificate object by browsing the NDS tree and selecting the parent container of the user license container object. With both the file name and the directory fields filled, install the license certificate.

A license container can contain one or more license certificates. This allows you to install more than one license at a time. For example, if you buy a software suite containing three separate pieces of software, you can install a license container that contains a separate license for each piece of software. Very cool.

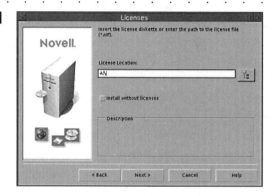

*Licensing your
NetWare 5 server in
Server Installation Step 11*

Once you legally license the NetWare 5 server, it comes to life. The supercar is charged up and ready to cruise the information superhighway. It's even equipped with NDS wings for "cloud surfing."

Wait . . . there's more! You can further customize the server with additional products and special fine-tuning tricks. Check them out in Stage 4. This is where we put the "*super*" in supercar.

Stage 4: Customization

In Stage 3, we entered GUI-land and refined the basic server foundation. We named the server, added networking protocols, and built a global NDS tree. In addition, we legalized our supercar with NetWare Licensing Services (NLS).

What's left?

In Stage 4, you can further customize the hot rod with additional products and special NetWare 5 tricks. Here is what's left:

▸ *Step 12*: Install additional products and services

▸ *Step 13*: Customize the server

▸ *Step 14*: Complete the installation

Remember: it's not over until the checkered flag falls.

Step 12: Install Additional Products and Services

Toward the end of the NetWare 5 Installation process, the Additional Products and Services dialog box will appear. Check it out in Figure 8.18. Here's a peek at the great new products and services you can add to your new NetWare 5 server:

▸ Novell Distributed Print Services (NDPS)

▸ LDAP Services

▸ NDS Catalog Services

▸ WAN Traffic Manager Services

▸ Secure Authentication Services (including SSL)

▸ Novell PKI Services

▸ Novell Internet Access Server

▸ Storage Management Services

▸ Novell DNS/DHCP Services

▸ · ◂

FIGURE 8.18

Installing additional products and services in Server Installation Step 12

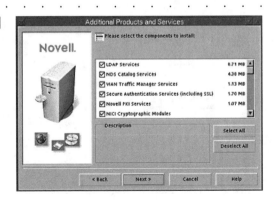

Mark the checkboxes of the additional products and services you'd like to install.

If you marked the LDAP Services checkbox on the Additional Products and Services screen shown in Figure 8.18, the LDAP Services for NDS Installation screen will appear. Click Yes to enable to use of the LDAP catalog on this server. Also, in the Catalog Usage for Searching section, make sure the "Search NDS if Requested Attributes are Not in Catalog" radio button is selected.

If you marked the Novell DNS/DHCP Services checkbox on the Additional Products and Services screen, the DNS/DHCP Installation screen will appear. Make sure the appropriate NDS context is listed in each field on this screen (for example: OU=LABS.OU=NORAD.O=ACME).

When the Summary screen appears, review the additional NetWare 5 products to be installed. When you are satisfied with the list of products, click Customize to be allowed to customize various installation parameters.

Step 13: Customize the Server

In Step 13, you can enhance the *basic* NetWare 5 server with some additional configurations. Most of this magic is accomplished in the Product Customization dialog box (see Figure 8.19). First, browse the tree to find the NetWare 5 components you wish to modify. Then, select the component and click Properties. Customize away!

FIGURE 8.19

Customizing the server in Server Installation Step 13

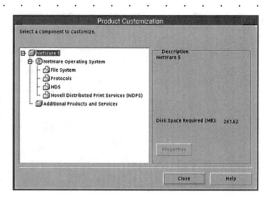

When you're finished supercharging your supercar, click Close to return to the Summary screen.

Step 14: Complete the Installation

On the Summary screen (see Figure 8.20), click Finish to complete the installation process. If a Disk Required dialog box appears, click the Browse button to the right of the Media Path field. When the next Disk Required screen appears, click the drive letter assigned to your CD-ROM drive, then click OK to return to the previous screen. When the Original Disk Required dialog box appears, click OK to continue.

Server Installation Summary screen at the end of Step 14

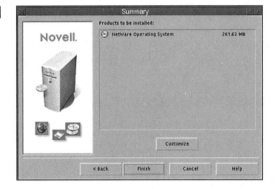

The Installation Wizard then performs the main file copy. (This step may take a while.) When the final copy is complete, the Installation Complete window appears—as shown in Figure 8.21. Click View Readme to display Release Notes. Click the Close button when you're finished reading them. Remove the NetWare 5 License diskette from the floppy drive. When the Installation Complete dialog box re-appears, click Yes to reboot the computer.

I Can't Believe It's Over!

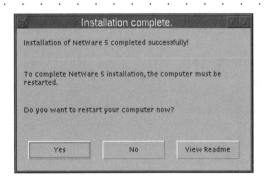

That's it — you've done it. You've successfully traversed the 4 stages and 14 steps of the NetWare 5 installation process — without too much pain and grease.

It all started with the Basic installation. This process involved some simple questions and NetWare-based defaults. Then, we got to customize the server with a variety of hotshot configurations — including server properties, languages, licensing, and additional components.

Well, that just about does it. You have built the NetWare 5 supercar. Now it's time to turn the key. You should feel proud about what you've accomplished here today.

STOP!

That concludes our exhaustive tour down Novell's newest information superhighway. As you can see, NetWare 5 is a powerful tool for saving the world and building a smaller Global Electronic Village. In this book, we've focused on the seven main features required for Novell's Course 560 (*NetWare 5 Administration*):

- ▸ Novell Directory Services (Chapter 2)

- ▸ NetWare 5 Connectivity (Chapter 3)

- ▸ NetWare 5 File System (Chapter 4)

- ▸ NetWare 5 Security (Chapter 5)

- ▸ NetWare 5 Workstation Management with Z.E.N.works (Chapter 6)

- ▸ NetWare 5 NDPS Printing (Chapter 7)

- ▸ NetWare 5 Installation (Chapter 8)

Boy, that's quite a deal. You're not only getting an award-winning network operating system but some great new applications as well. Don't ever say Novell never gave you anything.

Just in case you weren't paying attention during the previous 700 pages or so, I've summarized the most valuable NetWare 5 CNA/CNE features in Table 8.3. Knock yourself out.

TABLE 8.3

*Overview of the NetWare 5
Global Electronic Village*

FEATURE	NETWARE 4.11	NETWARE 5
Novell Directory Services (NDS)	NDS only	NDS and LDAP support
	Database parsing	Catalog Services
	Context-based login	Blue Sky Login
		WAN Traffic Manager
		NDS for NT (sold separately)
File System	2GB per file	8TB per file
	16 million directory entries	Trillions of directory entries
	One NetWare partition per disk	Four NetWare partitions per disk
	Eight volumes per partition	Unlimited volumes per partition
		Enhanced CD-ROM support
		High-performance access, regardless of file size
Security	Public-key authentication	Secure Authentication Services (SAS)
		Public Key Infrastructure Services (PKIS)
		Cryptographic services
Workstation Management	Novell Client 32	Z.E.N.works
	No remote control	Remote Control
		NDS Integration
		Desktop Maintenance
		Workstation Inventory

(continued)

TABLE 8.3

Overview of the NetWare 5 Global
Electronic Village (continued)

FEATURE	NETWARE 4.11	NETWARE 5
Printing	Queue-based printing	Novell Distributed Print Services (NDPS)
	Queues, print servers, and printers	Printer Agents
	Unidirectional communications	Bidirectional communications
		Plug-and-print
Installation	Text install	GUI install
		NLS Licensing
Java Support	JAVA.NLM	Java Virtual Machine (JVM)
		ConsoleOne
		OSA
IP Services	NetWare/IP Encapsulation	Pure IP
	DNS/DHCP	DNS/DHCP with NDS Integration
	SAP Discovery	SLP Discovery
		Compatibility Mode
Web Server	Novell Web Server	Netscape FastTrack Server
	FastTrack download	Administration Server Management
Application Server	Only real memory	Real memory and virtual memory
	No prioritization	Application prioritization
	Uni-processing kernel	Symmetrical multiprocessing
	Four processors, by default	32 processors, by default
	DOWN server for maintenance	HotPlug PCI
	Standard I/O	I_2O
		Network Management Agents (NMA)
		Oracle8 for NetWare

Oh, my goodness! Would you look at the time — where has it all gone? I've just been rambling away here . . . sorry, if you missed your train, plane, or supercar. I guess I'm done. There's not much more that can be said about NetWare 5. Are you interested in Golf? Aliens? Neurogenetic Recombination? We could talk about that for a while. Nah, I better save these topics for another book.

It's been quite a wild ride, and you should be very proud of yourself for surviving it in one piece — or so it seems. Do you still want to be a CNA? A NetWare 5 Superhero? Great. Because the world needs a few good CNAs, and you're a great place to start.

You are the final piece in our globe-trotting puzzle. You will save the world with NetWare 5. Your mission — should you choose to accept it — is to pass the *NetWare 5 Administration* exam. You will need courage, security, Z.E.N.works, and this book. If you succeed, you will save the world and become a CNA!

All in a day's work . . .

Well, that does it! The End . . . Finito . . . Kaput. Everything you wanted to know about NetWare 5, but were afraid to ask. I hope you've had as much fun reading this book as I've had writing it. It's been a long and winding road — a life-changer. Thanks for spending the last 700 pages with me, and I bid you a fond farewell in the only way I know how:

"See ya' later, alligator!"
"After a while, crocodile!"
"Hasta la vista, baby!"
"Live long and prosper!"
"So long and thanks for all the fish!"
"May the force be with you . . ."

GOOD LUCK, AND BY THE WAY....
THANKS FOR SAVING THE WORLD!!

BEST WISHES,
David James Clarke IV

LAB EXERCISE 8.1: INSTALLING THE CRIME-SRV1 SERVER IN TOKYO

Now that you've learned the basics of the NetWare 5 installation process, it's time to begin installing servers at ACME. The first server to be installed is located in the Crime Division at TOKYO.

To complete this exercise, you need the following:

- ▸ A computer that meets the minimum requirements for a NetWare 5 server.

- ▸ *NetWare 5 Operating System* CD-ROM.

Stage 1: Getting Started

The following tasks need to be completed before you install NetWare 5 on the server:

1. *Step 1: Complete pre-installation tasks*

   a. Select the computer to be used as a server, then create at least two verified backup copies of all data on tape or other storage media. Remember that all data on this computer will be destroyed during the pre-installation process. If this computer is currently being used as a server, be sure to back up the network security information (such as the bindery or NDS) as well as the file system.

   b. Install and configure network board(s) in the server. Refer to the network board manufacturer's documentation for configuration instructions.

   c. Boot the server using the version of DOS supplied by your computer manufacturer. (NetWare requires DOS 3.3 or higher.)

   d. Create a temporary boot disk. To format a disk and make it bootable, insert a diskette in Drive A:, type **FORMAT A: /S**, and press Enter.

   After the disk is formatted, use the DOS COPY command to copy the FDISK.EXE and FORMAT.COM utilities to the diskette. You may also want to copy the AUTOEXEC.BAT and CONFIG.SYS files, DOS CD-ROM drivers, and utilities such as EDIT.COM (to edit ASCII files), XCOPY.EXE (to copy files) and MEM.EXE (to display information about available RAM).

e. Use the DOS FDISK utility to delete existing hard disk partitions and create a new, active DOS partition of 30MB or more — leaving the rest of the hard disk space free.

f. After you've created the DOS partition, use the DOS FORMAT utility on the boot disk you made to format the new partition and make it bootable. To do so, type **FORMAT C: /S** and press Enter

g. On the server, install the CD-ROM drive as a DOS device, following the instructions provided by the drive manufacturer.

h. Use the DOS DATE and TIME commands to verify the computer's date and time, then modify them if necessary.

i. Make sure the server's CONFIG.SYS file contains the following parameters:

- FILES=40

- BUFFERS=30

2. *Step 2: Run INSTALL.BAT*

a. Insert the *NetWare 5 Operating System* CD-ROM in the server's CD-ROM drive.

b. Switch to the drive letter assigned to your CD-ROM drive. For instance, if the drive letter for your CD-ROM drive is E:, type the following and press Enter:

`E:`

c. Run the INSTALL.BAT batch file located in the root directory of the CD-ROM. To do so, type the following and press Enter:

`INSTALL`

Stage 2: C-Worthy Input Screens

3. *Step 3: Choose the type of installation*

a. While the Installation program is loading, the NetWare 5 title screen appears. Wait while the Installation program continues to load.

b. If a NetWare Installation screen appears, select the language to be used during the installation process and press Enter. In the initial release of NetWare 5, supported languages include English, French, German, Italian, Spanish, and Portuguese. (Note: This screen will only appear if you have an International version of the product.)

c. When the NetWare 5 Software License and Limited Warranty screen appears, read the agreement, then press F10 to accept the terms of the License Agreement.

d. On the "Welcome to the NetWare Server Installation" screen:

- In the "Is This a New Server or an Upgrade" field, make sure that "New Server" is selected.

- In the Startup Directory field, make sure that "C:\NWSERVER" is selected.

- Press F2 to gain access to the Advanced Settings menu.

e. On the Advanced Settings screen:

- In the "CD-ROM Driver to Access Install" field, make sure NetWare is listed. (If you know that you will need to use a DOS driver instead of a NetWare driver, type **D** to toggle the selection to DOS.)

- In the Server ID Number field, type **1001** and press Enter to replace the randomly generated number with a custom number.

- In the Load Server at Reboot field, verify that Yes is selected. (This will add the C:\NWSERVER\SERVER.EXE line to the server's AUTOEXEC.BAT file. The original version of the file will be saved with a .00X extension.)

- Leave the Server Set Parameters field unchanged.

- Press F10 to save these values and return to the previous screen.

f. When the "Welcome to the NetWare Server Installation" screen re-appears, select Continue from the Options menu and press Enter.

4. *Step 4: Select regional settings*

   Next, the Regional Settings screen will appear. Regional settings are used to customize server language and keyboard settings. If you are located in the United States, the default values are:

   - Country: 001 (USA)

   - Code Page: 437 (United States English)

   - Keyboard: United States

   Review the default settings and modify them if necessary. When the values are correct, select Continue from the Options menu and press Enter.

5. *Step 5: Modify selected drivers*

   During Step 5, the Installation Wizard attempts to automatically detect certain types of hardware and determine the appropriate drivers. Other drivers must be selected manually. Drivers that may be auto-detected include platform support, PCI HotPlug support, storage adapters, storage devices (such as hard disks, CD-ROMs, and tape drives), and LAN adapters. Drivers that are not auto-detected, and thus must be selected manually, include mouse type and display adapter. The drivers to be selected/confirmed appear on a series of three screens.

   a. The first driver screen lists mouse type and video mode parameters. Since these devices are not auto-detected by the installation program, you will need to select the appropriate settings manually.

      - *Mouse type* — Although the installation program supports PS/2 and serial mouse types, a mouse is not required.

      - *Video mode* — The installation program is optimized to use Super VGA and work with display hardware that is VESA 2-compliant. You should choose Standard VGA only if your video card does not support 256 colors.

Review the values listed on this screen and modify them if necessary. When the values are correct, select Continue from the Options menu and press Enter.

b. The system then automatically copies a number of server boot files from the CD-ROM to the startup directory indicated earlier. These include files such as SERVER.EXE, disk drivers, LAN drivers, NWCONFIG.NLM, NWSNUT.NLM, VREPAIR.NLM, and other NLMs. These files allow you to activate the NetWare operating system from the DOS partition and get things started.

c. The second driver screen lists the following types of drivers:

- *Platform Support Module* — The performance of servers with multiple processors and other configurations can be optimized by loading a platform support module driver. If no platform support module driver is detected, the server probably doesn't need one.

- *PCI HotPlug Support Module* — Computers that provide support for PCI HotPlug technology allow storage adapters and network boards to be inserted and removed while the computer is powered on. If your computer supports this technology, only one driver needs to be loaded, rather than one for each device. If no PCI HotPlug support driver is detected, your computer probably does not support PCI HotPlug technology.

- *Storage adapters* — The NetWare 5 installation program attempts to automatically detect storage adapters, then select the appropriate Host Adapter Module (HAM). If a particular storage adapter is not detected, choose the appropriate driver from the list provided or load it from a diskette or CD-ROM provided by the storage device manufacturer. Because a single storage adapter can control more than one type of storage device, only one HAM may be required. Make sure that any storage adapters are installed and configured properly, and that their settings do not conflict with other hardware devices in the same computer.

Review the values listed on this screen and modify them if necessary. When the values are correct, select Continue from the Options menu and press Enter.

TIP

If your computer does not support PCI HotPlug technology, do not attempt to remove network boards while the computer is powered on.

d. The third driver screen lists the following types of drivers that have been selected:

- *Storage devices* — The NetWare 5 Installation program attempts to automatically detect devices such as hard disks, CD-ROMs, and tape drives, then select the appropriate Custom Device Module (CDM) driver. If a particular storage device is not detected, choose the appropriate driver from the list provided or load it from a diskette or CD-ROM provided by the storage device manufacturer.

- *Network boards* — The NetWare 5 installation program attempts to automatically detect network adapters, then select the appropriate driver. If your LAN adapter is not detected, choose the appropriate driver from the list provided or load it from a diskette or CD-ROM provided by the LAN adapter manufacturer.

- *NetWare Loadable Modules* — Some servers and network configurations require that you load a NetWare Loadable Module (NLM) before completing the server installation. If so, add it in the NetWare Loadable Modules field.

Review the values listed on this screen and modify them if necessary. When the values are correct, select Continue from the Options menu and press Enter.

6. *Step 6: Create the NetWare partition and mount the SYS: volume*

a. Next, the Volume SYS and Partition Properties screen appears, displaying the defaults to be used for the creation of the default NetWare partition and SYS: volume. Parameters listed include the device, the NetWare partition size, the Hot Fix size, and the SYS:

volume size. To view the volume parameters for the SYS: volume, select Modify from the Options menu and press Enter, then press F3.

TIP

Don't forget that if you plan to use NSS, you will need to leave additional free space on the hard disk for the NSS partition, rather than using all of the free space for the NetWare partition.

b. The Volume Information screen appears. Typical values for these parameters are listed below. (Your values may be different):

- Volume Name: SYS

- Volume Block Size: 64KB Blocks

- Status: New, Not Mounted

- File Compression: On

- Block Suballocation: On

- Data Migration: Off

After you review the values, press Esc to return to the previous screen.

c. The "Volume SYS and Partition Properties" screen re-appears. If your SYS: volume is less than 1GB in size, skip to Step 6d. Otherwise, modify the value in the Volume SYS: Size (MB) field to be up to half the size of the existing SYS: volume, but in no case less than 850MB. Be sure to press Enter after you key in the new value.

If the values on the "Volume SYS and Partition Properties" screen are correct, press F10 to save them. Next, select Continue from the Options menu and press Enter.

d. The Installation program then creates a NetWare partition on your server's first hard disk consisting of all free space on that hard disk, unless you have specified otherwise. (If you have more than one hard disk, see the next Tip.) It also creates a SYS: volume on that NetWare partition consisting of all free space on the partition, unless you specified otherwise. Finally, the installation program mounts the SYS: volume.

REAL WORLD

NetWare 5 uses the following default procedure for creating NetWare partitions:

▸ **Single hard disk per server**—If the server contains only one hard disk, the INSTALL utility will create a single NetWare 5 partition consisting of all free disk space beyond the DOS partition.

▸ **Multiple hard disks per server**—On the first hard disk, the INSTALL utility will create a single NetWare 5 partition consisting of all free disk space beyond the DOS partition. On the remaining hard disks, the INSTALL utility will create one NetWare 5 partition per hard disk, where each partition consists of all of the available space on that disk.

Stage 3: GUI Input Screens

7. *Step 7: Name the NetWare 5 server*

   a. At this point, the installation program copies a number of files to the server (called the "preparatory file copy" process). A Java Virtual Machine will then be created on the server and the GUI portion of the Installation Wizard will be loaded. This step may take a while.

   b. When the Server Properties screen appears, type the following in the Server Name field, and then click Next:

     `CRIME-SRV1`

   c. When the Configure File System screen appears, review the information listed. If you modified the size of the SYS volume in an earlier step, skip to Step 7d. If not, click Next, then skip to Step 7g.

   d. On the Configure File System screen, click the Free Space icon, then click Create.

   e. When the New Volume screen appears, type the following in the Volume Name field and then click OK:

     `VOL1`

f. When the Configure File System screen re-appears, make sure the new volume is listed, then click Next.

g. When the Mount Volumes screen appears, you are asked whether to mount all volumes when the server reboots, or to mount them now. Make sure Yes is selected (to mount all volumes when the server reboots), then click Next.

8. *Step 8: Select networking protocols*

TIP

If your server will connect to the Internet, you must register with the Internet Network Information Center (InterNIC) and obtain a unique IP address. For information on receiving an IP address, contact your Internet Service Provider (ISP) or the Internetwork Information Center (InterNIC) directly at hostmaster@internic.net**.**

The Protocols screen will appear.

To configure the IP protocol:

- In the Network Boards pane on the left, click the icon for your network board.

- In the Protocols section on the right, mark the IP checkbox.

- Enter the IP address in the IP Address field. (If your server is not connected to the Internet, use 187.165.182.18)

- Enter the subnet mask in the Subnet Mask field. (If your server is not connected to the Internet, use 255.255.0.0)

- (Optional) Enter the router (gateway) address in the Router (Gateway) field.

To bind IPX:

- In the Protocols section on the right, mark the IPX checkbox.

When the values on this screen are correct, click Next.

9. *Step 9: Choose the server time zone*

When the Time Zone screen appears:

- Choose the correct server time zone for your location.

- Make sure the "Allow system to adjust for Daylight Saving Time" is marked, if applicable.

- When the values are correct, click Next.

10. *Step 10: Install Novell Directory Services (NDS)*

  a. On the NDS Install screen, select:

- "Create a New NDS Tree" to install this server into a new NDS tree. Take note of the fact that the resources available in the new tree will not be available to users that are logged into a different tree.

- Click Next.

  b. On the NDS screen, set up NDS by doing the following:

- Enter the following in the Tree Name field:

    `ACME_TREE`

- Enter the following as the location for the server in the Context for Server Object field:

    `CRIME.TOKYO.ACME`

- Enter the following as the Admin User object password in the "Password" and "Retype Password" fields.

    `ACME`

- When the values are correct, click Next. The installation program will check for duplicate tree names and install NDS.

  c. When the NDS Summary screen appears, write down the following information and store it in a safe place for future reference:

- NDS tree name

- Server context

- Administrator name

- (Password you entered on the previous screen)

Click Next to continue.

11. *Step 11: Install Novell Licensing Services (NLS)*

When the License screen appears:

- Normally, you would insert the appropriate NetWare 5 License disk in your floppy drive, browse to and select the appropriate license file, then click OK.

- Since this server is being installed for practice purposes only, mark the "Install without Licenses" checkbox.

- Click Next.

Stage 4: Customization

12. *Step 12: (Optional) Select Additional Products and Services*

a. When the Additional Products and Services screen appears:

- Click Select All to mark the checkboxes for all products and services listed.

- Click Next.

b. When the LDAP Services for NDS Installation screen appears:

- Click Yes to enable the use of the LDAP catalog on this server.

- In the Catalog Usage for Searching section, make sure the "Search NDS if Requested Attributes are Not in Catalog" radio button is selected.

- Click Next.

c. When the DNS/DHCP Installation screen appears:

- Make sure the following is listed in the Locator Object NDS Context field:

  `OU=CRIME.OU=TOKYO.O=ACME`

- Verify that the following is listed in the Group Object NDS Context field:

  `OU=CRIME.OU=TOKYO.O=ACME`

- Confirm that the following is listed in the RootSrvr Zone NDS Context field:

  `OU=CRIME.OU=TOKYO.O=ACME`

- Click Next.

d. When the Summary screen appears:

- Review the summary screen showing the NetWare 5 products to be installed. Since you deselected all of the selected products on the previous screen, the only product that should be listed is the NetWare Operating System.

- Click "Customize" to gain access to the Custom Hallway.

13. *Step 13: (Optional) Customize the Server*

a. On the Product Customization screen:

- Click Protocols.

- Click Properties.

b. When the Protocols Properties dialog box appears, the Protocols tab is selected by default:

- In the Network Boards pane on the left, click your network board.

- In the IPX section on the right, delete the value in the Network Address field next to the frame type selected, then type the following as the new value:

  1234

- Click OK to save your changes.

c. When the Product Customization screen re-appears, click Close to return to the Summary screen.

14. *Step 14: Complete the installation*

a. On the Summary screen, click Finish to complete the Installation process.

b. If a Disk Required dialog box appears:

- Click the Browse button to the right of the Media Path field.

- When the next Disk Required dialog box appears, click the drive letter associated with your CD-ROM drive in the left pane, then click OK.

- When the first Disk Required dialog box re-appears, click OK.

c. The Installation Wizard then performs the main file copy. (This step may take a while.)

d. When the copying is complete, the Installation Complete dialog box appears. Click View Readme to display the Release Notes

e. Read the Release Notes, then click Close when you're finished.

f. Remove the NetWare 5 License diskette from the floppy drive.

g. When the Installation Complete window re-appears, click Yes to reboot the computer.

LAB EXERCISE 8.2: NETWARE 5 CLIENT INSTALLATION

Now that you've successfully installed the CRIME-SRV1 ACME server in Tokyo, it's time to shift our focus to the distributed workstations. After all, the server won't have anyone to serve to if the clients can't speak NetWare.

In the next two sections, we'll explore the detailed Client Installation steps for two prominent workstation platforms:

▸ Windows 95/98

▸ Windows NT

Choose the section that relates to you . . . and we're off!

NetWare 5 Windows 95/98 Client Installation

To install the NetWare 5 client on a Windows 95/9 workstation, you will need the following components:

▸ A workstation that meets the minimum requirements for running the NetWare 5 Novell Client for Windows 95/98

▸ *NetWare 5 Novell Client Software* CD-ROM

Complete the following steps to perform a local installation of the NetWare 5 Windows 95/98 client on a workstation:

1. Exit any applications that you are running.

2. Install the NetWare 5 Windows 95 Client on your workstation:

  a. Insert the *NetWare 5 Novell Client Software* CD-ROM in your workstation's CD-ROM drive.

  b. When the first "WinSetup — Novell Clients" screen appears, click the language to be used for the Client installation, as shown in Figure 8.22.

► . . . . ◄

FIGURE 8.22

Choosing a language during Client installation

c. When the second "WinSetup — Novell Clients" screen appears, click Windows 95/98 Client, as seen in Figure 8.23.

► . . . . ◄

FIGURE 8.23

Choosing the Client type during Client installation

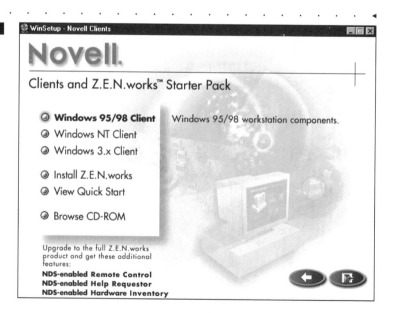

d. When the third "WinSetup — Novell Clients" screen appears, click Install Novell Client, as shown in Figure 8.24.

▶ · ◀

F I G U R E   8.24

Selecting the product during Client installation

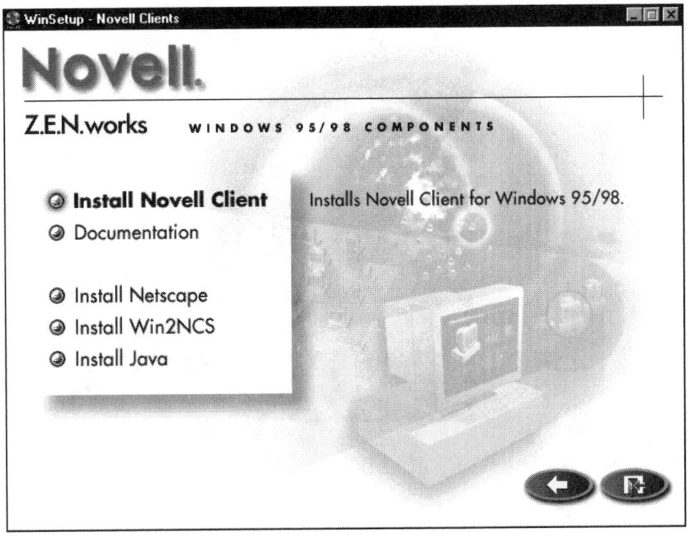

e. When the "Novell Client for Windows 95/98 License Agreement" window appears:

- Read the agreement

- Click Yes to accept its terms and conditions.

f. When the "Welcome to the Novell Client for Windows 95/98 Install" window appears:

- Click Custom to indicate that you'd like to perform a Custom installation, as seen in Figure 8.25.

- Click Next.

FIGURE 8.25

Selecting the installation type during Client installation

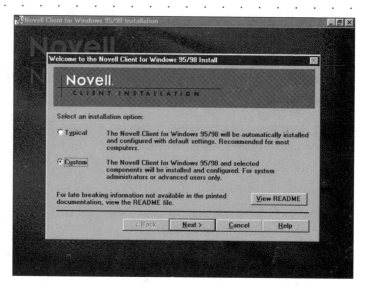

g. When the Protocol Preference window appears:

- Click IP and IPX to indicate that you'd like the Client to use the IP and IPX protocols, as shown in Figure 8.26.

- Click Next.

FIGURE 8.26

Selecting protocol(s) during Client Installation

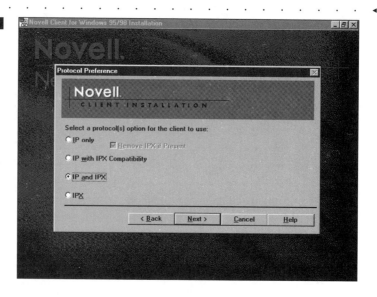

h. When the Login Authenticator window appears:

- Verify that the "NDS (NetWare 4.x or Higher)" radio button is selected, as seen in Figure 8.27.

- Click Next.

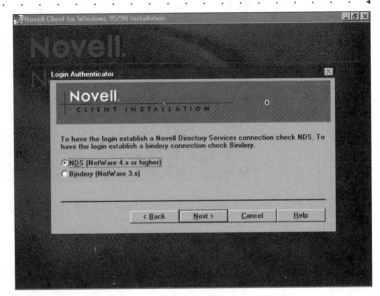

FIGURE 8.27

*Specifying an
NDS connection during
Client installation*

i. When the Novell Client for Windows 95/98 Custom Options window appears:

- Make sure that the following checkboxes are marked, as shown in Figure 8.28:

  Novell Workstation Manager

  Novell Distributed Print Services

  Novell NDS Provider—ADSI

- Click Install.

FIGURE 8.28

*Specifying optional
components during Client
installation*

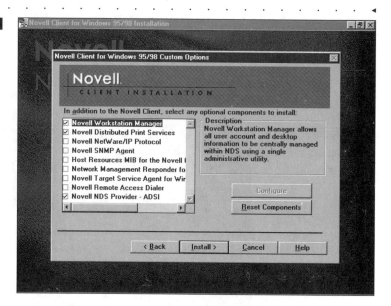

j. Wait while the NetWare 5 Client software is installed, as shown in
Figure 8.29.

FIGURE 8.29

*Copying files during Client
installation*

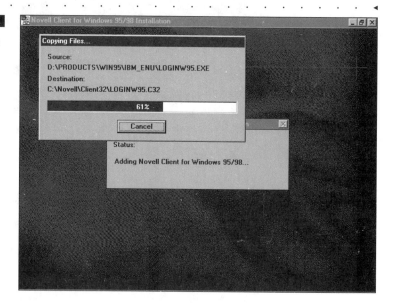

k. When the Novell Client for Windows 95/98 Installation window appears, click Reboot to reboot the computer, as seen in Figure 8.30.

▶ · ◀

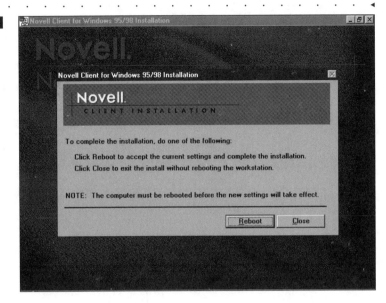

l. When the Novell Login dialog box appears, log into your tree as the Admin user.

NetWare 5 Windows NT Client Installation

To install the NetWare 5 client on a Windows NT workstation, you will need the following components:

▶ A workstation that meets the minimum requirements for running the NetWare 5 Novell Client for Windows NT

▶ *NetWare 5 Novell Client Software* CD-ROM

Complete the following steps to perform a local installation of the NetWare 5 Windows NT client on a workstation:

1. Exit any applications that you are running.

2. Install the NetWare 5 Windows NT Client on your workstation:

a. Insert the *NetWare 5 Novell Client Software* CD-ROM in your workstation's CD-ROM drive.

b. When the first "WinSetup — Novell Clients" screen appears, click the language to be used for the Client installation.

c. When the second "WinSetup — Novell Clients" screen appears, click Windows NT Client.

d. When the third "WinSetup — Novell Clients" screen appears, click Install Novell Client.

e. When the Novell Client Installation window appears:

- Click Custom Installation to indicate that you'd like to perform a Custom installation.

- Click Next.

f. When the Novell Client Installation window appears:

- Make sure that the following checkboxes are marked:

    `Novell Client for Windows NT (Required)`

    `Novell Distributed Print Services`

    `Novell Workstation Manager`

    `Z.E.N.works Application Launcher NT Serv`

- Click Finish.

g. Wait while the NetWare 5 Client software is installed.

h. When the Installation Complete window appears, click Reboot to reboot the computer.

i. When the Novell Login dialog box appears, log into your tree as the Admin user.

That's all there is . . . there isn't any more!

LAB EXERCISE 8.3:
START YOUR ENGINES

```
X  S  T  O  R  A  G  E  D  E  V  I  C  E  S  H  C  T  A  B
S  E  R  V  E  R  I  D  N  U  M  B  E  R  G  U  I  X  A  D
T  R  J  R  O  T  Y  R  H  P  C  U  S  T  O  M  V  S  U  F
O  V  P  Q  V  D  H  X  W  R  W  N  K  Y  E  X  I  P  T  D
R  E  L  E  A  S  E  N  O  T  E  S  I  Z  S  C  M  Y  O  G
A  R  A  U  S  D  M  M  G  H  B  D  O  M  C  F  Z  S  E  O
G  C  T  A  U  T  O  E  X  E  C  N  C  F  D  I  P  G  X  X
E  O  F  V  J  U  Q  L  I  E  E  B  X  X  N  A  T  V  E  H
A  N  O  L  S  T  A  R  T  U  P  N  C  F  R  D  L  P  C  E
D  T  R  E  G  I  O  N  A  L  S  E  T  T  I  N  G  S  B  G
A  E  M  H  O  T  P  L  U  G  P  C  I  T  C  V  Y  M  A  M
P  X  S  D  B  Q  W  L  R  C  V  T  Y  C  I  T  J  P  T  W
T  T  U  I  J  R  K  L  D  P  I  P  H  V  A  V  O  D  V  N
E  H  P  Y  Q  J  I  K  Y  O  B  T  D  B  C  X  T  U  C  I
R  V  P  B  X  C  O  W  N  R  K  K  L  E  O  D  V  L  S  F
S  J  O  W  P  E  Y  B  R  L  V  L  L  J  P  T  Z  M  H  E
W  X  R  V  Y  E  J  Y  N  S  W  W  M  X  I  Q  Z  I  U  O
K  U  T  K  X  G  X  G  W  H  N  T  S  V  L  D  J  S  R  F
```

Hints:

1. Name of default Administrator object.
2. DOS configuration boot file used to execute SERVER.EXE.
3. NetWare 5 configuration file that contains the server name and server ID number.
4. NetWare 5 installation method that uses pre-determined values for most configurable parameters.
5. NetWare 5 installation method where you install one server, then use the same profile to install other servers.
6. NetWare 5 installation method that allows you to modify values for most configurable parameters.

7. Home of the NWSERVER directory.
8. Type of user interface that is utilized in the second half of the NetWare 5 Installation process.
9. Type of support module that is auto-detected by the NetWare 5 Installation program.
10. Type of pointing device that is supported on NetWare 5 servers.
11. Another type of module that is auto-detected by the NetWare 5 Installation program.
12. Refers to country, code page, and keyboard settings.
13. Contains useful information regarding the NetWare 5 installation process.
14. Location of a server in the NDS tree.
15. New name for internal IPX number.
16. NetWare 5 configuration file that is used to load disk drivers.
17. Devices that use .HAM drivers.
18. Devices that use .CDM drivers.
19. Default NetWare 5 volume.
20. Selecting the wrong one may affect network time.

LAB EXERCISE 8.4: NETWARE 5 INSTALLATION

Across

1. NWPA device driver
2. Concurrently supported with IPX
3. Installation messages are displayed here
5. Traditional server programs
7. NetWare 5 installation utility
8. Traditional user interface type
10. Contains NetWare volumes
11. Auto-detected by the Install program
14. Uniquely identifies the server
17. Unsupported disk drivers
18. Loads NetWare 5 on the server

Down

1. Typical NetWare 5 installation media
2. Minimum server CPU type
4. NWPA storage adapter driver
6. Used to license the server
9. DOS partition utility
12. Operating system core
13. Default startup directory
15. Default installation language
16. Also known as server-to-server method

Appendixes

NetWare 5 Certification:
A World of Knowledge

In a world where people and businesses and organizations and governments and nations are being connected and sharing information at a dizzying rate, Novell's primary goal is to be the infrastructure that connects people and services together all over the world.

To help fulfill this goal, Novell Education is providing quality education programs and products to help create a strong support base of trained networking professionals. By itself, the Novell Education department isn't nearly large enough to provide high-quality training to the vast number of people who will require it. Therefore, Novell Education has developed training partnerships throughout the world to provide authorized training. In addition, Novell Education has created certification programs to help ensure that the standard for networking skills is maintained at a high level.

Today, Novell has more than 1,500 authorized education partners worldwide, including colleges, universities, professional training centers, and so on.

This appendix describes Novell Education and the CNA program. It also provides some practical tips, such as alternatives to formal classes, finding out how to take the test, and where to go from here. Specifically, we're going to learn how Novell Education and NetWare 5 will help you build your own on-ramp to the global Web — also known as a whole new "World of Knowledge."

Novell Certification

Every year, Novell certifies thousands of professionals around the world to manage and support its information technology (IT) products. Whether you are a network administrator, systems integrator, or other networking professional, you'll undoubtedly find that Novell offers one or more network certifications to meet your needs. If you want to learn more about the various types of certifications available, you should check out the information at `http://education.novell.com/certinfo/index.htm`.

NetWare 5 CNA Certification (New Candidates)

If you're new to the Novell certification process, you may find that the NetWare 5 CNA certification is the right one for you. This certification track consists of one course and one exam. Table A1 lists the course and associated test number that were valid as of the writing of this book.

T A B L E A.1	COURSE NUMBER	COURSE TITLE	TEST NUMBER
NetWare 5 CNA Exam Requirements	Course 560	NetWare 5 Administration	Test 50-639

While you're working toward your certification, you should always make sure that you have access to an up-to-date version of the progress chart relating to the certification you are interested in. If you plan to obtain a CNA certification, check out the CNA Progress Chart at `http://education.novell.com/cna/cnaprog.pdf`.

NetWare 5 CNE Certification (New Candidates)

If you're looking for a more comprehensive certification, you may find that the NetWare 5 CNE certification is the right one for you. This certification track consists of six courses, which map to six required exams. (You'll notice that one of the required courses, Course 560, is also a requirement for the CNA certification.) Five of the courses are preselected for you. You'll also be asked to select one of four electives. Table A2 lists the courses and test numbers that were valid as of the writing of this book.

TABLE A.2

*NetWare 5 CNE Exam
Requirements*

COURSE NUMBER	COURSE TITLE	TEST NUMBER
Course 560	NetWare 5 Administration	Test 50-639
Course 565	Networking Technologies	Test 50-632
Course 570	NetWare 5 Advanced Administration	Test 50-640
Course 575	NDS Design and Implementation	Test 50-634
Course 580	Service and Support	Test 50-635
	Electives: Select *one* of the following:	
Course 770	Intranet Security Management with BorderManager Enterprise Edition	Test 50-642
Course 730	Network Management Using ManageWise	Test 50-641
Course 555	NetWare: Integrating Windows NT	Test 50-644
Course 350	GroupWise 5 Administration	Test 50-633

When you're working toward your certification, it's very important that you always have access to an up-to-date version of the progress chart relating to the certification you are interested in. The CNE Progress Chart (which can be found at `http://education.novell.com/cne/cneprog.pdf`) includes a wealth of information, such as:

▸ Certification requirements (including current course numbers and exam numbers)

▸ A list of older exams that temporarily count toward certification

▸ Cross-certification information (for those who want to obtain CNE certifications for multiple Novell products)

NetWare 5 CNE Certification (Existing CNEs)

If you are currently a CNE, you can upgrade your certification to NetWare 5 using one of the following two options. Although either option can be used, note the specific recommendations from Novell for each type of existing CNE certification.

▶ *Option 1*: Pass the exam (test 50-638) for Course 529, "NetWare 4.11 to NetWare 5 Update." Novell recommends that NetWare 4 and IntranetWare CNEs use this option to upgrade their status to NetWare 5.

▶ *Option 2*: Pass the exam (test 50-640) for Course 570, "Advanced NetWare 5 Administration." Novell recommends that Classic, NetWare 3, and GroupWise CNEs use this option to upgrade their status to NetWare 5.

Training Options

You can obtain NetWare 5 certification by signing a Novell Education Certification Agreement (available at `http://education.novell.com/certinfo/certagrm.htm`) and passing the required exams. The following are among the many different training options available:

▶ Hands-on classroom training by Novell Authorized Education Centers (NAECs), which are Novell-approved commercial training centers, and Novell Educational Academic Partners (NEAPs), which are Novell-approved colleges and universities. (See the Authorized Training Locator at `http://db.netpub.com/nov_edu/x/naecloc.`)

▶ Novell Student Kit

▶ Novell Press books (See `http://www.novell.com/books` and `http://www.idgbooks.com.`)

▶ Online training

▶ Computer-based training (CBT)

▶ Videos

▶ Practice exams (such as The Clarke Tests at `http://www.Learning-Ware.com/`).

No matter which method(s) you use, just be sure that you have a thorough understanding of the technical concepts, as well as a firm grasp of the hands-on material.

▶ · ◀

The Testing Process

Okay. You've finished the course, you've studied this book, you've spent hours in the lab or on your own network using NetWare Administrator and other utilities to add users, change passwords, back up files, and the like. You're ready to show your stuff, and prove that you have the baseline of knowledge required to take on network administrator duties in the real world.

You're ready to take the test and become a CNA.

So, how do you sign up for the exam?

The NetWare 5 Administrator exam is offered at NAECs and NEAPs all over the world. The first thing you must do is find one of these centers to administer the exam.

How Do You Sign Up for an Exam?

All Novell exams are administered by one of two professional testing organizations: Sylvan Prometric or Virtual University Enterprises (VUE).

If you take a Novell-authorized course, you may be able to sign up to take the test at the same location, because some (but not all) NAECs are also affiliated with Sylvan Prometric. In fact, the instructor most likely can give you information about where to take the exam locally.

Otherwise, to find a location that administers this exam, simply call one of the following numbers:

- ▶ The Novell Education phone number at 1-800-233-EDUC (toll-free) or 1-801-222-7800

- ▶ Sylvan Prometric, at 1-800-RED-TEST (toll-free), 1-800-RED-EXAM (toll-free), or 1-410-880-8700

- ▶ VUE, at 1-800-511-8123 (toll-free), or 1-612-995-8800

Outside of the USA and Canada, contact your local Novell office, or a local Sylvan Prometric or VUE office.

What Is the Exam Like?

The NetWare 5 Administrator exam, like all Novell exams, is computer-based. In other words, you take the exam by answering questions on the computer. However, unlike more traditional tests, the NetWare 5 Administrator exam is *performance-based*. This means that instead of just asking you to regurgitate facts, the exam actually requires you to apply your knowledge to solve problems. For example, the exam may include simulations of network problems or tasks, such as adding a user. You must actually use NetWare utilities to complete the task or solve the problem.

The exam format, number of questions, and time limit will vary, depending on when you take the exam. Novell changes these parameters from time to time. If you take the exam early in the product's life cycle, you'll probably be given a *form test*, which means you'll be asked to answer a fixed number of questions in a specific time period (such as 80 questions in two hours).

An *adaptive test*, on the other hand, means that the exam offers easier or more difficult questions to you based on your last answer, in an effort to determine just how much you know. In other words, the exam starts off asking you a fairly easy question. If you answer it correctly, the next question will be slightly harder. If you answer that one correctly, too, it will offer you a slightly harder one again, and so on. If you answer a question incorrectly, on the other hand, the next question will be slightly easier. If you miss that one, too, the next will be easier yet, until you get one right. Then the questions will get more difficult again.

An adaptive exam typically has a 30, 45, or 60-minute time limit — depending on the exam. The number of questions you'll be asked in an adaptive exam will vary, depending on your level of knowledge. If you answer all of the questions correctly, you'll be presented with the minimum number of questions. If you answer any questions incorrectly, you'll be asked one or more additional questions — up to the maximum allowed. Obviously, the higher the level of knowledge the computer determines you have, the better score you'll receive.

The exam is closed-book and is graded on a pass/fail basis. The standard fee for the exam is $95. When you go to take the exam, remember to take two forms of identification with you (one must be a picture ID). You will not be allowed to take any notes into or out of the exam room.

If you fail the test, take heart. You can take it again. In fact, you can take it again as many times as you want — there are no limits to repeating it. You can repeat it as soon as you like, and as many times as it takes to pass (or until your checkbook runs dry, whichever comes first). Because of the way the exam is designed, questions are randomly pulled from a giant database. Therefore, chances are slim that you will ever get the same test questions twice, no matter how often you take the exam.

· ·

Checking Your Certification Status

Congratulations! You passed the exam with flying colors, just like we knew you would! Now comes the easiest part — getting your official CNA certification.

To receive your official certification status, you must sign a Novell Education Certification Agreement.

The certification agreement contains the usual legal jargon you might expect with such certification. Among other things, it grants you permission to use the trademarked name "CNA" on your resume or other advertising, as long as you use the name in connection with providing network administration services on a NetWare 5 network. It also reminds you that if the network administration services you offer don't live up to Novell's high standards of quality, Novell can require you to meet those standards within "a commercially reasonable time."

If you'd like to check your new or existing certification status, you can do so at `http://certification.novell.com/pinlogin.htm`. At this site, you can

▸ Update your personal information, such as name, address, phone, fax, e-mail address, and so on.

▸ View a list of certifications that you have already been awarded.

▸ Verify the exams that you have already completed.

This site requires a username and password, so you'll need to contact Novell CNA (or CNE) Administration if you don't know what those are.

For More Information

And, of course, you can always get more information about Novell products and services by surfing over to any of the Web sites described in Table A.3. Remember, we're here for you and *we care!*

TABLE A.3

For More Information

TYPE OF INFORMATION	WEB SITE URL
Novell Education	`http://education.novell.com/`
Novell Education Contact Information (Phone Numbers)	`http://education.novell.com/general/ eduphone.htm`
Novell Education Feedback (E-mail Addresses)	`http://education.novell.com/general/ feedback.htm`
Novell Certification Information	`http://education.novell.com/certinfo/`
Novell Certifications Available	`http://education.novell.com/certinfo/ index.htm.`
Certification Headline News	`http://education.novell.com/certinfo/ certnews.htm`
Novell CNA Program Information	`http://education.novell.com/cna/`
Novell CNE Program Information	`http://education.novell.com/cne/`
CNA Progress Chart	`http://education.novell.com/cna/cnaprog.pdf`
CNE Progress Chart	`http://education.novell.com/cne/cneprog.pdf`
NetWare 5 Certification FAQ	`http://education.novell.com/promos/ nw5faqs.htm`
CNA FAQ	`http://education.novell.com/faq/cnafaqs.htm`
Update Your CNE to NetWare 5	`http://education.novell.com/promos/529.htm`
Novell Training Options	`http://education.novell.com/general/ trainopt.htm`

(continued)

TABLE A.3

For More Information
(continued)

TYPE OF INFORMATION	WEB SITE URL
Authorized Training Locator	http://db.netpub.com/nov_edu/x/naecloc
Novell Press	http://www.novell.com/books
IDG Books	http://www.idgbooks.com/
IDG Books (Exclusively Novell section)	http://www.idgbooks.com/cgi-bin/ gatekeeper.pl?uidg3840:%2fnovell%2f
The Clarke Tests (interactive learning system)	http://www.learning-ware.com
Novell Education Certification Agreement	http://education.novell.com/certinfo/ certagrm.htm
Novell Testing Information	http://education.novell.com/testinfo/
CNENET (for current CNEs; requires username and PIN)	http://cnenet.novell.com/
Novell Education Personal Status Information (for current CNAs and CNEs; requires username and PIN)	http://certification.novell.com/ pinlogin.htm
Novell, Inc.	http://www.novell.com/
NetWare 5 Home Page	http://www.novell.com/netware5/
NetWare 5 Technical Papers	http://www.novell.com/netware5/ techpapers.html
NetWare 5 Online Documentation	http://www.novell.com/documentation/en/ nw5/nw5/docui/index.html
Novell Technical Support	http://support.novell.com/

Cross-Reference
to Novell Course Objectives

Novell's *CNA Study Guide* for NetWare 5 enables you to learn the Novell-authorized course objectives (see the page-number cross-references) in conjunction with Novell-authorized courseware. This appendix clarifies that relationship by pointing you in the right direction.

Have fun and good luck!

Section 1: Introduction to NetWare 5 and NDS

Section 2: Using a Workstation

4. Diagram a workstation dataflow model . . . . **(174)**

5. List the configuration options for the Novell Client and Windows . . . .
(176–178)

6. Install the Novell Client software . . . . **(176–183, 737–744)**

7. Explain and perform the login procedure . . . . **(178–183)**

8. Browse network resources . . . . **(210–219, 232–238)**

9. Install and configure a browser . . . . **(217–219, 232–238)**

Section 3: Setting Up and Managing Network Access for Users

1. Describe the function of the User object . . . . **(107–108, 115–117)**

2. Create and modify a user account using NetWare Administrator . . . .
(220–222, 239–256)

3. Create a User object using ConsoleOne . . . . **(222–224, 239–256)**

4. Create a User object using UIMPORT . . . . **(224–228, 239–256)**

5. Manage NetWare user licenses . . . . **(713–717)**

6. Identify the types of network security provided by NetWare . . . .
(340–348)

7. Describe and establish login security, including login restrictions for
users . . . . **(348–375, 442–450)**

Section 4: Printing with Novell Distributed Print Services

1. Describe network printing using NDPS . . . . (588–597)

2. Explain the four NDPS components and their functions . . . . (601–617)

3. List the NDPS printer types and explain the difference between public access printers and controlled access printers . . . . (598–601)

4. Configure the network for NDPS . . . . (618–635, 642–652)

5. Configure a workstation to print to NDPS printers . . . . (635–652)

6. Manage printer access and print jobs . . . . (653–665)

Section 5: Managing the File System

1. Identify the basic components of the network file system . . . . (262–264)

2. Identify the basic skills involved in managing the network file system . . . . (264–265, 303–311)

3. Use utilities to perform file system management tasks . . . . (264–311)

4. View file system information using NetWare Administrator and Windows . . . . (283–285, 292–296, 303–311)

5. Access the file system by configuring drive mappings . . . . (312–333)

6. Select the correct utilities for managing the directory structure . . . . (279–288, 303–311)

7. Select the correct utilities for managing files . . . . (288–311)

8. Manage volume space . . . . (273–279)

Section 6: Managing File System Security

1. Explain how file system security works . . . . (412–426)

2. Plan file system rights for your organization . . . . (437–450)

3. Plan and implement file and directory attribute security . . . . (426–432)

4. Create and implement file system security . . . . (437–450)

Section 7: Creating and Managing Login Scripts

1. Describe the types of login scripts and explain how they coordinate at login . . . . (184–190)

2. Design login scripts for containers, user groups, and users . . . . (190–208)

3. Use the MAP command in login scripts . . . . (196–197)

4. Create, execute, and debug login scripts . . . . (190–208)

5. Use the Login utility to edit login scripts . . . . (180, 182–183)

Section 8: Managing NDS Security

1. Define NDS security and how it differs from file system security . . . . (376–383, 413)

2. Control access to NDS objects . . . . (383–395, 442–450)

3. Determine rights granted to NDS objects . . . . (383–395, 442–450)

4. Block inherited rights . . . . (395–399, 442–450)

Section 9: Distributing and Managing Network Applications with Z.E.N.works

Section 10: Managing Workstations in an NDS Environment with Z.E.N.works

5. Register workstations in NDS and import them into the NDS tree . . . . (505–517)

6. Use policies to configure the desktop environment . . . . (547–551)

7. Establish and use remote control access to manage workstations . . . . (518–538)

8. Set up and use the Help Requester application . . . . (539–546)

Section 11: Managing Resources in a Multicontext Environment

1. Describe how the NDS tree structure affects network administration . . . . (97–105)

2. Identify NDS planning guidelines . . . . (126–127)

3. Provide users with access to resources . . . . (127–141, 179–180)

4. Create shortcuts to access and manage resources . . . . (228–231)

5. Identify guidelines for setting up resources in a multicontext environment . . . . (404–407, 228–231)

6. Identify the actions to take and the rights needed to grant a user access to NDS resources . . . . (404–407)

7. Create login scripts that identify resources in other contexts . . . . (190–208)

Section 12: Installing NetWare 5

1. Describe the function of a NetWare server and its interface, and identify the server components . . . . (672–689)

2. Perform a basic NetWare 5 server installation . . . . (689–736)

Solutions to Puzzles and Lab Exercises

Chapter 1: Saving the World with NetWare 5

Lab Exercise 1.1: ACME (A Cure for Mother Earth)

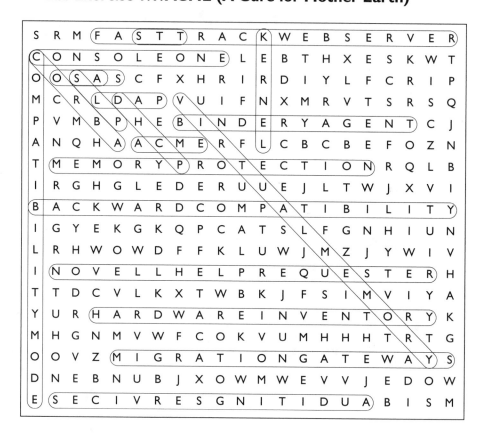

1. ACME
2. AUDITING SERVICES
3. BACKWARD COMPATIBILITY
4. BINDERY AGENT
5. COMPATIBILITY MODE
6. CONSOLEONE
7. CORBA
8. DHCP
9. FASTTRACK WEB SERVER
10. HARDWARE INVENTORY
11. KERNEL
12. LDAP
13. MEMORY PROTECTION
14. MIGRATION GATEWAYS
15. NOVELL HELP REQUESTER
16. OSA
17. SAS
18. SLP
19. TTS
20. VIRTUAL MEMORY

Lab Exercise 1.2: Saving the World with NetWare 5

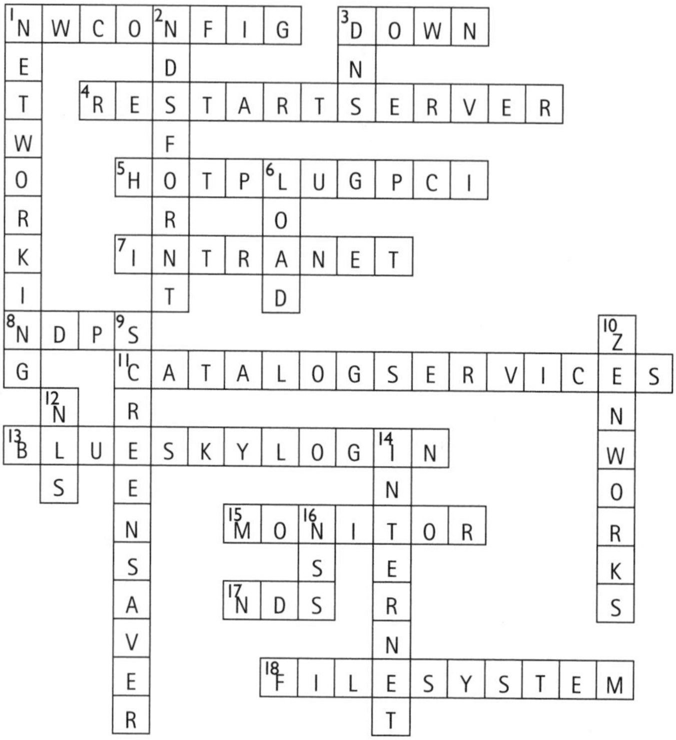
1 NWCONFIG
1 NETWORKING
2 NDSFORNT
3 DOWN
3 DN
4 RESTARTSERVER
5 HOTPLUGPCI
6 LOAD
7 INTRANET
8 NDPS
9 SCREENSAVER
10 ZENWORKS
11 CATALOGSERVICES
12 NLS
13 BLUESKYLOGIN
14 INTERNET
15 MONITOR
16 NS
17 NDS
18 FILESYSTEM

Chapter 2: Plant a Tree in a Cloud: Novell Directory Services

Lab Exercise 2.1: Getting to Know NDS

Part I

1. L
2. C
3. L

4. L
5. C
6. L
7. L
8. L
9. L
10. C

Part II

1. Container (Organizational Unit)
2. Leaf
3. Leaf
4. Leaf
5. Container (Organization)
6. Leaf
7. Container (Country or Organizational Unit)
8. Leaf
9. Organizational Unit
10. Leaf

Lab Exercise 2.2: Understanding NDS Naming

1. .BMasterson.BLUE.CRIME.TOKYO.ACME
2. .CN=RHood.OU=WHITE.OU=CRIME.OU=TOKYO.O=ACME
3. CRIME.TOKYO.ACME
4. CN=BLUE-SRV1.OU=BLUE.OU=CRIME.OU=TOKYO.O=ACME (since the default current context is the [Root])
5. SHolmes
6. LJohn.WHITE.CRIME
7. CN=SirKay.OU=CHARITY.
8. Admin...
9. CN=BThomas.OU=PR..
10. CN=BLUE-SRV1_SYS.OU=BLUE.OU=CRIME.OU=TOKYO.O=ACME....

11. .BLUE.CRIME.TOKYO.ACME (since it's the context of the server)
    LOGIN .DHolliday.BLUE.CRIME.TOKYO.ACME
    LOGIN DHolliday (since NetWare 4 searches the server's context by default)

12. CX CHARITY..

13. Add the following statement to his NET.CFG file (if he has an MS Windows workstation):

    NAME CONTEXT="OU=CHARITY.OU=TOKYO.O=ACME"

    Add the following to the Name Context field on the Client 32 page of the Novell NetWare Client 32 Properties dialog box:

    OU=CHARITY.OU=TOKYO.O=ACME

14. LOGIN .CN=SHolmes.OU=CRIME.OU=TOKYO.O=ACME
    LOGIN .SHolmes.CRIME.TOKYO.ACME
    LOGIN SHolmes.
    LOGIN CN=SHolmes.
    LOGIN SHolmes.CRIME..
    LOGIN CN=SHolmes.OU=CRIME..
    LOGIN SHolmes.CRIME.TOKYO...
    LOGIN CN=SHolmes.OU=CRIME.OU=TOKYO...
    LOGIN SHolmes.CRIME.TOKYO.ACME....
    LOGIN CN=SHolmes.OU=CRIME.OU=TOKYO.O=ACME....

15. CX /R

Lab Exercise 2.3: Plant a Tree in a Cloud

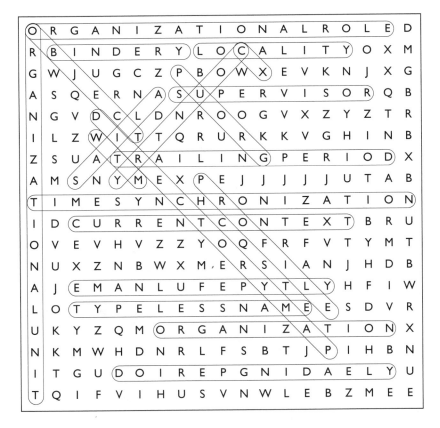

1. ALIAS
2. BINDERY
3. COUNTRY
4. CURRENT CONTEXT
5. CX
6. DIRECTORY MAP
7. GROUP
8. LEADING PERIOD
9. LOCALITY
10. OBJECT

11. ORGANIZATION
12. ORGANIZATIONAL ROLE
13. ORGANIZATIONAL UNIT
14. PROFILE
15. SUPERVISOR
16. TIME SYNCHRONIZATION
17. TRAILING PERIOD
18. TYPEFUL NAME
19. TYPELESS NAME
20. WTM

Lab Exercise 2.4: Novell Directory Services

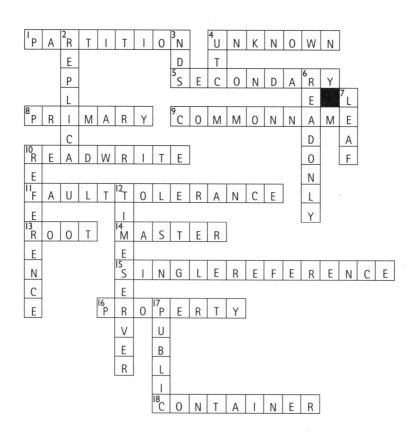

► · ◄

Chapter 3: Let Me In! NetWare 5 Connectivity

Lab Exercise 3.2: Configuring ACME's Login Scripts

```
REM This login Script was created by your name
REM On date at time.


REM TURN OFF THE DISPLAY OF DRIVE MAPPINGS
MAP DISPLAY OFF


REM MAP A SEARCH DRIVE TO SYS:PUBLIC
REM WITHOUT OVERWRITING THE DOS PATH
MAP INS S1:=SYS:\PUBLIC


REM MAP A SEARCH DRIVE TO THE TF-GP DIRECTORY
REM WITHOUT OVERWRITING THE DOS PATH
REM MAP S16:=SYS:\APPS\CRIME\TF-GP


REM A FALSE ROOT TO EACH USER'S HOME DIRECTORY
MAP ROOT U:=%HOME_DIRECTORY


REM DISPLAY A GREETING
WRITE "GOOD %GREETING_TIME, %LOGIN_NAME"
WRITE "TODAY IS %DAY_OF_WEEK, %MONTH_NAME %DAY, %YEAR"
WRITE "YOU HAVE LOGGED IN AT %HOUR:%MINUTE %AM_PM"


REM DISPLAY NEWS OF THE DAY
```

```
REM DISPLAY SHARED\CRIME\TF-GP\MESSAGE.NEW

PAUSE


REM REMIND TASKFORCE MEMBERS ABOUT WED STAFF MEETINGS

IF NDAY_OF_WEEK = "4" THEN BEGIN

  FIRE PHASERS 3

  WRITE "WEEKLY TASKFORCE MEETING IS AT 9:00 A.M."

  WRITE "IN CONFERENCE ROOM 3"

  PAUSE

END


REM RUN DR. WATSON'S LOGIN SCRIPT FOR TASKFORCE MANAGERS

REM IF MEMBER OF "TF-GPMGR" THEN INCLUDE
.DRWATSON.CRIME.TOKYO.ACME
```

Lab Exercise 3.3: "Tree Walking" for Toddlers
Part I: NetWare Administrator

3a. Answers will vary.

5a. The current context for the NetWare Administrator utility is the [Root].

5b. If you hadn't changed the context, the context would be whatever context was set when you previously used the utility.

5c. No; the context for each utility is set separately.

5d. Two.

5e. The objects are:

- ► ACME (Organization object)

- ► Security (special container that is created when Secure Authentication Services (SAS) is installed)

5f. Answers will vary.

Lab Exercise 3.4: Building ACME's NDS Tree
Part IV: Special Cases

We need a little help building ACME's NDS tree. In addition to the normal network resources, they have some special needs. Here's a quick list:

1. Each site needs a revolving administrator. This sounds like a job for Organizational Roles. Create an Organizational Role under each location OU. Use the following naming standard:

   `NORAD-Admin in OU=NORAD.O=ACME`

   `RIO-Admin in OU=RIO.O=ACME`

   `CAM-Admin in OU=CAMELOT.O=ACME`

   `SYD-Admin in OU=SYDNEY.O=ACME`

   `TOK-Admin in OU=TOKYO.O=ACME`

   Then, assign the divisional administrator as the first occupant in each location AEinstein, GWashington, KingArthur, Gandhi, and SHolmes, respectively.

2. Next, create a common Profile login script object for all the administrators to share. It should be called ADMIN-Profile and placed in the O=ACME container. Remember, shared objects are placed higher in the tree. Finally, attach each Organizational Role to the shared login script by referencing the Profile object within each Organizational Role's Login Script property.

3. The Directory Map object saves the day. If the Human Rights (HR) tracking program is constantly changing, consider creating a Directory Map object as a point of central control. Then, all the HR login scripts can point to the central object, not the physical application directory. In this case, create an HR Directory Map object called HR-App, and place it in the .OU=HR.OU=SYDNEY.O=ACME container. Then, place the following directory in the Directory Map object's Path property:

   `HR-SRV1/SYS:APPS\HRT`

4. In addition, each of the HR administrators need access to the Human Rights tracking application in HR-SRV1/SYS:APPS\HRT. Security could be a problem. The Group object is your friend. Create a Group leaf object called HR-Group, and place it in the .OU=HR.OU=SYDNEY.O=ACME

container. Then, create a Group Membership list containing each of the HR administrators—Gandhi, ASchweitzer, MTeresa, FNightingale, and Buddha.

5. The people in the Auditing department need easy access to the Financial resources. There's a simple solution, and it allows the auditors to access these resources from within their home OU=AUDIT container. Simply create an Alias object for .OU=FIN.OU=OPS.OU=CAMELOT.O=ACME, and place it in the OU=AUDIT container. The Alias will point to the original objects from within the auditor's home context. Clever, huh?

6. In addition, the auditors and financial accountants need access to the ever-changing financial database program. Once again, the Directory Map object saves the day. In this case, create a Directory Map object called FIN-App and place it in the .OU=AUDIT.OU=ADMIN.OU=RIO.O=ACME and .OU=FIN.OU=OPS.OU=CAMELOT.O=ACME containers. Then, place the following directory in the Directory Map object's Path property:

```
CAM-FIN-SRV1/SYS:APPS\FIN
```

7. The same holds true for the auditing application, except this time only the auditors need access to the Directory Map object. In this case, create a Directory Map object called AUD-App, and place it in the .OU=AUDIT. OU=ADMIN.OU=RIO.O=ACME container. Then, place the following directory in the Directory Map object's Path property:

```
AUDIT-SRV1/SYS:APPS\AUDIT
```

8. To accommodate traveling users, we will create corresponding Alias objects for them in the very top of the ACME tree. This way, they can log in from anywhere with a very simple name context. For example, MCurie's alias becomes .MCurie.ACME. That's a big improvement over MCurie.NUC.R&D. LABS.NORAD.ACME. To accomplish this, create three user Alias objects (MCurie, AEinstein, and DHoliday), and place them in the O=ACME container. All done.

9. Everyone in the Crime Fighting division needs access to a common login script. Simply create a global Profile Login Script property called CRIME-profile, and place it in the .OU=CRIME.OU=TOKYO.O=ACME container. Don't forget to add CRIME-profile to each user's Login Script property.

10. To empower Leonardo's scientists, you'll need to create an Organizational Role called R&D-Admin. Place it in the OU=R&D.OU=LABS.OU=NORAD.O=ACME

container, and give the Organizational Role Administrative rights over all R&D resources. Then, you can rotate the scientists through the Organizational Role, starting with LDaVinci. Make him the first occupant. It's as easy as 1-2-3.

Thanks for helping out. The world's in good hands with a CNA like you on the job!

Lab Exercise 3.5: Connecting to the NetWare 5 Network

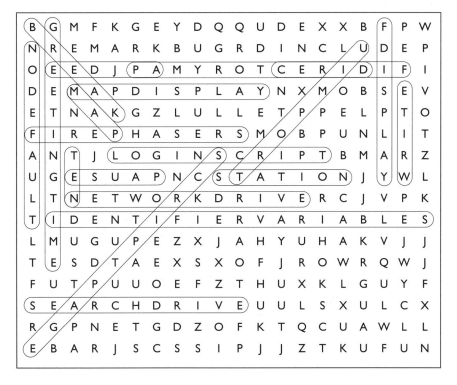

1. BREAK
2. DIRECTORY MAP
3. FDISPLAY
4. FIRE PHASERS
5. GREETING_TIME
6. IDENTIFIER VARIABLES
7. INCLUDE
8. LOGIN SCRIPT

9. MAP
10. MAP DISPLAY
11. NETWORK DRIVE
12. NO_DEFAULT
13. PAUSE
14. REMARK
15. SCRIPT PAGE
16. SEARCH DRIVE
17. STATION
18. TEN
19. UIMPORT
20. WRITE

Lab Exercise 3.6: Let Me In!

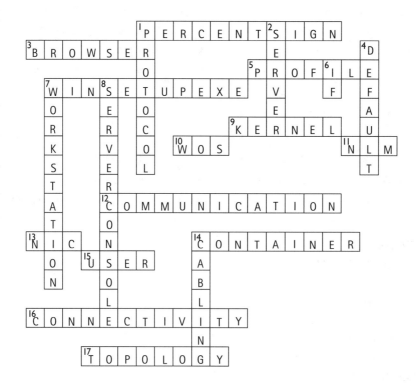

Chapter 4: File Cabinet of Life: NetWare File System

Lab Exercise 4.2: Mapping Drives with MAP

1. MAP /?
2. MAP
3. MAP F:=SYS:USERS
4. MAP G:=SYS:\SHARED\POL
5. MAP J:=F:
6. MAP S:=.WHITE.SRV1_SYS.WHITE.CRIME.TOKYO.ACME:SHARED
7. MAP INS S1:=SYS:\PUBLIC
8. MAP INS S2:=SYS:\PUBLIC\IBM_PC\MSDOS\V6.22
9. MAP S3:=APPS\SS30
10. MAP ROOT S4:=SYS:\APPS\DB50
11. MAP
    In the map list, the false root has no space after the volume name but does have a space followed by a backslash after the name of the directory it points to.
12. MAP S5:=W:=SYS:\APPS\WP70
    Yes.
13. The MAP command didn't work. To fix the problem, type **CD \PUBLIC**.
14. MAP DEL J:
15. MAP REM S3:
    The search drives with higher search drive numbers were renumbered accordingly.
    The network drive associated with the search drive was deleted.
16. MAP C S4:
    The search drive was deleted.
    The network drive associated with the search drive was moved to the top portion of the map list.

Lab Exercise 4.4: File Cabinet of Life

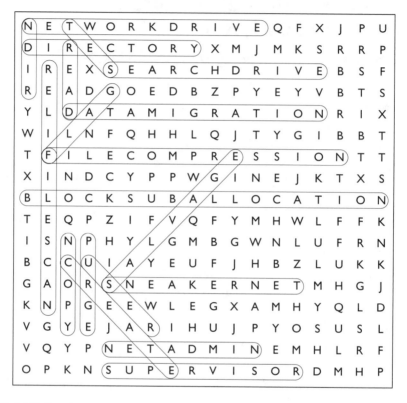

1. BLOCK SUBALLOCATION
2. CREATE
3. DATA MIGRATION
4. DIRECTORY
5. FILE COMPRESSION
6. FILE SCAN
7. FILER
8. FLAG
9. NCOPY
10. NDIR
11. NETADMIN
12. NETWORK DRIVE
13. PURGE

14. READ
15. SALVAGE
16. SEARCH DRIVE
17. SET
18. SNEAKERNET
19. SUPERVISOR
20. USER

Lab Exercise 4.5: NetWare 5 File System

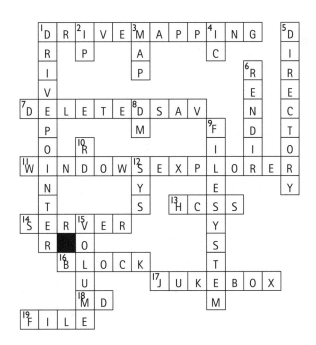

· ◄

Chapter 5: Keep the Bad Guys Out: NetWare 5 Security

Lab Exercise 5.1: Calculating NDS Effective Rights

OK, now that you're a pro with NetWare 5 NDS security, let's experiment with "modern math." In this exercise, we began Calculus 101 with NDS access rights.

Then, in Lab Exercise 5.2 (next), you'll get an opportunity to explore file system access rights. Also, we've included some beautiful graphic worksheets to help you follow along. You can create your own at home with a pencil, some paper, and a ruler.

So, without any further ado, let's get on with CASE #1.

CASE #1

In this case, we are helping Sherlock Holmes gain administrative rights to the Crime Fighting division of ACME. Refer to Figure C5.1 for the completed effective rights calculation worksheet.

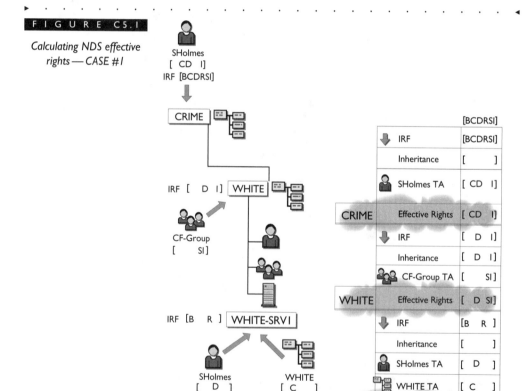

FIGURE C5.1

Calculating NDS effective rights — CASE #1

As you can see from the figure, Sherlock Holmes is granted [CD I] rights to the .OU=CRIME Organizational Unit. Since he has no rights from any other source, and explicit trustee assignments override the Inherited Rights Filter (IRF) for this container, his effective rights for the CRIME Organizational Unit are the same — [CD I].

These rights then flow down to the .OU=WHITE Organizational Unit as inherited rights, where they are partially blocked by an IRF of [D I] — leaving inherited rights of [D I]. Sherlock Holmes also gets the [SI] rights to the WHITE Organizational Unit as a member of the CF-Group object. If you add his individually-inherited rights of [D I] to the group-inherited [SI] rights, you'll find that his effective rights for the WHITE container are [D SI]. (Note: The fact that he has the [SI] object rights means that he implicitly has all object rights and all property rights for this object. However, the Supervisor right stands alone when it comes to the IRF . . . as you're about to see in the next section).

Finally, Sherlock's effective rights of [D SI] in the WHITE container flow down and become inherited rights at the WHITE-SRV1 server, where they are totally blocked by the IRF of [B R]. (Even though he implicitly had all rights to the WHITE container, implied rights do not flow down — only explicit rights. Also, remember, that the [S] right CAN be blocked by an IRF in the NDS tree.) Sherlock Holmes does, however, receive an explicit trustee assignment of [D   ] to the WHITE-SRV1 server as an individual. Also, his home container, the WHITE Organizational Unit, receives a trustee assignment of [C   ] — meaning that his effective rights for the WHITE-SRV1 server are [CD   ].

CASE #2

After careful consideration, you decide that the previous rights are inadequate for Sherlock and his administrative needs. So, let's try it one more time. But, in this case, we're going to use the "CF-Role" Organizational Role instead of the CF-Group. This gives us more administrative flexibility and narrows the scope of rights assignments. Refer to Figure C5.2 for the completed effective rights calculation worksheet.

In Case #2, Sherlock Holmes receives an explicit trustee assignment of [B R] to the CRIME Organizational Unit. Because he has no rights from other sources, and an explicit assignment overrides the IRF, his effective rights in the CRIME Organizational Unit are [B R].

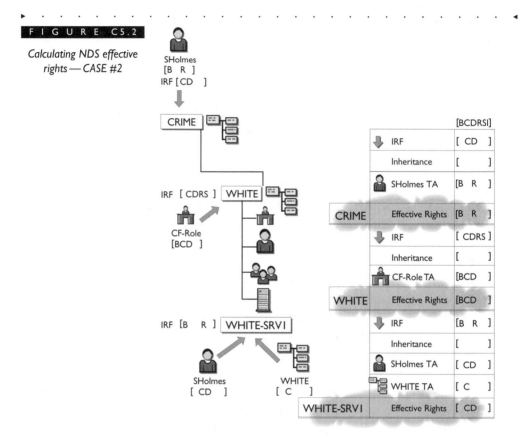

FIGURE C5.2

Calculating NDS effective rights — CASE #2

These rights would usually flow down and become inherited rights at the WHITE Organizational Unit. However, NetWare 5 requires the Inherited [I] right in order for rights to flow down the tree. Since Sherlock Holmes doesn't have the Inherited [I] right at CRIME, he won't inherit the [B R] rights in the WHITE sub-container. Interesting, huh? Therefore, his effective rights in WHITE are the same as his explicit rights from the CF-Role Organizational Role object — that is, [BCD].

Similarly, Sherlock's effective rights to the WHITE-SRV1 Server object are simply a combination of the individual rights he gains as SHolmes and the ancestral rights he gains from his home container (OU=WHITE). In this case, the

IRF is meaningless because there are no inherited rights due to the lack of the [I] right in the parent container.

Bottom line: Sherlock Holmes' effective rights to the WHITE-SRV1 object are [CD   ]. Viola!!

CASE #3

In this final case, let's bounce over to the .BLUE.CRIME.TOKYO.ACME container and help out Wyatt Earp — their administrator. Refer to Figure C5.3 for the completed effective rights calculation worksheet.

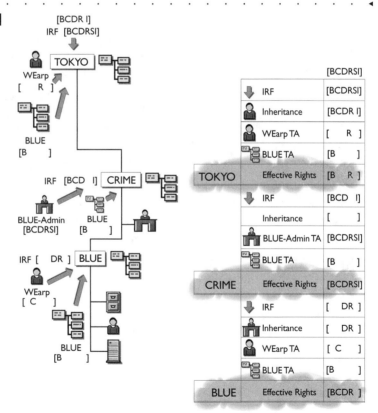

FIGURE C5.3

Calculating NDS effective rights — CASE #3

In Case #3, Wyatt Earp inherits [BCDR I] rights to the TOKYO Organizational Unit through a trustee assignment to his User object somewhere higher in the tree. These rights are then filtered by the Tokyo Organizational Unit's IRF of [BCDRSI] — which allows all five rights to flow through. He doesn't get to keep these rights, however, because his User object receives a new trustee assignment to the Tokyo Organizational Unit at this level — and such an assignment blocks inheritance from his User object from higher in the tree. Wyatt Earp does, however, receive the [B   ] trustee right for the TOKYO Organizational Unit from the Blue Organizational Unit, which is his home container, and the [R] right from his User object. This means that his inherited rights for the TOKYO container are [B   ] plus [R] or [B R].

None of these rights flows down to the CRIME sub-container because there's no Inherited [I] right in the TOKYO parent. It doesn't matter, though, because Wyatt Earp receives an explicit trustee assignment of all rights to CRIME through his BLUE-Admin Organizational Role object. This overshadows his [B   ] rights from BLUE and gives him effective rights for the CRIME Organizational Unit of [BCDRSI].

Finally, these rights flow down and become inherited rights at the BLUE Organizational Unit and are partially blocked by an IRF of [DR   ] — leaving inherited rights of [DR]. (Remember, the [S] right CAN be blocked by an IRF in the NDS tree.) Wyatt Earp also receives the [C   ] right to the BLUE Organizational Unit from his User object and the [B   ] right from the BLUE Organizational Unit, which is his home container. This means that his effective rights to the BLUE Organizational Unit are the [DR] rights, which he received through inheritance, plus the [C   ] right which he received from his User object, plus the [B   ] right which he received from the BLUE Organizational Unit — or [BCDR].

Well, there you have it. Great work. Now that you're an NDS security guru, let's rustle on over to Lab Exercise 5.2 — File System Access Rights.

Lab Exercise 5.2: Calculating File System Effective Rights

Case #1

See Figure C5.4 for the answer to this case.

▶ · ◀

FIGURE C5.4

Calculating file system effective rights — CASE #1

SYS: SHARED	S	R	W	C	E	M	F	A
Inherited Rights Filter	S	R	W	C	E	M	F	A
Inherited Rights — User								
Inherited Rights — Group								
Trustee Assignment — User		R	W	C			F	
Trustee Assignment — Group								
Effective Rights		R	W	C			F	

SYS: SHARED\CYBER	S	R	W	C	E	M	F	A
Inherited Rights Filter	S	R					F	
Inherited Rights — User		R					F	
Inherited Rights — Group								
Trustee Assignment — User								
Trustee Assignment — Group								
Effective Rights		R					F	

CYBER.DOC	S	R	W	C	E	M	F	A
Inherited Rights Filter		R	W	C			F	
Inherited Rights — User		R					F	
Inherited Rights — Group								
Trustee Assignment — User								
Trustee Assignment — Group								
Effective Rights		R					F	

Case #2

See Figure C5.5 for the answer to this case.

Calculating file system effective rights — CASE #2

SYS: SHARED	S	R	W	C	E	M	F	A
Inherited Rights Filter	S	R	W	C	E	M	F	A
Inherited Rights — User								
Inherited Rights — Group								
Trustee Assignment — User		R	W	C			F	
Trustee Assignment — Group								
Effective Rights		R	W	C			F	

SYS: SHARED\CRIME	S	R	W	C	E	M	F	A
Inherited Rights Filter	S							A
Inherited Rights — User								
Inherited Rights — Group								
Trustee Assignment — User								
Trustee Assignment — Group		R	W	C	E	M	F	
Effective Rights		R	W	C	E	M	F	

CRIME.DB	S	R	W	C	E	M	F	A
Inherited Rights Filter	S	R	W	C			F	
Inherited Rights — User								
Inherited Rights — Group								
Trustee Assignment — User								
Trustee Assignment — Group		R					F	
Effective Rights		R					F	

Case #3

See Figure C5.6 for the answer to this case.

FIGURE C5.6

Calculating file system effective rights — CASE #3

SYS: SHARED	S	R	W	C	E	M	F	A
Inherited Rights Filter	S	R	W	C	E	M	F	A
Inherited Rights — User								
Inherited Rights — Group								
Trustee Assignment — User								
Trustee Assignment — Group		R	W	C	E		F	
Effective Rights		R	W	C	E		F	

SYS: SHARED\POL	S	R	W	C	E	M	F	A
Inherited Rights Filter	S							
Inherited Rights — User								
Inherited Rights — Group								
Trustee Assignment — User						M		A
Trustee Assignment — Group		R	W	C	E		F	
Effective Rights		R	W	C	E	M	F	A

CRIME.RPT	S	R	W	C	E	M	F	A
Inherited Rights Filter	S	R	W	C	E	M	F	A
Inherited Rights — User						M		A
Inherited Rights — Group		R	W	C	E		F	
Trustee Assignment — User								
Trustee Assignment — Group								
Effective Rights		R	W	C	E	M	F	A

Case #4

See Figure C5.7 for the answer to this case.

▶ · ◀

FIGURE C5.7
Calculating file system effective rights — CASE #4

SYS: SHARED	S	R	W	C	E	M	F	A
Inherited Rights Filter	S	R	W	C	E	M	F	A
Inherited Rights — User								
Inherited Rights — Group								
Trustee Assignment — User	S	R	W	C	E	M	F	A
Trustee Assignment — Group								
Effective Rights	S	R	W	C	E	M	F	A

SYS: SHARED\CRIME	S	R	W	C	E	M	F	A
Inherited Rights Filter	S							
Inherited Rights — User	S							
Inherited Rights — Group								
Trustee Assignment — User								
Trustee Assignment — Group		R	W	C			F	
Effective Rights	S	R	W	C	(E)	(M)	F	(A)

CYBER.DB	S	R	W	C	E	M	F	A
Inherited Rights Filter	S	R					F	
Inherited Rights — User	S							
Inherited Rights — Group								
Trustee Assignment — User								
Trustee Assignment — Group		R					F	
Effective Rights	S	R	(W)	(C)	(E)	(M)	F	(A)

Lab Exercise 5.4: Keep the Bad Guys Out

```
T  S  L  R  W  G  R  A  C  E  L  O  G  I  N  S  C  I  L  B  U  P
R  T  I  M  E  R  E  S  T  R  I  C  T  I  O  N  S  F  Q  M  V  R
U  A  S  R  F  O  X  I  W  B  I  M  U  H  M  M  A  C  L  O  I  O
S  T  G  O  U  U  N  I  Q  U  E  P  A  S  S  W  O  R  D  S  N  P
T  I  E  I  V  P  S  N  T  I  J  G  F  B  F  Y  D  E  L  E  T  E
E  O  P  N  R  D  R  H  H  H  O  C  X  X  J  W  I  A  N  M  R  R
E  N  B  M  E  F  F  E  C  T  I  V  E  R  I  G  H  T  S  R  U  T
R  R  E  M  A  N  E  R  L  H  T  T  I  E  O  K  U  E  X  V  D  Y
I  E  Z  U  X  K  X  I  O  F  X  N  J  H  R  S  U  G  D  O  E  R
G  S  E  C  U  R  I  T  Y  E  Q  U  I  V  A  L  E  N  C  E  R  I
H  T  X  D  B  J  F  A  L  S  S  D  Y  O  C  P  Y  S  M  Z  D  G
T  R  I  H  I  H  G  N  I  T  J  D  R  C  S  M  L  I  J  L  E  H
S  I  F  M  X  E  F  C  J  A  U  U  J  Y  M  J  X  P  S  G  T  T
Q  C  N  Y  Z  L  I  E  I  X  Y  J  V  U  H  P  Q  A  Y  T  E  S
Q  T  R  E  S  H  H  C  E  R  I  S  K  V  K  U  O  M  M  Y  C  A
M  I  L  G  Y  K  S  T  K  J  O  B  J  E  C  T  R  I  G  H  T  S
M  O  S  C  Z  T  M  D  C  C  E  O  Q  C  H  E  I  R  Q  R  I  Y
H  N  R  H  I  G  V  X  A  U  T  H  E  N  T  I  C  A  T  I  O  N
I  S  S  G  O  G  Q  Q  D  K  Y  T  X  V  F  N  J  P  F  Z  N  Q
```

1. ACL
2. AUTHENTICATION
3. CREATE
4. DELETE
5. EFFECTIVE RIGHTS
6. GRACE LOGINS
7. GROUP
8. INHERITANCE
9. INTRUDER DETECTION
10. IRF
11. OBJECT RIGHTS

12. PROPERTY RIGHTS
13. [PUBLIC]
14. RENAME
15. SECURITY EQUIVALENCE
16. STATION RESTRICTIONS
17. TIME RESTRICTIONS
18. TRUSTEE RIGHTS
19. TTS
20. UNIQUE PASSWORDS

Lab Exercise 5.5: NetWare 5 Security

Chapter 6: The Zen of NetWare 5: NetWare 5 Workstation Management

Lab Exercise 6.1: Understanding Z.E.N.works

1. b (Realm 2: Desktop Management)
2. a (Realm 1: Workstation Maintenance)
3. c (Realm 3: Application Management)
4. a (Realm 1: Workstation Maintenance)
5. b (Realm 2: Desktop Management)
6. c (Realm 3: Application Management)
7. a (Realm 1: Workstation Maintenance)
8. c (Realm 3: Application Management)
9. b (Realm 2: Desktop Management)
10. a (Realm 1: Workstation Maintenance)
11. c (Realm 3: Application Management)
12. b (Realm 2: Desktop Management)
13. a (Realm 1: Workstation Maintenance)
14. a (Realm 1: Workstation Maintenance)
15. b (Realm 2: Desktop Management)
16. a (Realm 1: Workstation Maintenance)
17. b (Realm 2: Desktop Management)
18. a (Realm 1: Workstation Maintenance)
19. c (Realm 3: Application Management)
20. b (Realm 2: Desktop Management)
21. b (Realm 2: Desktop Management)
22. a (Realm 1: Workstation Maintenance)

Lab Exercise 6.6: The Zen of NetWare 5

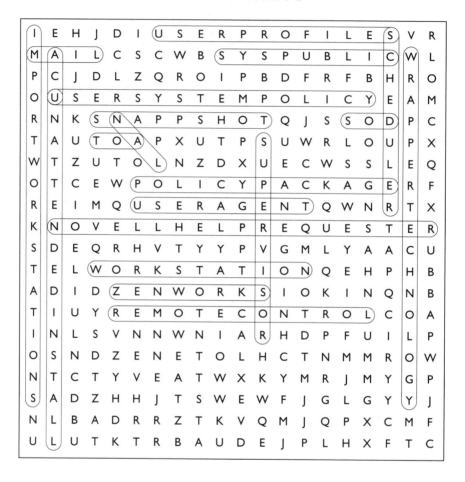

1. ACU
2. AOT
3. DOS
4. IMPORT WORKSTATIONS
5. MAIL
6. NAL
7. NOVELL HELP REQUESTER
8. POLICY PACKAGE
9. REMOTE CONTROL
10. SCHEDULER
11. SNAPPSHOT
12. SUPERVISOR
13. SYS:PUBLIC
14. UNATTENDED INSTALL
16. USER AGENT
15. USER PROFILES
17. USER SYSTEM POLICY
18. WORKSTATION
19. WRAPPER TECHNOLOGY
20. ZENWORKS

Lab Exercise 6.7: NetWare 5 Workstation Management

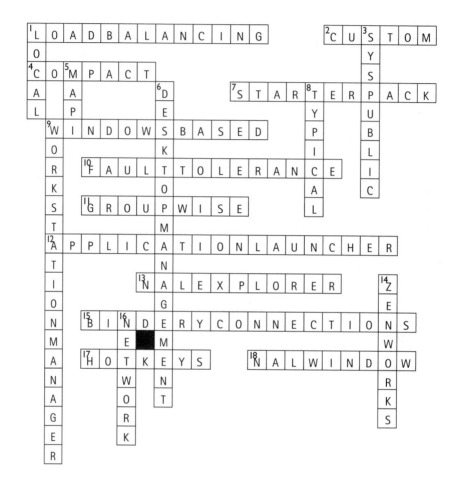

- - - - - - - -

Chapter 7: The Great Puzzle:
NetWare 5 Printing

Lab Exercise 7.1: Understanding NDPS

1. b (NDPS Manager)
2. d (Printer driver)

3. a (NDPS Broker)
4. f (Public Access printer)
5. c (Printer Agent)
6. g (Controlled Access printer)
7. e (Printer gateway)

Lab Exercise 7.3: The Great Puzzle

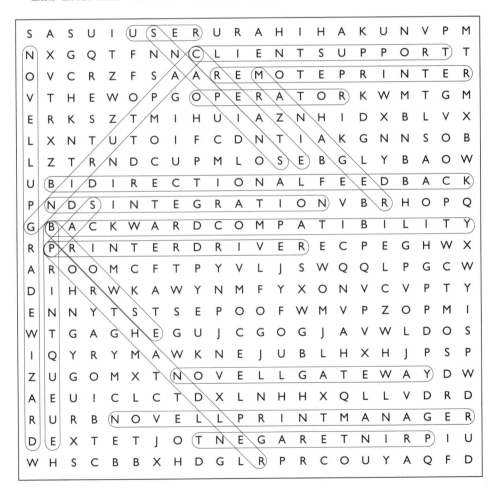

1. BACKWARD-COMPATIBILITY
2. BI-DIRECTIONAL FEEDBACK
3. BROWSE
4. CAPTURING
5. CLIENT SUPPORT
6. CREATE
7. MANAGER
8. NDS INTEGRATION
9. NOVELL GATEWAY
10. NOVELL PRINT MANAGER
11. NOVELL UPGRADE WIZARD
12. OPERATOR
13. PORT HANDLER
14. PRINT QUEUE
15. PRINTER AGENT
16. PRINTER DRIVER
17. REMOTE PRINTER
18. SAP
19. SNAP-INS
20. USER

Lab Exercise 7.4: NetWare 5 Printing

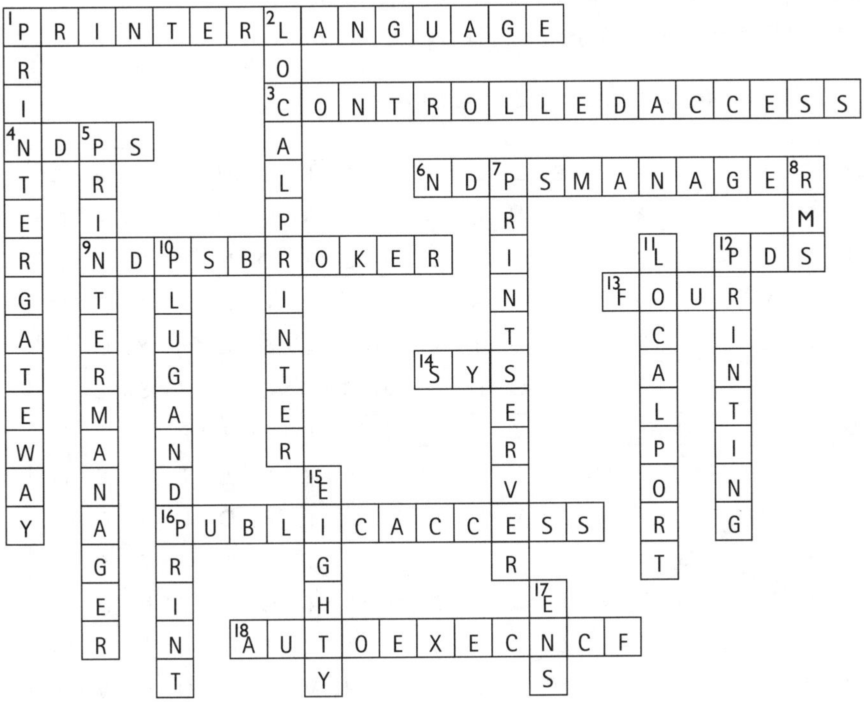
1 PRINTERLANGUAGE
1 PRINTERGATEWAY
2 LOCALPRINTER
3 CONTROLLEDACCESS
4 NDPS
5 PRINTERMANAGER
6 NDPSMANAGER
7 PRINTSERVER
8 RMS
9 NDPSBROKER
10 PLUGANDPRINT
11 LOCALPORT
12 PDS
12 PRINTING
13 FOUR
14 SYS
15 EIGHTY
16 PUBLICACCESS
17 ENS
18 AUTOEXECNCF

Chapter 8: Start Your Engines: NetWare 5 Installation

Lab Exercise 8.3: Start Your Engines

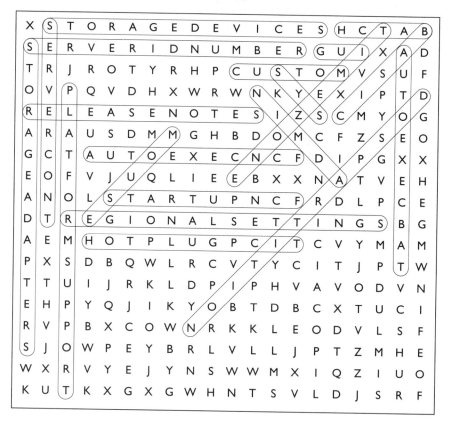

1. Admin
2. AUTOEXEC.BAT
3. AUTOEXEC.NCF
4. Basic
5. Batch
6. Custom
7. DOS Partition
8. GUI

9. Hotplug PCI
10. Mouse
11. Platform support
12. Regional settings
13. Release Notes
14. Server context
15. Server ID Number
16. STARTUP.NCF
17. Storage adapters
18. Storage devices
19. SYS:
20. Time zone

Lab Exercise 8.4: Netware 5 Installation

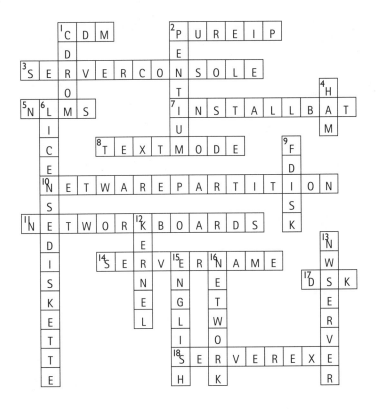

So You Wanna Be a CNA?

All over the world, NetWare 5 networks are being installed at a breathtaking pace. If you stop and think about how many thousands of users are being added to a NetWare 5 network every month, it's a rather staggering concept.

Over the past ten years, network computing has completely changed how the world communicates. Where were you a decade ago? If a business associate asked for your address back then, chances are good that you gave them a street address. If you wanted to send that person a document, you probably stuffed the document in an envelope, typed the address on the envelope, and pasted a stamp in the corner.

Today, when a business associate asks your addresses, you may be inclined to give him or her your e-mail address. It's a safe bet that you haven't touched a typewriter in years (and live in dread of having to find that bottle of white-out), and that you use the Postal Service only on those rare occasions when the recipient needs an honest-to-goodness signature on something.

The rest of the time, when you want to send someone a message or letter, your fingers skip across the keyboard, lightly and quickly typing up an e-mail message. Then, with a click of a button, the message is on its way through cyberspace, arriving within minutes in your colleague's electronic mailbox — no nasty stamp-taste on your tongue, no paper cuts from the envelope, no time wasted while the letter gets carried by trucks or airplanes to its destination.

And let's talk about the information in that letter you just sent via e-mail. A decade ago, you might have spent time at the corporate library (or in the city library downtown) to find the information you needed to write that letter. You would have leafed through stacks of periodicals, research reports, or other types of documents. You would have called experts and played phone-tag while you sat cooling your heels waiting for replies. You would have trekked through buildings, gone up and down elevators, and traipsed down long hallways looking for the person who'd borrowed the manila folder containing the Johannson files. You would have spent time at a terminal, accessing the company's database that was running on an astronomically expensive mainframe.

These days, you can do most or all of that research without leaving your desk. You can access on-line libraries of information, searching for your topic through hundreds of documents in moments. To avoid the phone-tag game (and some long-distance telephone charges), you can send e-mail to colleagues, asking them for the data they have. They, in turn, can send you the Johannson files via e-mail, or you can access them yourself from the document database that your company uses. And, better yet for your company's bottom line, you can get all this information from a NetWare 5 network, which is much less expensive than a mainframe.

Today's business world operates at a much higher speed than it did a decade ago. The breakneck rate at which communication travels from colleague to colleague, from customer to company, and from company to company is made possible in large part by the networking infrastructure that is spreading like a huge spiderweb over the planet.

Do you want to go back to where you were a decade ago? Most people don't. They may gripe about computers, and complain that they're at the mercy of those hunks of plastic and electronics taking up space on their desks. But just watch what happens when those hunks of plastic and electronics suddenly stop working. Mild-mannered accountants suddenly turn into irate bullies. Administrative assistants hide. Deals are put on hold. Transactions get stalled. Whole projects grind to a halt while everyone working on them wanders aimlessly out into the hallways to complain to each other. Frustration becomes tangible.

This is where you, the network administrator, come in.

As a network administrator, you are responsible for taking care of the NetWare 5 network on a day-to-day basis. You are the front line of defense for users who have problems. You are the gatekeeper who decides who gets to use the network, and how they get to use it. You are the person who installs new workstations on the network, and who updates old applications.

As a Certified Novell Administrator (CNA), you've not only learned how to do these types of tasks, you've also proven that you can do them to Novell's satisfaction. That can mean a great deal to your manager, and it can mean even more to a prospective employer who doesn't know much at all about you.

Knowledge is the important thing, of course. You can learn all about NetWare 5 and be a very competent network administrator without having to take a test to prove it. This book is designed to help you become a competent network administrator, regardless of whether you choose to take the test. But you may find that there is value in getting officially certified, anyway.

The Importance of Being Certified

As with most fields that offer the opportunity to become certified in a particular skill, the value of that certification varies somewhat with the person who gets it. There are two different ways to look at certification. For the individual who pursues the certification, it can mean:

- Tangible proof to show management you know what you're talking about

- Credibility with others in the company or industry

- A fast track to knowledge, as you take classes to prepare for the certification

- Potential college credit

- A valuable asset on your resume

- A competitive edge in the job hunt

- A valid reason to ask for a salary increase or promotion, or to ask for a high salary in a new job

- An admission ticket into user groups or professional organizations

For management, having an employee (or potential employee) with certification means:

- Reassurance that the employee really knows the product and has the recommended skills to work with the product

- A way to create a career path for employees

- A clear differentiator between job applicants

▸ A way to save money and time by dividing network support into two tiers — CNAs who provide the front-line support for users with their day-to-day networking needs, and CNEs who work on more technical issues (such as design and implementation of networking strategies)

CNA certification is no different in this regard. For the person who becomes a CNA, the certification can be the ticket to career advancement, credibility, or just a marginally impressive tidbit to work into conversations at social gatherings.

For management, hiring a CNA (or sending a current employee to class to become a CNA) means that the manager can be more confident in the employee's ability to keep the NetWare 5 network running smoothly.

The following sections delve a little deeper into ways you can use a CNA certification to your advantage, as well as how management benefits from having CNAs in the organization.

Tangible Proof

Managing a NetWare 5 network can be a challenge. It's even more of a challenge if you don't have the background knowledge required to keep it running smoothly. If you've received your CNA certification, you've proven that you were willing and able to learn about NetWare 5.

You spent time studying how NetWare 5 works. You learned the tools that make administration easier, the tricks that make each step go a little faster. You researched how your network works, and found ways to make it work more efficiently. You've made yourself available to people who have problems, and you've updated the applications that your people want to use.

Getting your CNA certification proves it. The certificate marks the fact that you've put in the hours and showed the tenacity required to learn how to run the network.

A piece of paper may not change how you do your job, but every once in a while, it's nice to be recognized for what you've accomplished. With your CNA certificate in hand, you can prove to your manager and colleagues that you know your stuff, and that you have earned the recognition of Novell.

Not to mention that it looks really cool hanging on your wall.

Fast Track to Knowledge

If you've been assigned to be your network's administrator, but your knowledge of NetWare 5 is fairly limited, you will eventually learn what you need to know. Either that, or you'll find another job fairly quickly.

You may learn by trial and error. You might tag along with someone else who understands the system and try to learn at that person's elbow. You can read all the manuals and try to make heads or tails of the correct processes and information that apply to your specific situation. You can experiment with the network (although, hopefully you experiment while everyone else is at home).

Regardless of the methods you use, you will eventually learn enough about the network to keep it going, at least marginally well. However, it's a good bet that it will take you several months (or more) to get to this point if you use these seat-of-the-pants methods.

If, on the other hand, you decide to really focus your attention and learn about NetWare 5 as quickly as you can, choosing the CNA route can be an efficient way to speed up your learning curve.

Take a look at the course objectives (see Appendix B) of the official NetWare 5 Administration course. The people who designed this Novell course believe that if you understand all the concepts and procedures described by each of the objectives, you will have a solid background of knowledge to help you run a NetWare 5 network.

The content of the NetWare 5 Administration test that qualifies you as a NetWare 5 CNA covers this broad range of information. If you can pass the test, you should have a good grasp of all the pertinent areas of network administration on a NetWare 5 network.

There will always be more to learn, of course, especially with regard to your individual network's specific characteristics. But these fundamentals will allow you to handle most situations, and will give you enough background to tackle new problems in a logical, educated approach.

How you learn these fundamentals is up to you. Armed with this book and the list of course objectives, the trial-and-error method of learning becomes much more efficient. Instead of a shotgun approach, you can plan the kinds of things you want to learn and tackle them one by one.

Taking the NetWare 5 Administration course from a Novell Authorized Education Center (NAEC) or from some other source can greatly shorten the time you'll need to learn about the network. A single class can't make you an expert in a week, but it can certainly give you a head start by giving you a broad overview of the necessary concepts. It can also give you hands-on experience on a lab network, where you don't have to worry about accidentally trashing your manager's account or deleting all the financial reports for 1998.

Whether you take an authorized course, an unauthorized course (there are plenty of people who teach similar courses, some of whom are very good, and some of whom are less so), or adopt some other method of learning, using the CNA objectives as a road map can help keep you in the fast lane.

Potential College Credit

There are two ways you might be able to get college credit for becoming a CNA.

First, you can take the NetWare 5 Administration course from an authorized college or university that offers the course. Such institutions are called Novell Educational Academic Partners (NEAPs). More than 100 such colleges and universities can be found in the United States, as well as some in Canada.

TIP

To receive a list of all the current NEAPs, you can call 800-233-EDUC or 801-222-7800. If you have a fax machine, you can use the Novell Education FaxBack feature. Call one of the same numbers, and follow the instructions to order the FaxBack master catalog of available documents, then order the Novell Educational Academic Partner (NEAP) List. Currently, the number of this document is 1235, but document numbers are subject to change.

Second, if you have taken the NetWare 5 Administration course from an NAEC, you may be able to get college credit for the course transferred from Novell to the college or university of your choice. College credit is also offered for other authorized Novell courses, as well. The Novell College Credit Program (NCCP) allows you to get an official transcript from Novell, showing the recommended college credit you may have earned by taking the course and passing the test. The American Council on Education (ACE) evaluates the Novell courses and recommends the amount of college credit that should be awarded for each course. Whether or not the college or university you're planning to attend accepts the credit is up to the college or university, however, and not up to Novell.

To apply for college credit, you must first take the full-length NetWare 5 Administration course from an NAEC. Only authorized courses taught by NAECs are accepted. Next, you must successfully pass the corresponding certification exam at a Sylvan Prometric or VUE testing center. (Details on how to find NAECs in your area and how to sign up for exams at Sylvan or VUE testing centers are presented in Appendix A.)

After you've successfully passed the corresponding exam, you can obtain a college credit transcript from the NAEC and have it sent directly to the college or university in which you're interested.

To request a transcript, you must present to the NAEC an original Novell Education course certificate and an original, embossed test score report that shows a passing score. The suggested price for obtaining a transcript is $30 for the first transcript, and $5 for each additional copy made at the same time, although prices are subject to change.

After the college or university receives your transcript, they will evaluate it and decide whether they will award the college credits recommended by the ACE. (Whether the credit is awarded, and how many credits are awarded, is entirely up to the college or university, as with all transferable credits.)

Fast Track to Jobs

Just about anyone you talk to these days will tell you that you must understand computers in order to compete in today's job market, regardless of the field you're in. This is largely true. Computer skills are rapidly becoming a basic requirement in many industries.

However, are general computer skills enough to guarantee you a job? No. Not having those skills may prevent you from landing a particular job, but having them just means you're in the running with everyone else. General computer skills don't differentiate you from the rest of the pack. That's where specialization and planning become important.

REAL WORLD

To make your resume stand out from the rest of the crowd, you must ensure that you have skills necessary in not just today's business world, but tomorrow's as well.

Obtaining your CNA certification can be a step in the right direction. With the range and reach of NetWare 5 networks growing rapidly all over the planet, the number of people needed to manage those networks is increasing at a rapid pace, too. Thousands of people have already recognized this and have begun pursuing their CNA and CNE certifications. The competition has begun.

Gaining a Competitive Edge

Many employers have started realizing that a CNA certification can be a differentiating factor in hiring. If a manager is trying to hire someone to administer a NetWare 5 network, the applicant with "CNA" on his or her resume will probably move higher up the list of potential interviewees than those without. This is because the employer recognizes that less training may be required for a CNA than for a non-CNA, and training costs money.

The term "CNA" on the resume also helps reassure the hiring manager that the applicant is probably being truthful about his or her knowledge of NetWare 5. Some employers have discovered too late that prospective applicants "enhanced" their resumes by claiming to understand NetWare 5 when all they really knew how to do was log in and out of the network.

Being Multitalented Helps, Too

Having CNA status doesn't just help you land a job as a network administrator. Many people running NetWare 5 networks are doing it as a special assignment, in addition to their "real" job. They may actually be accountants, dental hygienists, graphic artists, or account managers who showed an aptitude for computers and got the network administrator assignment as an afterthought.

With a CNA certification, you can make that special assignment a forethought rather than an afterthought. If you are applying for a job as an office manager, but you also let the employer know that you are a CNA, the employer may pick you over the competition because you can be of value in more than one area.

In this era of downsizing, more and more people are finding themselves in the sometimes uncomfortable position of having to cover more than one type of job in their company. The people who are surviving the layoffs and restructurings are often those who have more than one valuable skill. If you are capable not only of doing your regular job, but also of taking care of the network, this could possibly help you weather a layoff.

▶ · ◀

REAL WORLD

Take a gander at the help-wanted ads in a city newspaper these days. Every week, more and more positions are being advertised for people to run a company's computer operations. Many of these ads are requesting people who have experience managing Novell NetWare 5 networks, and many even specifically ask for people with CNA or CNE certifications. Your CNA certification will be the first step toward getting an interview at these companies.

There are no guarantees, of course, but it's always a smart idea to keep yourself diversified and versatile enough that you can move easily from one position to another. Then, even if you do find yourself back out in the job market, you'll still be ahead of much of your competition because you have the marketable quality of being a CNA, in addition to whatever else you have trained for.

Appendix E goes into more detail about career opportunities.

Going After the Big Bucks

Will getting your CNA certification translate immediately into an increase in salary? Possibly, or possibly not. Situations vary widely. It does, however, give you some real negotiating advantages.

If you're applying for a job with a new employer, you may be able to negotiate a higher salary because you are a CNA. The employer will spend less money training you and have more confidence in your abilities right from the start.

Becoming certified as a CNA may help you get a promotion at your current company. It shows a qualitative increase in your skill set, which usually translates into greater productivity for your company. Once again, it may help differentiate you from others in your company who are also vying for that promotion.

Keep in mind, however, that the value of the CNA isn't simply the certificate. It's how you apply the knowledge you received in your pursuit of the certificate. Whether or not you get that job, promotion, or salary increase will be up to you and the effort you show as a direct result of the CNA certification.

Joining Professional Organizations

As a CNA, you can join the Network Professional Association (NPA) as an associate member. This organization of network computing professionals strives to keep its members current with the latest technology and information about the networking industry. The NPA has more than 100 local chapters that meet regularly to see presentations and hands-on demonstrations of the latest technologies.

NetWare Users International (NUI) is an organization of NetWare 5 user groups. You don't have to be a CNA to join. NUI user groups also meet regularly and try to keep their users current with the latest networking trends.

You may find that because of their experience, members of such organizations can offer advice on issues you've been wrestling with, point out tricks they've found that will save you time and money, and steer you away from decisions that could negatively affect your network (such as buying troublesome hardware, installing incompatible applications, and so on). It may also just be nice to spend time socializing with others who have had the same types of experiences.

· ◀

How Management Benefits from Having CNAs

We've looked at how having CNA certification can benefit an individual. How does that CNA benefit the manager and the company? How do you convince an employer that having a CNA on board will be worth the investment?

One obvious benefit a manager gets from hiring a CNA is the reassurance that the employee has the fundamental background and recommended skills required to maintain a NetWare 5 network on a daily basis. Because of the training covered by the CNA program, the new employee will know how to connect workstations to the network, how to control security and access to files on the network, and how to monitor the network's performance. In addition, the CNA will know how to back up the network data and how to take care of the most common networking needs of users.

REAL WORLD

A real-world CNA, who is also an accounting manager in Washington, says that when she was convincing her company to pay for her CNA training, "We were paying consultants $95 per hour and travel, so it made sense to have someone [a CNA] in-house. I did not have much of a fight for them to agree to pay for it all."

CNA certification also provides employers with a clear differentiator between job applicants or between current employees who are working their way up the career ladder.

The biggest concerns of employers usually boil down to getting value for their investment. If your company is currently paying outside consultants to handle every support call or issue, you may be able to show how having a qualified CNA on staff could cut those expensive support calls drastically.

Alternatively, if your company doesn't use outside consultants, but does employ an expensive Information Services (IS) staff, you may be able to show them how having an entry-level CNA at the departmental level can benefit them. Such a CNA could provide on-site, personal attention to users' needs, thus improving solution turnaround time (key buzzwords here are "increased productivity in the department"), as well as off-loading many of the time-consuming (but routine) tasks from the more expensive IS employees (key buzzwords here are "efficient resource utilization").

When arguing dollars, do your homework and present an accurate picture. Try to get actual estimates of the costs of support calls, versus how much time you would realistically be able to devote to managing your network.

Also, make sure you're not comparing apples to oranges — as a CNA, you may not be qualified to accomplish everything the consultant does, so you might not be able to completely eliminate those support calls. Be practical and realistic. You don't want your eloquent arguments to backfire on you, setting up in your manager's mind some false expectations that you can't live up to.

As an extra benefit, users' confidence in the network may increase if they know they have an on-site CNA available to help them if a problem does arise.

For larger companies, another important benefit of having a CNA aboard is that it allows the company to divide network support tasks into two levels so that support can be managed more efficiently. CNAs can handle the day-to-day administration of the network and act as the front-line support for users' needs. This frees up the more technically advanced support personnel (such as CNEs) to concentrate on more technical, company-wide networking issues (such as design and implementation of networking strategies and research into new technologies).

This division between normal administrative tasks and more advanced issues also allows companies to create a clear career path for their IS departments, from entry-level employee at the CNA level, to advanced employees at the CNE level, to senior-level employees (Master CNEs).

Paper Certification Versus Real-World Experience

Every time someone starts talking about certification, or degrees, or official credentials of any kind, someone else starts arguing about the value of those credentials versus real-world experience. It's an argument that's worth looking into for a minute.

Official recognition (whether it's in the form of a college degree, a membership in an association, or a certificate) usually is designed to reward and recognize those people who have mastered a new skill or area of knowledge. The requirements to receive that recognition are established by experts in the field, experts who attempt to come up with a set of quantifiable or demonstrable skills or questions that indicate a certain level of proficiency.

REAL WORLD

Advice from a real-world CNA: "Use hands-on practice whenever possible. Don't try to be a paper CNA."

Because there is usually no way to absolutely determine a person's full depth of knowledge about anything, the set of requirements the experts establish are more representative than comprehensive.

This unavoidable weakness in the set of requirements can sometimes lead to a certain degree of abuse by some individuals—the kid in school who cheated on exams, the college buddy who could ace any written test but didn't have the common sense promised to a doorknob, or that character at work whose resume looks stellar, but who doesn't seem to have the foggiest grasp of real business sense.

There will always be those types of people in society.

Therefore, when someone argues that a CNA or CNE is a certification that isn't worth the paper it's printed on, it probably means they've encountered one of those individuals somewhere along the line. If this is the case, they have every right to be a little skeptical.

If all someone does is learn how to regurgitate facts, but never bothers to follow up with hands-on experience, then that person really isn't qualified to carry that certification. The CNA program attempts to prevent that situation, as much as possible, but there will always be a few people who manage to get around the system. Most CNAs don't ever fall into that trap, but there will certainly be a few.

So, is it worth it to get a CNA? Or any other degree or credential, for that matter?

Yes. Definitely, yes.

But it's a mistake to think that your education begins and ends with certification. Your CNA certification ensures that you have the foundation you need to do your job. How you build on that foundation is up to you.

▸ · ◂

REAL WORLD

Advice from a real-world CNA: "Never assume you know all the answers or that any problem will be just like the last. Often, CNEs and CNAs fall into this trap, getting complacent with problems. You need to look at problems with fresh eyes."

Building on the CNA Foundation

Once you've received your educational foundation of CNA skills, you will be able to start applying that education immediately on the job. You will quickly discover that what you do on the job will reinforce, enhance, and build upon the education you received. This is where you begin to dispel the argument that paper certification isn't worth as much as real-world experience.

As we've already discussed, pursuing a CNA through formal courses or by studying books such as this one will put you squarely on the fast track toward knowledge. You will eliminate much of the trial and error that comes with strictly sink-or-swim hands-on approaches. You can learn several months' worth of accidental discoveries in a few days. Then, once you have those basics down, the on-the-job learning will start at an already advanced point, and you will learn practical tricks and tips for your particular network much more quickly.

So, while the CNA certification is no substitute for hands-on experience, it gives you a definite advantage in achieving that experience rapidly.

Your response to the argument against "paper CNAs" will simply be your own experience. If you are a paper CNA (meaning you've received your CNA certification without much actual hands-on training), your response should be that your certification has prepared you for network administration by giving you the background of knowledge you need, and that you're looking forward to getting that hands-on experience that your challenger is extolling.

If you already have the real-world experience to go with your CNA certification, then your best defense against detractors is simply to show them that you really do know your stuff. That shouldn't be difficult.

Gaining Credibility

More often than encountering a skeptic, you'll probably encounter people who actually have higher expectations of you because you're a CNA.

There's something about credentials that may change many people's perceptions of you. It may not be a tremendous change, but it's one of those funny quirks of human nature that makes people raise their expectations a little higher when they know someone has a credential.

This can be good or bad, of course. If they raise their expectations of you, and you let them down, it can backfire for you. For example, if the only MBA in the office is the one who makes the most boneheaded decisions, the rest of the people in the office will probably not be impressed with other MBAs they meet in the future. This is similar to the "paper CNA" trap just discussed.

However, what will hopefully happen to you is that they will think to themselves, "Gee, that person is a CNA. I guess all that messing around with computers was beneficial after all. Maybe he/she can help me with my printing problems." Then you take one look at their printing setup, spot the problem (the wrong print driver being used by the application), fix it, and suddenly you've reinforced their new opinion of you.

This may sound silly at first, but think about the last time your company hired an outside consultant. Chances are good that some of the recommendations the consultant made were the same ones that your fellow employees were recommending. But, by virtue of being someone with "credentials," the consultant was listened to, while the regular employees were ignored.

What's going on here? A conspiracy? Not really. It boils down to the fact that some people unknowingly have higher expectations of "officially recognized" people than they do of "home-grown" people.

Becoming a CNA is your opportunity to make this quirk of human nature work for you. If you already have the knowledge, why not make it official and raise their opinion of you a little?

Getting What You Need Out of the CNA Program

In the CNA program, you will learn a great deal of information about NetWare 5. Because the program is trying to cover a representative amount of knowledge that will help the greatest number of people adequately manage their networks, you will find that not everything in the course objectives may apply to you. However, a significant portion of it will.

In addition, even though you may not immediately apply some of the information you learn, the education may have a more roundabout effect on your job performance. The more exposure you have to the different features and capabilities of NetWare 5, the more easily you can adapt that knowledge to new problems, even if those specific problems were never covered by the instructor.

> ## REAL WORLD
>
> What you'll have to remember is that you need to strike a balance between what the course objectives teach you, and what you'll need to learn and use on the job. Some of the information you learn in the course (or in this book) may not be of immediate use to you. Of course, you never know what the future will hold for you—the very skills you thought you could ignore in the class may be ones you need urgently in your next job.

In addition to learning some types of information you may not need right away, you might discover that your job involves aspects of NetWare 5 not covered in the CNA program. There are two reasons for this.

First, you may be encountering some of the more advanced, technical issues covered in other courses designed for the CNE program.

Second, your situation may be a less common one, which was simply not covered in either program. Again, this is probably because of the representative nature of the CNA program—the standardized courses attempt to give a broad foundation of knowledge about the most common situations that apply to the highest number of people.

Even if your particular problem isn't covered in the CNA program, the background of knowledge you learned there should help you formulate possible solutions.

Practical Education that Works

In this uncertain economy, where corporations are downsizing and layoffs are occurring with frightening frequency, it's often difficult to predict what skills and training will be in demand over the next few years.

There have been many stories of people who have trained for a skill or earned a degree that turns out to be obsolete (or at least less in demand) when they are finished with their education. This problem also has affected people who have participated in job retraining after a layoff. Too often, their job retraining has prepared them for jobs that will no longer exist when they graduate.

In addition, there are plenty of training programs out there that are catering to fads — certifying people for unique skills that may only have a shelf life of a year or two. This type of training may land you a job for now, but leave you high and dry when you've decided to advance your career to the next step.

There is no surefire way to avoid these fates, but with a little planning, you can better your chances at getting training that will stay in demand for a longer period of time. With the rampant growth of computing and communications, network administration appears to be a career choice that will be growing rapidly for many years to come.

Manufacturing jobs are giving way to computerized processes. The Internet is swelling by thousands of users every month. Businesses are looking for new ways to automate their work and increase the speed of communications. All of these trends appear to be gaining in strength, and show no signs of slowing for the foreseeable future.

Because of this growth, network administration (already a strong career choice) appears to be on the upward side of the growth cycle, poised for much more growth over the coming years. Demand for skilled network administrators is increasing daily, and should continue to rise rapidly as business becomes more and more dependent on communication and computerized processes.

With this kind of predicted growth, choosing to pursue a CNA certification now should be a very good move.

Paying for Your CNA Education

How much does it cost to become a CNA? The answer depends on the route you take to "CNA-dom." If you have been working in a NetWare 5 networking environment already, and you feel that this book has rounded out your knowledge sufficiently, then you may be able to simply take the exam and receive your authorization. The cost of the exam is in the neighborhood of $85–$95 at the time of this writing.

However, if you must get more formal education, you may want to look into taking a course from an instructor — either the Novell-authorized course, or a similar course from an independent trainer. In this case, you'll incur some additional expenses.

REAL WORLD

Because lawyers have long enjoyed a reputation for being able to charge astronomical fees, drive fancy cars, wear expensive Italian suits, and spend afternoons at the golf course, prospective law students have been flocking to law schools over the past several years without noticing that the law industry was reaching its saturation point. Now, record numbers of graduating law students are reporting that they are having a difficult time finding jobs.

The suggested retail price of the Novell-authorized, instructor-led NetWare 5 Administration course is currently $1,195. The price may vary somewhat. It's really up to the Novell Authorized Education Center (NAEC) that is offering the course.

Courses taught by independent instructors (which are not Novell-authorized) may be a little less expensive.

For many people, paying for the course may not be a problem. If you're fortunate enough to work for a company that understands the value of having a CNA on staff, then you probably will be successful in getting the company to pay for you to attend the necessary courses. Many CNA candidates do work for such an employer. For others, the cost may seem prohibitive at first. Let's look at some of the options you might have for funding your future. Because CNA candidates come from all walks of life, you'll find that the roads they took to get here run all over the map.

Financial Assistance

If you don't have the luxury of an employer who's willing to pay for your CNA education, you will probably have to foot the bill yourself.

The good news is, the money you spend on taking the course may be tax-deductible, depending on your particular circumstance. Be sure you do some research or talk to a tax planner about this possibility.

TIP In the United States, the IRS (Internal Revenue Service) has published a guide to claiming educational deductions on your tax return. To find out more information about this guide, call the IRS at 1-800-TAX-FORM, or write to the IRS Form Distribution Center nearest you. (You can find the address of the nearest office on the income tax package you receive every year.)

Another piece of good news is that you might be able to take advantage of some avenues for financial assistance.

If you're pursuing your CNA certification through a college or university, you may be able to get financial assistance through the school itself. If you aren't going the college route, but still need some financial assistance, you can check into federal programs that help provide funding for education and job retraining to see if you qualify for them.

In the United States, a variety of federal programs can help provide educational money, such as the Job Training Partnership Act (JTPA) and Trade Adjustment Assistance (TAA). These programs are administered at the state level, and are managed by local employment, job service, and rehabilitation agencies. Because these programs are administered locally, the services they offer may vary from state to state. You can contact any of these agencies in your local area to find out if you qualify for possible financial aid, as well as to find out about any employment opportunities.

TIP Your local **NAEC** or **NEAP** may also be able to point you to some possible sources for financial aid.

If you don't qualify for federal programs, you might try contacting your local banks and credit unions to see if they offer loans (possibly even low-interest student loans) that you can apply toward your educational expenses.

The following sections look at some of the options available in the United States. If you're not in the United States, contact your local government agencies, colleges, and universities for information about similar types of programs in your area.

Financial Aid at School

If you are considering taking the NetWare 5 Administration course through a college or university that is an NEAP, be sure you check with the school's financial aid office. You may discover that you are qualified to apply for a possible scholarship, low-interest loan, work-study program, or grant to help you pay for your education.

TIP **For more information about possible sources of financial aid at school, you can get a copy of The Student Guide by contacting the Federal Student Aid Information Line at 1-800-433-3243.**

In addition, some states have private institutions that may help provide financial assistance to students in matriculated schools. These institutions sometimes offer a variety of scholarships, grants, and fellowships based on religious, sports, or heritage affiliations. To find out if such a program exists in your state, talk to your local job service agency, or look for "College Academic Services" in the yellow pages of your telephone book.

Job Training Partnership Act (JTPA)

Job Training Partnership Act (JTPA) agencies are designed to help people get the education they need to find employment opportunities. These agencies assist the following types of people:

▸ Dislocated workers

▸ Veterans

▸ Youths and adults who are financially disadvantaged

▸ Youths and adults whose gross household income is less than government-established poverty levels

If you fall into one of these categories, contact your local job services agency (you can find them listed in the white pages) for information about JTPA programs and eligibility requirements in your area.

JTPA agencies offer financial assistance for education that is designed to land you a full-time career. In addition, they can help you find employment after you've completed your education. Some of the services they provide include:

▸ On-the-job training

- ▶ Classroom and customized training

- ▶ Internships

- ▶ Resume-writing assistance

- ▶ Financial assistance for education

- ▶ Help locating educational and professional resources

- ▶ Referrals for employment or educational institutions

Trade Adjustment Assistance (TAA)

If you and your coworkers have been displaced by foreign-import competition, you may qualify for additional unemployment insurance, job retraining, and financial assistance for job search and relocation expenses.

The Trade Adjustment Assistance (TAA) program was designed to help workers in the United States who have lost their jobs as a direct consequence of foreign import competition.

TIP

To be considered for TAA funds, an employer, a group of employees, or an employee representative (such as a labor union) must file a petition with the Department of Labor. If the Department of Labor finds that the claim is valid, the employees (and possibly the employer) can receive TAA services.

The North American Free Trade Agreement (NAFTA) is also connected with TAA. It specifies that employees who lost their jobs because of trade with Mexico or Canada, and who meet eligibility requirements, can receive similar NAFTA benefits.

If you think that you and your co-workers or your employer could be eligible for TAA assistance, contact your local job services agency. Ask for the TAA Coordinator for your state, who will be able to help you find out if you're eligible for TAA services.

Private Industry Councils (PICs)

Private Industry Councils (PICs) are organizations that control how funding is allocated for various government programs. Each PIC is made up of both government representatives and local business representatives. These people act as a governing board that approves contracts for state-allocated money targeted toward lower-income and disadvantaged people.

Because the PIC is run by both government and business representatives, theoretically a balance is maintained for determining the most appropriate and practical funding levels for the programs.

PICs represent many types of government programs. Job services, vocational rehabilitation, and JTPA are a few examples of these programs. For more information about possible opportunities or financial assistance through these or other programs, call your local PIC (listed in the yellow pages under "Private Industry Council").

Veterans' Administration

If you are a veteran, you should certainly check with your local Veterans' Affairs office for information about any Veterans' programs you may be eligible for. Veterans' programs exist that can provide assistance with education, job training, and vocational rehabilitation. The services you qualify to receive may vary, depending on such factors as your length of service, type of discharge, or a service-related disability.

Advancing Your Career

As a CNA, what are your options for the future?

Immediately, of course, you can apply your knowledge toward managing a NetWare 5 network for your company. The longer you experience the hands-on joys of network administration, the more you learn and the more valuable you will become as an employee.

But you may be wondering where you and the networking industry are headed in the future. Let's dust off the crystal ball and take a stab at some possibilities.

Current Outlook for the Networking Industry

Today's international forecast calls for widespread growth of the networking industry, increasing demand for people who understand networking, and widely scattered areas of specialization — an enticing forecast for prospective CNAs.

Want a more specific forecast? Okay. Pick up any recent survey on job trends for the next ten years or so. Then look through the top jobs. In almost all the recent surveys that have been coming out, jobs relating directly to computing (such as programmers, analysts, and IS personnel) are appearing in the highest-growth categories. Of those jobs that don't specifically deal with computing, most of them require knowledge of computers and software to get the job done.

The world is quickly being engulfed in a tightly woven network of communication. The sheer number of people that will be required to maintain that network is staggering.

Whereas large companies once were the bastion of computer and networking professionals, now everyone from your friendly neighborhood dentist, to your local car dealer, to your small-town church's office worker wants to connect up and dial in to the networked world. All of those businesses need help.

People are already answering the call for qualified networking professionals in large numbers. The CNA program is the fastest growing certification program around. About 10,000 to 12,000 new CNAs are certified every quarter, and the numbers are still growing.

This isn't just a North American phenomenon, either. Approximately 30 percent of the CNAs being certified as of this book's writing are from outside of the United States and Canada. That number is expected to grow sharply. Because the CNA program was introduced first in the United States, the rest of the world is still considered an emerging market.

REAL WORLD

Advice from a real-world CNA, on becoming a CNA: "Go for it! We may have to hire a computer person in the future and we would be looking for someone with CNA certification. The world is becoming more and more networked and it needs people with that expertise to guide those without."

The number of CNAs in Asia and Australia is growing incredibly fast. The European market is a little more mature, but numbers there are still growing dramatically. The worldwide growth rate is very impressive.

Does this mean the market will be saturated soon? Probably not. As fast as the CNA numbers are growing, the number of people and devices being hooked up together via computers and communication channels is outpacing them.

Current Outlook for Your Future

Even if the market for network administration skills is keeping pace (or outpacing) the number of CNAs available, you can't rest on your laurels if you want to stay marketable over the long haul.

Any certification has a limited shelf life, whether it is a CNA certificate or an engineering degree from the best university. These days, with the lightning speed of growth in the networking and computing industry, it's easy to feel like your entire base of knowledge and skills are obsolete in just a few years. You must take steps to ensure that this doesn't happen to you. Continuing education is vital.

The best way to plan out your continuing education needs is to consider your career goals over the long run. Today's goal is to become a network administrator. But then what? Where do you want to go next? Where do you want to be 10 or 20 years from now?

A Career in Network Administration

If network administration is right up your alley, and that's where you want to concentrate on building your career, then you must plan how you will stay current with networking technology over the coming years. For example, as Novell introduces future products, you will probably want to educate yourself in them and recertify on those products.

Additionally, you will most likely find that a great deal of your time as a CNA isn't just devoted to managing the NetWare 5 side of the network. Chances are very good that you'll exert a considerable amount of energy working with the applications that your users want to use. Staying current on those applications is vital.

Various software manufacturers offer certification programs for their specific applications.

Upping the Ante

As you begin to delve deeper into the technical workings of your network, you may decide that you want to focus more on design, strategy, and growth aspects of networking technologies. Perhaps you want to expand your depth of knowledge about NetWare 5 networking and advance up the career ladder to IS professional or possibly become a consultant.

If this is the case, you may decide to pursue a CNE, or Master CNE, certification.

CNEs are capable of handling jobs where they spend less time managing day-to-day network operations, and more time dealing with the larger, more technical issues of NetWare 5 network management. For example, CNEs are often involved in network design, installation, implementation, and troubleshooting. CNEs specialize in various Novell products (such as NetWare 5 or GroupWare), so that they can concentrate on developing their skills in those critical areas.

To become a CNE, you take additional classes and exams to learn (and demonstrate) advanced techniques and skills for planning and implementing NetWare 5 networks in any size organization.

The NetWare 5 Administration exam, which you must pass to receive your CNA certification, is one of the required classes for a NetWare 5 CNE certification. Therefore, you've already knocked one requirement off the list to becoming a CNE. Aren't you the clever one?

As a CNE, you may be able to move up in the IS hierarchy, moving into positions requiring greater technical backgrounds, and allowing you to get your hands on some of the more challenging technical aspects of networking. In addition, CNEs are often on the cutting edge of research, exploring new technologies and finding ways to keep their organizations in the fast lane.

A Master CNE has taken his or her education as a networking professional to an even higher level. Master CNEs declare a "graduate major" while they're pursuing their certification. These areas of specialization delve deeper into the integration- and solution-oriented aspects of running a network than the CNE level.

While CNEs provide support at the operating system and application levels, Master CNEs are expected to manage advanced access, management, and workgroup integration for multiple environments. Master CNEs can support complex networks that span several different platforms, and can perform upgrades, migration, and integration for various systems.

Periodically, as Novell introduces new generations of its products, Novell Education requires existing CNEs and Master CNEs to update their certification by learning about and demonstrating their proficiency in these new products. The need for such recertification is obvious. Without recertifying on new products, your skills can become dated, and your certification begins to lose its value.

A Stepping Stone to Other Careers

Of course, nothing says you must spend the rest of your life directly managing networks. Network administration may turn out to be the stepping stone that opens entirely new doors to you.

As we already mentioned, it is becoming increasingly difficult to find a good-paying job in a growing career field that isn't somehow tied into computers. Everywhere you look, knowledge of computers and how they affect your business and your life is becoming more and more important.

Being a network administrator can help you build that foundation of knowledge about business communications, tools, and resources. This background will become invaluable in nearly any aspect of the business world you pursue, whether you start your own business, hop onto a fast-growing startup company, or join a well-established organization.

Another benefit is that if you wisely apply the knowledge and skills you used to get your CNA certification, you will ideally establish a good reputation as a professional who is competent and productive. That reputation may help future employers recognize your ability to take on responsibilities in their organizations, even if the job they are offering is in a completely different area from network administration.

As with any certification, degree, or diploma, it is important to realize that what you make of that piece of paper is up to you. It will never be a free lunch ticket by itself. You must back up its validity by plunging into the real-world aspects of the field. Hard work, talent, skill, and knowledge go hand-in-hand with certification. With that combination, you will definitely have a strong edge over most of the rest of your competition.

Help! For More Information

Whenever a product becomes as popular and as widely used as NetWare, an entire support industry crops up around it. If you are looking for more information about NetWare 5, you're in luck. There are a wide variety of places you can go for help, advice, information, or even just camaraderie.

NetWare information is as local as your bookstore or local user group, and as international as the Internet forums that focus on Novell products. It can be as informal as articles in a magazine, or as structured as a college course. Best of all, it's easy to tap into most of these resources, wherever you may happen to be on the planet.

There is no point in trudging along through problems by yourself, when there is such a vast array of helpful people and tools at your fingertips.

This appendix describes the following ways you can get more information or technical support for NetWare. With a little digging, you can probably turn up even more resources than these, but these will get you started.

- General Novell product information

- The *Novell Buyer's Guide*

- The NetWare 5 manuals

- Novell information on the Internet

- Novell Technical Support

- Novell Support Connection

- DeveloperNet (Novell's developer support)

- *Novell Application Notes*

- NetWare Users International (NUI)

- Network Professional Association (NPA)

- Novell Press books and other publications

General Novell Product Information

The main Novell information number, 1-800-NETWARE, can be your inroad to all types of information about Novell and its products. By calling this number, you can obtain information about Novell products, the locations of your nearest resellers, pricing information, and so on.

The *Novell Buyer's Guide*

If you are responsible for helping find networking solutions for your organization, you may want to get a copy of the *Novell Buyer's Guide*. This guide is a complete book on everything you could possibly want to buy from Novell.

The *Novell Buyer's Guide* explains all the products Novell is currently offering, complete with rundowns on the technical specifications, features, and benefits of those products.

The *Novell Buyer's Guide* is available in a variety of formats, too. It is available on-line through Novell's on-line service on the Internet (**www.novell.com**) and through CompuServe (GO NETWIRE).

The *Novell Buyer's Guide* also comes on CD-ROM with *Novell's Support Connection* (formerly NSEPro) which is explained later in this chapter. If you prefer the written version, you can order the *Novell Buyer's Guide* by calling one of the following phone numbers (which are all toll-free in Canada and the USA):

- ▶ 1-800-NETWARE

- ▶ 1-800-544-4446

- ▶ 1-800-346-6855

There may be a small charge to purchase the printed version of *Novell Buyer's Guide*.

The NetWare 5 Manuals

The NetWare 5 manuals are the complete reference guides to the features and workings of NetWare 5. In your NetWare 5 package, you should have received one or two printed manuals (just enough to get you started), plus a CD-ROM containing the full set of manuals on-line.

If you install the on-line documentation on your server, you'll be able to access the manuals from any workstation on the network that has any HTML browser installed such as Netscape Navigator. If you have a laptop computer, you may want to install the on-line documentation on it, so that you can carry the entire set around with you.

If you really like having printed documentation, you can order the full printed set of manuals from Novell.

 TIP   **The only manual that is not included in the printed set is the *System Messages* manual. Believe me, you don't want to see how big that book would be if it were printed.**

To order the printed manuals for NetWare 5, you can use the order form that came in your NetWare 5 box, or call one of the following phone numbers:

- ▸ 1-800-336-3892 (toll-free in Canada and the USA)

- ▸ 1-512-834-6905

Novell on the Internet

A tremendous amount of information about Novell and NetWare products (both official and unofficial) is on the Internet. Officially, you can obtain the latest information about Novell from Novell's home page on the Internet, as well as from the Novell forums on CompuServe. Unofficially, there are several active user forums that deal specifically with Novell products, or generally with computers.

Novell's on-line forums offer you access to a wide variety of information and files dealing with NetWare 5 and other Novell products (such as GroupWise, LAN Workplace, intraNetWare, and ManageWise). You can receive information such as technical advice from SysOps (system operators) and other users, updated files and drivers, and the latest patches and workarounds for known problems in Novell products.

Novell's on-line sites also provide a database of technical information from the Novell Technical Support division, as well as information about programs such as Novell Education classes and NetWare Users International (NUI). In addition, you can find marketing and sales information about the various products that Novell produces.

Novell's Internet and CompuServe sites are very dynamic, well-done, and packed with information. They are frequently updated with new information about products, education programs, promotions, and the like. In fact, the technical support features of NetWire on the Internet even garnered a place on the "What's Cool" list of Internet sites from Netscape.

Novell's Internet site is managed by Novell employees and by SysOps who have extensive knowledge about NetWare. Public forums can be quite active, with many knowledgeable users offering advice to those who experience problems.

TIP

To get technical help with a problem, post a message and address the message to the SysOps. (But don't send the SysOps a personal e-mail message asking for help — the public forums are the approved avenue for help.)

To access the Novell forums on CompuServe, you need a CompuServe account. There is no additional monthly fee for using the Novell forums, although you are charged the connection fee (on an hourly rate) for accessing the service. To get to the Novell forums, use GO NETWIRE. There, you will find information for new users, telling you how the forums are set up, how to get technical help, and so on.

If you have a connection to the Internet, you can access Novell's Internet site in one of the following ways:

- World Wide Web: `http://www.novell.com`

- Gopher: `gopher.novell.com`

▶ File Transfer Protocol (FTP): anonymous FTP to `ftp.novell.com`

Users in Europe should replace ".com" with ".de".
To get to the Novell site on the Microsoft Network, use GO NETWIRE.

Novell Technical Support

If you encounter a problem with your network that you can't solve on your own, there are several places you can go for immediate technical help.
Try some of the following resources:

▶ Try calling your reseller or consultant.

▶ Go on-line, and check out the Technical Support areas of Novell's Internet site. There, you will find postings and databases of problems and solutions. Someone else may have already found and solved your problem for you.

▶ While you're on-line, see if anyone in the on-line forums or Usenet forums knows about the problem or can offer a solution. The knowledge of people in those forums is broad and deep. Don't hesitate to take advantage of it, and don't forget to return the favor if you know some tidbit that might help others.

▶ Call Novell Technical Support. You may want to reserve this for a last resort, simply because Novell Technical Support charges a fee for each incident (an "incident" may involve more than one phone call, if necessary). The fee depends on the product for which you're requesting support.

When you call Technical Support, be sure you have all the necessary information ready (such as the versions of NetWare and any utility or application you're using, the type of hardware you're using, network or node addresses and hardware settings for any workstations or other machines being affected, and so on). You'll also need a major credit card.

To get to Novell's Technical Support, call 1-800-858-4000 (or 1-801-861-4000 outside of the U.S.).

Novell Support Connection

A subscription to *Novell Support Connection,* formerly known as the *Novell Support Encyclopedia Professional Volume* (NSEPro), can update you every month with the latest technical information about Novell products. *Novell Support Connection* is a CD-ROM containing technical information such as:

- ▶ Novell technical information documents

- ▶ Novell Labs hardware and software test bulletins

- ▶ On-line product manuals

- ▶ *Novell Application Notes*

- ▶ All available NetWare patches, fixes, and drivers

- ▶ The *Novell Buyer's Guide*

- ▶ Novell corporate information (such as event calendars and press releases)

Novell Support Connection includes Folio information-retrieval software that allows you to access and search easily through the Novell Support Connection information from your workstation using DOS, Macintosh, or Microsoft Windows.

To subscribe to *Novell Support Connection,* contact your Novell Authorized Reseller or Novell directly at 1-800-377-4136 (in the United States and Canada) or 1-303-297-2725.

DeveloperNet Novell's Developer Support

If you or others in your organization develop applications that must run on a NetWare 5 network, you can tap into a special information resource created just for developers.

DeveloperNet is a support program specifically for professional developers who create applications designed to run on NetWare. Subscription fees for joining DeveloperNet vary, depending on the subscription level and options you choose. If you are a developer, some of the benefits you can receive by joining DeveloperNet include:

- The *Novell SDK (Software Development Kit)* CD-ROM, which contains development tools you can use to create and test your application

- The *DeveloperNet Handbook*

- Special Technical Support geared specifically toward developers

- *Novell Developer Notes*, a bimonthly publication from the Novell Research department that covers software-development topics for NetWare products

- Discounts on various events, products, and Novell Press books

For more information, to apply for membership, or to order an SDK, call 1-800-REDWORD or 1-801-861-5281, or contact the program administrator via e-mail at `devprog@novell.com`.

TIP

More information about DeveloperNet is available on-line on CompuServe (GO NETWIRE) or on the World Wide Web. On the Web, you can connect to the DeveloperNet information through Novell's home site, at `http://www.novell.com`**, or you can go directly to the DeveloperNet information at** `http://developer.novell.com`**. Both addresses get you to the same place.**

Novell Application Notes

Novell's Research department produces a monthly publication called the *Novell Application Notes*. Each issue of *Novell Application Notes* contains research reports and articles on a wide range of topics. The articles delve into topics such as network design, implementation, administration, and integration.

A year's subscription costs \$110 (\$129 outside the United States), which includes access to *Novell Application Notes* in their electronic form on CompuServe.

To order a subscription, call 1-800-377-4136 or 1-303-297-2725. You can also fax an order to 1-303-294-0930.

NetWare Users International (NUI)

NetWare Users International (NUI) is a nonprofit association for networking professionals. With more than 250 affiliated groups worldwide, NUI provides a forum for networking professionals to meet face-to-face, to learn from each other, to trade recommendations, or just to share "war stories."

By joining the NetWare user group in your area, you can take advantage of the following benefits:

▸ Local user groups that hold regularly scheduled meetings

▸ *NetWare Connection*, a bimonthly magazine that provides feature articles on new technologies, network management tips, product reviews, NUI news, and other helpful information

▸ A discount on Novell Press books through the NetWare 5 Connection magazine and also at NUI shows

▸ NUInet, NUI's home page on the World Wide Web (available through Novell's home site, under "Programs," or directly at `http://www.nuinet.com`), which provides NetWare technical information, a calendar of NUI events, and links to local user group home pages

▸ Regional NUI conferences, held in different major cities throughout the year (with a 15 percent discount for members).

The best news is, there's usually no fee or only a very low fee for joining an NUI user group.

▶ · ◀

REAL WORLD

You don't even have to officially join NUI to get a subscription to NetWare Connection, but don't let that stop you from joining. "Networking" with other NetWare administrators can help you in ways you probably can't even think of yet.

For more information or to join an NUI user group, call 1-800-228-4NUI or send a fax to 1-801-228-4577.

For a free subscription to *NetWare Connection*, fax your name, address, and request for a subscription to 1-801-228-4576. You can also mail NUI a request at:

NetWare Connection
P.O. Box 1928
Orem, UT 84059-1928
USA

▶ · ◀

Network Professional Association (NPA)

If you've achieved (or are working toward) your CNA or CNE certification, you may want to join the Network Professional Association (NPA), formerly called CNEPA. The NPA is an organization for network computing professionals. Its goal is to keep its members current with the latest technology and information in the industry.

If you're a certified CNE, you can join the NPA as a full member. If you're a CNA, or if you've started the certification process, but aren't finished yet, you can join as an associate member. Associate members have all the benefits of full membership, except that they cannot vote or hold offices in the NPA.

When you join the NPA you can enjoy the following benefits:

  ▶ Local NPA chapters (more than 100 worldwide) that hold regularly
    scheduled meetings that include presentations and hands-on
    demonstrations of the latest technology

▸ *Network News*, a monthly publication that offers technical tips for working with NetWare networks, NPA news, classified ads for positions, and articles aimed at helping CNEs make the most of their careers

▸ Discounts on NPA Satellite Labs (satellite broadcasts of presentations)

▸ Product discounts from vendors

▸ Hands-On Technology Labs (educational forums at major trade shows and other locations as sponsored by local NPA chapters)

▸ Discount or free admission to major trade shows and conferences

Membership in NPA costs $150 per year. For more information or to join NPA, call 1-801-379-0330.

Novell Press Books and Other Publications

Every year, more and more books are being published about NetWare and about networking in general. Whatever topic you can think up, someone's probably written a book about it.

Novell Press itself has an extensive selection of books written about NetWare and other Novell products. For an up-to-date Novell Press catalog, you can send an e-mail to Novell Press at `novellpress@novell.com`.

You can also peruse the selection of books on-line. From Novell's main Internet site (`http://www.novell.com`), you can get to the Novell Press area (located under "Programs"). You can also get to the same location by going directly to `http://www.novell.com/books`.

In addition to books, there are a wide variety of magazines that are geared specifically toward networking and general computing professionals, such as *Network News*, *NetWare Connection* (from NUI), *LAN Times*, *PCWeek*, and so on.

What's on the CD-ROM

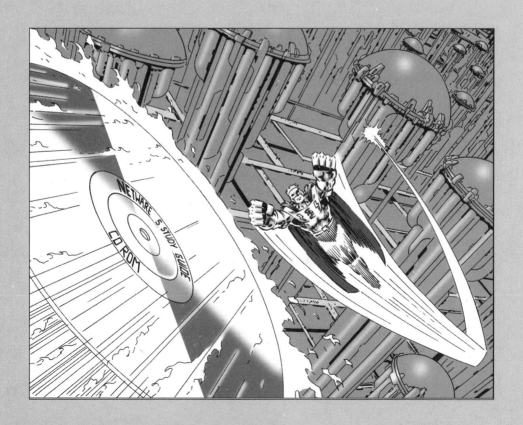

The CD-ROM included with *Novell's CNA Study Guide for NetWare 5* includes the NetWare 5 CNA module of The Clarke Tests v5.0. This appendix describes the contents, installation, and configuration of this unique interactive software for CNAs.

▶ · ◀

The Clarke Tests v5.0

Welcome to The Clarke Tests v5.0!

It is unlike anything you have ever seen. It is more than just sample test questions — this is an Interactive Learning System for CNAs.

The CD-ROM included with this book contains a special version of the NetWare 5 CNA module of The Clarke Tests v5.0. Here's a more detailed look at this wonderful multimedia learning system.

Four Study Modules to Choose From

Let us help you become a CNA or CNE! The entire Clarke Tests collection includes 12 courses, nearly 100 tests, and more than 4,000 study sessions on an interactive CD-ROM. Each test teaches you specific CNE objectives within a subsection of a required CNE course. The Clarke Tests v5.0 offers four different study modules covering four major Novell certifications — NetWare 5 Certified Novell Engineer (CNE-5), NetWare 3.12 CNE (CNE-3), and both Certified Novell Administrators (CNA-5 and CNA-3). Here's a breakdown of the four Clarke Tests modules and their corresponding certifications:

- ▶ NetWare 5 CNE Target Courses — Part 1 of CNE-5

- ▶ NetWare 3.12 CNE Target Courses — Part 1 of CNE-3

- ▶ Core Technologies and Electives — Part 2 of CNE-5/CNE-3

- ▶ NetWare 5 and 3.12 CNA — Covers CNA-5/CNA-3

The Interactive Learning System

The Clarke Tests v5.0 uses a multimedia, Windows-based interface to maximize your learning potential. This interface closely resembles the software used by Sylvan Prometric and Drake Technologies for actual CNE certification. The goal is to prepare you for the entire testing experience, not just the test objectives. In addition, LearningWare has enhanced the interface to create a complete Interactive Learning System.

Here's how it works.

The Tests

Each CNE course is divided into Study and Certification tests. Study Tests cover specific CNE objectives within a subsection of a required CNE course. They encompass 35 to 120 questions with the help of a proprietary Navigator. The Navigator allows you to answer questions in any order and return to previously answered questions for review. In addition, we've provided actual CNE Certification Tests for adaptive, form, simulation, and performance-based courses. Use the Study Tests to learn and the Certification Tests to prepare.

The Questions

Questions in The Clarke Tests are more than simple, one-dimensional brain teasers; they are complete interactive Study Sessions. They include a variety of learning tools to keep things interesting and make learning fun. Each of the following study session types presents the CNE study material in a slightly different way. This forces you to "truly" understand the testing objectives:

▶ *Hot Spots* — "Real life" graphical exhibits that test your hands-on knowledge.

▶ *Performance-based* — A new Novell testing strategy for Service and Support and NetWare 5 material. These questions test your ability to solve NetWare-related problems.

▶ *Traditional Multiple Choice* — One or more correct answers per question.

▶ *Matching* — Combine many NetWare topics in one interactive study session.

▶ *Fill-In* — Require tough "open-ended" answers.

In addition, many study sessions include graphical exhibits. These exhibits enhance your learning experience by providing screen shots, 3-D graphics, and professional case studies. Finally, if you're stuck along the way, The Clarke Tests v5.0 offers interactive Clues in a separate window. These clues allow you to continue studying without divulging the complete answer. We are with you every step of the way!

Interactive Answers

These are the real stars of the show. Each study session includes a full page or more of explanation and CNE study material. Instead of just displaying the answer, we explain it in detail. In addition, each Interactive Answer includes page references to Novell Authorized courseware, the CyberState University on-line CNE program, *Novell's CNE Study Guide*, *Novell's CNE Study Guide for NetWare 5*, *Novell's CNE Study Guide for Core Technologies*, *Novell's CNA Study Guide for NetWare 5*, NetWare documentation, and the "So You Wanna Be A CNE?!" video series.

Tracker Scoring

The Clarke Tests v5.0 includes an exciting new interactive scoring system called The Tracker. The Tracker is a separate module that gathers detailed information about your performance on individual CNE tests. It classifies your results according to key testing objectives and presents them in a table format. Here's how it works:

▸ *Certification Scoring* — All actual CNE certification exams are scored on an 800 scale. In order to pass, you must exceed a specific threshold for each course. The Clarke Tests v5.0 uses the same 800 scale and built-in thresholds as the actual exams. This allows you to accurately assess your chances of passing any given CNE exam.

▸ *Prescription Reports* — A series of detailed testing objectives are included with each exam. Your performance in each study area is tracked to help you identify your strengths and weaknesses. The Clarke Tests v5.0 also includes comprehensive Prescription Reports to help you isolate specific areas of study and track testing improvement.

▸ *Database Analysis* — The Tracker data can be exported to numerous database and spreadsheet programs for further graphical analysis. This is a great way to chart your CNE progress.

Tracker scoring is a great way to build custom CNE study sessions. You can trust that when the Clarke Professor says you're ready for the real CNE exam . . . you're ready! Good luck, and let us help you become a CNE!

Installing The Clarke Tests v5.0

To install The Clarke Tests v5.0, insert the CD-ROM into your CD drive (drive D:, for example).

1. If you are using Microsoft Windows 95/NT, select Start and Run. Type **D:\CNA95\SETUP** in the input window and click OK. (Remember that drive D: is the CD-ROM drive.)

2. If you are using Microsoft Windows 3.1, select File and Run. Type **D:\CNA31\SETUP** in the input window and click OK. (Remember that drive D: is the CD-ROM drive.)

3. The Clarke Tests v5.0 Setup will install the Delivery Module ("Clarke!!"), Tracker, and Administrator. By default, all tests will be highlighted. Click any tests you do not want to install and the system will deselect them.

4. As each test is installed, Setup will ask for a test directory. We recommend that you separate courses into different subdirectories and only install the tests on which you are currently working. In addition, The Clarke Tests v5.0 includes a "Save" feature that allows you to exit a test without losing your place.

5. Have fun!

See the `readme.txt` file on the CD-ROM for any updated information about the installation.

Using The Clarke Tests v5.0

Once The Clarke Tests v5.0 have been installed correctly, you will notice three icons in The Clarke Test program group. The "Clarke!" icon runs the interactive learning system, the "Admin Maker" is for test administration, and "Tracker" monitors your progress and prints Prescription Reports. Here are a few tips on using The Clarke Tests v5.0:

- ▶ *In the Beginning* — To begin The Clarke Tests, select "Clarke!" from the Start menu in Windows 95/NT, or double-click the "Clarke!" icon within Windows 3.1. Next, choose a test and enter your name. Let the tests begin.

- ▶ *Navigation* — To navigate questions, simply click on the question number or use the arrows at the bottom right-hand corner of the screen. Indicate your desired response by clicking on the appropriate radio button, or by entering text into the fill-in or matching spaces provided. The radio button is the white circle or square to the left of a selection.

- ▶ *Clues* — The "Help" button provides clues to guide you in the right direction. Don't worry, they don't give away the answer. When you are finished viewing the Clue, click the Done button to return to the question.

- ▶ *Interactive Answers* — The Info button provides a detailed answer for each question, including page references to numerous study aids. This is the Interactive Answer. When you are finished viewing the study material, click the Done button to return to the question.

- ▶ *Scoring* — Once you have completed a question, move to the next one. The Professor will automatically score your response. Correct answers will appear in green, while incorrect responses turn red. Look for lots of green!

- ▶ *Custom Reports* — Each test includes a detailed Prescription Report. The report helps you identify your strengths and weaknesses by comparing your results against actual CNA and CNE testing objectives. Also, the Professor will allow you to generate sophisticated custom reports using the Tracker Module.

With all this help, you are just moments away from an exciting new life as a NetWare 5 CNA or CNE.

Troubleshooting The Clarke Tests v5.0

If you run into any problems with The Clarke Tests v5.0, we're with you every step of the way. First, try any of the tips listed here. If that doesn't work, give us a call at 1-800-684-8858 or 1-801-423-2314 (internationally).

For Window 3.1 and Windows 95/98/NT Users

1. The interactive test screen will fill your monitor if the Windows driver is set to 640×480. The 640×480 setting is best for "hotspot" test question graphics.

2. If you are using a high-quality video driver (Viper VLB, for example), it may support a "large font" mode for high-quality text and graphics. This can cause the text of The Clarke Tests v5.0 to extend beyond designated areas. Avoid using "large fonts" mode.

3. If you have installed a previous version of The Clarke Tests, uninstall or delete the program before you install version 5.0. If you receive an error indicating previously used files, select "IGNORE" and continue. If you receive "Runtime Error 31037," consult the appropriate troubleshooting section that follows.

For Windows 3.1 Users Only

1. If you have a computer capable of playing .WAV files and you receive an error message indicating your computer is not capable of sound, copy the following file from the CD-ROM into the "TCS" directory on your hard drive:

D:\CNA31\TCS.SPT

2. Auto redraw — "Runtime Error 480" and/or "Unable to create auto redraw image." Windows 3.1 does not have enough system/memory resources to display the screen. Over time, the "memory leak" of Windows 3.1 will reduce system resources and available memory to draw the screen. Try this cure:

- Go to Program Manager and Help. View About Program Manager. You see that system resources are getting below 70 percent. A fresh install of Windows 3.1 yields 85 to 90 percent resource availability.

- We must increase system resources to allow enough memory for the screen to redraw. If you have any other programs running at startup, remove them and reboot your system. You may have given yourself more available resources. If so, you're finished.

- If not, you may try using Memmaker (go to DOS and type **MEMMAKER**). By following the instructions, you may free up some conventional memory. This may have minimal effect on the resources that the screen needs (GDI resources) to redraw the image. If it works for you, you're finished.

- If not, you may need to reinstall Windows 3.1. This may sound a bit drastic. However, it may be the fastest and easiest solution for many memory problems.

3. Share or Vshare — SHARE.EXE or VSHARE.386 errors. These programs may not be loading properly. Try these simple cures:

- SHARE and VSHARE cannot both be loaded at the same time. And, SHARE.EXE needs certain parameters to run.

- SHARE.EXE is loaded in your AUTOEXEC.BAT file. AUTOEXEC.BAT is in the root directory (C:\). The parameters should look like this: C:\DOS\SHARE.EXE /L:500 /F:5100

- VSHARE.386 is loaded from the SYSTEM.INI file. SYSTEM.INI is in the C:\WINDOWS\SYSTEM subdirectory. It is in the 386ENH section ("device=vshare.386").

4. Ensure that The Clarke Tests v5.0 files on your hard drive are not read-only. Ensure that TCSEMPTY.MDS exists on the hard drive in the directory that you installed TCS in, and it, too, is not read-only.

5. On some rare occasions, VESA local bus machines (typically 486s) using a VLB IDE controller with a special driver loading for higher performance (Dual Mode transfer, for example) may run into trouble. This driver may collide with VSHARE.EXE. In these instances, use SHARE.EXE.

For Windows 95/NT Users Only

1. Runtime Error 75 — "Path/file access error." After a certain percentage of The Clarke Tests v5.0 loads, you may get this error. This error is caused by one of the following problems: media failure (CD-ROM or drive), dirty CD-ROM drive, corrupted file, bad CD-ROM disk, hard drive failure, bad sector on the hard drive, not enough hard drive space, and/or compressed drives giving error for "true" space available. Here are some quick cures:

   - If the problem is caused by not enough drive space, delete the contents of the TCS directory. Next, free up enough hard drive space and reinstall The Clarke Tests v5.0 normally.

   - If that doesn't work, copy the contents of The Clarke Test v3.0 CD onto the hard drive in a TEMP directory. Use Explorer to make sure you do not have any 0 byte files (which means that it is not copying properly). Ensure that no file attributes of any file are set to read-only. Finally, run SETUP.EXE from TEMP and install The Clarke Tests v5.0 normally.

2. Runtime Error 31037 — "Registry error." Your Registry thinks that The Clarke Tests v5.0 can run from the CD-ROM. It cannot, because, as you take the tests, the program keeps track of your scores. Therefore, the computer must write to the default media. The CD is read-only. The Registry has "misplaced" the THREED32.OCX file. Try these cures:

   - Remove the TCS directory using "Add/Remove Programs" in the Control Panel. Go into Windows Explorer and check for any other directories containing The Clarke Test v3.0 files. Remove them.

   - Go to Start ⇨ Run.

   - Type REGEDIT and then press Enter.

   - In the Registry editor, search "My Computer" (using Edit ⇨ Find) for all references relating to The Clarke Tests v5.0 that may have been installed. Manually delete them (being sure to delete the entire reference). Here are some examples of what to look for: your CD-ROM

Drive D:\ (do not delete the Windows 95/NT CD references), \TCS\ directories (or other directory name you may have chosen), THREED32.OCX, DELIVERY.EXE, TCSADMIN.EXE, SETUP.EXE, and/or TRACKER.EXE.

- Copy REGCLN.EXE from the new Clarke Test CD into a temporary directory (it is D:\CNA95\REGCLN.EXE). This file is from Microsoft and is made to clean your Registry. It is a self-extracting file (which means that it may contain many files compressed into one, and that, when you execute it, it will decompress itself in the directory that it is in). Execute the command and let the files decompress.

- Run the Microsoft Registry Cleaner's SETUP.EXE program. This will clean your Registry.

- When you're finished, install The Clarke Tests v5.0 normally.

- Finally, you may need to let the Registry "know" some critical information about THREED32.OCX. Bring up a DOS prompt, and change to the directory in which you installed The Clarke Tests v5.0 (for example, C:\TCS). In this directory, type **REGOCX32\WINDOWS\ SYSTEM\THREED32.OCX**.

For More Information . . .

The Clarke Tests Professor is behind you every step of the way. Becoming a CNA or CNE has never been easier, or more fun. If you need a little more help:

- Try The Clarke Tests Tutorial—It's a great start!

- Check out the "README.CLK" file on the CD-ROM for installation instructions and last-minute changes or suggestions.

- Surf the Web at http://www.learning-ware.com.

- Fax us at 1-801-465-4755.

- If you must speak to a "real" person, call 1-800-684-8858 for orders and technical support.

Index

Continued

Continued

Continued

T

X

Z

Continued

IDG Books Worldwide, Inc.
End-User License Agreement

READ THIS. You should carefully read these terms and conditions before opening the software packet(s) included with this book ("Book"). This is a license agreement ("Agreement") between you and IDG Books Worldwide, Inc. ("IDGB"). By opening the accompanying software packet(s), you acknowledge that you have read and accept the following terms and conditions. If you do not agree and do not want to be bound by such terms and conditions, promptly return the Book and the unopened software packet(s) to the place you obtained them for a full refund.

1. **License Grant**. IDGB grants to you (either an individual or entity) a nonexclusive license to use one copy of the enclosed software program(s) (collectively, the "Software") solely for your own personal or business purposes on a single computer (whether a standard computer or a workstation component of a multiuser network). The Software is in use on a computer when it is loaded into temporary memory (RAM) or installed into permanent memory (hard disk, CD-ROM, or other storage device). IDGB reserves all rights not expressly granted herein.

2. **Ownership**. IDGB is the owner of all right, title, and interest, including copyright, in and to the compilation of the Software recorded on the disk(s) or CD-ROM ("Software Media"). Copyright to the individual programs recorded on the Software Media is owned by the author or other authorized copyright owner of each program. Ownership of the Software and all proprietary rights relating thereto remain with IDGB and its licensers.

3. **Restrictions On Use and Transfer**.

   a. You may only (i) make one copy of the Software for backup or archival purposes, or (ii) transfer the Software to a single hard disk, provided that you keep the original for backup or archival purposes. You may not (i) rent or lease the Software, (ii) copy or reproduce the Software through a LAN or other network system or through any computer subscriber system or bulletin-board system, or (iii) modify, adapt, or create derivative works based on the Software.

b. You may not reverse engineer, decompile, or disassemble the Software. You may transfer the Software and user documentation on a permanent basis, provided that the transferee agrees to accept the terms and conditions of this Agreement and you retain no copies. If the Software is an update or has been updated, any transfer must include the most recent update and all prior versions.

4. <u>**Restrictions On Use of Individual Programs**</u>. You must follow the individual requirements and restrictions detailed for each individual program in Appendix F of this Book. These limitations are also contained in the individual license agreements recorded on the Software Media. These limitations may include a requirement that after using the program for a specified period of time, the user must pay a registration fee or discontinue use. By opening the Software packet(s), you will be agreeing to abide by the licenses and restrictions for these individual programs that are detailed in Appendix F and on the Software Media. None of the material on this Software Media or listed in this Book may ever be redistributed, in original or modified form, for commercial purposes.

5. <u>**Limited Warranty**</u>.

a. IDGB warrants that the Software and Software Media are free from defects in materials and workmanship under normal use for a period of sixty (60) days from the date of purchase of this Book. If IDGB receives notification within the warranty period of defects in materials or workmanship, IDGB will replace the defective Software Media.

b. **IDGB AND THE AUTHORS OF THE BOOK DISCLAIM ALL OTHER WARRANTIES, EXPRESS OR IMPLIED, INCLUDING WITHOUT LIMITATION IMPLIED WARRANTIES OF MERCHANTABILITY AND FITNESS FOR A PARTICULAR PURPOSE, WITH RESPECT TO THE SOFTWARE, THE PROGRAMS, THE SOURCE CODE CONTAINED THEREIN, AND/OR THE TECHNIQUES DESCRIBED IN THIS BOOK. IDGB DOES NOT WARRANT THAT THE FUNCTIONS CONTAINED IN THE SOFTWARE WILL MEET YOUR REQUIREMENTS OR THAT THE OPERATION OF THE SOFTWARE WILL BE ERROR FREE.**

c. This limited warranty gives you specific legal rights, and you may have other rights that vary from jurisdiction to jurisdiction.

6. <u>Remedies</u>.

   a. IDGB's entire liability and your exclusive remedy for defects in materials and workmanship shall be limited to replacement of the Software Media, which may be returned to IDGB with a copy of your receipt at the following address: Software Media Fulfillment Department, Attn.: *Novell's CNA^{SM} Study Guide for NetWare 5*, IDG Books Worldwide, Inc., 7260 Shadeland Station, Ste. 100, Indianapolis, IN 46256, or call 1-800-762-2974. Please allow three to four weeks for delivery. This Limited Warranty is void if failure of the Software Media has resulted from accident, abuse, or misapplication. Any replacement Software Media will be warranted for the remainder of the original warranty period or thirty (30) days, whichever is longer.

   b. In no event shall IDGB or the authors be liable for any damages whatsoever (including without limitation damages for loss of business profits, business interruption, loss of business information, or any other pecuniary loss) arising from the use of or inability to use the Book or the Software, even if IDGB has been advised of the possibility of such damages.

   c. Because some jurisdictions do not allow the exclusion or limitation of liability for consequential or incidental damages, the above limitation or exclusion may not apply to you.

7. <u>U.S. Government Restricted Rights</u>. Use, duplication, or disclosure of the Software by the U.S. Government is subject to restrictions stated in paragraph (c)(1)(ii) of the Rights in Technical Data and Computer Software clause of DFARS 252.227-7013, and in subparagraphs (a) through (d) of the Commercial Computer — Restricted Rights clause at FAR 52.227-19, and in similar clauses in the NASA FAR supplement, when applicable.

8. <u>General</u>. This Agreement constitutes the entire understanding of the parties and revokes and supersedes all prior agreements, oral or written, between them and may not be modified or amended except in a writing signed by both parties hereto that specifically refers to this Agreement. This Agreement shall take precedence over any other documents that may be in conflict herewith. If any one or more provisions contained in this Agreement are held by any court or tribunal to be invalid, illegal, or otherwise unenforceable, each and every other provision shall remain in full force and effect.

WE WROTE THE BOOK ON NETWORKING

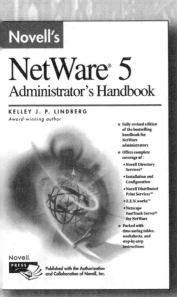
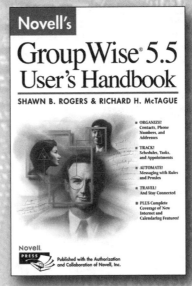
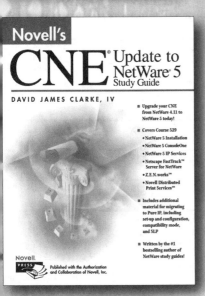
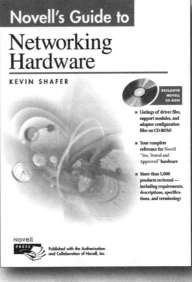

MORE BOOKS FROM NOVELL PRESS™

Study Guides:

Novell's CNE® Update to NetWare® 5 Study Guide	0-7645-4559-0	US $ 49.99 / CAN $ 69.99
Novell's CNA℠ Study Guide for NetWare® 5	0-7645-4542-6	US $ 74.99 / CAN $105.99
Novell's CNE® Study Guide for NetWare® 5	0-7645-4543-4	US $ 89.99 / CAN $126.99
Novell's Certified Internet Business Strategist℠ Study Guide	0-7645-4549-3	US $ 39.99 / CAN $ 56.99
Novell's Certified Web Designer℠ Study Guide	0-7645-4548-5	US $ 49.99 / CAN $ 69.99
Novell's CNE® Study Set IntranetWare/NetWare® 4.11	0-7645-4533-7	US $148.99 / CAN $209.99
Novell's CNE® Study Guide IntranetWare/NetWare® 4.11	0-7645-4512-4	US $ 89.99 / CAN $124.99
Novell's CNE® Study Guide for Core Technologies	0-7645-4501-9	US $ 74.99 / CAN $107.99
Novell's CNA℠ Study Guide IntranetWare/NetWare™ 4.11	0-7645-4513-2	US $ 69.99 / CAN $ 96.99

NetWare/intraNetWare:

Novell's Guide to NetWare® 5 Networks	0-7645-4544-2	US $ 74.99 / CAN $105.99
Novell's NetWare® 5 Administrator's Handbook	0-7645-4546-9	US $ 39.99 / CAN $ 56.99
Novell's Guide to NetWare® 5 and TCP/IP	0-7645-4564-7	US $ 49.99 / CAN $ 69.99
Novell's Guide to NetWare® for Small Business 4.11	0-7645-4504-3	US $ 34.99 / CAN $ 49.99
NDS™ for NT	0-7645-4551-5	US $ 39.99 / CAN $ 56.99
Novell's NDS™ Developer's Guide	0-7645-4557-4	US $ 59.99 / CAN $ 84.99
Novell's Guide to IntranetWare Networks	0-7645-4516-7	US $ 59.99 / CAN $ 84.99
Novell's IntranetWare Administrator's Handbook	0-7645-4517-5	US $ 39.99 / CAN $ 56.99
Novell's Introduction to intraNetWare	0-7645-4530-2	US $ 39.99 / CAN $ 56.99
Novell's Guide to Integrating IntranetWare and NT	0-7645-4523-X	US $ 44.99 / CAN $ 63.99
Novell's Guide to TCP/IP and IntranetWare	0-7645-4532-9	US $ 49.99 / CAN $ 69.99
Novell's Guide to NetWare® 4.1 Networks	1-56884-736-X	US $ 59.99 / CAN $ 84.99
Novell's NetWare® 4.1 Administrator's Handbook	1-56884-737-8	US $ 29.99 / CAN $ 42.99
Novell's Guide to Integrating NetWare® and TCP/IP	1-56884-818-8	US $ 44.99 / CAN $ 63.99
Novell's Guide to NetWare® Printing	0-7645-4514-0	US $ 44.99 / CAN $ 63.99

GroupWise:

Novell's GroupWise® 5.5 Administrator's Guide	0-7645-4556-6	US $ 44.99 / CAN $ 63.99
Novell's GroupWise® 5.5 User's Handbook	0-7645-4552-3	US $ 24.99 / CAN $ 35.99
Novell's GroupWise® 5 Administrator's Guide	0-7645-4521-3	US $ 44.99 / CAN $ 63.99
Novell's GroupWise® 5 User's Handbook	0-7645-4509-4	US $ 24.99 / CAN $ 34.99
Novell's GroupWise® 4 User's Guide	0-7645-4502-7	US $ 19.99 / CAN $ 28.99

ManageWise:

Novell's ManageWise® Administrator's Handbook	1-56884-817-X	US $ 29.99 / CAN $ 42.99

Border Manager:

Novell's Guide to BorderManager™	0-7645-4540-X	US $ 49.99 / CAN $ 69.99

Z.E.N. Works:

Novell's Z.E.N. works™ Administrator's Handbook	0-7645-4561-2	US $ 44.99 / CAN $ 63.99

Internet/Intranets:

Novell's Internet Plumbing Handbook	0-7645-4537-X	US $ 34.99 / CAN $ 49.99
Novell's Guide to Web Site Management	0-7645-4529-9	US $ 59.99 / CAN $ 84.99
Novell's Guide to Internet Access Solutions	0-7645-4515-9	US $ 39.99 / CAN $ 54.99
Novell's Guide to Creating IntranetWare Intranets	0-7645-4531-0	US $ 39.99 / CAN $ 54.99
Novell's The Web at Work	0-7645-4519-1	US $ 29.99 / CAN $ 42.99

Networking Connections/Network Management:

Novell's Guide to LAN/WAN Analysis: IPX/SPX™	0-7645-4508-6	US $ 59.99 / CAN $ 84.99
Novell's Guide to Resolving Critical Server Issues	0-7645-4550-7	US $ 59.99 / CAN $ 84.99

General Reference:

Novell's Encyclopedia of Networking	0-7645-4511-6	US $ 69.99 / CAN $ 96.99
Novell's Dictionary of Networking	0-7645-4528-0	US $ 24.99 / CAN $ 35.99
Novell's Guide to Networking Hardware	0-7645-4553-1	US $ 69.99 / CAN $ 98.99
Novell's Introduction to Networking	0-7645-4525-6	US $ 19.99 / CAN $ 27.99

www.novell.com/books   www.idgbooks.com

Available wherever books are sold
or call 1-800-762-2974 to order today.
Outside the U.S. call 1-317-596-5530

my2cents.idgbooks.com

CD-Rom Installation Instructions

To install the NetWare 5 CNA module of The Clarke Tests v5.0 included with this book, insert the CD-ROM into your CD drive (drive D:, for example).

1. If you are using Microsoft Windows 95/NT, select Start and Run. Type **D:\CNA95\SETUP** in the input window and click OK. (Remember that drive D: is the CD-ROM drive.)

2. If you are using Microsoft Windows 3.1, select File and Run. Type **D:\CNA31\SETUP** in the input window and click OK. (Remember that drive D: is the CD-ROM drive.)

3. The Clarke Tests v5.0 Setup will install the Delivery Module ("Clarke!!"), Tracker, and Administrator. By default, all tests will be highlighted. Click any tests you do not want to install and the system will deselect them.

4. As each test is installed, Setup will ask for a test directory. We recommend that you separate courses into different subdirectories and only install the tests on which you are currently working. In addition, The Clarke Tests v5.0 includes a "Save" feature that allows you to exit a test without losing your place.

For complete instructions on installation, configuration, and troubleshooting of the accompanying CD-ROM, please see Appendix F.